Islas Baleares

Ibiza, Formentera, Mallorca,
Cabrera and Menorca

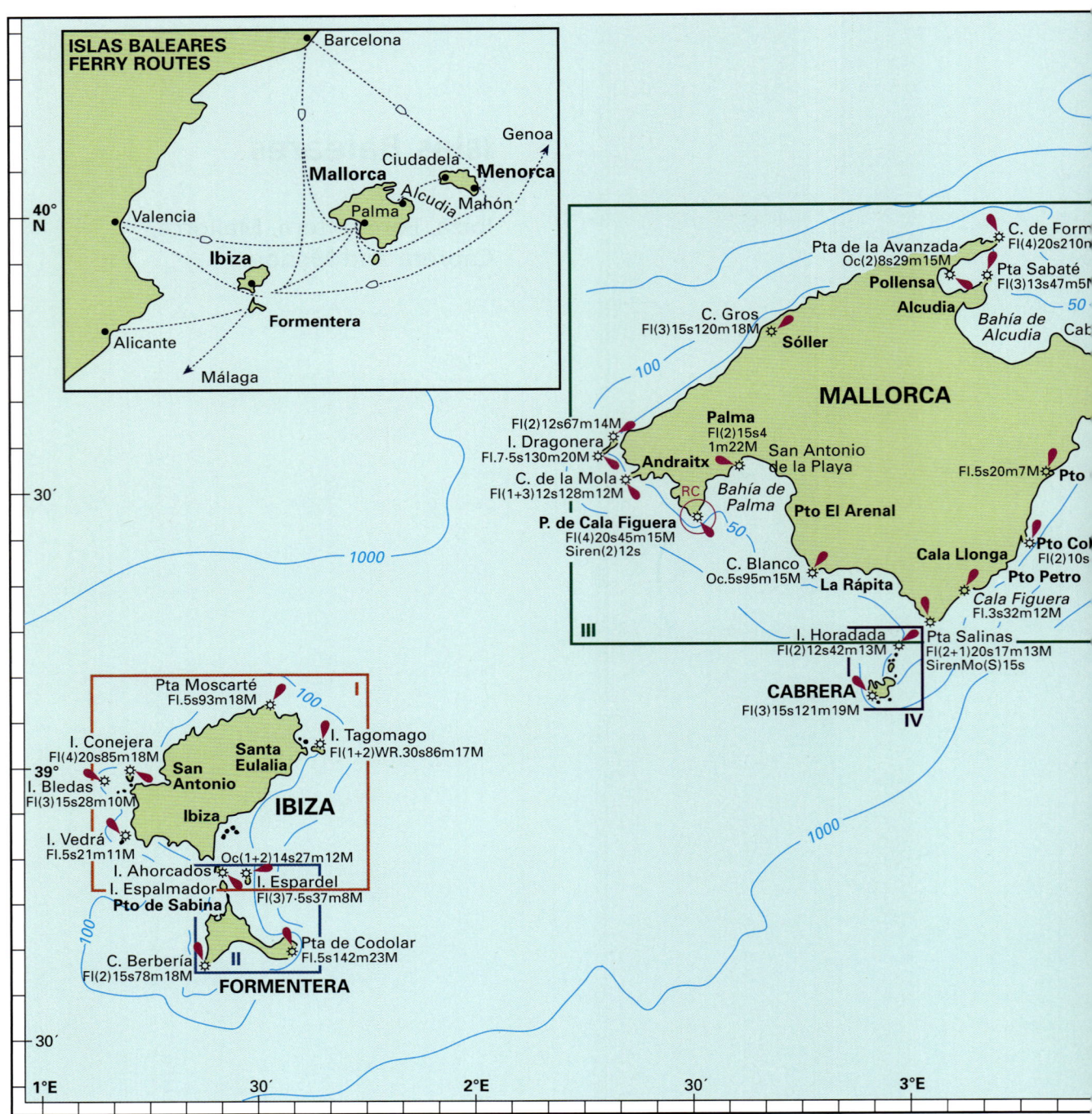

ISLAS BALEARES
FERRY ROUTES

Barcelona

Genoa

Ciudadela
Mallorca   Menorca
         Alcudia   Mahón
40°
N   Valencia   Palma

        Ibiza

      Formentera

   Alicante

        Málaga

Pta de la Avanzada   C. de Form
Oc(2)8s29m15M   Fl(4)20s210m

Pollensa   Pta Sabaté
              Alcudia Fl(3)13s47m5M
C. Gros   Bahía de
Fl(3)15s120m18M   Alcudia   Cab
         Sóller

                    MALLORCA   50

Fl(2)12s67m14M   Palma
I. Dragonera   Fl(2)15s4
Fl.7·5s130m20M   1m22M
                    San Antonio
C. de la Mola Andraitx de la Playa   Fl.5s20m7M   Pto
Fl(1+3)12s128m12M   Bahía de
                    RC   Palma   Pto El Arenal   Pto Co
P. de Cala Figuera   Fl(2)10s
Fl(4)20s45m15M   50   Cala Llonga
Siren(2)12s   C. Blanco   Pto Petro
                 Oc.5s95m15M   La Rápita   Cala Figuera
                                              Fl.3s32m12M
III
                    I. Horadada   Pta Salinas
                    Fl(2)12s42m13M Fl(2+1)20s17m13M
                                   SirenMo(S)15s
                CABRERA
                Fl(3)15s121m19M   IV

Pta Moscarté   I
Fl.5s93m18M   100
I. Conejera   I. Tagomago
Fl(4)20s85m18M Santa Fl(1+2)WR.30s86m17M
39°   San Eulalia
I. Bledas   Antonio
Fl(3)15s28m10M   IBIZA
I. Vedrá   Ibiza
Fl.5s21m11M
              Oc(1+2)14s27m12M
I. Ahorcados   I. Espardel
I. Espalmador   Fl(3)7·5s37m8M
Pto de Sabina
                  Pta de Codolar
100   Fl.5s142m23M
C. Berbería   II
Fl(2)15s78m18M
FORMENTERA

30′

30′
1°E   30′   2°E   30′   3°E

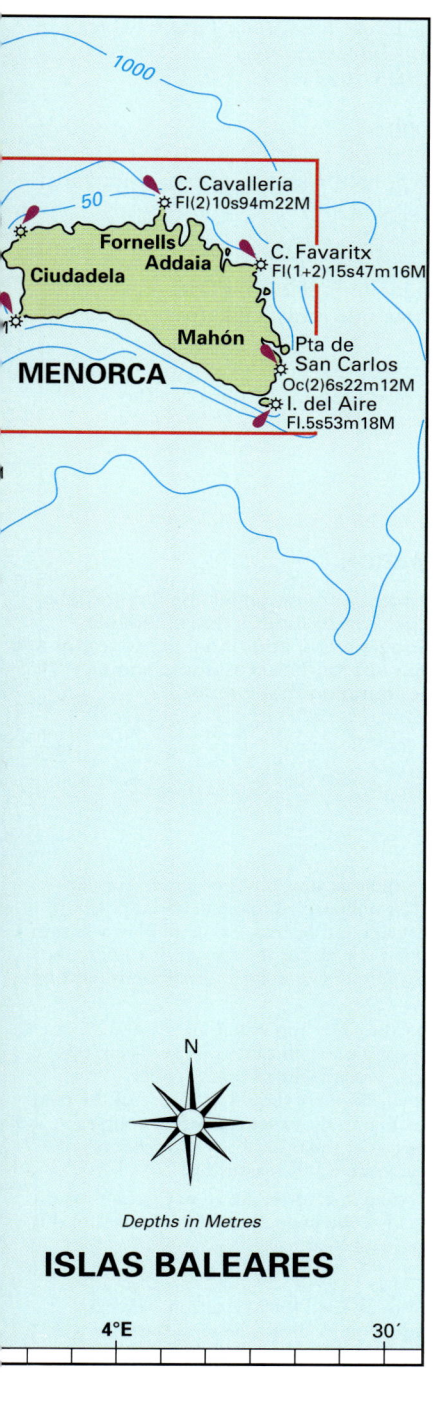

Islas Baleares

Ibiza, Formentera, Mallorca, Cabrera and Menorca

RCC PILOTAGE FOUNDATION

Graham Hutt

Imray Laurie Norie & Wilson

Published by
Imray Laurie Norie & Wilson Ltd
Wych House The Broadway St Ives
Cambridgeshire PE27 5BT England
☎ +44 (0)1480 462114
Fax +44 (0)1480 496109
www.imray.com
2011

© Text: RCC Pilotage Foundation 2011

© Plans: Imray Laurie Norie & Wilson Ltd 2011

© Photographs: Graham Hutt 2011

© Aerial photographs unless credited otherwise: Imray, Laurie, Norie & Wilson and Patrick Roach 2011

© Thumbnail positional photos: ESA2000–2005 Balearic Islands – ENVISAT MERIS – 02/Oct/2004

First edition 1977 (as *East Spain Pilot – Chapter VII, Islas Baleares*)
Second edition 1980
Third edition 1984
Fourth edition 1989 (including *East Spain Pilot Chapter I, Introduction and General Information*)
Fifth Edition 1991, updated 1995
Sixth Edition 1997
Sixth Edition revised 2000
Seventh Edition 2003
Eighth Edition 2006 (Reprinted with corrections, September)
Ninth edition 2011

ISBN 978 184623 283 1

British Library Cataloguing in Publication Data.
A catalogue record for this title is available from the British Library.

Printed in Singapore by Star Standard Industries Pte

CORRECTIONAL SUPPLEMENTS

This pilot book may be amended at intervals by the issue of correctional supplements. These are published on the internet at our website www.imray.com and also via www.rccpf.org.uk and may be downloaded free of charge. Printed copies are also available on request from the publishers at the above address. Like this pilot, supplements are selective. Navigators requiring the latest definitive information are advised to refer to official hydrographic office data.

ADDITIONAL INFORMATION

Additional information may be found under the Publications page at www.rccpf.org.uk. This includes a downloadable waypoint list, links to Google maps, additional photographs and mid season updates when appropriate. Passage planning information may also be found on that website.

CAUTION

Whilst the RCC Pilotage Foundation, the Author and the Publishers have used reasonable endeavours to ensure the accuracy of the content of this book, it contains selected information and thus is not definitive. It does not contain all known information on the subject in hand and should not be relied on alone for navigational use: it should only be used in conjunction with official hydrographic data. This is particularly relevant to the plans, which should not be used for navigation.

The RCC Pilotage Foundation, the Author and the Publishers believe that the information which they have included is a useful aid to prudent navigation, but the safety of a vessel depends ultimately on the judgment of the skipper, who should assess all information, published or unpublished.

The information provided in this pilot book may be out of date and may be changed or updated without notice. The RCC Pilotage Foundation cannot accept any liability for any error, omission or failure to update such information.

To the extent permitted by law, the RCC Pilotage Foundation, the Author(s) and the Publishers do not accept liability for any loss and/or damage howsoever caused that may arise from reliance on information contained in these pages.

POSITIONS

All positions in the text are to WGS 84 datum. They are supplied as aids to help orientation and to assist in locating and maintaining transits referred to in the book. As always, care must be exercised to work to the datum of the chart in use.

WAYPOINTS

The RCC Pilotage Foundation considers a waypoint to be a position likely to be helpful for navigation if entered into some form of electronic navigation system for use in conjunction with GPS. In this pilot they have been derived from electronic charts. They must be used with caution. All waypoints are given to datum WGS 84 and every

effort has been made to ensure their accuracy. Nevertheless, for each individual vessel, the standard of onboard equipment, aerial position, datum setting, correct entry of data and operator skill all play a part in their effectiveness. In particular it is vital for the navigator to note the datum of the chart in use and apply the necessary correction if plotting a GPS position on the chart.

Our use of the term 'waypoint' does not imply that all vessels can safely sail directly over those positions at all times. Some – as in this pilot – may be linked to indicate recommended routes under appropriate conditions. However, skippers should be aware of the risk of collision with another vessel plying the exact reciprocal course. Verification by observation, or use of radar to check the accuracy of a waypoint, may sometimes be advisable and reassuring.

We emphasise that we regard waypoints as an aid to navigation for use as the navigator or skipper decides. We hope that the waypoints in this pilot will help ease that navigational load.

PLANS

The plans in this guide are not to be used for navigation – they are designed to support the text and should always be used together with navigational charts. Waypoints should not be selected using the latitude and longitude scales of these plans.

It should be borne in mind that the characteristics of lights may be changed during the life of the book, and that in any case notification of such changes is unlikely to be reported immediately. Each light is identified in both the text and where possible on the plans (where it appears in magenta) by its international index number, as used in the *Admiralty List of Lights*, from which the book may be updated.

All bearings are given from seaward and refer to true north. Symbols are based on those used by the British Admiralty – users are referred to *Symbols and Abbreviations (NP 5011)*.

Contents

In 1976 an American member of the Royal Cruising Club, Dr Fred Ellis, indicated that he wished to make a gift to the Club in memory of his father, the late Robert E Ellis, of his friends Peter Pye and John Ives and as a mark of esteem for Roger Pinckney. An independent charity known as the RCC Pilotage Foundation was formed and Dr Ellis added his house to his already generous gift of money to form the Foundation's permanent endowment. The Foundation's charitable objective is 'to advance the education of the public in the science and practice of navigation', which is at present achieved through the writing and updating of pilot books covering many diffent parts of the world.

The Foundation is extremely grateful and privileged to have been given the copyrights to books written by a number of distinguished authors and yachtsmen including the late Adlard Coles, Robin Brandon and Malcolm Robson. In return, the Foundation has willingly accepted the task of keeping the original books up to date and many yachtsmen and women have helped (and are helping) the Foundation fulfil this commitment. In addition to the titles donated to the Foundation, several new books have been created and developed under the auspices of the Foundation. The Foundation works in close collaboration with three publishers – Imray Laurie Norie and Wilson, Adlard Coles Nautical and On Board Publications – and in addition publishes in its own name short run guides and pilot books for areas where limited demand does not justify large print runs. Several of the Foundation's books have been translated into French, German and Italian.

The Foundation runs its own website at www.rccpf.org.uk which not only lists all the publications but also contains free downloadable pilotage information.

The overall management of the Foundation is entrusted to trustees appointed by the Royal Cruising Club, with day-to-day operations being controlled by the Director. All these appointments are unpaid. In line with its charitable status, the Foundation distributes no profits; any surpluses are used to finance new books and developments and to subsidise those covering areas of low demand.

PUBLICATIONS OF THE RCC PILOTAGE FOUNDATION

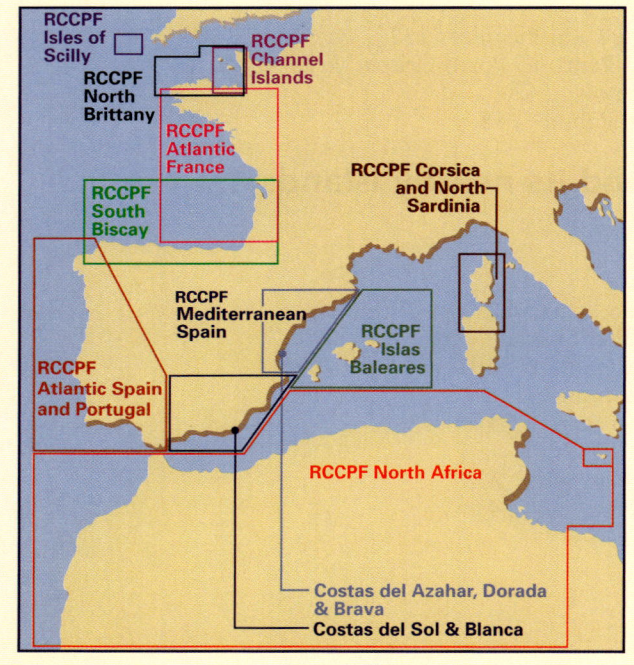

Imray
Faroe, Iceland and Greenland
Norway
The Baltic Sea
Channel Islands
North Brittany and the Channel Islands
Isles of Scilly
North Biscay
South Biscay
Atlantic Islands
Atlantic Spain & Portugal
Mediterranean Spain
   Costas del Sol and Blanca
   Costas del Azahar, Dorada & Brava
   Islas Baleares
Corsica and North Sardinia
North Africa
Chile

Adlard Coles Nautical
Atlantic Crossing Guide
Pacific Crossing Guide

On Board Publications
South Atlantic Circuit
Havens and Anchorages for the South American Coast

The RCC Pilotage Foundation
Supplement to Falkland Island Shores
Guide to West Africa
Argentina

RCCPF Website www.rccpf.org.uk
Supplements
Support files for books
Passage Planning Guides
ePilots

Foreword

The origins of this book go back to the late Robin Brandon's *East Spain Pilot*, in which Islas Baleares was first published after his detailed reconnaissance in 1977. When he revised that book in 1988 wealth and tourism were driving major changes. The RCC Pilotage Foundation was honoured to take on the regular updating of his books – the two volumes of *Mediterranean Spain*, from Gibraltar to Denia and Denia to the French Border, being the others amongst the Pilotage Foundation's coverage of the Western Mediterranean.

We were fortunate that Graham Hutt agreed to carry out a major revision on the book in 2005. His knowledge and fondness for the islands was reflected both in the content and the presentation of the Eighth Edition. Since then he has revisited the islands and maintained his close contacts there. His continuing attention to detail is reflected in this Ninth Edition.

The Balearic Islands offer wonderful sailing but it was interesting that by the mid 2000s the average yachtsman was becoming disenchanted by the high costs and unhelpfulness found in many marinas. More recently there have been signs that this is changing and information is now more readily available.

What is also changing is the emphasis given to marine conservation – a factor along the entire Spanish coastline. The overall policy may be interpreted in differing ways from place to place, ecological protected zones may move and mooring buoy arrangements may change during the year. This, coupled with the barring off of many beach areas for swimmers, means many of the traditional anchorages in these waters may no longer be available – particularly in the months of high summer. The best advice is to consult the websites listed and be flexible in planning.

The Pilotage Foundation is most grateful to Graham Hutt – and his assistant Di Stoddard – for the dedicated work undertaken to revise and maintain this book, and to Willie Wilson and his team at Imray for all their work to achieve this edition.

As always, the Pilotage Foundation welcomes feedback from yachtsmen so that we can continue to offer supplements via the Imray website. Additional information to support this book, including any important mid season corrections may be found on the Foundation's site at www.rccpf.org.uk.

Martin Walker
Director
RCC Pilotage Foundation
2011

Preface

Having sailed the Balearic Islands many times over the past few years, usually on my way to or from North Africa, it was an honour to be asked to revise the Eighth and Ninth editions. It was the first opportunity to explore inland, as I had previously ventured little further from the coasts than to the airports. The island interiors were very different to what I expected.

I hear many complaints about the ruin of the islands by tourist development and have to wonder if those complaining have actually travelled further than the main busy ports. There has certainly been a lot of tourist development, as in all the Mediterranean, but the islands are far from spoiled by this.

In Mallorca fine pine forests still thrive and have not given way to concrete jungles. I found that most of the inland private developments are tastefully done. Even coastal developments compared favourably with those of the Costa del Sol and the coastlines of Greece and Italy, which I am also familiar with. Some areas along the coast of Mallorca actually resemble the beautiful Tuscany area of Italy, with their narrow winding roads through the pine forests. In Mallorca, these roads are again peaceful, thanks to a huge investment in motorways which keep vehicles away from the coast.

I could not better many of the *cala* (cove) descriptions given in the previous seven editions which had been honed over the years by my predecessors. However, it has been a thorough and complete revision and hopefully, an easier book to use.

Several changes have taken place since my first review of the Islands in 2005/2006 for the eighth edition. First: the use of the internet. Almost all marinas and harbours now have internet and their own web sites. The URLs seem to change frequently, as do phone numbers, but a Google search usually rediscovers them. Additional and updated information on mooring fees and availability is now much more easily available. Many marinas allow online booking for a berth or a mooring buoy.

The governing authorities recently began publishing online maps of areas designated as marine reserve and conservation areas. Conservation is now a big issue – and big business – in the Islands. These conservation areas are regularly changed from one part of the coastline to another, so it is only by viewing the online sites that current information can be updated.

Most marinas now have Wi-Fi available to yachtsmen. Some charge per hour, but at least it is available to those of us who like to feel we are not missing the office while sailing!

Prices and the number of yachtsmen visiting in the high season have been considerably reduced since 2008, compared with previous years. Several friends told me that they were fed up with being overcharged and encountering rude port staff in the Islands and now go elsewhere. Recent indications and changes make me think that the hint has been taken, if belatedly.

German remains the most common language heard in many areas. Many shop workers speak German and English, but not Spanish or Catalan. Air Berlin has made a huge investment by making its hub in the Islands.

Another major change since the last edition is the 'seeding' of many wonderful anchorages with buoys. This has had a devastating affect on many yachtsmen's aspiration of freedom.

None of the above deters me from considering the Islas Baleares as one of the Mediterranean's prime cruising grounds, especially for out of season cruising.

Graham Hutt, 2011

Acknowledgements

I am indebted to those skippers living and working in the islands who contributed information and advice. Once again, as with my other books, Di Stoddard helped with every aspect in the preparation and checking, for which I am most grateful. I would like to thank John Hearney; David Evernden; Carolyn Ernst; Spencer Brown and Bob Parker of *Antigua Meloussa* (www.menorcaenvelero.com), who has been contributing information for some years from his base in Menorca.

The Baleares Tourist Information Office for a wealth of brochures and information provided. To Annette Ridout and Penny Scott-Bayfield who proof-read the book.

To Ros Hogbin and others behind the scenes at the Pilotage Foundation, who gave advice, help and checking of the text and layout to ensure that this edition is easier to navigate around and use.

The aerial photographers Patrick Roach and Geoff Williamson who provided many of the superb pictures. (Non-attributed pictures are the work of Patrick Roach. GW denotes Geoff Williamson.)

Graham Hutt
2011

Additional information about the author

Graham Hutt has been yacht-based in the Mediterranean for over 30 years, combining work as a medical anthropologist and practitioner of electromagnetic natural medicine, with sailing and writing. He also works as a consultant to an organisation translating ancient Aramaic, Hebrew and Greek Biblical texts into modern languages.

He has lived and worked continually in the Mediterranean since 1981, moving from the east to the west Mediterranean in 1990. His yachting experience began in Nicholson 55s, Windfalls and Contessas, while serving as a skipper at the Joint Services Sailing Centre in Gosport. His own yachts have included a 27ft mahogany clinker-built Stella sloop, a 31ft Golden Hind, the ferro Hartley Fijian yacht *Safwana*, an Ohlsen 38 and a 40ft Orion. Currently he owns a 43ft Westerly Ocean, which he sailed in summer 2010 around the Baleares Islands and to North Africa, updating both pilots.

List of ports

Isla de Ibiza

IB1 Puerto de Ibiza
IB2 Puerto de San Antonio
IB3 Puerto de Santa Eulalia

Isla de Formentera

F1 Puerto de Sabina (Marina Formentera Mar)

Isla de Mallorca

M1 Puerto de Palma de Mallorca
M2 Puerto de Cala Nova
M3 Puerto Portals
M4 Puerto de Palma Nova
M5 Porto Adriano
M6 Puerto de Santa Ponsa
M7 Puerto de Andraitx
M8 Puerto de Sóller
M9 Puerto de Pollensa
M10 Puerto del Barcarés
M11 Puerto/Marina de Bonaire
M12 Puerto de Alcudia
M13 Puerto de Ca'n Picafort
M14 Puerto de Serra Nova
M15 Puerto de Colonia de San Pedro
M16 Puerto de Cala Ratjada
M17 Puerto de Cala Bona
M18 Porto Cristo (Cala Manacor)
M19 Porto Colom
M20 Puerto de Cala Llonga (Marina de Cala d'Or)
M21 Porto Petro
M22 Puerto de Cala Figuera
M23 Puerto Colonia de Sant Jordi (Puerto de Campos)
M24 Puerto de la Rápita
M25 Puerto de S'Estanyol
M26 Puerto El Arenal
M27 Puerto de San Antonio de la Playa
M28 Puerto de Cala Gamba
M29 Puerto del Molinar de Levante
M30 Puerto de Cala Portixol

Isla de Cabrera

C1 Puerto de Cabrera

Isla de Menorca

ME1 Puerto de Mahón
ME2 Puerto de Tamarinda
ME3 Puerto de Ciudadela
ME4 Puerto de Fornells
ME5 Puerto (Deportivo) de Cala de Addaya

With the development and proliferation of Wi-Fi internet links, the world has become a very small place, where work can be carried out just about anywhere. Apart from providing a great platform for academic work, travelling by yacht and being based for extended periods in odd places, gives a true appreciation and insight into different cultures. His enduring love for the countries of the Mediterranean are a constant stimulus to continue all these activities.

Introduction

The Islas Baleares (Iles Balears, Ballerics, Balearics, etc.) consist of four main islands: Mallorca, Menorca, Ibiza and Formentera, along with a number of smaller islets in three separate groups. They form one of the most attractive and varied cruising grounds in the western Mediterranean. There are hundreds of pleasant anchorages and many harbours, ranging from large cosmopolitan ports such as Palma de Mallorca, to completely deserted anchorages in exquisitely beautiful bays.

The islands are under Spanish sovereignty and therefore within the European Union. The distances between islands are not great and those between ports, harbours and anchorages, often only a few miles, making the islands suitable for cruising throughout the year with shelter never far away.

Although the islands – and Mallorca in particular – have become a byword for all that is worst in holiday development, in practice this applies only to a small percentage of the coastline, notably the beaches running west from Palma. In other areas it is possible to sail for hours past apparently untouched and frequently dramatic coastline. The same may be said of western and northern Ibiza, while Menorca, though possibly less spectacular, has managed to preserve a great deal of its rural charm. Driving along the coastal roads which wind their way inland around mountainous areas through thick pine forests, is very pleasant.

The western group of islands lies less than 50 miles east of the Spanish mainland. This includes Ibiza, Espalmador, Formentera and half a dozen smaller islets (*islotes*) separated from the mainland and Mallorca by deep channels. These islands were recognised as a separate group in Roman times when they were called *Pityusae* (Pine Islands) and are still sometimes referred to as the *Islas Pitiusas*. They offer many secluded bays and *calas* (coves) where it is possible to anchor. The northern islands are high and rocky whereas the south is low-lying with sandy bays.

The second group, consisting of Mallorca, Cabrera, Menorca and some small inshore islands, was known by the Romans as *Insulae Baleares*, possibly from the Phoenician *baal laaron* meaning 'a man who throws stones' (apparently the islanders' favourite method of resisting attack). The names Mallorca and Menorca are derived from the Latin 'Major' and 'Minor'. Mallorca, the largest island of the group, is approximately 45 miles northeast of Ibiza. It has a major port, several harbours and many bays and *calas* where it is possible to anchor. The northern part is mountainous. There is one large offlying island to the south, Cabrera, which has a well protected bay, several *calas* and a number of offlying islets. It is a national park with restricted access. Anchoring is forbidden but mooring buoys have been laid. Menorca lies 25 miles northeast of Mallorca and is much lower and flatter than its neighbour. It is some 30 miles long, with few harbours but numerous *calas* where anchoring is possible. As in Mallorca, the northern part is higher and more rugged than the south.

The islands are attractive, particularly away from 'developed' areas, and form an excellent cruising ground. However some coastal areas have suffered from the rapid growth of tourism in the same way as the coast of mainland Spain. The days of empty anchorages and uncrowded harbours are long gone, particularly during July and August, when it is difficult to find a mooring in any of the harbours. A change was noted by many yachtsmen, including myself during the 2008 season. Many reports indicated far fewer yachtsmen visiting in the high season. Marina space was available and rates were very much reduced from those previously applied. Perhaps this is a positive side of the economic crisis.

By far the most significant change taking place all around the Baleares is the placement of mooring buoys in calas and the prohibition of anchoring. (See section on Anchoring and Moorings on page 16.)

Cala Pinar: rich pine forests stretch from the sea to the mountains

Traditional farming: near Montuiri, Mallorca *GW*

These buoys are not always laid well and are often too close together or placed too close to existing permanent private buoys. It is my view that the placement of buoys preventing anchoring is a key reason for the downturn in the number of yachts now visiting. Many feel they have lost their freedom.

CLIMATE AND SEASONS

For those accustomed to more northern latitudes a winter cruise has its attractions. There are many days with a good sailing breeze and the weather is warmer and sunnier than a normal English summer. Storms and heavy rain occur in winter, but in general the climate is mild and, particularly from January to March, reasonably pleasant most of the time.

Offshore, the Mediterranean weather in winter can be fearsome, but it is feasible to dodge bad weather and slip from harbour to harbour as they are seldom far apart. Sailing out of season not only has the great advantage that there are no crowds, but the shops and services are freer to serve the winter visitor. Local people can be met, places of interest enjoyed and the empty beaches and coves used in privacy. Many *club náuticos*, which in summer have to turn away cruising sailors, welcome visitors off-season.

LOCAL ECONOMY

Tourism is a significant contributor to the local economy, but agriculture and light industry manage to co-exist in the islands. An established boat building industry exists, drawing skilled labour from the industrial sectors. The yachting industry in the Balearic Islands generates almost half a billion Euros each year.

LANGUAGE

The islands have two official languages: Spanish Castilliano and Catalan. The latter is transformed into local dialects, referred to as *Mallorquín*,

Menorquín and *Ibicenco*, in Mallorca, Menorca and Ibiza. Examples of Catalan alternatives for Castilliano Spanish phrases include: *bondia* – good morning (rather than *buenos días*), *bona tarde* – good afternoon (*buenos tardes*), *s'es plau* – please (*por favor*). Many French and Italian words are integrated into the local dialects.

Many local people speak English or German, often learnt from tourists, and French is taught as a second language at school.

CULTURE AND RELIGION

Holidays and fiestas

As on the Spanish mainland, most inhabitants of the islands are Roman Catholic, though, as on many islands throughout the Mediterranean, practice may be more cultural than religious and quite different from that on the mainland. Perhaps the most overt manifestation of religious practice is the celebration of saints' days. There are literally hundreds of these throughout the islands and they can be a huge affair – always with a procession during which the saint, or an effigy of the Virgin Mary will be paraded down the main street or taken by boat, effectively closing down the town for several hours. One of the largest, *Fiesta del Virgen de la Carmen* is celebrated in many harbours during mid-July. When a national holiday falls on a Sunday it may be celebrated the following day.

Fiestas usually culminate with a firework display. Every city, town and village has its own saint's day and corresponding fiesta. Other celebrations are of historic events, commemorating the rich history of the islands.

A useful *Fiestas Guide* is published annually by the Balearic Tourist Institute and is available from tourist offices. There is also a monthly update including cultural events taking place locally, also available from tourist offices and from many hotel lobbies.

Addresses and websites for tourist offices in the Balearics are found later in this section, and overseas offices in the *Appendix*.

Ancient church in Banys de la Font Santa, Mallorca *Graham Hutt*

Maritime Information

METEOROLOGY

Regional weather in the Western Mediterranean

General

The weather pattern in the western Mediterranean basin is affected by many different systems and local topography. It is largely unpredictable, quick to change and often very different at places only a short distance apart (see *Appendix* for Spanish meteorological terms).

Winds most frequently blow from the west, northwest, north and east but are considerably altered by the effects of local topography. The Mediterranean is an area of calms and gales and the old saying that in summer there are nine days of light winds followed by a gale, is very close to reality. Near to the coast normal sea and land breezes are experienced on calm days.

The winds in the Mediterranean have been given names dependent on their direction and characteristics. Those which affect this area are detailed below.

Northwest: tramontana

This wind, also known as the *mestral* or *maestral* near Río Ebro and the *mistral* in France (where it usually originates), is a strong, dry wind, cold in winter, which can be dangerous. It is caused by a secondary depression forming in the Golfe de Lion or the Golfo di Génova on the cold front of a major depression crossing France. The northwesterly airflow generated is compressed between the Alps and the Pyrenees and flows into the Mediterranean basin. In Spain it chiefly affects the coast to the north of Barcelona, the Islas Baleares, and is strongest at the northern end of the Costa Brava.

The *tramontana* can be dangerous in that it can arrive and reach gale force in as little as 15 minutes on a calm sunny day, with virtually no warning. Signs to watch for are brilliant visibility, (sometimes two or three days in advance of a storm) clear sky – sometimes with cigar-shaped clouds, very dry air and a steady or slightly rising barometer. On rare occasions the sky may be cloudy when the wind first arrives, although it clears later. Sometimes the barometer will plunge in normal fashion, rising quickly after the gale has passed. If at sea and some way from land, a line of white on the horizon and a developing swell give a few minutes' warning. The only effective warning that can be obtained is by radio – Marseille (in French) and Monaco (in French and English) are probably the best.

The *tramontana* normally blows for at least three days and, on occasions, may last for a week or longer. It is very frequent in the winter months, blowing for a third of the time, and on occasions can reach Force 10 (50 knots) or above. In summer it is neither as strong nor as frequent.

West: vendaval

A depression crossing Spain or southern France creates a strong southwest to west wind, the *vendaval* or *poniente*, which funnels through the Strait of Gibraltar and along the south coast of Spain. Though normally confined to the south and southeast coasts, it occasionally blows in the northeast of the area. It is usually short-lived and at its strongest from late autumn to early spring.

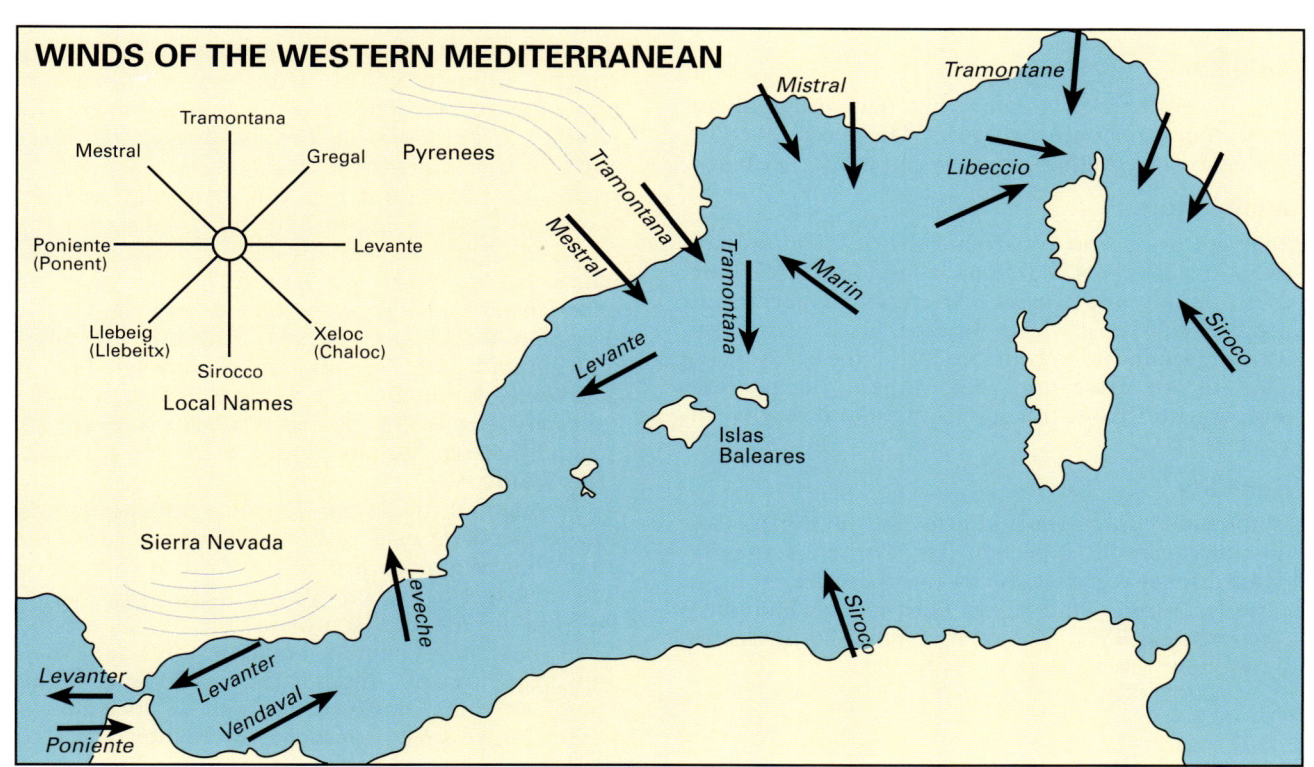

WINDS OF THE WESTERN MEDITERRANEAN

East: levante

Encountered from Gibraltar to Valencia and beyond, the *levante*, sometimes called the *llevantade* when it blows at gale force, is caused by a depression located between the Islas Baleares and the North African coast. It is preceded by a heavy swell (*las tascas*), cold damp air, poor visibility and low cloud which forms first around the higher hills. Heavy and prolonged rainfall is more likely in spring and autumn than summer. A *levante* may last for three or four days or more. It is usually preceded two or three days in advance by brilliantly clear weather and the formation of cigar or huge layered saucer-shaped clouds.

South: sirocco

The hot wind from the south is created by a depression moving east along or just south of the North African coast. By the time this dry wind reaches Spain or the Islas Baleares it can be very humid, with haze and cloud. If strong it carries dust, and should it rain when the cold front comes through the water may be red or brown and the dust will set like cement. This wind is sometimes called the *leveche* in southeast Spain. It occurs most frequently in summer, seldom lasting more than one or two days.

Precipitation

Annual rainfall is moderate, between 450mm and 500mm, and tends to be higher in the east of the area. It is heaviest in the last quarter of the year and lightest in the third quarter: July averages 4–5mm.

Thunderstorms

Thunderstorms are most frequent in the autumn – up to four or five each month, and can be accompanied by hail. High level cumulus clouds are frequent in winter.

Visibility

Fog is very rare in summer but may occur about three times a month in winter. On occasions dust carried by the southerly *sirocco* can reduce visibility.

Temperature

Temperatures drop to around 10–15°C in winter, rising steadily after March to around 20°C, reaching 29°C in July and August. Afternoon temperatures reach 30–33°C in these months, with occasional days higher, most likely in late July and early August. The usual afternoon sea breeze keeps the temperature from reaching mainland highs of around 40°C.

Humidity

With winds from west, northwest, or north, low humidity can be expected. The *sirocco* southerly winds bring exceptionally dry air: these are rare. An easterly *levante* wind brings with it high humidity, often around 95%. The relative humidity increases throughout the night and falls by day.

A storm rolling past the anchorage in Colom   *Graham Hutt*

LOCAL WEATHER IN THE ISLAS BALEARES

The two main weather areas in the Islas Baleares lie either side of a line roughly bisecting Mallorca from north–northwest to south–southeast.

The southwestern area is influenced by the weather over mainland Spain – winds are variable but, in general, those from the southeast semicircle prevail in summer and those from the northwest in winter. Gales are rare in summer (though sudden short term squalls are becoming increasingly common), but may blow for 5–10% of the time in winter. These are generally the result of a *tramontana* though they may blow from anywhere between west through north to northeast. Winds from the southeast can bring clouds, rain and poor visibility, though these are more frequent in the winter months.

In the Menorca area, northwest, north and northeast winds are most common, especially in winter, though winds from other directions frequently occur. This area is influenced by the weather in the Golfo de León and is in the direct path of the northwest *tramontana*, making it particularly important to listen to regular weather forecasts. Gales or increased winds forecast for the Golfo de León almost invariably mean stronger winds in the northeast Baleares. Gales may be experienced for 10% of the time during the winter, dropping to 2% in July and August, sometimes arriving with little warning and rapidly building to gale force. Although there is more rain than in the southwest sector of the archipelago, visibility is generally better. Menorca is sometimes described as 'The Windy Isle.'

Throughout the area, in calm weather a sea breeze (*brisa de mar*) will be experienced near the coast, blowing more strongly where it is channelled into a large bay such as the Bahías de Palma, Pollensa or Alcudia. It usually gets up at around 1300, is at its maximum between 1500 and 1600 and drops towards dusk. It can reach Force 5 (20 knots) or more at times. In spite of its name it seldom blows directly onshore – more often at 45° to the coast or even parallel to it.

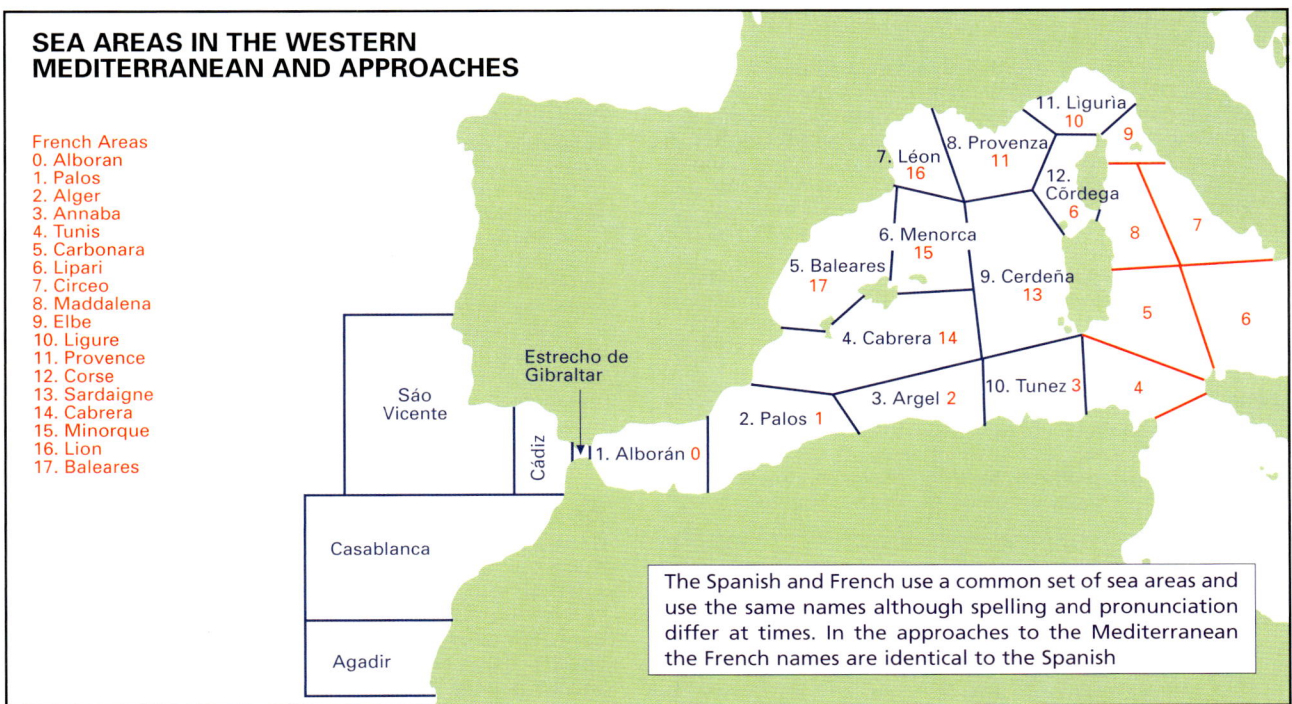

SEA AREAS IN THE WESTERN MEDITERRANEAN AND APPROACHES

French Areas
0. Alboran
1. Palos
2. Alger
3. Annaba
4. Tunis
5. Carbonara
6. Lipari
7. Circeo
8. Maddalena
9. Elbe
10. Ligure
11. Provence
12. Corse
13. Sardaigne
14. Cabrera
15. Minorque
16. Lion
17. Baleares

11. Liguria 10
8. Provenza 11
7. Léon 16
12. Côrdega 6
6. Menorca 15
5. Baleares 17
9. Cerdeña 13
4. Cabrera 14
3. Argel 2
10. Tunez 3
2. Palos 1
1. Alborán 0

Estrecho de Gibraltar
Sáo Vicente
Cádiz
Casablanca
Agadir

The Spanish and French use a common set of sea areas and use the same names although spelling and pronunciation differ at times. In the approaches to the Mediterranean the French names are identical to the Spanish

A land breeze is sometimes present during the latter half of the night and lasts until the sun has had time to warm the land. This breeze can be quite strong where there are valleys leading inland.

Precipitation and visibility

Annual rainfall at Palma averages 460mm, the wettest period being October to December. Fog sometimes occurs in winter but is almost unknown in summer.

WEATHER FORECASTS

It should be noted that visual signs and methods of forecasting using clouds and barometer, as is usual in Northern Europe, usually do not give the same indications in the Mediterranean. This is more noticeable as you travel east from the Strait of Gibraltar. It is common to see a fast falling or rising barometer, with no resulting change in conditions. Similarly, cloud formations that would normally indicate rain or storms approaching, often clear in minutes, leaving blue skies. Sudden winds or squalls can appear very quickly without any warning whatsoever. The good news is that these unannounced changes are normally short-lived.

Radio and other weather forecasts

Details of coast radio stations, weather forecasts, Weatherfax and Navtex follow. See individual harbour details for port and marina radio information. All times quoted are UT (universal time) unless otherwise specified. Only France Inter, Radio France International, BBC Radio 4 and one of the two Monaco stations observe local time (LT), thus altering the UT transmission times when the clocks change.

VHF

When calling a Spanish coast radio station on VHF use Ch 16. The station will then specify which channel to use for further communication. When calling a marina or another vessel, use Ch 09 unless stated otherwise in the text.

RADIO WEATHER FORECASTS IN SPANISH AND ENGLISH
Palma
Palma radio transmits a forecast on VHF in English and Spanish in Mallorca on Ch 10, in Ibiza on Ch 3 and in Menorca on Ch 85, announced on Ch 16 at about 0835, 1135, 1635, 2135 LT
Valencia
Valencia radio transmits a forecast on VHF Ch 10, announced on Ch 16, in English and Spanish at 15 minutes past every even hour.
Weather forecasts in French and English
Valencia
VHF Ch 10 at 0835 covering all the coastal waters around Mallorca
Monaco (3AC)
VHF transmits and receives on Ch 20, 22, 25, 23 (Navimet), 24 (winter 0600-2200; summer 0500–2100)
Weather messages
VHF Ch 20, 22 every H+03 and 0903, 1403, 1915 LT in French and English for areas 14, 15 and 17
Navigational warnings
VHF Ch 20, 22 at 0803 LT
France Inter (Bulletin Inter-Service-Mer)
On 162kHz at 2003 LT for areas 514-516. May be worth tape recording by the less fluent.
Radio France-Internationale
On 6175kHz at 1140 UT (gale warnings, synopsis, development, 24 hr forecast, in French)
Alger (7TA), Algeria (36°40'N 03°18'E)
On 1792kHz SSB at 0903, 1703 UT (12h forecast in French for area 3, followed by gale warnings, synopsis, 12h forecast and further 12h outlook, in French, for all areas (see diagram)

ENGLISH LANGUAGE
UK Maritime Mobile Net
In addition to 'official' weather forecasts, information given by the UK Maritime Mobile Net covering the Eastern Atlantic and Mediterranean are very useful, especially in forming an opinion from the general synopsis. The Net can be heard on 14303kHz SSB on the Upper Side Band at 0800 and 1800 UT daily, the full forecast following about 30 minutes later. On Saturday there is usually a preview of the coming week's weather prospects. It is not necessary to have a licence to listen to the Net, though an amateur radio licence is required to transmit.
BBC Radio 4, UK on 198kHz at 0048, 0555, 1355, 1750 LT. Occasionally the synopsis provides advance warning of the approach of an Atlantic depression which could lead to a northwest tramontana.

GERMAN LANGUAGE
Offenbach (Main)/Pinneberg (DDH)(DDK), Germany
On 4583, 7646kHz at 0415, 1610 for areas M1-M9; 1015, 2215. Two day prognosis for Western Mediterranean; 1115, 2315. Two day prognosis for Eastern Mediterranean.

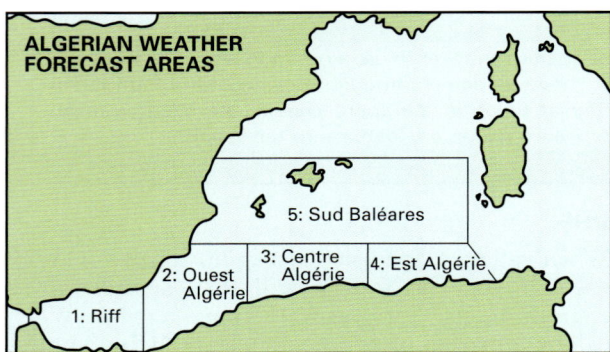

ALGERIAN WEATHER FORECAST AREAS

5: Sud Baléares
3: Centre Algérie
2: Ouest Algérie
4: Est Algérie
1: Riff

Non-radio weather forecasts
A forecast in Spanish can be obtained from the airport Met Office on each island (ask for *meteorologia*). Alternatively a pre-recorded marine forecast – the 'High Seas Bulletin' – includes the Islas Baleares and is available by telephoning Teletiempo (telephone numbers for meteorological maritime weather). By dialling the numbers below, a list of options will be given covering all Spanish sea areas.

Baleares   ☎ 807 17 03 70
Mediterranean   ☎ 807 17 03 71

An excellent forecast is given on all Spanish TV channels following the main morning and evening news. This is produced by the meteorological department of the Spanish military and are generally accurate. Channel TV1 gives best coverage with a full synoptic forecast, wind direction and 3-day outlook. News broadcast times vary depending on which channel is used and the length of the preceding adverts. Most national and local newspapers also carry some form of forecast.

All marinas and yacht harbours display a synoptic chart and forecast, generally updated daily (though often posted rather late to be of use if you want to get away early).

Weatherfax
Rome broadcast weatherfax transmissions covering the Islas Baleares and suitable for reception via SSB and computer or dedicated weatherfax receiver. Refer to the *Admiralty List of Radio Signals Vol 3 Part 1* (NP 283(1)) for times and frequencies.

Navtex
Navtex is transmitted on the standard frequency of 518kHz. The Mediterranean and Black Sea fall within NAVAREA III.

Valencia (Cabo de la Nao), Spain (Identification letter X)
Weather messages: 0750, 1950 (gale warnings, synopsis and 24-hr forecast, in English, for areas 8–12.
Navigational warnings: 0350, 0750, 1150, 1550, 1950, 2350 in English, for the Mediterranean coast of Spain and Islas Baleares.
La Garde (CROSS), France (Identification letter W)
Storm warnings: On receipt and at 0340, 0740, 1140, 1540, 1940, 2340, in English, for areas 14 (eastern part) 13, 6, 8, 9 and 10.
Weather messages: 1140, 2340 (gale or storm warnings, synopsis and 24-hr forecast, in English, for areas 514 eastern part-523, 531-534): see diagram for areas covered.
Navigational warnings: in English, for the northwestern Mediterranean only.

Weatherfax and RTTY
Northwood (RN) broadcasts a full set of UK Met Office charts out to five days ahead on 2618.5, 4610, 8040 and 11086.5kHz. (Schedule at 0236, surface analysis at three hourly intervals from 0300 to 2100 and 2300.)
Deutscher Wetterdienst broadcasts German weather charts on 3855,7880,13882.5kHz. (Schedule at 1111, surface analysis at 0430, 1050, 1600, 2200.)
DWD broadcasts forecasts using RTTY on 4583, 7646, and 10001.8kHz (in English at 0955 and 2155) 11039 and 14467.3kHz (in German at 0820, 1429, 2020). Alternatively, a dedicated receiver will record automatically – see 'weatherman' on www.nasamarine.com

Inmarsat
Broadcast times for weather for METAREA III are 1000 and 2200.

GRIB
This service enables arrow diagram forecasts for up to five days ahead, and other information, to be obtained in email form (or by marine HF and HAM radio). The data is highly compressed so that a great deal of information can be acquired quickly, even using a mobile phone connected to a laptop. For details of one popular service *Email* query@saildoc.com, subject 'any'.

Internet forecasts
Many internet sites give excellent forecasts. These are too numerous to mention and are added to daily. Few yacht skippers will be unfamiliar with these sites, but by typing into a search engine 'weather Med' many options will result. The Italian 'meteomar' is one of the best and http://meteonet.nl/aktueel/brackall.htm gives the latest UK Met office Bracknel synoptic chart of the whole Mediterranean. See also www.bbc.co.uk/weather/coast/pressure and www.inm.es. Of particular note are the sites:
www.inm.es/web/infmet/predi/metmar/bolmet.html
www.inm.es/web/infmet/predi/metmar/indpuer1.html
which give useful maps showing the wind speeds and wave heights for all of the coastal areas of Spain including the Balearic Islands and the Canaries).

See list of weather terms in English and Spanish in the *Appendix*.

SEA CONDITIONS

Currents

The current around the islands normally sets southeast, south or southwest at a rate of 0.5–1 knot, though stronger in the channels between them and off promontories. Its direction and strength can also be modified by the effects of strong or prolonged winds, those from the south tending to reduce or reverse the current and those from the north increasing the rate of flow.

Tides

Even at springs, tidal range is less than 0.3m, so can be disregarded. Sea level is more affected by the strength, direction and duration of winds and by variations in barometric pressure. In general, winds from the north combined with high pressure cause a fall in sea level and those from the south with low pressure cause a rise in the level. In addition, the levels in harbours or *calas* facing an onshore wind will be higher than in those experiencing offshore winds.

Even with these factors, the range of sea level is unlikely to exceed 1m, other than during a phenomenon known as *resaca* or *seiche*. This occurs rarely: usually when a depression and spring tide coincide. This causes a rise and fall of sea level by as much as 1.5m every ten or fifteen minutes; an oscillation which may last for several days. *Resaca* most often affects Puerto de Ciudadela, Menorca and the deeply indented harbours and *calas* on the southeast coast of Mallorca, but has also been experienced as far west as Puerto de Arenal in the Bahía de Palma.

For interest: an earthquake during 2004 in Al Hociema, Morocco, 400 miles away, caused a lot of damage in several marinas in the islands. Advance warning was given – though few understood its significance – when some harbours and the Mahón river suddenly dried out. The resultant surge of incoming water half an hour later was traumatic, leaving some boats several hundred metres inland and many trapped under pontoons.

Swell

Swell is not usually a problem in summer: winds are local and form a daily pattern of sea or land breezes, dropping at sunset. However, there are occasional gales which can quickly whip up high steep seas, though these usually are short lived. In early 2005, a large passenger ferry encountered 40-foot seas between Menorca and Corsica and sustained severe damage when the bridge windows were smashed and electrics disabled, but these conditions are rare. In July and August periods of flat calms are more often experienced. Swell from any direction can affect the Islas Baleares, and particularly the *cala* anchorages. A gale in the Golfo de León – common in winter – is likely to send a north or northeast swell of up to 2m down into the islands, possibly before the wind itself arrives. East or northwest winds can set in for days, making the east and north facing *calas* uncomfortable.

Scouring and silting

In passages and anchorages where the bottom is of loose sand, depths may change due to the effects of rainfall and wind.

Sea temperature

Sea temperature ranges from around 14°C in February to 25°C or more in August. Winds from the south and east tend to raise the temperature and those from the west and north to lower it.

Waterspouts

Waterspouts may occasionally be encountered in spring and autumn, usually near promontories and often associated with thunderstorms.

FLORA AND FAUNA ON THE ISLANDS

Much as on the Spanish mainland, pine trees and lavender can be smelled from miles offshore. Olive trees and several species of orchid, along with honeysuckle, abound. *Adelfa* (oleander) grow well in riverbeds, bringing colour throughout the summer season.

Birds

The Audouins Gull (rare elsewhere) can often be seen, particularly at San Antonio (Ibiza), Puerto de Andraitx, Puerto de Pollensa and Porto Colom (Mallorca), around Cabrera, and Mahón (Menorca). They are somewhat smaller than herring gulls, and have a large red beak with black tip and dark legs. Viewed from below in flight, the wingtips appear considerably blacker than those of a herring gull. The cry is a nasal 'gee-ow'. Herring gulls are common (though with yellow legs rather than the pink of their northern relatives), together with shearwaters and many land birds.

Poppies and daisies carpeting the earth in spring. Southeast Mallorca *GW*

An abundance of wildlife lives in the forests here, near Sóller
Graham Hutt

Birds of prey such as osprey and both species of peregrine and the very rare Eleanora's falcon favour the more wild and rocky stretches, including parts of Mallorca's north coast and that of the Cabrera group. Several species of owl, eagles, hawks and kites and the rare black vulture can be seen on the Formentor peninsula ridges.

The Albufera Nature Reserve, 4km south of Alcudia, is home to many rare waders and other water birds; a visit is recommended (and it is free!).

The publication *Essential Mallorca, Ibiza and Menorca* includes a particularly interesting section entitled 'Countryside and Wildlife on the Balearic Islands', detailing bird migration as well as the flora and fauna of the various habitats.

Animals

You can see sheep, goats, rabbits and horses throughout the islands. A rare frog-ferret can be found only on Formentor, Mallorca. Several different species of lizard abound on the islands, some being rare or none existent elsewhere.

Marine life

Several parts of the islands have been declared nature reserves and fishing is not permitted in those areas. This has done a lot to preserve fish stocks. Tuna and dolphins are often seen, along with grouper and sunfish.

NAVIGATIONAL INFORMATION

Buoyage

Buoys in the Balearics adhere to the IALA A system, based on the direction of the main flood tide. Yellow-topped black or red rusty buoys some 500m offshore mark raw sewage outlets.

Yellow or white buoys in line mark the seaward side of areas reserved for swimming. Narrow lanes for water-skiing and sailboarding, also buoyed, may lead out from the shore.

Harbour traffic signals

Traffic signals are rare, and in any case are designed for commercial traffic and seldom apply to yachts except in Ciudadela where everyone, including pleasure craft, must comply with the signals.

Storm signals

The signal stations at major ports and harbours may show storm signals, but many do not. With minor exceptions they are similar to the International System of Visual Storm Warnings.

Lights

The four-figure international numbering system has been used to identify lights in the text and on plans, the Mediterranean falling into Group E. As each light has its own number, correcting from *Notices to Mariners* or the annual *List of Lights and Fog Signals*, whether in Spanish or English, is straightforward.

Positions correspond to the largest-scale British Admiralty chart of the area currently available. All bearings are given from seaward and refer to true north. Where a visibility sector is stated this is always expressed in a clockwise direction.

Harbour lights, which in the Islas Baleares adhere to the IALA A system, are normally listed in the order in which they become relevant upon approach and entry.

Radio beacons

Many radio beacons are no longer maintained. Since the accuracy of GPS – even given the cautions below – is well above that which can be derived from radio beacons, this information is no longer included.

Depths around harbour entrances

Depths where known are shown on the harbour plans. It should be noted, however, that these can and do change, especially following onshore gales and if harbour entrances are open towards the prevailing wind sector. It also applies near rivers. Although most ports and harbours are dredged, there is no certainty about the depth to which dredging has taken place or when it was last done. Always proceed with caution, paying attention to the depth sounder on entry to any harbour.

Caution: important note on waypoints and location co-ordinates

Waypoints have been added in this edition to assist with passage planning and harbour approach. These should always be treated with caution.

The World Geodetic System 1984 is now the standard datum for all new charts and is used for all coordinates throughout this volume. Note, however, that many charts are in use with various datum systems. Ensure your GPS receiver is set to whatever datum the chart is using, or apply the appropriate correction as stated on the chart.

Positions given in the text and on plans are intended purely as an aid to locating the place in question on the chart.

Waypoint placements

Waypoints are named by the nearest charted point – usually a headland, harbour or *cala*. The coordinate given is usually located at least half a mile off the named point to act as a clearing coordinate or an approach coordinate.

Magnetic variation

Magnetic variation throughout the Balearics is now less than 001°W and decreasing further.

Charts

Current British Admiralty information is mostly obtained from Spanish sources. The Spanish Hydrographic Office re-issues and corrects its charts periodically, and issues weekly *Notices to Mariners*. Corrections are repeated by the British Admiralty, generally some months later. Spanish charts tend to be short on compass roses, so carry a chart plotter or rule which incorporates a protractor.

Before departure

Spanish charts can be obtained through certain British agents, notably

Imray Laurie Norie & Wilson Ltd, Wych House, The
  Broadway, St Ives, Cambs PE27 5BT
  ☎ +44 (0)1480 462114 *Fax* +44 (0)1480 496109
  www.imray.com

Orders can be made direct from

Instituto Hidrográfico de la Marina, Tolosa Latour 1, DP
  11007 Cádiz ☎ +34 956 59 94 12 *Fax* +34 956 25 85 84
Suisca SL, Avda Blas, Infante, Centro Blas Infante Local
  1,11201 Algeciras, Spain ☎ +34 902 22 00 7
  Fax +34 902 22 00 08 *Email* admiraltycharts@
  suiscasl.com

In Spain and Islas Baleares

The only British Admiralty chart agent in the Islas Baleares is

Rapid Transit Service SL, Network Yacht Team, Edificio
  Torremar, Paseo Marítimo, 44 – 07015, Palma de
  Mallorca ☎ 971 40 12 10 *Fax* 40 45 11
  Email rts@rapidtrans.com

In Mallorca, Spanish charts are stocked by

Libreria Fondevila, C/Costa de las Pols 18 Palma
  ☎ 971 72 56 16 *Fax* 971 71 33 26
  www.libfondevila.com
Casa del Mapa, Empresa Munic Informatica SA, Joan
  Maragall No 3, Palma ☎ 971 466061 *Fax* 971 77 16 16
Valnautica SL, Miquel Santadreu 10, Palma ☎ 971 46 49 90
  Fax 971 46 54 22

In Ibiza, Spanish charts of the islands are held by

Valnautica SL, Ibinave, Travesia del Mar, s/n, local 2, San
  Antonio ☎ 971 34 52 51 *Fax* 971 34 67 32
  Email ibinave@wanadoo.es

There is currently no approved Spanish chart stockist in Menorca.

Listing of a chart under both *Approach* and *Harbour* headings normally implies that a large-scale harbour plan appears as an insert on a smaller-scale approach chart. A complete list of available charts is included in the *Appendix*.

Pilot books

Details of principal harbours and some interesting background information appear in the British Admiralty Hydrographic Department's *Mediterranean Pilot Vol 1* (NP 45), updated and reissued in mid 2005. Harbour descriptions are also to be found in *Guia del Navegante – La Costa de España y el Algarve* (PubliNáutic Rilnvest SL) written in colloquial English with a Spanish translation. Published annually, it carries many potentially useful advertisements for marine-related businesses.

For French speakers, *Votre Livre de Bord – Méditerranée* (Bloc Marine) and *Les Guides Nautiques-Baléares* (Edition Eskis) may be helpful. In German there are *Spanische Gewässer, Lissabon bis Golfe du Lion* (Delius Klasing), *Die Baleares* (Edition Maritim) and others, though possibly out of date in some aspects. See *Appendix* for further details.

Presentation of information

Chart information

Much of the navigational information – lights, buoys, etc. – is better conveyed in the plans than by text. The text information has therefore been moved to the *Appendix* for those who want it.

Charts are the same for many adjacent ports. To avoid repeated lists of the same information, chart lists are given in the *Appendix* both by name and on island plans showing areas covered. Included are British Admiralty charts and those of the Spanish and French Hydrographic authorities. Imray M3 also covers the Balearic Islands.

Chart spellings, nomenclature and language

Charts and pilots are inconsistent in their spellings. Names appear in Castilliano, French, Catalan and English, often mixed or transliterated on the same chart.

An attempt has been made to standardise spellings to appear in Castilliano Spanish form where possible – the spelling normally used on British Admiralty charts – with local alternatives in brackets. Where there is no Castilliano form, the local name is used.

Many enterprises, including marinas, use different nomenclature to describe themselves. So, 'Puerto, Puerta and Port' can all be found along with 'Marina'. Since these are commercially registered names, these have been used. Many marine commercial enterprises are not quite what they seem. Several 'Marinas' are no more than a pontoon or two, with few facilities other than water and electricity. Some open beaches or *calas* (bays or coves) are also titled harbour, puerto or even sometimes, marina. To avoid confusion, since these are official names, they are named likewise here regardless of what they offer.

Words used to describe nautical locations are also variable, depending on which chart is used and even within the same chart. A cape may be called a 'point, punto, punta, pta, cabo, c', etc. As with island, which may be isl, isla, isloto, islota, the title used is as per the chart.

Information layout

Port information begins at the relevant capital, Palma, Puerto de Ibiza and Mahón, and moves in a clockwise direction around the island. With excellent international airports located close to these ports, this will be a natural starting point for the many who charter from, or keep their yachts in the islands.

Waypoints are noted in the text as they appear.

Harbour information

1. Co-ordinates of ports are usually taken from about midway in the entrance and given under *Location*. These should not be taken as waypoints.
2. Description of lights is sometimes changed from the *Admiralty List of Lights* if their description is not clear or is simply incorrect.
3. When two charts are listed for a port the first one is to scale (1:300,000) and the second to scale (1:60,000).
4. Some Admiralty charts give the tides as 'not exceeding 0.6m.' In practice the tides are usually less and are omitted.
5. Prices for harbour dues and hauling out, etc. are usually available on websites. Where known, web addresses are included.
6. Bearings are true and from seaward.
7. Depths are in metres.

PLANNING YOUR CRUISE

Time zone

Spain keeps Standard European Time (UT+1), advanced one hour in summer to UT+2 hours. Changeover dates are now standardised with the rest of the EU as the last weekends in March and October respectively.

Budgeting and finance

Though the islands are not cheap if harbours and marinas are used, most anchorages are free and cheap eating places can be found everywhere ashore. A Spanish custom, written into law, is that every restaurant must offer a *menu del dia* (lunch at a reasonable price). This is often a substantial meal with a set menu for less than €8, including wine. This law goes back to the Franco era when the country was poor. The islands' facilities cater for cruising yachtsmen on a tight budget to super-yachts, the latter abounding in places like Palma and Puerto Portals.

Credit cards can be used almost everywhere to draw cash from banks on presentation of a passport. ATM machines are fitted in most banks. Travellers cheques are taken in most banks. Cash in Dollars, Pounds Sterling and Euros is acceptable almost everywhere in banks and in many shops. €500 notes are not always accepted.

The unit of currency is the Euro, though prices are still often displayed using both the Euro and Peseta (€1=166.396 pesetas). Major credit cards are widely accepted. Bank hours are normally 0830 to 1400, Monday to Friday, with a few also open 0830 to 1300 on Saturday.

Medical advice

Vaccinations are not required. Take along any personal medicines or enquire about generic availability abroad via the internet. Many drugs normally restricted abroad are available here without prescription.

Though not a requirement, limited health insurance can be inexpensive and many yacht insurance policies include health cover for crew, particularly in the event of injury while on board. This can include repatriation to your home country for treatment.

Minor ailments may best be treated by consulting a *farmacía*, or by contacting a doctor (recommended by the *farmacía*, marina staff, a tourist office, the police or possibly a hotel). Medicines are expensive in Spain and often have different brand names from those used in Britain.

Apart from precautions against the well recognized hazards of sunburn and stomach upsets, heat exhaustion (or heat stroke) is most likely to affect newly joined crew not yet acclimatised to Mediterranean temperatures. Carry Dioralyte or similar to counteract dehydration. Insect deterrents, including mosquito coils, can be obtained locally.

Emergency medical treatment for EU/EEA nationals

The European Health Insurance card (EHIC) is valid for up to five years. This facilitates reduced cost or free emergency medical treatment under a reciprocal agreement between the countries of the EEA which in 2005 include the 25 EU member states plus Iceland, Norway and Lichtenstein.

If you are an EU/EEA national and qualify for a card, which is free, contact your Health Department several weeks before your planned departure date. UK nationals may apply to the Department of Health (DH) by post (forms available from post office branches), or phone ➀ 0845 606 2030, but the quickest method is via the DH website below (which also contains comprehensive information about the card and how to apply for it) whereby you should receive your EHIC within seven days:

www.dh.gov.uk/PolicyAndGuidance/ HealthAdviceForTravellers/fs/en

Be sure to see new EU regulations as of May 1st 2010.

(Other nationalities can run a web search: EHIC plus your country e.g. EHIC Italy.) For further enquiries, UK nationals may ring ➀ 08702 40 01 00 or from outside UK ➀ 0044 191203 55 55 or *Email* generalenquiries @cfsms.nhs.uk

For further details of Spanish medical protocols and emergency treatment access the DH webpage and click on: 'getting medical treatment around the world', followed by 'EEA and Switzerland', 'Country by country guide' and then select 'Spain (including the Canaries and Balearics Islands)'.

Medical emergency telephone numbers are ➀ 112 and ➀ 061. If you have an EHIC card, be sure to inform the medical authorities of this when first contacting them for emergency treatment or you may have to pay full private rates which might not not be reimbursed.

CRUISING THE ISLANDS

The whole island chain is a suitable cruising ground, though some areas have restricted access having been declared conservation zones. The island of Cabrera is one such place where buoys have been laid which must be used in lieu of anchoring in restricted zones, as is the National Park zone in Palma Bay. These zones are noted on the plans.

Anchorages

One of the main charms of the islands is the large number of attractive *cala* anchorages, although many are often crowded in summer. A down-sun approach using eyeball navigation with a lookout on the bow, equipped with Polaroid sunglasses greatly assists anchoring. Note that most of the anchorage plans (as opposed to those of marinas and commercial harbours) are derived from observation and virtually no official data is available. Depths, shapes, distances, etc. should be taken as approximate.

A number of *calas* have more than one name, whilst popular names, such as Cala Figuera, crop up several times.

The weather in the Islas Baleares can be unexpectedly changeable and can deteriorate very quickly. During the day the sea breeze can be strong, especially if there is a valley at the head of an anchorage. Similarly a strong land breeze can flow down a valley in the early hours of the morning. If anchored near the head of a *cala* backed by a river valley, should there be a thunderstorm or heavy downpour in the hills above, take precautions against the flood of water and debris which will descend into the *cala*.

Many *cala* anchorages suffer from swell even when not open to its apparent direction. This is because swell tends to run along the coast, curling around all but the most prominent headlands into the *cala* behind. Wash from boats entering and leaving, as well as from larger vessels passing outside, adds to the discomfort. If considering a second anchor or a line ashore in order to hold the yacht into the swell, first calculate the swinging room required by yachts on single anchors should the wind change.

In a high-sided *cala*, winds are often fluky and a sudden blow, even from the land, may make departure difficult. Plans for a swift and orderly exit – possibly in darkness – should be considered. This type of anchorage should only be used in settled weather and left in good time if swell or wind rise. It is unwise to leave an anchored yacht unattended for any length of time.

Anchoring technique

Choice of anchor: many popular anchorages are thoroughly ploughed up each year by the hundreds of anchors dropped and weighed by visiting yachts. Others are of weed-covered compacted sand and, not without reason, the four-pronged grab is the favourite anchor of local fishermen, though difficult to stow. A fisherman-type anchor is easier to stow and a useful ally. If using a patent anchor –

Danforth, CQR, Bruce, Fortress, etc. – an anchor weight (or Chum) is a worthwhile investment, encouraging the pull to remain horizontal.

Once in a suitable depth of water, if clarity permits, look for a weed-free patch to drop the anchor. In rocky or otherwise suspect areas, including those likely to contain wrecks, old chains, etc., use a sinking trip line with a float (an inviting buoy may be picked up by another yacht). Chain scope should be at least four times the maximum depth of water, for nylon scope double this. It is always worth setting the anchor by reversing slowly until it holds, but on a hard or compacted bottom this must be done very gently in order to give the anchor a chance to bite – over-enthusiasm with the throttle will cause it to skip without digging in.

Rescue and emergency services

In addition to VHF Ch 16 or 2182kHz on MW (MAYDAY or PAN PAN as appropriate) the marine emergency services can be contacted at all times on ☎ 900 202 202.

The National Centre for Sea Rescue is based in Madrid but has a string of communications towers, including one at Palma, Mallorca. On-the-spot responsibility for co-ordinating rescues lies with the Capitanías Marítimas with support from the Spanish Navy, Customs, Guardia Civil, etc. Lifeboats are stationed at some of the larger harbours but the majority do not appear to be all-weather boats.

The other emergency services can be contacted by dialling 003 for the operator and asking for *policía* (police), *bomberos* (fire service) or *Cruz Roja* (Red Cross). Alternatively the police can be contacted direct on 091.

Sea rescue/Rescate en alta mar emergency Salvamento notes

Search, rescue and salvage services at sea, as well as clean-up operations and the prevention of pollution, are undertaken by the National Society for Maritime Rescue and Safety (Salvamento y Seguridad

Puerto de Antraitx anchorage   *Graham Hutt*

INTRODUCTION

Marítima: SASEMAR). SASEMAR is co-ordinated by joint collaboration agreements between the following bodies:

The Spanish Navy, the Air Force SAR service – the Customs Coastguard Service, the Guardia Civil Maritime Services, the regional governments, the national telephone company's Maritime Service and the Spanish Red Cross.

SASEMAR works in close collaboration with the coastal stations of each town around the coast. These are equipped with rescue launches, 15m and 20m rapid intervention craft, small sized antipollution craft and rescue helicopters.

Anyone on shore who sees a boat in difficulties (signalling by waving arms or setting off flares, smoke or fire, etc.) should report to the appropriate rescue centre by calling Freephone ☎ 900 202 202.

Persons on board a ship in distress should radio for help on VHF Ch 16 or 2182kHz on MW. The correct procedure in Spanish is as follows:

1. MAYDAY ... MAYDAY ... MAYDAY ...
2. AQUI LA EMBARCACION ... (The name of your boat repeated three times)
3. ESTA EN LA SITUACION ... (Give your position) or ME ENCUENTRO A ... MILLAS DE ... (Give position as regards distance in miles or in journey time from any given point) Una (1), dos, tres, cuatro, cinco, seis, siete, ocho, nueve, diez (10))
4. NECESITO AYUDA URGENTE A CAUSA DE ... (Indicate nature of emergency)
   fire – *tengo fuego en mi barco*
   sinking – *mi barco esta hundimiento*
   man overboard – *hombre en agua*
   medical emergency – *urgencia medical*

Harbours of refuge

The following harbours and anchorages can be entered in severe weather, albeit with some difficulty. They are listed below with nearest waypoints.

Isla de Ibiza
Puerto de Ibiza	⊕2	38°53'.9N 01°26'.7E
Puerto de San Antonio	⊕10	38°58'.8N 01°17'.0E

Isla de Mallorca
Puerto de Palma	⊕31	39°33'.4N 02°38'.5E
Puerto Portals	⊕34	39°31'.5N 02°33'.8E
Puerto de Andraitx	⊕39	39°31'.6N 02°21'.4E
Puerto de Sóller	⊕44	39°48'.0N 02°41'.2E
Anchorage NW of Punta de la Avanzada, Bahía de Pollensa	⊕49	39°55'.0N 03°09'.0E
Puerto de Alcudia	⊕52	39°49'.9N 03°10'.3E
Porto Colom	⊕62	39°24'.7N 03°16'.2E
Cala Llonga	⊕63	39°22'.0N 03°14'.2E

Isla de Cabrera
Puerto de Cabrera (other than in a northwesterly gale)	⊕73	39°09'.5N 02°55'.6E

Isla de Menorca
Puerto de Mahón	⊕81	39°52'.0N 04°18'.6E
Puerto de Fornells	⊕96	40°04'.0N 04°08'.0E

Many other harbours and anchorages can safely be entered in strong offshore winds and even gales, and even more provide excellent shelter from most directions once inside.

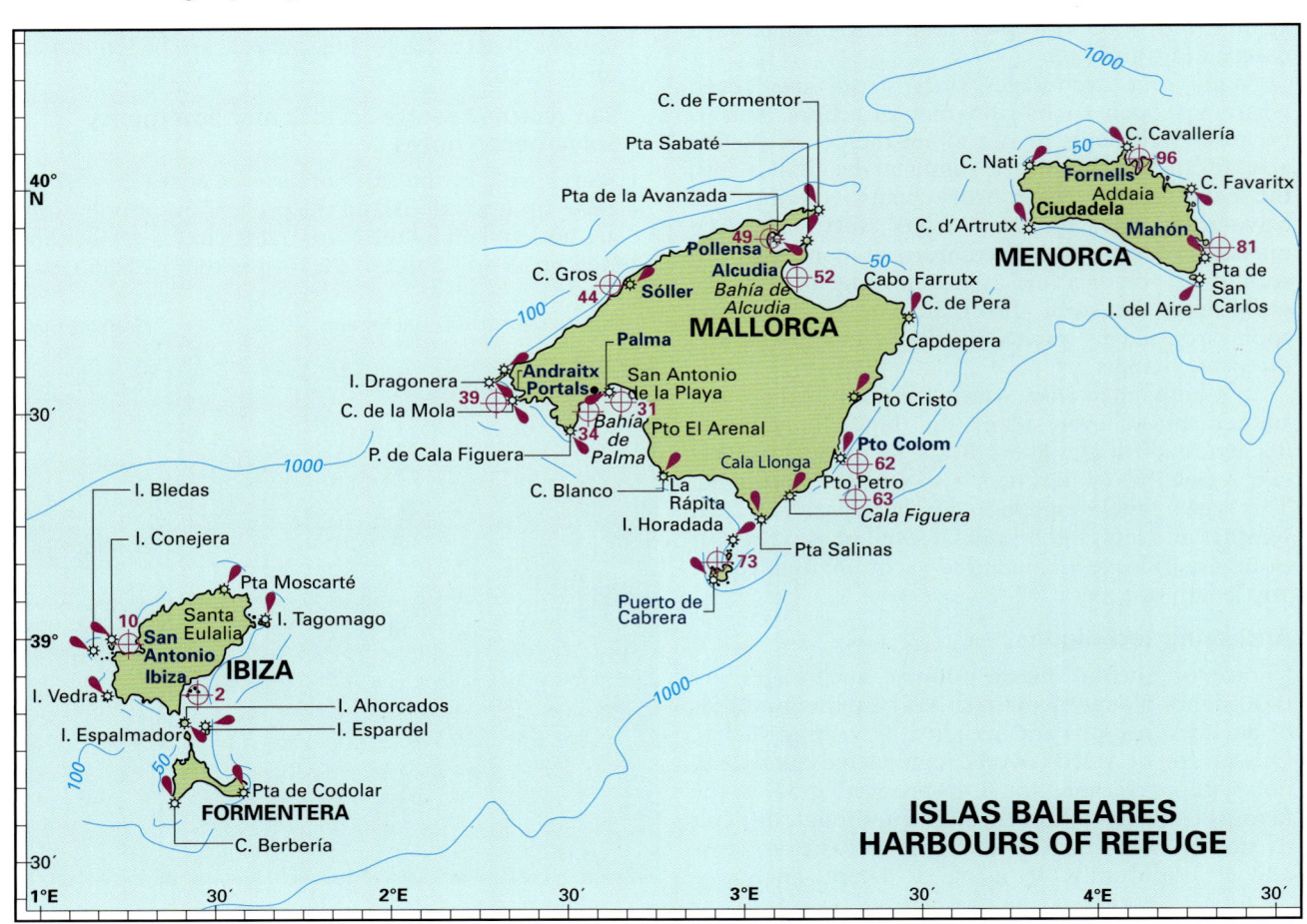

**ISLAS BALEARES
HARBOURS OF REFUGE**

The rescue centres lay particular emphasis on proper preparation as the best means of avoiding dangerous situations. It is essential to have the correct equipment, to have the necessary skill and experience, and to keep informed about weather conditions.

A shipping forecast is broadcast in Spanish, every two hours from Salvamento Marítimo's regional centres, and copies can be obtained from most yacht clubs.

The telephone and fax details of the sea rescue centre in Palma are ☎ 971 728322 / 722011 *Fax* 971 728352.

HAZARDS

Restricted areas

Anchoring and fishing is banned in the following areas due to submerged cables: Cala de Puerto Roig, Punta Grosa and north of Isla Vedrá in Ibiza, south of Cabo de Pera on the east coast of Mallorca and off Cabo Dartuch in southwest Menorca. Spanish naval vessels and submarines exercise around Isla de Cabrera and in the Bahía de Pollensa, Mallorca.

Night approaches

Approaches in darkness are often made more difficult by the plethora of background lights – fixed, flashing, occulting, interrupted – of all colours. Though there may be exceptions, this applies to nearly all harbours backed by a town of any size. Powerful shore lights make weaker navigation lights difficult to identify and mask unlit features such as exposed rocks or the line of a jetty. If at all possible, avoid closing an unknown harbour in darkness. A particular hazard is the green flashing light of the local pharmacy, which can be very confusing.

Skylines

Individual buildings on these developing islands – particularly prominent hotel blocks – do change with surprising frequency. With the greater use of waypoints and a more reliable accuracy of port coordinates, this should present no great problem these days.

Swimming areas

Many *calas* and beaches have large areas up to 50 metres from the shoreline roped and buoyed off during the summer. These areas are exclusion zones for all vessels and large penalties are extracted in fines for crossing them.

Tunny nets

In the past during summer and autumn, these nets anchored to the sea bed and up to six miles long, were a substantial hazard to yachts. Due to dwindling fish stocks and conservation zones, they no longer seem to be a problem around the Baleares Islands.

If found, they are normally laid inshore in depths of 15–40m but may extend several miles offshore. The outer end should be marked by a float or a boat carrying a white flag with an 'A' (in black) by day, and two red or red and white lights by night. There should also be markers along the line of the net. These nets, capable of stopping a small freighter, are expensive and are almost always accompanied by a patrol craft to ward off any unsuspecting vessels in the proximity.

Commercial fishing boats

Commercial fishing boats should be given a wide berth. They may be:
- trawling singly or in pairs with a net between the boats
- laying a long net, the top of which is supported by floats
- picking up or laying pots either singly or in groups or lines
- trolling with one or more lines out astern
- drifting, trailing nets to windward.

Do not assume they know, or will observe, the law of the sea – keep well clear on principle.

Small fishing boats

Small fishing boats, including the traditional double-ended *llauds*, either use nets or troll with lines astern and should be avoided as far as possible. At night many *lámparas* put to sea and, using powerful electric or gas lights, attract fish to the surface. When seen from a distance these lights appear to flash as the boat moves up and down in the waves and can give the appearance of a lighthouse.

Speedboats, etc.

Para-gliding, water ski-ing, speed boats and jet-skis are all popular, and are sometimes operated by unskilled and thoughtless drivers with small regard for collision risks. In theory they are not allowed to exceed 5kns within 100m of the coast or within 250m of bathing beaches. Water-skiing is restricted to buoyed areas.

Scuba divers and swimmers

A good watch should be kept for scuba divers and swimmers, with or without snorkel equipment, particularly around harbour entrances. If accompanied by a boat, the presence of divers may be indicated either by International Code Flag A or by a square red flag with a single yellow diagonal, as commonly seen in North America and the Caribbean.

PREPARATION AND PRACTICAL TIPS

Yacht and equipment

The type of yacht suitable depends entirely on the type of sailing envisaged, from a small motor yacht for coast hopping in good weather, to more adventurous voyages around the islands and to the mainland. Do bear in mind that there are often light winds, decreasing to no wind at night, or the occasional possibility of sudden strong or gale force winds, even in summer.

A yacht properly equipped for cruising in northern waters should need little extra gear, but the following items are worth considering if not already on board.

Batteries With sun all the year round, solar panels to keep the batteries charged will be useful, especially in summer if you cannot find a berth in a marina with services available.

Radio equipment In order to receive weather forecasts and navigational warnings from Coast Radio Stations, a radio capable of receiving short and medium wave Single Sideband (SSB) transmissions will be needed. Do not make the mistake of buying a radio capable only of receiving the AM transmissions broadcast by national radio stations, or assume that SSB is only applicable to transmitting radio tranceivers.

Most SSB receivers are capable of receiving either Upper Side Band (USB) or Lower Side Band (LSB) at the flick of a switch. Which band to use is determined by the frequency in use, as promulgated by international law and published by the UK Maritime Communications Agency. The UK Maritime Mobile Net covering the Eastern Atlantic and Mediterranean uses USB, and it is not necessary to have any licence to listen in. All Coast Radio Stations broadcast on SSB – whether on USB or LSB should be easy to determine by trial and error.

Digital tuning is very desirable, and the radio should be capable of resolving tuning to a minimum of 1kHz and preferably to 0.1kHz. Several companies (including Sony, Grundig and Roberts) market suitable SSB receivers in the UK via high street retailers and marine outlets. ICOM and Yaesu make more expensive marine receivers.

Ventilation Modern yachts are, as a rule, better ventilated than their older sisters though seldom better insulated. Consider adding an opening hatch in the main cabin, if not already fitted, and ideally another over the galley. A wind scoop for the forehatch helps increase the draught, particularly if the open hatch is not forward facing.

Awnings An awning covering at least the cockpit provides shade and protection for the crew, while an even better combination is a bimini which can be kept rigged whilst sailing, plus a larger 'harbour' awning, preferably at boom height or above and extending forward to the mast.

Cockpit tables It is pleasant to eat in the cockpit, particularly while at anchor. If nothing else can be arranged, a small folding table is an advantage.

Refrigerator/ice-box If a refrigerator is not fitted it may be possible to build in an ice-box (a plastic picnic coolbox is a poor substitute), but this will be useless without adequate insulation. An ice-box designed for northern climes will almost certainly benefit from extra insulation, if this can be fitted – 100mm (4in) is a desirable minimum, 150mm (6in) even better. A drain is also essential.

If a refrigerator is fitted but electricity precious, placing ice inside will help minimise battery drain.

Mosquito nets Some advocate fitting screens to all openings leading below. Others find this inconvenient, relying instead on mosquito coils and other insecticides and repellents. For some reason mosquitoes generally seem to bother new arrivals more than old hands, and anchoring well out will often decrease the problem.

Water A large extra water container or two should be carried in summer in case harbours are unable to offer a berth. Low cost watermakers are now available and could be considered.

Hose At least 25m. Standpipes tend to have bayonet couplings of a type unavailable in the UK so purchase them on arrival. Plenty of 5- or 10-litre plastic carriers will also be useful.

Deck shower If no shower is fitted below, a black plastic bag or even a bucket of water heats very quickly when hung in the rigging. (At least one proprietary model is available in the UK).

Communications

The GSM mobile phone system often functions several miles out to sea – particularly using one of the older types of handset – providing a link to the world even some miles offshore. With a computer interface, this can also provide Internet and email facilities. Ensure that the International Roaming facility is activated for use abroad. GSM call rates are usually cheaper than using local hotel phones.

Carry

Tools and equipment to hook up to continental-type electrical fittings. A selection of fittings and jubilee clips.

All charts, maps, guidebooks, and a Spanish dictionary.

Fenders and Warps

In marinas, mooring is usually bows or stern-to a quay or pontoon with a line tailed from the quay, so good clean fenders are required as it is often a tight squeeze.

PREPARATION – THE CREW

Clothing

The sun's rays at sea, especially in summer, are easy to underestimate and present a serious risk of burning. Direct sunlight, reflected light from the sea combined with salt air and wind, constitute a hazard to be avoided.

Lightweight, patterned cotton clothing is handy in this context – it washes and dries easily and the pattern camouflages the creases! Non-absorbent synthetic materials are best avoided. Until a good tan has been built up it may be wise to wear a T-shirt when swimming, while shoes give necessary protection against sea-urchin spines.

Some kind of headgear, preferably with a wide brim, is essential. A genuine Montecristi hat can be rolled up, shoved in a pocket and doesn't mind getting wet (they come from Ecuador, not Panama, which has usurped the name). A retaining string, tied either to clothing or around the neck, is a wise precaution whilst on the water.

Footwear at sea is a contentious subject. Many experienced cruisers habitually sail barefoot, but while this may be acceptable on a familiar vessel it would be courting injury on a less intimately known deck. In either case, proper sailing shoes should always be worn for harbour work or anchor handling. Decks (especially teak decks) may become unexpectedly hot and very painful to unprotected feet. If wearing sandals ashore, the upper part of the foot is a prime area for sunburn.

Winters can be wet and cold, and foul weather gear as well as warm sweaters, etc. will be needed. Even night sailing in summer can be unexpectedly cold due to precipitation.

Shore-going clothes should be on a par with what one might wear at home – beachwear is not usually acceptable in restaurants and yacht clubs.

AVAILABILITY OF SUPPLIES AND PROVISIONS

Fuel

Diesel (*gasoleo*, *gasoil* or simply *diesel*) is available in most marinas and yacht harbours in the Islas Baleares. A limited number also have a pump for petrol (*gasolina*). *Petróleo* is paraffin (kerosene). Credit cards are widely, but not universally, accepted – if in doubt, check before filling.

A concession for fishing boats that benefited yachts, was the provision of Gasoleo B. This carried a lower rate of tax making it considerably cheaper than the usual Gasoleo A. However, this tax exemption is being phased out to comply with EC tax laws.

Water

In many places drinking water (*agua potable*) is scarce and becoming increasingly more so each year. It is available at every berth, but expect to pay for it, particularly if supplied by hose, and do not wash sails and decks before checking that it is acceptable to do so. Many marinas insist on hoses being connected to a 'pistol' rather than being open-ended. In those harbours where a piped supply is not available for yachts a public tap can often be found.

Water quality in Mallorca and Menorca is generally good. However, water quality throughout all the islands varies from year to year. Locals nearly always drink bottled water, not so much because the *agua potable* is contaminated, but because it tastes better. Always check verbally and taste for salinity or over-chlorination before topping up tanks – the ideal is to have a tank specifically reserved for drinking water, with other tanks for general use. Failing this, earmark some cans for the purpose, but stow them in a dark locker to discourage algae. As most of the water in the islands is desalinated it can be quite corrosive, especially to stainless steel tanks and pumps, and a pre-tank in-line filter is highly recommended.

Bottled water is readily available in bars and supermarkets.

Note: Water quality in Ibiza has now been downgraded and is no longer considered fit for drinking.

Ice

Block ice for an icebox is widely obtainable – use the largest blocks that will fit – while chemical ice is sometimes available in blocks measuring 100x20x20cms. The latter must not be used in drinks, the former only after close inspection. Cube or 'small' ice is widely obtainable and generally of drinks quality, particularly if bought in a sealed bag. An increasing number of marinas and yacht clubs now have ice machines.

Gas

Camping Gaz is widely available from marinas, supermarkets or *ferreterias* (ironmongers); the 1.9kg bottles are identical to those in the UK. Its availability is therefore not usually listed in the text under individual harbour facilities.

REPSOL/CAMPSOL depots in Mallorca will not refill any UK (or any other country's) Calor Gas bottles even with a current test certificate. It is therefore essential to carry the appropriate regulator and fittings to permit the use of Camping Gaz bottles. Yachts fitted for propane systems should certainly follow this course. If in doubt consult Calor Services in the UK ☎ 0800 181 4530 www.calor.co.uk/customer-services/faqs/general-cylinder-queries.

Electricity

It is a good idea to be self-sufficient with solar panels and an inverter if planning to anchor a lot, or be prepared to run your engine on a regular basis.

Electricity is provided at every marina berth, the standard being 220V, 50Hz, generally via a two-pin socket for which an adapter will be needed. Some marinas provide 380V supplies to berths for yachts over 20m. If using 110V 60Hz equipment seek advice – cycles may be a greater problem than volts for some equipment, particularly those using motors. Even if the yacht is not wired for mains, a 25m length of cable and a trickle charger may be useful.

PROVISIONS

Food and drink

There are many well stocked stores, supermarkets and hypermarkets in the larger towns and cities and it may be worth doing the occasional major stock-up by taxi. Conversely, some isolated anchorages have quite literally nothing. As a rule, availability and choice varies in relation to the size of the town. Even the smallest has something and most older settlements (though not all tourist resorts) have a traditional-style market offering excellent local produce at very reasonable prices. Alcohol is cheap by UK standards with, not surprisingly, Spanish wines and spirits of particularly good value. Shop prices generally are noticeably lower away from tourist resorts.

Most shops, other than the largest supermarkets, close for siesta between 1400 and 1700 and remain closed on Sunday, though some smaller food shops do open on Sunday mornings. In larger towns the produce market may operate from 0800 to 1400, Monday to Saturday; in smaller towns it is more often a weekly affair.

Local gastronomic specialities include *ensaimadas*, flat spirals of flaky pastry ranging from one-person size to family-size – nearly two feet across! Everyone is familiar with *mahonésa* (mayonnaise), but possibly not with its cousin *aïoli* or *alioli*, a more powerful version made with garlic. An excellent way to sample unfamiliar delicacies in small portions is in the form of bar snacks or tapas, once served gratis but now almost invariably charged for, sometimes heavily.

Mallorca produces some local wines, including Binisalem and Felanitx, but most wine is imported from the mainland. Each island has its own apéritifs and liqueurs. Ibiza produces Hierbas, Rumaniseta and La Frigola, all made from herbs. Mallorca makes Palo from carob nuts, and Menorca specialises in gin: Bertram and Lord Nelson are the best known brands and are 70° proof.

EATING OUT

Every marina, port, harbour, village and even most semi-deserted bays have eating facilities too numerous to mention. In summer, *chiringhitos* spring up on every beach, offering fresh fish at decent prices.

Do consult some of the excellent guidebooks on the Balearics for more information.

HARBOURS AND MARINAS

The rapid growth of marinas in the 1990s was suddenly halted in 2000 because of environmental concerns. There are nearly 30,000 yacht berths in the islands and around 36,000 boats are cruising there in summer. During July and August, it is almost impossible to find a mooring in any of the harbours. The fact is that there are many more local yachts than berths available. Thus it is essential to radio (VHF Ch 09) or phone before arrival at a port to check if a berth may be available.

Future plans for new marinas or extensions

It is unlikely that any further major developments or new marinas will be permitted in the foreseeable future, though works are going on in several places to improve existing facilities.

Berthing

Due to the vast numbers of yachts and limited space available, berthing stern-to the quays and pontoons is normal (and allows easiest shore access). For greater privacy berth bow-to, which has the added advantage of keeping the rudder away from possible underwater obstructions near the quay and making the approach a much easier manoeuvre. An anchor may occasionally be needed, but more often a bow (or stern) line will be provided, usually via a lazyline to the pontoon, though sometimes buoyed. This line

may be both heavy and dirty and gloves will be useful. Either way, have plenty of fenders out and lines ready.

Most cruising skippers will have acquired some expertise at this manoeuvre before reaching the Islas Baleares, but if taking over a chartered or otherwise unfamiliar yacht it would be wise both to check handling characteristics and talk the manoeuvre through with the crew before attempting to enter a narrow berth. Detailed instructions regarding Mediterranean mooring techniques will be found in Imray's *Mediterranean Almanac*.

Mooring lines Surge in harbours is not uncommon and mooring lines must be both long and strong. It is sometimes useful to have a loop of chain made up at the shore end to slip over bollards, though in other places rings are in use. Carry plenty of mooring lines, especially if the boat is to be left unattended for any length of time.

Gangplanks If a gangplank is not already part of the boat's equipment, a builder's scaffolding plank, with a couple of holes drilled at either end to take lines, serves well. As it is cheap and easily replaced it can also be used outside fenders to deal with an awkward lie or ward off an oily quay. A short ladder may also have its uses, particularly if berthing bow-to.

Anchoring and Moorings

One of the principal attractions of the Islas, was the freedom to anchor almost anywhere: in a *cala*, approaches to harbours and often within the harbour itself. In order to capitalise on income to be gained from yachts anchoring, many marinas and harbours have laid moorings and prohibited the use of anchors altogether. This has now been extended to many of the calas around the islands.

A charge is made for the use of mooring buoys. Some are well served with rubbish collection and a water – taxi service to local restaurants, shops and other facilities. Others are quite isolated and served only by the local manager who turns up soon after arrival to collect mooring fees. Some complaints have been received about buoyage maintenance.

A colour coding exists to identify moorings for length of yacht. These are generally as follows: 'A' buoys are orange (up to 8m); 'B' are white (up to 15m).

Do note, however, that there is inconsistency in this, with some *calas* using red buoys to indicate yachts less than 10m and white for yachts over 10m. In Cabrera yet another colour coding system is in use with four bands, as noted in the relevant chapter.

Pricing for the use of buoys is different around the coasts and in some places, are free. There are nine additional areas where anchoring is forbidden and buoys have been placed, administered and run by the Baleareas government.

Reservations for the use of these buoys between June and September can be made at the web address on page 17, or ☏ +34 902 422 425 and enter No.1 to the voicemail prompt. It is advisable to book a few days in advance of arrival, particularly in high season. A pamphlet has been issued by the authorities showing buoyage zones and forbidden areas as well as giving booking information: www.balearslifeposidonia.eu (click on English – top right). Moorings covered on this site are free for the first two nights. Thereafter a fee is charged (if the warden collects it!) Clicking on each buoy will reveal its number and the maximum length of vessel permitted. See also Section 9 of the Appendix.

There is inconsistency in the prohibition of anchoring: some yachts have been fined for anchoring, whilst others have been permitted to stay in places marked as forbidden areas.

In some *calas*, buoys are seasonal, being removed during the low season. Buoys covering conservation areas are often moved, from one season to another, making it difficult to provide accurate information in this volume.

Note Anchor symbols have been deliberately left on the plans, even when buoys are laid, because these are often seasonal: laid between June and September.

Yacht clubs

Most harbours of any size support at least one *club náutico*. However, the grander ones in particular are basically social clubs – often with tennis courts, swimming pools and other facilities – and may not welcome the crews of visiting yachts. There is usually both a marina and a club, and unless there are special circumstances, the first option for a visitor is the marina. That said, many *club náutico*s have pleasant bars and excellent restaurants which appear to be open to all, while a few are notably helpful and friendly to visitors. The standard of dress and behaviour often appears to be somewhat more formal than that expected in a similar club in Britain.

Harbour charges

All harbours and marinas charge, at a scale which varies from season to season and year to year: sometimes even from day to day! Several marinas admit that prices increase if a regatta or some special event is in progress. July and August are normally considered to be 'high season', with some harbours citing May, June and September as 'mid-season' while others go directly to 'low-season' rates. During the low season, large discounts can often be negotiated, especially if paying in advance and with cash.

High-season charges vary from €35 to €200 per day for a 15m yacht and €20 to €70 for a 10m yacht but with berths at a premium in the islands, these figures may be greatly exceeded in some places. A banding system was used in the past to indicate prices, but it is so inaccurate and of little practical use, that it is now omitted. Many harbours and marinas have a website which gives up-to-date information of facilities, availability and prices. Use the web addresses supplied, 'Google' the name, or phone the marina for up-to-date information.

Public quays and club moorings

Many harbours have public quays, buoys or pontoons, administered by the port authority, rather than by the local *club náutico*. These are usually (though not always) charged at a lower rate. Anchoring is now prohibited or actively discouraged in all commercial (and some smaller) harbours. Where it is allowed, a charge will almost always be made.

Payment

Nearly all harbours accept payment by major credit cards (Amex, Visa, etc.) but where this is not the case it will be noted in the text. Multihulls are frequently charged up to 50% more than monohulls and some places are now charging by the (LOAxBeam) factor.

Large yachts

Many harbours in the Islas Baleares are too small, or too shallow for a large yacht, which must anchor outside whilst its crew visit the harbour by tender. It is essential that the skipper of such a yacht wishing to enter telephones or radios the harbour authorities well in advance to reserve a berth (if available) and receive necessary instructions.

Laying up

Laying up either afloat or ashore is possible at most marinas, though a few have no hard standing. Facilities and services provided vary considerably, as does the cost, and it is worth seeking local advice as to the quality of the services provided and the security of the berth or hard standing concerned.

The northwesterly *tramontana* (*mestral*) can be frequent and severe in winter and early spring, and this should be borne in mind when selecting the area and site to lay up. Yachts with wooden decks and varnished brightwork will need protection from the winter sun, and ideally arrangements should be made for the former to be hosed down each evening or covered with a tarpaulin. It may well prove cheaper to return to mainland Spain rather than to lay up in the Islas Baleares.

Repairs and chandlery

Many marinas are equipped to handle all aspects of yacht maintenance from laying up to changing a washer. Nearly all have travel-hoists and the larger marinas have specialist facilities – GRP work, electronics, sailmaking, stainless welding, etc. Charges may differ widely so, if possible, shop around.

The best-equipped chandleries will be found near the larger marinas, where they may equal anything to be found in the UK (though generally with higher prices). Smaller harbours or marinas are often without a chandlery, though some requirements may be found in the associated town. Basic items can sometimes be found in *ferreterias* (ironmongers).

Chartering

Chartering is a well-regulated business in the Islas Baleares with somewhat different regulations to those applied in mainland Spain: notably that there is no blanket restriction on foreign-owned and/or skippered vessels applying for charter authorisation. However the necessary paperwork is time-consuming and involved. See *Appendix* for further information.

Security

Crime afloat is not a major problem in most areas, and regrettably much of the theft which does occur can be laid at the door of other yachtsmen. It is sensible to take much the same precautions as at home: lock up before leaving the yacht, padlock the outboard to the dinghy, and secure the dinghy (particularly if an inflatable) with chain or wire rather than line. Folding bicycles are particularly vulnerable to theft, and should be chained up when not in use, even when on deck.

Ashore, the situation in the big towns is certainly no worse than in the UK, and providing common sense is applied to matters such as how handbags are carried, where not to go after the bars close, etc. there should be no problems.

The officials most likely to be seen are the *Guardia Civil*, who wear olive green uniforms and deal with immigration as well as more ordinary police work, the *Aduana* (customs) in navy blue uniforms, and the *Policía*, also in blue uniforms, who deal with traffic and civil disturbances rather than criminal matters.

FORMALITIES AND DOCUMENTATION

Formalities vary from place to place, but in general, if coming from another EC port, no formalities are expected other than checking in with the marina and officials, who are generally uninterested. If a vessel is entering from a non-EC country, or carrying non-EC nationals onboard, it is necessary to inform the local authorities, clear customs and complete immigration formalities when first entering the islands. Passports and the ship's registration papers will be required. A certificate of competence (or equivalent) and evidence of VAT status may also be requested.

Other documents sometimes requested are a crew list with passport details, the radio licence and evidence of insurance. Subsequently, at other ports, clearance need not be sought but the *Guardia Civil* (military police) may wish to see papers, particularly passports. Marina officials often ask to see yacht registration documents and the skipper's passport, and sometimes evidence of insurance.

Flag etiquette

A yacht in commission in foreign waters is legally required to fly her national maritime flag, normally the Red Ensign for a British yacht. If a special club ensign is displayed, it must be accompanied by the correct burgee. The courtesy flag of the country visited should be flown from the starboard signal halliard – note that in Spain, as in the UK, the maritime ensign and national flags are not the same. The Islas Baleares have their own regional flags which may be flown below the national courtesy flag if desired.

Under EU regulations, EU-registered vessels are not required to fly the Q flag on first arrival unless they have non-EU nationals or dutiable goods aboard. Nevertheless, clearance should be sought either by a visit to or from officials or through the offices of the larger marinas or yacht clubs.

Visas

As Spain is a member of the European Union, other EU nationals may now stay indefinitely. The requirement for a residence permit or visa was officially abolished as of 1 May 2006. However, some local authorities seem unaware of the changes and doubts have been raised about the working of the directive by some authorities.

Non-EU nationals wishing to remain in Spain may apply for a *permiso de residencia* and subsequent 90-day extensions.

With the high rate of illegal immigration and smuggling taking place throughout the Mediterranean, all yachts are now tracked by satellite. On entering harbour, a form is completed which often serves as the entry formality, with no officials involved.

Pet 'passports', along with up-to-date health check documents, are required but are rarely asked for.

Certificate of Competence

Like the pet 'passport', a Certificate of Competence, though a requirement by skippers of all Spanish vessels, is rarely asked of foreign visitors. Production of the RYA Yachtmaster's certificate is sufficient in most marinas for the form-filling. Note, however, that things are tightening up, principally as a result of the many jet-ski accidents, which has drawn attention to incompetent and unlicensed skippers of pleasure craft. The RYA will issue an internationally recognised Certificate of Competence on production of a Yachtmaster's certificate.

1. Given below is a transcription of a statement made by the Counsellor for Transport at the Spanish Embassy, London in March 1996. It is directed towards citizens of the UK but doubtless the principles apply to other EU citizens. One implication is that in a particular circumstance (paragraph 2a below) a UK citizen does not need a Certificate of Competence during the first 90 days of his visit.

2. a. British citizens visiting Spain in charge of a UK registered pleasure boat flying the UK flag need only fulfil UK law.

   b. British citizens visiting Spain in charge of a Spanish registered pleasure boat flying the Spanish flag have one of two options:

   i. To obtain a Certificate of Competence issued by the Spanish authorities. See *Normas reguladores para la obtención de titulos para el gobierno de embarcaciones de recreo* issued by the Ministerio de Obras Publicas, Transportes y Medio Ambiente.

   ii. To have the Spanish equivalent of a UK certificate issued. The following are used by the Spanish Maritime Administration:
   Yachtmaster Ocean: *Capitan de Yate*
   Yachtmaster Offshore: *Patron de Yate de altura*
   Coastal Skipper: *Patron de Yate*
   Day Skipper: *Patron de Yate embarcaciones de recreo*

Helmsman Overseas:* *Patron de embarcaciones de recreo restringido a motor*
*The Spanish authorities have been informed that this certificate has been replaced by the International Certificate of Competence.

3. The catch to para 2(a) above is that, in common with other EU citizens, after 90 days, a UK citizen is technically no longer a visitor, must apply for a *permiso de residencia* and must equip his boat to Spanish rules and licensing requirements.
In fact, many authorities refuse to grant residence to those living afloat because they are considered temporary. By the same token, the requirement for a British skipper in charge of a UK-registered pleasure boat flying the UK flag to carry a Certificate of Competence after their first 90 days in Spanish waters, also appears to be waived. However, since 2009 the Spanish authorities have changed these requirements but it is not known to which extent they are being implemented. See the *Taxation on foreign vessels in Spain* section.

4. The RYA suggests the following technique to obtain an equivalent Spanish certificate:
   a. Obtain two photocopies of your passport
   b. Have them notarised by a Spanish notary
   c. Obtain a copy of the UK Certificate of Competence and send it to the Consular Department, The Foreign and Commonwealth Office, King Charles Street, London SW1A 2AH, with a request that it be stamped with the Hague Stamp (this apparently validates the document). The FCO will probably charge a fee so it would be best to call the office first ✆ 020 7008 1500/0210 8438 www.fco.gov.uk
   d. Have the stamped copy notarised by a UK notary
   e. Send the lot to the Spanish Merchant Marine for the issue of the Spanish equivalent.

It may be both quicker and easier to take the Spanish examination!

VAT on yachts

Value Added Tax IVA – (*Impuesto sobre el valor añadido*), subject to certain exceptions, is levied at 16% of the value of the vessel unless it can be shown to have been paid or has an exemption certificate. To qualify for exemption, the vessel must have been launched before 1st January 1985 and have been in EU waters on 31st December 1992 (or, in the case of Austrian, Finnish and Swedish waters, 31 December 1994), with documents to verify these facts. A Single Administrative Document (SAD) certificate is issued if these credentials are ascertained.

Note that for VAT purposes the Canaries, Gibraltar, the Channel Islands and the Isle of Man are outside the EU fiscal area. See *Temporary import and laying up* below.

Any boat purchased outside the EU by an EU resident is liable for VAT on import to the EU.

EU owners of boats built within the EU, exported by them and which were outside EU fiscal waters at the cut-off date, may be entitled to Returned Goods Relief. In the latter case, HM Customs and Excise may be able to issue a 'tax opinion letter'. It is not, however, possible to obtain it from the UK authorities if the vessel is outside UK waters. All the rules change when a yacht is used commercially, most commonly for chartering.

Contact HM Customs and Excise ✆ 0845 010 9000 or +44 208929 0152 from outside UK. http://customs.hmrc.gov.uk

A boat registered outside the EU may stay in an EU port for up to six months before VAT must be paid, although this time period can often be extended.

All the above rules are open to differing interpretations and flexibility and the practices vary considerably from one country to another, and often from one harbour to another in Spanish waters.

Taxation on foreign vessels in Spain

During 2009, a new tax was implemented on foreign yachts based in Spain. The tax itself was not exactly new, but its enforcement and application to sailing craft was. The tax, known as *Impuesto de Matriculation* (IM), is a registration tax and is similar to that paid on motor vehicles when the owner has been in Spain for more than 183 days. The requirement is that the yacht be transferred to the Spanish register of craft following the payment of a 12% levy based on the Customs valuation – in exactly the same way as a motor vehicle is. Strangely, the authorities stopped short of demanding that the yacht be transferred to the Spanish register following collection of the IM. This is, however, the next step in the process. Please note that this has nothing whatsoever to do with VAT.

The tax is supposed to be applied to foreign residents of Spain with a yacht. However, another law entitles the authorities to consider anyone with property in Spain – including bricks and mortar, a yacht or car; or who has spent more than 183 days in the country – to be deemed 'Fiscally resident for the purposes of this tax' regardless of any other country residential status, or how long he spends in Spain.

Following the attachment of a sticker on the yacht by customs, (a *Precincto*) the onus is on the yacht-owner to prove that he cannot be considered fiscally resident i.e. he must not have property, (including the yacht in question!), accommodation – including rental accommodation – or a motor vehicle – to be considered free of the tax. This, as I discovered personally, is virtually impossible to prove. The authorities do not accept passport stamps in-and-out of the country (even if these are all outside of the EU). Neither would they accept a heap of airline tickets which were able to demonstrate frequent trips around North Africa totalling in excess of 183 days.

Finally, when pressed, I was informed that I had to obtain a *Certificate of non residence* from the British consulate in Malaga. I subsequently discovered that no such document exists. (And why would the British authorities hold such a register anyway!) Finally after much discussion and pushing, the local customs officer suggested that if I swore an affidavit in the local police station that I was neither a resident, nor with property in Spain; and had not spent more than the permitted 183 days of the year in the country in any year, I would be spared. Having completed this procedure, it was subsequently rejected by higher authorities!

Many foreigners have either moved their yachts out of Spain, with apparently thousands leaving the Costa Del Sol for Gibraltar, Morocco and the UK; or paid up. It can cost several thousand Euros to engage a lawyer to take care of the formalities and to arrange the full survey required by the authorities for their valuation. (I was quoted €4,000 as an 'advance.')

The *Aduana* (customs authorities) began their sweep and inspection of all yacht papers in the marinas on the Costa del Sol, in Southern Spain, but the intention is to sweep right through Spain. Islas Baleares are now the prime focus of the authorities, with many yachtmen having already left (late 2010).

To summarise: if you do not own or rent property in Spain, and do not own a car, and do not personally spend more than 183 days in a year in Spain or its waters, then your yacht should be spared this tax, however long it remains in Spain. You may, however, have to prove these negatives as facts, which is expensive and not straight forward.

Temporary import and laying up

A VAT paid or exempt yacht should apply for a *permiso aduanero* on arrival in Spanish waters. This is valid for 12 months and renewable annually, allowing for an almost indefinite stay. As well as establishing the status of a foreign-owned vessel, possession of a *permiso aduanero* should enable the owner to import equipment and spares from other EU countries free of duty.

A boat registered outside the EU fiscal area on which VAT has not been paid may be temporarily imported into the EU for a period not exceeding six months in any 12 before VAT is payable. This period may sometimes be extended by prior agreement with the local customs authorities (for instance, some do not count time laid up as part of the six months). While in EU waters the vessel may only be used by its owner, and may not be chartered or even lent to another person, on pain of paying VAT but see *Appendix* for further details. If kept in the EU longer than six months the vessel becomes liable for VAT, but there are huge differences in the way the rules are applied from one harbour to the next and in different countries, so check the local situation on arrival.

Insurance

Many marinas require vessels to have insurance cover, though third party only is usually all that is required. Many UK companies are willing to extend home waters cover to the Mediterranean, sometimes excluding certain areas.

On 1 July 1999 a requirement was introduced for all foreign yachts sailing in Spanish waters to carry third party insurance cover of at least £1,000,000 with all the details on the correct form in Spanish. UK insurance companies are aware of this requirement, and will issue, on request, the relevant document in Spanish. All kinds of unpleasantness, from a heavy fine to confiscation of the yacht can technically result from non-compliance. The law is not enforced currently, but would probably be in the event of an accident resulting in a claim.

Light dues

A charge known as Tarifa G5 is supposedly levied on all vessels in the islands. Locally based pleasure craft pay at the rate of €5 per square metre per year (area being calculated as LOA x Beam). Visiting pleasure craft pay one tenth of that sum on arrival, which covers a 10-day period, after which it is again due. Visiting vessels of less than 7m LOA and with engines of less than 25hp make a single payment of €30 per annum. The status of a charter yacht is not clear. In practice, this levy appears seldom to be requested and it is unclear to whom it should be paid.

MARITIME REGULATIONS AND RESTRICTIONS

Speed limit

All harbours have speed limits, usually 3kns or less. There is a blanket 5kn speed limit along the whole coast extending 100m offshore, increasing to 250m off bathing beaches.

Buoys

Yellow (usually) buoys are placed parallel to beaches in summer to indicate swimming areas. These can extend up to 100m off the beach, but are usually much closer. Anchoring or venturing beyond these towards the beach is strictly prohibited with heavy fines levied if contravened.

Water-skiing and jet-skis

There has been an explosive increase in the use of high powered outboards for water-skiing over the past decade, accompanied by a significant increase in accidents. In most of the main ports and at some beaches it is now controlled and enquiries should be made before skiing.

It is essential to have third party insurance and, if possible, a bail bond. If bathing and water skiing areas are buoyed, yachts are excluded.

Due to the number of fatal accidents in recent years, the use of jet-skis is now prohibited without a specific license to operate one.

Snorkelling

Spearfishing while using a snorkel is controlled and, in some places, prohibited.

Scuba diving

Inshore scuba diving is strictly controlled and a licence is required from the Comandancia Militar de Marina. This involves a certificate of competence, a medical certificate, two passport photographs, the passport itself (for inspection), knowledge of the relevant laws and a declaration that they will be obeyed. The simplest approach is to enquire through marina staff. Any attempt to remove archaeological material from the seabed will result in serious trouble.

Garbage

It is an international offence to dump garbage at sea and, while the arrangements of local authorities may not be perfect, garbage on land should be dumped in the proper containers. Many marinas now have facilities for the removal of holding tank waste (*agua negra*) and old engine oil.

Anchoring

It is prohibited to anchor within the confines of most harbours (except in an emergency or for a short period while sorting out a berth) and many authorities extend this prohibition to the bay areas outside. See under *Moorings* on page 16.

COMMUNICATIONS

Internet facilities

Internet cafés are located all over the islands with facilities also in many of the marinas. Modern mobile phones – especially those with GPRS access – can either connect to the internet directly, or through a computer. Wi-Fi is becoming more widespread. Some services are free, others are charged.

Telephone and Fax

International code +34
Local code for Balearics 971

Telephone kiosks are common, both local and *teléfono internacional*, and most carry instructions in English. Both coins and phonecards (available from tobacconists) are used – most kiosks accept either. American Express and Diners Club cards can also be used in some phone boxes, though oddly enough not VISA or Access. Mobile phones work throughout the islands.

Calls to the United Kingdom begin with the prefix 0044, followed by the area code (without the initial zero) and number; calls to North America with the prefix 001, plus area code and number. It may be necessary to pause after dialling the initial 00 to await a second dialling tone. The European International Operator can be accessed on 1008 and the Worldwide International Operator on 1005.

To call a Spanish number from abroad, dial that country's international access code (00 in the UK, 011 in North America) followed by 34, plus area code and number. If dialling within Spain it should be noted that the area code forms part of the number, with no digits dropped when dialling from abroad. A number prefixed with 6 denotes a mobile phone, e.g. 608 or 609.

Mail

Letters may be sent *poste restante* to any post office (*oficina de corréos*). They should be addressed with the surname of the recipient followed by *Lista de Corréos* and the town, island and Islas Baleares. Addresses of harbours can be found on the internet using the web address given in the text. Collection is a fairly cumbersome procedure and a passport is likely to be needed. Alternatively, most marinas and some *club náutico*s will hold mail for yachts, but it is always wise to check in advance if possible.

Uncollected letters are seldom returned.

Mail to and from the UK should be marked 'air mail' (*por avión*) but even so may take up to ten days, so if speed is important it may be better to arrange fax contact. Generally, mail speed in Spain is excellent, though some pockets of poor service remain. It takes much longer for mail sent locally to reach its desination than overseas mail. Post boxes are yellow, and stamps are available from tobacconists (*Estancos* or *Tabacos*) as well as post offices. Every town has a post office, so these are not listed under individual harbour facilities in the text.

Tourist offices

There is at least one tourist office in every major town or resort. They are graded as Provincial Tourist Office, one only in the Islas Baleares, at Plaça de la Reina 2, 07012 Palma de Mallorca ☎ 971 71 22 16 *Fax* 971 17 39 94 www.infomallorca.net; Insular Tourist Office, generally at the airport and well stocked with literature, maps, etc; and Municipal Tourist Office, to be found in most towns and usually listed at www.illesbalears.es

Of the many free handouts available, the A4-sized *I'd like to see you!* series published by The Balearic Institute for the Promotion of Tourism (IBATUR) is worth seeking out. Four beautifully illustrated booklets cover the main islands, giving a smattering of history, places to visit, fiestas, local folklore, island statistics and useful telephone numbers. Excellent value!

See *Appendix* for national tourist offices abroad.

Transport and travel

International airports Information is given in each island section. The three larger islands each have an international airport, Mallorca's being one of the busiest in Europe during the holiday season. There are still some real bargains to be found amongst charter flights from the UK.

Ferries Listed under each island. Ferries run to mainland Spain, France and Italy and there are frequent inter-island ferry and hydrofoil services. The largest ferry company is Trasmediterránea with offices at Palma, Ibiza and Mahón.

Almost every community has some form of public transport, if only one *autobús* a day.

Trains Surprisingly, Mallorca boasts two railway lines – one is narrow-gauge, dating back to Victorian times, which links Palma to the town of Sóller in the north, the final connection to Puerto de Sóller being completed by vintage tram. The other line runs from Palma to Inca, about halfway to Alcudia. Both are recommended for the experience and as a means of seeing some of Mallorca's unspoilt interior.

Taxis Are easily found in the tourist resorts though less common outside them, but can always be ordered by telephone. Car hire is simple, but a full national driving licence, preferably the new one with photo, must be shown.

Embassies

See *Appendix* for listing of British and American representation in the Balearics and Spain.

Approaches to the Islas Baleares

General

With the exception of a few inshore rocks and islands, and shallow water at the heads of bays, there is generally deep water up to the coast with few offshore dangers. The islands, by virtue of their height and the usual good visibility, can often be seen from many miles away and are well lit at night. The channels between the islands are free from obstructions, but in the strong winds that blow between Mallorca and Menorca, the sea can be rough due to a shallow and uneven bottom. The passage from the mainland to the islands presents no particular problems with the one exception of the north or northwest *tramontana* or *mestral* which can be dangerous in winter and unpleasant in summer.

From the Spanish coast

From west and southwest The shortest passage from mainland Spain is from Puerto de Jávea or Puerto de Denia to Puerto de San Antonio, Ibiza, at about 55 miles. Should a *tramontana* arise during the crossing it will be on the beam or the quarter and San Antonio can, if necessary, be entered under gale conditions. For a flatter approach and better protection once in harbour, it would be wise to continue around the island to Puerto de Santa Eulalia or Puerto de Ibiza.

From northwest and north From the Spanish coasts between Valencia and Barcelona, a choice of islands is offered at distances of 80 miles plus. The usual route is to leave the Spanish coast near Barcelona and to sail for Puerto de Andraitx (110 miles). If the *tramontana* or *mestral* blows it will be on the stern or quarter. Puerto de Andraitx can be entered in almost any conditions. In good and settled weather Puerto de Sóller is nearer but, because the coast on either side is very dangerous, accurate navigation is vital. Note also the *Caution* on the following page.

DISTANCES BETWEEN PORTS IN NAUTICAL MILES

MALLORCA	MENORCA Ciudadela	MENORCA Fornells	MENORCA Mahón	IBIZA Ibiza	IBIZA S Antonio	FORMENTERA Puerto de Sabina
Palma	87	106	100	69	77	78
Cala Bona	32	50	49	106	115	112
Cala d'Or	47	65	61	90	99	96
Cala Figuera	66	85	79	74	84	82
Cala Gamba	85	104	98	70	78	79
Cala Nova	87	106	100	67	75	76
Cala Ratjada	25	43	44	112	121	118
Ca'n Pastilla	84	103	97	70	78	79
Ca'n Picafort	34	51	56	121	125	129
Colonia San Jordi	63	82	76	77	87	85
Colonia San Pedro	32	49	54	122	126	130
El Arenal	82	101	95	71	79	80
Bonaire	35	51	62	119	123	127
Molinar de Levante	86	105	99	69	72	78
Islote El Toro	84	108	102	60	69	69
Estanyol	70	89	83	70	80	79
Palma Nova	87	106	100	65	73	74
P. d'Alcudia	35	51	60	119	123	127
P. Andraitx	81	96	108	59	63	67
P. Pollensa	35	61	62	119	123	127
P. Sóller	56	71	83	81	85	89
Portals Vells	86	105	99	61	69	70
Portixol	86	105	99	69	77	78
Porto Colom	44	62	60	93	101	99
Porto Cristo	36	54	52	101	110	107
Porto Petro	48	66	62	89	98	95
P. de la Rapita	67	86	80	74	84	82
Sta Ponsa	92	111	105	61	69	70
Serra Nova	32	49	54	122	126	130
Ciudadela		22	33	136	147	144
Fornells			20	155	166	163
Mahón				149	160	157
Ibiza					27	11
S Antonio						25
Puerto de Sabina						

From the French coast

Menorca is the nearest island to the French coast, being 170 miles from Port Vendres, 210 miles from Sète and Toulon and 270 miles from Nice. Probably the safest route is from the area of Cap Béar to Mahón, which can safely be entered in gale conditions. Should a *tramontana* blow it will be on the stern or quarter, and should this occur in the early part of the voyage the Spanish coast can be closed for shelter. Again, note the *Caution* below.

From the eastern Mediterranean

For yachts on passage from Sardinia, Tunisia, Malta or further east, Mahón is the obvious choice for arrival. Distances are approximately 200 miles from the west coast of Sardinia, 360 miles from Tunis and 550 from Valletta, Malta. Should a *tramontana* affect the last part of the passage it will of course be directly on the nose but the landfall will be relatively sheltered. Conversely a southerly *sirocco* will be on or aft of the beam but may give rise to poor visibility.

Caution

The two lights marking the north end of the channel between Mallorca and Menorca have similar characteristics and are easy to confuse. Cabo Formentor (Mallorca) shows Fl(4)20s while Cabo Nati (Menorca) is Fl(3+1)20s. When running towards the islands in a *tramontana*, mistaken identification could lead to a dangerous situation.

The Almudaina palace, Palma, displaying splendid Arab-style architecture from a bygone era   *GW*

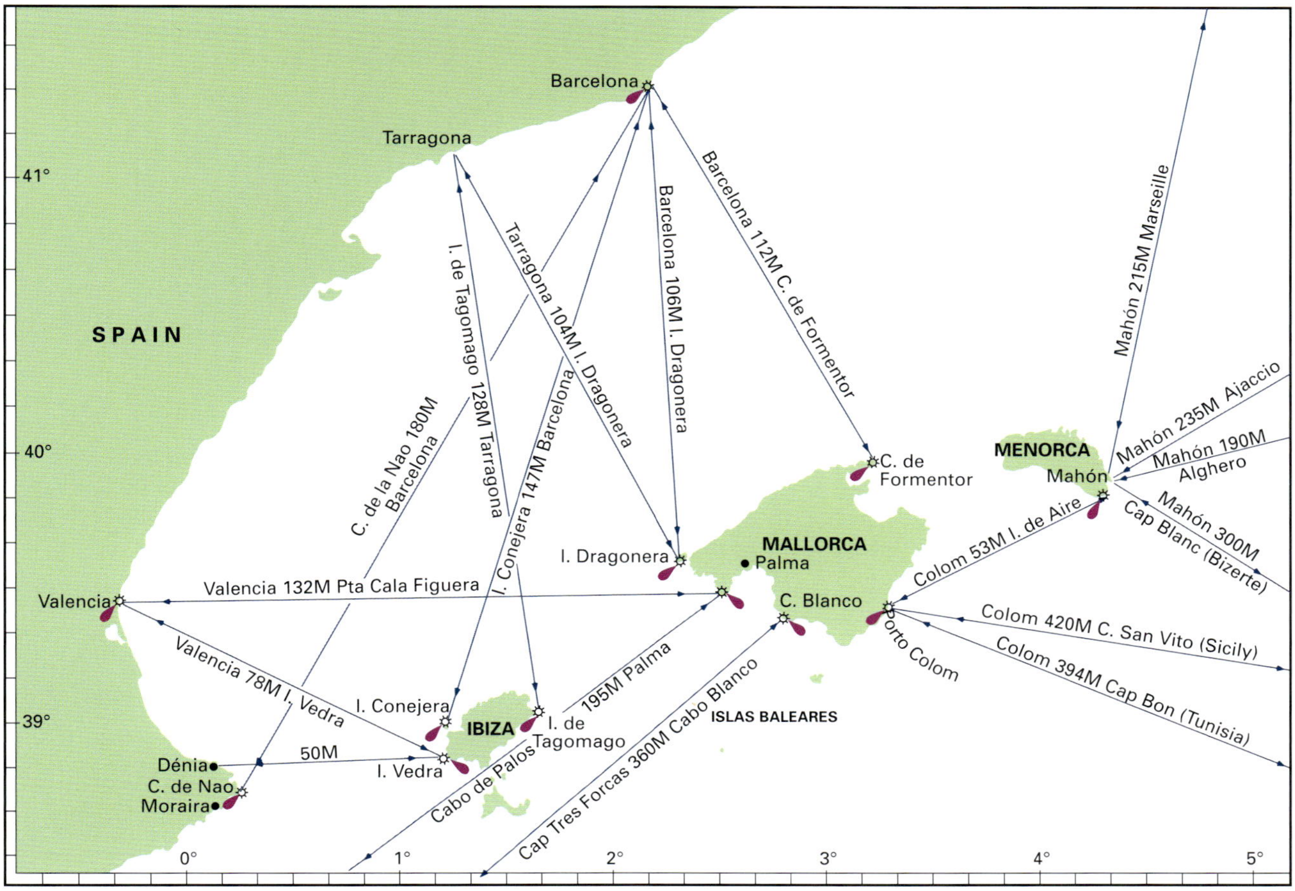

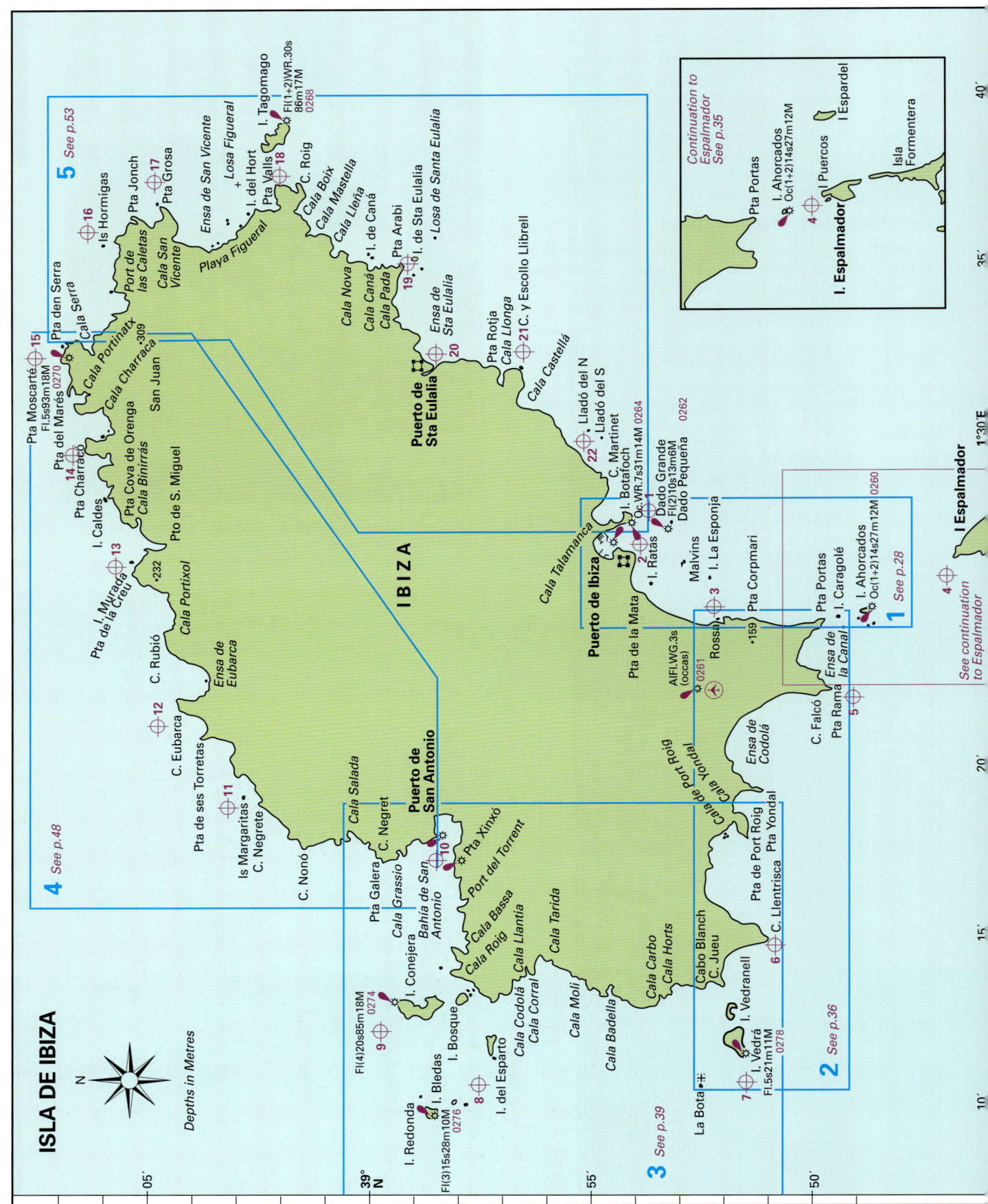

ISLA DE IBIZA

N

Depths in Metres

I B I Z A

Puerto de Ibiza

Puerto de Sta Eulalia

Puerto de San Antonio

39° N

05'

55'

50'

Continuation to Espalmador See p.35

Pta Portas

I. Ahorcados
Oc(1+2)14s27m12M

I Puercos

I Espardel

Isla Formentera

I. Espalmador

I Espalmador

See continuation to Espalmador

1 See p.28

2 See p.36

3 See p.39

4 See p.48

5 See p.53

Pta Moscarté 15
Fl.5s93m18M 0270

Pta del Marés
14 Pta Charraco

I. Caldes

13 I, Murada
Pta de la Creu

232

C. Eubarca
12

Pta de ses Torretas
11 Is Margaritas
C. Negrete

C. Nonó

I. Redonda
Fl(3)15s28m10M 0276

Fl(4)20s85m18M 0274
9 I. Bledas
8 I. del Esparto
I. Bosque

I. Conejera

Pta Galera
Cala Grassio
Bahia de San Antonio
10 Pta Xinxó
Port del Torrent

Cala Salada
C. Negret

Cala Bassa
Cala Roig
Cala Llantia
Cala Corral
Cala Codolá
Cala Moli
Cala Badella
Cala Tarida
Cala Horts
Cala Carbo

Cabo Blanch
C. Jueu

6 C. Llentrisca
Pta de Port Roig
Pta Yondal
Cala Yondal
Cala de port Roig

I. Vedranell
I. Vedrá
Fl.5s21m11M 0278
7

La Bota

C. Falcó
Ensa de Codolá

Pta Rama
Ensa de la Canal

Pta Portas
I. Caragolé
I. Caragolé

I. Ahorcados
Oc(1+2)14s27m12M 0260
4

5

Pta Corpmari
3 Rossa
159
AlFl.WG.3s (occas) 0261

Malvins
I. La Esponja
I. Ratas
2
I. Botafoch
Qc.WR.7s31m14M 0264
Dado Grande
Fl(2)10s13m6M
Dado Pequeña
0262

Cala Talamanca
Pta de la Mata

Lladó del N
22 Lladó del S
C. Martinet

21 C. y Escollo Llibrell
Cala Castellá
Cala Llonga
Pta Rotja
Ensa de Sta Eulalia
20 Losa de Santa Eulalia
I. de Sta Eulalia

19 Pta Arabi
I. de Caná
Cala Pada
Cala Caná
Cala Nova

Cala Lleña
Cala Mastella
Cala Boix
C. Roig 18 Pta Valls
I. del Hort
+ Losa Figueral
I. Tagomago
Fl(1+2)WR.30s 86m17M 0268

17 Pta Grosa
Pta Jonch
16 Is Hormigas

Ensa de San Vicente
Port de las Caletas
Cala San Vicente
Playa Figueral

Pta den Serra
Cala Serra
Cala Portinatx
309
Cala Charraca
Cala Binirás
San Juan
Pto de S. Miguel
Cala Cova de Orenga
Cala Portixol
Ensa de Eubarca
C. Rubió

40'
35'
20'
15'
10'
05'
1°30'E

I. Ibiza

Ensenada Codolar

Although a magnet for young nightclubbers and hordes of summer holiday-makers, Ibiza has much to offer the yachtsman year-round. Scenic anchorages abound and all facilities are available at the major marinas of Puerto de Ibiza and the breathtaking Puerto de San Antonio. The pine forests inland inspired the Romans to name the group Pityusae: the Pine Islands

SECTION HEADINGS

The coastline is considered in a clockwise direction around the island beginning at Puerto de Ibiza

1. **Puerto de Ibiza to Punta Portas (including Espalmador)**
2. **Ensenada de la Canal to Isla Vedrá**
3. **Cabo Jueu to Puerto de San Antonio**
4. **Cala Grassió to Pta Moscarté**
5. **Pta Den Serra to Islote Botafoch**

IBIZA WAYPOINTS

⊕1	E Approach to Puerto de Ibiza	38°53'.7N 01°27'.5E
⊕2	Puerto de Ibiza	38°53'.9N 01°26'.7E
⊕3	Isla Sal Rossa	38°52'.2N 01°24'.8E
⊕4	Freu Grande channel	38°48'.6N 01°25'.6E
⊕5	Punta Rama	38°49'.5N 01°22'.0E
⊕6	Cabo Llentrisca	38°51'.0N 01°14'.7E
⊕7	Isla Vedrá W	38°51'.7N 01°10'.8E
⊕8	Isla del Esparto W	38°57'.5N 01°10'.4E
⊕9	Isla Conejera NW	38°59'.7N 01°12'.5E
⊕10	Puerto de San Antonio	38°58'.8N 01°17'.0E
⊕11	Islas Margaritas (Margalides) W	39°03'.0N 01°18'.6E
⊕12	Cabo Eubarca	39°04'.6N 01°21'.4E
⊕13	Isla Murada	39°05'.8N 01°25'.9E
⊕14	Punta Charracó	39°06'.7N 01°29'.4E
⊕15	Punta Moscarté	39°07'.4N 01°32'.0E
⊕16	Islas Hormigas	39°06'.3N 01°35'.5E
⊕17	Punta Grosa	39°05'.0N 01°37'.0E
⊕18	Between Punta Valls and Isla Tagomago	39°02'.2N 01°37'.7E
⊕19	Isla de Santa Eulalia	38°59'.3N 01°34'.9E
⊕20	Puerto de Santa Eulalia	38°58'.6N 01°32'.5E
⊕21	Cabo y Escollo Llibrell	38°56'.6N 01°32'.0E
⊕22	Lladó del Norta W	38°55'.4N 01°29'.5E

Navigational information for approaches to Ibiza

All offlying dangers, including Islas Bledas and Isla Vedrá to the west and Isla Tagomago to the east are well covered in this chapter.

Magnetic variation

Ibiza – Now less than 1°W, decreasing (2010)

Approach and coastal passage charts

(See *Appendix* for full list of Balearic charts)
Imray	M3, M12, M13
Admiralty	1701, 1702, 2834
Spanish	7A, 478, 479
French	5505, 7114

Approach lights

0261 **Aeropuerto** 38°52'.7N 01°22'.3E Aero AlFl.WG.3s16m Control tower 9m Occas Situated 1M inland

0278 **Isla Vedrá** 38°51'.9N 01°11'.5E Fl.5s21m11M White conical tower 3m 262°-vis-134°

0276 **Islote Bleda Plana** 38°58'.9N 01°10'.5E Fl(3)15s28m10M White round tower 8m 349°-vis-239°

0274 **Isla Conejera** 38°59'.7N 01°12'.9E Fl(4)20s85m18M White tower and building 18m

0268 **Islote Tagomago** 39°02'.1N 01°38'.9E Fl(1+2)WR.30s86m17M White octagonal stone tower on building 23m 043.5°-W-037°-R-043.5° (red sector covers Losa de Santa Eulalia)

0270 **Punta Moscarté** 39°06'.8N 01°32'E Fl.5s93m18M White round tower, black diagonal stripes 52m 074°-vis-294°

INTRODUCTION

Ibiza, the most westerly of the Islas Baleares, lies 50 miles off Cabo de la Nao on the Spanish mainland. It is 26 miles long and 16 miles wide and covers an area of 22 square miles. The northern half and the southwestern extremity are mountainous, the highest point being Atalayasa at 475m. There are three true harbours and hundreds of small anchorages around the coast which, with the exception of some stretches of low sandy beaches on the south and southeast sides, is very rugged and broken. Rocky cliffs are interspersed with numerous *calas* (literally coves, but in practice often wide bays), many with small sandy beaches at their heads.

The Romans named the island group the Pityusae (Pine Islands), which is as appropriate today as it was 2,000 years ago. Inland, Ibiza is green and fertile with carpets of flowers in the spring and many pine forests throughout. In common with the rest of the archipelago, Ibiza receives huge numbers of holidaymakers each summer and many of the formerly deserted and exquisitely beautiful *calas* are now surrounded by hotels and holiday apartments as in all the Mediterranean. The permanent population of Ibiza is around 72,000, more than a third of whom live in the capital, Ibiza (Eivissa). Hotels, apartments and guest houses throughout the island have the capacity to accommodate a further 65,000 visitors.

The ancient Moorish castle and D'Alt Vila (old town), at the head of Ibiza port   *GW*

HISTORY

Like many parts of the Mediterranean, Ibiza has experienced waves of invasion and settlement throughout its history.

Neolithic pottery discovered in a cave near Cala Vicente indicates that the inhabitants at the time of the early Bronze Age were Iberian; this is borne out by drawings on the walls in a cave at the foot of Cabo Nono. But by 1200BC the civilisations of the eastern Mediterranean were spreading westwards and there are many objects of Phoenician and Carthaginian origin, such as bronze axes and discs from San Juan, Salinas and Formentera, as well as figures from the Cave of Es Cuyeram, once a temple dedicated to the goddess Tanit.

The city of Ibiza was founded during the 6th century BC by the Carthaginians, who are thought to have fortified the hill now known as D'Alt Vila (the old town) and to have given both town and island the name Ibasim. There is evidence to show that agriculture was improved, tunny fishing and olive cultivation were introduced and the manufacture of purple dye from murex molluscs commenced. By the 3rd century BC the island was minting its own coinage.

It is claimed that Isla Conejera, off the west coast of Ibiza, was the birthplace of the Carthaginian general Hannibal. Certainly the inhabitants of the Islas Planas, part of the Islas Bledas group, were known for their skill at stone slinging and a number of slingers were recruited for the armies of Hannibal in his fight against Rome. As Rome gradually became the victorious power, both Ibiza and Formentera recognised her sovereignty and became city states within the Roman Empire under the name Pityusae (the Pine Islands), as mentioned above.

Other than the name Ebysos there is little remaining evidence of the Greeks in Ibiza, but the Romans brought prosperity to the island, later renamed Ebusus, founding saltworks at Salinas and lead mines at San Carlos. They boosted agriculture by taking shipments of corn to Rome, also built an aqueduct, and a new citadel on the site of the old Carthaginian fortress.

With the fall of Rome, Ibiza suffered the same fate as other satellite countries, being occupied throughout the centuries by various different groups. Raids by the Vandals drove many inhabitants away to seek refuge on the mainland. In AD426 a Barbarian tribe called the Gunderic occupied the island until the great Byzantine sailor Admiral Belisarius captured it in 535.

The Moors, who at first found the island useful as a base for raids on shipping and the mainland, arrived from North Africa in 707 and remained for more than 500 years. To them the island was

Yebisah. The Vikings attempted an invasion in 857 as did Charlemagne in 798–801, but the Moors managed to hold on until 1235 when Ibiza was eventually reconquered by a force under Guillem de Montgrí, Bishop of Tarragona; backed by King Jaime I of Catalonia. The Moorish influence is still evident in the architecture, customs and traditional dress of the islanders and the presence of Catalonian in their language, from which the Ibizan dialect is derived; and the origin of the island name Eivissa.

Ibiza's return to Christian rule failed to bring peace, and the island was subject to much fighting during the period of Spanish internal strife. In 1492 the whole of Spain, including Ibiza, became united under King Ferdinand and Queen Isabella, but for another two centuries attacks on the island by Barbary pirates, Moors and Turks were frequent. Watchtowers were kept permanently manned, the present city walls were built and cavalry patrols were established. Even village churches were fortified.

After a period being part of the Kingdom of Mallorca, Ibiza reverted to Catalonian rule, but then backed the losing side in the War of the Spanish Succession (1702–14) and was made into a Spanish province as a result. It gradually became a cultural and economic backwater, emigration adding to a population decline begun by the Black Death 400 years earlier.

Recent history

During the Spanish Civil War Ibiza declared allegiance to Franco, only to be rebuffed by the Republicans and was occupied for a six-week period when considerable damage was done to churches and other buildings.

In the past, Ibiza's main wealth came from the export of 'red' salt which was particularly valued. Even today over 100,000 tons are exported each year. Fruit, grain and shellfish are other exports of importance. During the last fifty years the tourist trade has expanded into a major industry and the island, which was in the past a haven for the simple life and values, has been dragged into the 21st century. In particular both Ibiza and Formentera became favourites with the so-called 'hippie' culture, a legacy still evident in a marked tolerance towards unusual clothes and non-mainstream lifestyles. The construction of apartment blocks for tourists is finally slowing, together with large numbers of tourist shops, cafés, bars, restaurants and related services. The local authorities have realised, perhaps a little late, that ever-expanding tourism brings with it a heavy environmental price. It is hard, though, to dent the pleasure and joy the sea brings. Little changes that fact.

TOURIST INFORMATION

Places of particular interest on Ibiza

The church of Nostra Señora in the small village of Jesús just north of Ibiza city contains a famous (and very beautiful) altarpiece dating back to the early 16th century.

In the northern part of the island lie Balafia, a fortified Moorish village just outside San Lorenzo, and the Es Cuyeram cave which was once a Carthaginian temple to the goddess Tanit (also accessible from the anchorage at Cala de San Vicente). In the southwest, the Carthaginian and Roman remains at Ses Països de Cala d'Hort (near Cala Horts) make an interesting visit. Inland lies Ibiza's highest point, Atalayasa, near the village of San José. Further east, on the road to Ibiza, are the caves of Cova Santa, also accessible via a track from Cala Yondal.

For details of tourist offices see the *General Introduction*.

Embassies

See *Appendix*.

Cala Llonga. A sheltered anchorage in all but east winds, on the southeast side of the island   *GW*

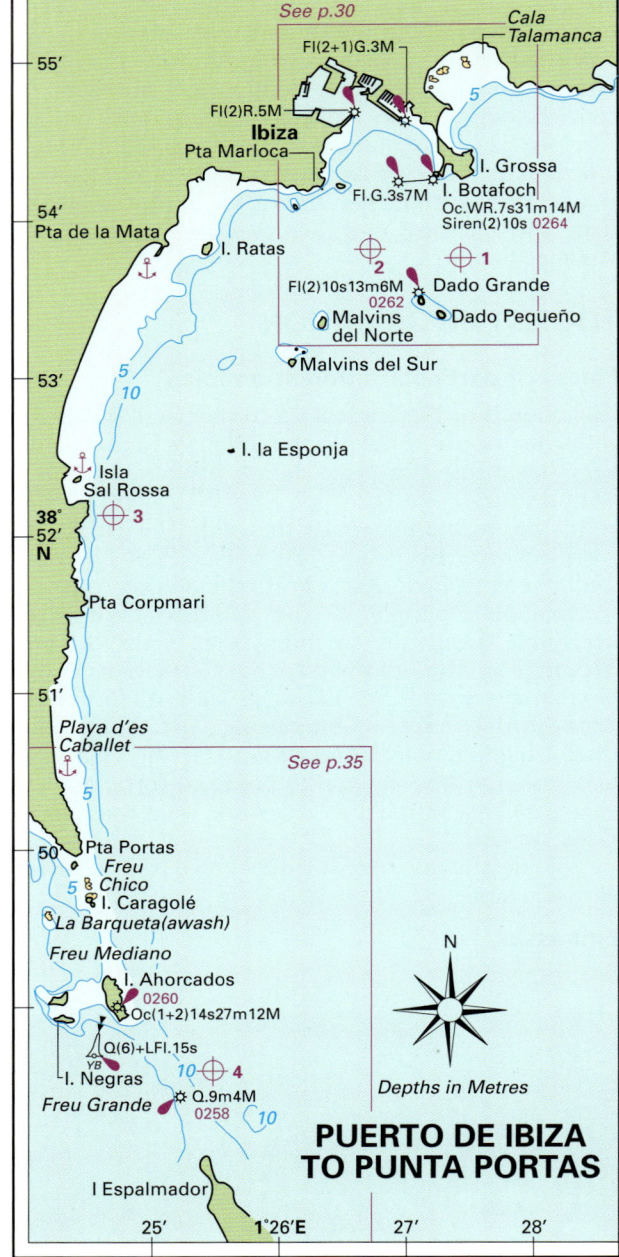

PUERTO DE IBIZA TO PUNTA PORTAS

Depths in Metres

⊕1	E Approach to Puerto de Ibiza	38°53'.7N 01°27'.5E
⊕2	Puerto de Ibiza	38°53'.9N 01°26'.7E
⊕3	Isla Sal Rossa	38°52'.2N 01°24'.8E
⊕4	Freu Grande channel	38°48'.6N 01°25'.6E

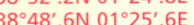

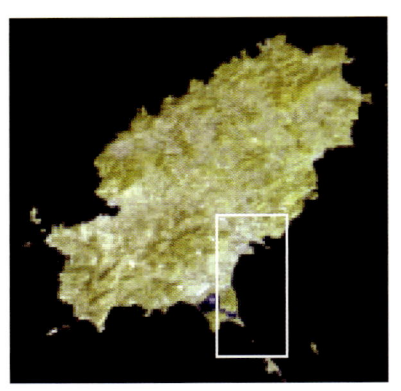

View along the southwest harbour wall towards the ancient town of Ibiza and the Cathedral of Our Lady of the Snows *GW*

IB1 Puerto de Ibiza (Eivissa)

An easy-to-enter harbour in almost any conditions, offering good shelter, with several commercial yachting facilities. Berthing for over 1,200 yachts up to 30m

Location
38°54'.7N 01°26'.7E

Communications
Pilots (*Ibiza Prácticos*) VHF Ch 12, 13, 14, 16
Port Authority Ch 09,16
℡ 971 31 06 11/31 33 63 *Fax* 971 31 04 00
See text for further internet information on other options

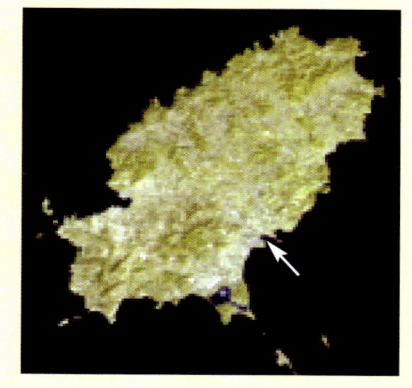

The port

Puerto de Ibiza is a large port offering excellent facilities for over 1,200 yachts. The harbour is easy to enter under most conditions, giving good shelter. Swell which used to enter the port has been considerably reduced by the extension of the breakwater extending west-southwest from Islote Botafoch. The harbour is expensive and in season a berth will be hard to find.

Puerto de Ibiza looking northwest. Marina Botafoch

PILOTAGE

Approach

⊕2 38°53'.9N 01°26'.7E Puerto de Ibiza

From south Several potential hazards litter the southern approach (see plan opposite). These are: Islote La Esponja (10m), one mile east of Isla Sal Rossa; Malvins del Sur (20m) and Malvins del Norte (12m), 1.1 and 0.9 miles south of Pta Marloca; Dado Grande (7m) and Dado Pequeño (9m) about 0.8 miles south of Isla Botafoch. All lie near or outside the 20m contour and in daylight can be left on either hand.

⊕1   E Approach to Puerto de Ibiza   38°53'.7N 01°27'.5E

I. IBIZA

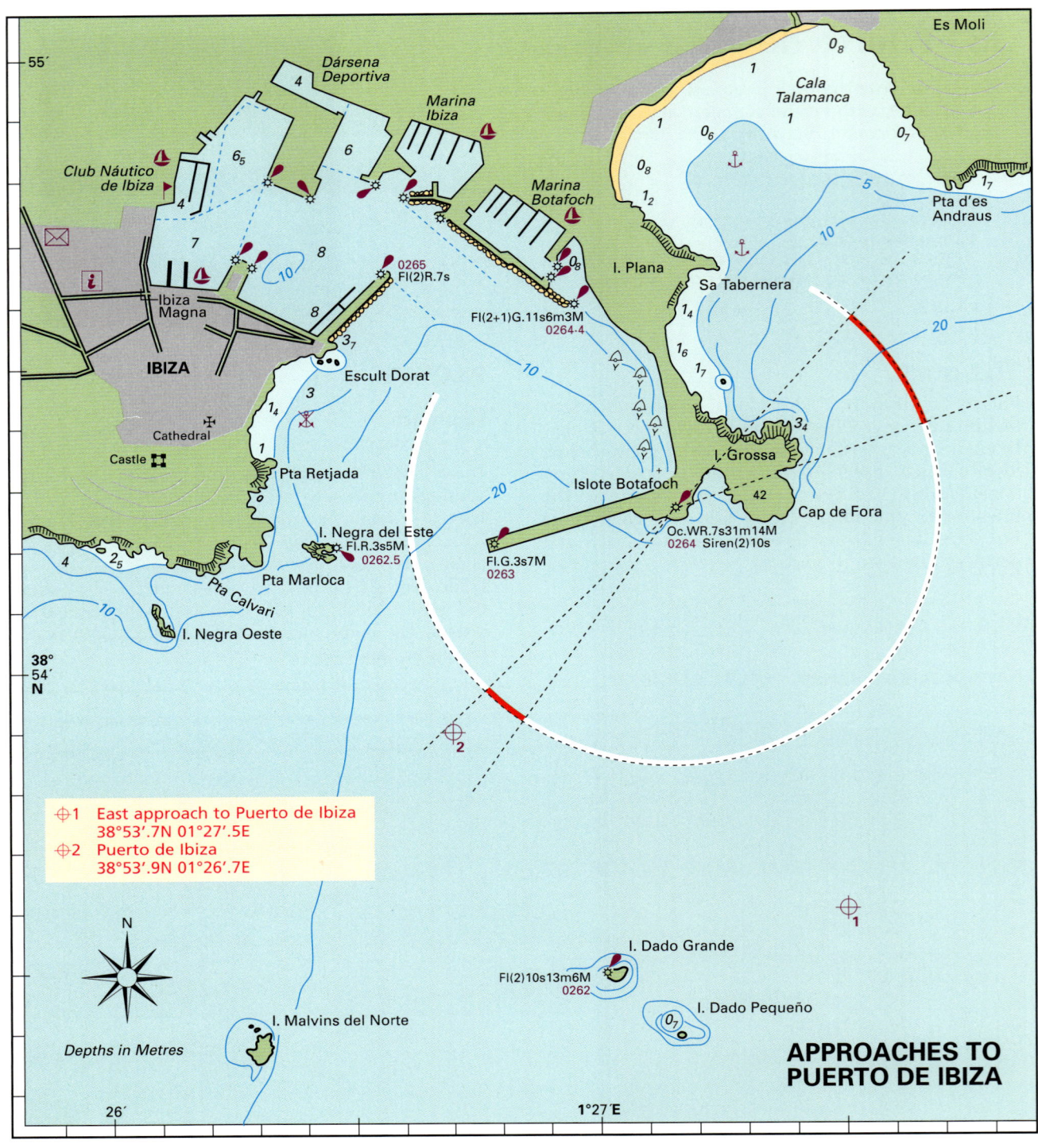

APPROACHES TO PUERTO DE IBIZA

⊕1 East approach to Puerto de Ibiza
38°53'.7N 01°27'.5E
⊕2 Puerto de Ibiza
38°53'.9N 01°26'.7E

Depths in Metres

If approaching at night it is wise to pass outside (east) of all these hazards – a bearing of 345° or less on Islote Botafoch ensures safe water. There is a Fl.G.3s5m7M light at the head of the newly extended breakwater.

From northeast Coastal sailing from the northeast end of the island, or approaching from the direction of Mallorca, see page 53 for details of the passage inside Isla Tagomago and page 56 for Isla de Santa Eulalia. After passing Puerto de Santa Eulalia, Cabo Llibrell should be given a least offing of 200m, then the two small islands Lladó del Norte (10m), and Lladó del Sur (6m) identified just under a mile northeast of Cabo Martinet. Once spotted they can safely be passed on either side. Cabo Martinet, Isla Grossa and Isla Botafoch are all steep-to, though the latter now has a 400m breakwater running west-southwest from the lighthouse, which must be rounded to starboard.

Anchorages in the approach

Anchoring on the northeast of the peninsula (east of the cathedral and north of Pta Retjada) is now prohibited. Since it is difficult to find a berth in the high season, bear this in mind if you are intending to pick up crew, as there are now no anchorages in the vicinity. A fine of up to €6,000 can be levied for anchoring.

Entrance

The outer harbour is entered on passing between the extended breakwater and Islote Negra del Este. An inner harbour half a mile further north, wherein lies Marina Ibiza, the *club náutico* and Marina Ibiza Magna, is formed by another mole on the west side; and Marina Botafoch to the northeast.

Large commercial ships and many ferries use the harbour; they have right of way and must not be obstructed. For this reason it is advisable to keep to the starboard side of the entrance but there are no other navigational hazards. Islote Negra del Este and the breakwater head are both steep-to and there are good depths (i.e. more than 5m) in the entrance and throughout the commercial harbour.

Berthing

Once in the harbour there are several options for berthing, though all are likely to be crowded in the high season.

1. Marina de Botafoch

An upmarket marina with 428 berths, able to take yachts of up to 30m, with excellent facilities. The office staff are helpful and several speak English.

The entrance lies outside the harbour proper, some 0.4M north of the Islote Botafoch, from which it takes its name. Although reasonably wide, the entrance does not open up until well inside a line from Islote Botafoch to the end of the northeast (Marina Botafoch) breakwater and can therefore be difficult to identify. The fuel and reception berth is on the starboard side on entry, with the marina offices nearby. When berths are not available, secure alongside the fuel dock when it closes at 1430, so long as you are away before it opens again at 0900 the next morning. A ferry plies across the harbour into town every half hour.

VHF Ch 09
① 971 31 17 11/31 30 13/31 22 31 *Fax* 971 31 15 57
Email info@marinabotafoch.com
www.marinabotafoch.com

2. Marina Ibiza
(formerly Deportivo Ibiza Nueva)

Extending into the old commercial basin to the west has made Marina Ibiza the largest marina in the port, with 536 berths for yachts up to 55m on two pontoons. The North Dock accommodates boats of 8–15m, providing optimum protection for vessels of that length. The South Dock caters to vessels 18–55m in length. Work has been underway through 2010 to upgrade the marina and facilities, to be completed by the summer of 2011. In the meantime,

the marina is still functioning – see the website for details. These include optimal parking, gardens, social club, fitness centre, restaurant, hairdressers, TV and conference rooms. Facilities for yachts include water and electricity, (400A/380V) internet, TV, bilge and sewage pumps, fuel station, dry dock for small vessels and smallscale repairs, as well as provision of a security service.

The dogleg entrance to the right of the yellow marina complex buildings presents no particular problems and has 3.5–4m depths. Secure on the north side of the north mole (where fuel is also available) to await allocation of a berth. There is a ferry service into town.

Note Berths near the commercial mole can be noisy with ships sometimes unloading all night.

Marina Ibiza VHF Ch 09
① 971 318 040 *Fax* 971 299 355
Email info@marinaibiza.com
www.marinaibiza.com/index_i.html

3. Club Náutico de Ibiza

Situated at the head of the harbour there is berthing for 300 vessels. The club normally reserves 20 outside berths for visiting yachts (berths inside the harbour are private). These can be oily and are exposed to ferry wash, so the use of 'spring coil'-type shock absorbers is recommended or use the club náutico lines which have car tyres as springs.

Club Náutico de Ibiza VHF Ch 09
① 971 33 97 54/31 33 63 *Fax* 971 33 28 10
Email info@clubnauticoibiza.com
www.clubnauticoibiza.com

4. Ibiza Magna
(formerly Port Authority pontoons)

This is now a fully functioning marina, situated in the extreme southwest corner of the harbour (at the foot of the historic D'Alt Vila, south of the *club nautico*); with 85 moorings for yachts up to 60m length and 10m draught. It consists of two pontoons for regular size vessels and one for superyachts. No depth restrictions. General facilities include *marineros* for assisted berthing, divers, weather forecasts, internet access, 24 hour security, a mini market, laundry, ATM, fax and postal services, bars and restaurants. See the website for full details, mooring fees and port plan. The picturesque cobbled streets of the old town, leading to the cathedral and punic necropolis, are close by. The area between the southwest breakwater and the inner mole (the ferry station) is devoted to RoRo ferries.

Ibiza Magna VHF Ch 09 (24 hours)
① 971 193 870 *Fax* 971 193 890
Email info@ibizamagna.com
www.ibizamagna.com

Puerto de Ibiza looking south. Isla Botafoch light top left of picture

Facilities

Water At all berths listed above. The water in Ibiza may not now be suitable for drinking, so if possible consult other yachtsmen before filling tanks.

Electricity At all berths. Normally 220v, but 380v available at large yacht (25m) berths in the two marinas.

Fuel At marinas. Marina Ibiza has two fuelling points.

Bottled gas Camping Gaz exchanges at chandleries or in town. Note that Calor Gas bottles are not refillable on the islands now.

Provisions Supermarkets at the marinas plus an excellent choice in the town. There is an all-day market on Fridays in summer.

Ice In the supermarkets at the marinas and in the *club náutico* bar.

Chandlery Well-stocked chandleries at the Marina Botafoch and across the road from the *club náutico*.

Repairs The largest boatyard is situated just north of the *club náutico* but is actually part of the Marina Ibiza, as is the yard at the head of their west basin ☎ 971 310617 *Fax* 971 311377. A smaller concern at Marina Botafoch. There are 160-tonne (max beam 10m) and 27-tonne travel-lifts at Marina Ibiza yards, 62-tonnes at Marina Botafoch and a slipway close north of the *club náutico*. Ibiza Yacht Service ☎ 971 312920 *Email* comercial@ibizayachtservice.com

Engineers Marina Botafoch and Marina Ibiza boatyards, also Yates Ibiza ☎/*Fax* +34 971 19 03 26 just north of the *club náutico* and Ibiza Yacht Service ☎ +34 971 31 06 17 *Fax* 971 31 06 56 at the head of the Marina Ibiza west basin.

Official service agents include: Auto Recambios Isla ☎ +34 971 31 10 12, 31 37 00 *Fax* +34 971 31 69 66 – Yamaha; Ibiza Yachting ☎ +34 971 341159 – Johnson; Marina Marbella Ibiza SA ☎ +34 971 31 08 11 – Mercury/MerCruiser, Volvo Penta; Motonautica ☎ +34 971 30 66 65 *Fax* +34 971 30 66 62 – Honda, Mercury/MerCruiser, Soler, Suzuki, Yanmar; Servinautic ☎/*Fax* +34 971 31 19 63 – Mariner, MerCruiser, Volvo Penta. ☎ +34 971 19 19 59 – Englishman located by the casino north of the Nueva Marina.

Electronic and radio repairs Both marina boatyards, Nautronic at Marina Botafoch, Yates Ibiza and Ibiza Yacht Service. Dews Marine.

Sailmaker At the Polígono Eurocentro ☎ +34 971 31 16 60. Also services inflatable dinghies and liferafts.

Yacht club The Club Náutico de Ibiza has a bar, lounge, terrace, showers and restaurant.

Showers At the marinas and the *club náutico*.

Launderettes At the marinas and in the town.

Banks In the town, many with credit card facilities.

Post office In the town.

Hospital/medical services In the town.

Transport

Car hire/taxis In the town, or arrange through marina offices.

Buses Regular services over most of the island.

Ferries Car ferries to mainland Spain and Mallorca. Frequent tourist ferries and hydrofoils to Formentera and various beaches.

Air services International airport three miles south of the harbour. The hourly bus service from the airport to the terminus on Avenida Isidoro Macabich in the centre takes 20 minutes and runs between 0730–2230 from the airport.

Sights ashore locally

Although a small part of the old town and citadel is still unspoilt, the city has become an international tourist centre, very overcrowded in the summer, and even in winter the locals are outnumbered by foreign visitors and residents.

It was founded during the 6th century BC by the Carthaginians, who are thought to have occupied the hill now known as D'Alt Vila (the old town) and to have referred to both town and island as Ibasim.

The city is well worth a visit and contains, amongst many other interesting buildings, including the cathedral and the Archaeological Museum.

On the western slopes of the hill is the Puig des Molins necropolis, a subterranean burial place which served the city from the Phoenician era (7th century BC) until Roman times. It is open to the public, together with a museum. Parts of the cathedral date back to the 13th century, shortly after the island was reconquered for Spain, but the great citadel walls were built in the late 16th century and bear the arms of King Phillip II.

If travelling by car, take the road north from Ibiza city towards San Juan Bautista and Cala Portinatx or to the tranquil Cala San Vicente, a pleasant drive along windy coastal roads, where you will find a shrine to the goddess Tanit who was worshipped by the Phoenicians at the Cueva Culleram.

Local events

Fiestas are held on the Friday night of Holy Week (Good Friday), on 24 June to celebrate the king's name saint (San Juan), and 1 August in honour of La Virgen de las Nieves, patron saint of the island. On 16 August there is a sea procession as part of the Fiesta del Virgen del Carmen.

Eating out

Restaurants, cafés and bars at both marinas plus vast numbers in the town.

Islets south of Puerto de Ibiza

Several small islets lie in the bay south of Puerto de Ibiza (see *Approach* above). From north to south these are: Dado Grande (Dau Gran) (7m) and Dado Pequeño (Dau Petit) (9m) about 0.8 miles south of Islote Botafoch; Malvins del Norte (12m) and Malvins del Sur (20m) 0.9 and 1.1 miles south of Pta Marloca; and Islote La Esponja (10m), one mile east of Isla Sal Rossa. All lie near or outside the 20m contour and can be left on either hand.

Ibiza viewed southwest across Marina Botafoch and the ferry terminal towards the old town GW

ANCHORAGES AND FEATURES SOUTH OF PUERTO DE IBIZA

⚓ PUNTA DE LA MATA (PLAYA D'EN BOSSA)
38°53'.7N 01°25'E

A small and shallow harbour of little use to yachts about one mile southwest of Puerto de Ibiza, tucked southwest of the *punta* and partially enclosed by a rough breakwater and short jetty. Small fishing boats and motor boats lie to crowded moorings in ±1m over sand and weed.

It is overlooked by hotels and high-rise tourist apartments, with a main road nearby.

⊕3 38°52'.2N 01°24'.8E Isla Sal Rossa

⚓ CALAS DE SAL ROSSA
38°52'.3N 01°24'.4E

Two small anchorages either side of Isla Sal Rossa, open northeast–east–southeast. Anchor in 2–3.5m over weed, sand and rock. The conspicuous (28m) Torre Sal Rossa stands to the northwest.

The area is still unspoilt, with only some local fishing craft and net stores ashore. Ibiza airport is little more than a mile away but noise is not really a problem. There is a rough track to the main road.

⚓ PLAYA D'ES CABALLET (ES CAVALLET)
38°50'.7N 01°24'.3E

A long sandy beach open from north–east–south. There are developments at either end, a small jetty to the north and a track to the road. Anchor in 5m or less over sand and rock.

ISLA ESPALMADOR
38°47'.8N 01°25'.3E (N tip)

This 1.5M long rocky island is the largest of a chain forming the long south-southeast-going reef that connects (with passages between) Ibiza with the island of Formentera. Anchorages and features around Espalmador and Espardel are described separately under *Formentera* on page 71.

I. IBIZA

Passages between Ibiza and Espalmador

PILOTAGE

This whole area is a marine reserve (effectively meaning no fishing or anchoring) and marked by six yellow conical buoys Fl.Y.5s with × topmark. Three are to the east and three to the west of the chain of islands.

There are three possible passages (*freus*) between Isla de Ibiza and Isla Espalmador, which are separated by a series of small islands and rocky banks strung along a ridge running south from Ibiza through Espalmador to Formentera.

Only one, the Freu Grande, is usable in all conditions, day or night; though the northern Freu Mediano makes a useful short cut in good weather in daylight. The lights in the area are reliable and a night passage through Freu Grande should not present any problems. See plans on pages 28, 35 and 64.

Approach

From east or northeast Approach the *freus* on a southwest course following the coast of Ibiza and leaving Isla Espardel (lit) to port. Two hills, Corpmari (159m) and Falcón (145m), lie near the southern extremity of Ibiza though Punta Portas itself is low. The black-and- white-banded lighthouses of Isla Ahorcados and Isla Puercos (or Los Pou) are unmistakable, with the lit north cardinal beacon of Bajo d'en Pou between them.

From west or northwest If approaching the passages from the Spanish mainland, the mountains of southern Ibiza will be first to rise above the horizon, followed by the spectacular cliffs of Isla Vedrá (lit). On closer approach the higher southern parts of Formentera will be seen, but the smaller islands of the freus will not become visible until much closer in, when the black-and-white-banded lighthouses of Isla Ahorcados and Isla Puercos (or Los Pou) can be identified with the lit north cardinal beacon of Bajo d'en Pou between them.

TRANSITING THE PASSAGES

FREU GRANDE
38°48'.5N 01°25'E
⊕4 38°48'.6N 01°25'.6E E entrance to Freu Grande channel

Freu Grande is located between the lighthouses of Isla Ahorcados to the north and Isla Puercos (or Los Pou) to the south and is just over a mile wide and 6–7m deep. Slightly to the south of its centre is the north cardinal beacon marking Bajo d'en Pou, also lit. In heavy seas keep clear of Bajo Ahorcados, 550m southwest of Isla Ahorcados, and pass just north of Bajo d'en Pou. It is the only passage recommended for use after dark, but in that case be careful to avoid the two Islas Negras del Freu, about 500m west of Isla Ahorcados, unlit, and only 2m and 4m high.

FREU MEDIANO

38°49'.4N 01°24'.6E

Freu Mediano lies between Isla Ahorcados to the south and Islote Caragolé, a small rock 8m high, to the north. Watch out for La Barqueta, an unmarked rock awash 500m west-southwest of Islote Caragolé: though often indicated by breaking seas, in calm weather it does not show clearly. Depths of 3–4m are to be found in the centre of the channel. Isla Ahorcados was once the site of the gallows where condemned prisoners were executed.

FREU CHICO

38°49'.8N 01°24'.4E

The furthest north, narrowest and shallowest of the northern *freus*, for use only by shallow-draught vessels in calm weather and with care. Depths may shoal to less than 1m. Careful eyeball navigation is required in order to avoid a rocky patch north of Islote Caragolé; a course a little north of halfway between Islote Caragolé and Punta Portas appears the optimum. La Barqueta rock (see *Freu Mediano* above) is also a potential hazard when using this *freu*.

Freu Grande passage from the southwest. Lighthouses on Isla Puercos (right) and Isla Ahorcados (left) are clear for a night passage

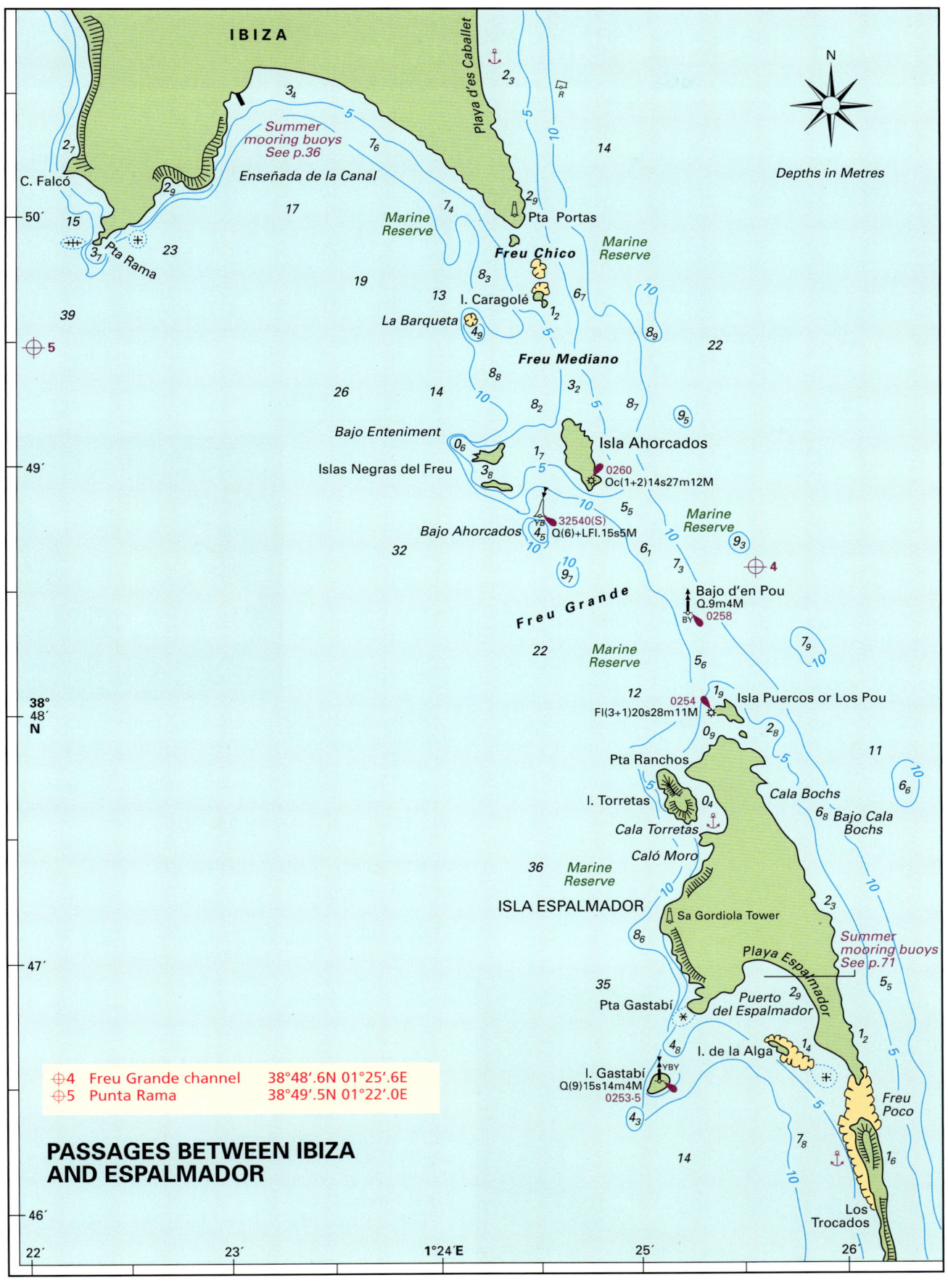

IBIZA

Playa d'es Caballet

2_3

R

2_7

C. Falcó

2_9

3_4

Summer
mooring buoys
See p.36

Enseñada de la Canal

7_6

5

10

14

Depths in Metres

N

50′

15

23

Pta Rama

3_7

17

7_4

2_9
Pta Portas

Marine
Reserve

Freu Chico

Marine
Reserve

39

5

19

8_3

13 I. Caragolé

6_7

10

La Barqueta

4_9

1_2

5

8_9

22

Freu Mediano

49′

26

14

8_8

8_2

10

3_2

8_7

9_5

Bajo Eteniment

0_6

1_7

Isla Ahorcados

Islas Negras del Freu

3_8

5

●0260
Oc(1+2)14s27m12M

32

Bajo Ahorcados

YB ●32540(S)
4_5 Q(6)+LFl.15s5M

10

5_5

Marine
Reserve

9_3

6_1

7_3

⊕4

9_7

10

Freu Grande

Bajo d'en Pou
Q.9m4M
BY ●0258

7_9

10

38°
48′
N

22

Marine
Reserve

5_6

12

1_9

●0254
Fl(3+1)20s28m11M

Isla Puercos or Los Pou

2_8

11

0_9

Pta Ranchos

5

6_6

10

I. Torretas

0_4

Cala Bochs

Cala Torretas

6_8 Bajo Cala
Bochs

Caló Moro

36

Marine
Reserve

ISLA ESPALMADOR

10

2_3

Sa Gordiola Tower

8_6

Summer
mooring buoys
See p.71

47′

35

Pta Gastabí

Puerto
del Espalmador

2_9

5_5

1_2

4_8

I. de la Alga

1_4

I. Gastabí
Q(9)15s14m4M
●0253·5
4_3

YBY

Freu
Poco

7_8

1_6

14

Los
Trocados

10

⊕4 Freu Grande channel   38°48′.6N 01°25′.6E
⊕5 Punta Rama   38°49′.5N 01°22′.0E

PASSAGES BETWEEN IBIZA
AND ESPALMADOR

46′

22′   23′   1°24′E   25′   26′

I. IBIZA

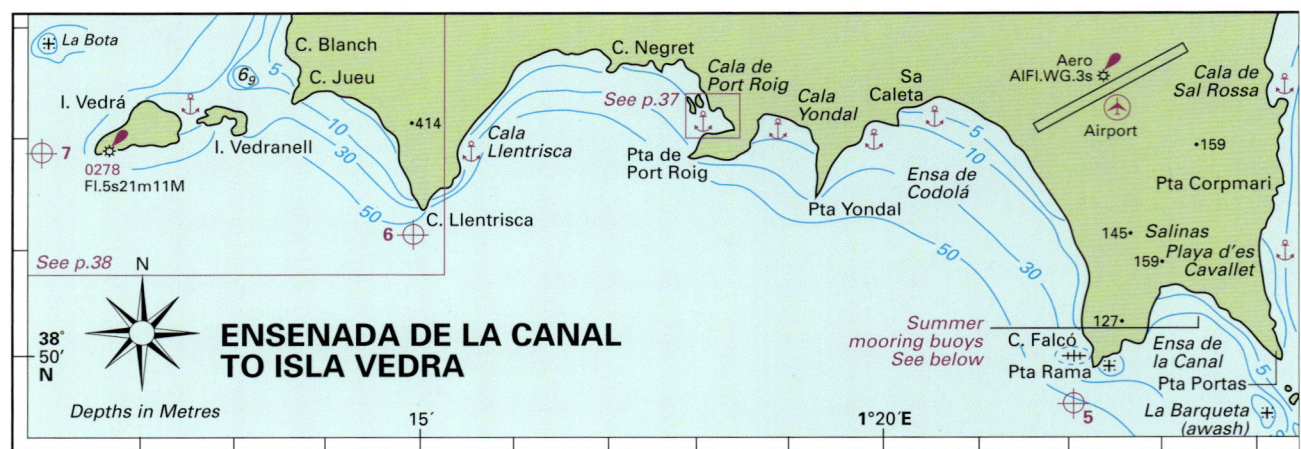

ENSENADA DE LA CANAL TO ISLA VEDRA

Depths in Metres

WAYPOINTS
⊕5 Punta Rama   38°49'.5N 01°22'.0E
⊕6 Cabo Llentrisca   38°51'.0N 01°14'.7E
⊕7 Isla Vedrá W   38°51'.7N 01°10'.8E

⚓ ENSENADA DE LA CANAL

38°50'.4N 01°23'.2E

A large sandy bay south of the National Park Ses Salines, between Punta Portas and Punta Rama; on the southern tip of Ibiza. Mooring buoys have been placed in the north east corner of the bay and can be reserved in advance from the 1st June to 30th September, for a maximum stay of two nights per week. Please see www.balearslifeposidonia.eu/index.php?register_vars[lang]=en and the plan above. See also the Anchoring and Moorings section on page 16. A pier for loading salt is sited in the northwest corner, backed by a factory complex ashore.

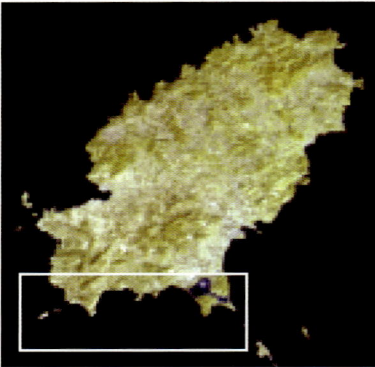

Relatively undeveloped ashore other than a few beach restaurants, but the beach itself (the Playa de Mitjorn) can get very crowded, due to frequent ferries and buses from Ibiza. The nearby *salinas* (salt pans) are a protected area, attracting many migrating birds in spring and autumn.

PUNTA RAMA AND CABO FALCÓ

38°50'.1N 01°22'.3E
⊕5 38°49'.5N 01°22'.0E Punta Rama

A prominent double headland with various offlying hazards. The isolated Bajo Morenallet lies 350m east of Punta Rama, several islets to the south and a wreck some 100m west of the punta. Allow an offing of at least 500m.

⚓ ENSENADA DE CODOLÁ (SA CALETA)

38°51'.8N 01°20'.3E

A long bay shielded by Punta Yondal and Cabo Falcó at either end. Anchor in 10m over sand and weed off the sand and stone beach. The village of Sa Caleta lies at the northwest end, backed by several tower blocks.

The centre of the bay lies under the airport flight path, making the area noisy – it is 1.5 miles from Sa Caleta to the terminal buildings. The southern part of the beach is backed by salt pans.

Ensenada de la Canal anchorage. Note the salt loading pier

PUNTA YONDAL (DES JONDAL)
38°51′.4N 01°19′.3E

A serrated headland running out to a low promontory with a hole through it. Rocks extend up to 300m south of the point. Phoenician remains have been found on the peninsula west of Sa Caleta, including the foundations of a village dated at around the 7th century BC.

⚓ CALA YONDAL (DES JONDAL)
38°51′.8N 01°18′.9E

A wide but relatively sheltered bay lying between Punta de Port Roig and Punta Yondal, open south and southwest. Anchor about 100m off the beach in 6–10m over sand and weed. Beach café and other buildings inland, and a track to the road.

Cala de Port Roig: a remarkably tranquil place to anchor

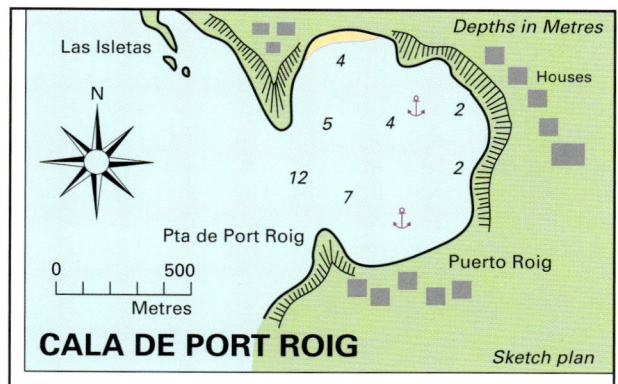
CALA DE PORT ROIG
Sketch plan

Cala Yondal

PUNTA DE PORT ROIG (PUNTA PORROIG)
38°51′.7N 01°17′.9E

A low flat point with a hole through it and some scattered buildings on the summit.

⚓ CALA DE PORT ROIG (CALA PORROIG)
38°52′.1N 01°18′.3E

In no way a port, but rather a delightful sheltered anchorage between Punta de Port Roig and Las Isletas, surrounded by sloping reddish cliffs and well protected from all winds except southwest. Anchor in 6–10m over sand, weed and rock, taking care to avoid cables from the Spanish mainland which come ashore in the bay.

Fishermen's huts line the eastern shore but otherwise there are few buildings and currently no bars or restaurants, though a small beach bar will be found under Cabo Negret about a mile to the northwest (best reached by dinghy).

⚓ CALA LLENTRISCA
38°51′.8N 01°15′.4E

A small anchorage with a stony beach tucked under scrub-covered cliffs. Exposed from northeast to southeast and to swell from the south. Anchor in

Cala Llentrisca: a small sheltered anchorage northeast of Cape Llentrisca

I. IBIZA

4–6m over sand and stone, though there are depths of up to 23m off the entrance. Boats and fishermen's huts line the beach, with a steep track up to the road.

This is a useful anchorage while awaiting favourable weather for the passage to the mainland but keep well clear of the fishermen's moorings.

CABO LLENTRISCA

38°51'.4N 01°15'E
⊕6 38°51'.0N 01°14'.7E Cabo Llentrisca

A steep, white-cliffed headland (148m) free of offlying dangers.

⚓ ISLA VEDRÁ

38°51'.7N 01°11'.3E (light)
⊕7 38°51'.7N 01°10'.8E Isla Vedrá

A lofty (382m), spectacular, rocky island, steep sided and steep-to, of a reddish colour. The lighthouse (Fl.5s21m11M, white conical tower 3m) is on the south coast and obscured when bearing between 134° and 262°.

There are two possible anchorages: one close north of the island in 12m, with landing feasible in a small inlet, the other off the northeast coast in 15m, just west of a group of rocks. Both have poor holding over stone and rock. Approach with care, and only in good conditions. The island was used as the location for the *South Pacific* 'Bali Hai' photography.

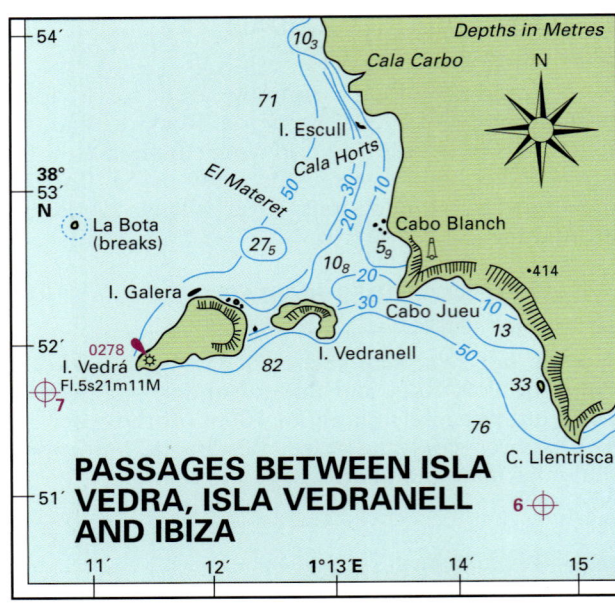

Isla Vedra, Isla Vedranell and the passages to the mainland
GW

⚓ ISLA VEDRANELL

38°52'.4N 01°12'.8E

Considerably lower (125m) and smaller than its neighbour, but equally steep-to, particularly to the south. Anchor in 12m over sand and rock close off the north coast. Again, a strictly fair weather spot.

Passages between Isla Vedrá, Isla Vedranell and Ibiza

A channel 750m wide and with a minimum depth of 10.8m runs between Isla Vedranell and Cabo Jueu on the mainland. A much narrower passage, some

⊕6	Cabo Llentrisca	38°51'.0N 01°14'.7E
⊕7	Isla Vedrá W	38°51'.7N 01°10'.8E

200m wide but also carrying a good 10m, separates Isla Vedranell and Isla Vedrá. However, attention must be paid to the following dangers:

- La Bota, a breaking rock 1M north-northwest of Isla Vedrá light
- A series of small rocky islets on the northeast and east coasts of Isla Vedrá
- El Materet, 10.8m deep, 800m southwest of Cabo Blanch.

A course of 125°/305° down the centre of the passage between Isla Vedranell and Cabo Jueu, keeping the point of Cabo Llentrisca equidistant between the two, clears El Materet. The inside passage is prone to sudden, strong gusts, and in heavy weather it is advisable to pass well outside Isla Vedrá and La Bota.

Isla Vedranell with deep-water passages either side

WAYPOINTS
⊕6 Cabo Llentrisca   38°51'.0N 01°14'.7E
⊕7 Isla Vedrá W   38°51'.7N 01°10'.8E
⊕8 Isla del Esparto W   38°57'.5N 01°10'.4E
⊕9 Isla Conejera NW   38°59'.7N 01°12'.5E
⊕10 Puerto de San Antonio 38°58'.8N 01°17'.0E

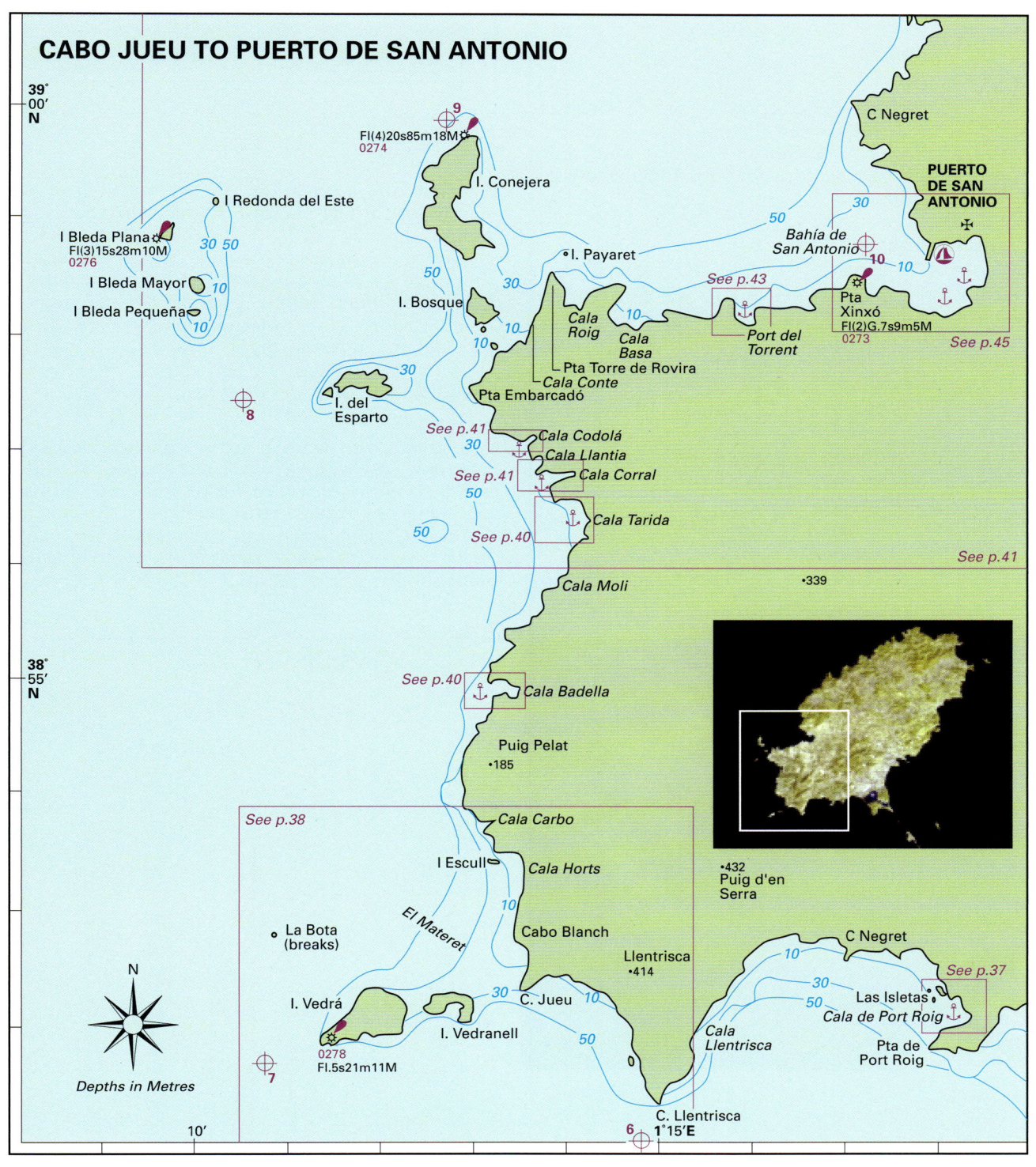

CABO JUEU TO PUERTO DE SAN ANTONIO

I. IBIZA

39°00'N

C Negret

9
Fl(4)20s85m18M
0274

I. Conejera

PUERTO DE SAN ANTONIO

o I Redonda del Este

30 50

I Bleda Plana
Fl(3)15s28m10M
0276

I Bleda Mayor
10

I Bleda Pequeña
10

50

30

50

50

Bahía de San Antonio

See p.43

10
10

Pta Xinxó
Fl(2)G.7s9m5M
0273

See p.45

o I. Payaret

I. Bosque

Cala Roig
Cala Basa

Port del Torrent

10

Pta Torre de Rovira

Cala Conte

30

I. del Esparto

Pta Embarcadó

See p.41
30

Cala Codolá
Cala Llantia

8

See p.41

Cala Corral

50

Cala Tarida

50

See p.40

See p.41

Cala Moli
•339

38°55'N

See p.40

Cala Badella

Puig Pelat
•185

See p.38

Cala Carbo

I Escull

Cala Horts

El Materet

10

La Bota (breaks)

Cabo Blanch

Llentrisca
•414

N

•432
Puig d'en Serra

C Negret

10

See p.37

30
50

Las Isletas
Cala de Port Roig

I. Vedrá

30

C. Jueu
10

0278
Fl.5s21m11M

I. Vedranell

50

Cala Llentrisca

Pta de Port Roig

7

Depths in Metres

10'

6
1°15'E
C. Llentrisca

⚓ CALA HORTS (D'HORT)

38°53'.3N 01°13'.4E

A popular anchorage in 5–10m over sand, open to south and southwest, but sheltered by high cliffs and the two offshore islands. The long stony beach has two beach restaurants, one high-rise building and some smaller buildings.

Remains from the Carthaginian and Roman periods, including the foundations of a substantial villa, have been excavated at ses Països de Cala d'Hort, a short distance inland.

⚓ CALA CARBO

38°53'.7N 01°13'.0E

A small angled *cala* between low reddish headlands, which may be difficult to identify from offshore. Sound-in carefully to anchor in ±3m over sand and weed, off a fine sandy beach sporting the usual beach restaurant.

⚓ CALA BADELLA (VADELLA)

38°54'.9N 01°13'.2E

A deep and attractive *cala* with an excellent beach, well protected by high wooded cliffs and offering a safe but often crowded anchorage with many permanent moorings. The north headland extends underwater and should be given minimum clearance of 25m, otherwise depths are considerable until well inside the *cala*. Anchor in 3–10m as space permits over sand and weed; it may be necessary to use two anchors to limit swinging. Larger yachts sometimes moor with a line to the rocks on the southern headland. No shortage of restaurants, cafés and bars behind the beach, plus a small supermarket in the village.

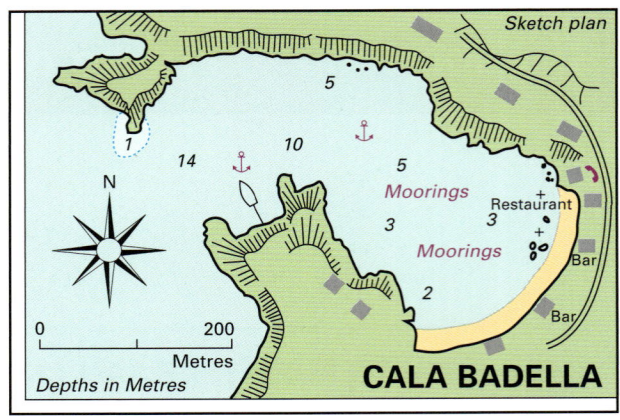

⚓ CALA MOLI

38°55'.9N 01°13'.8E

A small *cala* with a fine sandy beach, open to southwest through northwest but otherwise well protected by high cliffs. A distinctive pink building stands on the southern headland, its curved façade supported by columns. Anchor in 5m over sand. A beach restaurant ashore, catering for the tourist boats from San Antonio, plus some new development to the north.

⚓ CALA TARIDA

38°56'.4N 01°14'E

A long bay with sandy beaches separated by rocky outcrops, and with two low, inshore islands. Cala Tarida is easily identified by the extensive tourist developments to both north and south. Anchor in 4–5m over sand, weed and rock. There are many beach restaurants and cafés ashore, together with some shops.

Cala Badella: fine anchorage with restaurant on the beach

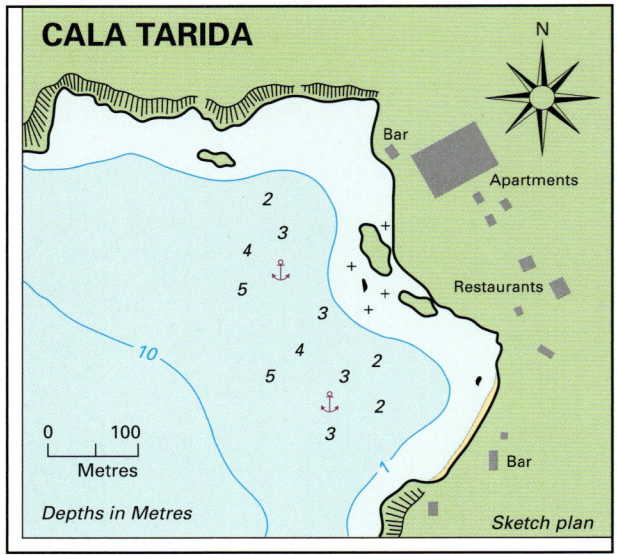

Cala Tarida

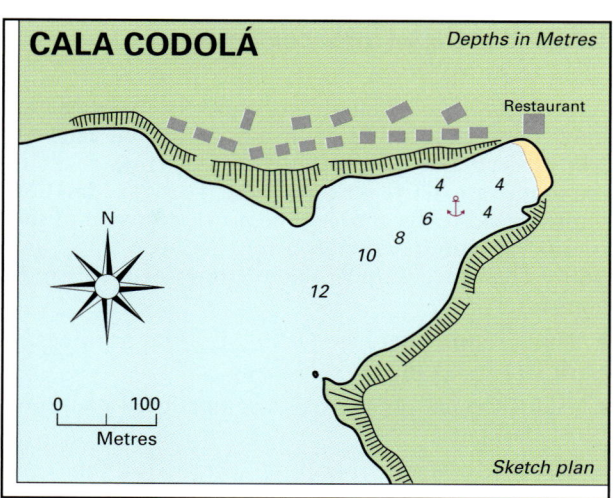

⚓ CALA CORRAL

38°56'.8N 01°13'.8E

A rocky-sided *cala* open southwest through northwest and with a small and shallow private harbour (Coralmar) tucked behind a rocky wall at its head. Anchor in 5–6m over sand and rock. A large tourist development stands behind and somewhat above the beach, itself fringed by fishermen's huts. A restaurant and supermarket will be found amongst the buildings to the north.

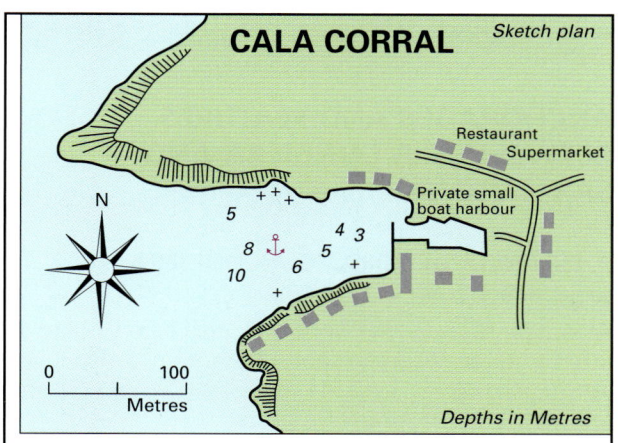

⚓ CALA LLANTIA

38°56'.8N 01°13'.7E

A rocky-sided *cala* open southwest and west, with a beach at its head and a line of white houses on a cliff to the northwest. Anchor off the beach in 5m over sand.

⚓ CALA CODOLÁ (CODOLAR)

38°57'N 01°13'.5E

A cliff-sided *cala* with a stony beach at its head, open to southwest through northwest. Anchor in 4–6m

over sand and weed near the head of the *cala*, where a restaurant and beach bar will be found. Low-rise white houses line the clifftop to the north, together with a few shops. Tourist boats visit daily in season.

Passage between Isla del Esparto (Illa de s'Espart) and Ibiza

The north–south passage between Isla del Esparto (68m) and Ibiza is more than 1,000m wide with a minimum depth of 30m. A small rocky islet stands just off the northeast point of the island.

⊕ 8 38°57'.3N 01°10'.4E Islote Espardel W (off Isla Esparto)

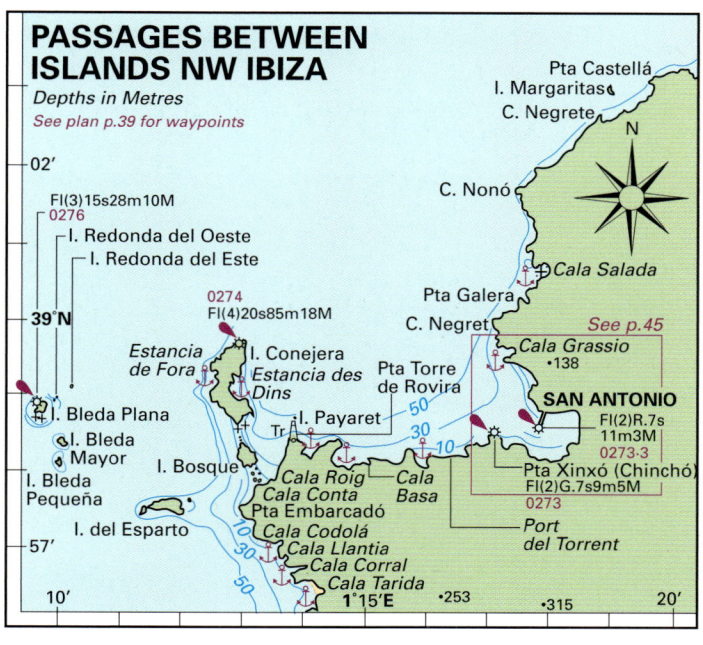

I. IBIZA

Islas Bledas (Ses Bledes)

38°58'.8N 01°09'.6E

A group of five uninhabited rocky islets lying two miles northwest of Isla del Esparto. At their centre is Isla Bleda Plana (23m), which has offlying rocks to the southwest. There is a lighthouse (Fl(3)15s28m10M, white round tower 8m) on the northwest side of this island, obscured when bearing between 239° and 349°. The other islands, taken from north to south, comprise:

- Isla Redonda del Este (13m), 1,000m northeast of Isla Bleda Plana
- Isla Redonda del Oeste, close northeast of Isla Bleda Plana
- Isla Bleda Mayor (Na Bose) (39m), 1,000m south-southeast of Isla Bleda Plana
- Isla Bleda Pequeña (Na Gorra) (29m), sometimes referred to as Porros, about 400m south of Isla Bleda Mayor and with foul ground between the two.

Explore the area with care and a bow lookout. In settled conditions it is reported possible to anchor in 5m near the lighthouse landing on Isla Bleda Plana, taking a sternline ashore.

⊕9 38°59'.7N 01°12'.5E Isla Conejera (NW)

Passage between Isla Conejera (Sa Conillera) and Isla Bosque (de Bosc)

A passage 200m wide exists between Isla Conejera (69m) and Isla Bosque (67m). It is generally deep, except where a narrow sandbar links the two islands, leaving minimum depths of 3.4m mid-way between islands (clearly visible on photo below). In good light the paler colours of the bar should be clearly visible. Rocks extend from both islands, those off Isla Conejera barely breaking while those

Isla Conejera (larger island) and Isla Bosque: the bar clearly visible

Isla Bosque: the rocky reef between Ibiza and the island is clear

off Isla Bosque stand well above the water (though with a few breaking outliers).

Take the passage in an east–west direction halfway between the two islands with a bias towards Isla Bosque. It becomes unsafe with any sea running, when it would be wise to pass outside Isla Conejera (⊕9).

Passage between Isla Bosque and Ibiza

The passage between Isla Bosque and Ibiza is a dangerous mass of awash and barely-covered rocks (see photo) and really only suitable for dinghies in calm conditions, though a 2m passage is said to exist.

ANCHORAGES AND FEATURES BETWEEN ISLA CONEJERA AND SAN ANTONIO

⚓ ESTANCIA DE FORA, ISLA CONEJERA

38°59'.1N 01°12'.4E

A small *cala* on the west side of Isla Conejera. Strictly a fair-weather spot. Anchor in 5–7m over sand and rock.

⚓ ESTANCIA DES DINS, ISLA CONEJERA

38°59'.0N 01°12'.6E

A large sandy bay on the east of the island, open to the northeast and with a three mile plus fetch to east and southeast. Anchor in 3m or more over sand and rock. There is a landing and miniature boat harbour at the north end of the bay, with a track to the lighthouse (Fl(4)20s85m18M, white tower and building 18m) which stands at the north end of the island.

There are no facilities ashore, though temporary beach restaurants do set up in summer when the island is a popular destination with tourist boats. The protected green lizard abounds.

⚓ CALA CONTA (COMTE)

38°57′.9N 01°13′.4E

A small *cala* on the mainland shore just north of the shoals running out to Isla Bosque, but exposed. Anchor in 5–6m over sand, off a fine beach fringed by fishermen's huts.

⚓ CALA ROIG (ROJA)

38°58′.3N 01°14′.1E

A rocky-sided *cala* open to the north sector, not recommended unless conditions are good. The impressive Torre de Rovira, built in 1763 to protect Ibiza's west coast, stands on the headland of that name west of the *cala*. Shoals run out towards Isla Payaret some 200m northeast of the point.

⚓ CALA BASA

38°58′.2N 01°14′.6E

A large and attractive *cala* with a sandy beach at its head, surrounded by pine woods and low cliffs, open to north and northeast. Anchor in 5–8m over sand. There is a landing stage used by tourist boats, several beach restaurants and cafés, and a nearby camp site. Though often crowded during the day, the beach is usually deserted by evening.

Cala Basa: yachts anchored on west side. Note the swimmers' buoys   *GW*

⚓ PORT DEL TORRENT

38°58′.2N 01°15′.9E

A large angled *cala* with low rocky sides and a sandy beach at its head, open to the north sector. Anchor in 4–6m over sand, rock and weed. Small yachts may be able to tuck into the sheltered east arm, though this is now partly occupied by permanent moorings. A careful watch should be kept for swimmers and water-skiers, as well as on the depth. Larger vessels should anchor further northwest (see plan) where the holding is also somewhat better, but be ready to depart at the threat of onshore winds.

Port del Torrent: only a *cala*, but offering shelter deep inside

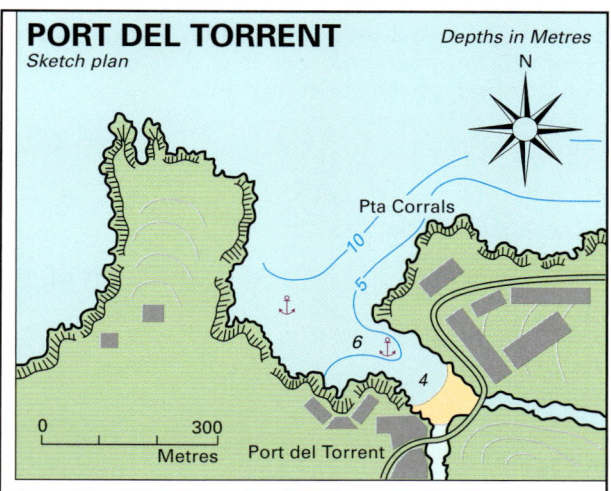

Beach bars and restaurants abound, with a supermarket some 100m to the south. Hotels and apartment blocks fringe the bay to the east and south.

PUNTA XINXÓ (Chinchó)

38°58′.5N 01°17′.1E

A very low, rocky-cliffed promontory, difficult to identify except for the lighthouse on the point (Fl(2)G.7s9m5M green column on white base displaying a green triangle). A road and buildings lie behind.

IB2 Puerto de San Antonio (Sant Antoni de Portmany)

A harbour easy to enter in all conditions, tucked into the N end of a large bay, with berthing for 330 yachts at Club Náutico, San Antonio, though all usually occupied

Location
38°58'.5N 01°17'.9E

Communications
Yacht harbour (San Antonio Náutico) VHF Ch 09 (0830–1330 and 1600–2100).
Port Authority ☎ 971 340503
Club Náutico San Antonio ☎ 971 340645
Fax 971 345607
Email Info@nauticsantantoni.com
www.nauticsantantoni.com

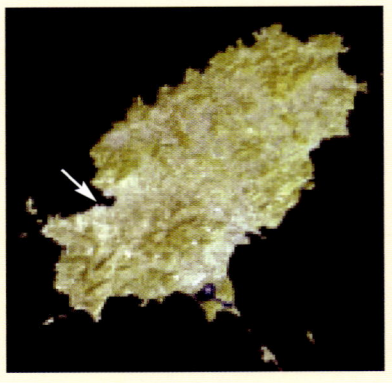

The harbour

A yachting and fishing harbour in a deep bay partially protected by a breakwater. Several private moorings line the shore but it is difficult to get a berth or find space here at any time.

PILOTAGE

Approach

⊕10 38°58'.8N 01°17'.0E Puerto de San Antonio

From northeast and north Cabo Eubarca, which has a cone-shaped top, and Cabo Nonó, which is covered with pine woods, are high, steep headlands and easy to identify (see plan on page 48). The Islas Margaritas can be left on either side. Enter the bay of San Antonio on a southerly course, steering

Bahía de San Antonio

PUERTO DE SAN ANTONIO

⊕10 Puerto de San Antonio
38°58'.8N 01°17'.0E

Depths in Metres

initally towards a group of distant mountains. When well inside the bay the head of the breakwater with its red column and white base will open up.

From west and south Isla Conejera with its conspicuous lighthouse is easily seen (see plan on page 39). In bad weather it is advisable to pass outside this island with an offing of at least 200m before setting a southeast course towards the harbour. In settled conditions the passage between Isla Conejera and Isla Bosque can be used. If approaching from the Iberian mainland note that the Islas Bledas lie some 2½ miles west of Isla Conejera, only the largest having a lighthouse.

Anchorage in the approach

There are several possible *cala* anchorages on the south side of the Bahía de San Antonio, as detailed in the preceding pages.

Entrance

Underwater obstructions extend a short distance beyond the end of the breakwater, so allow at least 50m. Otherwise the entrance is wide and without hazards, though shoals run out a short way beyond Punta Xinxó (Chinchó) and its equally inconspicuous eastern neighbour: keep at least the first two starboard-hand buoys to starboard.

Berthing

Club Náutico San Antonio has 330 berths, but even with the latest extension, vacant berths are seldom available in high season.

A small dinghy quay administered by the Port Authority exists in the extreme northeast of the bay. It is forbidden for yachts to berth alongside the breakwater.

Anchorage in the bay

Anchor to the south and east of the green buoys marking the access channel in 5m or less, in sand and weed. Holding is poor in patches, with the best holding in the north of the bay.

Ro-Ro ferries which berth near the root of the breakwater and on the widened area must not be impeded, and a channel must also be left for the fishing boats and tourist ferries which berth east of the *club náutico* pontoons. As much of the bay is occupied by moorings this leaves limited space for anchoring in the northern part of the bay but even in the height of summer there is usually room to be found further south.

Puerto de San Antonio

San Antonio: a view along the promenade *GW*

Moorings

There are a few private moorings, some of which may be available. However one can never be sure of intended maximum tonnage, state of repair, or when the owner will return. Certainly a yacht on a borrowed mooring should never be left unattended.

Facilities

Water Taps on the pontoons and at the *club náutico*, available 1000-1300 on payment of a fee. It is very brackish and unsuitable for drinking.

Electricity On the pontoons.

Fuel Diesel and petrol from pumps on the breakwater. Diesel at the *club náutico*.

Provisions A wide range of shops and supermarkets in the town, several on the road leading from opposite the *club náutico*. Also two small supermarkets behind the prominent Hotel Hawaii on the southeast shore of the bay. A produce market on the Carrer Vara del Rey.

Ice From the *club náutico* bar.

Chandlery On the road opposite the *club náutico*.

Charts The only agent for Spanish charts on the island is Valnautica SL, Ibinave, Travesia del Mar s/n, local 2, San Antonio ② 971 34 52 51 *Fax* 971 34 67 32 *Email* ibnave@wanadoo.es.

Repairs A small yard at the *club náutico* able to handle routine maintenance, painting, etc. and other craftsmen and engineers are also available – enquire at the club. A 6.5-tonne mobile crane.

Yacht club The Club Náutico San Antonio welcomes visiting yachtsmen, including those anchored off. It has a pleasant bar/restaurant, and an excellent view from its terrace. Several of the staff speak English. ☎ 971 34 06 45.

Showers At the *club náutico*. The crews of yachts anchored off are charged a small fee.

Banks In the town, most with credit card facilities.

Hospital/medical services In the town.

Transport

Car hire/taxis In the town, or arrange through the *club náutico*.

Buses Regular bus service to Ibiza and elsewhere.

Ferries Ferry service to the Spanish mainland.

History

The harbour has probably been in use since prehistoric times, and certainly since the Phoenician and Carthaginian eras. In Roman times it was called Portús Magnus, changed by the Ibizencos to Portmany (meaning 'big bay'). It is claimed that Isla Conejera ('rabbit's burrow') was the birthplace of the Carthaginian warrior Hannibal – not impossible, since the island was in the hands of the Carthaginians at the time. Certainly, many of the stone-slingers in his army came from the nearby Islas Bledas.

Sights ashore locally

Little is now evident of the original fishing village, which has given way to tourist development and the bay is now lined with high-rise apartment buildings and hotels, mainly for young English tourists. Although the town itself is without charm, the bay is still surprisingly attractive and largely surrounded by rolling, tree-covered hills.

In spite of its reputation as a noisy and crowded holiday resort, San Antonio still makes a good base for exploring the western and northern coasts.

There are cave paintings of disputed date at the cave 'des Vi' near Cabo Nonó, and a subterranean chapel dedicated to Santa Inés (Santa Agnès in Ibicenco) close north of the town. The church of San Antonio de Portmany, parts of which date back to 1305, is also worth a visit.

Local events

On 17 January a fiesta is held in honour of San Antonio (patron saint), while on 16 July there is the fiesta of Our Lady of Mont Carmel, with a regatta on the following Sunday. 24 August sees the fiesta of San Bartolomé.

Eating Out

An enormous range of cafés and restaurants to suit all purses.

I. IBIZA

View across Bahía de San Antonio *GW*

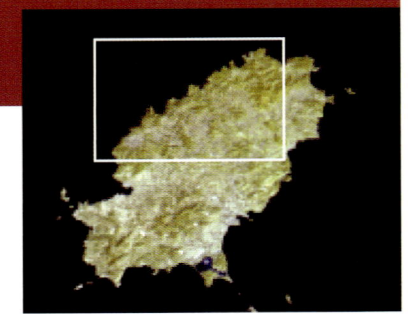

WAYPOINTS

⊕11 Islas Margaritas
    (Margalides) W   39°03'.0N 01°18'.6E
⊕12 Cabo Eubarca   39°04'.6N 01°21'.4E
⊕13 Isla Murada   39°05'.8N 01°25'.9E
⊕14 Punta Charracó   39°06'.7N 01°29'.4E

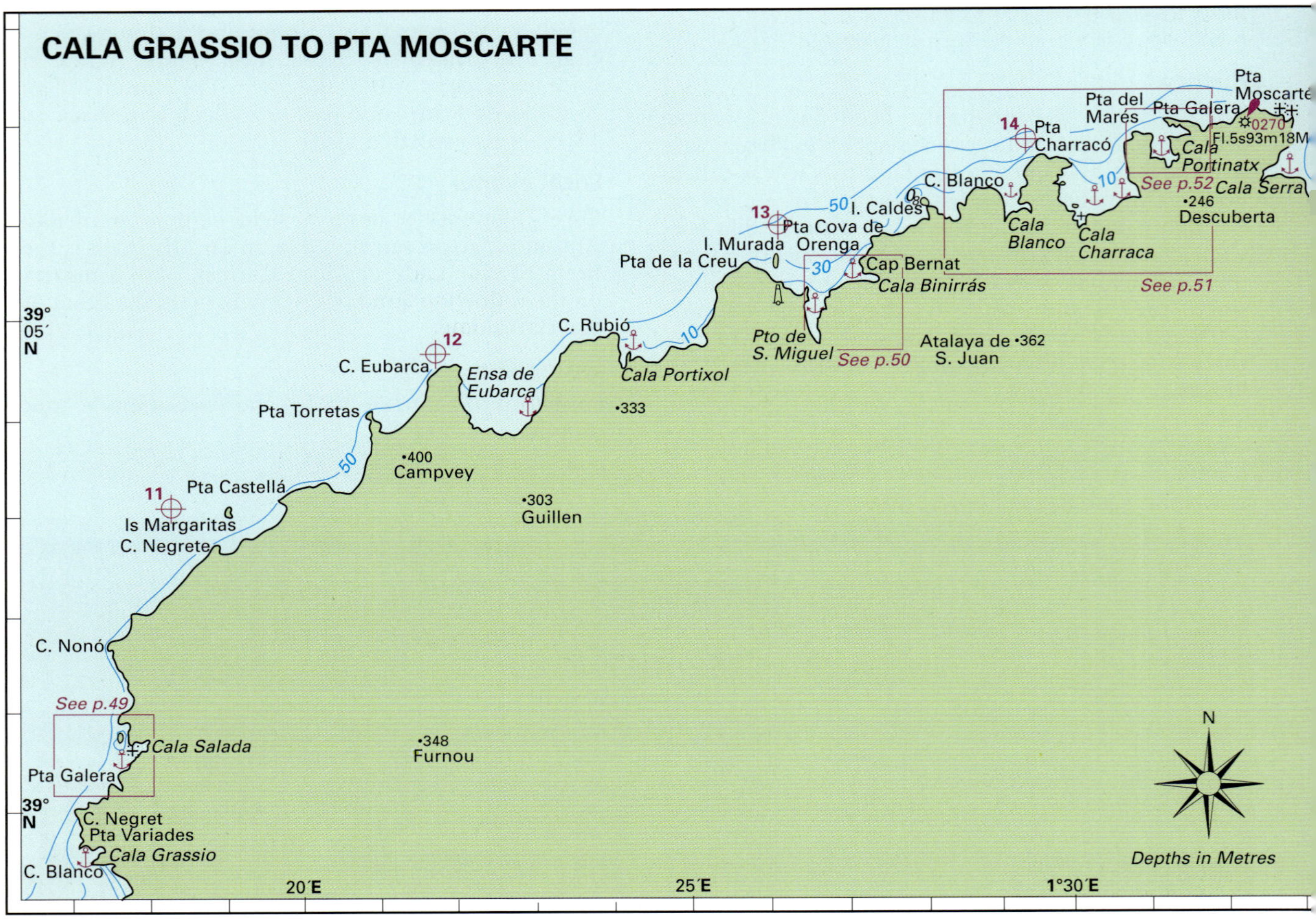

CALA GRASSIO TO PTA MOSCARTE

Pta Moscarté
Pta del Marés
Pta Galera
✳02701
Fl.5s93m18M
14 Pta Charracó
Cala Portinatx
See p.52
Cala Serra
C. Blanco
Cala Blanco
Cala Charraca
•246 Descuberta
See p.51
13 Pta Cova de
I. Caldés
50
I. Murada Orenga
30
Cap Bernat
Pta de la Creu
Cala Binirrás
C. Rubió
10
Pto de S. Miguel
See p.50
Atalaya de •362 S. Juan
12 C. Eubarca
Ensa de Eubarca
Cala Portixol
•333
Pta Torretas
50
•400 Campvey
•303 Guillen
11 Pta Castellá
Is Margaritas
C. Negrete
C. Nonó
See p.49
Cala Salada
Pta Galera
C. Negret
Pta Variades
Cala Grassio
C. Blanco
•348 Furnou

39°05'N
39°N

20'E   25'E   1°30'E

N

Depths in Metres

⚓ CALA GRASSIÓ (GRACIÓ)

38°59'.5N 01°17'.3E

A *cala* surrounded by low cliffs, splitting into two branches near its head, both with sandy beaches. Open to west and southwest. Anchor in 4–6m over sand. The immediate surroundings are wooded, with houses and apartments set further back. Both beaches are popular with tourist boats and the usual bars and restaurant will be found ashore.

Looking north over Pto Variades from Cala Grassio towards Pto Galera

Cala Salada: still an unspoilt spot to anchor

⚓ CALA SALADA
39°00′.6N 01°17′.8E

A narrow, largely unspoilt *cala* with steep rocky sides and woods above. The small island of S'Illeta lies close inshore to the north. Anchor in 4–8m over sand and thin weed, taking care to avoid an unmarked rock carrying some 2.8m in the north of the *cala*. Fishermen's huts line the south side where there is a small quay.

The beaches are popular with day tourists from San Antonio, and there are beach bars and restaurants ashore. Part of the beach, marked by a line of white buoys, is marked off for swimmers as a defence against the many water-skiers.

⊕11 Islas Margaritas (Margalides) W 39°03′.0N 01°18′.6E

ISLAS MARGARITAS (SES MARGALIDES)
39°03′N 01°19′E

A horseshoe-shaped group of rocks with a low arch through their centre. They can be left on either side when coastal sailing, an offing of 350m ensuring good water.

PUNTA TORRETAS
39°04′.0N 01°20′.6E

A relatively low promontory running out as an apparent afterthought from the surrounding 150-200m cliffs. From some directions it appears as two towers or a small fort. A natural arch runs through the point.

CABO EUBARCA (CAP DES MOSSONS)
39°04′.5N 01°21′.5E

A high, steep-cliffed promontory topped by a regular cone (262m).

⊕12 39°04′.6N 01°21′.4E Cap Eubarca

⚓ ENSENADA DE EUBARCA (D'ALBARCA)
39°04′.0N 01°22′.4E

A large, high-cliffed bay with shallowish rocky sides, sheltered by Cabo Eubarca to the west and Cabo Rubió to the east. The holding is mostly rock with sand patches; use with care. The *cala* itself is deserted, but there is a village up the track leading inland.

CABO RUBIÓ
39°04′.8N 01°23′.8E

A high, steep-cliffed promontory.

Punta Torretas: a rugged coastline

I. IBIZA

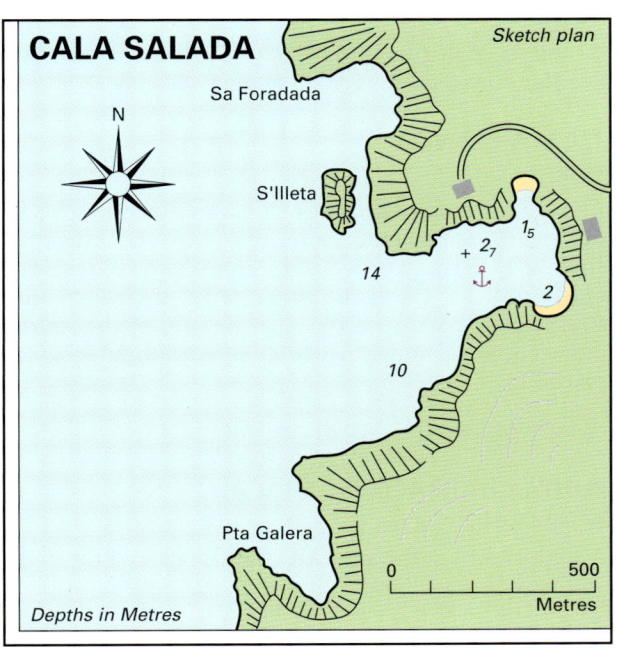

Cala Portixol: a bay cut into rugged scenery

⚓ CALA PORTIXOL

39°04'.6N 01°23'.9E

A very small horseshoe *cala* just east of Cabo Rubió, open to north and northeast but otherwise surrounded by high cliffs. Anchor in 4–5m over sand and rock (there is a sand patch near the centre of the *cala*) off the sand and stone beach.

⊕ 13 39°05'.8N 01°25'.9E Isla Murada

⚓ PUERTO DE SAN MIGUEL

39°05'.2N 01°26'.5E

Not a true port but a deeply indented *cala*, well protected by Isla Bosch (a rocky peninsula stretching nearly halfway across the inner entrance on the west side) and surrounded by cliffs. If approaching from

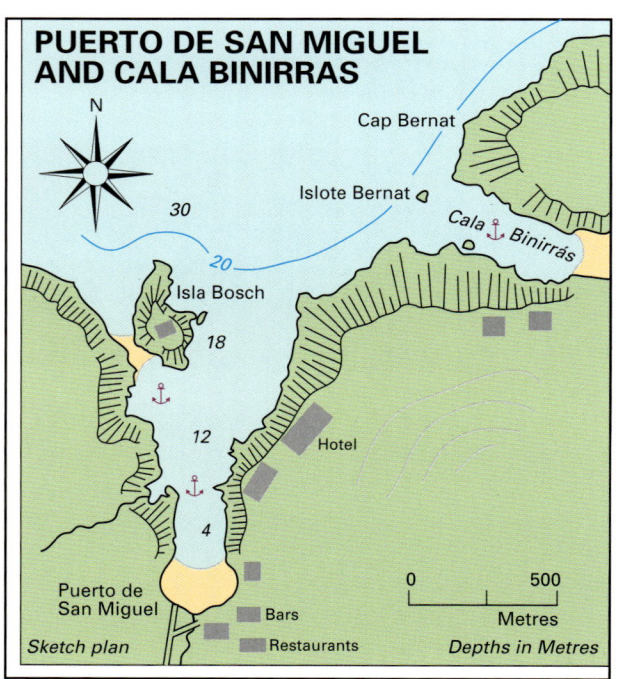

the west and planning to pass inside Isla Murada, (⊕13) watch out for an isolated rock 1.5–2m high which lies in the passage between the island and the shore towards Punta de la Creu.

Anchor in 4–8m over sand behind the peninsula or off the larger of the two beaches, open only to north and northeast. There are some permanent moorings and a buoyed-off area reserved for the water-ski school.

At the head of the *cala* are apartment blocks and hotels. The beach is usually crowded in season, with beach bars and restaurants flourishing. There is a good supermarket on the west side of the *cala*.

⚓ CALA BINIRRÁS (BENIRRÁS)

39°05'.3N 01°27'.1E

A small *cala* between steep cliffs, less than 1,000m east of Puerto de San Miguel. The rocky, pinnacled Islote Bernat (27m) lies in the middle of the entrance, from some angles looking uncannily like the elderly Queen Victoria on her throne! It is without outliers and can safely be passed on either hand.

Anchor in 5–8m over sand near the head of the *cala*, avoiding some rocky shallows in the southeast corner. Although as yet still undeveloped other than a few bars and restaurants, the beach is often crowded.

PUNTA COVA DE ORENGA

39°05'.8N 01°27'.2E

A high, cliffed point with a cave at its foot.

ISLAS CALDES (D'EN CALDERS)

39°06'.2N 01°27'.8E

A group of rocky islands close off Punta Caldes, itself between Punta Cova de Orenga and Cabo Blanco, with offliers up to 350m offshore.

CABO BLANCO

39°06'.3N 01°28'.5E

A spit is reported to stretch northeast from this headland, extending some distance offshore.

⚓ CALA BLANCO

39°06'.2N 01°29'E

A small, attractive *cala* east of Cabo Blanco, open to the north sector and with two distinct 'corners'. Anchor in either corner over sand; some 5–6m will be found to the southwest with 4–5m to the southeast. Apart from two private houses the *cala* is deserted, and much of the surrounding land is private.

⊕ 14 39°06'.7N 01°29'.4E Pta Charracó

PUNTA CHARRACÓ (XARRACA)

39°06'.6N 01°29'.4E

A high (73m) cliff-edged headland, covered by trees.

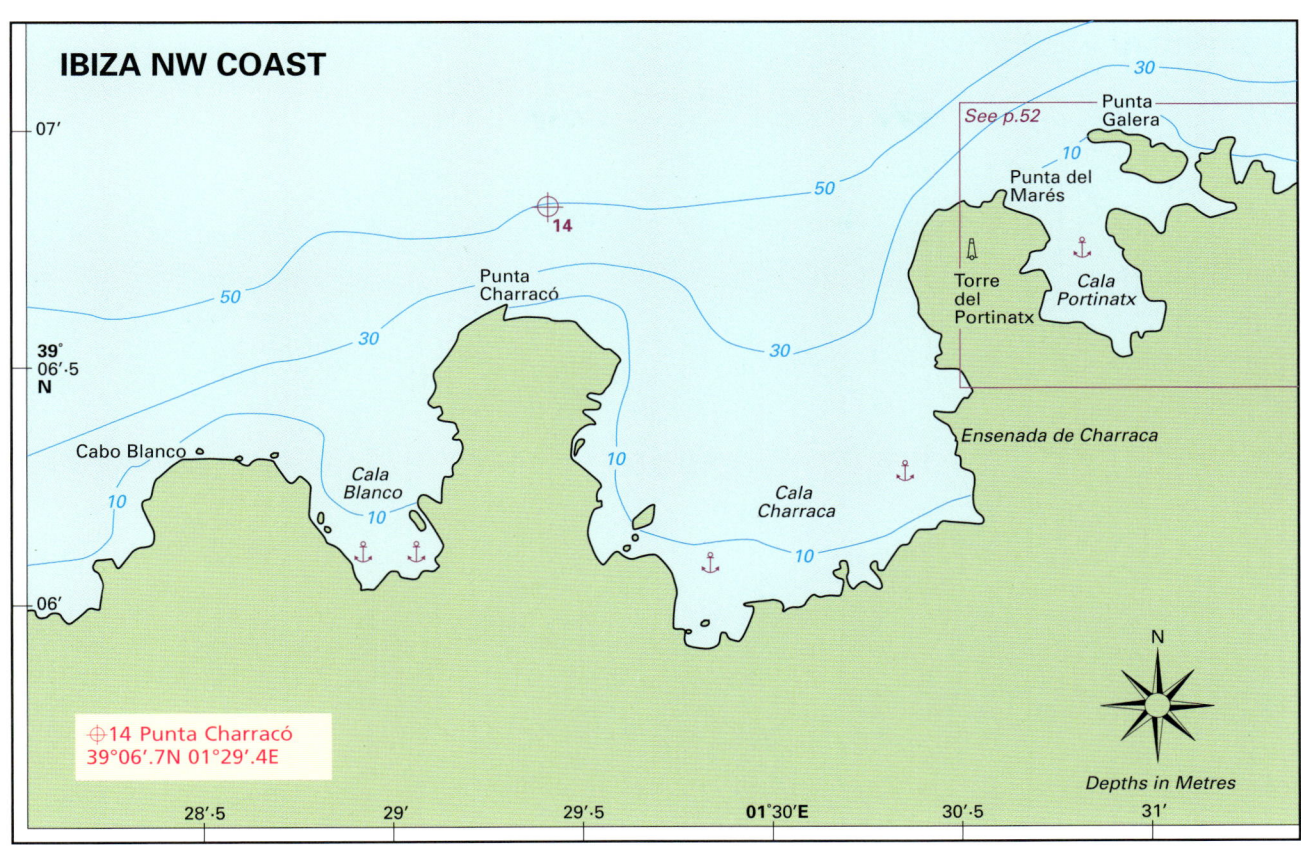

IBIZA NW COAST

07'

See p.52

Punta Galera

30

Punta del Marés

50

Torre del Portinatx

Cala Portinatx

Punta Charracó

39°06'·5 N

50

30

30

Ensenada de Charraca

Cabo Blanco

30

10

Cala Blanco

10

10

Cala Charraca

10

06'

N

⊕14 Punta Charracó
39°06'.7N 01°29'.4E

Depths in Metres

28'·5   29'   29'·5   01°30'E   30'·5   31'

⚓ CALA CHARRACA (XARRACA)

39°06'.2N 01°30'E

A large, square bay surrounded by forested cliffs and offering several possible anchorages, open north–northeast. There are two small rock-fringed islands near the west side of the *cala* plus a rock awash in the centre of the southwest cove, so approach slowly with a lookout on the bow. A rock lies in the southeast corner in approximately 14m, rising to 1.8m. Position: 39°06'.21N 01°30'.43E. Anchor in 5–6m over stones and sand to suit wind direction.

A road runs down to the southwest corner where there are fishermen's huts, a few houses and a restaurant.

PUNTA DEL MARÉS

39°06'.9N 01°30'.7E

A 54m headland crowned by a 9m watchtower. The 'cliffs' are set well back from the present shoreline.

⚓ CALA PORTINATX

39°06'.8N 01°30'.8E

An attractive multiple *cala* against a backdrop of wooded mountains, Cala Portinatx has seen considerable tourist development over recent years. There are three arms, each with a sandy beach.

Cala Portinatx: looking northeast over Punta Moscarté and its unusual lighthouse

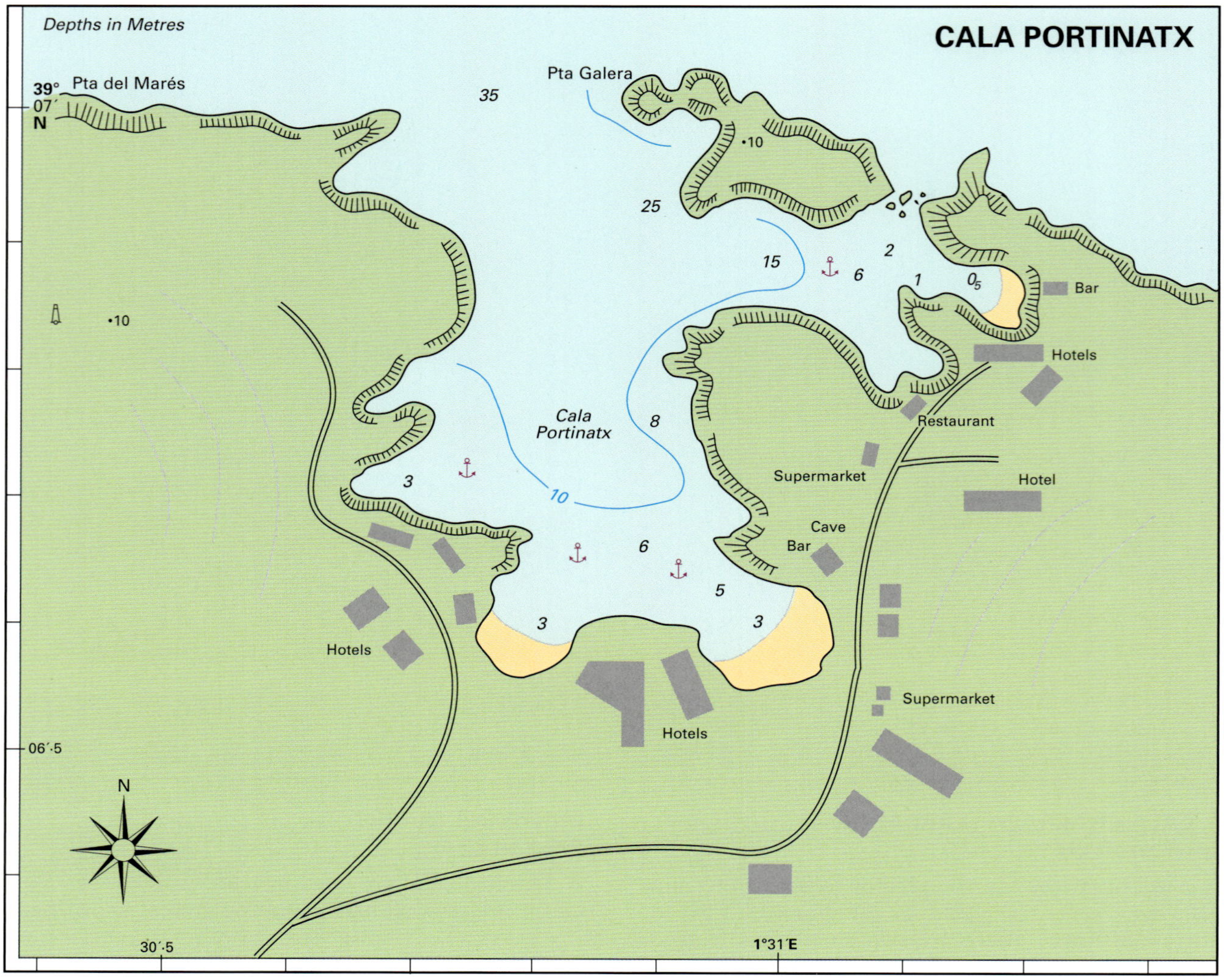

Depths in Metres

CALA PORTINATX

Pta del Marés

Pta Galera

35

Pta del Marés

39° 07′ N

•10

25

15

2

6

1

0 5

Bar

Cala Portinatx

8

•10

Hotels

Restaurant

Supermarket

Hotel

3

Cave Bar

6

5

Supermarket

3

3

Hotels

Hotels

06′·5

N

30′·5

1°31′E

There are bars, restaurants; and discos at night (and sometimes during the day).

Anchor in 3–15m over sand and weed as space permits (but note that holding is patchy and very poor in places); open to northwest and north. There are some private moorings, mostly in the eastern arm, and each beach has an area roped off for swimmers.

Amongst the surrounding hotels and apartment blocks are many restaurants, supermarkets and other shops, plus a dive centre on the central beach where scuba bottles can be refilled.

The Torre de Portanix (or Torre de sa Plana) stands on Punta del Marés to the west of the *cala*. Like most of Ibiza's defensive towers it was built in the second half of the 18th century, but was never fitted with artillery and was later used as a dwelling.

⊕ 15 39°07′.4N 01°32′.0E Pta Moscarté

PUNTA MOSCARTÉ (DES MOSCARTER)

39°07′.2N 01°32′.1E

A prominent rocky headland topped by an unusual lighthouse (Fl.5s93m18M, white round tower with black diagonal stripes 52m: *see photo*).

Pta Moscarté light with its strange diagonal black stripes

5. Punta Den Serra to Islote Botafoch

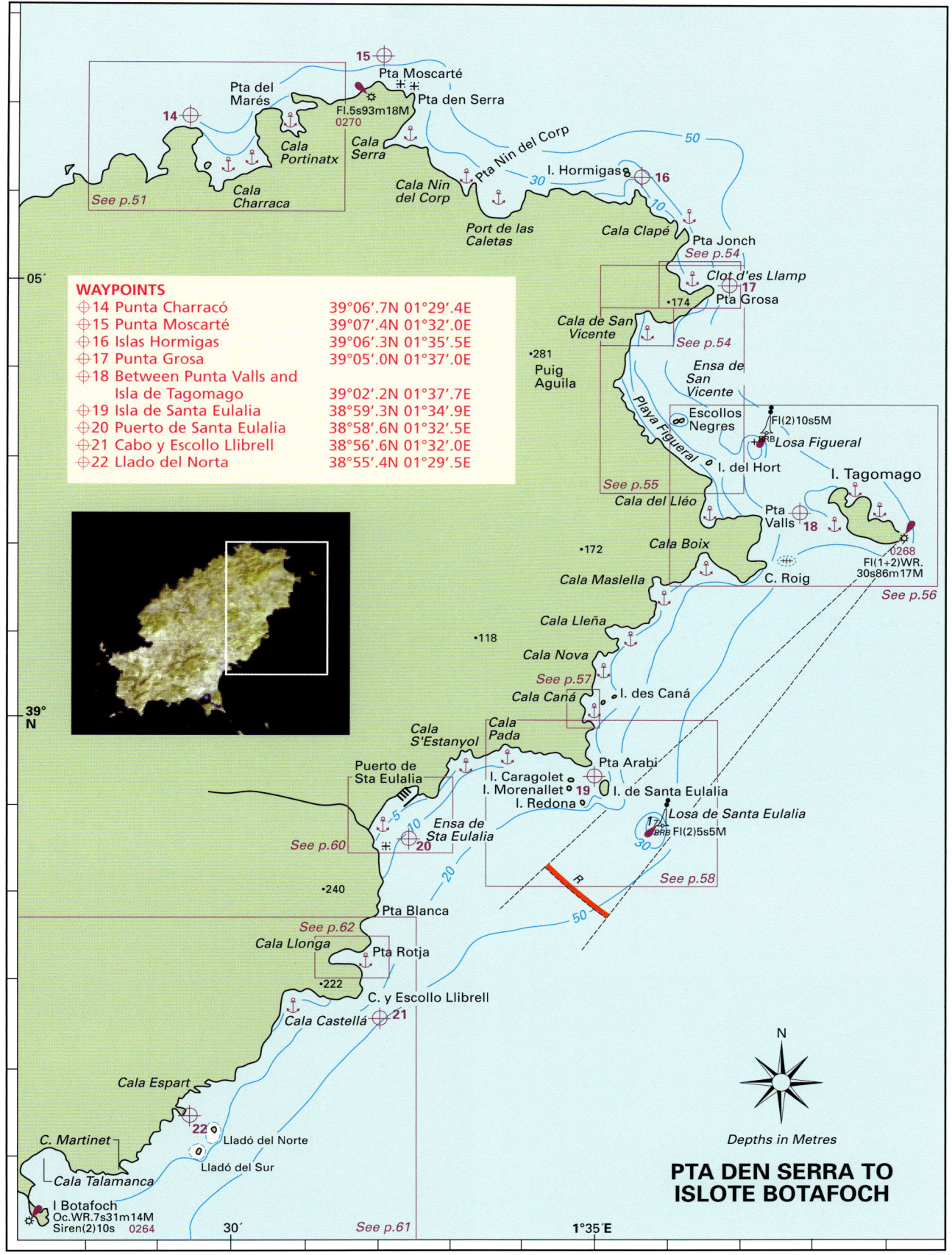

WAYPOINTS

⊕14	Punta Charracó	39°06'.7N 01°29'.4E
⊕15	Punta Moscarté	39°07'.4N 01°32'.0E
⊕16	Islas Hormigas	39°06'.3N 01°35'.5E
⊕17	Punta Grosa	39°05'.0N 01°37'.0E
⊕18	Between Punta Valls and	
	Isla de Tagomago	39°02'.2N 01°37'.7E
⊕19	Isla de Santa Eulalia	38°59'.3N 01°34'.9E
⊕20	Puerto de Santa Eulalia	38°58'.6N 01°32'.5E
⊕21	Cabo y Escollo Llibrell	38°56'.6N 01°32'.0E
⊕22	Llado del Norta	38°55'.4N 01°29'.5E

Pta del Marés · Cala Portinatx · Cala Charraca · *See p.51* · Cala Serra · Pta Moscarté · Fl.5s93m18M · 0270 · Pta den Serra · Pta Nin del Corp · Cala Nin del Corp · Port de las Caletas · Cala Clapé · 50 · 30 · I. Hormigas · ⊕16 · 10 · Pta Jonch · *See p.54* · Clot d'es Llamp · Pta Grosa · 17 · •174 · Cala de San Vicente · *See p.54* · Ensa de San Vicente · •281 Puig Aguila · Playa Figueral · Escollos Negres · Fl(2)10s5M · RB Losa Figueral · I. del Hort · I. Tagomago · *See p.55* · Cala del Lléo · Pta Valls · 18 · 0268 · Fl(1+2)WR. 30s86m17M · •172 · Cala Boix · C. Roig · *See p.56* · Cala Maslella · •118 · Cala Lleña · Cala Nova · *See p.57* · Cala Caná · I. des Caná · Cala S'Estanyol · Cala Pada · Pta Arabí · Puerto de Sta Eulalia · I. Caragolet · I. Morenallet · 19 · I. de Santa Eulalia · I. Redona · Losa de Santa Eulalia · 17 RB Fl(2)5s5M · Ensa de Sta Eulalia · *See p.60* · 5 · 10 · 20 · •240 · R · 50 · *See p.58* · Pta Blanca · *See p.62* · Cala Llonga · Pta Rotja · •222 · C. y Escollo Llibrell · Cala Castellá · 21 · Cala Espart · C. Martinet · 22 · Lladó del Norte · Lladó del Sur · Cala Talamanca · I Botafoch Oc.WR.7s31m14M Siren(2)10s 0264 · 30' · *See p.61* · 1°35'E

05' · 39° N

N

Depths in Metres

PTA DEN SERRA TO ISLOTE BOTAFOCH

⚓ CALA SERRA
39°06'.5N 01°32'.5E

An attractive rocky *cala* open to northeast and east and surrounded by wooded hills. Anchor in 4–5m over sand and rock close to the small stony beach, possibly taking a line to the rocks to limit swinging. Deserted until recently, a tourist development has taken shape to the northwest of the *cala*; this has done little to disturb the remoteness of this bay.

⚓ CALA NIN DEL CORP
39°06'N 01°33'.2E

A small, narrow *cala* to the west of Punta Nin del Corp, which can be difficult to identify from offshore. Anchor in 3–4m near the head of the *cala* over rock, stones and weed; open to the north sector. A second anchor or a line ashore may be needed to limit swinging. Some fishermen's huts will be found on the beach but there are no other buildings.

⚓ PORT DE LAS CALETAS (RACÓ DE SA TALAIA)
39°05'.9N 01°33'.6E

Another misnomer, being a wide but undeveloped *cala* lying beneath high rocky cliffs and open to the north sector. Houses line the zigzag road up from the small beach. Anchor in the west part of the *cala* close inshore in 10m over rock, stone or sand; a breaking shoal lies between this anchorage and the beach.

⊕ 16 39°06'.3N 01°35'.5E Islas Hormigas

⚓ CALA CLAPÉ (CALA JONE)
39°05'.5N 01°36'.2E

A small *cala* northwest of Punta Jonch (Punta Jone), open to north sector and fringed by rocks on its south side. Anchor in the middle of the *cala* over sand.

⚓ CLOT D'ES LLAMP
39°04'.9N 01°36'.4E

A coastal anchorage on the north side of Punta Grosa, useful for the crossing to and from Mallorca. Anchor inshore in 4–6m over sand and stone. Open to the north sector and the east, but protected from other directions by high cliffs containing some fantastic rock formations, including a large stalactite cave. Beware of sudden catabalic winds off the cliffs.

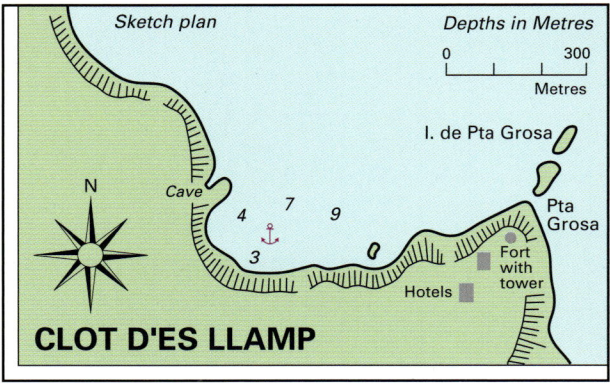

Landing can be difficult, but once ashore there are steps up to some hotels and a supermarket.

⊕ 17 39°05'.0N 01°37'.0E Pta Grosa

PUNTA GROSA
39°04'.9N 01°36'.7E

A high (174m), rocky, cliffed point with two offlying islands. A small square fort with a distinctive single tower stands on the headland.

⚓ CALA DE SAN VICENTE (SANT VICENC)
39°04'.5N 01°35'.6E

A well-protected anchorage at the north end of a long bay, the Ensenada de San Vicente, open to the southeast and with some fetch from the south. Anchor close inshore in 3–6m over sand and weed, being careful to avoid an underwater cable from Palma which terminates near the road (see plan below). *Note* The Losa Figueral isolated danger mark in the south end of Ensenada de San Vicente

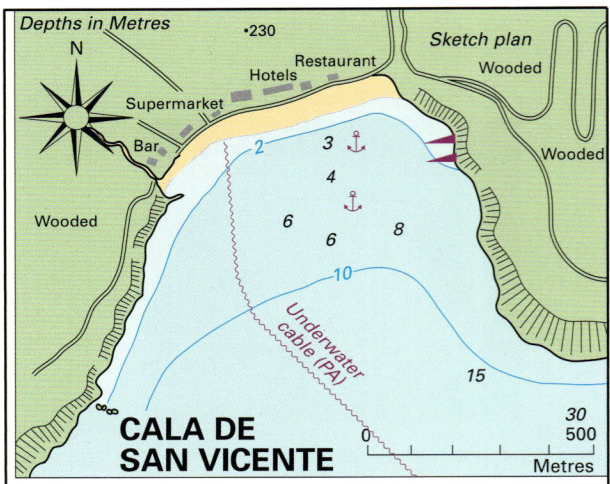

Cala de San Vicente: again showing the spectacular countryside

was reported out of position during 2009. (See plan below.) The beach is lined by hotels and tourist apartments against a backdrop of high wooded hills. The beach gets crowded in season and the usual bars and restaurants will be found ashore.

The cave temple of Es Cuyeram, dating back to the 5th century BC and later dedicated to the Carthaginian goddess Tanit, lies in the hills to the north. Excavated in 1907, most of the artefacts have now been moved to the Archaeological Museum of Ibiza.

PLAYA FIGUERAL

Centred on 39°03'.4N 01°36'E

A long stony beach occupying the south part of the Ensenada de San Vicente; and with various offlying dangers. Taken from north to south these are:

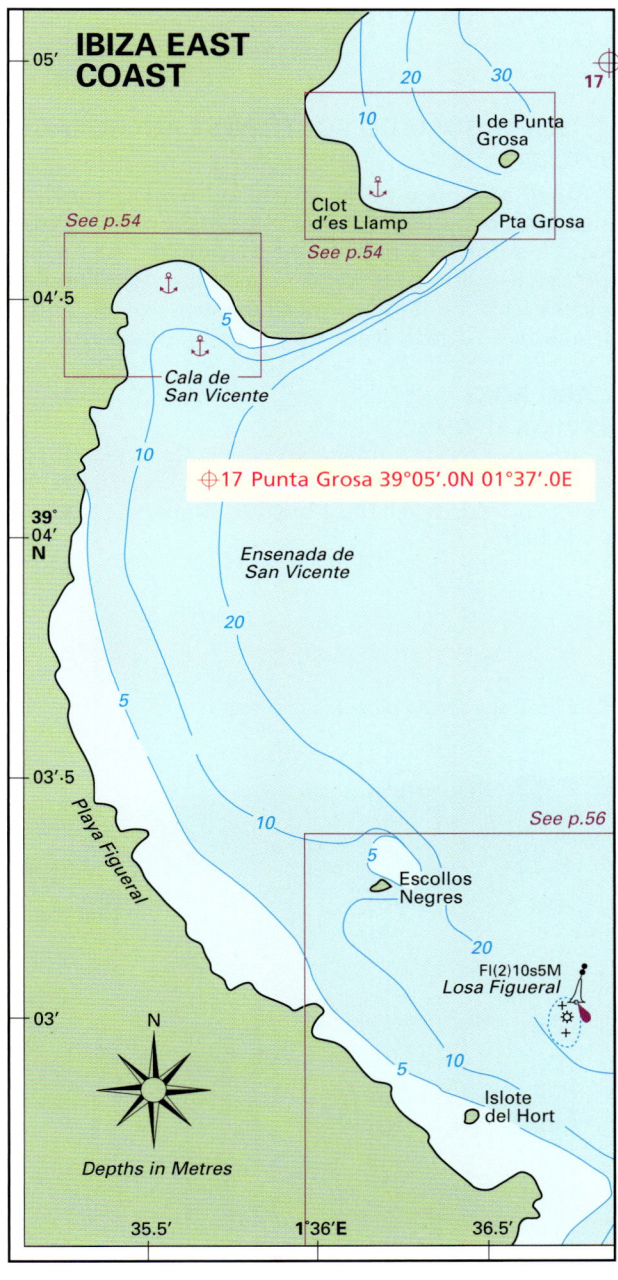

- The Escollos Negres, three small, low, black rocky islands lying up to 0.4 miles offshore
- Losa Figueral (39°03'.1N 01°37'.3E), is an awash rock 0.6 miles off the beach. An isolated, lit (Fl(2)10s5M), danger pillar buoy has been laid nearby with ⁞ topmark. Note that dangerous, rocky shoals extend 500m north and south of the Losa itself
- Isla del Hort, 20m in height, lying 200m off the coast inshore of Losa Figueral.

Small inshore rocky islets line much of the playa, in addition to the above.

⚓ CALA DEL LLÉO (CALA SAN CARLOS)

39°02'.3N 01°36'.6E

An open bay anchorage under high cliffs, south of Playa Figueral and northwest of Punta Valls. There are dangerous rocks on either side of the bay – approach the centre of the sandy beach on a bearing of 220° to anchor in 4–6m over sand and rock. A few fishermen's huts will be found at the head of the *cala* with a café a short walk inland.

PUNTA VALLS

39°02'.3N 01°37'.3E

A 67m cliffed promontory with a 9m stone tower.

ISLA TAGOMAGO

39°01'.9N 01°39'.0E (lighthouse)

A very conspicuous island nearly one mile long which resembles a huge dolphin heading out to sea. The lighthouse at its southeast tip (Fl(1+2)WR.30s 86m17M White octagonal tower on building 23m) has a red sector 037° to 043.5° over Losa de Santa Eulalia (see plan on page 56) and is obscured from the west by a 114m hill. A large white house occupies the centre of the island.

Passage between Isla Tagomago and Ibiza

⊕18 39°02'.2N 01°37'.7E Between Pta Valls and Isla Tagomago

A clear passage 0.8 miles wide and around 40m deep separates Isla Tagomago from Ibiza. However, be aware of the unmarked wreck off Cabo Roig (see plan on page 56).

⚓ ISLA TAGOMAGO, NORTHEAST ANCHORAGES

39°02'.4N 01°38'.5E and 39°02'.2N 01°38'.8E

Two small *calas* open to the northeast sector, the northeast *cala* tucked in behind breaking rocks. Approach with care: the water is deep until very close in, so anchor close inshore in 8–10m over rock with a few sand patches.

I. IBIZA

Isla Tagomago: looking east-southeast into the west anchorage

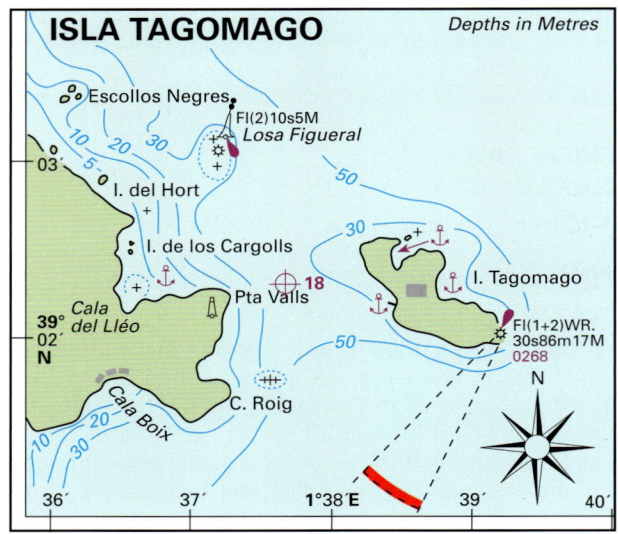

ISLA TAGOMAGO — Depths in Metres

Escollos Negres
Fl(2)10s5M
Losa Figueral
I. del Hort
I. de los Cargolls
Pta Valls — 18
Cala del Lléo
39° 02' N
Cala Boix
C. Roig
I. Tagomago
Fl(1+2)WR. 30s86m17M
0268
36' 37' 1°38'E 39' 40'

⊕18 Between Punta Valls and Isla Tagomago
39°02'.2N 01°37'.7E

Isla Tagomago: southwest anchorage

Looking northwest across Isla Tagomago towards Cala de San Vicente

⚓ ISLA TAGOMAGO SOUTHWEST ANCHORAGE
39°02'.2N 01°38'.4E

A small *cala* open to the south and west sectors and susceptible to swell. Anchor close inshore in 5m over sand – a line to a rock may be required – or further off in 8–10m over weed. There are two landing places used by daily tourist boats in season, and a beach bar. A track leads up to the lighthouse.

CABO ROIG
39°01'.5N 01°37'.0E

A grey and reddish rocky cliffed headland (138m). A dangerous wreck, awash but unmarked, lies some 350m northeast of the point. It should be given a wide berth.

Cala Boix: the fertile plain highlighted in the sun

⚓ CALA BOIX
39°01'.7N 01°36'.5E

A good anchorage west of Cabo Roig, surrounded by high rocky cliffs and open to the south sector. Anchor off the sandy beach in 3–8m over sand. There is a small jetty, a beach bar and a few houses ashore, plus a track to the main road.

⚓ CALA MASTELLA
39°01'.3N 01°35'.8E

A pleasant little *cala* with a beach at its head, surrounded by trees and some houses. Anchor in the centre of the *cala* in 2–4m over sand, weed and occasional rock patches. There is a beach bar and fish restaurant ashore, and the village of Ca'n Jordi about ½ mile away.

Cala Mastella: a tiny *cala* with a development at its head

Cala Lleña: an attractive beach

⚓ CALA LLEÑA (LLENYA)
39°00'.9N 01°35'.4E

A wide *cala* with an attractive beach, often crowded, in an outcrop of square white hotels and apartment buildings; the Club Cala Lleña, amongst the pine trees to the south. Anchor off the beach in 5m over sand, open to the east–southeast–south.

⚓ CALA NOVA
39°00'.5N 01°35'.1E

Another wide *cala* with a long beach and pine trees, but somewhat less built up than Cala Lleña. Even so there are beach bars, etc. to cater for the tourists staying in nearby resort of Es Caná. Anchor in 4–6m over sand. If approaching from the south be sure to avoid the Islas des Caná, described below.

ISLAS DES CANÁ
39°00'.2N 01°35'.2E

The Islas des Caná comprise Isla de Caná (2.3m) and the smaller Sa Galera, plus some offlying rocks. Shoals run out from the headland north of Cala Caná to about halfway to the islands, and the inside passage should not be attempted without local knowledge.

⚓ CALA CANÁ (CANAR)
39°00'.1N 01°34'.7E

A popular open *cala* with a sandy beach and low rocky sides, surrounded by hotels and apartment blocks. There is a tiny harbour for speedboats and small fishing craft on the south shore. Anchor off the centre of the beach in 4–6m over sand as fringing rocks, covered to a depth of 2m or so, extend from either side. The Islas des Caná lie some 600m offshore due east of the *cala*, but are easily seen on approach.

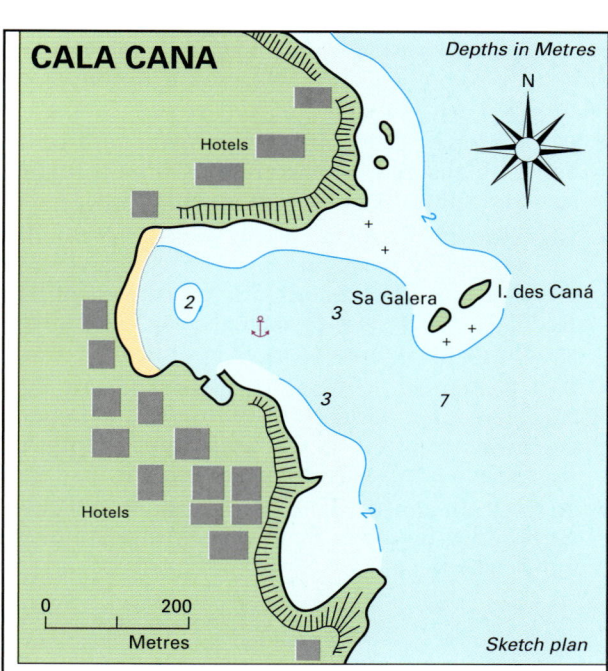

CALA CANA — Depths in Metres

Hotels

Sa Galera — I. des Caná

Hotels

0 — 200 — Metres

Sketch plan

Cala Caná: surrounded by the usual tourist development, but still a good anchorage

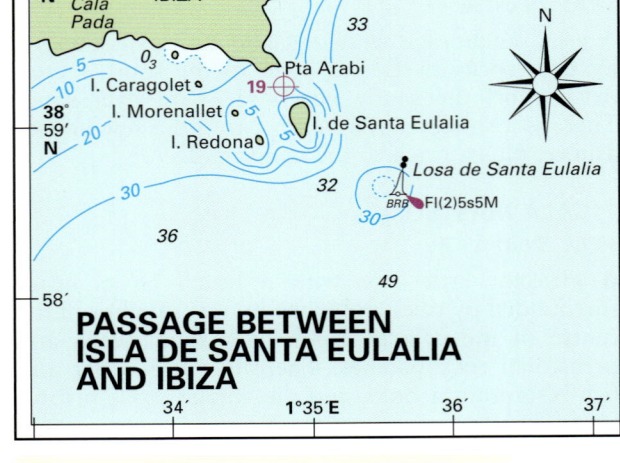

⊕19 Isla de Santa Eulalia 38°59'.3N 01°34'.9E

PUNTA ARABI

38°59'.4N 01°35'E

A low (22m) whitish rocky point surmounted by buildings and dark trees.

ISLA DE SANTA EULALIA

38°59'.1N 01°35'.2E

A peardrop-shaped island, 37m in height and measuring some 350m along its north/south axis.

Passages between Isla de Santa Eulalia and Ibiza

The passage itself should present no problems, being at least 400m wide and with depths of more than 5m throughout. However, a possible hazard is posed by four small rocky islands which straddle the western approach/exit (see plan). Taken from northeast to northwest these comprise:

- Isla Redona (22m), 400m southwest of Isla de Santa Eulalia and easily seen. Close in it is foul to east and south. It can be left on either side.
- Isla Morenallet, a low, black, rocky islet usually surrounded by breaking seas, some 650m west of Isla de Santa Eulalia and 550m northwest of Isla Redona. Easily seen in daylight but difficult to spot at night. Again, it can be left on either side.
- Isla Caragolet, similar in appearance to Isla Morenallet but 450m to the northwest and about that distance offshore. On no account attempt to pass inside Isla Caragolet, due to shoals.
- A small unnamed island close inshore, which is surrounded by rocky shallows and should not be approached.

LOSA DE SANTA EULALIA

38°58'.8N 01°35'.7E

This rocky patch 1.7m deep lies 1,000m southeast of Isla Santa Eulalia and is often marked by broken water. A buoy has been laid at 110° from the rock at 38°58'.7N 01°35'.5E, (Fl(2)5s5M Pillar buoy with topmark). This isolated danger buoy has been reported closer inshore (2010).

Other than a few nearby rocks the Losa de Santa Eulalia is surrounded by clear water, and a 32m deep passage separates it from Isla Santa Eulalia. It is covered by the red sector of the Islote Tagomago light to the northeast. See plan on page 56.

⚓ CALA PADA

38°59'.5N 01°33'.7E

A very small anchorage in a tiny *cala*, surrounded by trees and open southeast–south–southwest. The eastern part of the bay is reserved for boardsailors. Anchor in 3m over sand off the small beach, avoiding the many permanent moorings. A beach restaurant lies directly behind the short wooden jetty.

⚓ CALA S'ESTANYOL

38°59'.5N 01°33'.2E

A small, wooded anchorage near the mouth of a river, off a sand and stone beach. Anchor in 3m over sand, stones and weed, open to east–southeast–south. Two large white hotel or apartment buildings mark the southern end of the beach.

IB3 Puerto de Santa Eulalia del Río (Santa Eulària des Riu)

A safe and friendly harbour, 50M from Mallorca, easy to enter in most conditions, with berths for 755 vessels up to 25m

Location
38°58′.9N 01°32′.3E

Communications
Puerto Deportivo de Santa Eulalia VHF Ch 09
Club náutico ① 971 339754/336161 *Fax* 971 332810
Email ptostaeulalia@interbook.net

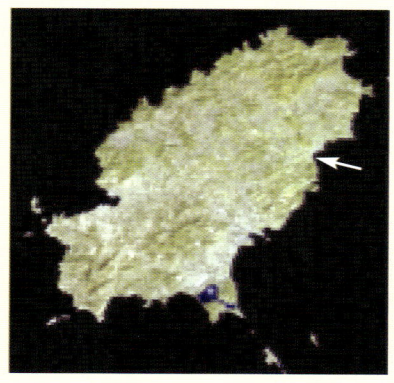

The marina

Santa Eulalia Marina is a large (755-berth) marina completed in 1991, with an easy approach and entrance except in strong winds from southeast and south. The staff are helpful and several speak good English.

PILOTAGE

Approach

⊕20 38°58′.6N 01°32′.5E Puerto de Santa Eulalia

From southwest If coming from Puerto de Ibiza or Formentera be sure to identify the two small islands

Lladó del Sur (6m), and Lladó del Norte (10m), which lie 0.8 and one mile respectively northeast of Cabo Martinet, near the 30m contour (see plan on page 53). Once identified, they can safely be passed on either side. Cabo Llibrell can be rounded at 200m, after which the houses and high-rise buildings of Santa Eulalia will be seen. The harbour lies at the northern end of the town, near the middle of the wide bay.

From northeast If approaching the island from the direction of Mallorca and intending to make Puerto de Santa Eulalia the first port of call, Isla Tagomago may be passed on either side. However, if taking the inshore passage give a wide berth to the wreck, awash but unmarked, 350m northeast of Cabo

Puerto de Santa Eulalia viewed from southeast

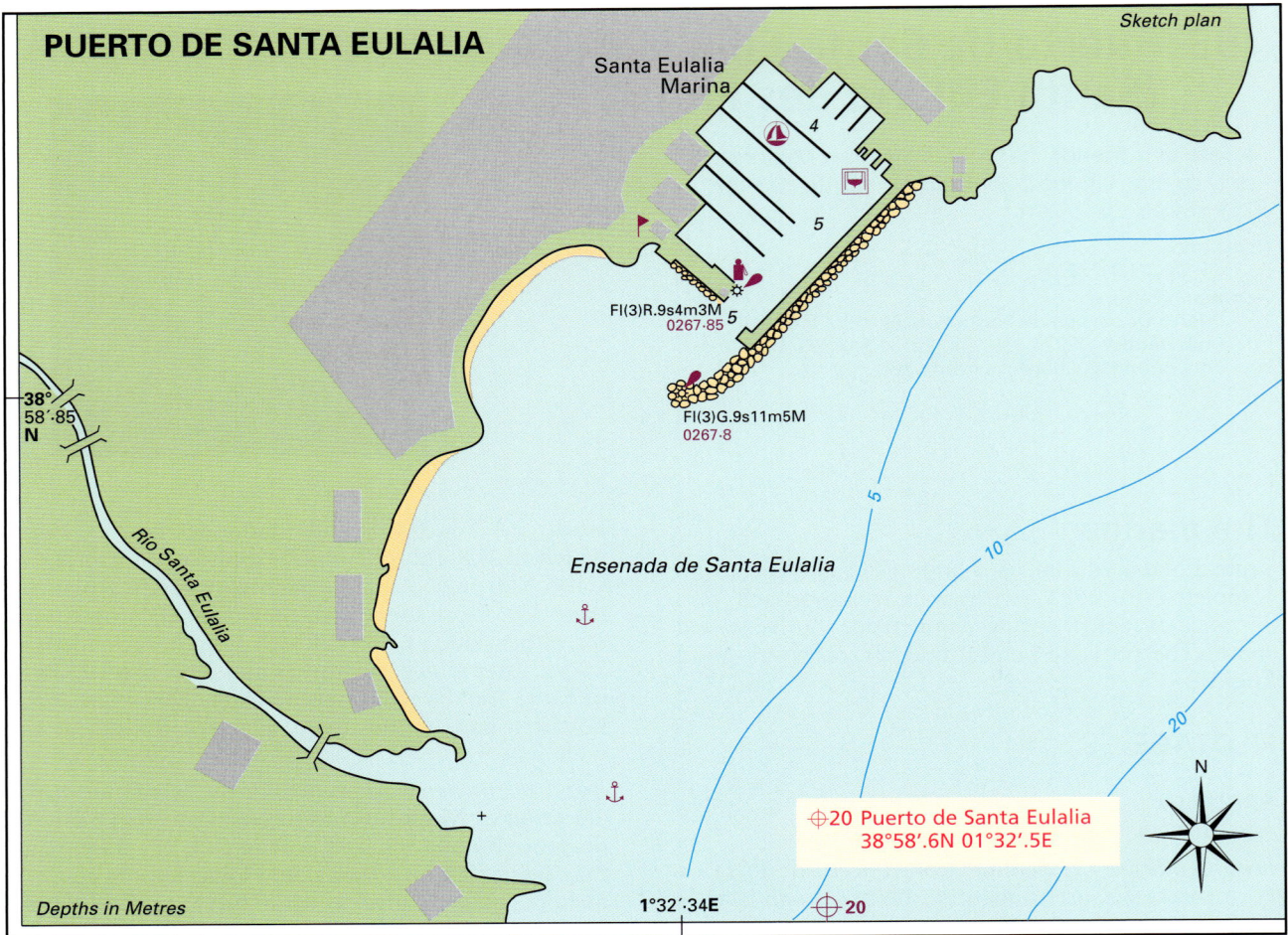

PUERTO DE SANTA EULALIA

Sketch plan

Santa Eulalia Marina

4

5

Fl(3)R.9s4m3M
0267·85 5

Fl(3)G.9s11m5M
0267·8

Río Santa Eulalia

38°
58'·85
N

Ensenada de Santa Eulalia

⊕20 Puerto de Santa Eulalia
38°58'.6N 01°32'.5E

N

Depths in Metres

1°32'·34E

⊕ 20

Roig. The headland itself is steep-to. Off Punta Arabi, either set a course between Isla de Santa Eulalia and Losa de Santa Eulalia, or take one of the passages between Isla de Santa Eulalia and the mainland as described earlier. The harbour lies at the north end of the town, near the middle of the wide bay.

Anchorage in the approach

There are two small calas, Cala Pada and Cala S'Estanyol (detailed above and marked on the plan on page 53), in the north part of the bay. However, the anchorage most convenient for the town is that in the southwest corner of the bay, near the mouth of the Río Santa Eulalia (see *Ensenada de Santa Eulalia* anchorage above). Anchoring outside the marina entrance is forbidden.

Entrance

At the end of the west mole is situated a round, white, three-storey tower which houses, amongst other things, the marina offices. Approach from anywhere in the bay keeping well clear of the end of the southeast breakwater. The marina entrance is kept dredged to at least 5m.

Berthing

Berth alongside the fuel/reception pontoon, beneath the white tower, to be allocated a berth. There is a 3-knot speed limit. The marina can accommodate yachts of up to 25m LOA and 4.5m draught. However, like many marinas in the Islas Baleares, it is frequently full to capacity during the high season.

Facilities

Water Taps on pontoons and quays. The water in Ibiza is of variable quality so if possible consult other yachtsmen before filling tanks.

Electricity 220v AC points on pontoons and quays.

Fuel Diesel and petrol pumps close beneath the tower on the west mole.

Provisions Shops and supermarkets in Santa Eulalia del Río nearby, where most requirements can be met. All-day market on Wednesdays in summer. There is also a supermarket at the harbour.

Ice From the marina office.

Chandlery In the marina complex.

Repairs Marina Río boatyard can handle all usual work including GRP repairs ☏ 971 33 04 53 *Fax* 971 33 21 11. Travel-lift 60 tonnes.

Engineers At Marina Río, Boat Service Germany ☏/*Fax* 971 33 01 21 is a local service agent for Volvo Penta.

Showers In the 'control tower' building and behind the diving school at the northwest end of the marina.

Launderette In the town.

Banks In the marina complex and in town.

Hospital In the town.

Transport

Car hire/taxis Can be arranged via the marina office.
Buses Regular service to Ibiza town (15 minute journey) and elsewhere.
Ferries Tourist ferries berth outside the harbour, near the root of the west mole.
Air services Ibiza airport 15 miles.

Sights ashore locally

Previously a fishing village and market centre based on the fortified 16th-century church at Puig de Missa, the hill above the river mouth, Santa Eulalia later became a centre for artists but is now a major tourist resort. The bay has been overwhelmed by hotels and other buildings in recent years, but still offers good, if crowded, sand and rock beaches.

There are many interesting buildings in the old town, plus the remains of a Roman aqueduct across the Río Santa Eulalia. The Ethnological Museum of the Pitiusan Islands is situated in the town.

Local events

Santa Eulalia's day is celebrated on 12 February. There is a Holy Week procession on the afternoon of Good Friday and a Festival of Flowers on the first Sunday in May. The Fiesta de Jesus is held on 8 September.

Eating out

Many, cafés and restaurants of all grades, including several in the marina itself.

Paella chef near Santa Eulalia   *GW*

ANCHORAGES AND FEATURES FROM PUERTO STA EULALIA TO PUERTO IBIZA

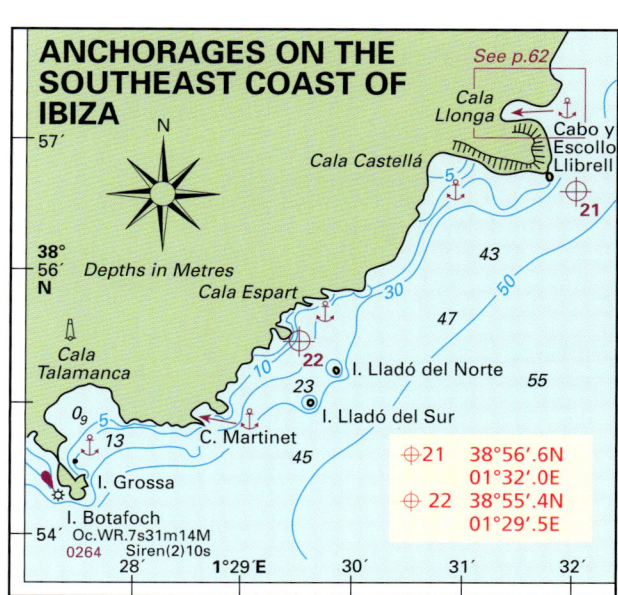

ANCHORAGES ON THE SOUTHEAST COAST OF IBIZA

See p.62

Cala Llonga
Cabo y Escollo Llibrell
Cala Castellá
Depths in Metres
Cala Espart
Cala Talamanca
I. Lladó del Norte
I. Lladó del Sur
C. Martinet
I. Grossa
I. Botafoch
Oc.WR.7s31m14M
Siren(2)10s
0264

⊕21	38°56′.6N 01°32′.0E
⊕22	38°55′.4N 01°29′.5E

I. IBIZA

⚓ ENSENADA DE SANTA EULALIA (SANTA EULÀRIA)

38°58′.7N 01°32′.1E

Anchor in the southwest corner of this large bay, near the mouth of Río Santa Eulalia, in 3–5m over sand and mud. A sandy beach runs northeast, with several large hotels a short distance inland. All the facilities of Puerto de Santa Eulalia are available within half a mile. There are rocks awash near the shore south of the river mouth.

PUNTA ROTJA (ROJA)

38°57′.4N 01°31′.9E

A high (100m) red and whitish cliffed point with houses on the top.

⚓ CALA LLONGA

38°57′.2N 01°31′.6E

A long, high-sided *cala* with an excellent but often crowded beach at its head. The entrance can be difficult to spot until almost due east of the *cala*, when the huge blocks of flats and other buildings which line the wooded cliffs will be seen.

Anchor in 4–6 m over sand about halfway up the *cala* but keep clear of the swimmers' buoys at the west end of the *cala*. Although open only to the east and offering good protection, it can be gusty at times when west winds funnel down the valley. Swell from the east quadrant also works in, rebounding off the sides and setting yachts rolling.

Daily tourist boats visit from Santa Eulalia, causing some wash. Bars, restaurants and a supermarket will be found ashore. Buses run to Santa Eulalia. On 15 August Cala Llonga celebrates the anniversary of its patron saint.

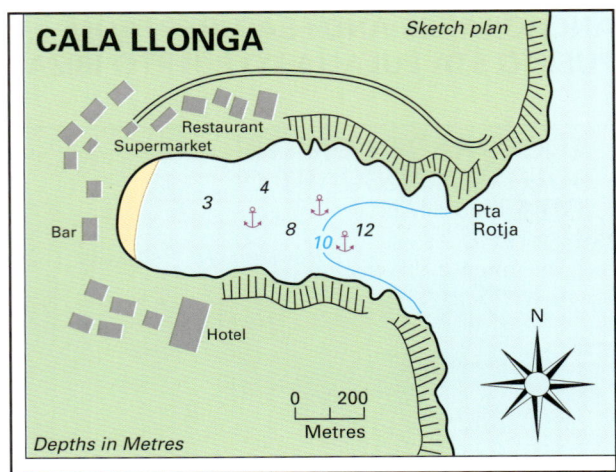

CALA LLONGA
Sketch plan

Restaurant
Supermarket

3   4

Bar   8   12
10

Hotel

Pta
Rotja

N

0   200
Metres

Depths in Metres

⊕ 21 38°56'.6N 01°32'.0E Cabo y Escollo Llibrell

CABO Y ESCOLLO LLIBRELL
38°56'.8N 01°31'.8E

A high (220m) headland of whitish rock with a small outlying islet.

⚓ CALA CASTELLÁ (SÓL D'EN SERRA)
38°56'.8N 01°30'.9E

A wide bay just south of Cabo y Escollo Llibrell, open to east through south to southwest. Anchor in 5m over sand off the long sandy beach.

⚓ CALA ESPART
38°55'.6N 01°29'.4E

A small open bay with a sandy beach track to the road. Anchor in 5m over sand off the beach.

Cala Llonga: a popular anchorage in summer

⊕ 22 38°55′.4N 01°29′.5E Between Lladó del Norte and the mainland

LLADÓ DEL NORTE AND LLADÓ DEL SUR
38°55′.2N 01°29′.8E

Two small islands, 10m and 6m high respectively, which lie 0.5 and 0.7 miles south of Cala Espart, near the 30m contour. They may be left on either side.

⚓ CALA NORTHEAST OF CABO MARTINET
38°54′.9N 01°28′.6E

A small unnamed *cala* on the northeast side of the cape, to be used with care. Anchor off the small beach in 5m over sand and rock, open to east through south. There is a road at the top of the cliff.

CABO MARTINET
38°54′.8N 01°28′.7E

A low headland of dark rock with trees and houses on the top. An aero radiobeacon, inconspicuous, lies 700m to the west-northwest.

⚓ CALA TALAMANCA
38°54′.9N 01°27′.6E

A large open *cala* with a long sandy beach at its head. The head of the *cala* is shallow and has some reefs; anchor with care off Punta Sa Tabernera in 3–6m over sand and weed, although with careful sounding, a spot can be found further north in the middle of the *cala*.

Land in the northwest corner of the bay – from which it is about 20 minutes' walk into Ibiza or a mere 350m to the facilities of Marina Botafoch – or on the isthmus leading to Isla Grossa. (See plan on page 61.)

I. IBIZA

Ibiza Town, viewed towards Marina Botafoch and Cala Talamanca *GW*

II. Formentera

Smaller than Ibiza and without an airport, Formentera is less developed and enjoys a slower pace of life. Nudism is an accepted feature. The low-lying plain in the north with its associated saltpans and lagoons are of interest. The only port, Puerto de Sabina, has limited facilities. There are a few pleasant anchorages around the island, and a large bay in which to drop anchor in the adjacent Isla Espalmador, linked to Formentera via a long sandy spit, broken by a rocky passage.

FORMENTERA WAYPOINTS
⊕4   Freu Grande channel   38°48'.6N 01°25'.6E
⊕23 Puerto de Sabina   38°44'.2N 01°25'.3E
⊕24 Isla del Gastabí (SW)   38°46'.3N 01°24'.7E
⊕25 Pta Single Mal   38°39'.8N 01°36'.0E
⊕26 Cabo Berbería   38°37'.7N 01°23'.2E
⊕27 Pta Gabina   38°43'.1N 01°22'.1E

Note Many anchorages are now laid with buoys for part of the year

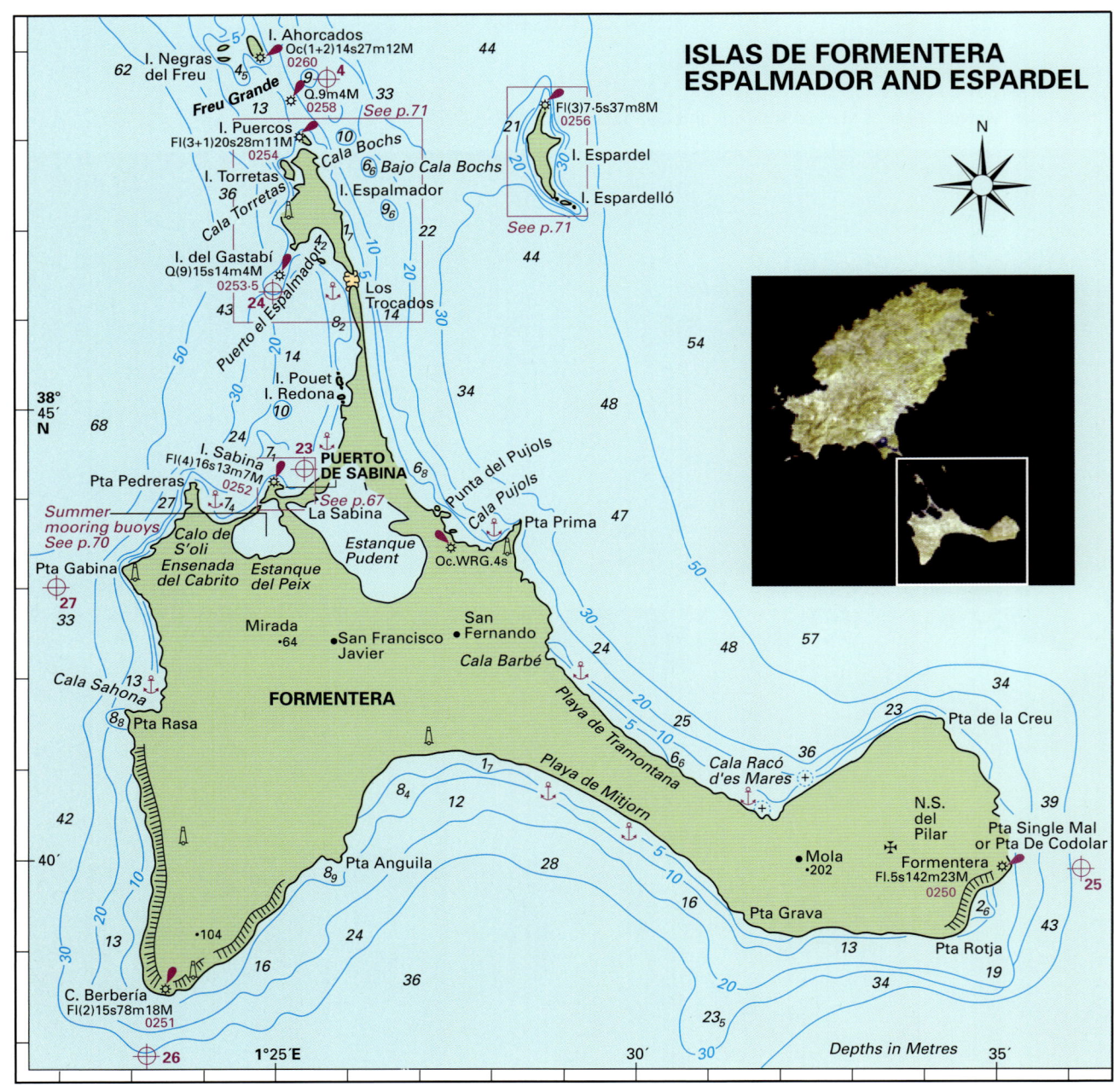

ISLAS DE FORMENTERA ESPALMADOR AND ESPARDEL

NAVIGATIONAL INFORMATION FOR APPROACHES TO FORMENTERA

Coming up from North Africa or the Eastern Mediterranean and heading for Spain, Formentera is a good first landfall if west winds have hindered a westerly passage. In which case, head either for one of the anchorages described on the east side of the island, or for the only port on the island, Puerto de Sabina.

Magnetic variation

Formentera –00°42'W (decreasing 6'E annually).

Approach and coastal passage charts
(See *Appendix* for a full list of Balearic charts)

Imray	M3, M12, M13
Admiralty	1701, 1702, 2834
Spanish	7A, 478, 479, 479A
French	5505, 7114

Approach lights
0256 **Isla Espardel, north point** 38°48'.2N 01°28'.6E
Fl(3)7.5s37m8M White truncated conical tower 16m
0250 **Formentera (Punta Single Mal or Punta de Codolà)**
38°39'.7N 01°35'E Fl.5s142m23M White tower on white building 22m 150°-vis-050°
0251 **Cabo Berbería** 38°38'.4N 01°23'.3E Fl(2)15s78m18M White round tower 19m 234°-vis-170°
0252 **Isla Sabina** 38°44'.1N 01°24'.9E Fl(4)16s13m7M White truncated conical tower 11m
0253.5 **Isla del Gastabí** 38°46'.5N 01°25'.1E Q(9)15s14m4M W cardinal tower, ⚡ topmark 8m

Buoys in the approach to Puerto de Sabina
32841(S) **Buoy 1** 38°44'.2N 01°25'.1E Fl.G.4s5M lateral starboard, green cylindrical buoy.
32842(S) **Buoy 2** 38°44'.3N 01°25'.5E Fl.R.4s5M lateral port, ■ topmark

Introduction

Formentera and the small island of Espalmador to its north (*see plan on* page 35), lie two miles south off Punta Portas, the most southerly tip of Ibiza. These islands remain underdeveloped as compared with the rest of the Balearic Islands, with just one harbour serving Formentera.

Espalmador, by far the smaller of the two and virtually deserted, is 1.5 miles long and less than a mile wide, rising to a height of 24m on its west side where there is a conspicuous tower. It is joined to Formentera by a long sandy spit broken by a shallow rocky passage, the Freu Poco, which separates the two islands.

Formentera is 10 miles long and eight miles wide at its extremes, but being an elongated S-shape, covers an area of only 37 square miles. It comprises two high features: La Mola (192m), an island-like area to the east, and the peninsula running out to Cabo Berbería (107m) to the southwest. These two higher regions are attached by a long, low neck of land. There is a large, low-lying plain in the northern part of the island, the greater part of it occupied by lagoons and salt pans. Salt has long been a major export. Around the two high features the coast is made up of rocky cliffs, but in the north and northeast it is flat and sandy. Much of the island is cultivated and there are pine forests around La Mola.

There is a permanent population of around 5,000 (according to some sources, favoured with the longest life expectancy in Spain), most of whom are involved in some aspect of the tourist industry. Nudism has long been accepted on the beaches of Formentera. Do not be surprised to see sailboarders, waterskiers and yacht crews sailing around naked.

HISTORY

The history of Formentera and Espalmador parallels that of Ibiza. The oldest evidence of human occupation is the 2000BC megalithic tomb at Cana Costa. In Roman times they formed part of the Pityusae (Pine Islands): Espalmador was known as Ophioussa and Formentera as Frumentum or Frumentaria (a reference to the large amount of wheat it supplied), since corrupted into Formentera.

During the hundreds of years following the downfall of Rome the island became depopulated as it was frequently raided by Barbarians, Moors, Saracens and even Scandinavians on their way home after taking part in one of the Crusades. It was not until 1697 that the island was repopulated, but even so was still subject to raids by pirates. The local inhabitants even turned to piracy themselves on occasion, and in 1806 captured the British 12-gun brig *Felicity* and sailed her into Ibiza.

TOURIST INFORMATION

Places of interest

San Francisco Javier is an attractive small town with a fortified church which once mounted guns on its tower, from which fine views can now be enjoyed. The ravine running down to Cala Sahona on the west coast and the area around La Mola in the east are worth visiting if time permits, with the caves of d'en Xeroni also of interest.

For details of tourist offices see the *General Introduction*.

Embassies

See *Appendix* for list of embassies.

One of the many anchorages around Formentera

F1 Puerto de Sabina (Port de sa Savina)

Puerto de Sabina is the only harbour on Formentera. It provides good protection from swell but not from the wind as it is a low-lying island. The two marinas within the harbour provide just over 200 yacht berths between them, for yachts up to 22m. Both are always full during the summer

Location
38°44'.1N 01°25'.1E

Distance from Spanish mainland
Javier 60M

Buoys
32843(S) **Buoy 3** 38°44'.2N 01°25'.4E Fl(2)R.15s3M lateral port, ■ topmark
32844(S) **Buoy 4** 38°44'.1N 01°25'.4E Fl(3)R.19s3M lateral port, ■ topmark

Communications
Marina de Formentera VHF Ch 09
Port Authority ☎ 971 32 31 32 *Fax* 971 32 32 52
www.marinadeformentera.com
Email info@marinadeformentera.com
Marina Formentera Mar
☎ 971 32 32 35/32 29 63
Fax 971 32 22 22
Email info@formenteramar.com
www.formenteramar.com

The port

Puerto de Sabina is the only harbour on Isla de Formentera and is in constant use by ferries, commercial shipping and fishing craft. Even so, it has maintained an attractive atmosphere and is not yet overrun with tourists. No room will be found for visiting yachts during the summer season. Even getting water may take a day or two of waiting at the anchorage. The harbour is easy to approach and enter, well sheltered once inside, though the breakwaters offer little protection from the wind. As with many harbours in the Islands, more than one marina operates within the same basin.

Formentera viewed from northwest across Puerto de Sabina

PILOTAGE

Approach

⊕23 Puerto de Sabina 38°44'.2N 01°25'.3E

From east and northeast Approach to the marina can be made either through the Freu Grande between Ibiza and Espalmador (see *Passages between Ibiza and Espalmador* on page 34) or around the south side of the island.

From west Approach from the Spanish mainland is straightforward with no offlying dangers.

From west, northwest and north There are no hazards in the approach to Puerto de Sabina over an arc between Punta Pedreras (unlit) to the west and Isla Gastabí (lit) to the north (see plan on page 64). The white buildings behind the harbour show up well, as does the white tower of Isla Sabina lighthouse. Note that this lighthouse is situated near the end of a projecting rocky spur with shallow water to either side.

Entrance

Entrance to the main harbour is generally straightforward, though it can become dangerous in strong northerly or northwesterly winds due to shoaling depths. This has been alleviated with the aid of the four laid buoys noted above and shown on the plan below, but care is still needed in the entrance in rough weather. Normally the greatest hazard is posed by the many ferries which enter and leave at speed. Both Marina de Formentera in the southwest corner of the basin and Marina Formentera Mar to the east are reached through relatively narrow inner entrances.

Berthing

Marina de Formentera at the southwest end of the harbour. 108 berths up to 20m.
VHF Ch 09
☎ 971 32 31 32 *Fax* 971 32 10 33
Email reservas@marinadeformentera.com
www.marinadeformentera.com

Marina Formentera Mar to the east end berths 90 vessels.

Contact the marina office on approach or occupy any convenient vacant berth until allocated a spot by marina staff. Staff are usually prompt at any time of the day or night in summer, in turning away most new arrivals!
☎ 971 32 32 35/32 29 63 *Fax* 971 32 22 22
Email info@formenteramar.com
www.formenteramar.com

Facilities

Water Metered taps on pontoons and quays.
Electricity 220v AC points on pontoons and quays, charged by the day.
Fuel Diesel pump on the central mole (see plan).
Repairs A small boatyard centred around the travel-lift and slipway. Boat repairs and engineering services can be arranged via the marina office. A 35-tonne travel-lift and slipway near the office. Oil collection facility.

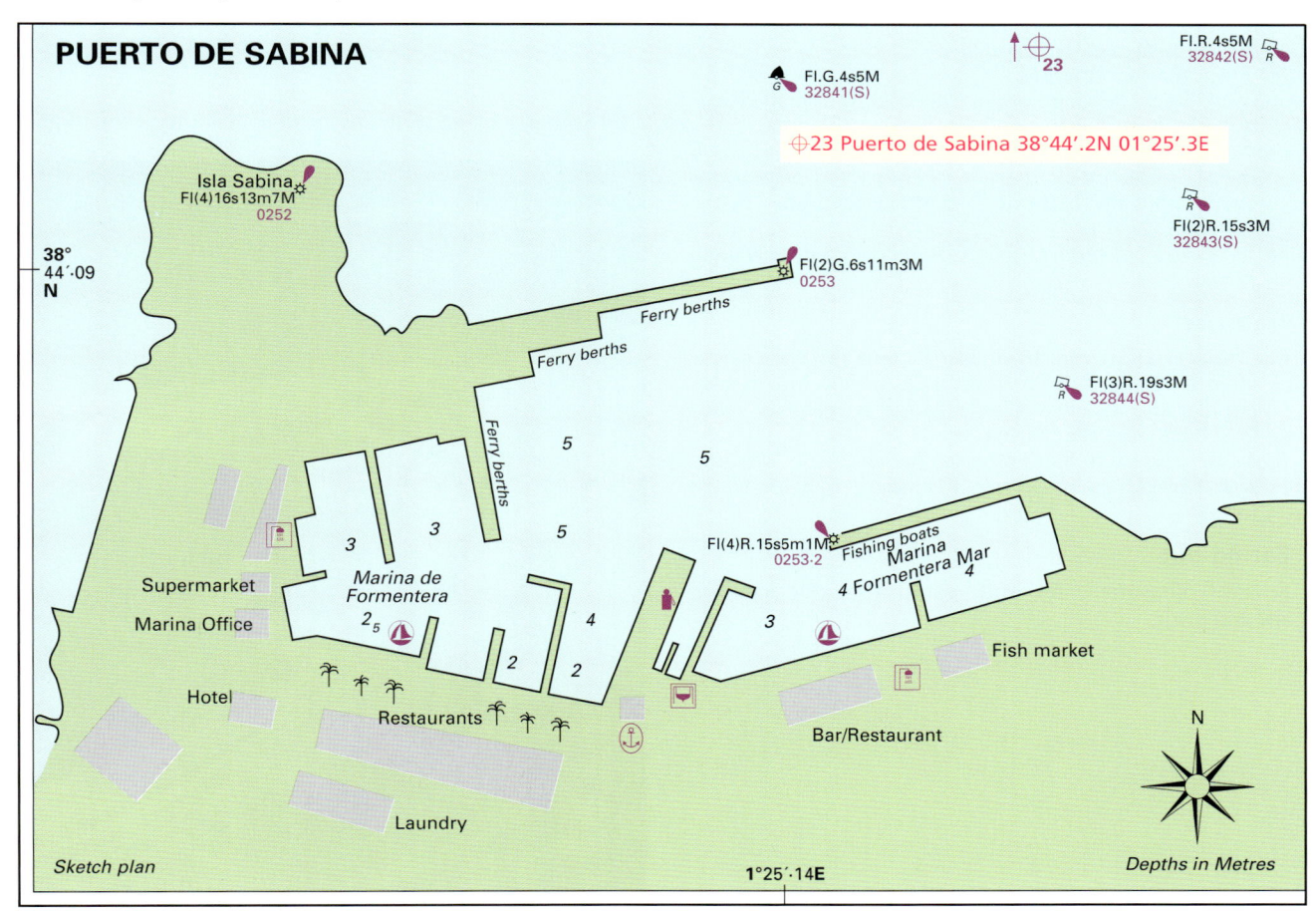

PUERTO DE SABINA

II. FORMENTERA AND ESPALMADOR

Puerto de Sabina. Good protection from the seas, but the low-lying surroundings give little shelter from the wind

Cala Sabina, looking west. Ensenada del Cabrito at top of photo *GW*

Chandlery To the west of the main harbour.

Provisions Two supermarkets near the harbour, plus more in San Francisco Javier a couple of miles inland. A fish market near the east basin.

Ice From the supermarket.

Showers Blocks serving both marina basins, a small charge is made. Basins at the *club nautique* in the port.

Banks and post office None closer than San Francisco Javier; ATMs on the parade of shops and restaurants overlooking the harbour. Post office facililities in the marina.

Hospital/medical services Small hospital in San Francisco Javier.

Transport

Car hire/taxis Car hire from an office to the west of the main harbour ✆ 971 32 20 02. Bicycle hire is also popular and widely available. Motor scooters may also be rented from the marina.

Buses Bus service to San Francisco Javier.

Ferries Very frequent ferries (including hydrofoils) to Ibiza.

Eating out

Several pleasant cafés and restaurants overlooking the harbour.

ANCHORAGES AND FEATURES AROUND FORMENTERA

⚓ CALA SABINA
38°44′.2N 01°25′.4E

A wide *cala* east of Puerto de Sabina has been encroached by the extended harbour development, but leaves an anchorage extending to the beach, Playa del Cabali Borras. Anchor in 3–5m over sand and rocky beach. This area is open to west and north. There is a restaurant in the ruined windmill at the northern end of the beach.

⚓ ISLAS REDONA AND POUET (PONET)
38°45′.2N 01°25′.9E

Two small islands north of Puerto de Sabina (see page 64) which, together with three even smaller islets, give some shelter to a shallow (2–3m) anchorage in a sandy bay otherwise open west–northwest–north. The restaurant in the old windmill to the south is near a landing pontoon for local tourist ferries.

⚓ PLAYA TROCADOS (TROCADORS)
38°45′.7N 01°25′.9E

A long sand and rock beach open southwest–west–northwest. Anchor near the centre of the beach in 5m or less over sand: there are rocky outcrops near each end. A nature reserve has been enforced at the north end of the beach. Playa Trocados is popular with local boats and tourist ferries.

⚓ FREU POCO (PAS DE TROCADORS)
38°46′.5N 01°26′E

A very shallow channel separating Espalmador from Formentera, Freu Poco lies at the north end of the Playa Trocados, east of Isla Gastabí. (See plan on page 71.)

⊕24 38°46′.3N 01°24′.7E Isla del Gastabí

Espalmador looking northeast. The shallow Freu Poco passage right and Freu Grande left of picture above Isla del Gastabí

The channel can only be transited by dinghy and sometimes it is possible to wade between the islands, though either of these would be unwise if any swell is breaking.

⚓ CALA PUJOLS
38°43′.6N 01°28′.1E

A rocky-sided *cala* on the northeast coast, tucked between the Punta and Islas del Pujols, and Punta Prima; littered with shallows, and with rocks on its northwest side. Approach with care and anchor in the southeast corner in 8m over sand, northwest of the old watchtower. There is a large holiday village nearby, complete with supermarkets and restaurants. There are leading marks for the fishing boat slipway northwest of the anchorage, but these are not relevant for deep keeled vessels.

⚓ PLAYA DE TRAMONTANA
Centred on 38°41′.4N 01°30′.2E

A long sand and rock bay (more rock than sand) stretching for three miles between Cala Barbé and Cala Racó d'es Mares. Open to north and east sectors. There are some interesting sea caves. Anchor close inshore in 5–10m over sand.

⚓ CALA RACÓ D'ES MARES (RECO DEL CALÓ)
38°40′.6N 01°31′.6E

A small fishing-boat *cala*, with steep rocky sides and a 1.5m deep rock 100m north of the entrance. There is a small jetty and a beach restaurant ashore.

⊕25 38°39′.8N 01°36′.0E Pta Single Mal

PUNTA SINGLE MAL (PUNTA DE CODOLAR OR DE SA RUDA)
38°39′.9N 01°35′.1E

The headland is 120m high with a tall white lighthouse (Fl.5s142m23M, white tower on white building 22m). It has steep rocky cliffs, as do Punta de la Creu to the north and Punta Rotja to the south. The light is obscured when bearing between 50° and 150°.

⚓ PLAYA DE MITJORN (MIGJORN)

Centred on 38°40'.6N 01°29'E

A 4-mile long sandy beach which is open to the south sector. Anchor in 5m over sand and rock in settled weather only. Unsuitable for an overnight stay.

CABO BERBERÍA

38°38'.5N 01°23'.5E

⊕26 38°47'.7N 01°23'.2E Cabo Berbería

A steep-to, rocky cliffed headland (55m) with a lighthouse (Fl(2)15s78m18M, round white tower 19m) and a watchtower 650m to the northeast. The light is obscured when bearing between 170° and 234°.

⚓ CALA SAHONA (SAONA)

38°41'.8N 01°23'.3E

An excellent anchorage off a sandy beach with rocky sides, somewhat spoilt by a large hotel and other buildings ashore. Open to west–northwest–north but protected from the south by Punta Rasa. Anchor off the beach in 3–5m over sand. There is a beach bar and restaurant ashore, and fishermen's huts to the south.

⊕27 38°43'.1N 01°22'.1E Pta Gabina

PUNTA GABINA (GAVINA)

38°43'.1N 01°22'.9E

A 14m cliffed headland topped by a 9m tower.

⚓ ENSENADA DEL CABRITO (CALÓ DE S'OLI)

38°43'.8N 01°24'.2E

Just west of the marina lies a large bay between Isla Sabina and Punta Pedreras: Ensenada del Cabrito. Mooring buoys have been placed where it was previously possible to anchor. These may be reserved in advance for a maximum stay of two nights per week from the 1st June to 30th September www.balearslifeposidonia.eu/index.php?register_vars[lang]=en. See plan on page 64 and the Anchoring and Moorings section on page 16. It is open to the north-northwest through northeast, but gives good protection from the south and west. Tucked in behind Pta Pedreras, swell is usually not a problem unless the wind turns to the north. This is a good spot if the marinas are full, while waiting for fuel or water.

⚓ ESTANQUE DEL PEIX (ESTANY DES PEIX)

38°43'.9N 01°24'.8E (entrance)

A large saltwater lagoon with a narrow entrance, carrying a scant 1m depth. Once inside depths are

Espalmador: looking north-northeast. Puerto El Espalmador centre, Ibiza top, with a yacht passing through Freu Grande passage

ISLA ESPALMADOR

⊕24 Isla del Gastabí (SW)
38°46'.3N 01°24'.7E

Freu Grande

Fl(3+1)20s 28m11M
0254
Isla Puercos or Pou

Pta Ranchos

I Torretas

Cala Bochs

Bajo Cala Bochs

Caló Moro

Isla Espalmador

(34)

Pta Gastabí

Puerto El Espalmador

Summer mooring buoys see below

I del Gastabí Q(9)15s14m4M
0253.5

I de la Alga

Freu Poco

N

⊕24

Los Trocados

Depths in Metres

24'   25'   1°26'E   27'

reported to increase, and many dinghies and other small pleasure and fishing craft are moored there. The larger Estanque (Estany) Pudent further east has no outlet to the sea.

ISLA ESPALMADOR

PUERTO EL ESPALMADOR

38°46'.8N 01°25'.7E

Puerto and *marina* in Spanish can mean any place to accommodate a vessel, even, sometimes, an anchorage off a beach. This bay is by no means a port, but it does give excellent shelter from the north and east, though it is open to the southwest.

From the south, enter between Isla del Gastabí (lit, ⊕24) and Isla de la Alga. Two small white buoys between Pta Gastabí and Isla de la Alga mark the entrance, and keep you clear of the shallow patch. Do not attempt to cut between Isla de la Alga and Espalmador itself. From north or west, enter between Punta Gastabí and Isla del Gastabí, keeping at least 200m off Punta Gastabí to avoid shoals. Mooring buoys have been placed in the bay north of Isla de la Alga. These may be reserved in advance from the 1st June to 30th September, for a maximum free stay of two nights per week at www.balearslifeposidonia.eu/index.php?register_vars[lang]=en. See plan above and the Anchoring and Moorings section on page 16 for further details.

It remains a tranquil and sheltered spot, probably because it is privately owned. There appears to be no serious attempt to prevent visitors using the beaches, though the owners' privacy should be respected.

SA GORDIOLA TOWER (TORRE ESPALMADOR)

38°47'.1N 01°25'.1E

A large (9.6m) and very conspicuous stone tower standing near the cliff edge (at a total elevation of 34m) on the west coast of Espalmador.

⚓ CALÓ MORO (CALA MORROS)

38°47'.4N 01°25'.3E

A tiny anchorage capable of taking one yacht in fair weather. Open to the south through to west. Anchor in 4m over rock and sand with a line ashore.

⚓ CALA BOCHS (CALA BOC OR CALA ROJA)

38°47'.6N 01°25'.6E

A small and shallow anchorage near the northern end of Espalmador. Anchor in 1.5m over sand off the small beach; otherwise, the shore is mostly rock.

ISLA ESPARDEL

The island is a mile long with an elevation of 29m. It is low to the west and cliffed to the east, with outlying rocks and islets extending 300m northwards (Piedra Espardelló Tramontana awash) and 500m southeast from Punta Mitjorn to Islote Espardelló. There is no navigable passage between the latter. This island is now a nature reserve and marked by four yellow conical buoys Fl.Y.5s5M with × topmark. No swimming or fishing is allowed and the passage of any pleasure craft is prohibited inside the buoys.

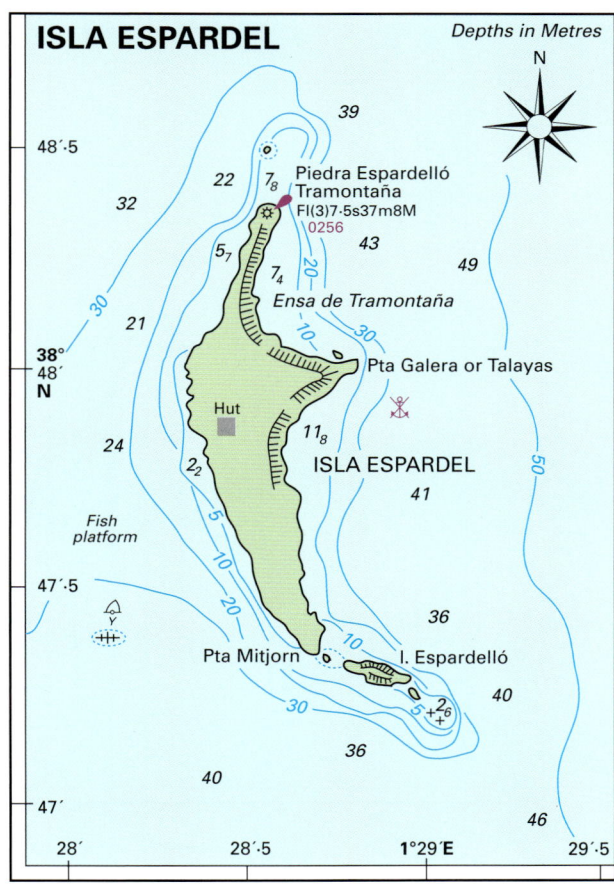

ISLA ESPARDEL

Depths in Metres

N

48'.5

Piedra Espardelló Tramontaña Fl(3)7.5s37m8M
0256

Ensa de Tramontaña

Pta Galera or Talayas

38° 48' N

Hut

ISLA ESPARDEL

Fish platform

Pta Mitjorn

I. Espardelló

47'.5

47'

28'   28'.5   1°29'E   29'.5

II. FORMENTERA AND ESPALMADOR

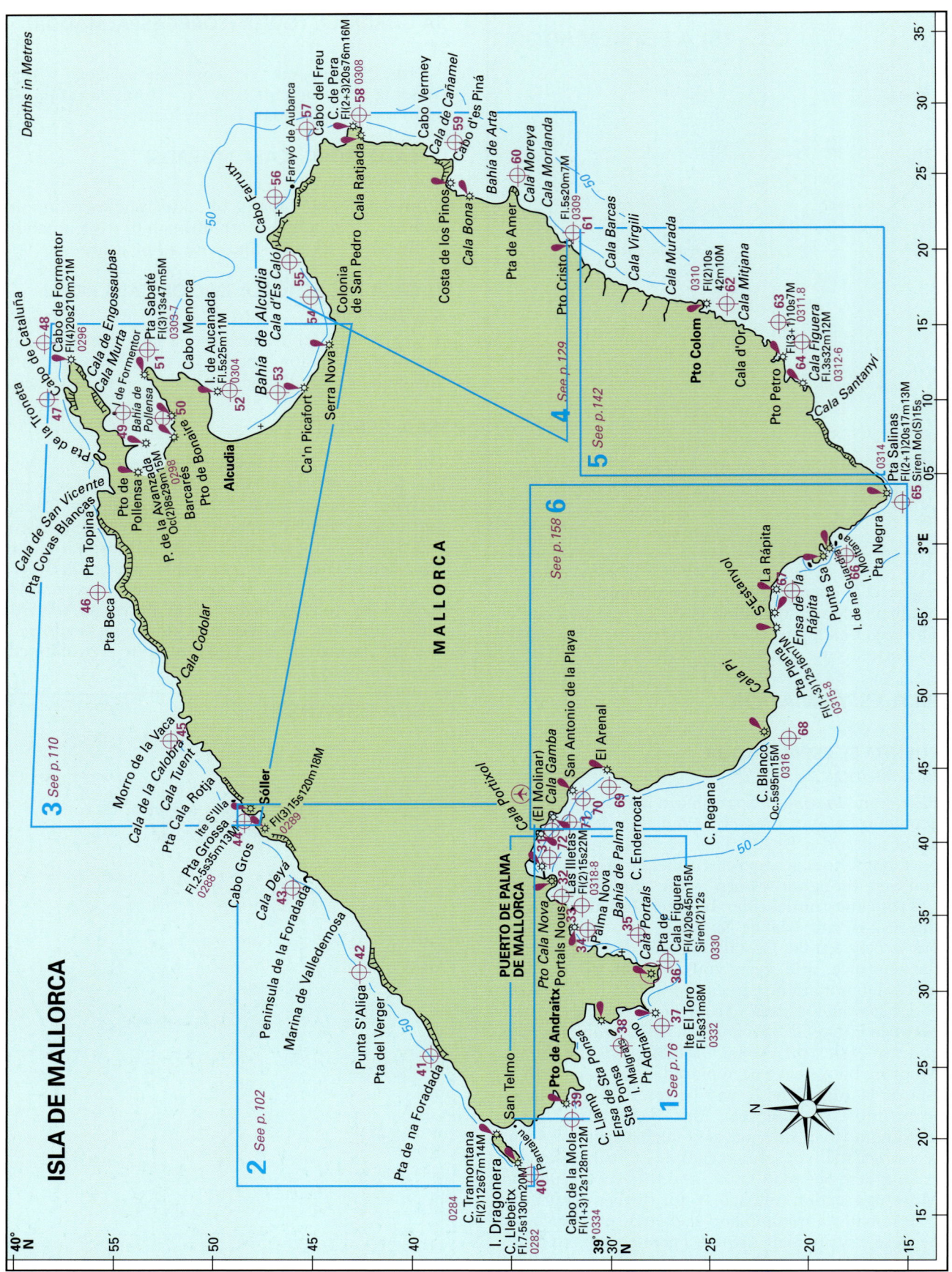

Depths in Metres

ISLA DE MALLORCA

MALLORCA

3 See p.110

2 See p.102

4 See p.129

5 See p.142

6 See p.158

1 See p.76

C. Tramontana
Fl(2)12s67m14M
0284
I. Dragonera
C. Llebeitx
Fl.7.5s130m20M
0282 0334

Cabo de la Mola
Fl(1+3)12s128m12M

C. Llamp
Ensa de Sta Ponsa
Sta Malgrat 38
I. Malgrat
Pt Adriano 39

San Telmo

Pto de Andraitx 40 (Pantaleu)

Pta de na Foradada

Pta del Verger
Punta S'Aliga 41

Marina de Valledemosa 42

Peninsula de la Foradada

Cala Deyá 43

Morro de la Vaca 45
Cala de la Calobra
Cala Tuent
Pta Cala Rotja
Ite S'Illa
Pta Grossa
Fl.2.5s35m13M
0288
Cabo Gros 44
Söller
Ite Fl(3)15s120m18M
LFl Fl(3)15s120m18M
0289

Pta Beca
Pta Topina 46

Cala Codolar

Cala de San Vicente
Pta Covas Blancas

Trioneta de Cataluña
Cabo de Formentor
Fl(4)20s210m21M
0296
Cabo de Formentor 48
C. el ap de 47
Pta el ap de

Cala de Engossaubas
Cala Murta
I. de Formentor
Pto de 49
Pollensa
Bahia de
Pollensa
Pta Sabaté
Fl(3)13s47m5M
0303·7 51
Cabo Menorca
Pto de la Avanzada
P. de Formentor
Oc(2)8s29m15M
0298
Barcarés 50
Pto de Bonaire
Alcudia

I. de Aucanada
Fl.5s25m11M
0304 52

Bahia de Alcudia
Cala d'Es Caló 55
53
54
Serra Nova
Ca'n Picafort

Colonia
de San Pedro

Cala Ratjada
Faravó de Aubarca 56
Cabo Farrutx 57
C. de Pera 58
Cabo del Freu
Fl(2+3)20s76m16M
0308

Cabo Vermey
Cala Vermey
Cabo d'es Pinä 59
Bahia de Arta
Pta de Amer
Cala Moreya 60
Cala Morlanda
Pto Cristo 61
Fl.5s20m7M
0309

Costa de los Pinos
Cala Bona

Cala Barcas
Cala Virgili
Cala Murada

Cala Mitjana 62
Fl(2)10s
42m10M
0310
Cala Figuera 63
Fl(3+1)10s7M
0311.8
Pto Colom
Cala d'Or
Pto Petro 64
Fl.3s32m12M
0312·6
Cala Santanyi

Pta Salinas 65
Fl(2+1)20s17m13M
Siren Mol(S)15s
0314

Pta Negra
Pta de Guerra 66
I. de na Guerra
I. Molina
Punta Sa

La Rápita 67
S'Estanyol
Ensa de la
Rápita
Pta (3)12s(3)m16m13M
0315·8
Cala Pi

C. Blanco
Oc.5s95m15M
0316 68
C. Regana

El Arenal
San Antonio de la Playa
C. Enderrocat 69
Pta de
Cala Figuera
Fl(4)20s45m15M
Siren(2)12s 70
0330

Cala Nova
Portals Nous
Pto Cala Nova
Portals
Illetas
Fl(2)15s22M
0318·8
las Illetas
Cala Portals
PUERTO DE PALMA
DE MALLORCA
Bahia de Palma
Palma Nova
Cala Gamba
(El Molinar)
Cala Portixol
Cala Figuera 35
36 37
Ite El Toro
Fl.5s31m8M
0332

N
N
40°
N
55'
50'
45'
40'
35'
30'
25'
20'
39°
30'
N

15'
20'
25'
30'
35'
40'
45'
50'
55'
3°E
55'
50'
45'
40'
35'
30'
25'
20'
15'

III. Mallorca

Mallorca, the capital of the Balearics, is the largest and most cosmopolitan of the group. There are many historical sites to visit, including the capital port of Palma which provides excellent berthing and every nautical requirement, including the necessary permits for the neighbouring island of Cabrera. There are many superb ports and anchorages around its coasts. Puerto de Sóller is of particular interest with its vintage tramway and Victorian train linking the port with Palma. Inland there are orange groves and pine forests; and restored windmills: a unique feature of the island.

SECTIONS

The coastline is considered in a clockwise direction around the island beginning at Palma. Cabrera is dealt with in Chapter IV.

1. **Puerto de Palma to Puerto de Andraitx**

2. **Cala Egos to Sóller**

3. **Punta Grossa to Puerto de Ca'n Picafort**

4. **Puerto de Colonia de San Pedro to Porto Cristo**

5. **Cala Murta to Cala Marmols**

6. **Punta Salinas to Bahiá de Palma**

NAVIGATIONAL INFORMATION ON APPROACHES TO MALLORCA

Coming from the south from North Africa or the eastern Mediterranean and heading for northern Spain or France; or for a crew change, Mallorca may be the preferred landfall because of its size, international airport or the safe port of Palma. With many ports and anchorages to choose from and the huge Bahía de Palma, calmer waters in any weather conditions are assured. Passages to and from the other islands are described.

Magnetic variation

Insignificant – almost zero.

MALLORCA WAYPOINTS

⊕31	Puerto de Palma	39°33'.4N 02°38'.5E
⊕32	Puerto de Cala Nova	39°32'.8N 02°36'.1E
⊕33	Las Illetas	39°31'.8N 02°35'.5E
⊕34	Puerto Portals	39°31'.5N 02°33'.8E
⊕35	Isla del Sech	39°28'.7N 02°32'.8E
⊕36	Punta de Cala Figuera	39°27'.2N 02°31'.5E
⊕37	Islote el Toro	39°27'.5N 02°28'.0E
⊕38	Isla Malgrats	39°29'.5N 02°26'.5E
⊕39	Cabo de la Mola	39°31'.6N 02°21'.4E
⊕40	Isla Dragonera (S)	39°33'.8N 02°18'.5E
⊕41	Punta de na Foradada	39°38'.5N 02°25'.2E
⊕42	Punta S'Aliga	39°42'.4N 02°31'.5E
⊕43	Peninsula de la Foradada	39°45'.6N 02°37'.2E
⊕44	Approach to Puerto Sóller	39°48'.0N 02°41'.2E
⊕45	Morro de la Vaca	39°52'.0N 02°48'.3E
⊕46	Punta Beca	39°55'.6N 02°57'.0E
⊕47	Cabo de Cataluña	39°58'.0N 03°10'.7E
⊕48	Cabo de Formentor	39°57'.8N 03°13'.0E
⊕49	Isla de Formentor (S)	39°55'.0N 03°09'.0E
⊕50	Puerto de Bonaire	39°52'.2N 03°08'.5E
⊕51	Cabo del Pinar	39°53'.5N 03°12'.7E
⊕52	Isla de Aucanada (S)	39°49'.9N 03°10'.3E
⊕53	Off C'an Picafort	39°46'.2N 03°09'.5E
⊕54	Off Puerto de Colonia de San Pedro	39°44'.5N 03°16'.3E
⊕55	SW of Cala Es Calo	39°46'.3N 03°19'.8E
⊕56	Farayó de Aubarca (W)	39°46'.2N 03°24'.3E
⊕57	Cabo del Freu	39°45'.0N 03°28'.0E
⊕58	Cabo de Pera	39°43'.0N 03°29'.2E
⊕59	Cabo d'es Piná (Del Pinar)	39°38'.0N 03°26'.5E
⊕60	Punta de Amer	39°34'.8N 03°24'.5E
⊕61	Cala Manacor (Porto Cristo)	39°32'.2N 03°20'.5E
⊕62	Punta de ses Crestas (Approach to Puerto Colom)	39°24'.7N 03°16'.2E
⊕63	Cala Llonga (Approach to Puerto de Cala D'or)	39°22'.0N 03°14'.2E
⊕64	Off Porto Petro	39°21'.3N 03°13'.2E
⊕65	Punta Salinas	39°15'.5N 03°03'.2E
⊕66	Off Puerto Colonia de Sant Jordi	39°18'.5N 02°59'.7E
⊕67	Puerto de la Rápita	39°21'.7N 02°57'.3E
⊕68	Cabo Blanco	39°21'.6N 02°47'.0E
⊕69	Off El Arenal	39°30'.3N 02°44'.5E
⊕70	Puerto de San Antonio	39°31'.7N 02°43'.0E
⊕71	Puerto de Cala Gamba	39°32'.7N 02°41'.7E
⊕72	Off Puerto de Cala Portixol	39°33'.4N 02°40'.1E

Approach and coastal passage charts
(See *Appendix* for a full list of Baleares charts)

Imray	M3
Admiralty	1702, 1703, 2831, 2832
Spanish	48E, 900, 965, 970, 421, 422, 423, 424, 425, 426, 427
French	5505, 7115, 7116, 7118

Approach lights

0318.8 **Puerto de Palma** 39°33'N 02°37'.5E Fl(2)15s41m22M Square brown stone tower, visible outside Bahía de Palma 327°-040°

0330 **Punta de Cala Figuera** 39°27'.5N 02°31'.4E Fl(4)20s45m15M Siren(2)12s White round tower, black diagonal stripes, on building 24m

0334 **Cabo de la Mola** 39°32'N 02°21'.9 Fl(1+3)12s128m12M White column, black bands, on white square tower 10m

0282 **Cabo Llebeitx** 39°34'.5N 02°18'.3E Fl.7.5s130m20M Masonry tower on stone building with red roof 15m 313°-vis-150°

III. MALLORCA

0284 **Cabo Tramontana** 39°36′N 02°20′.4E Fl(2)12s67m14M
Round masonry tower on stone building with red roof
15m 095°-vis-230° and 346°-vis-027°

0289 **Cabo Gros** 39°47′.9N 02°41′E Fl(3)15s120m18M White
tower and house, red roof 22m 054°-vis-232°

0296 **Cabo Formentor** 39°57′.7N 03°12′.8E Fl(4)20s210m21M
White tower and house 22m

Note The characteristics of Cabo Formentor are almost
identical to those of Cabo Nati, Menorca

0303.7 **Punta Sabaté (Cabo del Pina)** 39°53′.6N 03°11′.8E
Fl(3)13s47m5M White triangular tower, black band 12m

0308 **Cabo de Pera** 39°43′N 03°28′.7E Fl(2+3)20s76m16M
White tower on white building with dark corners and
red roof 21m 148°-vis-010°

0310 **Punta de ses Crestas/Punta de la Farola** 39°24′.9N
03°16′.3E Fl(2)10s42m10M White round tower, three
black bands, on white building with red roof 25m 207°-
vis-006°

0312.6 **Torre d'en Beu** 39°19′.8N 03°10′.7E Fl.3s32m12M
White octagonal tower, vertical black stripes 6m

0314 **Punta Salinas** 39°16′N 03°03′.3E Fl(2+1)20s17m13M
SirenMo(S)15s White tower and building 17m 265°-vis-
116°

0316 **Cabo Blanco** 39°21′.9N 02°47′.3E Oc.5s95m15M White
tower and building 12m 336°-vis-115°

INTRODUCTION

Isla de Mallorca (also spelled Majorca and
pronounced as Mayorca) is the largest island of the
Baleares group, being some 62 miles long and 47
miles wide. The north and east coasts are
mountainous with numerous coves, whilst the south
coast has rolling hills and sandy beaches. The central
plain is flat with huge expanses of fertile agricultural
terrain. Mallorca has a very large port, several
harbours and many anchorages in *calas*. There is one
large offlying island to the south (Cabrera),
described in the next chapter.

The mountain range that fringes the northwest-
facing coast is high, culminating in the 1,445m peak
of Puig Mayor. This stretch of coast is very rugged,
with steep rocky cliffs broken by a number of
indentations, nearly all located in the northeastern
section and providing some spectacular anchorages
for use in settled weather. Puerto de Sóller offers the
only harbour on the northwest coast and a refuge in
the event of a northwest *tramontana* or *mestral*,
turning the entire coastline into one long leeshore.

The coast that faces northeast towards Menorca
consists of two large sandy bays, each with a major
harbour and a number of anchorages and smaller
harbours. While not as dramatic as the northwest
coast, parts are attractive and safe harbours and
anchorages can be found in most conditions.

The southeast coastline comprises the 'Coast of
the calas'. In general this 35 mile section has low
rocky cliffs with ranges of hills several miles inland.
The relatively straight run of the coast is broken by
numerous inlets in which lie small harbours and
anchorages, the majority very attractive. Notable on
this coast is the large but relatively shallow inlet of
Porto Colom, the best natural harbour and
anchorage in Mallorca and possibly in the whole
Islas Baleares. It was also the cheapest until now.

The remaining coast, facing the southwest, is
centred around the large Bahía de Palma, where the
majority of the industry and population of the island
is situated. Palma de Mallorca, the capital and a
major port, can supply most material, cultural and
holiday requirements but, like all cities, it is busy,
crowded and noisy. On the southeast side of this bay
are high, white cliffs and on the opposite side high,
rocky cliffs broken by a number of small bays and
calas.

With the exception of the heads of the large sandy
bays, deep water can generally be carried very close
to the shore. Other than Isla de Cabrera and Isla
Dragonera there are no offshore dangers, and the few
smaller islands that exist are generally very close in.

Inland, Mallorca is unexpectedly beautiful, with
large areas of fruit orchards, in addition to olive
groves and fields of wheat and vegetables. In the
more hilly areas Moorish methods of terraced
cultivation are still to be seen. The mountains of the
northwest provide dramatic views and some
challenging hill walks. Away from the coast – and
particularly in the eastern half of the island – many
of the smaller walled towns remain relatively
unspoilt. One feels saddened, and at the same time
relieved, that so few tourists appear to venture far
beyond the nearest beach and their package holiday
hotel.

Two factors have tended to make the Mallorcans
more cosmopolitan and subtly different from the
inhabitants of the other islands in the group – firstly,
wide intermarriage with the Moors, who remained
in greater numbers than on the other islands; and
secondly, the rise in power and prosperity of Palma
in the 14th and 15th centuries, which brought a flow
of riches and contact with the outside world which
the other islands lacked. Palma is still the seat of the
government and parliament of the Autonomous
Community of the Balearic Islands, and home to
well over half of the island's current population of
around 530,000 people.

HISTORY

Mallorca appears to have been inhabited for at least
6,000 years, with some of the earliest human traces
found in a cave near Sóller on the north coast. Later,
from around 1200BC, the bronze age *talayot* (tower)
culture flourished in both Mallorca and Menorca,
with sites near Artá on the east coast and
Lluchmayor further south. Little is known about
these early peoples, though successive invasions by
Phoenicians, Carthaginians and Greeks have left
some traces. According to the 1st century BC Greek
writer Diodorus, the inhabitants of both Mallorca
and Menorca wore few clothes and were called
gymnetes ('naked men'), their islands being
collectively known as Gymnesia.

The Romans conquered Mallorca in 123BC and
remained until the 5th century. It was known to
them as Major, as opposed to Menorca, which was
called Minor, and these two formed, together with
Cabrera, the Insulae Baleares. The city of Pollentia,
now called Alcudia, became their capital, and they
also founded the harbours of Palma and Pollensa.

However, the Romans used the island more as a staging post than as a permanent settlement and there are few remains of buildings to be found. A notable exception is the Roman theatre at Alcudia, easily reached from the yacht harbour. After the departure of the Romans the island entered the dark ages, overrun by the Vandals and a favoured base for pirates and Corsairs.

Mallorca's next taste of prosperity was under the Moors, who arrived early in the 10th century. Roman Palma was renamed Medina Mayurqa and grew into a bustling city of some 25,000 inhabitants, while throughout the island agriculture was improved and irrigation canals built. However, almost equally little remains of this period, other than the delightful Arabian Baths and the Almudaina arch in Palma.

The destruction of Moorish Palma can fairly be laid at the door of King Jaime I (Rey Jaime Conquistador), who drove the Moors out in 1229, backed by the combined armies of Catalonia and Aragon. A monument to their landing stands on the headland overlooking Puerto de Santa Ponsa on the southwest coast. With them the conquering army brought the Catalan language, which gradually evolved into the Mallorquín dialect spoken by many islanders today.

The 13th to 15th centuries were a golden age, with a vast increase in population and wealth. Palma, with its imposing Gothic cathedral, new castle and growing dock system, became a centre for trade inside the Mediterranean. However, as Spain gradually turned her attention westward towards the New World, her Mediterranean possessions became something of a backwater. Frequent attacks by

North of Mallorca lush green pine forests and olive orchards *Graham Hutt*

pirates resulted in coastal villages and towns being rebuilt several miles inland, with only a few huts on the shore or at the harbour. In this way the damage and loss caused by surprise raids were minimised. During the next few centuries little of historical importance took place in Mallorca, other than the building of many churches and of houses for the nobility.

Recent history

During the Spanish Civil War the island supported the Nationalists and suffered little damage. Greater changes have come about with the post-war advent of mass tourism. Not only are there now areas in which the ground can barely be seen for high-rise hotels or the beach for sunbeds; but the many support services, from tourist shops to smart restaurants, have revived Mallorca's fortunes and changed its former agricultural-based economy for ever.

TOURIST INFORMATION

Places of interest

In addition to places of interest described in the harbour sections, there are many other sites further inland which can be visited by taxi, bus or in some cases rail, from almost any port. Mallorca is one place where it is well worth hiring a car. Car rental in the town centres is considerably cheaper than at the airports. There are spectacular mountain ranges and old *pueblos* (towns) to visit, along with the ancient remains of Moorish and Roman architecture.

High in the mountains near the northwest coast is the Carthusian monastery at Valldemosa, which was once the palace of the Kings of Mallorca and has fine views. The road running east towards Sóller passes the Peninsula de la Foradada and the Son Marroig estate (once owned by Archduke Luis Salvador of Austria), before winding through Deya, famous for its associations with the writer Robert Graves. Further northeast, Lluch boasts a monastery built in the 14th century; is 305m high and provides excellent views.

In the southern part of the island, Campos has Roman baths and a 15th-century church, while nearby Lluchmayor has prehistoric and Roman remains and is also the site of the battle where Mallorca lost her independence.

Look up the tourist information offices, where a wealth of information will be found on all the sites of interest. These are listed in the *General Introduction* and at www.illesbalears.es. See also www.infomallorca.net for current events. Many books have been published on the sites of the island, a number of which are available at airports throughout Europe.

Embassies

For details of embassies see that section in the *Appendix*.

PUERTO DE PALMA TO PUERTO DE ANDRAITX

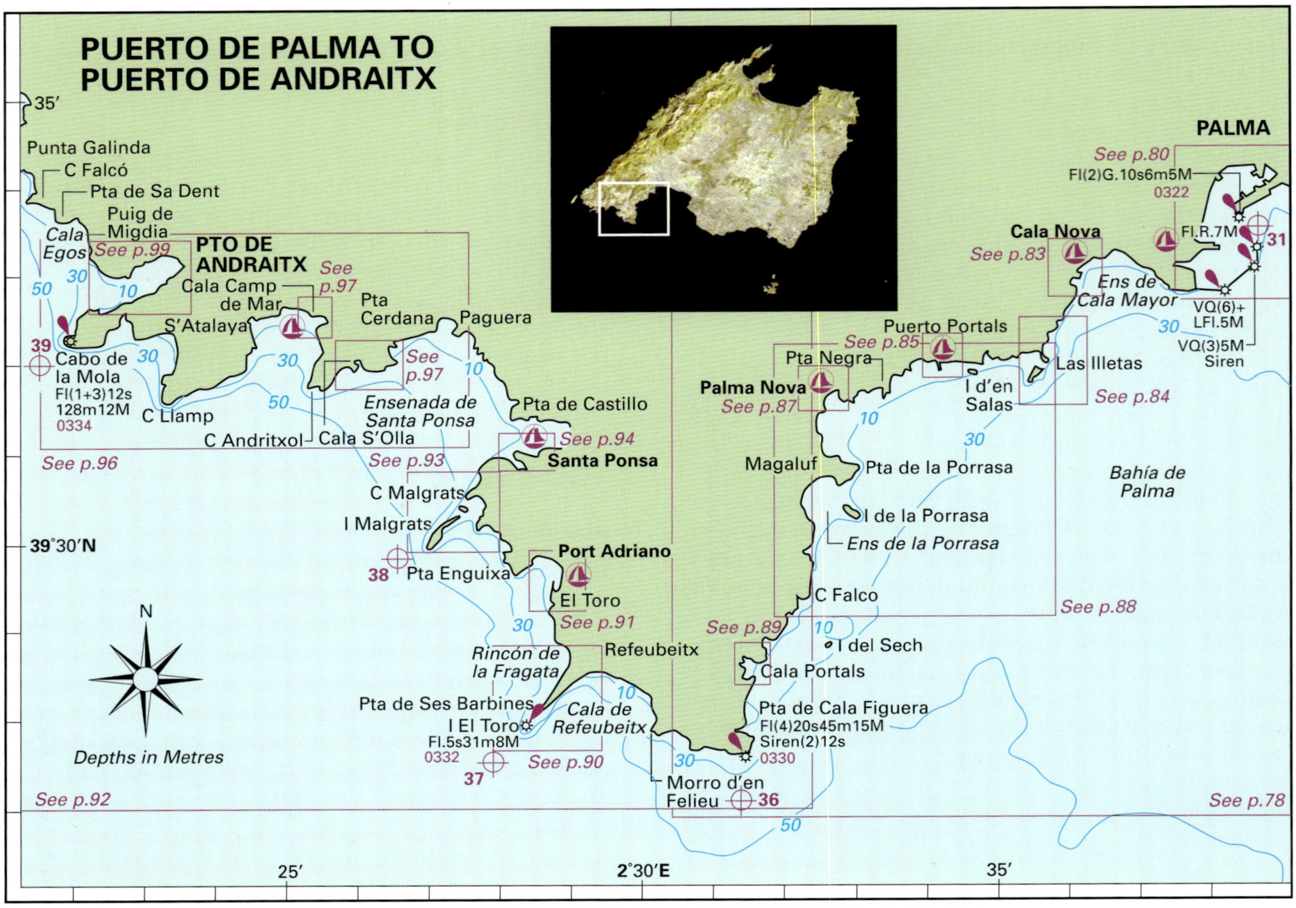

35'

Punta Galinda
C Falcó
Pta de Sa Dent
Puig de Migdia
Cala Egos *See p.99*
50 30 10

PTO DE ANDRAITX
Cala Camp de Mar
See p.97
S'Atalaya
Pta Cerdana Paguera

39
Cabo de la Mola
Fl(1+3)12s
128m12M
0334
30
C Llamp
50
C Andritxol
Cala S'Olla
Ensenada de Santa Ponsa
See p.97
10
Pta de Castillo

See p.96
See p.93
See p.94
Santa Ponsa

39°30'N
C Malgrats
I Malgrats
38 Pta Enguixa
Port Adriano
El Toro
30 *See p.91*

N
Rincón de la Fragata Refeubeitx
Pta de Ses Barbines
I El Toro
Fl.5s31m8M
0332 *Cala de Refeubeitx*
10
See p.90
37
Morro d'en Felieu 36

Depths in Metres

See p.92
50

25' 2°30'E 35'

PALMA
See p.80
Fl(2)G.10s6m5M
0322
Fl.R.7M 31
VQ(6)+ LFl.5M
VQ(3)5M
Siren

Cala Nova
See p.83
Ens de Cala Mayor
30

Puerto Portals
See p.85
Pta Negra
Palma Nova
See p.87
I d'en Salas
Las Illetas
See p.84

Magaluf
Pta de la Porrasa
I de la Porrasa
Ens de la Porrasa
C Falco
See p.88

See p.89
10
I del Sech
Cala Portals
Pta de Cala Figuera
Fl(4)20s45m15M
Siren(2)12s
0330
30
See p.78

Bahía de Palma

WAYPOINTS:
⊕		
31	Puerto de Palma	39°33'.4N 02°38'.5E
36	Punta de Cala Figuera	39°27'.2N 02°31'.5E
37	Islote el Toro	39°27'.5N 02°28'.0E
38	Isla Malgrats	39°29'.5N 02°26'.5E
39	Cabo de la Mola	39°31'.6N 02°21'.4E

Palma: looking over Muelle Viejo, the ancient cathedral is still well able to dominate the skyline after hundreds of years   *GW*

M1 Puerto de Palma de Mallorca

Within this major commercial port lie several marinas with facilities for several thousand yachts of any size, including super-yachts. However, it is difficult to find a place to berth during July and August. Safe to enter in any weather

Location
39°33'.5N 02°38'E

Distances
Ibiza 60M
Barcelona 120M

Communications
VHF Ch 6, 7,9, 14,16.
Port office ✆ 971 72 68 48 *Fax* 71 86 36
Pilots (Palma Prácticos) 971 71 19 37
Email rcnp@pml.servicom.es or
club@realclubnauticopalma.com
www.realclubnauticopalma.com
See text for further internet information on other options

The port

Puerto de Palma shelters several yachting facilities, most called marinas even if only a pontoon. Set in a huge bay, it is one of the largest collective yachting centres in the Mediterranean, with berthing for several thousand yachts.

The port comprises naval, commercial, fishing and yachting harbours, which are clean and can be entered in all weathers, providing good shelter. Amenities are excellent and there is an attractive town nearby with extensive shops and markets. There are two large principal yacht marinas, both with palatial clubhouses and all facilities. Pier 46 and a Port Authority quay, along with several more 'marinas' – some offering not much more than a berth with water and electricity – complement the

The commercial mole of Palma de Mallorca harbour, with several of the inner harbours visible

o de Mar   La Cuarentina   Port Authority Moorings   Réal Club Náutico   Pier 46

Marina de la Mediterraneo   Marina Port de Mallorca   Marina Alboran

III. MALLORCA

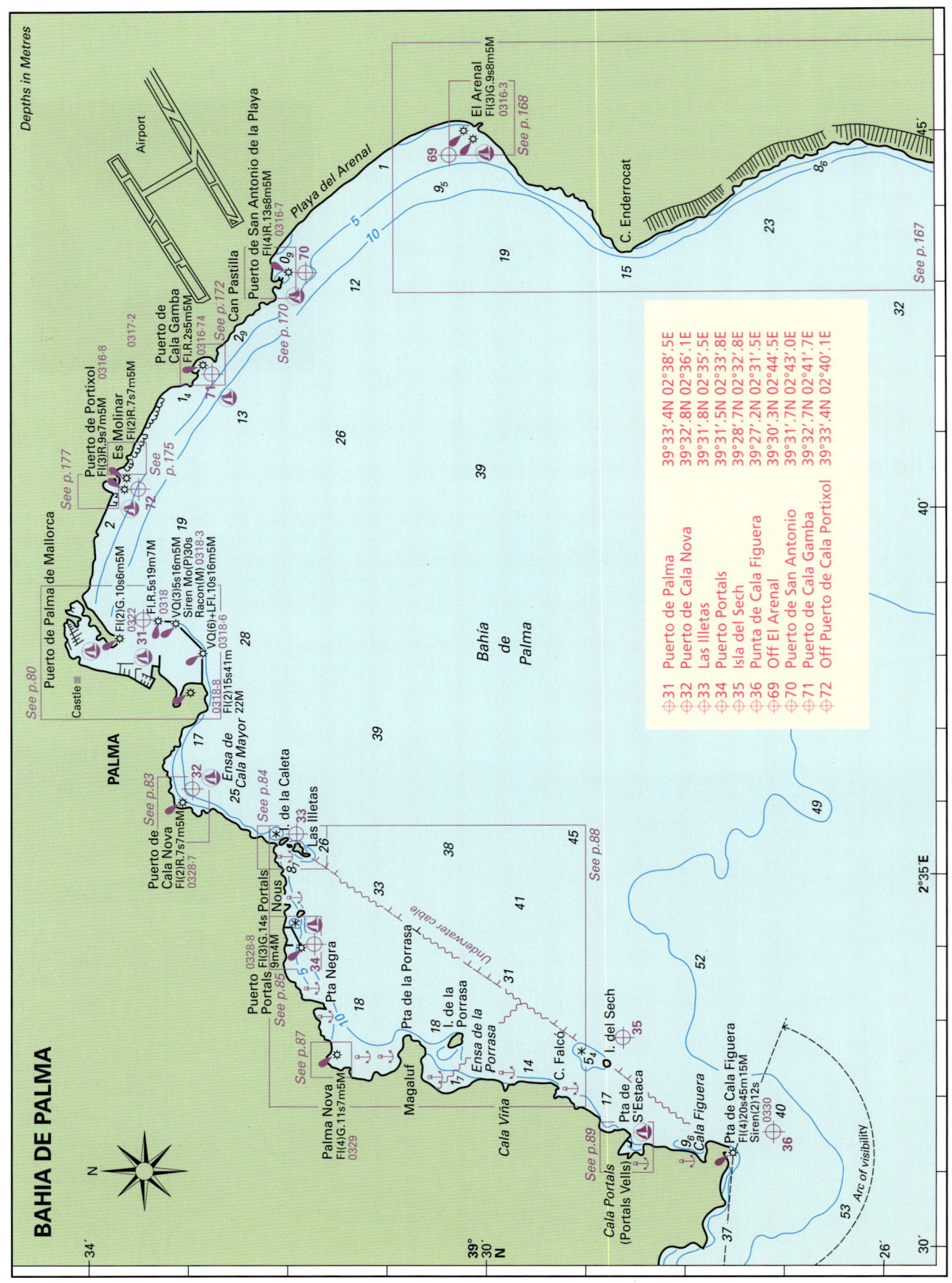

⊕31	Puerto de Palma	39°33'.4N 02°38'.5E
⊕32	Puerto de Cala Nova	39°32'.8N 02°36'.1E
⊕33	Las Illetas	39°31'.8N 02°35'.5E
⊕34	Puerto Portals	39°31'.5N 02°33'.8E
⊕35	Isla del Sech	39°28'.7N 02°32'.8E
⊕36	Punta de Cala Figuera	39°27'.2N 02°31'.5E
⊕69	Off El Arenal	39°30'.3N 02°44'.5E
⊕70	Puerto de San Antonio	39°31'.7N 02°43'.0E
⊕71	Puerto de Cala Gamba	39°32'.7N 02°41'.7E
⊕72	Off Puerto de Cala Portixol	39°33'.4N 02°40'.1E

harbour. The Port Authority moorings (there are 2,300 of them) were traditionally a cheaper alternative to the marinas, but are now about the same price, despite their lack of security or services. The harbour becomes very crowded in summer and vacant berths may be difficult to find but there are other yacht harbours in the Bahía de Palma where berths are usually available, and many possible anchorages can be found.

This is one of the few places where a major expansion plan for the commercial port is planned and work is already underway to almost double the size of 'Muelles Commerciales,' the main commercial mole.

PILOTAGE

Approach

⊕31 39°33'.4N 02°38'.5E Puerto de Palma

From west Round the very prominent Punta de Cala Figuera which has a lighthouse (Fl(4)20s45m15M white round tower with black diagonal stripes on building 24m) and radio masts on its steep cliffs (see plan opposite). Cross the Bahía de Palma heading northeast towards Palma Cathedral, a very large building with small twin spires. Castillo de Bellver (140m) is also conspicuous. The breakwaters will be seen on closer approach. There are no offlying dangers for day or night entry, except shipping in the entrance to beware of.

From east Round Cabo Blanco, which is high with steep light brown cliffs topped by a lighthouse (Oc.5s95m15M, white tower and building 12m) and an old watchtower (see plan on page 158). Follow the coast northwest until the buildings of Palma, including the cathedral and Castillo de Bellver, described above, come into view. The breakwaters will be seen on closer approach.

Anchorage in the approach

Anchor in 10–12m over mud and sand south of the northeast breakwater, exposed to the southerly quadrant. Keep well out of the channel, and display an anchor light at night. Note that anchoring within the harbour is prohibited.

Entrance

Puerto de Palma is a busy harbour in which ferries and other commercial vessels have right of way. Round the end of the south breakwater with an offing of at least 100m. The Club de Mar will be seen ahead with the Réal Club Náutico de Palma to starboard behind the northeast breakwater (which should be given a similar offing).

There is a 5-knot speed limit in the harbour, decreasing to 3kns in the marinas.

In fog

If navigating without GPS or the equivalent, the radiobeacon and siren on Punta de Cala Figuera (the siren at the outer elbow of the south breakwater and the racon at Puerto de Palma lighthouse), may be of assistance.

Berthing (see plan on page 80).

Although there are so many moorings, the harbour still becomes very crowded in high season and it is essential to book ahead in one or other of the available amenities. Going clockwise from the southwest corner, moorings are as follows.

1. **Darsena de Porto Pi**
   A commercial quay tucked into the southwest corner of the harbour, which allows yachts to moor on the south side. It offers few facilities.

2. **Club de Mar**
   A very large and well equipped marina due west of the entrance, offering more than 600 berths ranging in size from 8m up to 120m. Facilities are excellent, with charges to match. There is no reception pontoon; call on VHF Ch 09 to be allocated a berth. Note that the marina is divided into two sections with separate entrances (see plan).
   ☎ 971 40 36 11 *Fax* 971 40 36 18
   Email secretaria@clubdemar-mallorca.com
   www.clubdemar-mallorca.com

3. **Pontelle/Pantelan de la Cuarentina**
   A long single pontoon located just north of Club de Mar. It is prone to surging during winds from the west sector.
   ☎ 971 45 43 95 *Fax* 971 28 84 14

4. **Marina del Mediterraneo**
   A single long pontoon just north of Pontelle Cuarentina, offering little protection during winds from the west sector.
   www.mallorcaonline.com

5. **Marina Port de Mallorca**
   Just north of the Port Authority pontoon on the Paseo Marítimo, in front of Hotel Melia Victoria, with berthing for 152 yachts. Although privately owned with all berths being used by locals, visitors are welcome to use any vacant berths. It is expensive but has water and electricity on the pontoons and free showers, with the office on the southeast corner of the shore pontoon. Security is excellent but there is no fuel or reception dock. The concrete pontoons are unusually high, the lower edge of their sides being some 1.25m above water. Thus even quite large craft are in danger of being pushed under the pontoons in a crosswind as fending off may not be possible. Also, despite addition of extra wave breaks under the north/south pontoon, swell and wash from passing craft is still a problem.
   ☎ 971 28 96 93 / 8 *Fax* 971 28 63 11
   Email recepcion@portdemallorca.com or comercial@portdemallorca.com
   www.portdemallorca.com

6. **Port Authority berthing: Paseo Marítimo**
   For many years yachts have anchored and moored bow or stern-to along the main thoroughfare: the Paseo Marítimo. The entire length of the Paseo Marítimo has been paved, giving it a clean look and increased security by the addition of a stainless steel fence. It is convenient for the town but lacks the security of the marinas.

III. MALLORCA

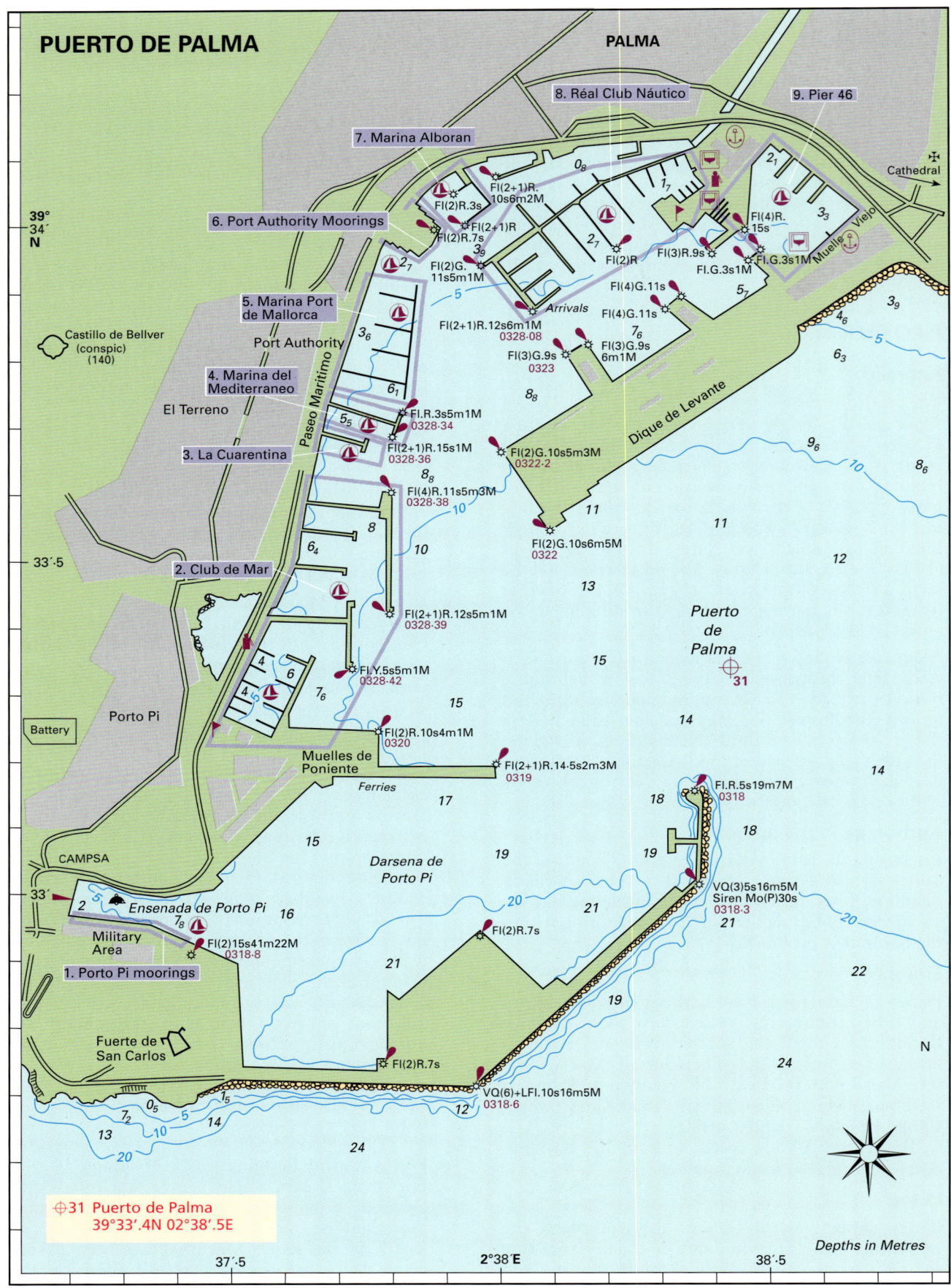

PUERTO DE PALMA

PALMA

8. Réal Club Náutico

9. Pier 46

7. Marina Alboran

Cathedral

39°
34′
N

Fl(2+1)R.
10s6m2M

Fl(2)R.3s

6. Port Authority Moorings

Fl(2+1)R
Fl(2)R.7s
3_9

0_8

1_7

2_1

3_3

Fl(4)R.
15s

Fl(2)R

Fl(3)R.9s

Fl(4)R.
15s

Muelle Viejo

2_7

Fl(2)G.
11s5m1M

3_9

Fl.G.3s1M

5. Marina Port
de Mallorca

2_7

Arrivals

Fl(4)G.11s

Fl.G.3s1M

4_6

Castillo de Bellver
(conspic)
(140)

3_6

Port Authority

Fl(2+1)R.12s6m1M
0328·08

Fl(4)G.11s

7_6

Fl(3)G.9s
6m1M

3_9

5_7

El Terreno

4. Marina del
Mediterraneo

6_1

Fl(3)G.9s
0323

6_3

5

3. La Cuarentina

5_5

Fl.R.3s5m1M
0328·34

Fl(2+1)R.15s1M
0328·36

8_8

Fl(2)G.10s5m3M
0322-2

8_8

9_6

8_6

8

6_4

Fl(4)R.11s5m3M
0328·38

10

11

11

12

2. Club de Mar

10

13

15

Puerto
de
Palma

Fl(2+1)R.12s5m1M
0328·39

15

31

14

4

6

Fl.Y.5s5m1M
0328·42

Battery

Porto Pi

4_5

7_6

15

14

14

Muelles de
Poniente

Fl(2)R.10s4m1M
0320

18

Fl.R.5s19m7M
0318

Ferries

Fl(2+1)R.14·5s2m3M
0319

17

Darsena de
Porto Pi

19

19

18

CAMPSA

15

5

20

21

VQ(3)5s16m5M
Siren Mo(P)30s
0318·3

2

Ensenada de Porto Pi

16

7_8

Fl(2)R.7s

21

20

Military
Area

Fl(2)15s41m22M
0318-8

21

22

1. Porto Pi moorings

21

19

24

Fuerte de
San Carlos

7_2

0_5

1_5

Fl(2)R.7s

12

VQ(6)+LFl.10s16m5M
0318-6

N

24

13

10

5

14

20

24

Depths in Metres

⊕31 Puerto de Palma
39°33′.4N 02°38′.5E

37′·5

2°38′E

38′·5

Port de Mallorca: one of the many facilities within Puerto de Palma *GW*

There are no facilities, though buoys have been laid along the entire length of the Paseo providing moorings for 2,300 yachts. In strong east or southeast winds surging is evident, but some protection is afforded by the several marina pontoons which now run parallel to the quayside.

PA berthing includes most of the quay areas west of all the marinas and includes a large quay marked 'Terminal para pasajeros de la trafico local' (passenger quay) just north of the marina Port de Mallorca. This is a large car park around which boats engaged in local chartering moor. It also includes a single pontoon just east of Marina Alboran for fishing boats.

☎ 971 71 51 00/72 47 49 *Fax* 971 72 69 48

Palma: Overlooking Castillo de Bellver into Réal Club Náutico de Palma and Pier 46 (top end of commercial quay) *GW*

7. Marina Alboran

This consists of two pontoons on the north Paseo Marítimo (opposite Hotel Miramar) which runs around the port. This new facility offers security and parking via the use of a large glass sliding door frontage accessed by an electronic key.

8. Réal Club Náutico de Palma

Situated in the northeast of the harbour at the root of a long mole with many side spurs, this huge marina has berthing for 850 yachts from 8m to 20m. There is a reception quay on the outside of the southwest arm (see '*Arrivals*' on plan) and visiting yachts usually lie alongside or bow/stern-to on one of the fingers in the basin to the north. A splendid backdrop is the ancient cathedral a short distance away.

Harbourmaster VHF Ch 07 or 09
Marina ☎ 971 72 68 48 *Fax* 971 71 86 36
Email rcnp@pmi.servicom.es or
club@realclubnauticopalma.com
www.realclubnauticopalma.com

9. Pier 46

This marina has moved to the northeast corner of Dique de Levante, just east of Réal Club Náutico from its former position along the Paseo Marítimo. This is one of the most sheltered positions within the harbour.

☎ Pier 46 971 72 49 49 *Fax* 971 72 52 08

Facilities

Palma de Mallorca has by far the best facilities for yachts in the Islas Baleares and many of the services listed are not readily available elsewhere in the islands.

Water Water points at all yacht berthing locations including the Port Authority jetties at intervals along the Paseo Marítimo.

Electricity 220v and 380v AC available at both marinas and the two Pier 46 berthing areas. Some power points on the Port Authority jetty.

Fuel Diesel and petrol pumps at the Club de Mar and on the quay. The Réal Club Náutico has a fuel berth near the end of the main northwest-going pontoon.

Bottled gas It is understood that CAMPSA will not now fill any gas bottles, even with a current test certificate. Camping Gaz is, however, widely available.

Repairs See *Appendix* for list of chandleries and repair facilities.

Provisions A massive Carrefour hypermarket in the Porto Pí shopping centre five minutes' walk from the Club de Mar, with another of similar size on the road to the airport. Small supermarket at Club de Mar. A wide variety of other shops, as one would expect of a major city. A produce market at Santa Catalina, ten minutes from the Réal Club Náutico and Pier 46 berths.

Ice Cube ice from the Réal Club Náutico, the fuel berth at the Club de Mar and many supermarkets. Block ice (not for use in drinks) from *la lonja*.

Yacht clubs The Réal Club Náutico de Palma was founded nearly fifty years ago and has bars, a restaurant, bedrooms, a swimming pool, showers, repair workshops, etc. The Club de Mar is a much newer 'marina' yacht club with similar facilities. Apply to the secretary before using either club.

Showers At both marinas and Port de Mallorca. No showers on public jetties.

III. MALLORCA

Communications Wi-Fi is free at the Real Club Nautico, but in 2007 it was not working properly on the new visitors' berth pontoon as the signal did not appear to have any booster system for that part of the marina.

Banks One in the Club de Mar complex, with many more throughout the city. Most (including the Club de Mar unit) have ATMs.

Launderettes Facilities at both marinas and others in the city.

Hospital/medical services Medical Office in Club de Mar and several in the city.

Transport

Car hire A wide choice, with the cheapest rates to be found around the Paseo Marítimo.

Taxis Can be found everywhere.

Buses and trains Bus service throughout the island plus trains to Sóller (recommended) and Inca. Timetables available from tourist offices.

Ferries Car ferries to mainland Spain, Ibiza and Menorca. (See *General Introduction*.)

Air services Busy international airport four miles east of the city and the hub for Air Berlin. (A bus links Plaza de España in the city centre to the airport four times an hour. Times from the airport are between 0610–0215.)

History

The city of Palma is thought to have been founded by the Romans, who knew it as Palmaria and built its first city walls during the 4th century. It flourished under the Moors, who renamed it Medina Mayurqa and whose legacy includes the Arabian Baths and the Almudaina arch. Subsequently it became the Spanish capital of the islands and the centre of a Mediterranean trading empire, giving rise to the first proper harbour works some time in the 14th century.

Sights ashore locally

First amongst Palma's treasures must be its soaring Gothic cathedral, begun in 1230 and still able to dominate the eastern part of the city at the north end of the port. Opposite is the Almudaina palace, built by the Moors but swiftly taken over by their Christian conquerors. Behind and slightly inland lies the oldest and most fascinating part of the city, where narrow flagged alleyways lined by shops, bars and restaurants can only be explored on foot. All are within comfortable walking distance of the harbour. Further out of the city on a hillside to the northwest stands the Castillo de Bellver, also built in the 13th century and entered by a drawbridge across the moat. As with any major city there are museums, churches and historic buildings by the score. Do refer to the list of guide books (see *Appendix*) or visit the tourist office for information or you will miss a lot.

Local events

Fiestas are held on 5 January with the Procession of the Three Kings and on 17 January to celebrate the Blessing of St Anthony. Two days later are the Revels of St Sebastian. February sees Carnival Week and March or April the Fair of Ramos. Religious processions are held during Easter Week, with the Fiesta of the Angel on the first Sunday after Easter. The Fiesta de Santa Catalina Tomás, the island's own saint, is held on the first Sunday after 28 July, with the Procession of Sta Beateta on 28 October. On 31 December the old year is rounded off with the Fiesta of the Standard.

Many of the elegant courtyards, which are a feature of the Old Town, are open to the public over the summer and some host musical events.

Eating out

Bars, cafés and restaurants abound all around the harbour and in the city. Of the latter, some of the most intriguing are in the old part of the city behind the cathedral. Many specialist high class Indian, Sushi, Chinese, Malasian, Thai and French restaurants can be found. Both main marinas have their own restaurants and indoor/outdoor bars.

ANCHORAGE WEST OF PUERTO DE PALMA

⚓ ENSENADA DE CALA MAYOR

39°33'.0N 02°36'.23E

An open bay close to and west of Puerto de Palma, with Puerto de Cala Nova yacht harbour tucked in on its western side. Anchor in 5m+ over sand and stone about 200m northeast of the harbour entrance and well clear of the approach, open to southeast through southwest. Five underwater cables run in a south–southeast direction from a point near the centre of the bay, where anchoring is prohibited. The anchorage is backed by large apartment blocks, houses and shops. (See plan on page 76.)

Victorian mahogany train, still in daily service
Patricia Chung

M2 Puerto de Cala Nova

A small friendly harbour a short distance W of Palma but with doubtful space for visitors. It has berths for 215 yachts, most of which are taken up by locals all year round

Location
39°33'N 02°36'E

Communications
Escola Nacional de Vela Cala Nova VHF Ch 09
☎ 971 40 25 12 *Fax* 971 40 39 11

The harbour

A small and rather shallow artificial harbour, built by the Balearic authorities as a base for the national sailing school, the Escola Nacional de Vela, where children and adults learn windsurfing, dinghy and keelboat sailing. Although technically a private harbour, visitors' berths are occasionally available. Cala Nova is pleasant with good facilities. It is easy to enter with good protection once inside, though a swell works in with strong east or southeast winds.

PILOTAGE

Approach

⊕32 39°32'.8N 02°36'.1E Puerto de Cala Nova

For outer approaches see *Puerto de Palma*.

From west (See plan on page 78.) After rounding Punta de Cala Figuera cross the Bahía de Palma heading northeast, leaving the low-lying Isla del Sech to port. When past Las Illetas follow the coast at 200m for one mile when Puerto de Cala Nova will easily be seen.

From east (See plan on page 78.) Leave Puerto de Palma's long south breakwater to starboard to enter the Ensenada de Cala Mayor. Puerto de Cala Nova will be seen in the northwest corner.

Anchorage in the approach

In the Ensa de Cala Mayor (see plan below).

Entrance

Keep to the middle of the 55m-wide entrance maintaining a careful watch for sailing school craft (novices) entering or leaving. There is a 2-knot speed limit inside the harbour.

Berthing

Secure to the inside of the south breakwater unless a berth has already been allocated.

Facilities

Water Taps on quays and pontoons.
Electricity 220v AC points on the quays and pontoons.
Fuel For the sailing school's use only, and not on public sale.
Provisions All normal supplies are available from supermarkets and shops in Cala Nova and nearby San Augustin.
Ice From the *club náutico* bar.
Chandlery By the harbour.
Repairs A 35-tonne travel-lift at the west end of the harbour and a 2.5 tonne crane. A wide but shallow dinghy slipway backed by an area of hard standing.

Puerto de Cala Nova from south

Engineers Available: enquire at the *club náutico* or the Escola Nacional.

Yacht club The Club Náutico de Cala Nova has a pleasant clubhouse on the north mole with a restaurant, bar, terrace, swimming pool, showers, etc.

Showers At the *club náutico*.

Launderette Near the harbour.

Hospital/medical services In Palma.

Transport

Car hire/taxis ☎ 971 75 54 40 or from Palma.

Buses To Palma and elsewhere regularly pass the port.

Sights ashore locally

As for Palma.

Eating out

Many eating places of all grades, including a restaurant and bar at the *club náutico*.

ANCHORAGES WEST OF CALA NOVA

⊕33 39°31'.8N 02°35'.5E Las Illetas

⚓ LAS ILLETAS ANCHORAGES

39°31'.5N 02°35'.5E

An attractive group of anchorages best viewed on the chart, surrounded by the exclusive Bendinat holiday development. There are a few dangerous rocks awash between Islote de s'Estenedor (actually a low peninsula) and Illeta, and southwest of Islote de la Caleta. Islote de s'Estenedor is a military area and landing on the beach may not be permitted. Fishing nets supported by lines of floats are sometimes laid in the approaches.

Note From Las Illetas south to Cabo Falcó there are several fish farms, noted on Spanish charts as obstructions. All are easily seen.

⚓ **North anchorage** Enter heading west or southwest to anchor in 3m over sand, open northeast through east to southeast.

⚓ **Central anchorage** Enter from northeast (inside Islote de la Caleta) or southeast, in which case take care to avoid Bajo Calafat and other rocks southwest of the island. Anchor in 2–3m over sand, open to northeast and southeast, off a small beach.

⚓ **South anchorage** A small, well protected anchorage between Islote de s'Estenedor and Illeta, open only to the east and to swell from northeast and southeast. Anchor in 3–5m over sand.

⚓ **West anchorage** The largest of the four anchorages, off a good beach (the property of the holiday complex and technically private). Enter heading northeast to anchor in ±5m over sand, open to southwest and west.

⚓ PORTALS NOUS

39°31'9.N 02°34'.6E

A deeply indented *cala*, close east of Islote d'en Salas. Anchor in 5m over sand, open to south and southwest. There are shops, restaurants, etc. ashore.

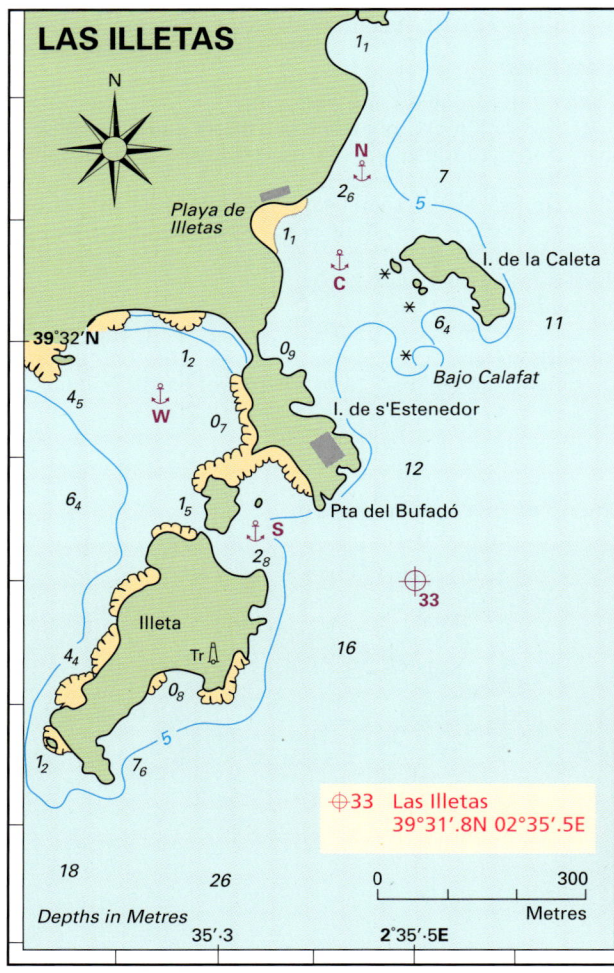

Puerto Portals foreground, looking east over Isla D'En Salas and Las Illetas to Cala Major and the Bay of Palma *GW*

M3 Puerto Portals

One of the most luxurious and expensive marinas in the Mediterranean with facilities for 670 yachts from 8–80m

Location
39°31'.46N 02°35'50E

Communications
VHF Ch 09
Puerto Portals ☏ 971 17 11 00 *Fax* 971 17 11 17
Email marina@puertoportals.com and
puertoportals@oninet.es
www.puertoportals.com

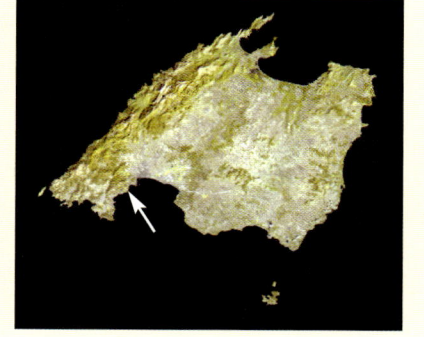

The marina

Opened in 1986 Puerto Portals is, in the words of its brochure 'modern and sophisticated' – as are many of the 670 yachts berthed there. Like Puerto de Palma four miles to the northwest, it is capable of taking super-yachts up to 80m overall, and claims to have minimum depths of 4–5m throughout. Staff here are quite indifferent to visitors, though I suspect they would be more accommodating to a super-yacht arrival.

The immediate surroundings include restaurants, cafés, boutiques and various marine-related businesses, against a backdrop of bare sandy cliffs topped by white apartment blocks and hotels. Approach and entrance are straightforward except with a southeasterly gale when care must be taken.

PILOTAGE

Approach

⊕34 39°31'5.N 02°33'.8E Puerto Portals

For details of the outer approaches see *Puerto de Palma* and page 79.

From west After rounding Punta de Cala Figuera follow the coast north–northeast, leaving the low-lying Isla del Sech on either side but then maintaining an offing of about ½ mile. Isla and Punta de la Porrasa are unmistakeable, while Portals Nous's orange cliffs surmounted by white buildings can be seen from afar. In the close approach the long south breakwater will be seen, as will the distinctive square tower on the north mole, which houses the marina offices.

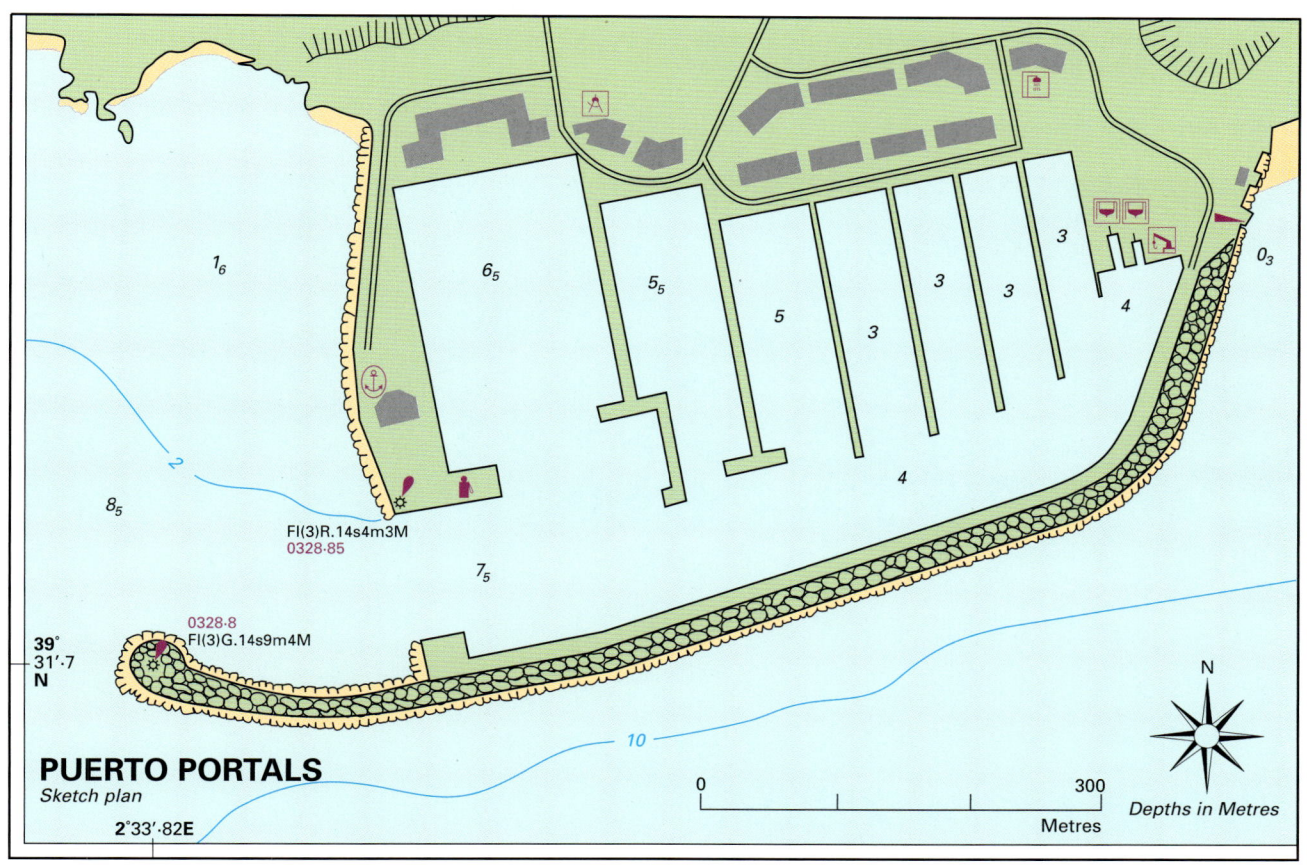

PUERTO PORTALS
Sketch plan

Fl(3)R.14s4m3M
0328·85

0328·8
Fl(3)G.14s9m4M

39°
31'·7
N

2°33'·82E

0   300
Metres

Depths in Metres

III. MALLORCA

From east Round Cabo Blanco (see page 158) onto a northwest course across the Bahía de Palma. See page 78 for the final approach.

Anchorage in the approach

Anchor 200m west of the tower in 5m over sand, taking care not to impede the entrance channel. Watch for buoys off the beach.

Entrance

Swing wide around the head of the south breakwater onto an easterly heading, ready to berth alongside the reception quay at the south end of the north mole. There is a 3-knot speed limit in the harbour.

Berthing

The harbour is frequently full to capacity in summer, and it is wise to call before arrival (telephone or VHF) to ascertain that a berth will be available.

Facilities

Water Taps on all quays and pontoons. Check for quality before filling tanks.

Electricity 220v and 380v AC points on all quays and pontoons.

Fuel Diesel and petrol from pumps at the head of the north mole. Direct supply available to yachts over 18m requiring more than 1,000 litres.

Provisions The shops on the north side of the harbour include a small supermarket. More shops in Portals Nous a short distance inland.

Ice At the fuel berth.

Chandlery Multi-Marine ☎ 971 67 56 62/67 72 29 *Fax* 971 67 72 44 and Nauti Parts ☎ 971 67 77 30 *Fax* 971 67 74 95.

Repairs Mundimar Boatyard: Portals SA ☎ 971 676369 *Fax* 971 676409 at the northeast end of the harbour can handle most jobs on yachts up to 80 tonnes. It has two travel-lifts 80 and 30 tonnes, with 2- and 10-tonne cranes near the travel-lifts. A dinghy slip at the root of the south breakwater.

Engineers Danbrit ☎ 971 67 72 01 *Fax* 971 67 73 28. Official service agents include: Danbrit – Lugger; Motornautica Portals Nous ☎ 971 67 77 95 *Fax* 971 67 77 94 – Mercury/MerCruiser, Quicksilver, Volvo Penta; Mundimar Portals SA (see *Repairs*) – Volvo Penta.

Electronic & radio repairs Danbrit ☎ 971 72 39 77.

Showers Two shower blocks in the marina complex, for which a key is required.

Launderette In Portals Nous.

Banks Bank with ATM in the marina complex.

Hospital/medical services In Portals Nous and Palma.

Transport

Car hire Four car hire firms around the harbour.

Taxis Via the marina office or ☎ 971 68 09 70.

Buses Bus service along the coast.

Sights ashore locally

As for Palma.

Eating out

Many restaurants and a few cheaper eating houses in the vicinity. There are more than twenty restaurants, cafés, bars and ice cream parlours around the harbour alone. Some of the most expensive restaurants in Mallorca are in this harbour.

ANCHORAGE SOUTHWEST OF PUERTO PORTALS

⚓ ANCHORAGE PUNTA NEGRA

39°31'.8N 02°33'.4E & 02°33'.1E

Anchor on either side of the headland in 2–3m over sand and stone. Punta Negra is remarkably unspoilt, with few houses ashore.

Puerto Portals: one of the most expensive marinas in the Mediterranean

M4 Puerto de Palma Nova

A small harbour with 82 berths and a restricted entrance due to silting. Hardly worth a mention, but it may spring to life if dredged

Location
  39°31'.5N 02°32'.6E

Communications
  Club Náutico Palma Nova ☎ 971 68 10 55
  Fax 971 68 24 37

The harbour

This very small harbour has been partially silted up for years and does not seem to have the funds to dredge. At present it can only be used by local shallow draught vessels. Depths in the entrance are reported (July 2010) to be around 1–1.5m. Harbour facilities for the 82 boats it can accommodate are very limited.

PILOTAGE

Approach

Details of the outer approaches as for Puerto de Palma.

From west (See plan on page 76.) After rounding Punta de Cala Figuera follow the coast north–northeast, leaving the low-lying Isla del Sech on either side. Round Isla and then Punta de la Porrasa, after which Puerto de Palma Nova will been seen at the north end of the long beach, Playa de Palma Nova.

From east (See plans on pages 158 and 72.) Round Cabo Blanco onto a northwesterly course across the Bahía de Palma. Puerto de Palma Nova will be seen at the north end of the long beach.

Anchorage in the approach

Anchor in 3–5m over sand south of the harbour, open to southeast.

Entrance

Due to the silting problem (sand rather than mud) it would be unwise to enter the harbour in any boat drawing more than 1m without first making a recce by dinghy. The water is generally too cloudy to read depths visually. There is a 2-knot speed limit.

Berthing

Secure in an empty berth and report to the harbour office by the slipway (closed Thursday and Saturday, otherwise open 0930–1300 daily).

Facilities

Water Taps around the harbour.
Electricity A few 220v AC points.
Fuel By can from a filling station on the road to Palma.
Provisions Supermarket and other shops nearby.
Repairs A 6-tonne crane beside the slipway at the north of the harbour, which has 1m depth.
Yacht club The Club Náutico Palma Nova ☎ 971 68 10 55 has a small clubhouse and bar near the slipway.
Banks In Palma Nova.
Hospital/medical services In Palma Nova and Palma itself.

Transport

Car hire/taxis In Palma Nova or taxi ☎ 971 68 07 80
Buses Bus service along the coast.

Eating out

A vast number of restaurants and cafés (Palma Nova is at the northern end of the Magaluf holiday area).

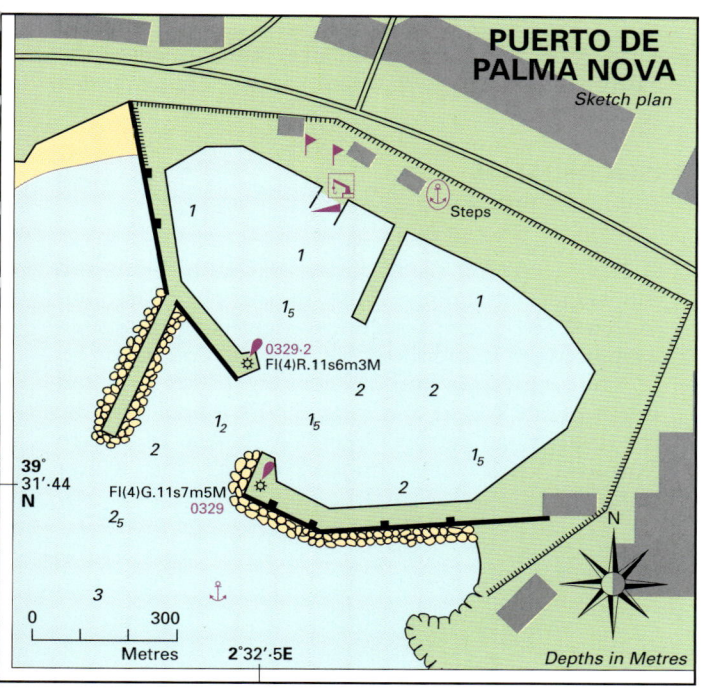

PUERTO DE
PALMA NOVA
Sketch plan

Steps

0329·2
Fl(4)R.11s6m3M

39°
31'·44
N

Fl(4)G.11s7m5M
0329

0

300

Metres   2°32'·5E

N

Depths in Metres

III. MALLORCA

ANCHORAGES BETWEEN PALMA NOVA AND PORT ADRIANO

⚓ PLAYA DE PALMA NOVA

39°31'.0N 02°32'.5E

A long and often crowded sandy beach, broken into three by a pair of low rocky promontories, each occupied by a large hotel. Anchor in 2–4m over sand, open to the eastern quadrant. Behind the beaches there are many hotels, restaurants and shops.

View over Torre Nova and Playa de Palma Nova, with Magaluf behind   *GW*

⚓ PLAYA DE MAGALUF

39°30'.3N 02°32'.3E

An anchorage off a long beach in the northern part of the Ensenada de la Porrasa, tucked in behind Isla de la Porrasa. The beach is lined with apartment blocks, hotels, beach cafés, shops, etc. but the island is deserted and landing there is possible on the southwest coast.

The island (which is unlit) can be left on either side on entry, though 2.5m shoals extend northwest for 200m. Anchor in 3–5m over sand, open to the east and southeast. Holding is reported to be poor. A submarine cable runs southeast from a point just south of the centre of the bay.

A marina with 1,500 berths is supposedly planned for this bay, but it appears unlikely to be built in the foreseeable future.

Isla de la Porrasa is rocky and scrub-covered: 425m long, 220m wide and 36m high. The southeast point is steep-to, but the northwest end of the island has a 2.5m shoal extending as described above. There is a 200m passage with 5–6m depths between Isla de la Porrasa and Punta de la Porrasa to the north.

Long fishing nets supported by small white or pink floats are sometimes laid near the island.

⚓ CALA VIÑA

39°29'.6N 02°32'.2E

A small, narrow *cala* surrounded by high-rise buildings, with a small sandy beach. The inner half of the bay is roped off for swimmers. Anchor in 4–5m over sand, open to the east.

⚓ SOUTH OF CABO FALCÓ

39°29'.1N 02°32'.1E

Two very small *calas* lie south of Cabo Falcó (note the 0.4m shoal 100m southeast of the headland). Both anchorages are in 3m over sand, open to the eastern quadrant, with small sandy beaches and a few houses.

ISLA DEL SECH

Bisected by 39°28.8'N 02°32'.5E

⊕35 39°28.7'N 02°32'.8E Isla del Sech

A low (10m) flat black rocky islet with 4–6m and 4m shoals extending 500m to the northeast, but with a 0.5M wide passage with depths of more than 10m between it and the shore. (See plan on page 78.)

Unlit buoys are laid in February 150m west and north of the island, marking the dive area used by the tourist submarine *Nemo I* (based in Puerto Portals). These are removed during the winter months.

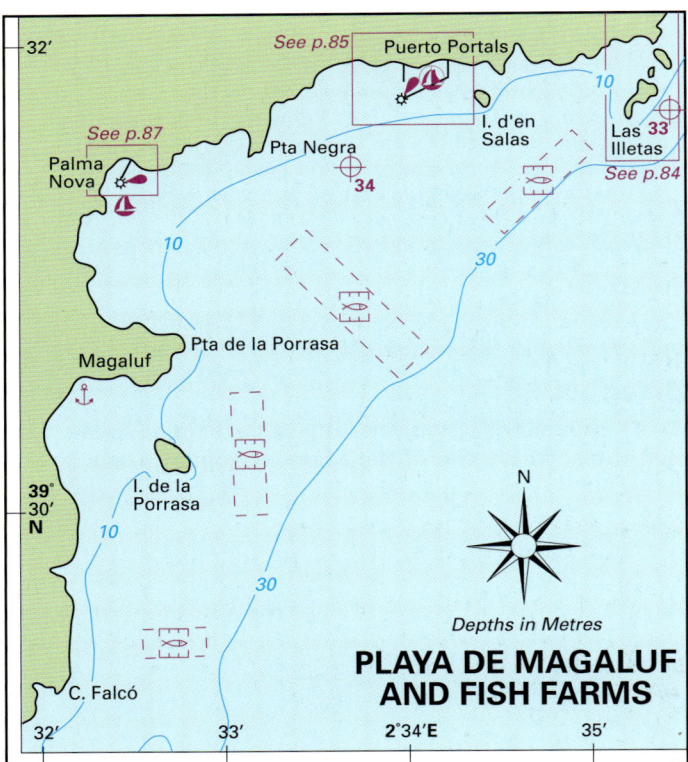

PLAYA DE MAGALUF AND FISH FARMS

⊕33	Las Illetas	39°31'.8N 02°35'.5E
⊕34	Puerto Portals	39°31'.5N 02°33'.8E

⚓ CALA PORTALS (PORTALS VELLS)

39°28'.4N 02°31'.5E

An attractive triple *cala* a mile north of Punta de Cala Figuera, approached between steep-to cliffs and popular with the tourist operators who visit by ferry (road access is poor). The tiny private harbour is lit (Fl.G.3s5m5M: 39°28'.9N 02°31'.5E, green column on white base). The harbour is shallow and can only take craft of less than 9m overall. There are water taps on the quay.

Anchor as space permits in 2–8m over sand and weed, with poor holding. Open to east.

There are tombs dating back to Phoenician times cut into the caves in the southern cliffs, one of which has been turned into a small shrine (take a torch). Several beach cafés and restaurants, some of which close for the evening after the tourists depart, overlook the bay. Parts of the beach are designated nudist areas.

Harbour ☎ 971 68 05 56.

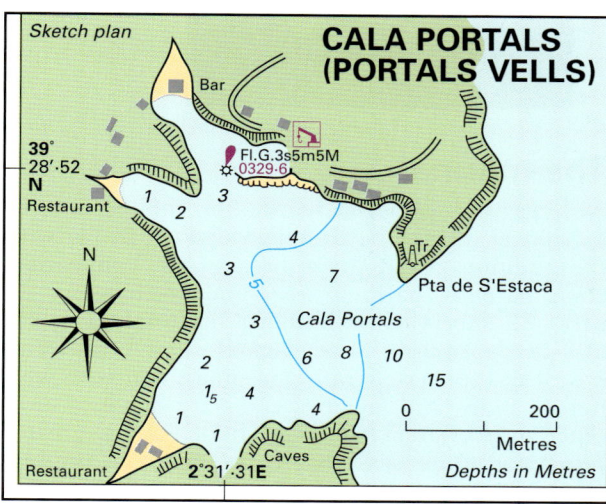

Cala Portals (Portals Vells)

⚓ CALA FIGUERA

39°27'.8N 02°31'.4E

A small *cala* close north of Punta de Cala Figuera. Its steep sides are wooded, with few houses. Anchor in 5m over sand and rock, open to northeast and east. (See plan on page 78.)

⊕36 39°27.2'N 02°31'.5E Pta de Cala Figuera

PUNTA DE CALA FIGUERA

39°27'.5N 02°31'.4E

A very prominent headland with a lighthouse (Fl(4)20s45m15M, white round tower with black diagonal stripes on building 24m) and radio masts on its steep cliffs. The light is only visible when bearing between 293° and 094° – not from within the Bahía de Palma.

⊕37 39°27'.5N 02°28'.0E Islote el Toro

View over Punta de Cala Figuera looking northeast into the Bay of Palma *GW*

Passage between Islote El Toro and Punta de Ses Barbines

39°27'.9N 02°28'.4E

A passage 200m wide and carrying 3m+ depths, leads on a northwest–southeast axis between a small rock just northeast of Islote El Toro (Fl.5s31m8M, white round tower 7m) and the double-humped Islote Banco de Ibiza off Punta de Ses Barbines. This latter promontory is very low and difficult to see from a distance, which can be confusing on the approach. Best depths (±4m) are reported about two-thirds of the way from Islote Banco de Ibiza out towards the rock. (See plan on page 90.)

III. MALLORCA

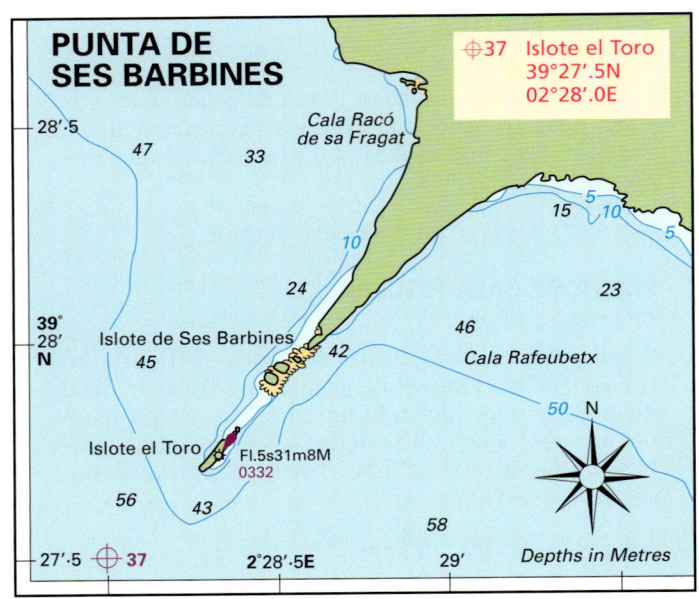

PUNTA DE SES BARBINES

⊕37 Islote el Toro
39°27'.5N
02°28'.0E

28'.5

47

33

Cala Racó de sa Fragat

15 10

10

5

24

23

46

Cala Rafeubetx

Islote de Ses Barbines

45 42

50 N

Islote el Toro Fl.5s31m8M
0332

56 43

58

27'.5 ⊕ 37

2°28'.5E 29' Depths in Metres

Islote El Toro and Punta de Ses Barbines showing clearly the bar. Port Adriano is tucked inside the bay on the far side of the peninsula

Port Adriano

⚓ CALO RACÓ DE SA FRAGAT

39°28'.5N 02°28'.7E

An attractive anchorage close inshore at the root of the long promontory leading to Punta de Ses Barbines, exposed to west and south sectors. The cliffs are steep-to. Anchor in 10–15m over sand and rock, open from southwest to northwest. A trip line is advisable.

M5 Port Adriano

A large yet quiet and pleasant harbour with berthing for over 400 yachts up to 18m. Set in the E side of the Cala de Peñas Rojas, it is easy to enter in most conditions and safe inside

Location
39°29'.5N 02°28'.7E

Communications
VHF Ch 09 and 16
℡ 971 23 24 94 *Fax* 971 23 25 66
Email info@portadriano.com
www.portadriano.com

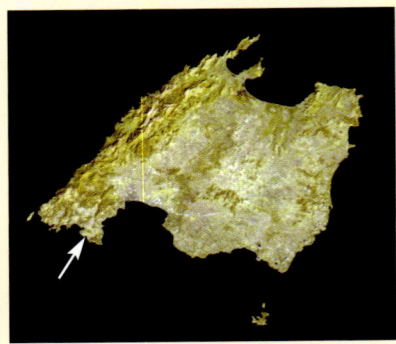

The marina

A large and pleasant marina in the process of expansion (due to be completed Spring 2011) with the addition of an outer breakwater, commercial zone, gardens, parking areas and berthing for an extra 82 superyachts (bringing the total to nearly 500 berths overall). The original outer breakwater has been converted into an inner pontoon with luxury shops and facilities along its length. A new outer breakwater has been built giving greater protection from seas that came over the original structure and provides additional moorings for superyahcts.

In November 2010 the expansion was nearly finished and most of the moorings already available. The backdrop of bare reddish cliffs, hotels and apartment buildings is somewhat barren but the marina itself is quite attractive. Above is the luxury holiday development of El Toro, with the 5-star Hotel Port Adriano providing a good landmark north of the port.

The marina is often very full especially in summer and contact should be made before arrival to check that a berth will be available.

The diving school, Escuela Buceo, in the marina complex covers all aspects of the sport including beginners' tuition. It stocks diving equipment, and has full decompression facilities.

Port Adriano is simple to approach and enter with reasonable protection once inside.

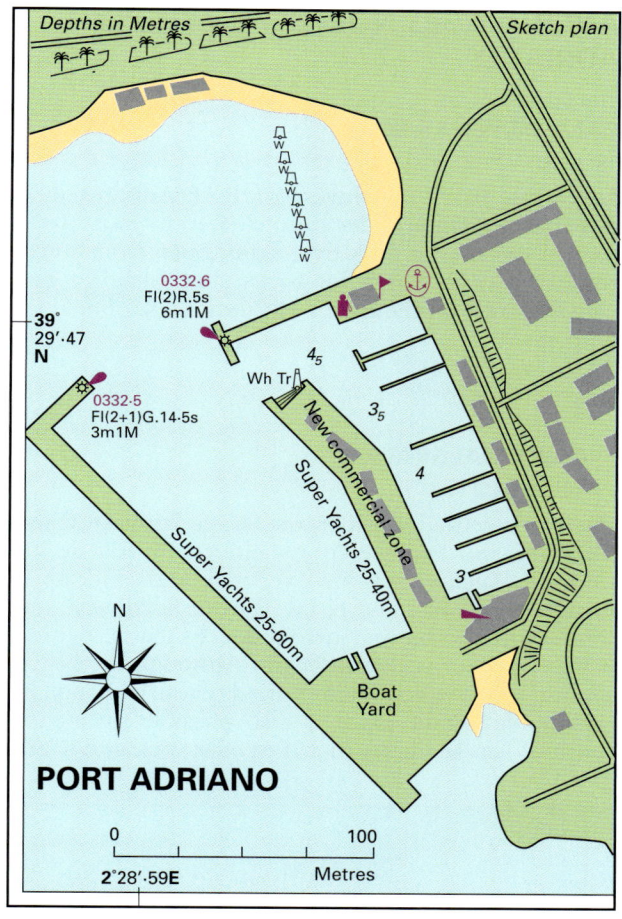

Depths in Metres   Sketch plan

0332·6
Fl(2)R.5s
6m1M

39°
29'.47
N

Wh Tr

0332·5
Fl(2+1)G.14·5s
3m1M

New commercial zone

Super Yachts 25-40m

Super Yachts 25-60m

4 5

3 5

4

3

Boat Yard

N

PORT ADRIANO

0   100

2°28'·59E   Metres

PILOTAGE

Approach

From the northwest Round Cabo de la Mola, a high headland terminating in sheer cliffs topped by a lighthouse (Fl(1+3)12s128m12M, white column with black bands on a square white tower 10m) and Cabo Llamp (unlit) (See plan on page 76.) Then steer southeast across the wide mouth of Ensenada de Santa Ponsa towards Islote El Toro leaving Isla Malgrats to port. Port Adriano will open up on rounding Punta Enguixa.

From the southeast Round the very prominent Punta de Cala Figuera (see plan on page 92) which has a lighthouse (Fl(4)20s45m15M, white round tower with black diagonal stripes on building 24m) and radio masts on its steep cliffs, continuing west to

leave Islote El Toro (Fl.5s31m8M, white round tower) to starboard, or see page 89 for details of the passage between Islote El Toro and the peninsula. Port Adriano will then be visible just under two miles north, tucked well into the aptly named Cala de Peñas Rojas, 'the bay with red cliffs'.

Anchorage in the approach

Anchor off the beach close north of the entrance in 3m+ over sand, open to the westerly quadrant, or see *Cala de Peñas Rojas* on page 92.

Entrance

Entrance is straightforward, but do not cut the west breakwater too closely as stones slope downwards from its end. There is a reception pontoon at the end of the east mole, near the large brown and cream office building. There is a 2-knot speed limit in the harbour. After strong south or west winds have been blowing there is a possibility that the entrance depth may be reduced due to silting; careful sounding in the approach is needed following these strong onshore winds.

Berthing

The marina is often very full and if possible contact should be made before arrival to check that a berth will be available.

Secure port side-to at the reception pontoon until a berth is allocated.

Facilities

Water Water points on the pontoons and breakwater.
Electricity 220v and 380v AC points on the pontoons and breakwater.
Fuel Diesel and petrol pumps at the fuel berth on the east mole (by the reception pontoon).
Provisions Supermarket in the marina complex and another at the top of the steep hill up from the marina, but otherwise mainly tourist shops.
Ice Cube ice from bars and supermarkets.
Chandlery In the marina complex.
Repairs Boatyard Mar Adriano (☎ 971 10 26 65) at the southern end of the harbour is able to handle all normal work. A 50-tonne lift and slipway in the boatyard. A new commercial zone is being built (November 2010) on the central quay. See website for details: http://portadriano.com/servicios_puerto.php

Porto Adriano: almost complete (2010). View from the north with new breakwater on the right-hand side
Patricia Chung

Engineers At Mar Adriano (see *Repairs* above).

Electronic & radio repairs At Mar Adriano (see *Repairs* above).

Yacht club The Club Náutico Porto Adriano has good facilities including a large restaurant and a swimming pool.

Showers In the marina office building.

Launderette In El Toro.

Bank/bureau de change In the nearby holiday town of El Toro.

Hospital/medical services In El Toro and Palma (the latter about eight miles by road).

Transport

Car hire/taxis Arrange via the marina office or taxi ☎ 68 09 70

Buses Bus service to Santa Ponsa and Palma from a stop near the top of the marina access road.

Sights ashore locally

Spectacular countryside with huge expanses of pine forests, especially to the northeast. See *Palma* for attractions.

Eating out

Restaurants and cafés overlooking the marina and in the new commercial zone on the central quay; hotels and more restaurants in the surrounding tourist development.

ANCHORAGES NORTHWEST OF PORT ADRIANO

CALA DE PEÑAS ROJAS

39°29'.6N 02°28'.5E

Less than 0.5M northwest of Port Adriano it is possible to anchor under steep cliffs in the northwest part of the *cala* in 5m+ over sand, open from south round to west. Watch for rocks close inshore. The *cala* is shown on the photo of *Punta de Ses Barbines* on page 90.

⊕38 39°29'.5N 02°26'.5E Isla Malgrats

⚓ CABO MALGRATS

39°30'.2N 02°27'.5E

There is a settled-weather anchorage between Cabo Malgrats and Punta Negra sheltered by Isla de los Conejos. Anchor in 4–5m over rock and sand, open to south and west and to swell from northwest and southeast. The bay is surrounded by cliffs, behind which is a tourist development. Although the beach is poor, the area is popular with day tourist boats. In favourable conditions it is also possible to anchor south of Isla Malgrats in ±10m over rock and sand.

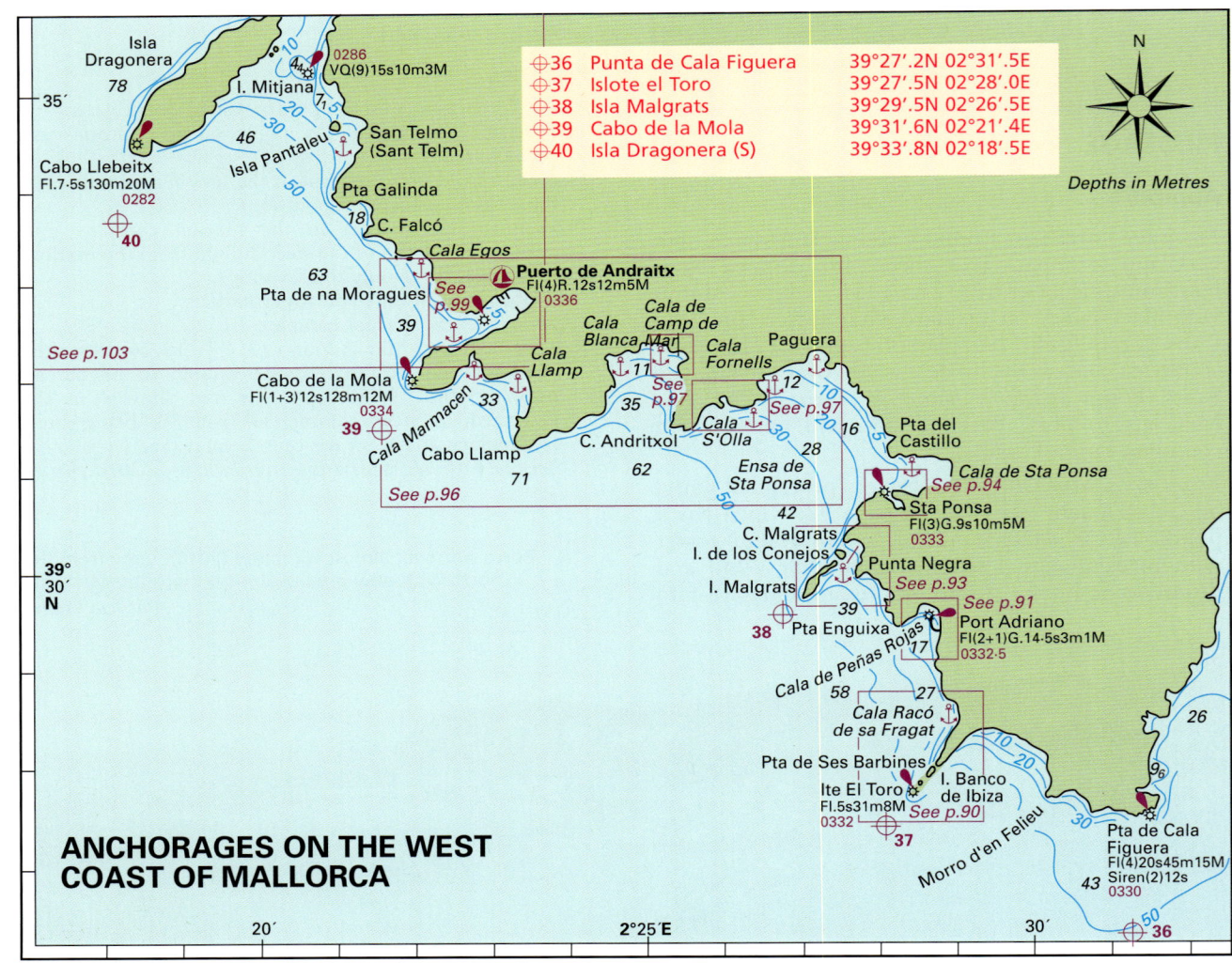

⊕36	Punta de Cala Figuera	39°27'.2N 02°31'.5E
⊕37	Islote el Toro	39°27'.5N 02°28'.0E
⊕38	Isla Malgrats	39°29'.5N 02°26'.5E
⊕39	Cabo de la Mola	39°31'.6N 02°21'.4E
⊕40	Isla Dragonera (S)	39°33'.8N 02°18'.5E

Depths in Metres

ANCHORAGES ON THE WEST COAST OF MALLORCA

Passages either side of Isla de los Conejos

39°30'.2N 02°27'.4E

Spectacular passages 100m wide exist either side of Isla de los Conejos. The southern passage has a minimum of 6m and should be taken on a northwest–southeast axis keeping to the centre of the channel. For the northern passage, less than 5m deep, and approaching from the south, leave Punta Negra some 100m to starboard and steer north for Cabo Malgrats. When the northeast point of the island is about 100m on the port beam, steer to follow the island's coast keeping 100m off until a course of northwest is attained and then depart on that course. Coming from the north use the reciprocal.

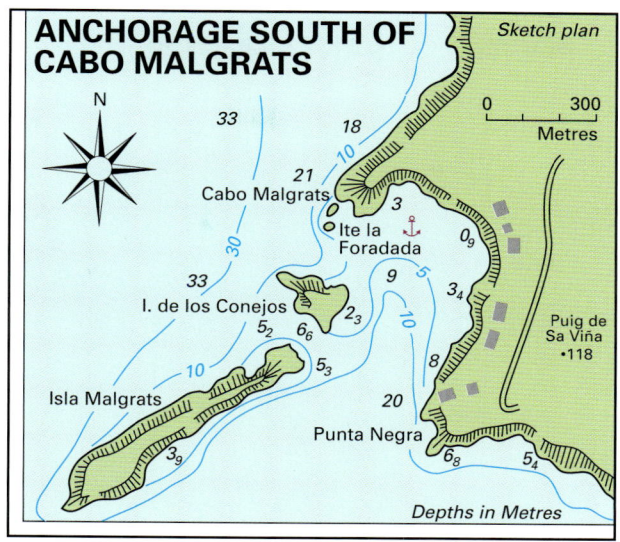

M6 Puerto de Santa Ponsa

A very attractive harbour with berths for over 500 yachts up to 20m

Location
  39°30'.8N 02°28'E
Communications
  VHF Ch 09
  Club Náutico Santa Ponsa ☏ 971 69 49 50
  Fax 971 69 44 88
  Email cnsp@sertebal.com or cnsp@arrakis.es

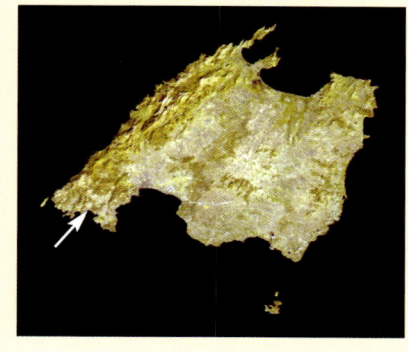

The harbour

On an island with so many attractive harbours, Santa Ponsa (Santa Ponça) must be one of the most picturesque, in spite of the many surrounding buildings. Long and narrow, guarded at its northwestern end by a curved breakwater, the inlet gives excellent protection, though it can get rather hot and airless in summer. There are 522 berths for yachts up to 20m, but even so it is necessary to contact the *club náutico* before arrival as most of the berths are permanently occupied and there is often no room for visitors.

Approach and entry are straightforward, but care should be taken in strong winds from the westerly quadrant. Space for manoeuvring larger yachts is very restricted once inside the harbour.

PILOTAGE

Approach

From northwest Round Cabo de la Mola, a high headland terminating in sheer cliffs topped by a lighthouse (Fl(1+3)12s128m12M, white column with black bands on a square white tower 10m) and Cabo Llamp (unlit). Then head east towards the long Playa de Santa Ponsa – the tall stone memorial to Jaime I and the breakwater below will be seen to starboard, near the mouth of the bay, on closer approach. A fish conservation area has been created near the entrance to the *cala* which is clearly visible when in place.

From southeast Round the very prominent Punta de Cala Figuera which has a lighthouse (Fl(4)20s45m15M, white round tower with black diagonal stripes on building 24m) and radio masts on its steep cliffs, continuing west to leave Islote El Toro (Fl.5s31m8M, white round tower) to starboard. Settle onto a northwest course to round Isla Malgrats (or in good weather use the inshore passage as previously described), then follow the coast northeast. Soon after rounding Morro d'en Grosser, the tall stone memorial to Jaime I and the breakwater below will be seen to starboard.

Anchorage in the approach

See *Cala Santa Ponsa* under *Anchorages* on page 95.

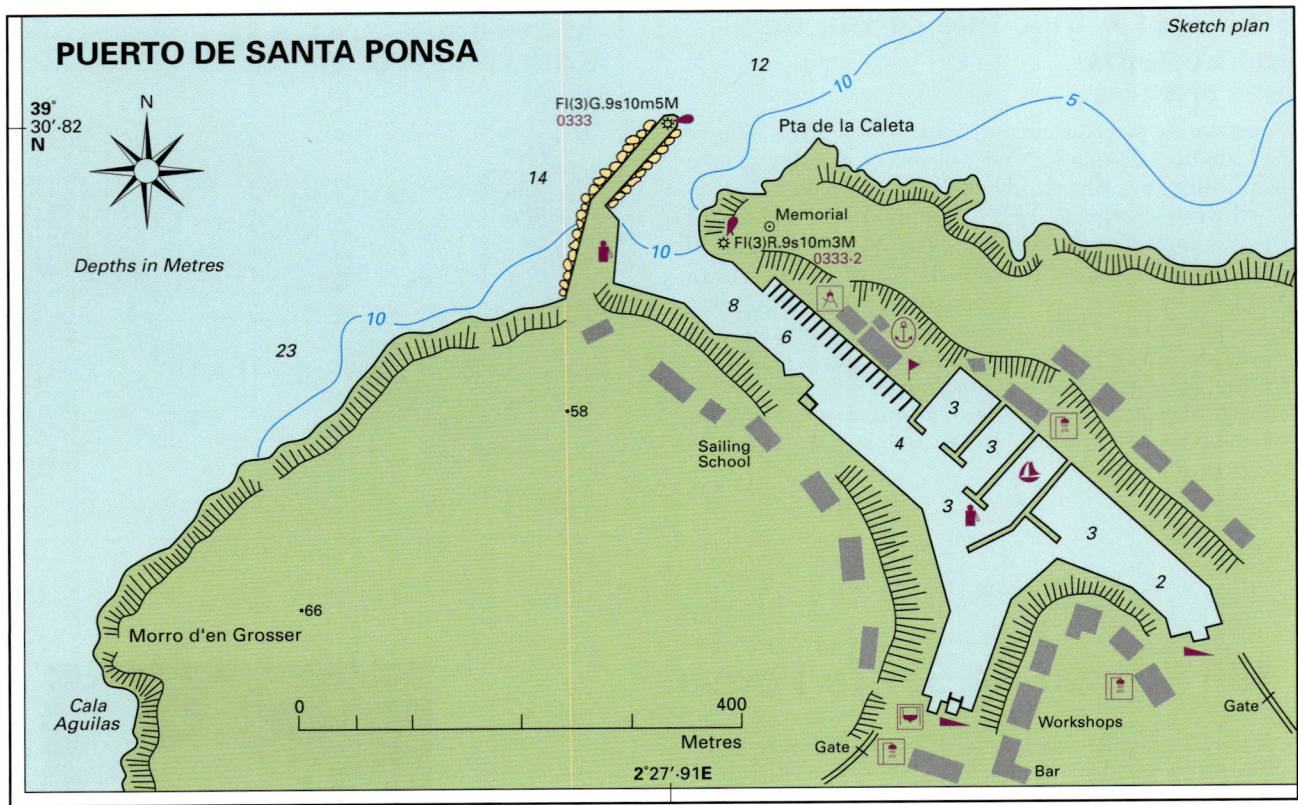

PUERTO DE SANTA PONSA

Sketch plan

Depths in Metres

Entrance

Approach the head of the northwest breakwater on a south or southeast course. Enter keeping to the starboard side of the channel, ready to berth starboardside-to on the reception quay at the root of the breakwater. There is a 2-knot speed limit.

Berthing

It is advisable to contact the *club náutico* before arrival as most of the berths are permanently occupied and there is often no room for visitors.

A berth will be allocated (if available). The marina office can be contacted on VHF Ch 09, or by dialling 9 at one of the four telephone booths around the inlet (the nearest one to the reception pontoon is situated by the sailing school).

Facilities

Water Taps on quays and pontoons.
Electricity 220v AC points on quays and pontoons. 380v AC available in the boatyard.
Fuel Pumps on the reception quay at the root of the breakwater and on one of the inner pontoons.
Provisioning Small supermarket near the *club náutico* and many shops in Santa Ponsa less than a mile away.
Ice At the fuel berth.
Chandlery In the block containing the *club náutico* and marina office.
Repairs Boatyard at the head of the southwest arm with a 50-tonne lift. A 2.5-tonne crane at the sailing school. Three slipways, one in each of the southern arms of the harbour and one at the sailing school.
Engineers At the boatyard and Port Fairline Santa Ponsa ☎ 971 69 07 17 (official service agents for Volvo Penta).

Metalwork Metalnox SL ☎ 971 69 40 11 *Fax* 971 69 56 91.
Electronic & radio repairs Can be organised via the boatyard or *club náutico*.
Sail repairs In the block containing the *club náutico* and marina office.
Yacht club The Club Náutico de Santa Ponsa has a palatial clubhouse on the northeast side of the harbour with lounge, terrace, restaurant, bar, etc.
Showers Below the *club náutico* and at the heads of both the southern arms.
Launderette At the *club náutico*.
Banks Several in Santa Ponsa.
Hospital/medical services In Santa Ponsa and Palma (about 7M by road).

Transport

Car hire/taxis At the marina office or in Santa Ponsa.
Buses Bus services from Santa Ponsa to Palma and elsewhere.

History

This is a place of great historical interest. The area is celebrated for the fact that the combined fleets of Catalonia and Aragon dropped anchor here in 1229 under the command of King Jaime I (Rey Jaime Conquistador), landing an army which eventually drove the Moors from Mallorca.

Sights ashore locally

A stone cross with scenes commemorating the events above stands on Punta de la Caleta, just inside the harbour entrance and is well worth the short stroll for closer inspection. A fiesta to celebrate the anniversary is held from 9–16 September.

Santa Ponsa Marina looking southeast: a well-sheltered harbour in pleasant surroundings *GW*

Cala de Santa Ponsa anchorage viewed from west *Patricia Chung*

Eating out

Many eating establishments of all grades, including a restaurant at the *club náutico*.

ANCHORAGES AROUND ENSENADA DE SANTA PONSA

Cala de Santa Ponsa looking across the harbour entrance. Note shoal patch markers just visible centre of *cala* *GW*

⚓ CALA DE SANTA PONSA
39°31′N 02°28′.3E

There are several good anchorages in Cala de Santa Ponsa, a wide bay to the northeast of the harbour surrounded by apartments, houses and hotels (see plan on page 92). It is shallow around the sides and near the head – where there is a long but often crowded beach – with two 0.5m shoal patches (Las Secas) near the centre, marked by a west card light buoy YBY(9)15s at its seaward end and an unlit east card beacon BYB 250m to the east.

An underwater cable runs from the southern end of the beach towards Las Secas before continuing westward.

III. MALLORCA

Anchor about 200m north of Caló de Pellicer on the southern shore in 2–4m over sand, open to west and northwest, or on the north side in 4–6m over sand, open to west and southwest. Shallow-draught yachts may be able to work closer in towards the head of the bay but a careful watch on the depth will be necessary.

Routine shopping requirements can be met in the tourist developments surrounding the bay, and there are many restaurants, cafés and bars. If anchored on the north side, a walk out to the fortified Gothic tower and the smaller watchtower on the northern headland might be enjoyed.

⚓ PLAYA DE PAGUERA

39°32'.2N 02°27'.1E

A large semicircular bay with an excellent beach, backed by apartment buildings and hotels. Rocks run out some distance from the southeast side of the entrance. Anchor as space permits in 3–5m over sand, open to south and southwest.

⚓ CALA FORNELLS (PUERTO DE PAGUERA)

39°32'N 02°26'.4E

An attractive anchorage just north of Pta Cerdana, but not in any sense a port; the most sheltered part is occupied by moorings. It is open to east and southeast and from swell from the south. The *cala* is surrounded by wooded cliffs and a growing number of low-rise apartment buildings plus a few shops. The small sandy beach at the head of the *cala* is often crowded. A fish conservation farm is usually laid just off Pta Cerdana running southeast. Anchor as space allows in 5–10m over sand and weed. A tripline is advised as there is reported to be considerable debris on the bottom.

⚓ CALA S'OLLA

39°31'.7N 02°26'E

A fascinating small *cala* between rocky cliffs, surrounded by unspoilt woodland. Approach with a lookout on the bow to anchor near the entrance in 3–5m over sand as there are several isolated rocks further in. Space is very restricted and two anchors will probably be required. Although open only to the south, the *cala* would quickly become dangerous in any wind from this direction and should be vacated immediately.

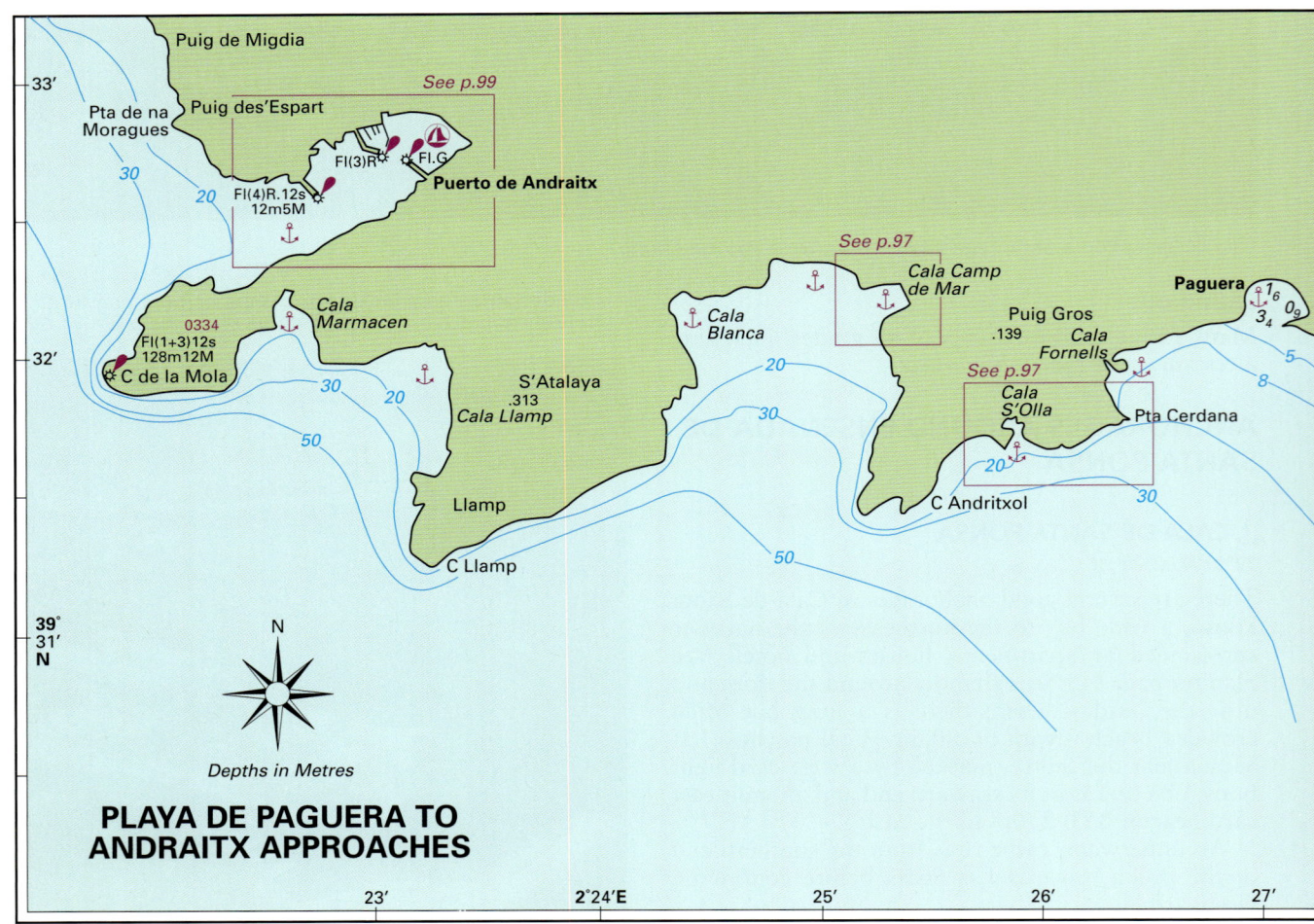

PLAYA DE PAGUERA TO ANDRAITX APPROACHES

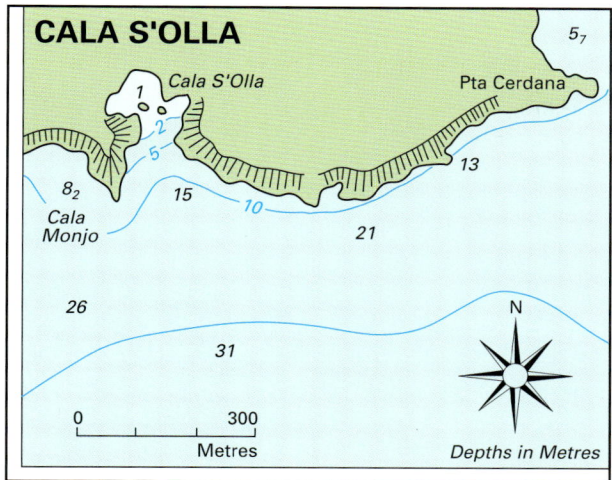

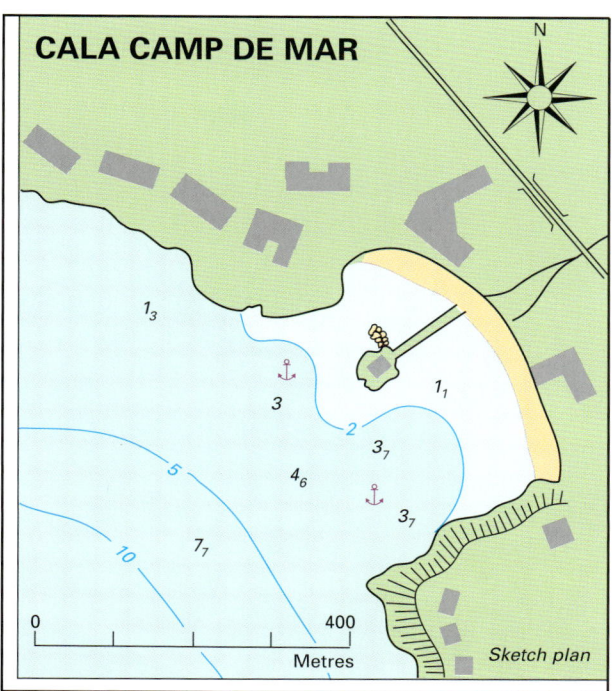

Cala Camp de Mar island and restaurant *GW*

Cala S'Olla from the south. Submerged rocks further in can be clearly seen

Cala Camp de Mar viewed from west. Note island and restaurant left *Graham Hutt*

⚓ CALA CAMP DE MAR

39°32′.3N 02°25′.4E

A pleasant bay which has become a popular tourist resort, partly due to a small island in its centre reached by a narrow wooden bridge and housing an outdoor bar/restaurant. A tourist ferry is often moored stern-to the restaurant island. There are several high-rise hotels behind the beach and more close northwest, plus a few tourist shops.

Anchor southeast of the island in 2–4m over sand and rock (shoals extend northwards from the heel of the island towards the white hotel); open to south and southwest.

III. MALLORCA

View over Cala Marmacen and Cabo de la Mola to Andraitx harbour

Cala Blanca: a pleasant but very busy bay in the high season
GW

⚓ CALA BLANCA
39°32'.2N 02°24'.5E

A small *cala* with cliffed sides and a sand and stone beach, as yet undeveloped. Anchor in 2–3.5m over sand off the beach, open to east through south.

⚓ CALA LLAMP
39°32'N 02°23'.3E

A somewhat unappealing anchorage, very open and with much development despite having no beach. Anchor close to the northeast corner in 4m over sand and stone, open south through southwest to west. (See plan of *Approaches to Andraitx* on page 96.)

⚓ CALA MARMACEN
39°32'.2N 02°22'.7E

A spectacular anchorage surrounded by cliffs in the approach and narrow at its head. Anchor in 5m over sand and stone near the head of the *cala*, open to the southern quadrant. Much new development surrounds the *cala*.

⊕39 39°31'.6N 02°21'.4E Cabo de la Mola

CABO DE LA MOLA
39°32'N 02°21'.9E

A high headland terminating in sheer cliffs topped by a rather inconspicuous lighthouse (Fl(1+3)12s128m12M, white column with black bands on a square white tower 10m). The light is only visible when bearing between 304.4° and 158.2° and is obscured during the final approach to Puerto de Andraitx.

⚓ SOUTHEAST OF PUNTA DEL MURTÉ
39°32'.3N 02°22'.4E

A small anchorage under steep cliffs, suitable for use in settled southerly weather. Anchor off the beach in 3m over sand and stone, open to north and northeast.

M7 Puerto de Andraitx (Club de Vela)

One of the oldest yachting marinas in Mallorca, in a fine setting. It offers nearly 500 berths for yachts up to 25m, with easy access through a buoyed channel. The harbour is often full

Location
39°32'.7N 02°22'.8E

Communications
Call *Andraitx Vela* VHF Ch 10 to avoid confusion with Puerto de Santa Ponsa (Ch 09)
Port Authority ☎ 971 46 62 12
Club de Vela Puerto de Andraitx
☎ 971 67 17 21 *Fax* 971 67 42 71
Email cvpa@sertebal.com
www.cvpa.es

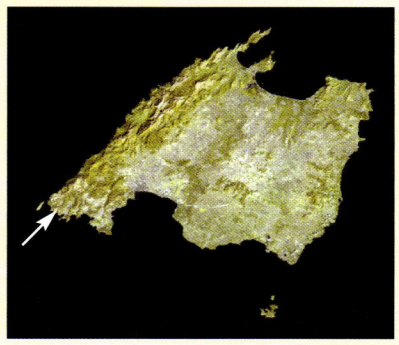

The harbour

A yachting and fishing harbour set in most attractive surroundings with a pleasant village nearby and a larger (and much more atmospheric) town some two miles inland. Inevitably a good deal of housing development is taking place around the bay, but this has not ruined its beauty and charm.

The harbour is easy to approach and enter and offers good protection, though strong gusts of wind can flow down from the surrounding hills. A heavy swell sets in with strong winds from west and southwest. Very occasionally the phenomenon known as *resaca* or *seiche* occurs (see *Tides* section in the *General Introduction*): particularly dangerous to yachts berthed on the quays.

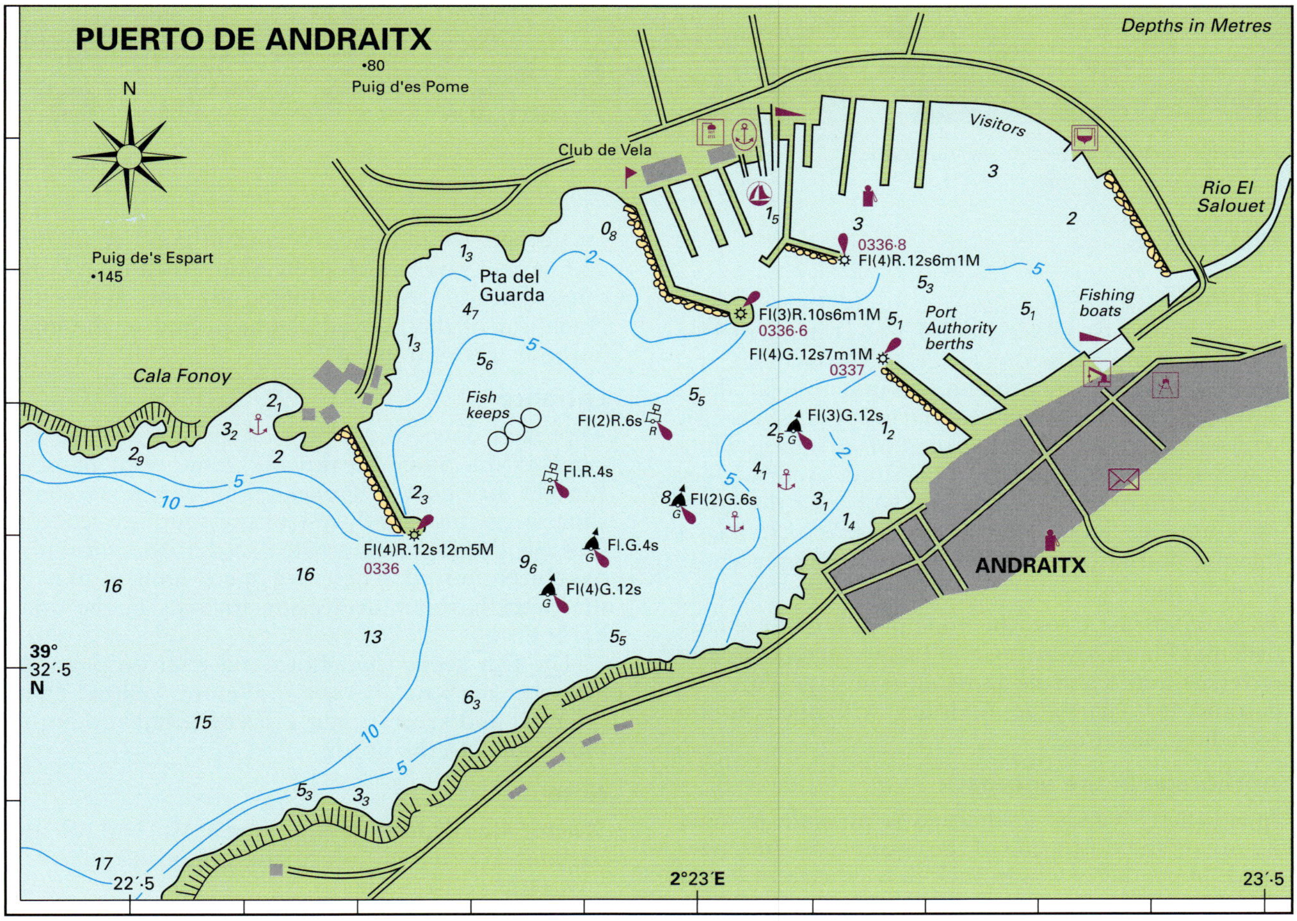

III. MALLORCA

PUERTO DE ANDRAITX

Depths in Metres

•80
Puig d'es Pome

N

Club de Vela

Visitors

3

Rio El Salouet

Puig de's Espart
•145

1₃

Pta del Guarda

0₈

1₅

3

0336·8
Fl(4)R.12s6m1M

2

5

4₇

5₆

Fl(3)R.10s6m1M
0336·6

5₃

Port Authority berths

5₁

Fishing boats

Cala Fonoy

1₃

Fl(4)G.12s7m1M
0337

2₁

3₂

Fish keeps

5₅

Fl(3)G.12s
1₂

2₉

2

Fl(2)R.6s

2₅ G

2₃

Fl.R.4s
R

4₁

2

Fl(4)R.12s12m5M
0336

8 Fl(2)G.6s
G

3₁

1₄

ANDRAITX

16

16

9₆

Fl.G.4s
G

13

Fl(4)G.12s
G

5₅

5₅

39°
32'·5
N

15

6₃

10

5

5₃

3₃

17

22'·5

2°23'E

23'·5

Andraitx Harbour viewed from southeast

PILOTAGE

Approach

From north Pass either side of Isla Dragonera (see separate plan of island on page 103) towards Cabo de la Mola, a high headland terminating in sheer cliffs topped by a lighthouse (Fl(1+3)12s128m12M, white column with black bands on a square white tower 10m). The entrance to Puerto de Andraitx lies to the north of the headland and will come into view on rounding Punta de las Brescas, which has a massive housing development on its sloping face (see plan on page 92).

From southeast Cross the wide mouth of Ensenada de Santa Ponsa towards Cabo Llamp (high and pine-covered) and Cabo de la Mola (see page 96). The entrance to Puerto de Andraitx will open up on rounding the latter.

Anchorage in the approach

In northerly winds, anchorage is possible in Cala Fonoy on the north side of the entrance in 2m+ over sand. In southerly winds, tuck in southeast of Punta del Murté in 3m over sand and stone. These anchorages should only be used in good conditions and neither gives much protection. Anchoring in the outer harbour is discouraged by the authorities (keep out of the buoyed channel), and in the inner harbour it is prohibited.

Entrance

Approach down the centre of the bay leaving the head of the outer breakwater some 50m to port. Keep to the buoyed channel, taking care to avoid the shoal area close southwest of the south mole. Note that the original buoys listed in the *Appendix* may have been moved. There is a speed limit of 5kns in the outer harbour decreasing to 3kns in the inner harbour.

The fish keeps (see photo and plan on page 99) may be marked by one or more yellow lights (Fl.Y.4s) and several unlit reflectors, but are out of the channel to the north.

Note

Where 4m depths at the northeast end of the harbour are shown, information indicates that it is now reduced to 2.3m.

Berthing

If intending to stay in the yacht harbour run by the Club de Vela Puerto de Andraitx, secure to the inner side of the head of the north mole until a berth is allocated (assuming one is available – the Club de Vela has 475 berths for yachts up to 25m, but is often full). Visitors are often allocated berths on the quay in the northeast of the harbour, between the pontoons and the travel-lift (which is near the end of the stone wall). Yachts lie bow or stern-to, and a mooring line is provided tailed to the quay.

Alternatively, the Port Authority oversees an area on the south side of the harbour, with berthing bow or stern-to along the inside of the end section of the south mole (no mooring lines, so an anchor will be needed) or on the floating pontoon just beyond it (mooring lines provided, tailed to the pontoon). About 125 Port Authority berths are available, nominally able to take yachts to 25m but these are mainly taken by local residents.

Note that there are 3m depths along the visitors' quay itself but care should be exercised at the far eastern end where the depth is reported to be less than 2.3m.

Moorings

The area between the outer breakwater and the north mole is filled with moorings, but it is unlikely that any will be free.

Facilities

Water On the Club de Vela pontoons and at the fuel berth. The quality is reported to be poor – brackish and over-chlorinated.

Electricity 220v AC points at the Club de Vela and on the south mole and adjacent pontoon.

Diesel and petrol At the fuel berth on the furthest but one pontoon at the Club de Vela. There is a diesel pump on the fish quay but it is for fishing vessels only.

Provisions Good supermarket just behind the fuel berth on the fish quay with other food shops nearby, plus many tourist shops. Two small supermarkets north of the harbour. The town of Andraitx two miles inland has many more shops and a good market. Good fish market in the southeast corner of the harbour after the boats return each day. Regular Wednesday market at Andraitx, 2½ miles inland.

Ice From Tim's Bar close southwest of the south mole and from some supermarkets.

Chandlery One at the Club de Vela plus a chandlery/hardware store south of the harbour.

Repairs Can be carried out at the yacht harbour boatyard – enquire at the Club de Vela office. A 50-tonne capacity lift and a 3-tonne crane in the yacht harbour. A large slipway at the yacht harbour and another at the southeast corner of the inner harbour.

Engineers Phoenix Marine ☎ 971 67 20 12 *Fax* 971 67 29 66 are official service agents for Mercury/MerCruiser and Volvo Penta. Taller Náutico Toni Mas ☎ 971 67 36 03, 105565 *Fax* 971 67 36 03 are official service agents for Mercury/MerCruiser and Yanmar.

Electronic & radio repairs Enquire at the Club de Vela office.

View down *cala* hosting Andraitx harbour. Note circular fish keeps northeast of the outer dique   *GW*

Yacht club The Club de Vela Puerto de Andraitx ☎ 971 67 23 37 *Fax* 971 67 42 71 occupies an impressive building north of the yacht harbour with lounge, bar, restaurant, swimming pool and showers.

Showers At the Club de Vela, free to those staying in their marina but with restricted hours.

Laundry/launderette In the town.

Banks In the town south of the harbour.

Hospital/medical services In Andraitx and Palma (about 15 miles by road).

Transport

Car hire/taxis In the town or arranged through the Club de Vela.

Buses Frequent buses to Andraitx 2½ miles inland and several each day to Palma.

Ferries A tourist ferry makes the trip to Isla Dragonera via San Telmo.

Sights ashore locally

In addition to the old town, where there is an interesting church, a walk along the upper roads and tracks on either side of the harbour is rewarded with excellent views.

Local Events

Fiestas are held on or about 29 June (a public holiday), in honour of San Pedro, with waterborne processions; 15–16 July, Fiesta de la Virgen del Carmen, again with waterborne processions, and the two weekends around 19–20 and 26–28 August, S'Arracó El Santo Cristo (also a public holiday).

Eating out

Many eating places around the harbour, with the southern waterfront seemingly wall-to-wall with cafés and restaurants.

III. MALLORCA

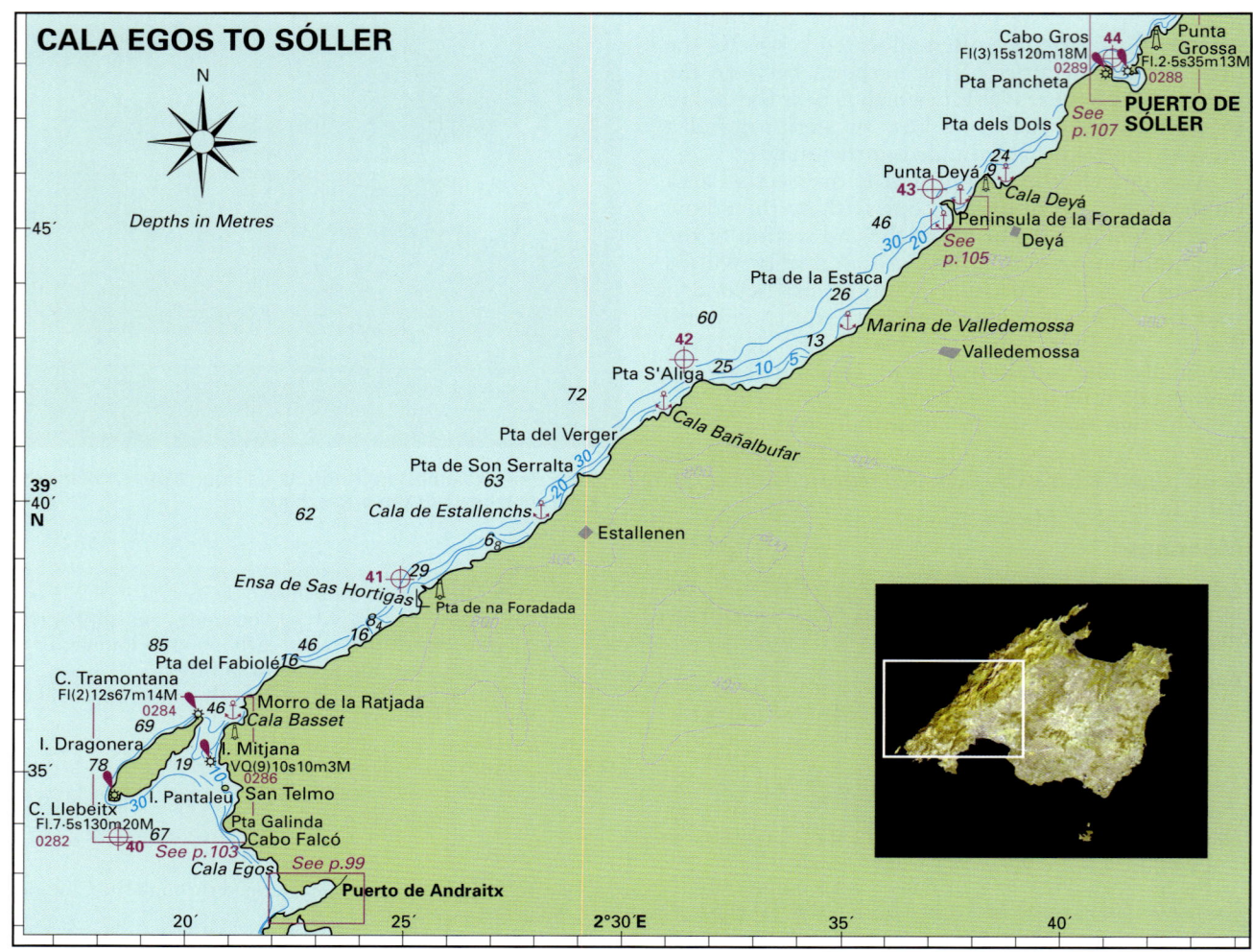

CALA EGOS TO SÓLLER

N

Depths in Metres

45′

39°
40′
N

35′

20′   25′   2°30′E   35′   40′

⚓ CALA EGOS

39°33′.2N 02°22′E

A small, unspoilt *cala* and beach surrounded by rocky cliffs southeast of Pta de sa Dent. Anchor in 4m over sand and rocks off the beach, open to south through west.

⚓ PLAYA DE SAN TELMO
(SANT TELM OR SAN ELM)

39°34′.7N 02°21′.1E

A pleasant bay with sandy beaches and a small tourist resort. Isla Pantaleu (29m) 220m long by 200m wide in the mouth of the bay gives protection from the west, as does Isla Dragonera further offshore. Parts of the beach are buoyed off for swimmers.

Mooring buoys have now been laid here, which can be booked in advance, for 1st June to 30th September at: www.balearslifeposidonia.eu/index.php?register_vars[lang]=en. See the plan above and the Anchoring and Moorings section on page 16 for

WAYPOINTS:
⊕40	Isla Dragonera (S)	39°33′.8N 02°18′.5E
⊕41	Punta de na Foradada	39°38′.5N 02°25′.2E
⊕42	Punta S'Aliga	39°42′.4N 02°31′.5E
⊕43	Peninsula de la Foradada	39°45′.6N 02°37′.2E
⊕44	Approach to Puerto Sóller	39°48′.0N 02°41′.2E

details. Enter the bay from the southwest to pick up your mooring.

Be aware that the bay is open to the southwest with a mile or more's fetch to the northwest. The winds can also funnel down from the mountains, causing local disturbances on the water.

The approach from the northwest is shallow, and may be obstructed by the stern anchors of tourist ferries lying bows-on at the quay as well as moored smallcraft. Several years ago plans were drawn up to construct a large yacht harbour in the bay north of Isla Pantaleu but these appear to have been dropped, along with most expansion plans for the island, due to environmental considerations.

San Telmo from southwest. Isla Pantaleu centre, north tip of Isla Dragonera left

Isla Pantaleu was the first landfall of King Jaime I of Aragon on his way to liberate Mallorca from the Moors in 1229, though his troops were finally disembarked near Santa Ponsa.

Isla Dragonera and the Dragonera Passage

Location
39°35'.3N 02°20'.2E

⊕40 39°33'.8N 02°18'.5E Isla Dragonera (S)

The island

Isla Dragonera is an island of spectacular and unique shape, being almost sheer on the northwest side and steeply sloping to the southeast. It is just over two miles long but only 0.6 miles wide with an old signal station and tower on Puig de Sa Popi, the pyramid-shaped 360m summit. Lighthouses mark each end of the island.

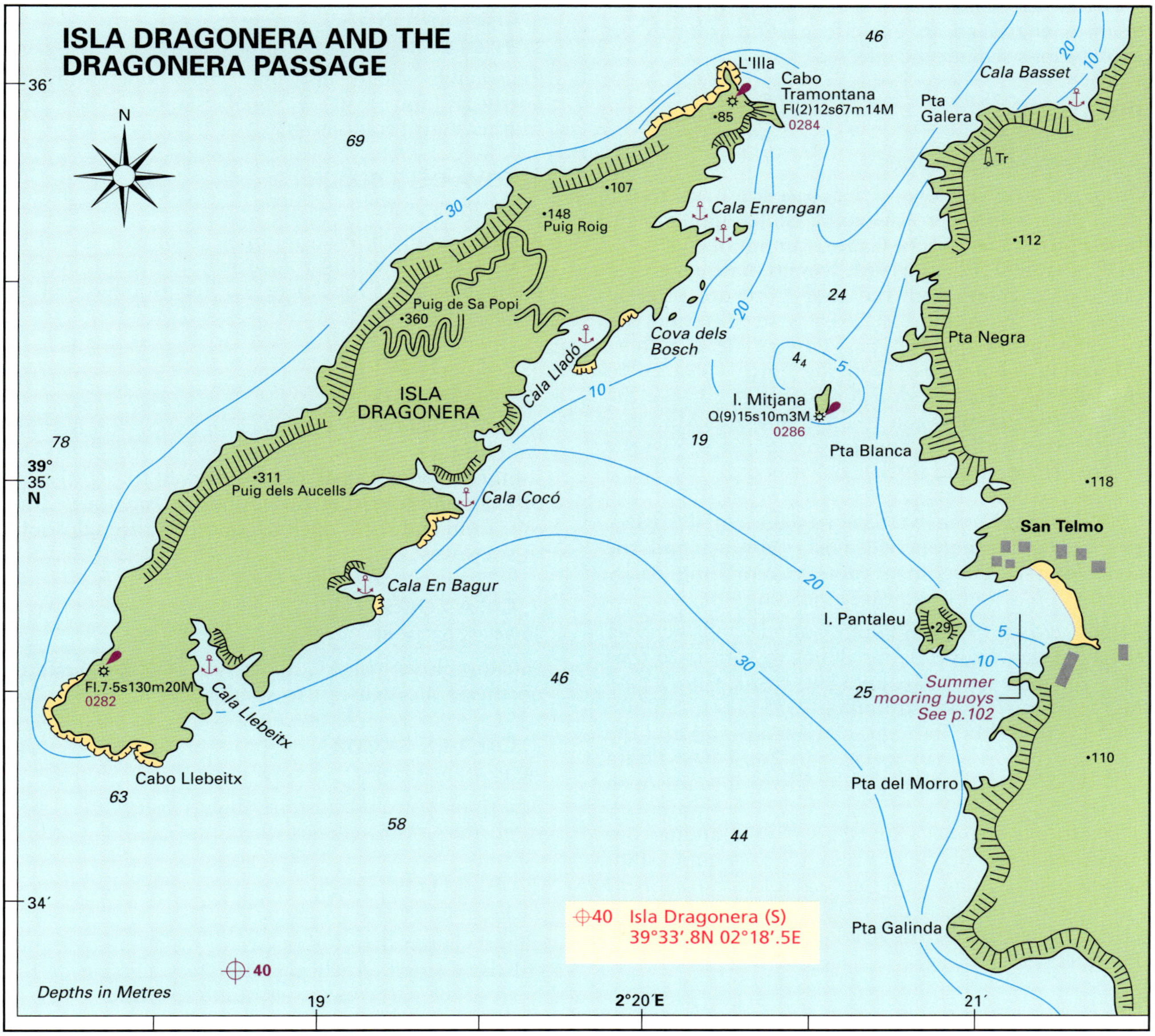

ISLA DRAGONERA AND THE DRAGONERA PASSAGE

36'

N

69

46

L'Illa
Cabo Tramontana
Fl(2)12s67m14M
0284
•85

Pta Galera

Cala Basset

•107

•148
Puig Roig

⚓ Cala Enrengan

⚓ Tr

•112

Puig de Sa Popi
•360

ISLA DRAGONERA

Cala Lladó

Cova dels Bosch

24

4 4
5

Pta Negra

I. Mitjana
Q(9)15s10m3M
0286

78

39°
35'
N

•311
Puig dels Aucells

⚓ Cala Cocó

19

Pta Blanca

•118

Cala En Bagur ⚓

San Telmo

⚓

Fl.7·5s130m20M
0282

Cala Llebeitx

46

20

I. Pantaleu
•29

30

25

5

10

Summer mooring buoys
See p.102

•110

Cabo Llebeitx
63

58

44

Pta del Morro

34'

⊕40 Isla Dragonera (S)
39°33'.8N 02°18'.5E

Pta Galinda

Depths in Metres

⊕ 40

19'

2°20'E

21'

III. MALLORCA

The passages

The passage between Isla Dragonera and Mallorca should present no problems to yachtsmen: the height of the surrounding hills make it appear much more alarming than it really is. The passage is funnel-shaped, opening to the south, with shoals and small rocky islets on either side of the narrows at the northern end. There are effectively two passages, either side of the 8m Isla Mitjana. The main channel is that to the west, which although wider has unmarked foul ground on both sides stretching some 200m from both Isla Mitjana and Isla Dragonera, leaving a passage 350m wide and 19m deep. The eastern channel, though much narrower at less than 200m, has a good depth of water (10m+) close to both Isla Mitjana and Mallorca.

Heavy gusts can descend from the high land around the passage without warning, while strong currents may flow through it in either direction after a gale; the direction dictated by the wind. Fishing nets supported by small white or pink buoys may be laid from either shore of the passage. The area between the island and mainland is marked on Spanish charts as an exercise ground, though no prohibitions seem to be effected.

PILOTAGE

Approach and passages

From northeast Following the coast southwestwards from Puerto de Sóller or beyond; Isla Dragonera will be seen from afar. (Light Cabo Tramontana 39°36′N 02°20′.4E Fl(2)12s67m14M. Round masonry tower on stone building with red roof 15m) See plan on page 102. The Mallorcan coast is steep-to and can be followed close inshore past Punta Galera, with its prominent watchtower, into the north entrance to the passage. Then work 200m offshore to take the eastern passage between Isla Mitjana and Mallorca in a north–south direction, approximately down the centre. There are no further hazards once the island has been passed.

Alternatively the western passage can be used, passing equidistant between Isla Mitjana and the coast of Isla Dragonera (note the offlying rocky islands) on a south–southwest heading.

From southeast Round Punta Galinda and then Isla Pantaleu, leaving the latter 300m to starboard (See plan on page 103). To take the east channel pass halfway between Isla Mitjana (39°35′.2N 02°20′.6E Q(9)15s10m3M Y beacon, black band 5m) and the Mallorcan coast, then follow this coast past Punta Galera with its prominent watchtower, into the open sea.

The west channel can be used by standing out into the centre of the passage to pass equidistant between Isla Mitjana and the coast of Isla Dragonera (note the offlying rocky islands) on a north-northeast bearing before heading northeast to round Punta Galera.

At night

Transiting either passage after dark is not recommended unless the area is already familiar. It would be safer to sail the extra few miles around Cabo Llebeitx at the southwest end of Isla Dragonera.

Sites ashore locally

There is very little ashore, but tracks link Cala Lladó to the lighthouses and the northwest coast and offer some memorable walks.

ANCHORAGES AROUND ISLA DRAGONERA

There are several possible daytime anchorages on the southeast coast of Isla Dragonera, all framed by spectacular cliffs. Without exception they are small with sand and rock bottoms, and tenable only in settled conditions. Taken from northeast to southwest they are as follows. (See plan on page 103.)

⚓ CALA ENRENGAN

39°35′.6N 02°20′.1E

Reasonable shelter for one yacht, open only to northeast and east. A small island lies off the southeastern promontory.

⚓ COVA DELS BOSCH

39°35′.3N 02°20′.0E

A wide open, cliffed *cala*, open from east round to south and to swell from southwest. Careful eyeball pilotage is called for. There is a low, isolated rock to the east.

⚓ CALA LLADÓ

39°35′.2N 02°19′.7E

A narrow *cala* with a 2m rock in the centre. A stone watchtower stands on the promontory to the southeast, with a small quay (reserved for lighthouse officials and tourist ferries) opposite. Anchor in 2m+ over sand and rock, open to southeast through south to southwest.

⚓ CALA COCÓ

39°34′.9N 02°19′.4E

Anchor close inshore under steep cliffs, open to northeast through east to southeast.

⚓ CALA EN BAGUR

39°34′.7N 02°19′.2E

Again anchor close inshore under steep cliffs, open to northeast through east to southeast.

⚓ CALA LLEBEITX

39°34′.4N 02°18′.5E

Slightly larger than Cala Cocó or Cala En Bagur, but still very small. Anchor under steep cliffs near the head of the *cala*, open east round to south.

Dragonera Island light with San Telmo behind   *GW*

ANCHORAGES FROM ISLA DRAGONERA TO SÓLLER

There are a small number of rocky anchorages on this stretch of the northwest coast of Mallorca, only suitable for use with great care in settled conditions. The only shelter is the port of Sóller in the event of sudden weather deterioration. The mountains and sheer cliffs which form much of the Costa Mirador offer spectacular scenery but also a totally unforgiving lee shore in the wrong conditions – in particular the northwest *tramontana* (see *General Introduction* on page 3). The mountains and narrow valleys influence the wind in both strength and direction, and a generous offing must be allowed in these conditions. See plan on page 102.

⚓ CALA BASSET
39°35'.8N 02°21'.3E

Close north of Punta Galera, which has a tower, a small house and track to the road. Enter with a lookout forward as there are several isolated breaking rocks. Open west–north. Holding is reported to be poor.

⊕41 39°38'.5N 02°25'.2E Pta de na Foradada

⚓ CALA DE ESTALLENCHS
39°39'.7N 02°28'.3E

A very open *cala* under the village of the same name, totally exposed to the entire west sector. There is a track up to the village. Reports mention a small rock awash close northeast of the small stone jetty.

⚓ CALA BAÑALBUFAR
39°41'.6N 02°31'E

Another open *cala*, exposed to the west sector, with a track up to the village.

⊕42 39°42'.4N 02°31'.5E Pta S'Aliga

⚓ CALA DE VALLEDEMOSSA
39°43'.2N 02°35'.3E

Very little shelter, but there is a tiny quay backed by a small village, both dwarfed by breathtaking pine-covered mountains. Worth a detour inshore if time and weather conditions permit.

Peninsula de la Foradada
39°45'.4N 02°37'.3E (N tip of peninsula)
⊕43 39°45'.6N 02°37'.2E Peninsula de la Foradada

This extraordinary inverted boot-shaped promontory 600m in length has anchorages on either side, though the most sheltered area is now full of moorings. It is possible to land at the northwest corner where there is a path up to a white house. A track inland leads to a large and conspicuous house known as Son Marroig, once owned by Archduke Luis Salvador of Austria who kept his steam yacht in the anchorage below. See plan.

⚓ West anchorage

The most sheltered area, in the angle of the 'L', is now occupied by moorings; anchor as close in as these permit in 5–10m over rock and weed with a few sand patches, open (depending on position) to southwest–west–northwest. Holding is generally poor. The spectacular hole through the end of the outcrop is best seen from this angle.

⚓ East anchorage

This anchorage, tucked between the peninsula and the coast, is open through northwest–north–northeast. Approach from the northwest, following the coast of the peninsula, to avoid a line of breaking and submerged rocks which extend 100m or so from the mainland coast. The easternmost rock is about 100m from the anchorage. Anchor in 7–10m over rock and sand. There is a track uphill to the road.

⚓ CALA DEYA (DEIA)
39°45'.8N 02°38'.5E

A small, picturesque *cala* northeast of the Peninsula de la Foradada, with a tiny quay at its head. Anchor near the middle in 4–6m over sand and rock, open to the northerly quadrant. There are fishermen's huts and several restaurants near the water, but little else. Deya itself, about a mile inland, is celebrated as the home of Robert Graves for many years prior to his death in 1985. It is also amongst the loveliest of Mallorca's villages and the antithesis of the tourist resorts that abound on much of the coastline. See page 102.

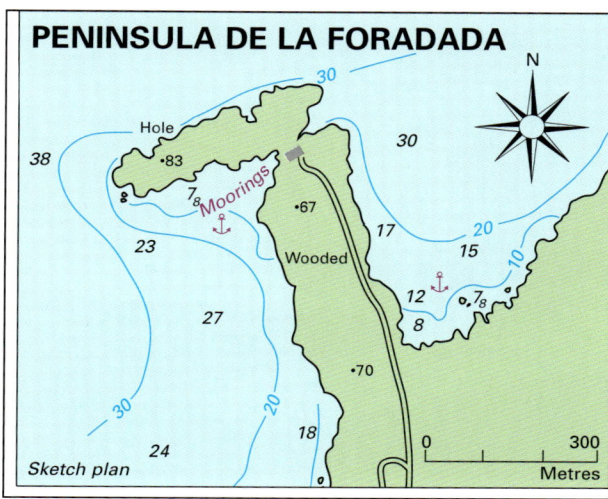

III. MALLORCA

M8 Puerto de Sóller

A very attractive harbour with a long history, tucked well inside a large *cala*. It is surrounded by mountains and pine forests. This is the only harbour on this stretch of coast and easy to enter in most conditions

Location
  39°47'.7N 02°41'.6E

Communications
  Port Authority ℡ 971 63 13 26 or ℡/*Fax* 971 63 33 16
  Email webmaster@solleronline.com
  www.SollerOnline.com

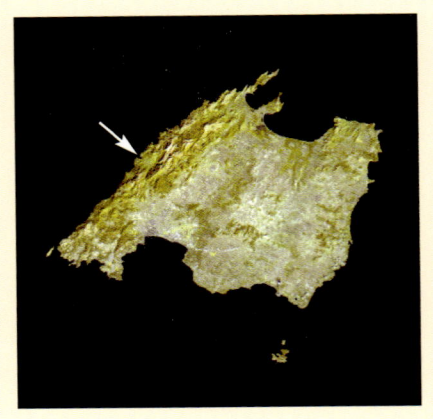

The port

Lying at the northeast end of a beautiful bay, in the midst of spectacular mountainous scenery, Puerto de Sóller is a commercial and fishing harbour with some space for yachts. With the addition of a new pontoon and refurbished town quay, more yachts have made this a prime place to visit, and from which to make excursions to the surrounding spectacular countryside.

This is the only harbour of refuge on the whole 50 mile stretch of the rugged, inhospitable northwest coast of Mallorca, although there are a number of fair-weather anchorages. Facilities for yachtsmen are somewhat limited and it is often difficult to find a vacant space on the commercial mole. Improvements have been made by addition and rearrangement of the moles with berths reserved for visitors. The anchorage west of the port has been laid to buoys.

PILOTAGE

Approach

⊕44 39°48'.0N 02°41'.2E Approach to Puerto Sóller

The approach and entrance present no problems in normal conditions, but could become difficult and perhaps dangerous in a gale from the northwest, north or northeast.

From northeast From Cabo de Formentor, which can be recognised by its lighthouse (Fl(4)20s210m21M, white tower and house 22m), the coast comprises high rocky cliffs, very rugged and broken (see plan on page 110). Careful pilotage is necessary because many of the headlands are similar. The following may be recognised: Cala de San Vicente, which has a tourist development at its head, Punta Beca with a long beak-like extension, and Morro de la Vaca, looking like the head of a cow from some directions. In the last three miles two conspicuous watchtowers and the small Islote S'Illa will be seen and, in the close approach, the two lighthouses at the harbour entrance. Puig Mayor (1,445m), the highest point on Mallorca with radio towers (F.R) and two radomes on its summit, is just under five miles east of the entrance.

From southwest From Isla Dragonera, a large, high and conspicuous island with two lighthouses (Fl.7.5s130m20M and Fl(2)12s67m14M), the coast

Puerto de Sóller, set in mountainous surroundings, looking north-northeast (prior to improvements for visitors)

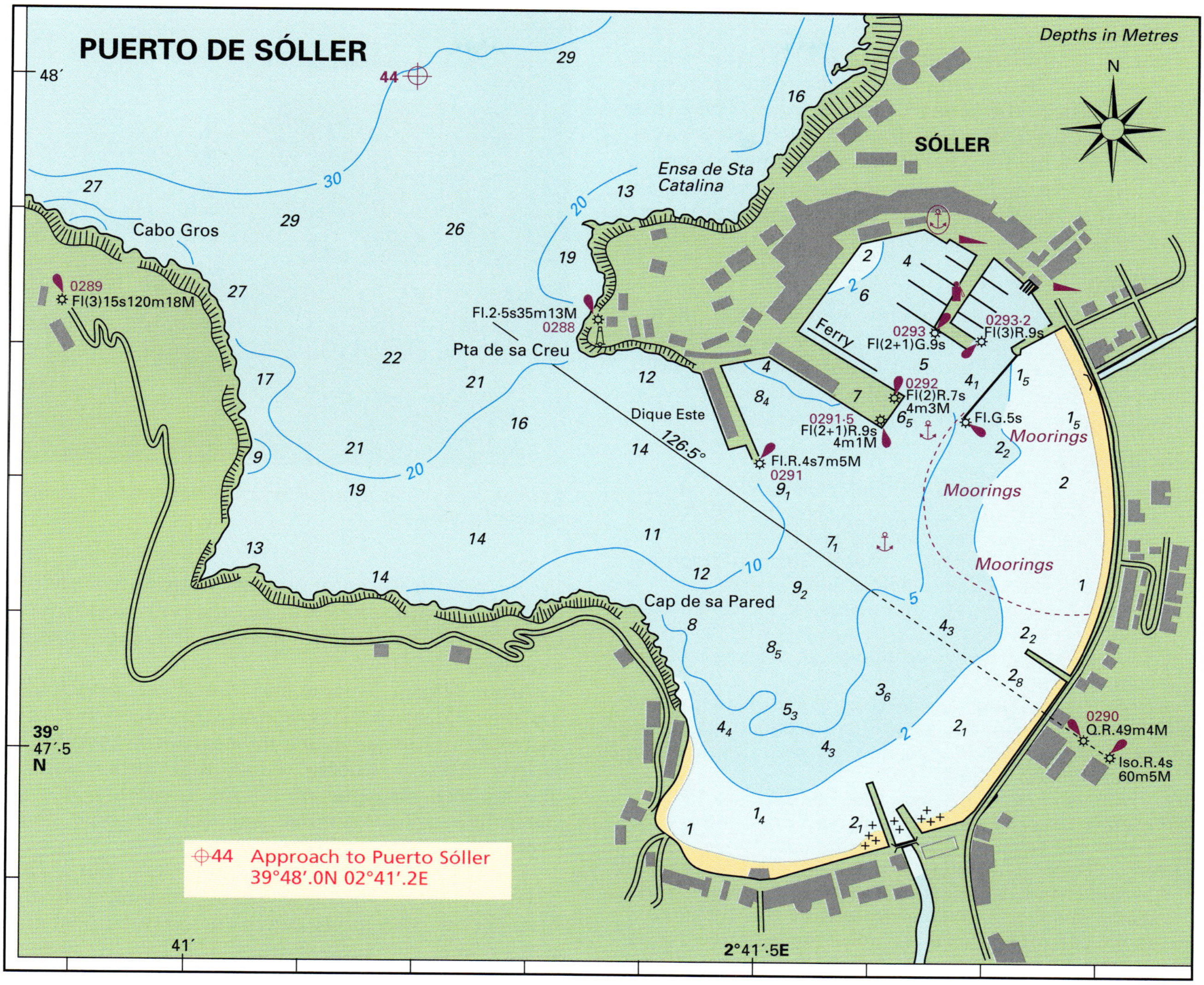

PUERTO DE SÓLLER

Depths in Metres

48′

44 ⊕

29

16

N

SÓLLER

Ensa de Sta Catalina

30

27

13

20

19

Cabo Gros

29

26

27

0289
✺ Fl(3)15s120m18M

22

21

Fl.2·5s35m13M
0288
Pta de sa Creu

12

5

4

2

6

Ferry

2

4

0293
Fl(2+1)G.9s

0293-2
✺ Fl(3)R.9s

17

21

16

Dique Este

8₄

7

0292
✺ Fl(2)R.7s
4m3M

0291·5
Fl(2+1)R.9s
4m1M

6₅

4₁

2₂

1₅

1₅

Fl.G.5s

Moorings

9

20

19

14

126·5°

Fl.R.4s7m5M
0291

9₁

7₁

2

Moorings

13

14

11

12

10

Cap de sa Pared

9₂

5

Moorings

1

14

8

4₃

2₂

2₈

5₃

8₅

3₆

2₁

0290
Q.R.49m4M

39°
47′·5
N

4₄

4₃

2

Iso.R.4s
60m5M

1

1₄

2₁

⊕44 Approach to Puerto Sóller
39°48′.0N 02°41′.2E

41′

2°41′·5E

Puerto de Sóller: a new pontoon and refurbished town quay facilitate more berthing for visiting yachts   *David Evernden*

is very high with broken rocky cliffs backed by mountains inland (see plan on page 102). The unmistakable Peninsula de la Foradada will be seen if coasting close inshore, with Cabo Gros and its white lighthouse 3.8 miles beyond. Punta de Sa Creu on the east side of the entrance is considerably lower and will not open until Cabo Gros has been rounded.

Anchorage in the approach

Anchor as space permits in 5–10m over mud and sand. Moorings extend to the 5m line, but appear too light for all but the smallest yachts. In summer the anchorage may become very full.

Entrance

Enter on a southerly course between Cabo Gros and Punta de sa Creu, swinging southeast and then east to remain near the centre of the channel. There is a 4kn speed limit. Keep well clear of the two naval moles if looking for a berth on the commerical mole.

Entrance at night should not present problems in reasonable weather: follow the leading lights into the anchorage.

Berthing

There is now more room for visiting yachts (September 2010) following the addition of a new pontoon and refurbishment of the town quay. Both moles on the northwest side of the harbour are in the naval zone and should not be approached.

Facilities

Water Taps on the commercial mole, but only operational for a few hours each day (currently 0900–1100 weekdays). Also from a public water fountain up the hill behind the commercial mole. Reports regarding quality vary: seek advice before filling tanks.

Electricity 220v and 380v AC points on the commercial mole.

Fuel Diesel and petrol from pumps at the angle of the commercial mole.

Provisions Shops and supermarkets in the village around the harbour, with a much greater selection in the town two miles inland. Produce/fish market every morning except Sunday in Sóller town.

Ice From the fishermen's quay, bars and supermarkets.

Chandlery Small chandlery/fishing tackle/hardware shop up the hill behind the commercial mole.

Repairs There is no boatyard, but local craftsmen are available and should be able to carry out minor work. Three small slipways either side of the commercial mole, one of which has a cradle. However, there is no more than 2m depth at its foot. A 1-tonne crane near one of the slipways.

Engineers Available, but more accustomed to fishing boats.

Yacht club There is a small *club náutico*.

Launderette In the village.

Banks In the village and at Sóller town.

Hospital/medical services In Sóller town. Medical Emergencies ☏ 971 63 30 11 or 63 30 50. Other emergency and useful local numbers on the marina website.

Transport

Car hire/taxis In Sóller town.

Buses Bus service to Sóller and elsewhere.

Trams A quaint old wooden tram provides transport between the port and the town. The 2-mile journey takes about 20 minutes.

Trains Rail link from Sóller town to Palma by Victorian train (1 hour).

Ferries Tourist ferries to several of the *calas* along the coast to the northeast.

History

Several prehistoric artifacts have been found in the town indicating its ancient past. In the 13th century under Moorish Arab power it was known as Puerto de Santa Catalina. Some years later King Jaime I conquered the island and the port was renamed Puerto de Sóller.

Ancient tram still in service, linking Sóller town to the port
Patricia Chung

The port has been of crucial importance since the thirteenth century when it was the only stopover on this coast between the islands and the Spanish mainland.

After 1399 it became a trading post, principally for the sale of local agricultural produce and raw materials destined for Spain, South of France, Italy, North Africa, Puerto Rico and other closer destinations. Because of its inaccessibility it was generally easier to move supplies by boat than overland to the port of Palma.

The construction of several towers along this coast, including Torre Picada, are testimony to the frequent and continous attacks by Arab bandits and pirates since the 13th century. The Es Firo festival celebrates a rebuffed pirate attack.

From the Middle Ages onwards Sóller had a huge fleet of merchant, fishing vessels and passenger ferries.

The port was rebuilt in the 18th century, and the splendid quays were used from 1936–39 by Franco as a major military base. It later became the centre of learning for the submarine service.

After the civil war the shipping trade was in decline but tourism created new oportunities. The whole region has been transformed by the construction of hotels, restaurants, bars and other trades, though the charm and originality of this port remains.

A small naval fleet remained until recently and the port is becoming more accommodating to yachtsmen.

Sights ashore locally

The attractive old rural town of Sóller – the name derived from the Arabic Sulliar, meaning 'golden valley' – was set well back from the sea as a first defence against pirate raids. It was long known for its oranges and lemons, which were exported in the famous *balancelles* (small, single-masted vessels). Even with the loss of that trade to Valencia the

Bay of Sóller. Note dredger at work in bay

orange groves surrounding the little town remain. Sóller is linked to its port by a vintage tramway, an excursion highly recommended, as is a trip on the Victorian train which connects Sóller to Palma. Sóller, along with numerous other places in the western Mediterranean, claims to have been the birthplace of Christopher Columbus.

Further information is available from the tourist office in Sóller: Calle Calonge Oliver No.10 ☎/Fax 971 63 30 42. Open between March and October 1000–1300 and 1500–1830 weekdays, Saturday 1000–1300.

Tickets for bus excursions may be found at change offices, car rental and tourist agencies in the port.

Local events

The fiesta and pageant of Nuestra Señora de la Victoria is held on the second Sunday in May to commemorate a victory over Moorish pirates in 1561; 15–16 July sees the Fiesta de la Virgen del Carmen with a waterborne procession; 25 July a fiesta in honour of Santiago (St James), and 24 August a fiesta in honour of San Bartolomé.

Eating out

A number of hotels and many restaurants, bars and cafés around the harbour.

Overlooking the port from the northeast *Patricia Chung*

III. MALLORCA

PUNTA GROSSA TO PUERTO DE CA'N PICAFORT

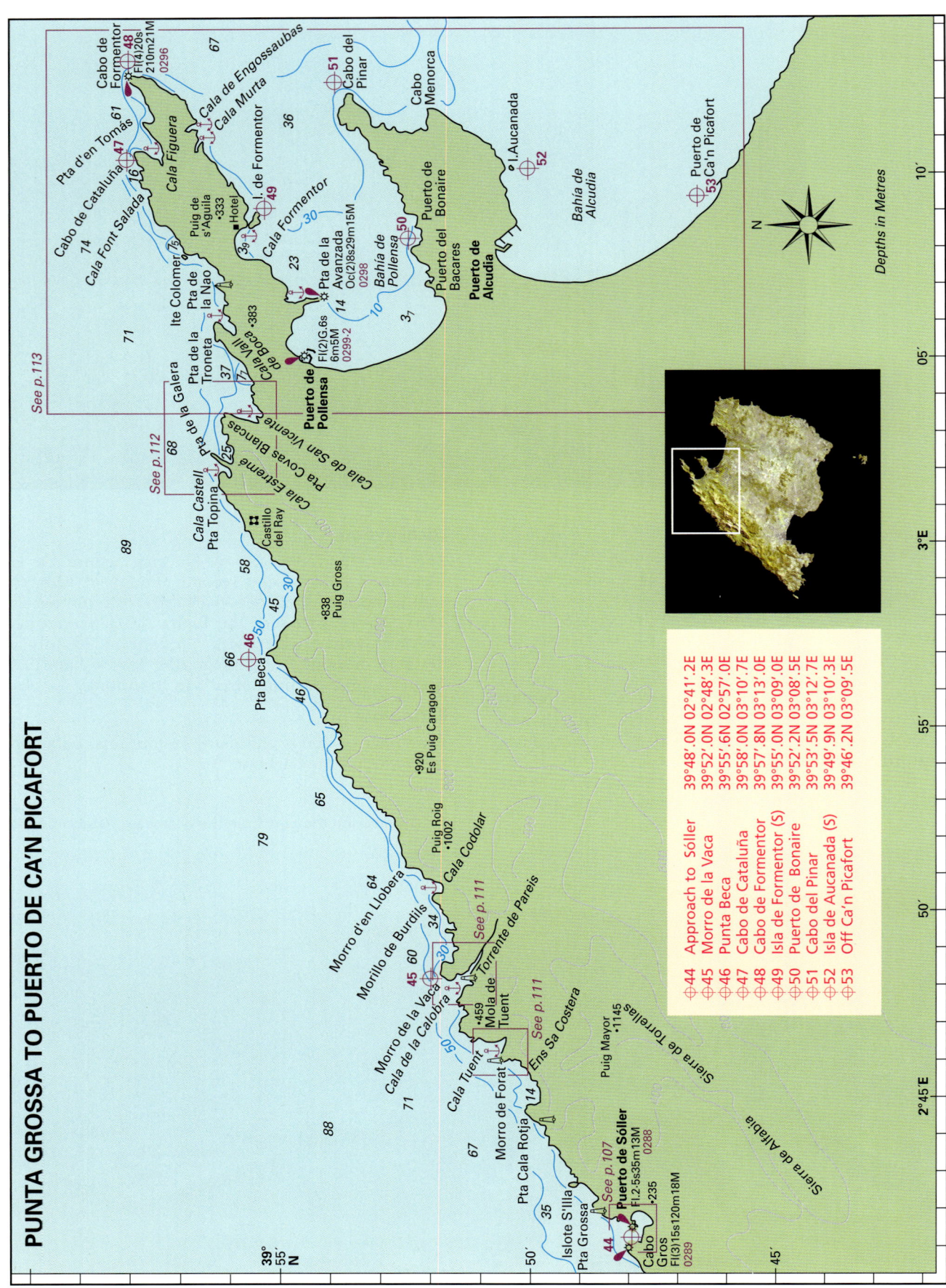

Depths in Metres

⊕44	Approach to Sóller	39°48'.0N 02°41'.2E
⊕45	Morro de la Vaca	39°52'.0N 02°48'.3E
⊕46	Punta Beca	39°55'.6N 02°57'.0E
⊕47	Cabo de Cataluña	39°58'.0N 03°10'.7E
⊕48	Cabo de Formentor	39°57'.8N 03°13'.0E
⊕49	Isla de Formentor (S)	39°55'.0N 03°09'.0E
⊕50	Puerto de Bonaire	39°52'.2N 03°08'.5E
⊕51	Cabo del Pinar	39°53'.5N 03°12'.7E
⊕52	Isla de Aucanada (S)	39°49'.9N 03°10'.3E
⊕53	Off Ca'n Picafort	39°46'.2N 03°09'.5E

3. Punta Grossa to Puerto de Ca'n Picafort

ANCHORAGES ALONG THE NORTHWEST COAST

⚓ ENSENADA SA COSTERA

39°49'.8N 02°45'E

A wide, deep bay and a pleasant anchorage in settled conditions. Rocks line the shore but the water is usually very clear; approach carefully with a bow lookout, to anchor in 12–15m in the southwest corner, open to north and northeast. Puig Mayor (1,445m), the highest point on Mallorca with radio towers (F.R) and two radomes on its summit, lies just over two miles inland.

⚓ CALA TUENT

39°50'.6N 02°46'.4E

A small *cala* with a wide sand and stone beach, amidst spectacular surroundings 4.8 miles northeast of Puerto de Sóller. Morro de Forat, close southwest, has a ruined watchtower and offlying rocks. Anchor in 5–10m over sand and rock, open to northwest and north. There are a few houses and a restaurant on the slopes overlooking the *cala* and a very winding road.

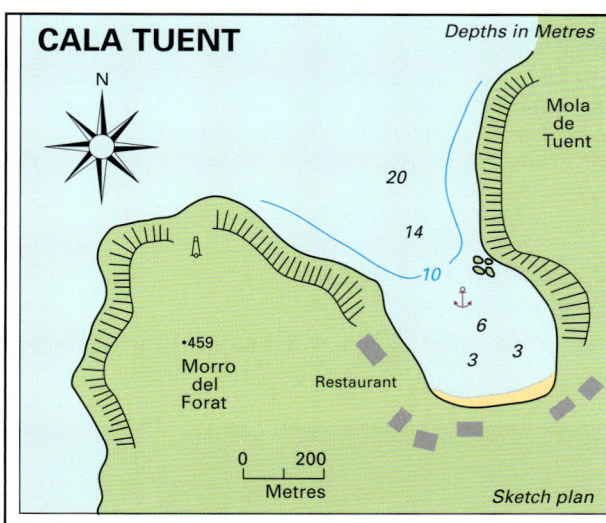

Cala Tuent viewed from northwest

⚓ CALA DE LA CALOBRA (TORRENTE DE PAREIS)

39°51'.4N 02°48'.1E

A large and spectacular *cala* just south of Morro de la Vaca, with several mini bays and a slit in the high rocky cliffs behind, through which the Torrente de Pareis (more often a gentle stream) enters the sea. Anchor in 5–10m over sand and stones, open to northwest and north. Tourist ferries land their passengers near the hotel overlooking the southwest beach and should not be impeded.

The Torrente de Pareis is considered one of the sights of Mallorca and is a popular destination by road and sea, resulting in the usual restaurants and beach cafés. A tunnel through the rock links the two beaches.

⊕45 39°52'.0N 02°48'.3E Morro de la Vaca

Cala de la Calobra (Torrente de Pareis) from southeast

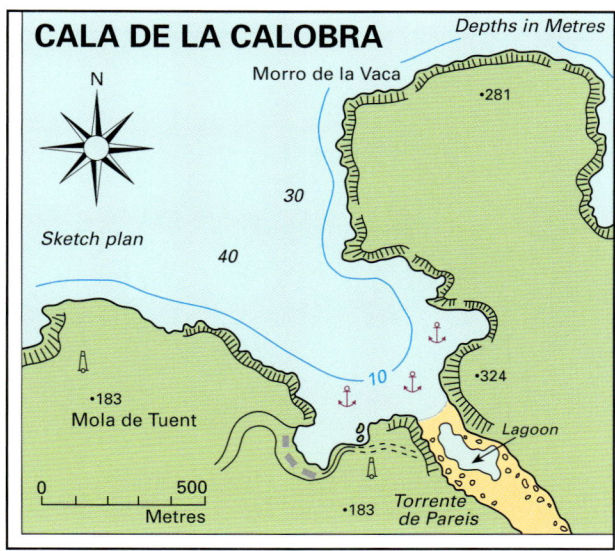

III. MALLORCA

Cala de la Calobra viewed from northwest

Cala Estremé

⚓ CALA CODOLAR

39°51'.8N 02°50'.6E

A small *cala* surrounded by high cliffs close east of Morillo de Burdils. The water is deep (10m or so) up to the shore and the bottom is very rocky. If anchoring, it is essential to use a tripline.

⊕46 39°55'.6N 02°57'.0E Punta Beca

⚓ CALA CASTELL

39°56'N 03°02'.1E

A narrow *cala* open to the northeast, separated from Cala Estreme by Punta de la Galera, a narrow rocky peninsula. Punta Topina close west, is a distinctive wedge shape when seen from the northeast. Anchor in 5m over rock in the centre of the *cala* or in 3m over sand near the beach. Rocks line the eastern side. There is a small building behind the beach at the head of the *cala*, and a road leading inland.

⚓ CALA ESTREMÉ

39°56'N 03°02'.5E

Close east of Punta de la Galera and less sheltered than its neighbour, Cala Castell. Anchor over rock and sand near the small beach, open to northeast and east.

⚓ CALA DE SAN VICENTE

39°55'.4N 03°03'.6E

A large *cala* backed by holiday developments. At its head there are two sandy beaches separated by a rocky point with a hole in it, fringed by hotels and apartments plus the usual cafés and restaurants. Anchor off either beach in 5m over sand. There is a very small stone quay in the southwest corner of the western *cala*. A fiesta in honour of La Virgen del Mar is held on the first Sunday in July.

⚓ CALA VALL DE BOCA

39°55'.8N 03°05'.9E

A narrow *cala* with a small stony beach between

Cala de San Vicente

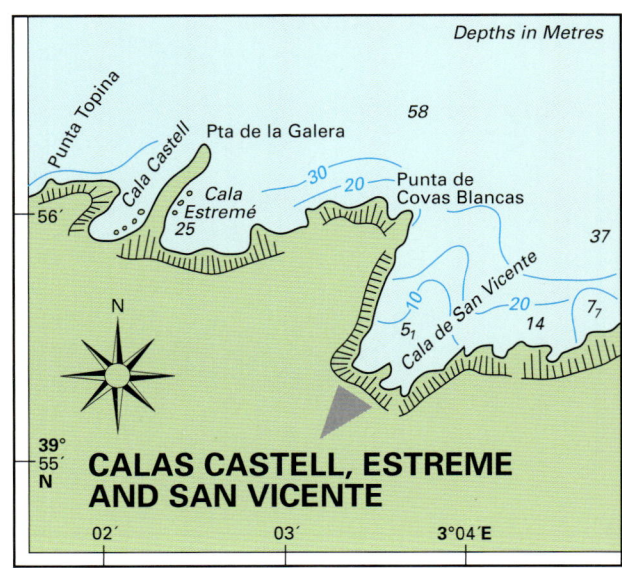

CALAS CASTELL, ESTREME AND SAN VICENTE

ANCHORAGES ON THE NORTHEAST COAST OF MALLORCA

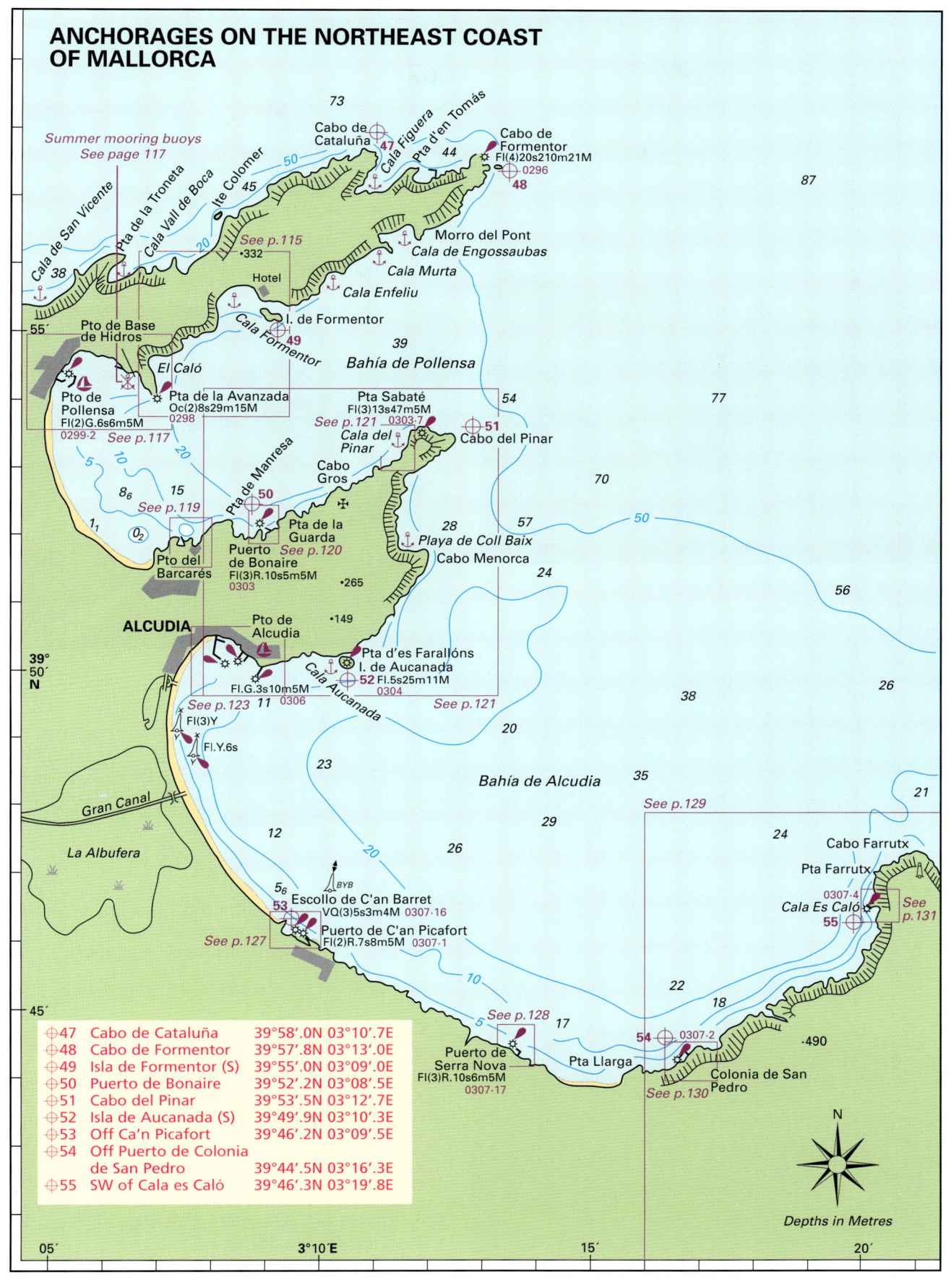

Summer mooring buoys
See page 117

Cala de San Vicente

Pta de la Troneta

Cala Vall de Boca

Ite Colomer

Cabo de Cataluña 47

Cala Figuera

Pta d'en Tomás

Cabo de Formentor
Fl(4)20s210m21M
0296 48

73

44

87

50

45

20

38

55′

Pto de Base
de Hidros

•332

See p.115

Hotel

Cala Formentor

Cala de Engossaubas

Morro del Pont

Cala Murta

Cala Enfeliu

I. de Formentor 49

El Caló

Pto de
Pollensa
Fl(2)G.6s6m5M
0299·2

Pta de la Avanzada
Oc(2)8s29m15M
0298

See p.117

39

Bahía de Pollensa

Pta Sabaté
Fl(3)13s47m5M

See p.121 0303·7

Cala del
Pinar

Cabo del Pinar 51

54

77

70

5

10

20

Pta de Manresa

50

Pto del
Barcarés

8₆ 15

See p.119

1₁

0₂

Pta de la
Guarda
See p.120

Puerto
de Bonaire
Fl(3)R.10s5m5M
0303

Cabo
Gros

•265

Playa de Coll Baix

Cabo Menorca

28

57

24

50

56

ALCUDIA

Pto de
Alcudia

•149

Fl.G.3s10m5M 0306

See p.123 11

Fl(3)Y

Fl.Y.6s

Cala Aucanada

Pta d'es Faralllóns
I. de Aucanada
52 Fl.5s25m11M
0304

See p.121

38

26

20

23

Gran Canal

La Albufera

12

Bahía de Alcudia

29

35

See p.129

24

21

Cabo Farrutx

Pta Farrutx

0307·4

Cala Es Caló
55

See
p.131

5₆

53

BYB

Escollo de C'an Barret
VQ(3)5s3m4M 0307·16

Puerto de C'an Picafort
Fl(2)R.7s8m5M 0307·1

26

20

10

22

18

See p.127

See p.128 17

Puerto de
Serra Nova
Fl(3)R.10s6m5M
0307·17

Pta Llarga

See p.130

54 0307·2

Colonia de San
Pedro

•490

39°
50′
N

45′

N

Depths in Metres

05′ 3°10′E 15′ 20′

III. MALLORCA

high rocky cliffs. Anchor in ±5m over rock, open to north and northeast. There is an overland track to Puerto de Pollensa. See plan on page 113.

⊕47 39°58'.0N 03°10'.7E Cabo de Cataluña

⚓ CALA FIGUERA
39°57'.2N 03°10'.7E

Cala Val de Boca. Spectacular view looking from northeast between the cliffs

A large deserted *cala* 1.6M west of Cabo de Formentor, surrounded by rocky hills and cliffs and with a small stone and sand beach at its head. Anchor in 5m over sand and rock, open to north and northeast. There is a rough road leading up from the beach but little else.

This is one of three Cala Figueras around the coast of Mallorca, the others being at the southwest end of the Bahía de Palma and on the southeast coast near Punta Salinas.

⊕48 39°57'.8N 03°13'.0E Cabo de Formentor

Rounding Cabo de Formentor looking southwest: Cala de Engossaubas to the left

⚓ CALA DE ENGOSSAUBAS (CALA EN GOSSALBA)
39°56'.5N 03°11'.4E

A very beautiful and deserted *cala* 1.7M southwest of the tip of Cabo de Formentor, reasonably wide and completely unspoilt; between high steep cliffs. Anchor close to the head in 2.5m over sand, or further out in 6m over weed and rock. Open to southeast round to southwest though an east or even northeast swell may work in. Ashore there is a track up to the road.

⚓ CALA MURTA

Cala Engossaubas: crystal clear waters

39°56'.4N 03°11'E

Another pleasant and unspoilt small *cala* with rocky sides (37m) and a stony beach. There is a small castle-like rock at the entrance and very clear water. Anchor in 3–5m over sand.

⚓ CALA ENFELIU
39°55'.8N 03°09'.9E

A tiny *cala* with rocky sides and a small stony beach. Enter with care to anchor in 3–5m over rock and sand, open to northeast–southeast–southwest.

⊕49 39°55'.0N 03°09'.0E Isla de Formentor (S end)

⚓ CALA FORMENTOR (CALA PINO)
39°55'.6N 03°08'.4E

This used to be a very popular open anchorage northwest of Isla de Formentor (34m). The narrow passage inside Isla de Formentor now has a depth of only 1m.

The whole *cala* has been laid with buoys and it is now forbidden to anchor inside the (approximately) 15m contour. Anchoring is permitted outside the bay but there is little protection in that area from wind and swell from any direction.

The beaches are popular with day tourists, speedboats, jet-skis and water-skiers weaving

Cala Formentor looking northwest over Isla de Formentor. Note mooring buoys

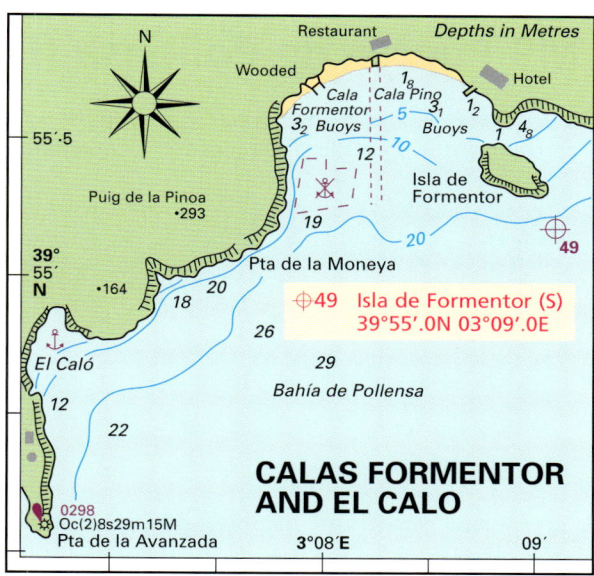

Depths in Metres

CALAS FORMENTOR AND EL CALO

⊕49 Isla de Formentor (S) 39°55'.0N 03°09'.0E

amongst the anchored yachts. Some areas may be buoyed off for bathers. As a contrast to the five-star hotel there are various beach bars and restaurants. The small jetties and quays in the northwest corner are privately owned.

⚓ EL CALÓ
39°54'.7N 03°06'.7E

A small *cala* close east of the root of Punta de la Avanzada. Anchor in ±5m over sand.

⚓ BEHIND PUNTA DE LA AVANZADA
39°54'.3N 03°06'.4E

A well-sheltered former anchorage close west of Punta de la Avanzada (Oc(2)8s29m15M, octagonal stone tower on building 18m) and only a mile east of Puerto de Pollensa. Mooring buoys have now been

Looking across Pta de la Avanzada towards Puerto de Pollensa

laid here which can be reserved in advance at www.balearslifeposidonia.eu/index.php?register_vars[lang]=en for 1st June to 30th September. See plan on page 117 and the Anchoring and Moorings section on page 16 for further details. Apart from the considerable daytime disturbance from speedboats and jet-skis, the anchorage is calm. Unfortunately the old castle on the promontory, known as La Fortaleza, is privately owned and explorations ashore are said to be unwelcome.

PUERTO DE BASE DE HIDROS (SEAPLANE BASE)
39°54'.5N 03°6'.1E

This small and very shallow harbour belongs to the Spanish Navy and is a seaplane base. For obvious reasons it does not welcome yachts.

The harbour/marina

Anchorage southwest of Pta de la Avanzada: note seaplane base right and buoyed exclusion zone along the coast

III. MALLORCA

M9 Puerto de Pollensa (Pollença)

A very friendly and sheltered harbour with
berthing for 375 yachts, 100 miles from Barcelona

Location
39°54'.1N 03°05'.1E

Distances
Barcelona 100M
Menorca 35M

Communications
VHF: Ch 09
Real Club Náutico de Pollensa ℡ 971 86 46 35
Fax 971 86 46 36
Email oficina@rcnpp.net
www.rcnpp.net

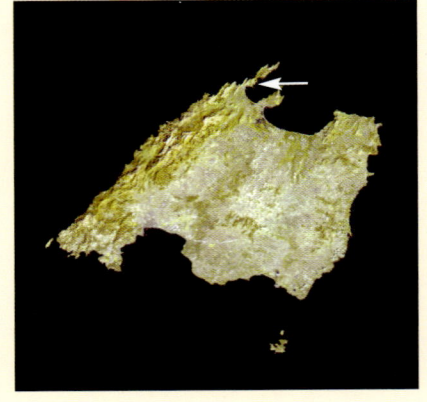

A good-sized yacht and fishing harbour with 375
berths. Puerto de Pollensa is at the head of a
beautiful wide bay surrounded by spectacular
mountains. The approach and harbour are both
somewhat shallow, but should present no problems
other than in strong east winds. The bay is open to
the sea from northeast through east to southeast,
and in heavy winds or swell from these directions,
the head of the bay is best avoided. The anchorage
behind Punta de Avanzada provides a sheltered
alternative, though during gales from the north
quadrant violent gusts may be experienced. (See
page 115 for details.)

PILOTAGE

Approach

From south Cross the wide Bahía de Alcudia (see
page 113) towards Cabo del Pinar and Punta Sabaté
– conspicuous, with high rocky cliffs
(Fl(3)9s47m5M, white triangular tower, black band
12m). Cabo de Formentor will be seen beyond.
Round Punta Negra onto a westerly course towards
Punta de la Avanzada (Oc(2)8s29m15M, octagonal
stone tower on building 18m), after which Puerto de
Pollensa will open up.

From north Round the almost vertical rocky cliffs of
Cabo de Formentor (Fl(4)20s210m21M, white tower
and house 22m), then follow the coast southwest
past the lower Punta de la Avanzada. Puerto de
Pollensa will be seen once past this headland.

Anchorage in the approach

See *Anchorage behind Punta de la Avanzada* on page
115. Anchoring is now prohibited in the bay
northeast of the harbour as moorings have now been
laid, for which there is a charge.

Less protection can be had southwest of the harbour
towards the two training walls (see plan) in 2m+ over
sand, mud and weed. There are some moorings in this
area. In strong southeast winds the best shelter will be
found close west of Puerto de Bonaire, some 3.5M
across the bay, in 4–6m over sand.

Entrance

Approach the head of the northeast breakwater
from east or southeast, leaving it 30–40m to
starboard on entry. There are shoals close southwest
of the entrance (see plan) and the wreck of a yacht is
noted on some charts, unmarked at 39°54'.1N
03°05'.01E just south of the entrance, apparently
covered by only 1m of water. The fuel berth at the
end of the southwest mole doubles as a reception
quay. There is a 4-knot speed limit.

Berthing

The *club náutico* visitors' berths are on the outside
of the north quay, exposed to northeast and east.
Mooring lines are provided, tailed to the quay.

Inside the harbour there is a Port Authority quay

Puerto de Pollensa from northeast: protected in the bay
and in spectacular surroundings   *GW*

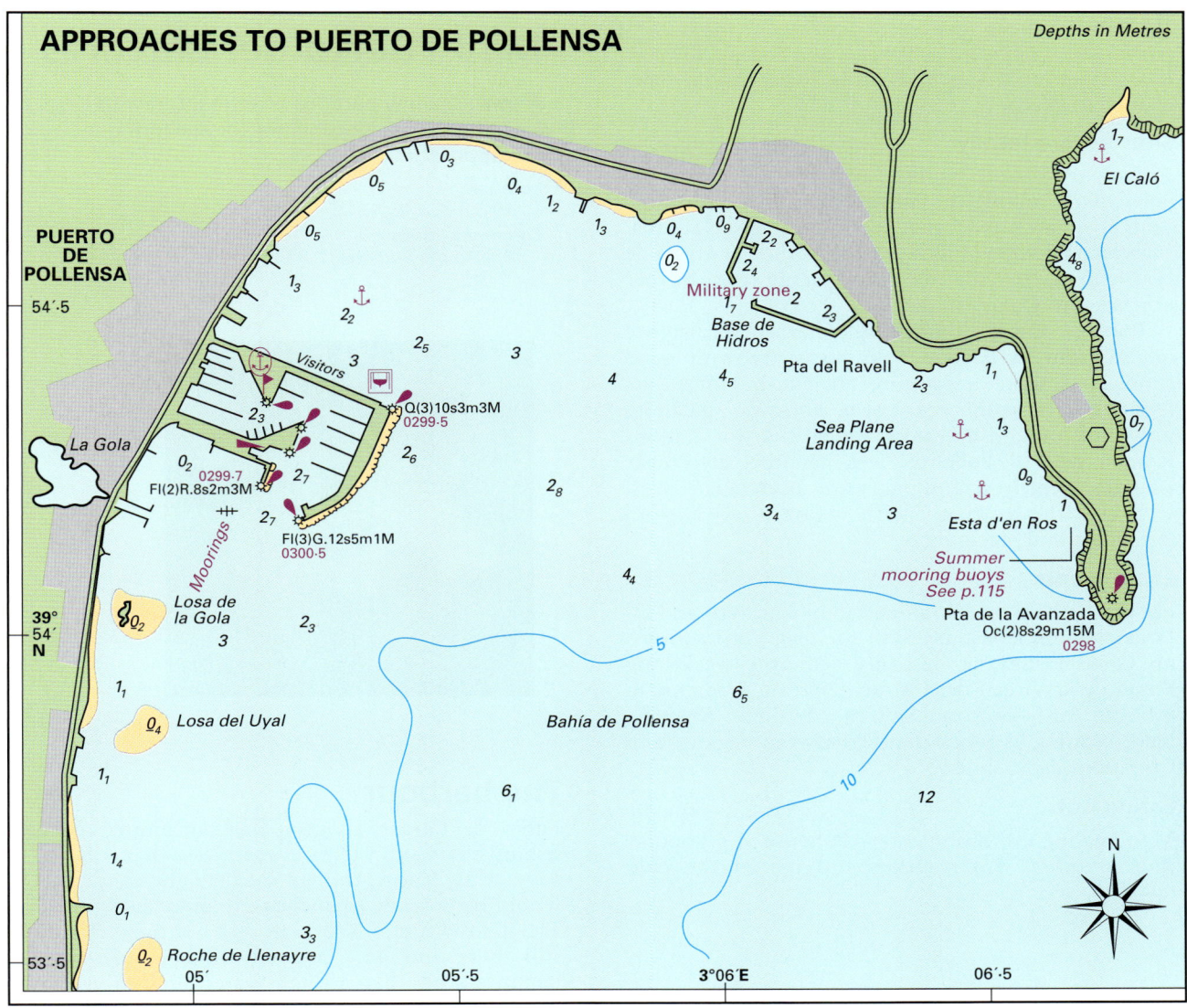

APPROACHES TO PUERTO DE POLLENSA

Depths in Metres

PUERTO DE POLLENSA

El Caló

Military zone

Base de Hidros

Pta del Ravell

Sea Plane Landing Area

Esta d'en Ros

Summer mooring buoys See p.115

Pta de la Avanzada
Oc(2)8s29m15M
0298

La Gola

Visitors

Q(3)10s3m3M 0299·5

Fl(2)R.8s2m3M 0299·7

Moorings

Fl(3)G.12s5m1M 0300·5

Losa de la Gola

Losa del Uyal

Bahía de Pollensa

Roche de Llenayre

III. MALLORCA

on the north side of the southwest mole, and visitors may also use the outer section of the nearby pontoon (see plan). These berths also have mooring lines with water and electricity.

Facilities

Water Taps on quays and pontoons. There is a tap by Hotel Diana's swimming pool – and a place for a dinghy!

Electricity 220v AC points on all quays and pontoons, plus some 380v points.

Fuel Diesel and petrol pumps on the head of the southwest mole.

Provisions Two supermarkets and other specialist food shops able to supply all normal requirements. An open-air market on Wednesday mornings in Puerto de Pollensa and Sunday in Pollensa town nearby, where there are also good shops.

Ice At the fuel berth, the Réal Club Náutico bar and a shop opposite the harbour.

Chandleries Náutica Brúixola SL ① 971 53 11 93 *Fax* 53 48 18 and others. Maritime International ① 971 86 72 99 *Fax* 971 86 69 96 offer a total boat care and maintenance service as well as selling chandlery from

an office/shop close to the marina.

Repairs Astilleros Cabanellas boatyard on the southwest mole can handle all normal work. A 50-tonne lift at the northeast breakwater elbow. A 1-tonne crane on the northeast breakwater and 4-tonne crane at the boatyard. A small slipway in the interior of the harbour and a larger one, with cradle able to take vessels up to 21m, at the boatyard.

Engineers At the boatyard. Motonautica Bonaire ① 971 53 04 62/89 23 01 *Fax* 971 53 04 66 are official service agents for Mercury/MerCruiser, Sole Diesel, Tohatsu, Volvo Penta and Yamaha.

Sailmaking and repairs Wilson Yachts ① 971 86 40 67 *Fax* 971 86 40 59; Plana Velámenes ①/*Fax* 971 86 60 61.

Yacht club The Club Náutico de Puerto de Pollensa has a smart, modern clubhouse on the northeast breakwater with lounge, terrace, bar, restaurant, swimming pool and showers.

Showers At the *club náutico* free to visitors using their berths, otherwise a small fee is charged.

Launderette Near the harbour.

Banks In Puerto de Pollensa and Pollensa town.

Hospital/medical services In Puerto de Pollensa and Pollensa town three miles inland.

Transport

Car hire/taxis In Puerto de Pollensa and Pollensa town.
Buses Frequent service to Pollensa town, several times daily to Palma.

Sites ashore locally

There are good walks around the harbour, particularly among the hills to the north with some dramatic views over the north coast of Mallorca. Two recommended hikes are across the Peninsula de Formentera to Cala de San Vicente and further northeast to Cala Vall de Boca.

Pollensa town – built, like Sóller, some distance inland from its harbour – is attractive with good shops and some interesting ancient buildings. Its name comes from the Latin *pollentia* meaning powerful, though it is now agreed that the famous Roman city of Pollentia was actually sited near Alcudia. Nearby at Campanet are spectacular caves, well worth a visit; with 50-million-year-old stalactites and stalagmites.

Local events

Fiestas are held on 17 January (San Antonio) and 20 January (San Sebastian) with the usual processions; on Good Friday, in mid-July, with the week-long Fiesta de la Virgen del Carmen; and on 2 August in honour of Nuestra Señora de los Angeles, incorporating a mock battle between Moors and Christians as in Sóller.

Eating out

Many eating establishments – Pollensa is a popular tourist resort. A restaurant and bar at the *club náutico*.

M10 Puerto del Barcarés

A small shallow harbour of little interest to yachts, but with possibilities for anchoring in the approach

Location
39°51'.85N 03°07'.2E
Communications
Puerto del Barcarés ☎ 971 53 18 67

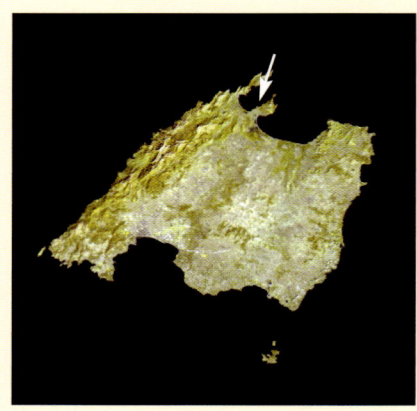

The harbour

Puerto del Barcarés is a tiny harbour limited to small fishing boats and yachts drawing less than 1m and is in no way a port, though in the right conditions it would be possible to anchor off and visit by dinghy. The light was removed years ago but the structure is still there and now painted white. There are no facilities other than a single water tap on the quay.

Puerto del Barcarés from northwest: shallows easily seen left of small harbour

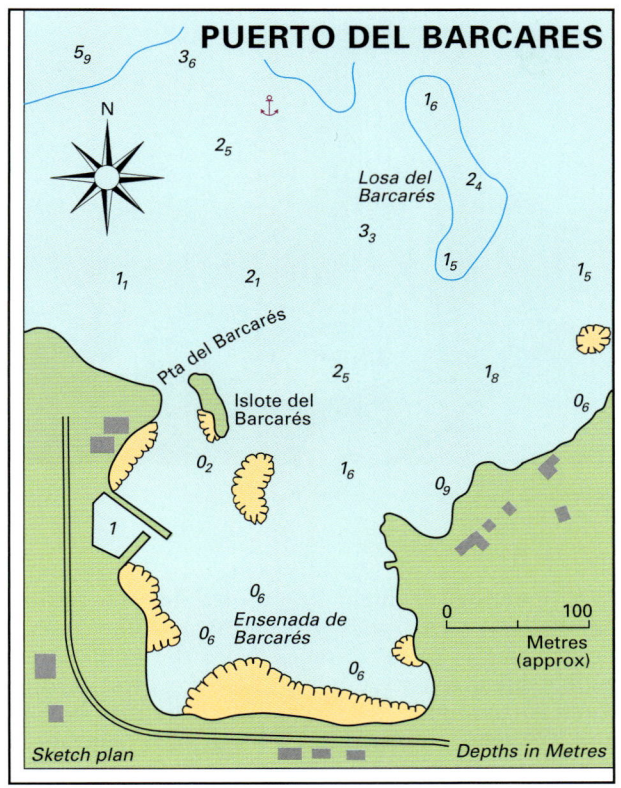

PUERTO DEL BARCARES

Losa del Barcarés

Pta del Barcarés

Islote del Barcarés

Ensenada de Barcarés

0   100

Metres (approx)

Sketch plan   Depths in Metres

M11 Puerto/Marina de Bonaire (Cocodrilo)

A well sheltered marina on the S side of Bahía de Pollensa with 352 moorings up to 17m, most occupied by local boats. It is easy to approach and is pleasantly located in a deeply forested region of the bay

Location
39°52'.1N 03°08'.5E

Communications
VHF Ch 09
Marina de Bonaire ☎ 971 54 69 55
Fax 971 54 85 64 *Email* marinabonaire@terra.es

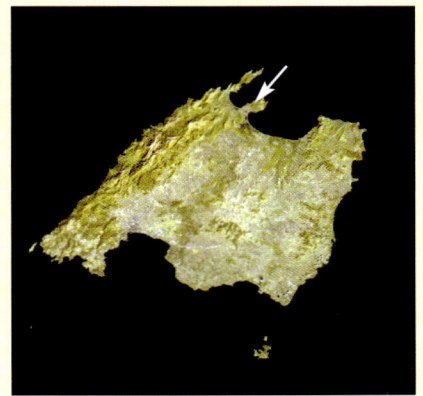

PILOTAGE

Approach

Punta del Barcarés lies near the southwest corner of the Bahía de Pollensa (see plan on page 113), west of Punta de Manresa and some three miles southeast of Puerto de Pollensa. There are shoals in the approach, including the 1.5m Losa del Barcarés 400m northeast of the entrance and an unnamed breaking patch southeast of Islote del Bacarés (itself only a low rocky ledge).

Anchorage in the approach

Anchor north of Islote del Bacarés in 2–5m over sand and weed, open to west–north–northeast.

Entrance

(Inadvisable except by dinghy).

Swing wide of the unnamed shoal mentioned above to round the north mole at slow speed. The entrance is no more than 2.5m wide and less than 1m deep.

Berthing

There is a dinghy slipway opposite the entrance.

Facilities

Water A tap on the quay

The harbour

Formerly known as Port del Cocodrilo, and still called by that name on several road signs locally and some charts, Puerto de Bonaire is an attractive, purpose-built yacht harbour amongst pleasantly wooded surroundings; believed to be on the site of one of the original Phoenician landings. The harbour is simple to approach and enter and offers excellent shelter. Most of the 352 berths for yachts up to 17m

Puerto de Bonaire: an attractive purpose-built marina

III. MALLORCA

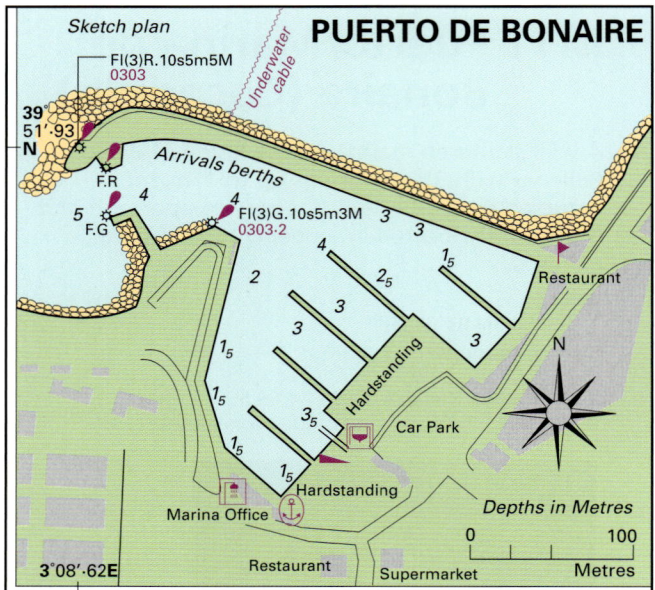

Puerto de Bonaire from within the marina   GW

are permanently occupied. Unlike many similar harbours in the Islas Baleares there is no commercial or fishing usage.

In December 2001, during a hurricane of over 100 knots, the sea wall was breached and partially destroyed, the restaurant at the breakwater root was blown away and 22 boats sank. Extensive reconstruction has included the raising of the sea wall by 2m and reshaping the entrance, providing excellent shelter and comfort.

PILOTAGE

Approach

⊕50 39°52'.2N 03°08'.5E Puerto de Bonaire

From south Cross the wide Bahía de Alcudia towards Cabo del Pinar and Punta Sabaté – conspicuous, with high rocky cliffs (Fl(3)9s47m5M, white triangular tower, black band 12m). Round Punta Negra to follow the south coast of the Bahía de Pollensa past Cabo Gros and Punta de la Guarda. Puerto de Bonaire lies 0.5M further west. (See plan on page 113.)

From north Round the almost vertical rocky cliffs of Cabo de Formentor (Fl(4)20s210m21M, white tower and house 22m), then steer southwest towards Punta de Manresa, a low, dark rocky point surmounted by a castle. Puerto de Bonaire lies 0.5M east of this headland.

Anchorage in the approach

Anchor in the bay west of the harbour entrance in 5m over sand, open to the northern quadrant.

Entrance

The entrance is relatively narrow with a distinct dogleg. Approach on a southerly course, slowly closing the coast west of the north breakwater until the west mole comes into view. Then swing east and northeast to remain in the centre of the channel. The reception quay is to port immediately inside the entrance.

If entering at night (quite feasible in settled conditions) note that the light on the north breakwater is some distance from the end of the rubble breakwater. A bow lookout with a strong torch is recommended. In summer there may be F.R and F.G lights on the spurs each side of the entrance.

Berthing

Berth at the reception quay until directed elsewhere by marina staff, preferably having already called on VHF Ch 09.

Facilities

Water Taps on quays and pontoons.
Electricity 220v AC points on quays and pontoons.
Fuel Available end of south jetty.
Provisions Small supermarket just south of the harbour (opposite a restaurant) and many shops in Alcudia a mile southwest.
Ice From the bar/restaurant at the root of the north breakwater.
Chandlery Next to the marina office.
Repairs Workshops near the marina office. Motonautica Bonaire ☎ 971 53 04 62 *Fax* 971 53 04 66. A 30-tonne lift in the south part of the harbour. Slipway next to the travel-lift.
Engineers Engineering workshop near the marina office and Motonautica Bonaire (see above).
Electronic & radio repairs Enquire at the marina office.
Showers Near the marina office.
Launderette By the shower block.
Hospital/medical services In Alcudia.
Banks In Alcudia.

Transport

Car hire/taxis From Alcudia. Enquire at the marina office.

Sites ashore locally

There are excellent walks in the area and good views from Punta de Manresa, while the old Roman city of Alcudia is just over a mile away.

Eating out

Bar/restaurant at the root of the north breakwater and another south of the harbour. Others in the vicinity.

ANCHORAGES ON PENINSULA CABO DEL PINAR

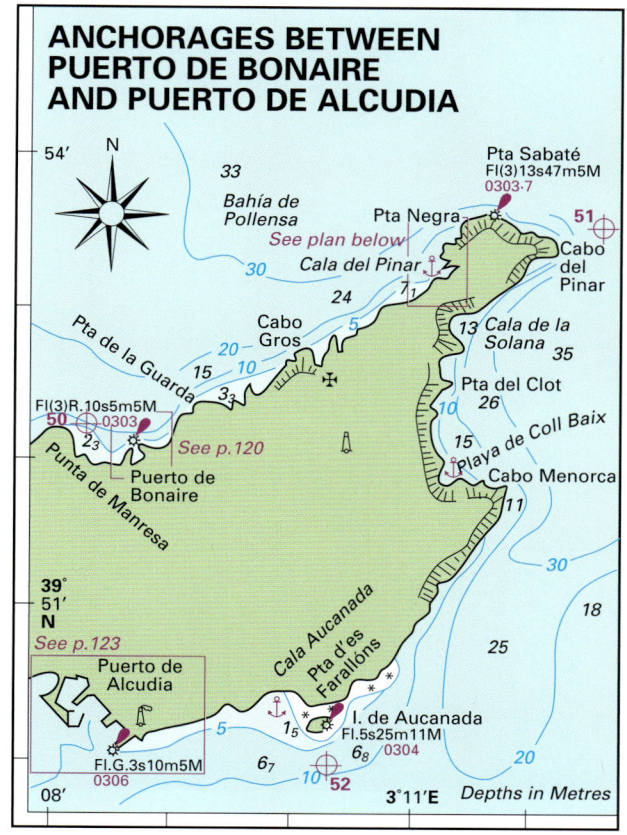

ANCHORAGES BETWEEN PUERTO DE BONAIRE AND PUERTO DE ALCUDIA

⊕50	Puerto de Bonaire	39°52'.2N 03°08'.5E
⊕51	Cabo del Pinar	39°53'.5N 03°12'.7E
⊕52	Isla de Aucanada (S)	39°49'.9N 03°10'.3E

⚓ CALA DEL PINAR (SES CALETAS)

39°53'.3N 03°11'.3E

An anchorage behind Punta Negra on the north side of the peninsula Cabo del Pinar, consisting of a

Looking east over Cala del Pinar to Pta Sabate and Cabo del Pinar

Playa de Coll Baix with Cabo Menorca looming left

double *cala* plus a smaller one to the north. Cabo del Pinar is a military area, with landing in the *calas* forbidden and access sometimes restricted by buoys. Anchor in 5–7m (less if it is permitted to enter the calas) over sand and weed. Holding is patchy. It is a popular place for day visitors from Pollensa and can become crowded.

⊕51 39°53'.5N 03°12'.7E Cabo del Pinar

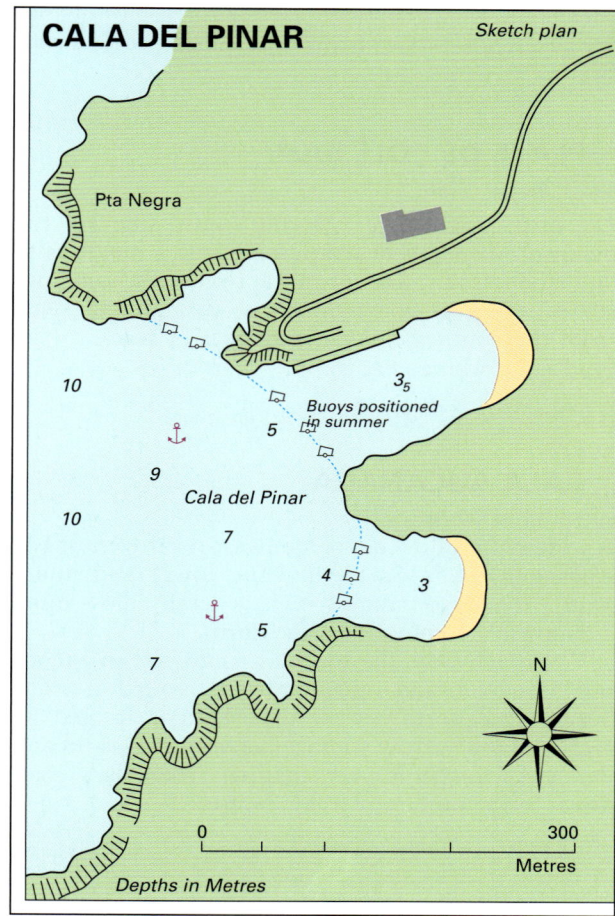

III. MALLORCA

Bahía de Alcudia viewed from north, with Isla de Aucanada left

⚓ PLAYA DE COLL BAIX

39°51'.9N 03°11'.4E

An open anchorage on the south side of the peninsula beneath dramatic cliffs off a small sand and stone beach. Anchor in 5m over rock, sand and stones, open to north–northeast–east and to swell from the southeast. Ashore there is a track to the road but nothing else.

⊕52 39°49'.9N 03°10'.3E Isla de Aucanada (S)

⚓ CALA AUCANADA

39°50'.3N 03°09'.9E

A wide but shallow bay 600m west-northwest of Isla Aucanada (Fl.5s25m11M, white tower and house 15m). The surrounding land is generally flat – quite a contrast if coming from the north.

Approach from the south or southwest to anchor in 1.5m+ over sand, open to the south quadrant. The beach close northwest of the island is fringed by reefs and the narrow passage between the island and Punta Aucanada is very shallow. There is a road down to the point and a few houses.

Isla de Aucanada looking west with anchorage behind

M12 Puerto de Alcudia (Marina Alcúdiamar)

A very sheltered marina with easy access and berthing for over 700 yachts, but shallow at the N end of the harbour. A commercial and naval port lie just outside the marina

Location
39°50'.3N 03°08'.2E

Communications
Pilots (*Alcudia Prácticos*) VHF Ch 11, 13, 14, 16
Marina Alcúdiamar VHF Ch 09 ① 971 54 60 00/04
Fax 971 54 89 20
Email alcudiamar@alcudiamar.es
www.alcudiamar.es

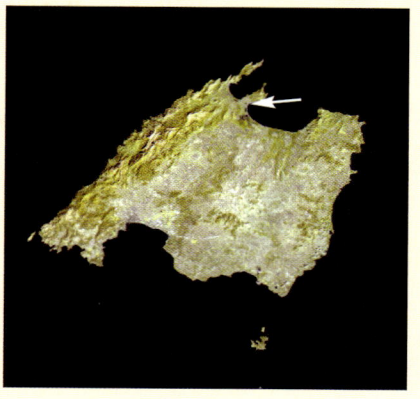

The marina

Alcúdiamar, a large, well-equipped but rather shallow marina able to accommodate 744 yachts of up to 30m; lies northwest of a small commercial port handling cargo ships and ferries, with a small naval zone sandwiched between the two. The marina is easy to approach and enter and well sheltered once inside, though public access to the many restaurants and cafés on the west breakwater means that security is virtually nil. It shares its location with an old fishing harbour but this is no longer busy.

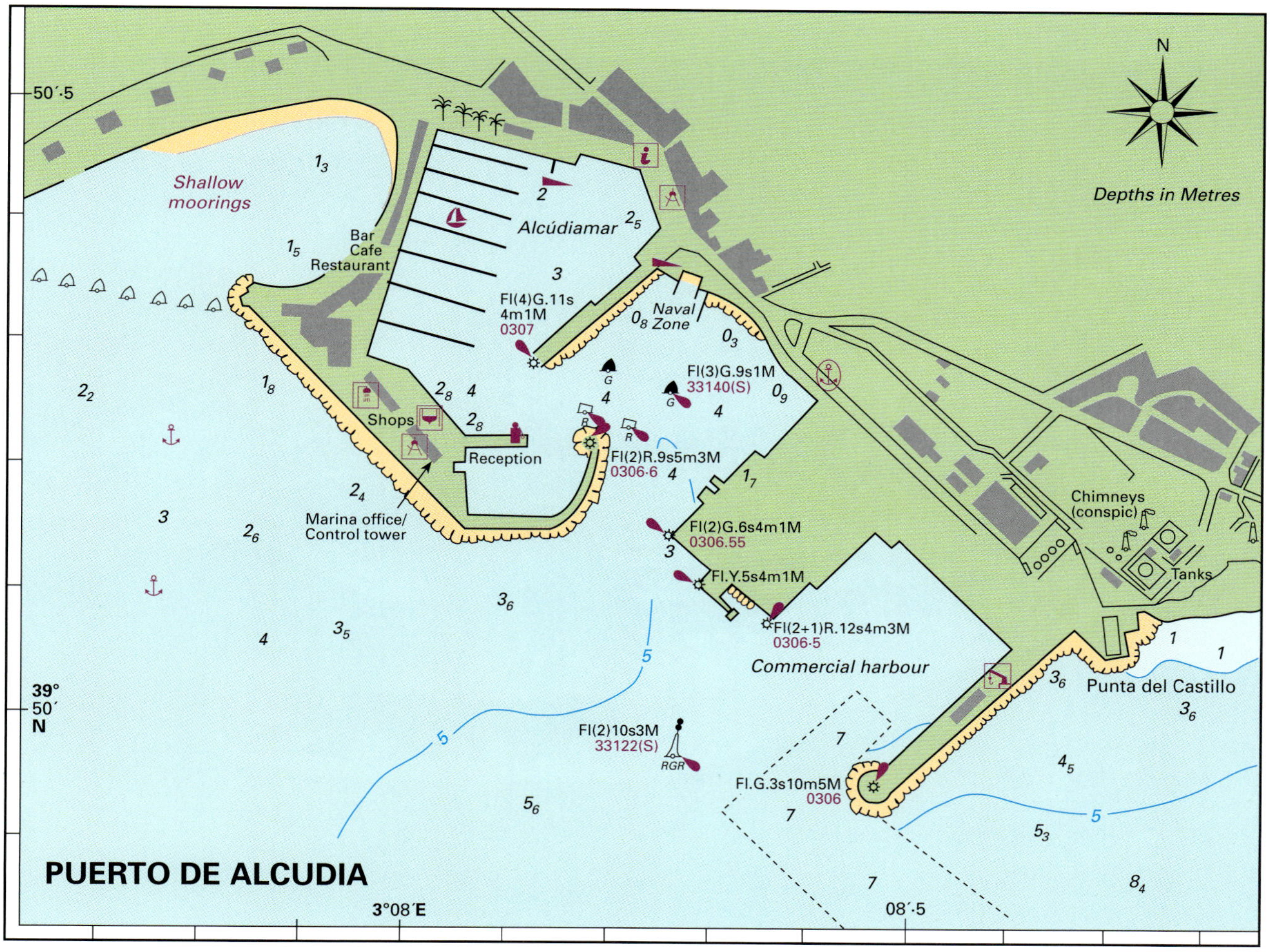

PUERTO DE ALCUDIA

PILOTAGE

Approach

From south The high headland of Cabo de Pera (Fl(2+3)20s76m16M, white tower on white building with dark corners and red roof 21m) and the even higher (272m) Cabo del Freu, which has a long low rocky projection at its foot, are both unmistakeable. (See plans on pages 129 and 113.) Follow the coast northwest towards Cabo Farrutx, passing the islet of Farayó de Aubarca (23m high and about 750m offshore) en route. There is good water on either side of the island.

On rounding Cabo Farrutx (unlit, though there are red lights on Puig Tudosa 1.5M to the south) the Bahía de Alcudia opens up, with Puerto de Alcudia in the northwest corner. Pass *outside* Isla de Aucanada (Fl.5s25m11M, white tower and house 15m) and leave the head of the southeast breakwater at least 50m to starboard. The two tall chimneys near the root of the breakwater are conspicuous.

From north Cross the Bahía de Pollensa and round first the steep reddish-cliffed Cabo del Pinar and then the even higher, but not so prominent, Cabo Menorca. Follow the coast (now becoming low and flat) at 500m to pass *outside* Isla de Aucanada and proceed as above.

Puerto de Alcudia and southwest anchorage looking north into Bahía de Pollensa

Note The approach and entrance to the yacht harbour are relatively shallow and can be dangerous in heavy seas from east and southeast. The area is prone to silting up and charted depths should not be relied upon.

Submarines occasionally exercise in the Bahía de Alcudia and its approaches. Commercial ships may be anchored south of the harbour.

Anchorage in the approach

Anchor southwest of the marina in 2–4m over sand and weed, open to southeast and south, keeping well clear of the entrance. Some moorings have been laid out to about 100m from the breakwater.

Entrance

Leave the head of the southeast (commercial) breakwater (Fl.G.3s10m5M) a good 50m to starboard and also the buoy (Fl(2)10s3M) just to starboard. Keep well clear of any commercial ship or ferry movement by leaving the RGR buoy to starboard. Then steer north to pass between the marina breakwater light (Fl(2)R.7s5m3M) and the starboard hand buoy (Fl(3)G.9s1M). When halfway between the two lights, come round to port, leaving the breakwater end 50m or so to port to approach the marina entrance on a westerly heading. Depth at the entrance is dredged to 4m but silting can occur after strong winds, so proceed with caution. There is a 3-knot speed limit in the harbour.

Berthing

There is a reception area on the south side of the fuelling quay, but it is preferable to contact the marina office on VHF Ch 09 before arrival so that a permanent berth can be allocated. Anchoring is not allowed inside the yacht harbour.

Facilities

Water Taps on quays and pontoons, and at the fuelling berth.

Electricity 220v AC at all berths plus 380v AC at berths over 14m.

Fuel Diesel and petrol pumps on the inner arm of the southwest breakwater.

Gas No Calor gas cylinders can be refilled in Mallorca now, but Náutica Mahón stocks Camping Gaz.

Provisions Small supermarket on the southwest breakwater, many more in Puerto de Alcudia and Alcudia town. A produce market Sunday and Tuesday mornings in Alcudia town.

Ice From the fuel berth.

Chandleries Enmartor ☎ 971 54 84 15, EMO's Ship-Shop ☎/*Fax* 971 54 71 10 and others.

Repairs Construcciones Navales Benassar SA boatyard ☎/*Fax* 971 54 67 00. All repair work can also be undertaken by Náutica Mahón ☎ 971 54 67 50 *Fax* 971 54 67 54 which has its offices in the marina complex. A 150-tonne lift and an 80-tonne lift are available on the southwest breakwater. An 8-tonne mobile crane is also available. Small slipway in shallow (0.7m) water on the north side of the yacht harbour.

Engineers Náutica Mahón (see *Repairs* above) and Motonáutica Alcudia ☎ 971 54 61 30. The latter is the official service agent for MerCruiser, Tohatsu, Volvo Penta, Yanmar. Europa Marine Services (Balearics) S.L. ☎ 971 54 92 15 can service inboard/outboard engines and refrigeration units.

Electronic & radio repairs Náutica Mahón (see above) and others.

Sailmaker Plana Velámenes ☎/*Fax* 971 86 60 61.

Rigging Yacht-Rigger ☎ 908 43 59 75.

Showers On the southwest breakwater.

Laundry In the marina.

Banks In Puerto de Alcudia and Alcudia town.

Hospital/medical services Medical services via marina office, hospital in Alcudia town.

Transport

Car hire/taxis In both Puerto de Alcudia and Alcudia town. A taxi rank at the root of the southwest breakwater.

Buses Bus service to Alcudia town, Palma and elsewhere.

Ferries Regular service to Ciudadela in Menorca and Port Vendres in France.

History

Both the port and the old town a mile inland date back to Phoenician times, the latter a typical settlement site on a hilly peninsula served by two harbours on opposite sides of the isthmus. In due course the Romans took it over, calling the area Pollentia ('powerful') and making it the capital of the island; however, the Vandals occupied the town after the fall of Rome and destroyed most of the Roman buildings. Little evidence is left of the Moorish occupation except the name, Al Kudia, which means 'the hill'. After the Christian re-conquest, walls were built around the town.

Sights ashore locally

Sections of the walls can still be seen, together with the remains of the Roman theatre. In addition to the theatre (on the road between the harbour and the town), St Martin's cave, the castle and the museum are worth visiting.

For those who are interested in birds, the Albufera Nature Reserve behind the beach to the southwest is a most important site. Follow the coast road south for about three miles, cross the Gran Canal and the entrance to the park is clearly labelled. There is an entry fee, but bird hides, etc. are provided. The Bahía de Alcudia is a popular tourist area, largely due to its excellent beaches.

Local events

Fiestas are held on 29 June in honour of San Pedro, with land and sea processions. On 2 July the Romería a la Virgen de la Victória includes a pilgrimage to the Santuari de la Victória on a peak three miles away, and on 25 July a fiesta in honour of Santiago (St James), the patron saint of the town, includes a parade on horseback.

Eating out

Many restaurants and cafés line the marina. There is a 4-star hotel in the northwest corner of the marina, offering special rates for visiting yachtsmen.

III. MALLORCA

Post-storm seascape in the Bay of Pollensa looking southeast towards Alcudia Old Town *GW*

M13 Puerto de Ca'n Picafort

A small harbour with 470 yacht berths, easy to enter and offering excellent protection. It is 4M S of Alcúdimar with superb beaches on either side

Location
39°46'.1N 03°09'.6E

Communications
VHF Ch 09
Puerto Deportivo de Ca'n Picafort ☎/Fax 971 85 00 10
Club Náutico Ca'n Picafort ☎/Fax 971 85 01 85
Email pdcanpicafort@futurnet.es

The harbour

Ca'n Picafort is a fairly small yacht harbour able to take 470 boats up to 12m, built onto a small, old fishing harbour. It is backed by a popular tourist resort of fairly recent origin, the first hotel having been built in 1933 when building controls were lifted.

Approach is straightforward, but entrance is dangerous with even moderate seas from the east or northeast quadrant, due to shoaling water around the entrance. These are well marked.

PILOTAGE

Approach

⊕53 39°46'.2N 03°09'.5E Off Ca'n Picafort
For outer approaches see *Puerto de Alcudia* on page 124.

From south Round the high (432m) Cabo Farrutx on to a course just south of west. (See plan on page 113.) Puerto de Ca'n Picafort lies nine miles away, near the south end of the hotels which line much of the Bahía de Alcudia. There is a day-mark (see *Lights* in *Appendix*) close to the harbour entrance, but it may be lost against the high-rise buildings behind.

From north After rounding Cabo Menorca head south-southwest across the Bahía de Alcudia, Puerto de Ca'n Picafort lies six miles away, identified as above.

Anchorage in the approach

The bottom is rocky near the harbour. Anchor in 5m over sand, 700m from the shore and some 1,000m northwest of the harbour, with the two No.3 beacons in line; open to northeast and east. Sound carefully.

Entrance

A dangerous breaking reef, Escollo de Ca'n Barret, marked by an east cardinal beacon (Q(3)10s3m4M, BYB post on wide yellow base, ♦ topmark) lies 300m west-northwest of the entrance.

Puerto de Ca'n Picafort. Seas breaking over the Escollo de Ca'n Barret reef

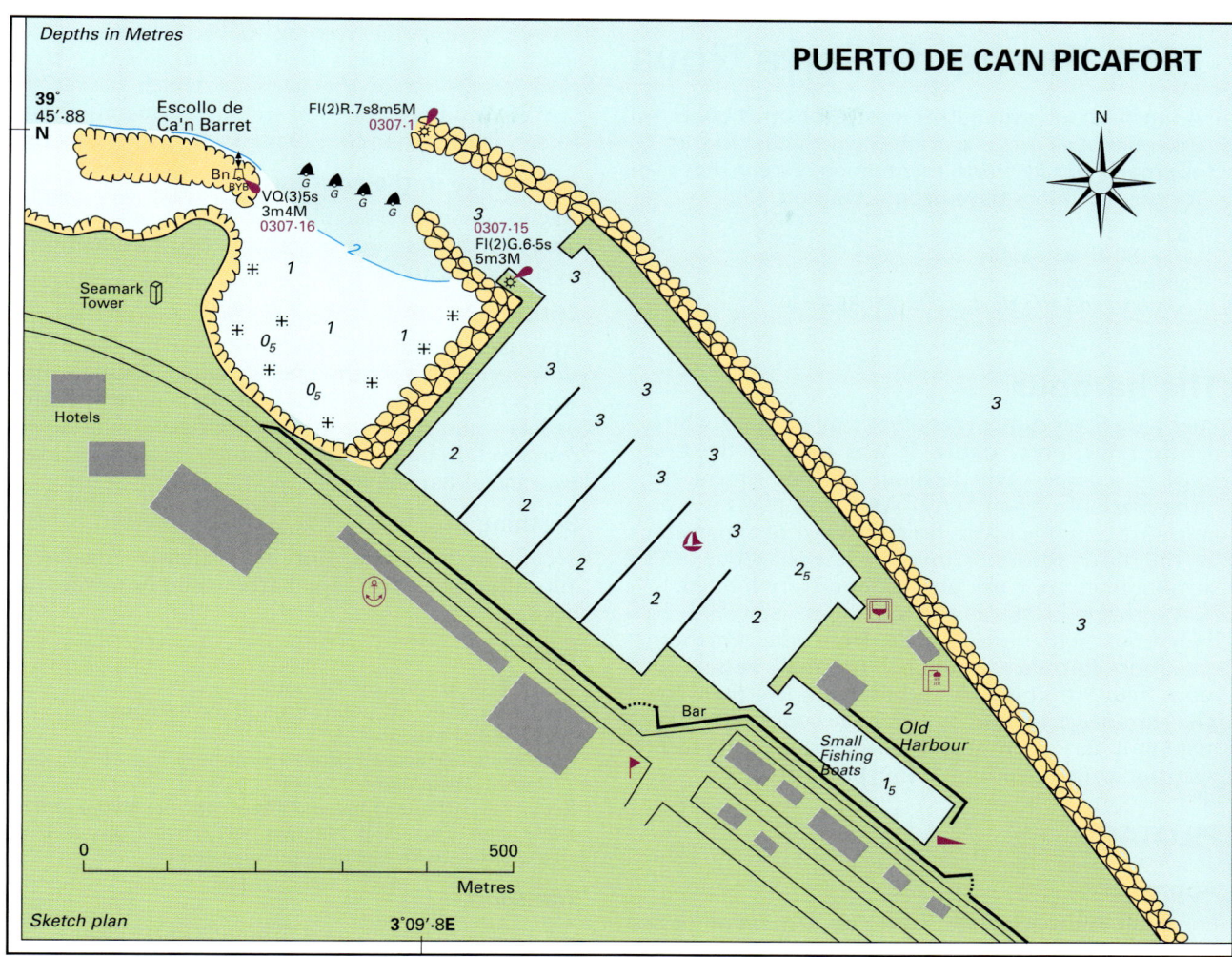

Depths in Metres

PUERTO DE CA'N PICAFORT

39°
45'·88
N

Escollo de
Ca'n Barret

Fl(2)R.7s8m5M
0307·1

Bn
BYB
VQ(3)5s
3m4M
0307·16

G G G G G

3
0307·15
Fl(2)G.6·5s
5m3M

Seamark
Tower

Hotels

Bar

Small
Fishing
Boats

Old
Harbour

0   500

Metres

Sketch plan   3°09'·8E

Approach the head of the northeast breakwater on a southerly course at slow speed, watching the depth-sounder. A line of four green buoys indicate the west side of the channel (July 2010), though these were red in previous years. Round the breakwater at about 20m and turn sharply to port to line up for the centre of the entrance, where at least 3m should be found. Entrance after dark is not recommended.

Berthing

Secure to the inner side of the northeast breakwater until a berth can be allocated. The harbour office will be found near the root of the west mole.

Facilities

Water Taps on quays and pontoons. Check quality before filling tanks.
Electricity 220v AC points on quays and pontoons, 380v on hardstanding.
Fuel Still no fuel pumps (July 2010).
Provisions Many shops and supermarkets in the town. Market on Tuesday afternoons in Calle Cervantes.
Ice Available from bars and the *club náutico*.
Repairs Basic boatyard services near the 20-tonne travel-lift beside the old harbour. An 8-tonne mobile crane. A small slipway at the head of the old harbour.
Yacht club The Club Náutico de Ca'n Picafort has a lounge and bar.

Showers Shower block near the travel-lift.
Laundry In the town.
Banks In the town.
Hospital/medical services Doctor in the town, otherwise in Alcudia.

Transport

Car hire/taxis In the town.
Buses Bus service to Alcudia, Palma and elsewhere.

Sites ashore locally

The name Picafort is from the Spanish words meaning 'hew strongly', presumably referring to the cutting of stone from nearby quarries. The Necropolis de Son Real (a Bronze Age cemetery dating back to 700BC) is only ten minutes' walk along the shore to the southeast. There are excellent beaches on either side of the harbour which understandably become crowded in summer.

Local Events

The fiesta of Mare de Deu d'Agost is held on 15 August each year.

Eating out

An outdoor bar near the old harbour and many restaurants and cafés in the town.

M14 Puerto de Serra Nova

A tiny harbour with berths mostly for small boats. An exceptionally narrow entrance, with silting in the approach: hardly worth mentioning, except that plans for greater things have been submitted

Location
39°44'.4N 03°13'.4E

Communications
Puerto de Serra Nova ①/Fax 971 85 40 30

The harbour

Puerto de Serra Nova is another tiny harbour which hardly rates 'port' status. It was built as the first stage of a large yacht harbour to complement the 'urbanisation' of Son Serra Nova, but plans are on hold for the project with little prospect of expansion in the near future. Currently the harbour and surroundings are bleak and facilities very limited.

Approach is straightforward but it would be dangerous with heavy seas from the northern quadrant. Entrance is limited to small vessels no more than 9m in length and drawing less than 2m. The entrance is formed by two huge concrete blocks, making it very narrow and intimidating, and recent visits indicate a depth of 1.4m (July 2010).

PILOTAGE

Approach

For outer approaches see *Puerto de Alcudia* on page 124.

From south Round the high (432m) Cabo Farrutx (see plan on page 113) and follow the coast westwards at a distance of 500m once past Colonia de San Pedro. Puerto de Serra Nova lies three miles beyond, at the northern end of an area of scattered houses backed by pine forest.

From north After passing Cabo Menorca, head south across the Bahía de Alcudia to close the coast close northwest of the harbour, which lies at the northern end of the area of scattered houses and pine forest. The surrounding countryside is generally flat.

Anchorage in the approach

Anchor in 5m over sand about 400m from the shore, north of the harbour entrance; open to northwest–north–northeast.

Entrance

Approach the head of the northwest breakwater at slow speed on a southwesterly course. The entrance, which lies a short distance beyond, is narrow – 10m or less – and room to manoeuvre once inside is very restricted. In bad weather the entrance can be closed by a metal barrier.

Berthing

Secure in a vacant slot as available and await allocation of a berth. The harbour shoals towards its head.

Facilities

Water Taps around the harbour.
Electricity 220v AC points around the harbour.
Fuel No fuel available.
Provisions The nearest shops are in the village of Son Serra 1.25 miles inland.
Repairs A 3-tonne crane and slipway at the *club náutico*.
Yacht club The Club Náutico Serra Nova has a small clubhouse with bar near the west mole.

Transport

Car hire/taxis Taxi from Ca'n Picafort by telephone.
Buses Bus service along the main road a mile inland.

Eating out

Friendly bar at the *club náutico* and a café or two in the 'urbanisation'. No restaurants nearby.

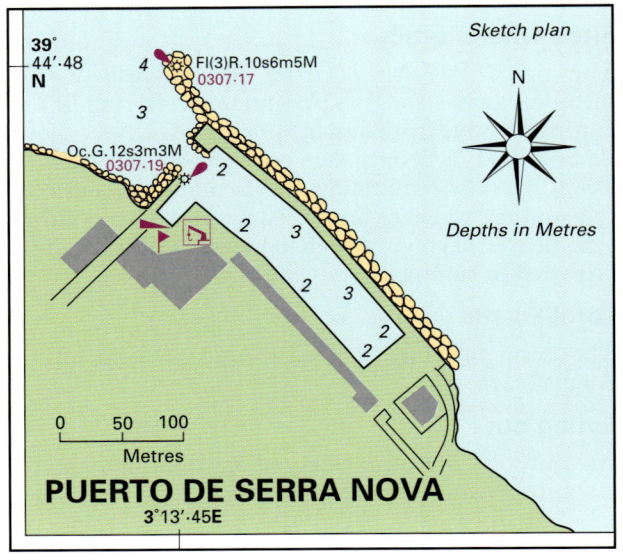

Puerto de Serra Nova: insignificant except that there are plans for expansion of this harbour into a major marina

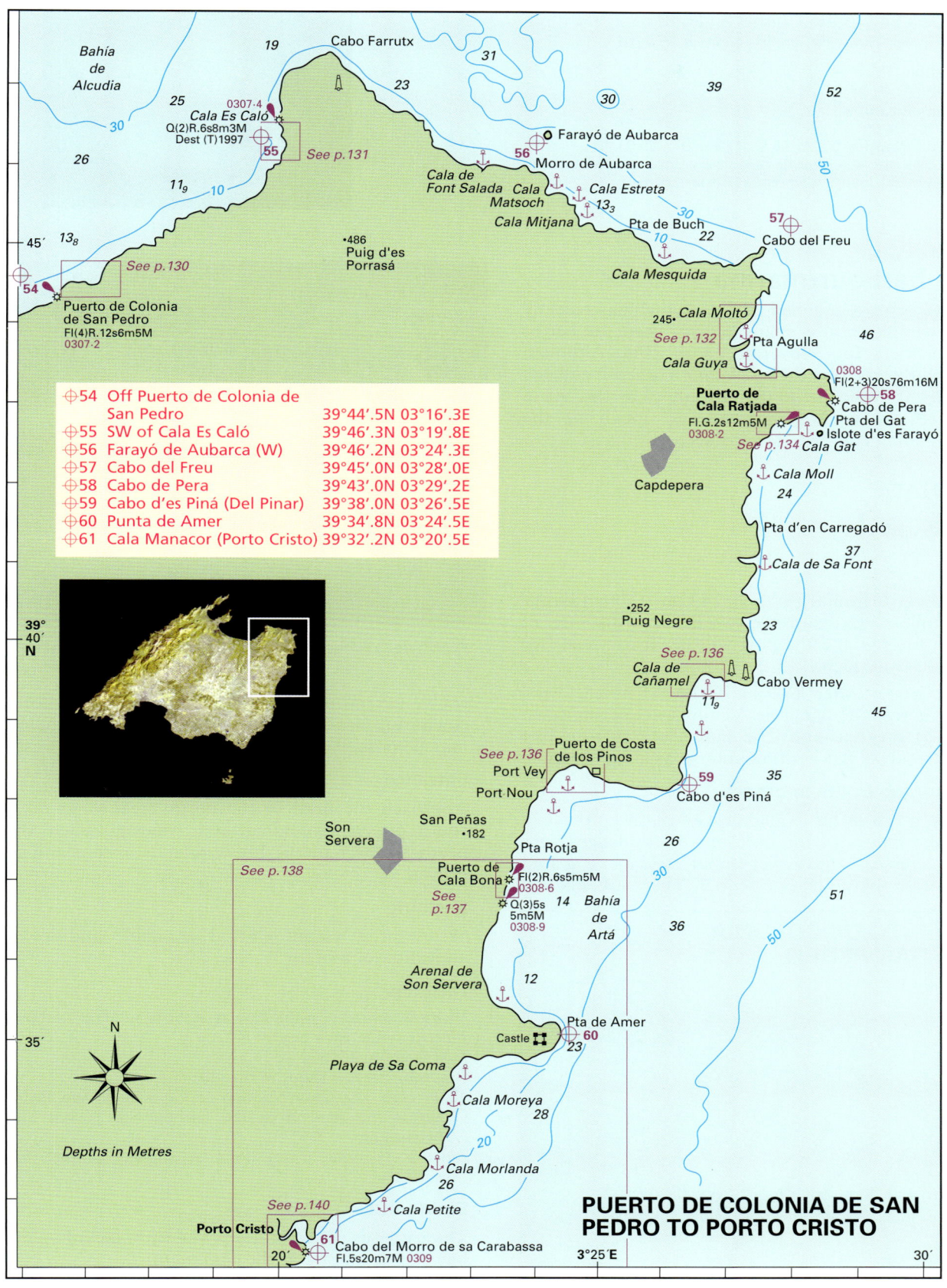

Bahía de Alcudia

Cabo Farrutx

19

23

31

30

39

52

25

30

0307·4

Cala Es Caló
Q(2)R.6s8m3M
Dest (T)1997

55

See p.131

26

11₉

10

Farayó de Aubarca

56

Morro de Aubarca

Cala de Font Salada

Cala Matsoch

Cala Estreta

Cala Mitjana

13₃

Pta de Buch

10

22

57

Cabo del Freu

45′

13₈

See p.130

•486
Puig d'es Porrasá

Cala Mesquida

54

Puerto de Colonia de San Pedro
Fl(4)R.12s6m5M
0307·2

245•

Cala Moltó

See p.132

Pta Agulla

46

Cala Guya

0308
Fl(2+3)20s76m16M

Puerto de Cala Ratjada

58

Cabo de Pera

Fl.G.2s12m5M
0308·2

Pta del Gat

Islote d'es Farayó

See p.134

Cala Gat

Cala Moll

24

Capdepera

Pta d'en Carregadó

37

Cala de Sa Font

•252
Puig Negre

23

See p.136

Cala de Cañamel

Cabo Vermey

11₉

45

Puerto de Costa de los Pinos

See p.136

Port Vey

Port Nou

59

Cabo d'es Piná

35

San Peñas
•182

26

Son Servera

See p.138

Pta Rotja

Puerto de Cala Bona

Fl(2)R.6s5m5M
0308·6

See p.137

Q(3)5s 5m5M
0308·9

14

Bahía de Artá

36

30

51

50

Arenal de Son Servera

12

35′

N

Pta de Amer

Castle

60

23

Playa de Sa Coma

Cala Moreya

28

20

Depths in Metres

Cala Morlanda

26

See p.140

Cala Petite

Porto Cristo

61

20′

Cabo del Morro de sa Carabassa
Fl.5s20m7M 0309

3°25′E

30′

Waypoint list

No.	Name	Coordinates
54	Off Puerto de Colonia de San Pedro	39°44′.5N 03°16′.3E
55	SW of Cala Es Caló	39°46′.3N 03°19′.8E
56	Farayó de Aubarca (W)	39°46′.2N 03°24′.3E
57	Cabo del Freu	39°45′.0N 03°28′.0E
58	Cabo de Pera	39°43′.0N 03°29′.2E
59	Cabo d'es Piná (Del Pinar)	39°38′.0N 03°26′.5E
60	Punta de Amer	39°34′.8N 03°24′.5E
61	Cala Manacor (Porto Cristo)	39°32′.2N 03°20′.5E

39° 40′ N

35′

PUERTO DE COLONIA DE SAN PEDRO TO PORTO CRISTO

III. MALLORCA

M15 Puerto de Colonia de San Pedro (Sant Pere)

A recently completed private marina in the E of Alcudia Bay, located within a nature park; with berths for over 300 yachts from 6 to 20m

Location
39°44'.3N 03°16'.2E

Communications
VHF: Ch 09
Club Náutico ✆ 971 58 91 47 *Fax* 971 58 91 18
Email info@clubnautic-coloniadesantpere.com
www.clubnautic-coloniadesantpere.com

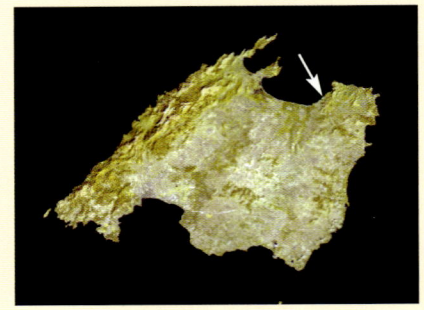

The harbour/marina

A new, privately funded marina, which has recently been completed after many delays. There are berths and services for 308 craft up to 20m. Although privately owned by the local *club náutico* members, visitors are welcome to use any empty berths. Set in an area of natural beauty, and much of the surrounding countryside is protected.

PILOTAGE

Approach

⊕54 39°44'.5N 03°16'.3E Off Puerto de Colonia de San Pedro

From south Round the high (432m) Cabo Farrutx and follow the coast westwards at a distance of 500m for 4M and the port will be clearly seen (see plan on page 113).

From north After passing Cabo Menorca, head south across the Bahía de Alcudia to close the coast near to the harbour. The immediate surrounding countryside is flat with mountains as a backdrop.

Anchorage in the approach

Whilst it is possible to anchor west of the entrance in 6m, the nature of the bottom – rocky ledges with many crevices – gives very poor holding or a foul anchor so a tripline is essential. There are shallow

Puerto de Colonia de San Pedro viewed from northeast

rocks extending out to 75m from the shore. Anchoring has been discouraged since 2005 but it may be possible to anchor 0.5M further northwest.

Entrance

Approach the head of the north breakwater on a south course, rounding and entering when the northeast part of the breakwater is abeam and in transit.

Berthing

Secure in a vacant slot as available and await allocation of a berth.

Facilities

Water Water tap near the slipway at the head of the harbour.
Electricity On each berth
Fuel Is not available.
Provisions A few shops in the village.
Yacht club The Club Náutico de Colonia de San Pedro across the road from the harbour has a bar and restaurant.
Repairs 35-tonne travel hoist. A slipway at the *club náutico*.

Eating out

There are several restaurants and cafés including the bar and restaurant at the *club náutico*.

PUERTO DE COLONIA DE SAN PEDRO

N

Depths in Metres

5 Fl(4)R.12s6m5M
0307·2
6

Fl(4)G.12s4m3M
0307·25
3
5
3

Sketch plan. Not to scale

ANCHORAGES BETWEEN PUERTO DE COLONIA AND PUERTO DE CALA RATJADA

⊕55 39°46'.3N 03°19'.8E SW of Cala Es Caló

⚓ CALA ES CALÓ

39°46'.5N 03°20'E

An isolated anchorage 1.2 miles southwest of Cabo Farrutx (see plan on page 129) set against a dramatic rocky backdrop, Cala Es Caló offers a useful anchorage if waiting to round the cape. There is a short mole but no harbour. The single light was destroyed some years ago and has not functioned since. There are no facilities and only a track ashore.

Approach from west or northwest to anchor in 5–6m over sand, weed and stones south or southeast of the molehead; open to west and northwest with some fetch from southwest and south. Holding is poor in places. The short mole has underwater projections near its head and its east (inner) side is

sometimes used by fishing vessels, which must not be obstructed. Nets may also be laid in the vicinity.

There are good walks in the surrounding hills, and for the fit the climb to the top of Atalaya de Morey (432m), overlooking Cabo Farrutx, is rewarding. The Cueva (cave) des Vells Marins some 600m south of the anchorage, is also worth visiting.

⚓ CALA DE FONT SALADA

39°46'N 03°23'.2E

One of several similar *calas* in a large shallow bay southeast of Cabo Farrutx. Anchor off a white sandy beach in 4–6m over sand, exposed to northwest–north–northeast. A track leads to a road some distance inland.

⊕56 39°46'.2N 03°24'.3E Farayó de Aubarca (W)

FARAYÓ DE AUBARCA

39°46'.3N 03°24'.5E

A small nobbly islet 23m high and some 750m offshore, off the headland of Morro de Aubarca, which is topped by a watchtower. There is good water on either side: the inshore passage has depths of 20m or more and is free of dangers.

⚓ CALAS MATSOCH, ESTRETA AND MITJANA

Around 39°45'.5N 03°24'.8E

Three small open anchorages off narrow white sand and stone beaches, backed by sand dunes. Anchor in 3–5m over hard sand, open northwest–north–east. All three can be reached by road and are frequented by tourists. Cala Mitjana has a beach café.

⚓ CALA MESQUIDA

39°44'.8N 03°26'.1E

An open anchorage off a long white sandy beach, with a growing tourist resort behind. Anchor in 3–5m over sand, open through north, northeast and east and to swell from the northwest. Water and basic provisions are available.

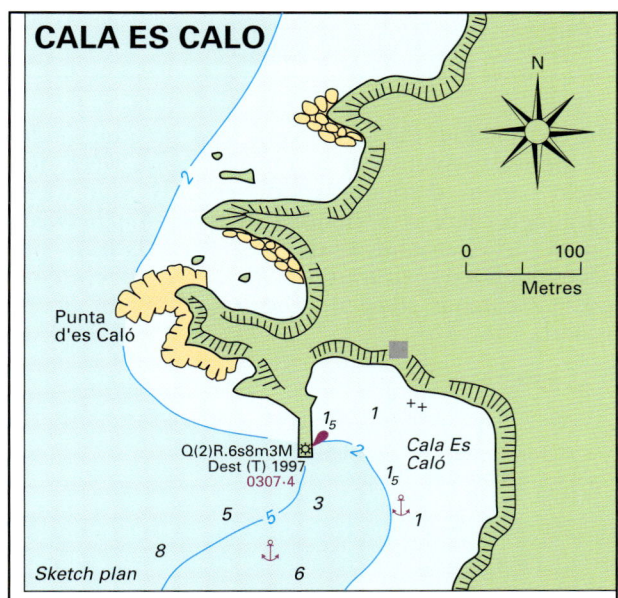

CALA ES CALO

Punta d'es Caló

Q(2)R.6s8m3M
Dest (T) 1997
0307·4

Cala Es Caló

Sketch plan

Cala Es Caló viewed from southwest, nestling on south side of Cabo Farrutx

Cala Torta: between Cala Mitjana and Cala Mesquida, south of Pta de Buch   *GW*

⊕57 39°45'.0N 03°28'.0E Cabo del Freu

⚓ CALAS MOLTÓ AND GUYA (CALAS MOLTA AND DE S'AGULLA)

39°43'.6N 03°27'.3E

Two *calas* either side of a narrow rocky promontory terminating in Punta Agulla, Cala Moltó has a very small beach and no facilites whereas Cala Guya has a much longer sandy beach, which is popular with holidaymakers. There is a growing tourist development on its south shore.

Anchor in 3–5m over sand off either beach, taking particular care in Cala Moltó to avoid a pipeline running northeast towards Menorca. Cala Moltó is open to the northeast, Cala Guya to northeast and east.

⚓ CALA GAT (CAT)

39°42'.7N 03°28'.3E

A *cala* tucked well into the northwest side of Punta del Gat with Islote d'es Farayó to the east and Puerto de Cala Ratjada to the west. Cliffed and wooded slopes are overlooked by several houses, including

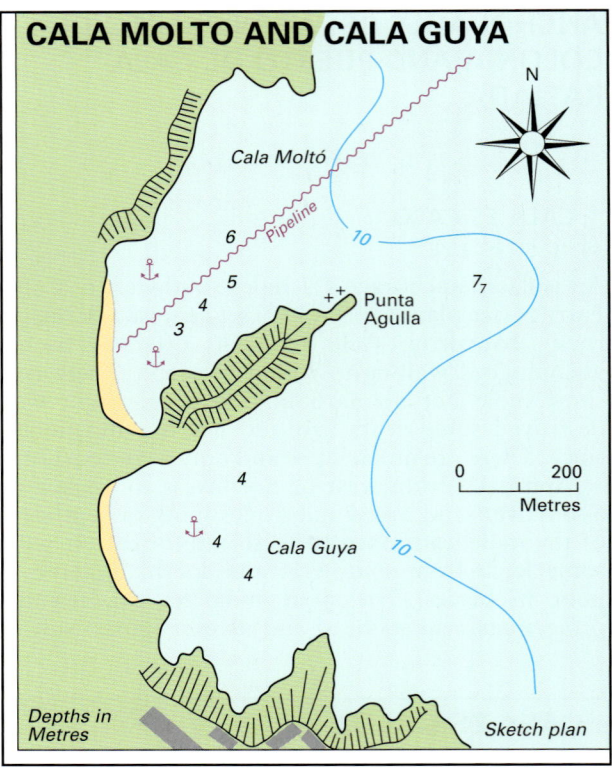

CALA MOLTO AND CALA GUYA

the conspicuous Palacio Torre Ciega, on a hill 200m to the west. Anchor in 3–5m over sand, weed and rock, open through southwest to southeast. Although there is a channel carrying 4m between Punta del Gat and Islote d'es Farayó, it is not recommended without local knowledge. Foul ground extends some distance to the south of the island.

⊕58 39°43'.0N 03°29'.2E Cabo de Pera

View from southeast over Cala Guya.
Cala Moltó far side of Punto Agulla

M16 Puerto de Cala Ratjada

A small and very friendly harbour tucked under Cabo de Pera, offering berthing and facilities for 100 small yachts inside and larger vessels on the sheltered outer mole. The closest harbour to Menorca (23 miles away)

Location
39°42'.7N 03°27'.9E

Communications
Port Authority ☎/*Fax* 971 56 50 67
Club Náutico de Cala Ratjada ☎ 971 56 40 19
Fax 971 81 90 08
Email clubnautico@calaratjada.e.telefonica

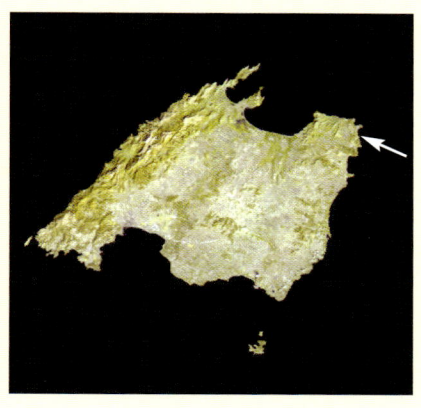

The harbour/marina

Once a little fishing harbour but now a thriving (and rather pleasant) tourist resort with a strong German influence. The vast majority of local boats are small and the *club náutico* pontoons can only take craft up to 12m or so. However, yachts up to 20m can lie alongside the breakwater outside the harbour proper, which is well sheltered in most conditions. Menorca is only 23 miles to the east, making Puerto de Cala Ratjada a popular destination or departure point for the inter-island passage.

Approach is straightforward but the entrance to the inner harbour is narrow and the harbour congested with fishing craft. Strong winds from between east and south create a heavy swell in both entrance and harbour, and the outside berths might become untenable.

Ratjada port entrance. Note new visitors berths either side of the entrance *Patricia Chung*

PILOTAGE

Approach

From south The coast is very broken, with high rocky cliffs backed by even higher tree-covered hills (see plan on page 129). Cabo Vermey is high (252m sloping down to 185m) and has a rounded profile of reddish rocks with two towers on the top. Puerto de Cala Ratjada lies 4.4 miles north of this headland and about 0.8 miles west of Cabo de Pera (Fl(2+3)20s76m16M, white tower on white building with dark corners and red roof 21m).

From north Cross the wide Bahía de Alcudia towards Cabo Farrutx (see page 113), a high sloping promontory (unlit, though there are red lights on Puig Tudosa 1.5M to the south). Follow the coast southeast to Cabo del Freu (⊕57, see plan on page 129) – a low, narrow, pointed promontory, also unlit – passing en route Farayó de Aubarca islet (⊕56, 23m high and about 750m offshore). There is good water on either side of the island.

PUERTO DE CALA RATJADA

Cabo de Pera (⊕58) 2.1 miles south-southeast of Cabo del Freu is easily identified by its lighthouse. Follow its steep rocky cliffs southwest to round Islote d'es Farayó off Punta del Gat, after which the harbour will be seen 0.7M to the west.

Anchorage in the approach
Anchor 500m southwest of the end of the breakwater in 5m over sand, open to east through southeast to south. Closer to the entrance the bottom is of rock, stone and weed and unsuitable for anchoring. There are a few sand patches opposite the breakwater head in 2–5m, but they may be occupied by moorings.

Entrance
Round the end of the breakwater at 30–40m to seek a berth on the inner side. There is a 3-knot speed limit. A rock carrying less than 3m has been reported 90–100m south-southwest of the breakwater head.

Sea levels
The level of the water increases by about 0.5m with onshore winds and decreases by the same amount with offshore winds.

Berthing
New arrangements made in 2010 have increased spaces for visitors.

The south side of the inner harbour is usually occupied with tourist day trip boats and more permanent yachts. Larger visiting yachts can use the southwest mole along with a catamaran ferry, which runs between Rataja and Ciudadela.

Yachts up to 12m can use the new moorings – bows to- on the outer side of the jetties either side of the entrance to the harbour, where lines are tailed to the quay. This is sheltered except in west sector winds. These moorings can be booked at www.portsib.es.

Facilities
Water Points on all quays and pontoons.
Electricity 220v AC points on the pontoons and at visitors' berths on the inner side of the breakwater.
Fuel Diesel from pumps at the head of the breakwater spur (fishermen's quay), not open on Sundays and public holidays. Petrol from a garage ¾ mile northwest of the harbour.
Provisions Several supermarkets and specialist food shops in the town, with more in Capdepera about 1½ miles away. Markets are Saturdays in Puerto de Cala Ratjada and Wednesdays in Capdepera.

Ice There is an ice factory at the back of the town just south of the *plaza*.

Chandlery Small chandlery/hardware store on the east side of the harbour.

Repairs No boatyard as such, though basic repairs can be carried out. Two cranes 10 and 7.5-tonnes are by the *club náutico* on the west side of the harbour. The slipway for fishing craft in the northeast corner of the harbour may be available for yachts. There are two cradles, maximum draught 2m. Other slipways around the harbour.

Engineers Ask advice from local fishermen.

Yacht club The Club Náutico de Cala Ratjada is small, but has showers and a bar.

Showers At the *club náutico*.

Laundry In the town.

Banks In the town, with credit card facilities.

Hospital/medical services In the town.

Transport

Car hire/taxis In the town.

Buses Bus service to Capdepera and onward to Palma, etc.

Ferries Tourist ferries make daily trips to a number of popular beaches in the area.

Sights ashore locally

Little of the original town has survived the tourist building boom, but both Artá five miles inland and Capdepera 1½ miles away have retained many of their old buildings, the latter including an interesting castle with particularly good views.

The Cuevas (caves) de Artá at Cabo Vermey are well worth visiting and the garden museum of Sa Torre Cega has an interesting collection of sculptures.

Restored windmills abound in the area – most have been converted from water pumps for the agricultural area to electricity generators, though many do both. They are no longer in active use, because of supplies from the grid and mains water systems.

Local specialities

An enclave of Moors remained in this area much longer than elsewhere and the local people show more traces of Moorish descent than do those in other parts of the island. They also practise the old Moorish art of palmetto (palm work).

Local events

A fiesta is held at Puerto de Cala Ratjada in mid-August in honour of San Roc, patron saint of the town, and events include sailing races. On 24 August Capdepera honours its patron saint, San Bartolomé, this time with horse races among the revelry.

Eating out

Many eating houses of all descriptions, with the harbour surrounded by pleasant cafés and restaurants.

Restored windmills: once used for pumping water and generating electicity, rather than as mills *Graham Hutt*

ANCHORAGES BETWEEN PUERTO DE CALA RATJADA AND PUERTO DE COSTA DE LOS PINOS

⚓ CALA MOLL
39°42′.3N 03°27′.5E

A wide bay off a popular sandy beach ¾ mile southwest of Puerto de Cala Ratjada (see page 129), Cala Moll has low rocky sides and is largely surrounded by buildings. Anchor about 150m off the beach in 2.5m over sand, open to the east quadrant. The small Islote Forana lies to the southeast and should be left on the landward side.

⚓ CALA DE SA FONT (CALA DE SAN GERONI)
39°40′.9N 03°27′.3E

A sizeable, attractive *cala* with a fine sandy beach and some apartment buildings nearby. Anchor off the beach in 5m over sand and stone, open to the east quadrant. Some facilities ashore, otherwise Capdepera is less than two miles by road.

Cala de Sa Font viewed from east

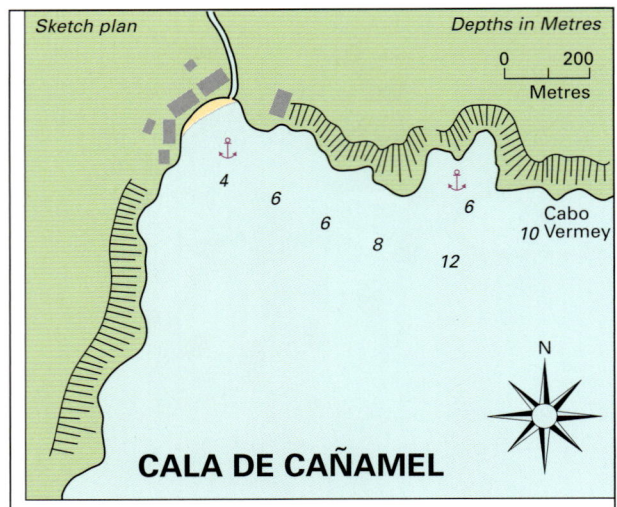

Sketch plan — *Depths in Metres*

0 — 200 Metres

4

6

6

6

8

12

Cabo 10 Vermey

N

CALA DE CAÑAMEL

Cala de Cañamel looking west, with Cabo Vermey dominating right of picture

⚓ CALA DE CAÑAMEL

39°39'.4N 03°26'.6E

Rather an open anchorage in a bay just south and west of Cabo Vermey (reddish, with little vegetation) and the famous Cuevas (caves) de Artá (see page 129). The sandy beach at the head of the *cala* is backed by hotels and apartments, but a good deal of greenery has been retained. A river flows through the beach on its northern side. Anchor in 3–5m of very clear water over sand, open to east, southeast and south. The bottom shelves gradually and in heavy weather waves break some distance offshore. There are some shops in the tourist complex, including a small supermarket.

A second anchorage, with less swell but having room for only two boats, will be found in a very small *cala* halfway to Cabo Vermey. A spherical yellow buoy (Fl(5)Y.20s) is positioned 1.4 miles east of the cape itself.

⊕59 39°38'.0N 03°26'.5E Cabo d'es Piná (Del Pinar)

PUERTO DE COSTA DE LOS PINOS

A jetty rather than a port, but with a pleasant anchorage with easy access ashore nearby.

Location
39°38'.2N 03°24'.8E

The jetty and anchorage

A very small, shallow facility that is not much more than a broad quay with a short protective extension. Built as an amenity for guests of the four-star Hotel Golf Punta Rotja, the 'Puerto' offers little shelter and can take only the smallest craft. The bay is often used for water-skiing, etc. but it nevertheless makes a pleasant anchorage.

PILOTAGE

Approach

The jetty and anchorage lie close west of Cabo d'es Piná (Cabo d'es Ratx), itself some 5.4 miles south of Cabo de Pera and 3.6 miles north of Punta de Amer. The square, white hotel overlooking the harbour will be seen for many miles.

Anchorage in the approach

Anchor in 2–4m over sand and weed west of the molehead, open to south and west. The bottom is uneven with some rocks and a careful watch on the depth sounder will be necessary.

PUERTO DE COSTA DE LOS PINOS
Sketch plan

Supermarket

Cafe

Hotel (conspic)

0₅

2

2

1

2

2

1₅

Dique

3

2

0 — 50 Metres

N

Depths in Metres

Entrance

Approach the northwest corner of the quay, sounding continuously.

Berthing

Secure as space permits. There are a few projecting underwater rocks. Officials may appear, otherwise visit the hotel reception desk.

Facilities

Water Tap on the quay.
Provisions Supermarket behind the hotel.
Repairs Two small dinghy slipways.

Eating out

A choice of restaurants and cafés.

ANCHORAGES OFF PUERTO DE COSTA DE LOS PINOS

The long stretch of sandy beaches and small *calas* between Puerto de Costa de los Pinos and Puerto de Cala Bona make good anchorages in settled weather. Port Vey (Vell) and Port Nou are marked on the plan at the beginning of this section on page 129. Far from being ports, these are pleasant anchorages off the open beach. Anchor in 3–4m over sand and weed. A few houses, hotels, shops and cafés line the road behind the beach.

M17 Puerto de Cala Bona

A small but safe harbour with the recent addition of diesel and petrol, and 20 berths allocated for visitors

Location
39°36'.9N 03°23'.7E
Communications
Puerto de Cala Bona ☏/Fax 971 58 62 56

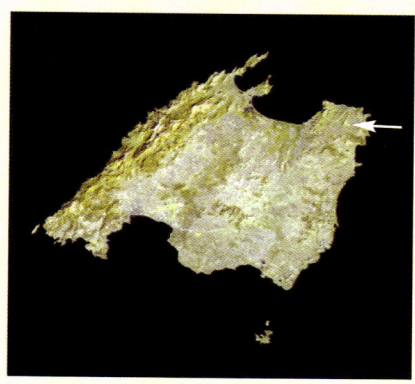

The harbour

Originally a small fishing harbour with an even tinier inner harbour, Puerto de Cala Bona has been improved by the construction of two outer breakwaters. Even so it is not large, with a total of 192 berths. The approach is straightforward but should not be attempted in strong onshore winds. The harbour is home to a number of glass-bottomed and other tourist excursion boats.

Puerto de Cala Bona: still a small harbour, despite the extensions

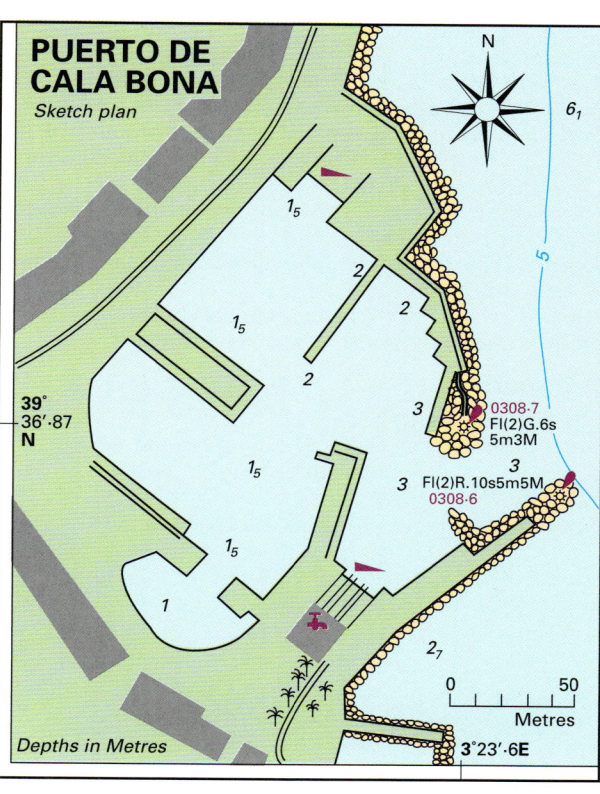

PUERTO DE CALA BONA
Sketch plan

Depths in Metres

III. MALLORCA

PILOTAGE

Approach

From south Punta de Amer is a low, rocky-cliffed promontory with a small castle on its summit. The wide Bahía de Artá stretches northwards from it as far as Cabo d'es Piná and the harbour is located near its centre, at the northern end of the heavily built up area.

From north The high, rounded profile of Cabo Vermey, which has reddish rocks, is recognisable as is the dark-cliffed Cabo d'es Piná. South of Cabo d'es Piná lies the wide Bahía de Artá, with Puerto de Cala Bona near its centre, at the northern end of the heavily built up area. See plan on page 129.

Anchorage in the approach

There are sand patches off the harbour entrance in 5m+, but it would be distinctly exposed.

Entrance

There are a number of rocky breakwaters close south of the harbour, established to retain sand on the beaches, so ensure that the harbour entrance is identified beyond all doubt. Enter at slow speed on a southwesterly course. Once inside there is little room to manoeuvre and parts are shallow.

Berthing

Secure bow or stern-to on the inside of the south breakwater. This position is exposed to wind or swell from east or northeast but well protected from the southeast quadrant.

Facilities

Water In containers from the fishermen's co-operative near the old inner harbour, or from one of the bars or restaurants.
Electricity A few 220v AC points around the harbour.
Fuel Diesel and petrol now available.
Provisions Shops and supermarkets to the south of the harbour, more in Son Servera, two miles inland. Friday market in Son Servera.
Ice From the fishermen's co-operative or from one of the bars or restaurants.
Repairs Three slipways around the harbour, but little more than dinghy size.
Banks To the south of the harbour and in Son Servera.
Hospital/medical services In Son Servera.

Transport

Car hire/taxis In the town.
Buses Bus service to Son Servera and beyond.

Eating out

Many eating places around the harbour.

ANCHORAGES FROM PUERTO DE CALA BONA TO PORTO CRISTO

⊕60 Punta de Amer   39°34'.8N 03°24'.5E
⊕61 Cala Manacor (Porto Cristo)   39°32'.2N 03°20'.5E

CALA MILLOR

39°36'.3N 03°23'.4E

The large holiday development of Cala Millor lies half a mile south of Cala Bona. A small lit pier (Q(3)5s5m5M black column, yellow band with ⧫ topmark) is present. It is not recommended to moor there but is included here in case the light confuses passing yachtsmen.

⚓ ARENAL DE SON SERVERA

39°35'.6N 03°23'.3E

A long sand and stone beach immediately north of Punta de Amer. Anchor in 5m over sand and rock near the southern end of the Cala Millor holiday development. There are numerous restaurants and cafés ashore plus a few shops.

⊕60 39°34'.8N 03°24'.5E Punta de Amer

⚓ PLAYA DE SA COMA

39°34'.5N 03°22'.8E

A wide and often crowded sandy beach close south of Punta de Amer. Anchor in 2–4m over sand, with some rock and weed further out, open to southwest–south–east.

⚓ CALA MOREYA

39°34'.1N 03°22'.6E

A sandy bay close south of Playa de Sa Coma but surrounded by the much denser development of the S'Illot holiday town. Anchor in 2–4m over sand. Open to the east sector.

Cala Morlanda viewed from northeast across Punta de Sa Roca

⚓ CALA MORLANDA

39°33'.4N 03°22'.3E

A double *cala* at the south end of the S'Illot holiday development but still largely unspoilt, with rocky sides and two small stony beaches. Anchor in 4–5m over sand. Open to the east.

⚓ CALA PETITE

39°32'.9N 03°21'.4E

A narrow, dog-legged *cala* with space for no more than two boats, enclosed by rocky cliffs and with nothing ashore beyond a rough track. Anchor in 3–6m over sand and rock in the centre of the *cala*, using two anchors to restrict swinging room; open to the east and southeast.

There are a number of isolated rocks awash just off the small beach.

Cala Petite, bottom right-hand, looking southwest to Porto Cristo

M18 Porto Cristo (Port de Manacor)

A very sheltered harbour with a total of 500 berths up to 16m, tucked well into the Cap de Estoy river

Location
39°32'.1N 03°20'.4E

Communications
Puerto de Porto Cristo VHF Ch 16
℡ 971 82 04 19
Club Náutico de Porto Cristo VHF Ch 09
℡ 971 82 12 53 *Fax* 971 82 06 50
Email lequio18@yahoo.es
www.cnpc@maptel.es

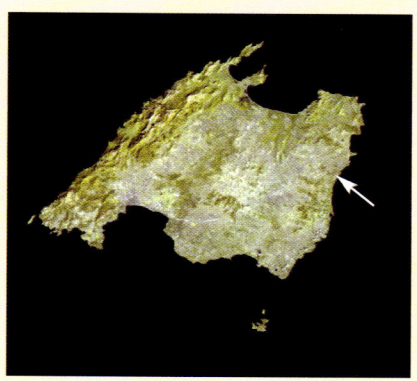

The harbour

A long and well-sheltered inlet with several doglegs, which has managed to retain a good deal of its charm despite the growth of the town. Approach and entrance present no problems other than in strong onshore winds. There are a total of 497 berths, with facilities on both banks of the river: at *club náutico* on the southeast side, and the public quays on the northwest side. Even so, the harbour is often full in summer and berths cannot be reserved in advance.

PILOTAGE

Approach

⊕61 39°32'.2N 03°20'.5E Cala Manacor (Porto Cristo)

From south The coast from Porto Colom is of low rocky cliffs which are broken by many calas, all very similar and difficult to identify. However, at Porto Cristo the conspicuous lighthouse tower on Cabo del Morro, with black and white vertical stripes is easily seen. See plan on page 142.

From north Cross the wide Bahía de Artá which terminates on its south side at Punta de Amer, which is relatively low but prominent. Porto Cristo lies four miles to the southwest and can be identified as above. See plan on page 138.

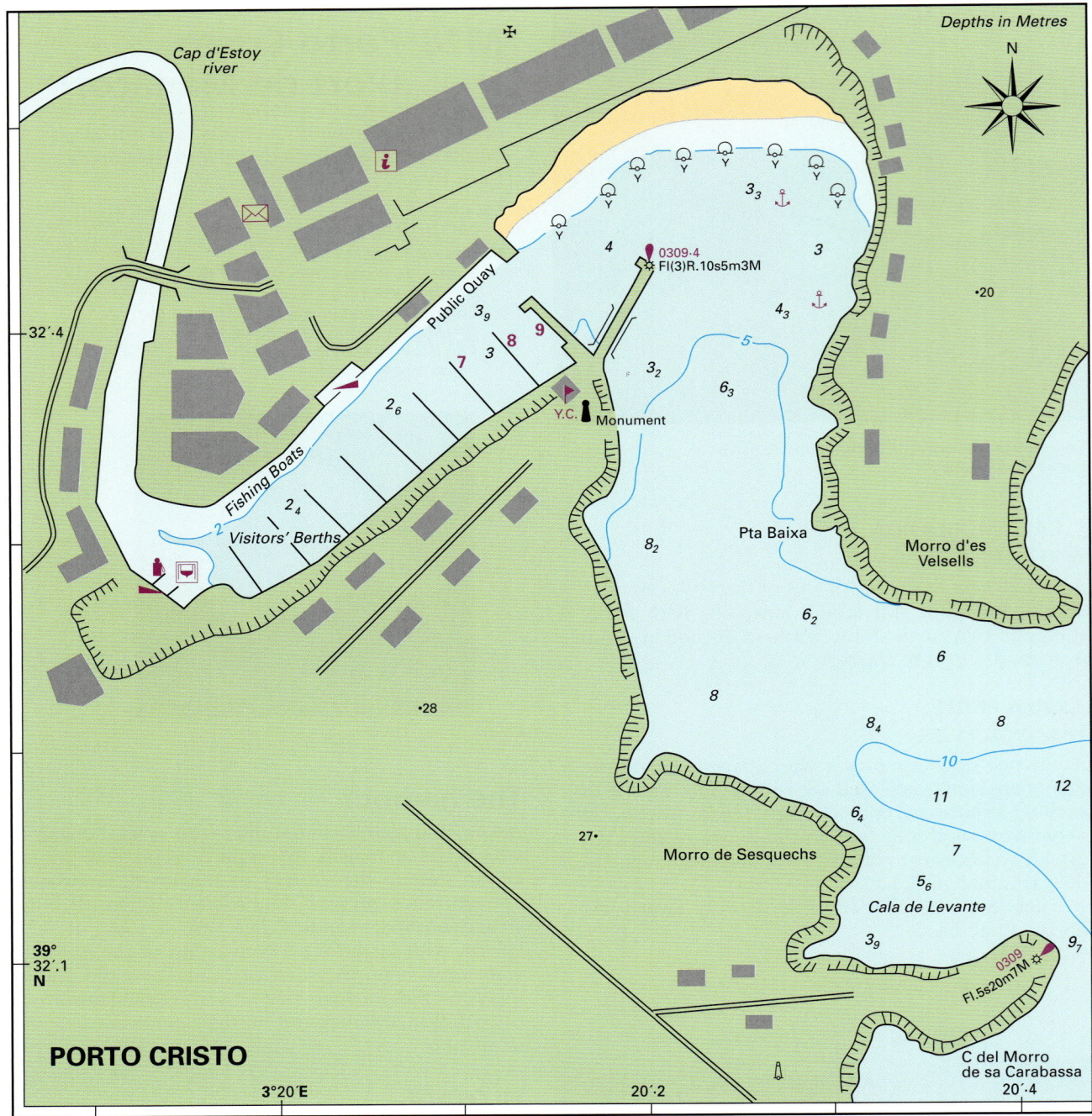

PORTO CRISTO

Anchorage in the approach

It is possible to anchor under the cliffs on the east side of the channel opposite the monument, or further north outside a line of yellow buoys marking the bathing area, in 3–5m over sand, mud and weed. Both spots can be roly, due either to swell or to wash from passing speedboats, and may be affected by a circular current in low pressure weather. Anchoring in the harbour itself is not permitted.

Entrance

The entrance channel is both wide and deep. Keep to the centre or slightly to starboard before rounding the northeast mole into the yacht harbour (this mole is not completely solid but includes a bridge near the

shore). Strong currents can occur when the river Cap d'Estoy is in spate and in heavy weather a strong surge may build up. In pleasant conditions it is not unusual to find swimmers and snorkellers virtually under the bow! A series of yellow buoys with a connecting line lies some way off the bathing beach. There is a 3-knot speed limit.

Berthing

The *club náutico* reserves the three easternmost pontoons (7, 8, 9) for visiting yachts. Moorings and lazy lines are provided and a berthing master is usually on duty. However the harbour is often full in summer, so it is advisable to call on VHF Ch 09 to check whether a berth will be available, even though

Porto Cristo: a very safe and sheltered harbour

they cannot be reserved before arrival. The visitors' pontoons have 3m or more at the outer ends, shoaling towards the quay.

If there is no space available at the *club náutico* it may be possible to lie stern-to on the Port Authority public quay opposite, southwest of the beach. There are the usual lazy lines running out from the quay.

Facilities

Water Water points on the quay, pontoons and at the *club náutico*.
Electricity 220v AC points on quays and pontoons.
Fuel Diesel and petrol from pumps next to the travel-lift.
Provisions Shops of all types in the town including several small supermarkets, but a long walk round from the yacht pontoons (alternatively use the dinghy). Produce/fish markets Sunday in Porto Cristo and Monday in Manacor six miles inland.
Ice Delivered to the quay daily, also from the *club náutico* bar.
Chandlery Two well-stocked chandleries either side of the channel north of the boatyard.
Repairs A 50-tonne travel-lift and 12.5-tonne crane in the boatyard. Small slipways on both sides of the harbour. Jaume Vermell Náutica boatyard ✆ 971 82 20 22 *Fax* 82 20 21 at the southwest end of the harbour has most facilities including a very protected winter lay-up area.
Engineers At the boatyard. Marina Marbella Balear SA ✆ 971 82 05 90 is official service agent for Mercury/ MerCruiser and Volvo Penta.
Yacht club The Club Náutico de Porto Cristo has a smart clubhouse with bar, restaurant, swimming pool, terrace, showers, etc.

Showers At the *club náutico*.
Launderettes In the town.
Banks Several in the town, mostly with credit card facilities.
Hospital/medical services Medical services in Porto Cristo, hospital in Manacor six miles inland.

Transport

Car hire/taxis In the town.
Buses Regular service to Manacor, Palma, etc.

Sights ashore locally

The area is famous for the caves discovered by MEA Martel in 1896, and for an unsuccessful landing by Communist forces during the civil war. There are two monuments to this landing, one near the root of the northeast mole and another at the northwest end of the town. It was also favoured by the kings of Mallorca for their summer holidays.

The spectacular Cuevas del Drach (Caves of the Dragon) and Cuevas del Hams south of the town should not be missed (open 1000 to 1700). There is also a wildlife park nearby. Spectacular views of the coast can be seen from the tower southwest of the lighthouse.

Local event

The Fiesta de la Virgen del Carmen, with waterborne processions, is held on 16 July.

Eating out

A large number of restaurants, cafés and bars.

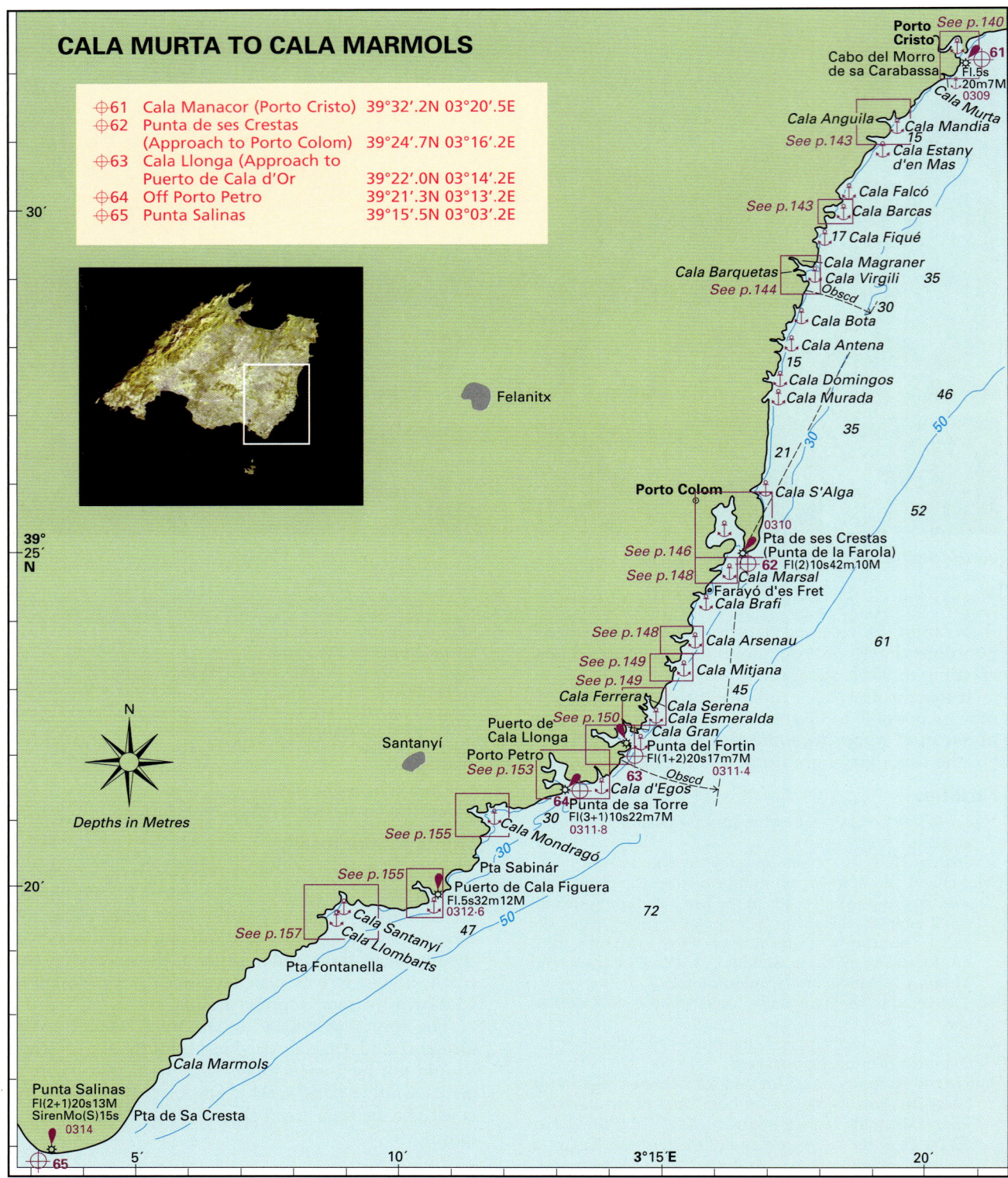

CALA MURTA TO CALA MARMOLS

⊕61	Cala Manacor (Porto Cristo)	39°32'.2N 03°20'.5E
⊕62	Punta de ses Crestas (Approach to Porto Colom)	39°24'.7N 03°16'.2E
⊕63	Cala Llonga (Approach to Puerto de Cala d'Or)	39°22'.0N 03°14'.2E
⊕64	Off Porto Petro	39°21'.3N 03°13'.2E
⊕65	Punta Salinas	39°15'.5N 03°03'.2E

Depths in Metres

Felanitx

Santanyí

Porto Cristo
Cabo del Morro de sa Carabassa
See p.140
61
Fl.5s 20m7M
0309
Cala Murta

Cala Anguila
See p.143
Cala Mandia
15
Cala Estany d'en Mas

Cala Falcó
See p.143
Cala Barcas
17 Cala Fiqué

Cala Barquetas
See p.144
Cala Magraner
Cala Virgili
Obscd
30
35

Cala Bota
Cala Antena
15
Cala Dòmingos
Cala Murada
46
35
21
30
50

Cala S'Alga
52

Porto Colom
0310
Pta de ses Crestas (Punta de la Farola)
See p.146
See p.148
62 Fl(2)10s42m10M
Cala Marsal
Farayó d'es Fret
Cala Brafi

See p.148
Cala Arsenau
61

See p.149
Cala Mitjana
See p.149
45
Cala Ferrera
See p.150
Cala Serena
Cala Esmeralda
Cala Gran
Punta del Fortin
Fl(1+2)20s17m7M
Obscd
0311·4

Puerto de Cala Llonga
Porto Petro
See p.153
Cala d'Egos
63
64 Punta de sa Torre
Fl(3+1)10s22m7M
0311·8
30
Cala Mondragó

See p.155
Pta Sabinár
See p.155
Puerto de Cala Figuera
Fl.5s32m12M
0312·6
30
72

See p.157
Cala Santanyí
Cala Llombarts
47
50
Pta Fontanella

Cala Marmols

Punta Salinas
Fl(2+1)20s13M
SirenMo(S)15s
0314
Pta de Sa Cresta
65

ANCHORAGES BETWEEN PORTO CRISTO AND PORTO COLOM

⚓ CALA MURTA

39°31'.9N 03°20'.1E

A narrow *cala* between steep rocky sides, with some new buildings to the north. Anchor in 3–5m over sand, open to the east and southeast. See plan on page 142.

⚓ CALAS ANGUILA AND MANDIA

39°31'.3N 03°19'.1E

A small double *cala* with sandy beaches. A holiday development, Porto Cristo Nova, lies on the north side and there are others to the south. Anchor off either beach in 3–5m over sand, open to the east. Several nearby restaurants and cafés.

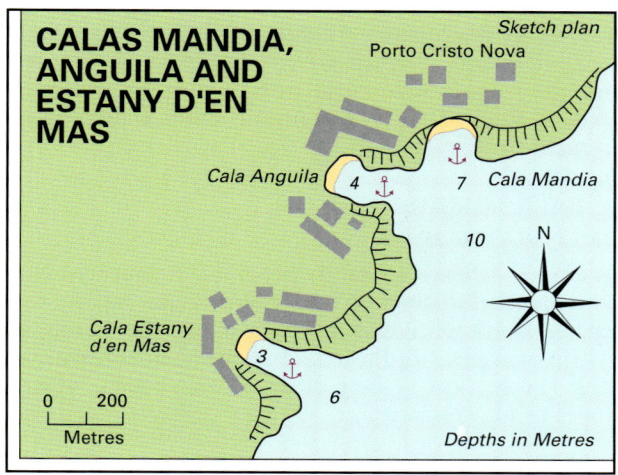

⚓ CALA ESTANY D'EN MAS

39°31'N 03°18'.9E

A small *cala* with rocky sides, the northern one almost completely covered with low-rise buildings. Anchor in 2–4m over sand off the crowded beach,

Calas Mandia (right), Anguila (centre), and Cala Estany d'en Mas (left)

Cala Barcas: there are several nearby *calas* with good anchoring

open to the east and southeast. Beach bars and *chiringhito* (summer beach restaurant).

⚓ CALA FALCÓ

39°30'.2N 03°18'.2E

A very open, totally deserted *cala*, with a track to the Cuevas del Pirata about a mile inland. Anchor in 2–5m over sand off the small stony beach, open to the eastern quadrant.

⚓ CALA BARCAS

39°29'.9N 03°17'.9E

A wide, square, undeveloped *cala*, the two sandy beaches at its head separated by a stretch of dark rocks. There is a shallow rocky outcrop projecting from the cliffs to the north, which have many sea caves. Keep to the centre of the entrance to anchor off either beach in 3–5m over sand, open to the northeast and east. There is only a very rough track ashore, but the *cala* is popular with tourist boats and can become crowded in summer.

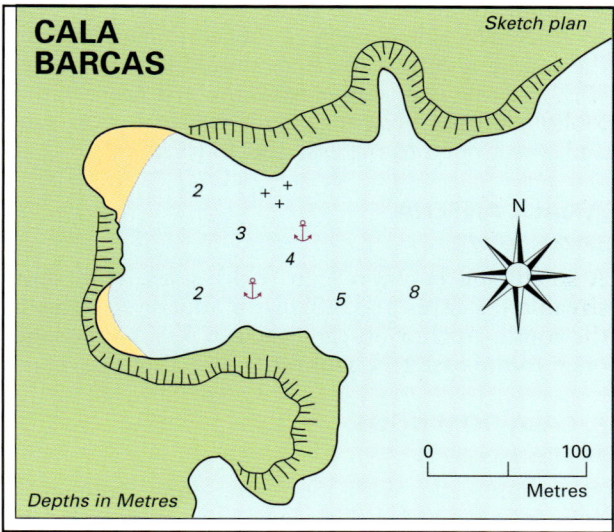

III. MALLORCA

⚓ CALA FIQUÉ (CALA SERRAT)

39°29'.6N 03°17'.7E

More accurately three very small, deserted *calas* with rocky headlands between. Anchor in 3–5m over sand, open to the eastern quadrant.

⚓ CALAS MAGRANER, BARQUETAS AND VIRGILI

39°29'.0N 03°17'.4E

Twin *calas* with sandy beaches, offering good protection near their heads. Anchor in 2–4m over sand; also just south of the projecting headland in Cala Virgili, in 3.5m. Other than a small grey hut on the northern headland there are no buildings, and the development shown behind the *calas* on several local maps does not appear to have taken place. Tracks ashore lead inland but few tourists seem to venture here.

Calas Magraner (right), Barquetas and Virgili, (left) viewed from southeast

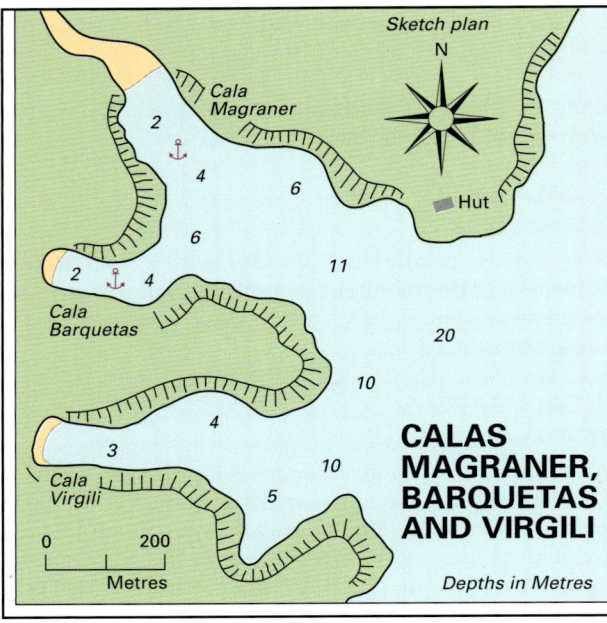

⚓ CALA BOTA

39°28'.4N 03°17'.3E

A small undeveloped *cala*, its mouth partially obstructed by a breaking rocky shoal running out from the southern cliffs, Cala Bota should be approached with extreme care. Enter from the northeast with a lookout on the bow, to anchor in 4–5m over sand and weed, open to the east and southeast.

⚓ CALA ANTENA

39°28'N 03°17'E

A small *cala* between high rocky sides, with some sizeable sea caves and a high-rise tourist complex to the south. Anchor off the beach in 3–5m over sand, open to the eastern quadrant.

⚓ CALA DOMINGOS

39°27'.5N 03°16'.8E

A double *cala* with two fine (and frequently crowded) sandy beaches, inevitably surrounded by tourist development. Anchor in 3–5m over sand, open through northeast–east–southeast. There are several large hotels close north, and the southern arm is backed by a restaurant with a distinctive conical roof.

⚓ CALA MURADA

39°27'.3N 03°16'.8E

A curved *cala* with a sandy beach at its southern end and dense housing on the point: once again, the beach is often crowded. Anchor off the beach in 3–5m over sand and weed, open to the northeast and east. Protection is best close to the beach, where there is a bar/restaurant.

⚓ CALA S'ALGA

39°25'.8N 03°16'.6E

A large open *cala* with rocky sides and a very small stony beach, one mile north of the entrance to Porto Colom. Anchor in 3–5m over sand and weed, open to northeast and east. There is a road across the headland to Porto Colom where supplies are available.

The conspicuous banded lighthouse on Punta de ses Crestas guards the eastern side of the entrance to Porto Colom

M19 Porto Colom

A large natural and well protected harbour with berthing for 250 yachts and many mooring buoys. One of the most pleasant places to visit in Mallorca

Location
 39°25'N 03°16'.2E (entrance)
 39°25'.4N 03°15'.8E (public pontoons)
Communications
 VHF Ch 09
 Club Náutico de Porto Colom ☎ 971 82 46 58
 Fax 971 82 53 99
 Email tomeu.tejedor@zagal.es

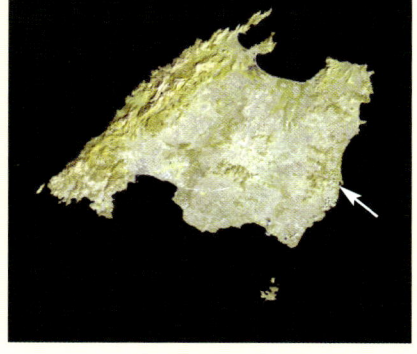

The harbour and anchorage

A large natural harbour with moorings for over 200 vessels in the Club Náutico de Porto Colom, operating in the northwest corner of the harbour. With many more mooring buoys laid south of the port, anchoring is now technically prohibited, though many yachts do still anchor away from the port as described below. The port is well protected with a deep and narrow entrance, though much of the interior is relatively shallow: under 2.5m.

Although there is a low-rise housing development around the harbour, the area is surprisingly undeveloped.

The *club náutico* staff are not particularly friendly or helpful but since there are usually no berths available for visitors this is not important. By contrast, the Port Authority staff are very helpful and have their office close to the fuelling berth.

Approaches to Colom: note buoys laid southwest of port where anchoring is prohibited

III. MALLORCA

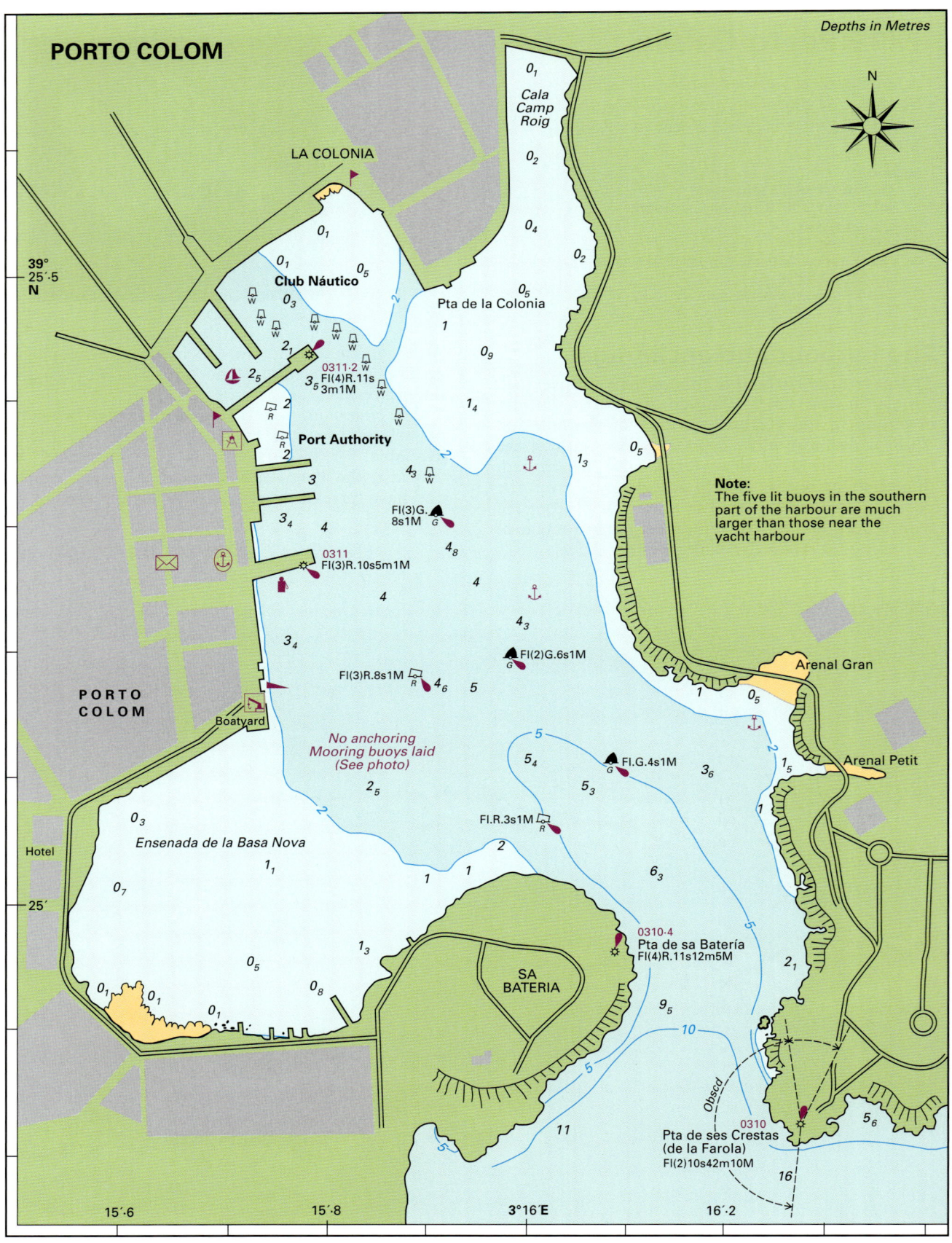

PORTO COLOM

Depths in Metres

Cala Camp Roig

LA COLONIA

Club Náutico

Pta de la Colonia

39°
25´·5
N

0311·2
Fl(4)R.11s
3m1M

Port Authority

Fl(3)G.
8s1M

0311
Fl(3)R.10s5m1M

Note:
The five lit buoys in the southern part of the harbour are much larger than those near the yacht harbour

Arenal Gran

Fl(2)G.6s1M

Fl(3)R.8s1M

PORTO COLOM

Boatyard

Arenal Petit

Fl.G.4s1M

*No anchoring
Mooring buoys laid
(See photo)*

Ensenada de la Basa Nova

Fl.R.3s1M

Hotel

25´

0310·4
Pta de sa Batería
Fl(4)R.11s12m5M

SA BATERIA

Obscd

0310
Pta de ses Crestas
(de la Farola)
Fl(2)10s42m10M

15´·6   15´·8   3°16´E   16´·2

Porto Colom looking northwest. Mooring buoys, Club Náutico top and two Port Authority pontoons centre. The wide fuelling jetty left

PILOTAGE

Approach

⊕62 39°24'.7N 03°16'.2E Pta de ses Crestas (Approach to Porto Colom)

From south The coast from Porto Petro and beyond (⊕64 on page 142) is of low rocky cliffs broken by many calas. The distinctive lighthouse on Punta de ses Crestas (Fl(2)10s42m10M, ⊕62) white round tower with three black bands on white building with red roof 25m) on the east side of the entrance can be seen from many miles off, though if sailing close inshore the light itself will be obscured when bearing more than 006°. There is a small islet, Farayó d'es Fret (11m), 0.8 miles southwest of the entrance.

From north The coast from Porto Cristo also consists of low rocky cliffs broken by many calas. When very close inshore the lighthouse on Punta de ses Crestas (see page 144) is obscured when bearing less than 207° but is otherwise clearly seen from many miles. The entrance itself does not open until around this headland.

Entrance and buoyed channel

The entrance is deep and unobstructed, other than a small rocky islet against the eastern shore. As the harbour widens out, follow the (unlit) buoyed channel to remain in depths of 4–5m. Unlit fish cages may be anchored to the east of the channel. (See photo above.)

Much of the harbour is shallow and all manoeuvring outside the buoyed channel should be done with one eye on the depth-sounder, particularly since some of the banks appear to be unusually steep-sided.

Berthing

Secure bow or stern-to the south side of the yacht harbour south mole, or to one of the two Port Authority pontoons close south. The former has no more than 2.2m at its outer end and all three shoal towards the shore. Lazy lines are tailed to both mole and pontoons. None of these berths are viable in strong southeast winds. Another option is on the fuel jetty, which is close to the harbour office.

The area south of the fuel jetty is now completely full of Port Authority moorings and although yachts do still anchor east of the channel, the harbourmaster discourages this when there are vacant moorings. The charge for the mooring buoys includes showers and water from the jetty tap (although reported to be very brackish in summer).

Anchorages

These are becoming scarce in the harbour as buoys are being laid in order to facilitate higher charges. One possibility is close to Arenal Gran and Arenal Petit, though south and southeast swell affects the area. The Port Authority has been allowing anchoring due east of their finger pontoon moorings by arrangement. All mooring buoys are taken up by permanent residents with a waiting list.

Facilities

Water Taps on yacht harbour mole and pontoons, Port Authority pontoons and near the Port Authority office. Also a tap by the fuel berth, for which a charge is made. Yachtsmen are advised not to drink the water, which in any case tastes very bad. This is probably a seasonal problem, as in many other ports.

Electricity 220v AC points on yacht harbour mole and pontoons, and on the public pontoons.

Fuel Diesel from pumps on the south side of the west mole (claimed to have 4m alongside). Petrol from a garage near the root of the mole.

Provisions Two supermarkets near the Ensenada de la Basa Nova, south of the yacht pontoons. Many other shops in the town.

Wi-Fi There are no Wi-Fi facilities anywhere near the port.

Ice From the *club náutico* and from the above filling station.

Chandlery Near the *club náutico*.

Repairs A boatyard on the corner north of the Ensenada de la Basa Nova capable of straightforward work in wood or GRP. Also engine repairs. 10-tonne and 5-tonne mobile cranes at the boatyard. A 1.5m slipway at the boatyard and several others around the harbour.

Yacht clubs The Club Náutico de Porto Colom at the northwest corner of the harbour has a bar, lounge, terrace and showers. The Club Náutico de Pescadores is northeast of the harbour.

Showers By the Port Authority office just north of the west mole, and at the *club náutico*.

Post office A mobile post office visits a site near the Port Authority office (see plan) between 1150 and 1220, weekdays only. Times appear to change periodically.

Hospital/medical services Medical services in the town, hospital in Manacor 11 miles away.

Transport

Car hire/taxis In the town.
Buses Bus service to Felanitx, Manacor and beyond.

Sights ashore locally

The Monastery of San Salvador four miles inland is interesting and has a fine view, as has the ruined Castillo de San Tueri three miles inland.

Local event

A fiesta in honour of the Virgen del Carmen is held on 16 July, when the local fishing boats parade around the harbour dressed overall.

Eating out

The usual range of restaurants, cafés and bars.

ANCHORAGES FROM PORTO COLOM TO PUERTO DE CALA LLONGA

⚓ CALA MARSAL AND CALÓ D'EN MANUELL

39°24'.6N 03°15'.8E

A double *cala* with rocky cliffs close south of Porto Colom (see plan on page 142). Cala Marsal has a sandy beach at its head. Anchor in 3–5m over sand off the beach, open to northeast and east, or tuck into Caló d'en Manuell which has a sand and rock bottom, open to the southeast. Both *calas* are surrounded by apartment blocks and hotels.

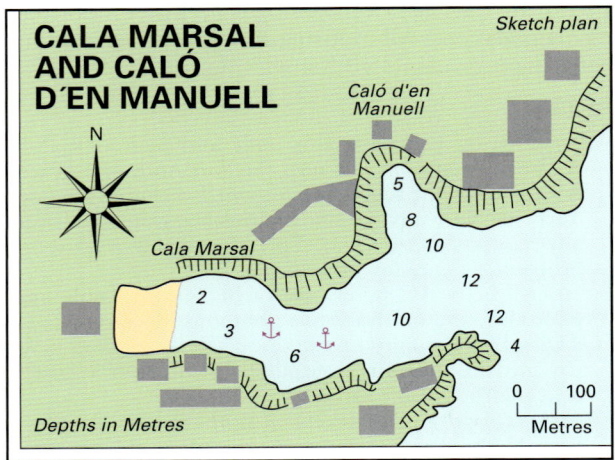

⚓ CALA BRAFI

39°24'.2N 03°15'.5E

A small, narrow, dog-legged *cala* between rocky cliffs, with a stone boathouse at its head but no other buildings nearby. Anchor in 3–4m over sand, stone and weed. The small islet of Farayó d'es Fret lies close northeast of the *cala*. It consists of a flat shelf of rock just above sea-level, with a narrow, vertical-sided 11m high rock on the top. In time erosion will probably displace this and convert it into a dangerous breaking ledge.

⚓ CALA ARSENAU (CALA SA NAU OR CALA DE RAS)

39°23'.6N 03°15'.2E

A narrow, angled *cala* offering relatively good protection, particularly near its head where there is a sandy beach, boathouse and café. There are breaking rocks close to the headland north of the *cala*. Anchor in 3–6m over sand and weed, open to the east and (depending on position) northeast. One option is to take a sternline ashore to the northern bank behind the central promontory. In settled conditions Cala Arsenau makes a feasible overnight anchorage.

⚓ CALA MITJANA

39°23'.2N 03°15'E

A very attractive triple *cala* with two sandy beaches and room for at least ten yachts. A tall white

Cala Arsenau viewed from southeast

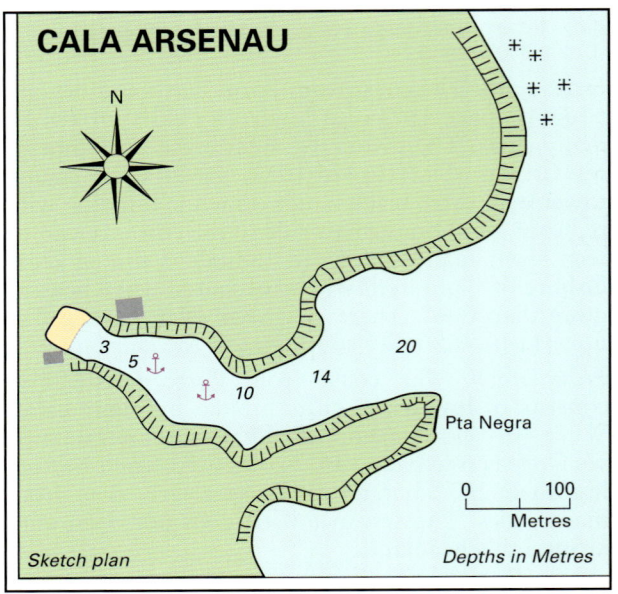

Cala Mitjana looking north with Cala Arsenau beyond. One of the most attractive anchorages in the Islands

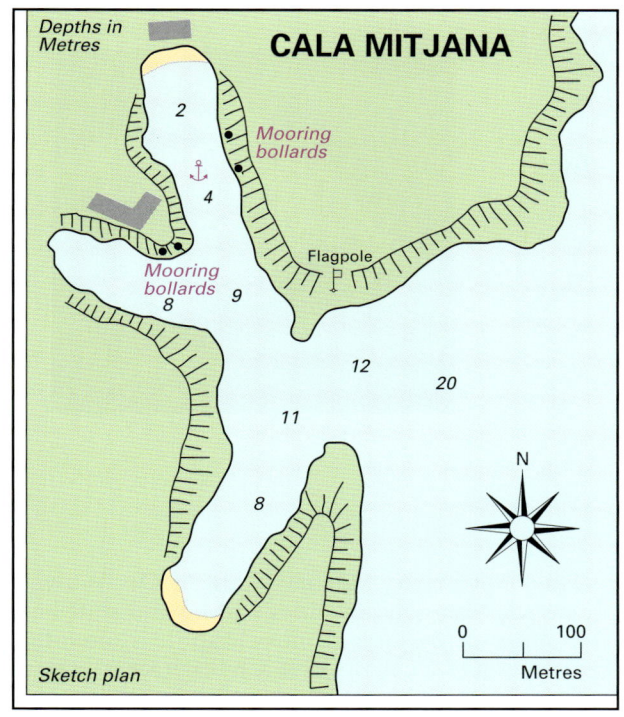

CALA MITJANA

Depths in Metres

Mooring bollards

Mooring bollards

Flagpole

Sketch plan

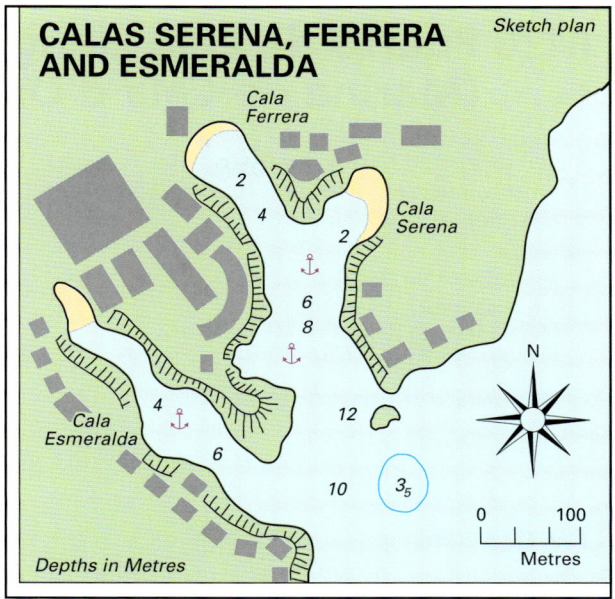

CALAS SERENA, FERRERA AND ESMERALDA

Sketch plan

Cala Ferrera

Cala Serena

Cala Esmeralda

Depths in Metres

flagstaff (often with flags) stands on the north side of the entrance and a pink-roofed building occupies the central headland. Swing wide of the rocky promontory below the flagstaff – a blind turn.

Anchor in 5m or less over sand and weed in the northern arm, setting a second anchor to limit swinging room, or take a line to the bollards set into the cliffs (see plan). This spot offers all-round protection.

⚓ CALAS SERENA, FERRERA AND ESMERALDA

39°22'.6N 03°14'.5E

A treble *cala* with sandy beaches surrounded by hotels and apartments, with a prominent island off the northern headland and breaking rocks to the south. There is an isolated shoal patch carrying 3.5–4m in the centre of the entrance.

Anchor in 3–6m over sand and weed, open (depending on position) to southeast and either east or south. Supermarkets and other shops nearby plus innumerable restaurants and cafés.

Looking northwest into Cala Esmeralda (left) with Cala Ferrera (centre) and Cala Serena (right)

III. MALLORCA

M20 Puerto de Cala Llonga (Marina de Cala d'Or)

A well protected harbour, easy to enter in most conditions and with berthing for over 500 vessels in very pleasant surroundings

Location
39°22'.2N 03°14'.2E

Communications
Marina (Puerto Deportivo Marina) VHF Ch 09
Marina Cala d'Or ☎ 971 65 70 70
Fax 971 65 70 68
Club Náutico de Cala d'Or ☎ 971 64 82 03
Fax 64 81 30
Email marinacalador@ctv.es

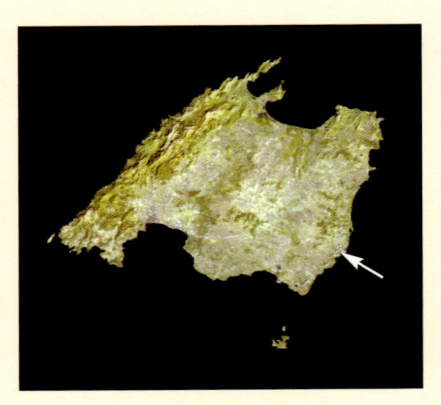

The marina

A single entrance from the sea leads to three calas: Cala Gran, Cala d'Or and Cala Llonga. Confusingly, the Marina Cala d'Or is located in the southernmost, Cala Llonga, rather than in Cala d'Or itself. Developers have not spoiled the very special nature of this place: it retains much of its original charm, and is still counted amongst the most beautiful *calas* on this coast of Mallorca.

The 565-berth Marina Cala d'Or is well protected, with good facilities and helpful staff but, as in most of Mallorca, is not cheap. It is often full in summer and a call on VHF Ch 09 prior to arrival would be wise. Approach and entrance are straightforward and good shelter is obtained, though in an east or southeast wind a heavy swell enters all three calas.

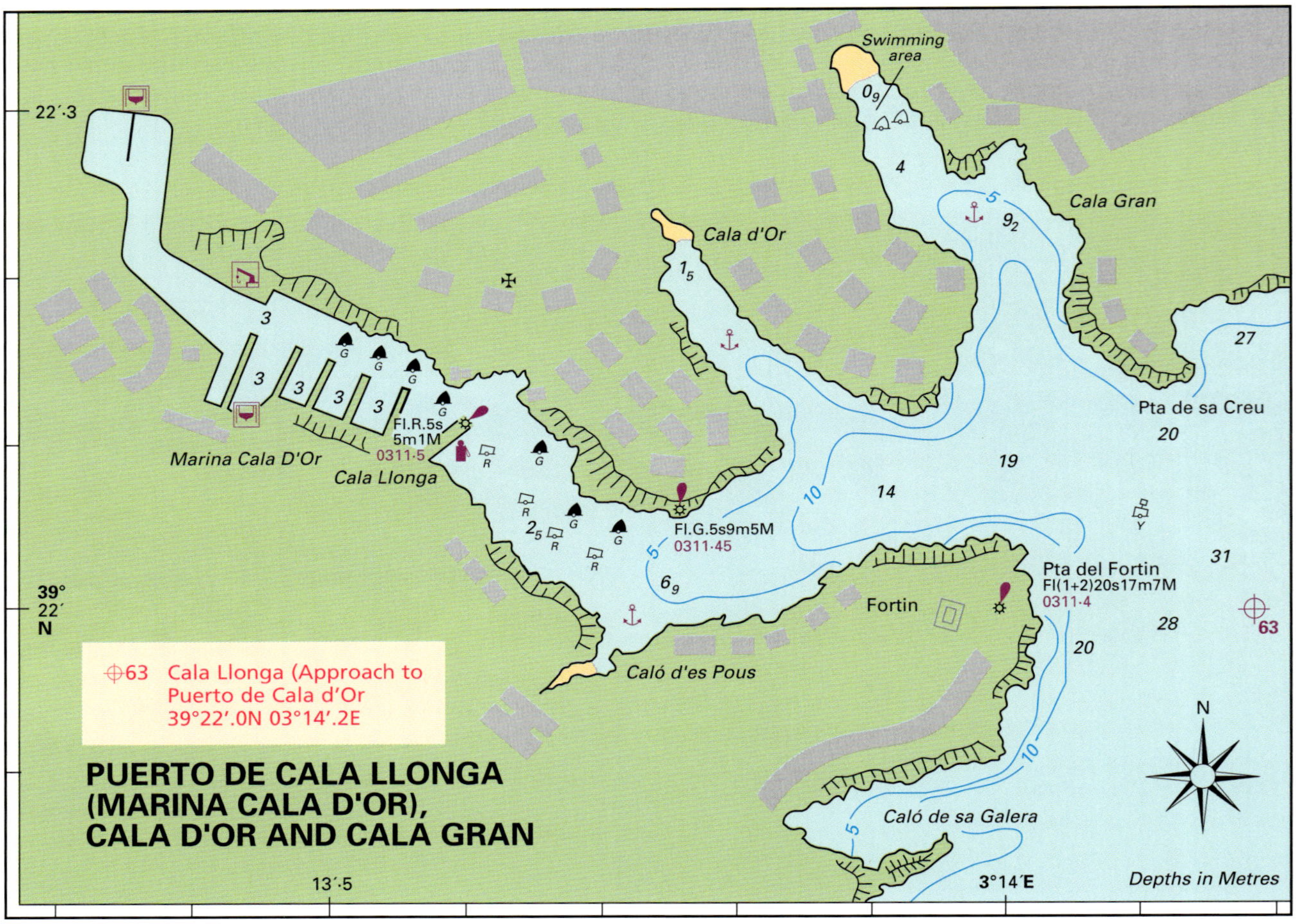

⊕63 Cala Llonga (Approach to Puerto de Cala d'Or 39°22'.0N 03°14'.2E

PUERTO DE CALA LLONGA (MARINA CALA D'OR), CALA D'OR AND CALA GRAN

View west into Cala Llonga

Cala Llonga Marina viewed from southeast

PILOTAGE

Approach

⊕63 39°22'.0N 03°14'.2E Cala Llonga (Approach to Puerto de Cala D'or)

From south Low rocky cliffs broken by two small *calas* extend northwards from Porto Petro (see plan on page 142). The low, square pinkish-brown fort on Punta del Fortin with its nearby lighthouse (Fl(1+2)20s17m7M, round white column on square white base, both with vertical black stripes, 6m) are easily identified.

From north There are five small *calas* in the low rocky cliffs that extend from Porto Colom southwards. Again the fort and lighthouse are easy to identify.

Anchorages in the approach

- *Cala Gran* Anchor in 5–6m over sand and weed in the middle of the *cala*, opposite a small squarish *cala* on the starboard side, open to the south and to swell from the southeast and east.

Anchorage in Cala Gran, Cala d'Or *GW*

There is a fine sandy beach which is buoyed-off for bathing.

- *Cala d'Or* This *cala* is sometimes closed in the summer by means of buoys, when anchoring is prohibited. Otherwise anchor in the centre of the *cala* in 3–5m over sand and weed patches off a small sandy beach, open to east and southeast and to swell from the east. This is the least sheltered of the three calas.
- *Cala Llonga* Anchor in the entrance to Caló d'es Pous in 2.5m over sand and weed, well out of the marina approach channel, open to the east.

Entrance

The outer entrance is straightforward with good depths. After passing the light structure on the north side of the entrance to Cala Llonga (Fl.G.5s9m5M, green column on white base 6m) and crossing the 5m contour, the buoyed channel into the marina will open up. A minimum depth of 2.5m should be found in the channel.

Berthing

Secure temporarily to the fuelling berth at the end of the marina south mole, having already called on VHF Ch 09. In this case a berth may be allocated over the radio.

Facilities

Water On the pontoons and the marina south mole.
Electricity 220v AC points on all pontoons, some 380v points.
Fuel Fuelling berth at the end of the marina south mole.
Provisions Supermarket and other shops nearby, with more at Porto Petro about one mile away. Produce markets on Wednesday and Saturday mornings in Santanyí, about seven miles away by road.
Ice From the supermarket.
Chandlery In the marina complex.
Repairs Small repairs to GRP and wood hulls and engineering jobs can be handled by the marina boatyard. Outside contractors are not allowed to work in the marina without permission. A 50-tonne travel-lift at the marina plus a new one at the head of the *cala* and a 5-tonne crane.
Sail repairs Can be arranged via the marina office.
Yacht club The Club Náutico de Cala d'Or has a clubhouse on the northeast side of Cala Llonga with bar, lounge, terraces and showers.

III. MALLORCA

Showers In the marina complex and the *club náutico*.
Laundry In the nearby tourist complex.
Banks Several in the nearby tourist complex.
Medical services In Cala d'Or and Santanyí.

Transport

Car hire/taxis In the town.
Buses Bus service to Santanyí, Palma, etc.

Sights ashore locally

The old fort on the headland is worth the walk. The unusual Punta de Fortin light structure can be seen from here.

Local event

A fiesta with waterborne processions is held on 15 August in honour of the area's patron saint, Santa Maria del Mar.

Eating out

Many restaurants, cafés and bars.

ANCHORAGES SOUTH OF PUERTO DE CALA LLONGA

⚓ CALA D'EGOS

39°21'.5N 03°13'.5E

A twisty, rocky-cliffed *cala*, surrounded by mainly luxurious detached houses plus a large hotel overlooking the beach at its head. Anchor in 3–5m over sand and weed, open to southeast and south.

⚓ CALA DEL LLAMP

39°21'.5N 03°13'.2E

A small *cala* between rocky cliffs on the northeast side of the entrance to Porto Petro (see plan on page 142). Anchor near the head in 3m over stone and weed, open to southeast and south. The area is also occupied by very luxurious detached houses, many with large gardens and pools.

Entrance to Porto Petro: Cala d'els Homos Morts and Cala de Sa Torre east on left, Cala del Llamp and Cala dels Mats right; Porto Petro centre

Cala de Sa Torre
Cala d'els Homos Morts
Cala del Llamp
Cala dels Mats
Porto Petro

M21 Porto Petro

A small and friendly harbour which has recently been expanded to berth 230 vessels up to 15m.

Location
39°21'.5N 03°13'E
Communications
VHF Ch 09
Port Authority ✆/*Fax* 971 65 70 12
Yacht harbour (Real Club Náutico Porto Petro)
✆ 971 65 76 57 *Fax* 971 65 92 16
Email rcnportopetro@btlink.net

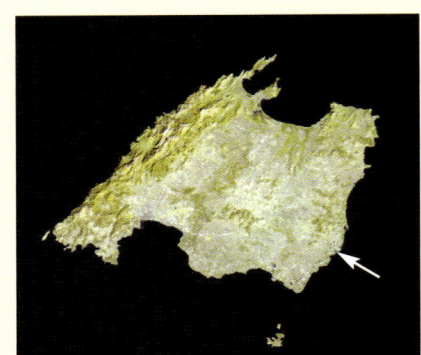

The harbour

A small but attractive yacht and fishing harbour occupying only one corner of a good-sized *cala* amidst relatively undeveloped surroundings and good anchorages. Porto Petro yacht harbour can berth 230 or so vessels up to 15m. In the past depth was a problem with much of the yacht harbour having less than 2m, but dredging has approximately doubled previous figures (and charges have increased to match!). A new mole has been built northeast from the rocky headland south of the harbour, increasing the number of deeper berths and blocking any southeasterly swell.

There is a sailing school and a branch of the Club Méditerranée in the *cala*. Facilities for visitors are still improving, but as usual the small yacht harbour is frequently crowded in summer. A preliminary call on VHF Ch 09 is advisable.

PILOTAGE

Approach

⊕64 39°21'.3N 03°13'.2E Off Porto Petro

From south Porto Petro lies 9.5 miles northeast of Punta Salinas (Fl(2+1)20s17m13M, white tower and building, narrow stone bands 17m), much of the coastline between comprising rough cliffs with few *calas* of any size until Calas Llombarts and Santanyí are reached (see plan on page 142). From Puerto de Cala Figuera with its conspicuous lighthouse (Fl.3s32m12M, white octagonal tower with vertical black stripes 6m) the coast is of low rocky cliffs. There is one small bay and a large deep *cala* before Porto Petro is reached. The Torre de Porto Petro and lighthouse (Fl(3+1)10s22m7M, white tower on square base with two vertical black stripes 9m) are obscured from west of south, and the entrance will be visible before they are seen.

From north From Cala Llonga and its low, square pinkish-brown fort and nearby lighthouse (Fl(1+2)20s17m7M, round white column on square white base, both with vertical black stripes, 6m), the coast is of low rocky cliffs broken by two small calas. The Torre de Porto Petro is very conspicuous from this direction, as is the lighthouse described above.

Anchorages in the approach

Anchorages in Cala del Mats, Cala d'els Homos Morts and Cala se sa Torre have now been replaced by mooring buoys which can be reserved in advance at www.balearslifeposidonia.eu/index.php?register_vars[lang]=en between 1st June and 30th September; for a maximum of two free nights per week. All may be affected by swell from the south, southeast or east. See Anchoring and Moorings on page 16.

Entrance

The *cala* entrance is wide and unencumbered. Buoys are sometimes laid in the approach to the yacht harbour, otherwise remain near the middle of the *cala* until the south mole is abeam before swinging to pass between it and the hammerhead. On no account venture beyond the north end of the hammerhead as depths shoal rapidly.

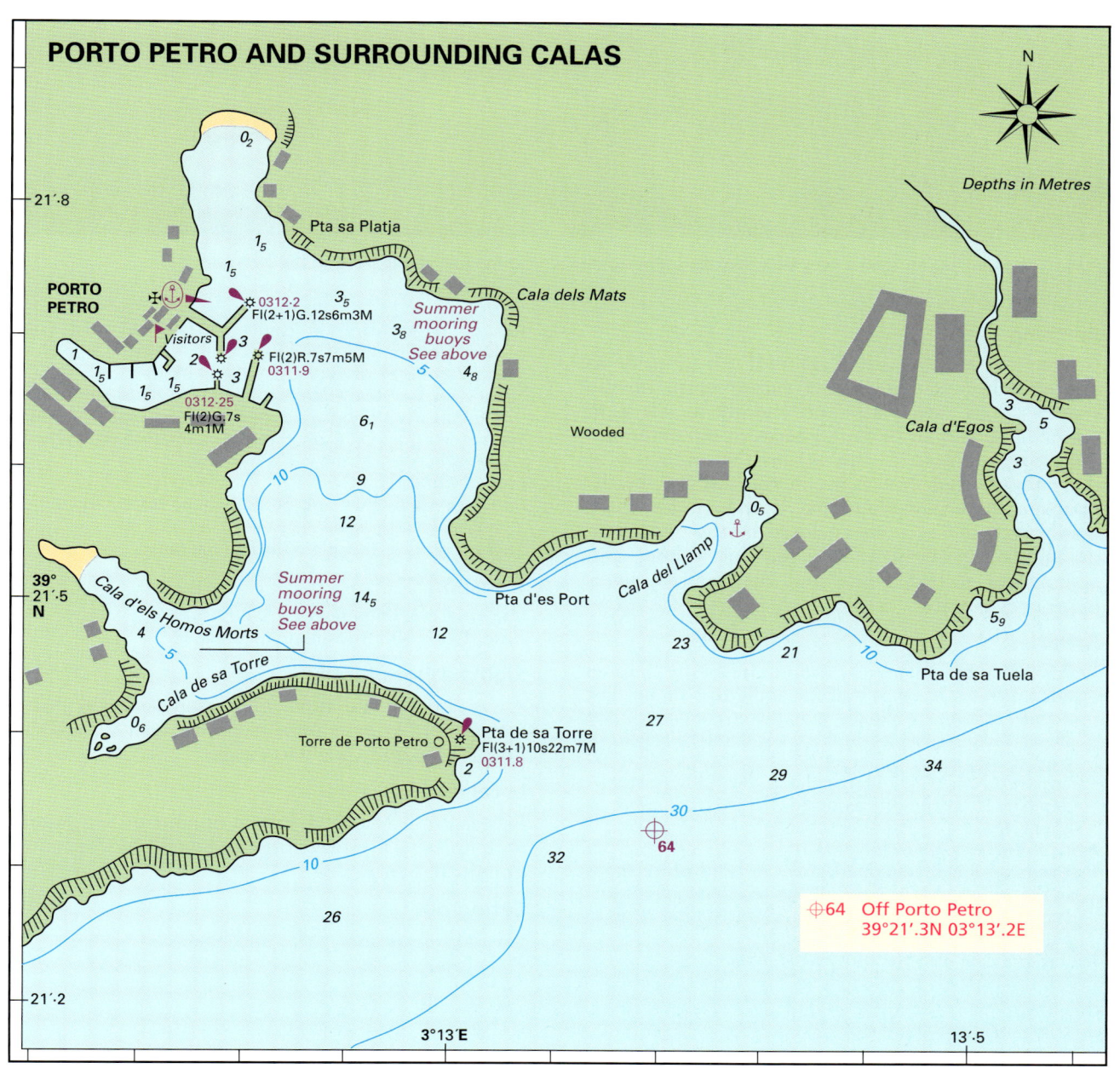

PORTO PETRO AND SURROUNDING CALAS

Porto Petro looking northeast over Cala dels Mats. Puerto de Cala Llonga just visible beyond the peninsula

Berthing

Contact the harbour office on VHF Ch 09 prior to arrival, otherwise look for a vacant berth on the visitors' quay (see plan) and enquire at the *club náutico*. 3m should be found between the outer and inner south moles, 2.5–3m against the south arm of the hammerhead and 2.5m in the visitors' berths opposite. Otherwise watch the depth-sounder whilst manoeuvring. The angle enclosed by the north arm of the hammerhead is reserved for fishing and commercial tourist boats and the shallow inner harbour is private.

Facilities

Water All water connectors ashore are of the push-in adaptor type. It seems that the authorities do not like people visiting by dinghy and filling containers, but prefer them to berth to take on water (for which, of course, they make a charge).

Electricity 220v AC on quays plus a few 380v points. A deposit is normally required before the cable is connected.

Fuel No fuel available (July 2010).

Provisioning Small supermarket nearby plus other shops in the village able to meet all day-to-day requirements. Produce markets Wednesday and Saturday mornings in Santanyí, some 5M away.

Ice From a café near the root of the mole.

Repairs Basic work on engines, woodwork and GRP possible. Enquire at the Réal Club Náutico. A shallow slipway north of the hammerhead mole.

Yacht club The Réal Club Náutico Porto Petro has a small clubhouse on the quay overlooking the yacht harbour.

Showers At the Réal Club Náutico. A small charge is made if not berthed in the yacht harbour.

Laundry In Cala d'Or.

Banks In Cala d'Or and Santanyí, the latter about five miles away by road.

Medical services In Cala d'Or and Santanyí.

Transport

Car hire/taxis Enquire at the *club náutico*.

Buses Bus service to Santanyí, Palma, etc.

Sights ashore locally

A visit to the old town of Santanyí should prove interesting. A '*petit train*' runs between Cala d'Or, Porto Petro and Cala Mondragó.

Local events

Fiestas are held on 25 July in honour of San Jaime, with horseback processions, and on 30 November in honour of San Andrés.

Eating out

Several restaurants, cafés and bars.

CALA BETWEEN PORTO PETRO AND PUERTO DE CALA FIGUERA

⚓ CALA MONDRAGÓ

39°21'N 03°11'.5E

A wide, attractive and largely unspoilt *cala* between low rocky cliffs, Cala Mondragó has four arms, two of which are buoyed off in summer for swimmers. Anchor in 4–8m over sand and some weed. There are café/bars on both the tourist beaches.

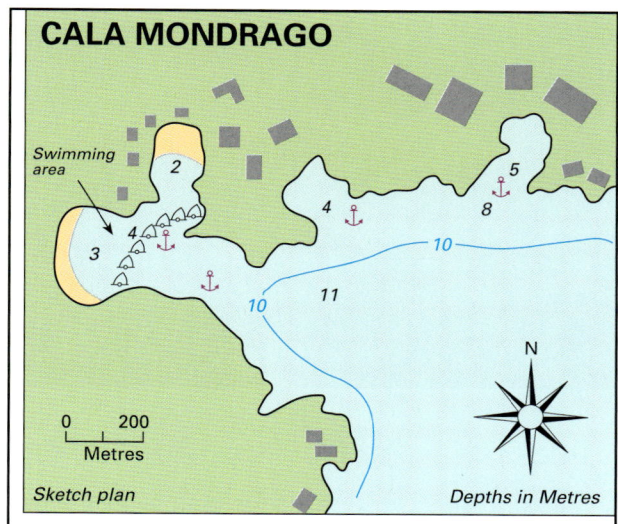

Cala Mondragó viewed from southwest, showing nearby bays

M22 Puerto de Cala Figuera (de Santanyí)

A very tiny harbour offering good shelter but with visitors' berths for only six vessels. Cabrera is 15M from here

Location
39°19'.8N 03°10'.5E

Communications
Puerto de Cala Figuera ☎ 971 64 52 42

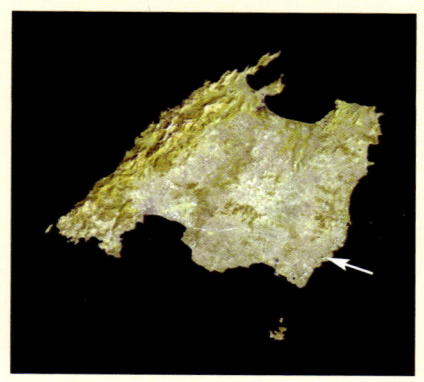

The harbour

A very small, attractive harbour devoted to fishing and a small day tourist trade. There is little space for yachts in the sheltered areas although six berths are reserved for visitors stern-to at the short mole. These would become untenable with strong wind or swell from east, southeast or south, as would the anchorage further out. For this reason the *cala* is only suitable for a night stop in settled weather. The approach is straightforward but the entrance can be difficult to locate as it is narrow and lies between cliffs. Facilities are very limited.

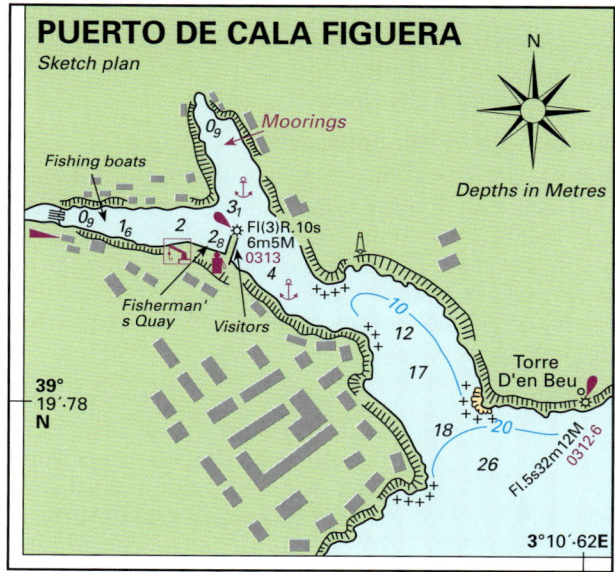

Puerto de Cala Figuera: small harbour with little space for visitors

PILOTAGE

From south Puerto de Cala Figuera lies seven miles northeast of Punta Salinas (Fl(2+1)20s17m13M, white tower and building, narrow stone bands 17m) see plan on page 142. Much of the coastline comprises rough cliffs with few *calas* of any size until Cala Llombarts is reached. The entrance to Cala Figuera can be identified in the close approach by the lighthouse (Fl.3s32m12M, white octagonal tower with vertical black stripes 6m) in front of a brownish stone watchtower on the northeast side of the entrance.

From north From Porto Petro the coast is of low, broken rocky cliffs with a wide, deep indentation at Cala Mondragó. If sailing close inshore the lighthouse and tower at Cala Figuera are screened by hills and not visible until the closer approach.

Anchorage in the approach

Anchor in the middle of the *cala* well clear of the mole in 4–8m over muddy sand and rock, possibly with a line ashore to limit swinging, open to east and southeast. If space and draught permit, anchorage may be found north of the mole, but this area is usually taken up by large fishing boats. Holding is reported to be poor in places.

Entrance

The red column on the end of the molehead can be seen from outside the entrance. Follow an S-shaped course, remaining near the centre of the *cala* and swinging wide of the foul ground extending from the two rocky points (see plan and photo). The wind can be fluky between the high cliffs and the seas heavy and confused, making it difficult for craft with limited auxiliary power.

Berthing

Six berths are reserved for visiting yachts on the southeast side of the mole, which require laying an anchor ahead and taking a stern line ashore. Holding is poor with weed on soft, shallow, muddy sand over rock; and plenty of scope is required. The inner end of the small breakwater to which visiting yachts may secure shoals to below 2m near the root and there is a rock with 0.3m over it close to the root. This position is completely exposed to onshore winds from between east and southeast, which bring in a nasty swell and the *cala* is therefore only suitable as a night stop in very settled conditions.

Yachts are not normally permitted to berth at the fishermen's quay inside the mole, though from Friday evening to Sunday evening it may be possible to lie alongside a fishing boat – which will probably wish to leave at 0600 on Monday morning. A small yacht can sometimes find a slot in the narrow northern arm. The western arm is very tight and is further obstructed by lines across the harbour. Plans to create a yacht harbour have been shelved for now.

Moorings

There are a few moorings in the northern arm but they are private and usually occupied.

Facilities

Water Tap at the (wholesale) fish market near the root of the mole.
Electricity Not available.

Fuel Diesel from a pump near the root of the mole. Petrol by can from a filling station at Santanyí some 2½ miles inland.

Provisions Supermarket 10 minutes' walk up the hill south of the harbour. A few small shops provide everyday requirements. There are many more shops in Santanyí and a market is held there on Wednesday and Saturday mornings.

Ice From one of the restaurants.

Repairs A 5-tonne crane on the fishermen's quay. Small slipway at the head of the western arm.

Banks In Santanyí.

Medical services In the village and at Santanyí, 2½ miles inland.

Transport

Car hire/taxis In Santanyí.
Buses Summer service to Santanyí and beyond.

Sights ashore locally

See *Porto Petro* on page 154.

Local events

Puerto de Cala Figuera is one of many harbours in Mallorca to honour Nuestra Señora del Carmen on 16 July with a fiesta including waterborne processions.

Eating out

Several restaurants and some cafés/bars near the harbour.

ANCHORAGES BETWEEN PUERTO DE CALA FIGUERA AND PUERTO COLONIA DE SANT JORDI

⚓ CALA SANTANYÍ

39°19'.7N 03°08'.9E

A *cala* surrounded by houses and hotels, its sandy beach roped off for swimming. There is a small tower on the east side of entrance and a small island on the west side, plus some breaking rocks inshore. Anchor in the middle of the *cala* in 5–10m over sand, open to east and southeast. In addition to the many swimmers there is a windsurfing school. See plan below, and page 158.

Cala Santanyí (right) viewed from southeast, with Cala Llombarts left

Cala Llombarts from southeast. The sea undercutting rock and creating caves is typical in this area

⚓ CALA LLOMBARTS

39°19'.5N 03°08'.6E

A double *cala*, though the northern arm is much the smaller, with rocky sides and a roped-off beach to the south. Mooring buoys have been laid, but it is not known if these are permanent. There is foul ground off the headland between the two. Anchor in 4–6m over sand and weed, open to east, southeast and possibly south.

⚓ CALA MARMOLS

39°17'.3N 03°05'.6E

A small and completely deserted *cala* between rocky cliffs, just over two miles northeast of Punta Salinas. Anchor in 3–6m over sand, open from east round to south.

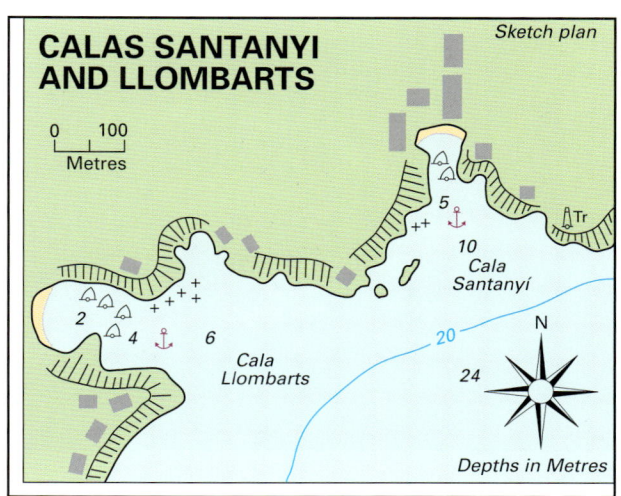

CALAS SANTANYI AND LLOMBARTS

Sketch plan

0   100
Metres

5
10
Cala Santanyí
20
24
N

2   4   6
Cala Llombarts

Tr

Depths in Metres

III. MALLORCA

See p.80
Palma
Cala Portixol *See p.177*
Fl(3)R.9s
El Molinar de Levante *See p.175*
Fl(2)R.7s
Cala Gamba *See p.172*
Fl.R
San Antonio de la Playa
See p.170

PUNTA SALINAS TO BAHIA DE PALMA

31
0318.8
Fl(2)15s41m22M
10

Bahia de Palma

Fl(4)R.11s
Puerto El Arenal
Fl.Y.5s 69
See p.168
Cala Blava
C Enderrocat
Fl(2)Y.10s
Pta Negra
Fl(2)Y.10s

30'

⊕31	Puerto de Palma	39°33'.4N 02°38'.5E
⊕65	Punta Salinas	39°15'.5N 03°03'.2E
⊕66	Off Puerto Colonia de Sant Jordi	39°18'.5N 02°59'.7E
⊕67	Puerto de la Rápita	39°21'.7N 02°57'.3E
⊕68	Cabo Blanco	39°21'.6N 02°47'.3E
⊕69	Off El Arenal approach	39°30'.3N 02°44'.5E

39°
25'
N

El Dorado
C Regana
Fl.Y.5s

50

See p.167

Pta Plana
Fl(1+3)12s16m7M
0315.8
S'Estanyol
Fl(2)R.6s7m5M
La Rápita
Fl.R.2.5s7m5M
See p.162

C Blanco
Oc.5s15M
0316
See p.166
See p.165

68
Cala Beltran/
Cala Pi
Ensenada de la Rápita
67
Pta Colonia de Sant Jordi

See p.162

Cala Santanyi

20'

50

See p.160
Pta Sal
See p.159
Fl(3)10.5s7M
Fl(4)G.12s5M
Playa des Carbo

See p.162
I Moltana
I Pelada
66
Cala Entugores
Cala Caragol
Cala Marmols
30
50

N

I des Caragol
Marine Reserve
Pta Negra
Pta Salinas
Fl(2+1)20s13M
Siren Mo(S)15s
0314
65

50
Freu de Cabrera

Depths in Metres

| 40' | 45' | 50' | 55' | **3°00'E** | 05' | 10' |

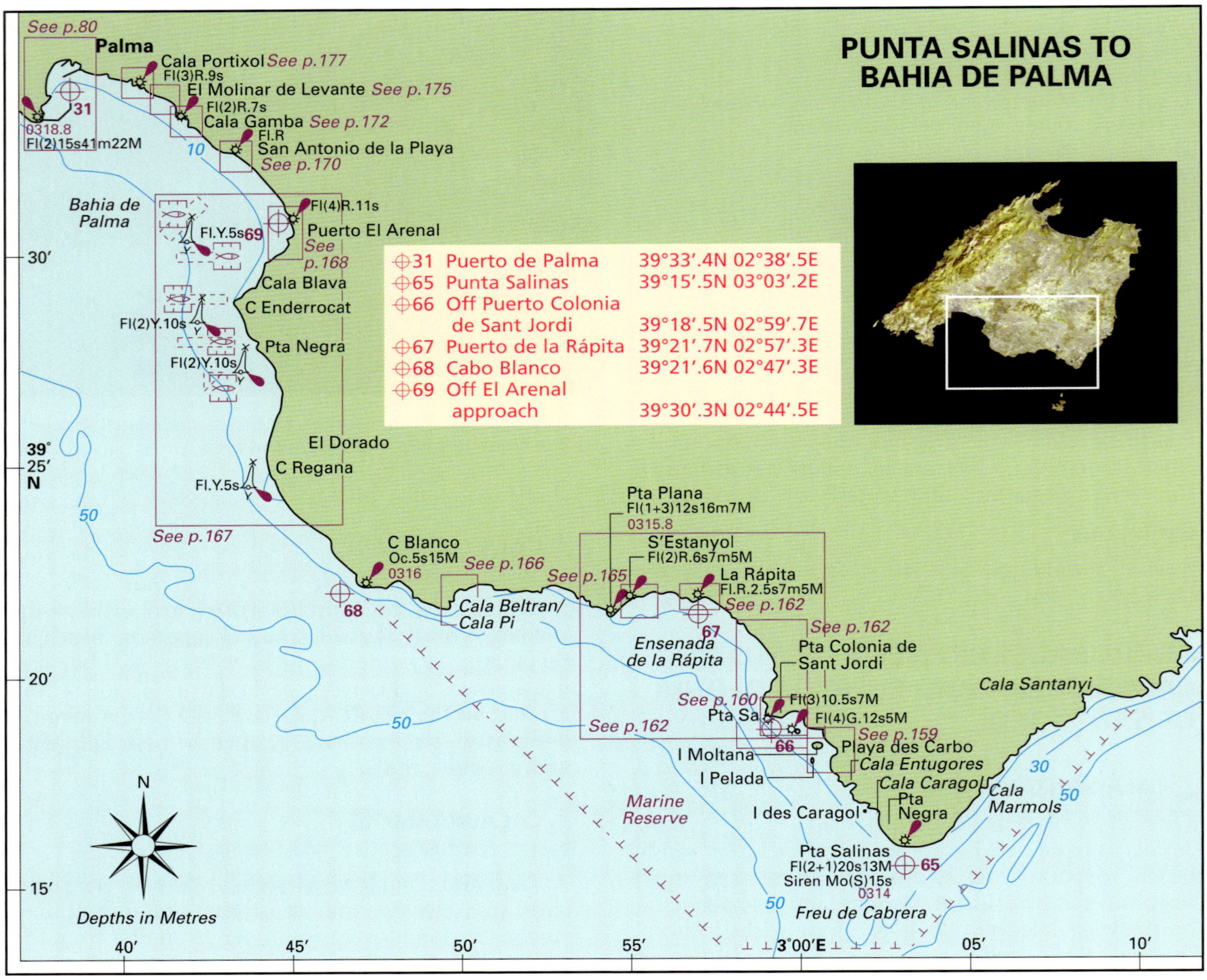

Punta Salinas looking northwest over the lighthouse

⊕65 39°15'.5N 03°03'.2E Punta Salinas

PUNTA SALINAS

39°16'N 03°03'.5E

A low, flat, wooded promontory edged by stony beaches and marked by a conspicuous lighthouse (Fl(2+1)20s17m13M, white tower and building with narrow stone bands 17m).

⚓ CALA CARAGOL

39°16'.7N 03°02'.5E

A wide bay one mile northwest of Punta Salinas and backed by pine woods, Cala Caragol has a particularly fine beach bounded to the southeast by the low rocky Punta Negra and to the northwest by Islote Caragol. Anchor in 2–5m over sand and weed, open to the south sector. The bay is often full of yachts during summer, but otherwise appears little visited. There are a few houses and a rough road.

Close to Punta Salinas lie these salt pans, worked since before Roman times *Graham Hutt*

Approaches to Puerto Colonia de Sant Jordi viewed northwest over Isla de na Guardia

⚓ CALA ENTUGORES

39°17'.4N 03°01'.8E

Much smaller and narrower than its neighbour Cala Caragol, Cala Entugores has no beach and is very shallow. Enter carefully watching the depth-sounder – it is reported to shoal to below 2.5m not far from the entrance. Anchor as depth dictates, open to south and west.

ANCHORAGES BETWEEN ISLA PELADA AND ISLA DE NA GUARDIA

⚓ PLAYA DES CARBÓ

39°18'.6N 03°00'.8E

⚓ PLAYA DE SA ROQUETAS

39°18'.3N 03°01'.1E

Playa des Carbó and Sa Roquetas (right-hand) with Islas Pelada and Moltana shown, viewed from south-southeast

Less than 1M northwest of Cala Entugores lies a long sandy beach with a spit running out to several small islands and rocky shoals close to the shore. These are Isla Pelada, Isla Moltana and Isla de na Guardia, the latter being the only one lit (Fl(4)G.12s7m5M), marking the approach to Puerto Colonia de Sant Jordi (see plan on page 160). Do not attempt to pass between these islands and the mainland with a keeled yacht (see plan).

Anchor in the northern bay (Playa des Carbó) in 3–4m over mainly sand, or further south (Playa de sa Roquetas) in 2–4m over sand and weed. There can be considerable disturbance from jet-skis and small speedboats in both anchorages.

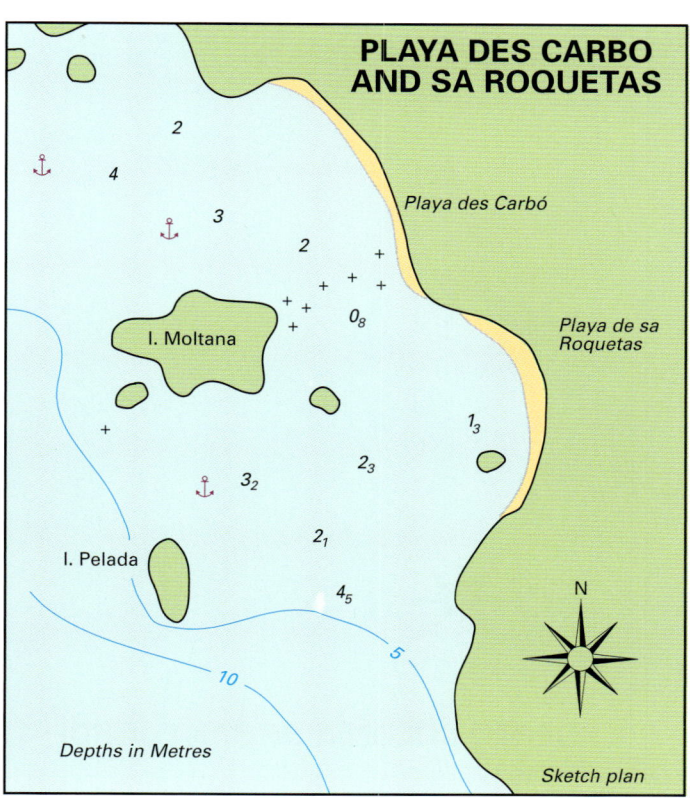

PLAYA DES CARBO AND SA ROQUETAS

I. Moltana

Playa des Carbó

Playa de sa Roquetas

I. Pelada

Depths in Metres

N

Sketch plan

III. MALLORCA

M23 Puerto Colonia de Sant Jordi (Puerto de Campos)

A small friendly fishing harbour with berths for over 300 vessels, usually full with local craft

Location
39°19'N 03°00'E

Communications
Puerto Colonia de Sant Jordi ☏/Fax 971 65 51 48

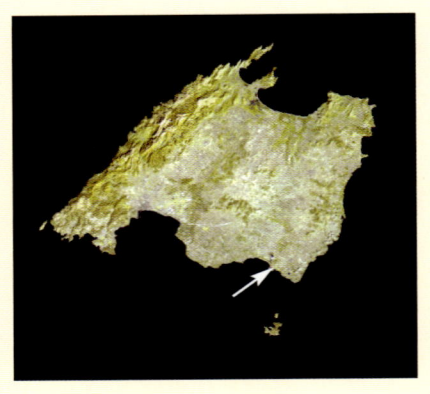

The harbour

A medium-sized fishing and yachting harbour, with 322 berths, mostly for small vessels. Much of the harbour is shallow and occupied by local craft. This is still basically a fishing port with nets being mended on the quayside. Facilities are limited but do include fuel, water and reasonable shopping. The approach is between low islands, some unmarked, and care is necessary.

Tourist ferries taking visitors to Cabrera berth inshore of the fuelling pontoon and leave the harbour at speed. This is a particular hazard if coming in by dinghy.

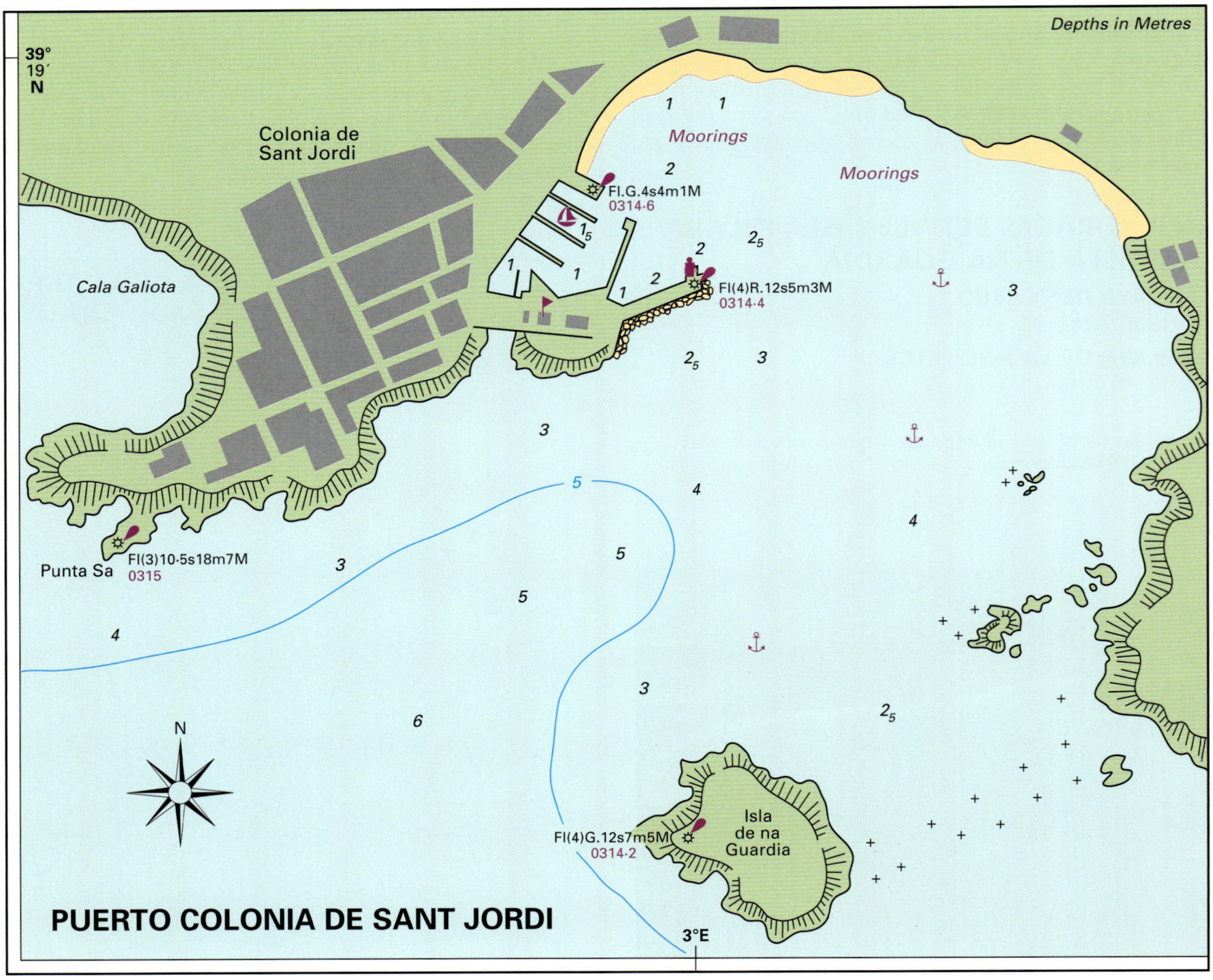

Depths in Metres

39° 19' N

Colonia de Sant Jordi

Moorings

Moorings

Fl.G.4s4m1M
0314·6

Cala Galiota

Fl(4)R.12s5m3M
0314·4

Punta Sa   Fl(3)10·5s18m7M
0315

N

Isla de na Guardia

Fl(4)G.12s7m5M
0314·2

PUERTO COLONIA DE SANT JORDI

3°E

Puerto Colonia de Sant Jordi and the anchorage east of the port

PILOTAGE

Approach

⊕66 39°18'.5N 02°59'.7E Off Puerto Colonia de Sant Jordi

From west From Cabo Blanco – a high promontory of steep light brown cliffs topped by a lighthouse (Oc.5s95m15M, white tower and building 12m) and an old watchtower – the coast is of low rocky cliffs with a long sandy bay, Playa del Trench, followed by more low rocky cliffs and the houses and apartment blocks of Colonia de Sant Jordi (see plan on page 158). Punta Sa may be identified by its conspicuous lighthouse (Fl(3)10.5s18m7M, white round tower with three black bands 12m) on the very end of the headland, though it is partially hidden if viewed from further north. The low and inconspicuous Isla Corberana some 550m offshore presents a potential hazard, particularly when sailing at night, though there is good water on either side.

From east Round the low, tree-covered Punta Salinas with its lighthouse (Fl(2+1)20s17m13M, white tower and building with narrow stone bands 17m) and follow the coast past several sandy bays and low inconspicuous islands until south of the lighthouse on Punta Sa (see above). Do not attempt to pass inside either Isla Moltona or Isla de na Guardia.

Anchorage in the approach

The northeast part of the bay between the harbour entrance and Isla de na Guardia is occupied by moorings; anchor further southwest in 3–5m over sand and weed, open to southwest and south, but with partial shelter from the southeast. Areas of the bottom are foul and a trip line is advisable.

Entrance

From a point south of the lighthouse on Punta Sa, enter the bay on a northeast course leaving Isla de la Guardia to starboard. Depths shoal as the harbour is approached, so sound carefully. Note that the end of the southeast breakwater projects some distance beyond the light structure (though entry at night is not recommended).

Berthing

Much of the inner harbour has depths of less than 1.5m, though the fuel berth and the southern side of the marina south mole are reported to have 2m. Secure at the fuel berth and consult harbour staff.

Facilities

Water Taps on quays and pontoons, and at the fuel berth.
Electricity 220v AC on quays and pontoons.
Fuel Diesel and petrol pumps inside the end of the south breakwater, but no more than 2m depth. Access can be difficult due to nearby tourist boats.
Provisions Supermarket and other shops in the town.
Ice From the fuel berth.
Repairs Small boatyard west of the *club náutico*. Two slipways, both very shallow. Engineer at the yard.
Yacht club The Club Náutico de Sant Jordi has a small clubhouse at the south end of the harbour.
Laundry In the town.
Banks In the town.
Medical services Basic medical services available.

Transport

Car hire/taxis In the town.
Buses Bus service to Ses Salinas and on to Palma, etc.
Ferries Ferries to the nearby island of Cabrera 12M south. See page 178.

ANCHORAGES BETWEEN PUERTO COLONIA DE SANT JORDI AND PUERTO DE LA RÁPITA

The headland southwest of Puerto Colonia de Sant Jordi southeast has several anchorages and offlying islands as follows. See plan on page 158 and below.

⚓ ENSENADA DE LA RÁPITA, SOUTHEAST CORNER

39°19'.7N 02°59'.4E

A well-sheltered anchorage close north of the headland on which Colonia Sant Jordi stands, and south of Playa del Trench. Anchor in 3m or more over sand and weed northeast of an old and dilapidated quay, open to northwest (short fetch) and west. There is a fine beach to the east and a large hotel near the root of the quay.

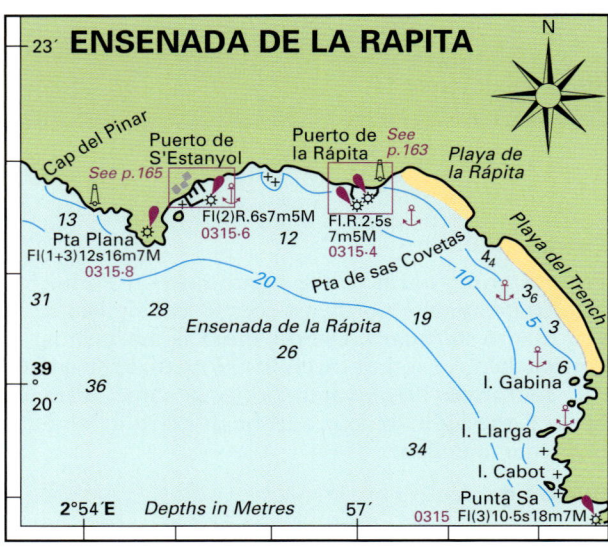

Ensenada de la Rápita: Isla Gabina can just be seen right of picture

⚓ BAY SOUTH OF ISLA GABINA

39°20'N 02°59'.5E

Similar to the above, but with much less shelter from the southwest.

⚓ PLAYA DEL TRENCH

39°20'.8N 02°59'E

An open bay anchorage off a fine sandy beach. Anchor in 3m+ over sand and weed. A submarine cable runs in a west-southwest direction from Punta de sas Covetas at the north end of the beach.

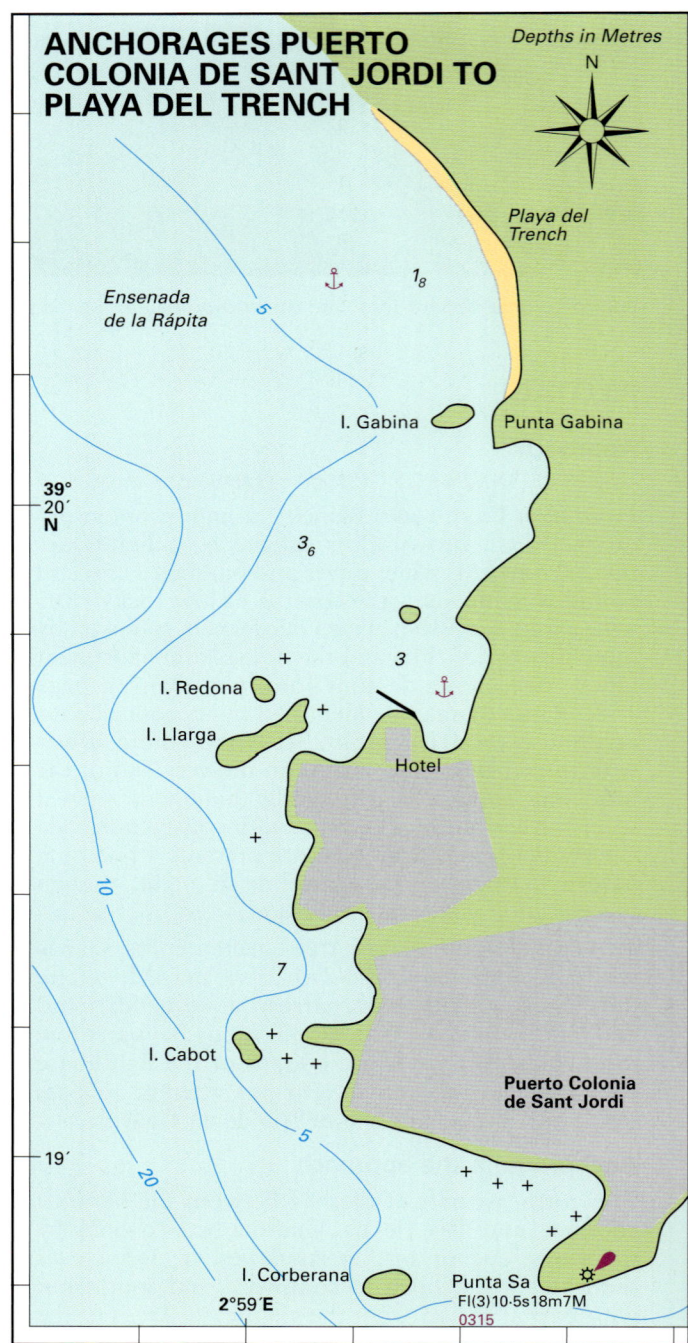

M24 Puerto de la Rápita

A large, safe and friendly yacht habour with berthing for 460 yachts just W of the finest beach in Mallorca: Playa del Trench. A good departure point for Isla de Cabrera

Location
39°21'.7N 02°57'.4E

Distances
Cabrera 12M

Communications
VHF Ch 09
Club Náutico de la Rápita ① 971 64 00 01
Fax 971 64 08 21
Email velarapita@webhouse.es

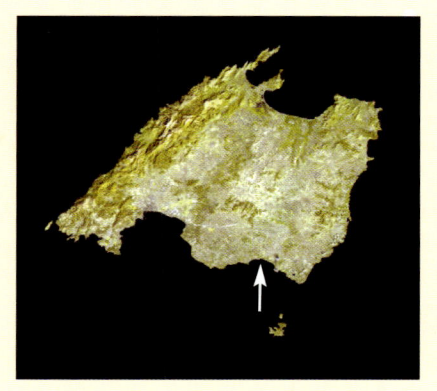

The port

Puerto de la Rápita is a large and modern artificial yacht harbour with 460 berths and excellent facilities, situated at the northwest end of the long Playa del Trench. It is easy to enter and offers good protection once inside, though a heavy swell from southeast or south could make the final approach dangerous due to shoaling water.

Puerto de la Rápita is a favourite departure point for Isla de Cabrera, just 12 miles south, and the marina staff are happy to help visitors apply for the necessary permit. (For details of *Isla* and *Puerto de Cabrera* see the following chapter.)

PILOTAGE

Approach

⊕67 39°21'.7N 02°57'.3E S Puerto de la Rápita

From west Round Punta Plana (Fl(1+3)12s16m7M, white tower with black bands on building 12m) and pass Puerto de S'Estanyol in the northwest corner of the bay; a northeast course should then be set towards the far end of the houses of La Rápita. On closer approach the harbour breakwater will be seen with an old watchtower (18m) behind.

From east Allow Punta Sa (Fl(3)10.5s18m7M, white round tower with three black bands 12m) an offing

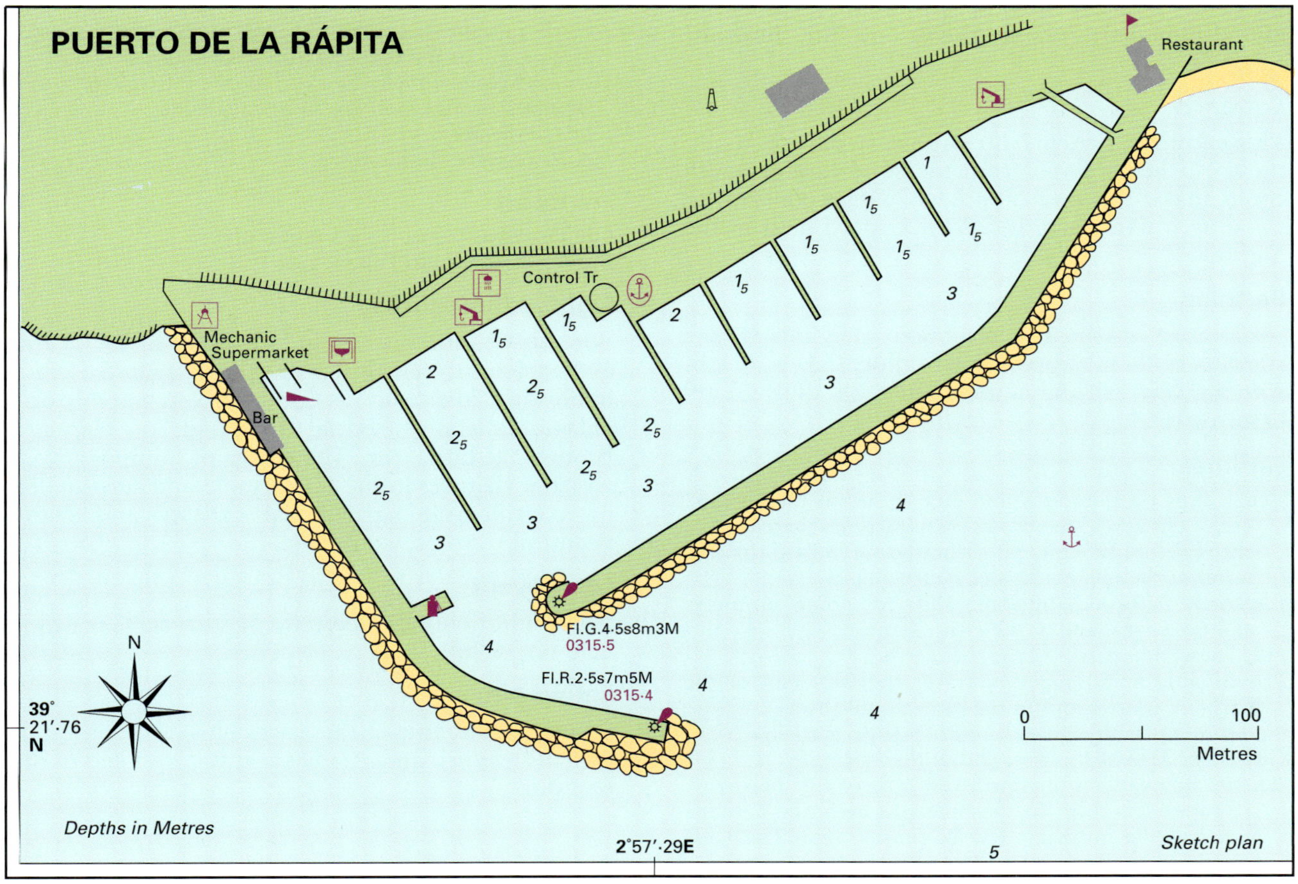

PUERTO DE LA RÁPITA

Restaurant

Control Tr

Mechanic
Supermarket

Bar

Fl.G.4·5s8m3M
0315·5

Fl.R.2·5s7m5M
0315·4

N

39°
21'·76
N

Depths in Metres

2°57'·29**E**

0   100
Metres

Sketch plan

5

Puerto de la Rápita looking north

of at least ½ mile in order to clear Isla Corberana, then steer northwest into the wide Ensenada de la Rápita towards the houses of La Rápita. On nearing the harbour, the breakwater and watchtower will come into view.

Anchorage in the approach

In calm weather anchor in 4–5m over sand, 200–300m east or southeast of the harbour entrance.

Entrance

The entrance presents no problems day or night, though a heavy swell from the southeast or south could make the final approach dangerous due to shoaling water. There is a 2-knot speed limit in the harbour.

Berthing

Secure stern-to at the reception quay inside the southwest breakwater until allocated a berth. Alternatively call the marina office on VHF Ch 09 before arrival.

Facilities

Water Taps on pontoons and quays, and at the visitors' quay. However, the water is sometimes brackish so check before filling tanks. It has been reported that the water at the fuel berth is of better quality.

Electricity 220v AC and some 380v AC points on quays and pontoons, and at the visitors' quay.

Fuel Diesel and petrol at the fuel berth.

Provisioning Small supermarket at the west end of the harbour, more shops in the town ½ mile away.

Ice From a machine near the marina supermarket.

Chandlery Two at the west end of the harbour.

Repairs Boatyard in the northwest area of the marina. A 50-tonne travel-lift in the boatyard area and 7-tonne crane at the northeast end of the harbour. The wide slipway nearby has been rendered inaccessible by a fixed walkway.

Engineers Cosme Oliver ① 971 64 01 99 *Fax* 971 64 00 21 at the west end of the harbour are official service agents for Caterpillar, Honda, Perkins, Tohatsu, Vetus, Volvo Penta and Yamaha.

Yacht club The Club Náutico de la Rápita has a large and well-appointed clubhouse with a bar and terrace restaurant at the east end of the harbour.

Showers Several shower blocks opposite the control tower.

Communications Good free Wi-Fi available.

Bank In the town.

Medical services In the town.

Transport

Car hire/taxis Consult the marina office.

Buses Bus service to Palma, etc.

Sights ashore locally

For those interested in ancient history and archaeological remains, this area is littered with interesting 'finds' such as Capicorp Vey, a prehistoric village, Sollerich (a burial cave) and Son Herue, a Bronze Age burial site. The village of Campos is well worth a visit, set in the countryside and surrounded by considerable agricultural activity and many beautiful restored windmills.

Local event

A fiesta in honour of Nuestra Señora del Carmen is held on 16 July.

Eating out

Several restaurants in the town, plus a restaurant at the *club náutico* and a café/bar at the west end of the harbour.

M25 Puerto de S'Estanyol de Migjorn (El Estañol)

A small harbour less than 2M W of Puerto de la Rápita, but usually full with local vessels

Location
39°21'.7N 02°55'.3E

Communications
VHF Ch 09
Club Náutico de S'Estanyol ☎ 971 64 00 85
Fax 971 64 06 82
Email cne@cnestanyol.com
www.cnestanyol.com

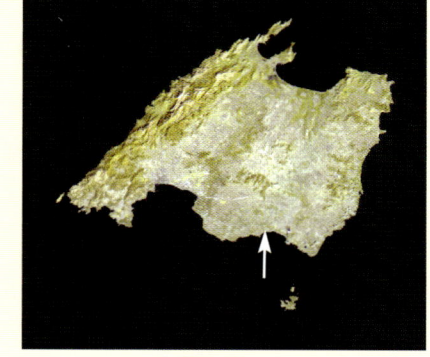

The harbour

A small, square, artificial harbour close east of Punta Plana, occupied by fishing boats and a few yachts under 12m or so. Approach and entrance are not usually difficult but would be dangerous in strong winds and swell from southeast or south due to shallow water in the approach. Facilities are fair and everyday shopping requirements can be met in the strip of coastal development which joins up with La Rápita to the east.

Ambitious plans to more than double the size of the harbour by means of a new breakwater enclosure have been under discussion for years. Work had still not started in July 2010 and it is unlikely that permission will be granted (as in other places, because of environmental concerns).

PILOTAGE

Approach

From west Once past Punta Plana (see plan on page 158), Puerto de S'Estanyol lies 0.6 miles north-northeast of the headland past a small, low-lying island which should be left to port.

From east Heading northwest through Ensenada de la Rápita, Puerto de S'Estanyol lies 0.6 miles north-northeast of the headland.

Entrance

Approach the eastern corner of the harbour heading northwest to round the head of the south breakwater at slow speed. The entrance is narrow and may be partially blocked by moored boats. There is a 2-knot speed limit. Note that the close approach and entrance are shallow, making it dangerous in heavy swell from south or southeast.

Berthing

Secure to the inner side of the south breakwater as space permits and visit the harbour office for

Puerto de S'Estanyol. Some development around the port, but plans for a much larger marina have been shelved for now due to environmental concerns

III. MALLORCA

Sketch plan

0   100
Metres

Fl(2)G.7s8m1M
0315·7

Fl(2)R.6s7m5M
0315·6

N

PUERTO DE S'ESTANYOL

Depths in Metres

39°21'·65N

2°55'·17E

allocation of a berth. Depths are 2.5–3m near the breakwater head shoaling to 2m or so at the elbow.

Facilities

Water Taps on quays and pontoons.

Electricity 220v AC points at foot of lamp-posts and at normal supply points.

Fuel Diesel pump at the head of the north mole, petrol pump at its root (i.e. by can only).

Provisioning Everyday supplies from a supermarket and other shops in the nearby town.

Ice From the bar.

Repairs A 12.5-tonne crane, and slipway near the root of the north mole. Motor mechanic available for engine repairs.

Yacht club The Club Náutico S'Estanyol has a small clubhouse with restaurant, bar, terrace and two tennis courts.

Showers In the west corner of the harbour.

Bank In La Rápita, about 1½ miles away.

Hospital/medical services In Lluchmayor, eight miles inland.

Transport

Car hire/taxis Consult the harbour office.

Buses Bus service to Palma, etc.

Eating out

A few restaurants and several café/bars.

ANCHORAGES WEST OF PUERTO DE S'ESTANYOL

⚓ CALA PI

39°21'.6N 02°50'.1E (entrance to *cala*).

A beautiful and very popular *cala* between high cliffs, but extremely narrow and often crowded (avoid weekends when charter yachts are setting out or returning). See plan on page 158. There is a conspicuous stone tower on the headland southeast of the entrance. Anchor in 2–8m over sand and some weed either using a stern anchor or taking a line ashore, to restrict swinging. At about 3.5m depth beware an isolated rock, with 1.3m clearance, close

Cala Pi right and the smaller Cala Beltran left, viewed from the north

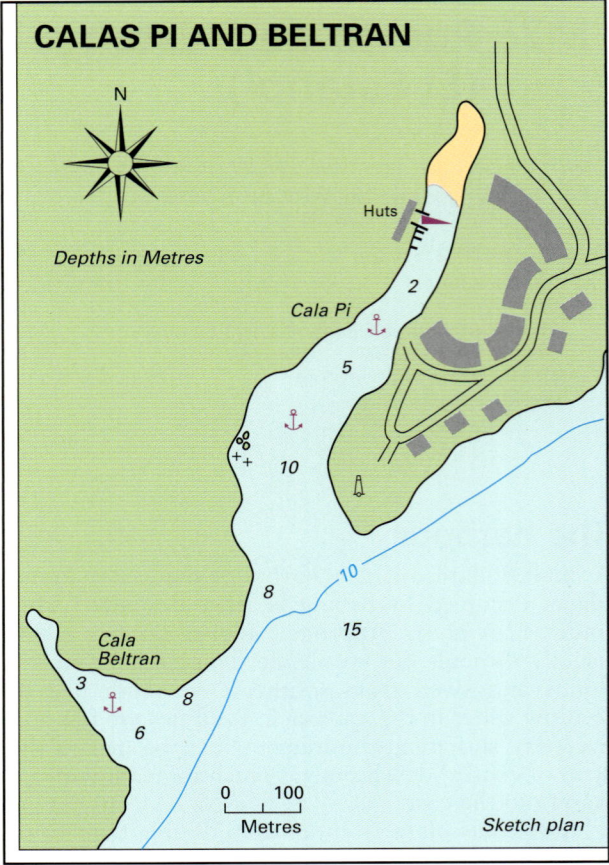

CALAS PI AND BELTRAN

N

Depths in Metres

Huts

Cala Pi

2

5

10

10

8

15

Cala Beltran

3

8

6

0   100

Metres

Sketch plan

to the cliff where rope tails from old shorelines abound. There is also a substantial mooring block and ground tackle in the centre of the *cala* at this same depth, which may be a mooring in season but could be used as a swing limiter in low season. There are fishermen's huts and a rough slipway by the sandy beach at the head of the *cala*, and a small tourist development with cafés and restaurants, etc. to the east.

⚓ CALA BELTRAN

39°21'.6N 02°50'E

A small *cala* between rocky cliffs just west of Cala Pi, where it is possible to anchor in 3–5m over sand, open to east and southeast.

⊕68 39°21'.6N 02°47'.3E Cabo Blanco

BAHÍA DE PALMA MARINE RESERVE

A marine reserve area has been created off Cabo Enderrocat, 3M north of Cabo Blanco, with four lightbuoys indicating the extremities. Vessels should keep outside these buoys.

Buoys

34190(S) **Buoy A** 39°24'.7N 02°43'.8E Fl.Y.5s5M pillar with × topmark (S marker)

34191(S) **Buoy 2** 39°25'.5N 02°43'.6E Fl(2)Y.10s3M can with × topmark

34192(S) **Buoy 1** 39°28'.4N 02°42'.2E Fl(2)Y.10s3M can with × topmark

34193(S) **Buoy C** 39°29'.9N 02°42'.1E Fl.Y.5s5M pillar with × topmark. (N marker)

CALA BLAVA MOORING BUOYS

Mooring buoys have been laid in Cala Blava, about 1.5km south of Puerto El Arenal in the Bay of Palma, which may be reserved in advance at www.balearslifeposidonia.eu/index.php?register_vars[lang]=en for 1st June to 30th September. See plan below and the Anchoring and Moorings section on page 16 for further details.

⊕69 Off El Arenal approach
39°30'.3N 02°44'.5E

N

Depths in Metres

BAHIA DE PALMA MARINE RESERVE

M26 Puerto El Arenal

A large yacht harbour at the southeast end of the Playa de Arenal, with berthing for over 600 yachts up to 25m

Location
39°30'.2N 02°44'.9E

Communications
VHF Ch 09
Club Náutico El Arenal ☎ 971 44 01 42 / 44 02 67
Fax 971 44 05 68
Email administracion@cnarenal.com
www.cnarenal.com

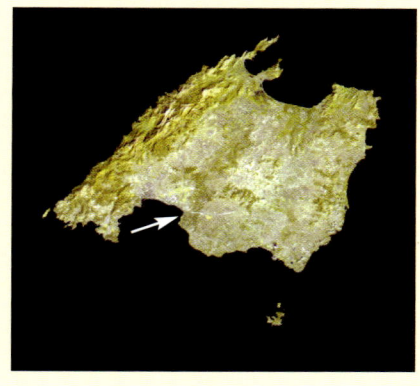

The harbour

A large, modern yacht harbour with 667 berths for vessels up to 25m and with 3m+ depths throughout. Built at the southeast end of another spectacular and popular beach: Playa de Arenal, the new harbour is built alongside the small old harbour which has now been improved.

To the south a low rocky coast is backed initially by large houses and, further on, by unspoilt open countryside.

The harbour offers first class facilities including a lovely clubhouse with restaurant and pool and is far enough away from the tourist areas not to suffer from traffic or other noise. El Arenal is now full of charter craft and has become very expensive – even the Cabrera permit is now charged for! This is a useful place for a crew change as the airport is close by.

Approach and entrance are normally without problem, but heavy winds and swell from the southwest quadrant could render the close approach and entrance dangerous.

Puerto El Arenal is one of many suitable departure points for Isla de Cabrera and the *club náutico* are happy to help visitors apply for the necessary permit.

For details of Isla and Puerto de Cabrera see the following chapter.

III. MALLORCA

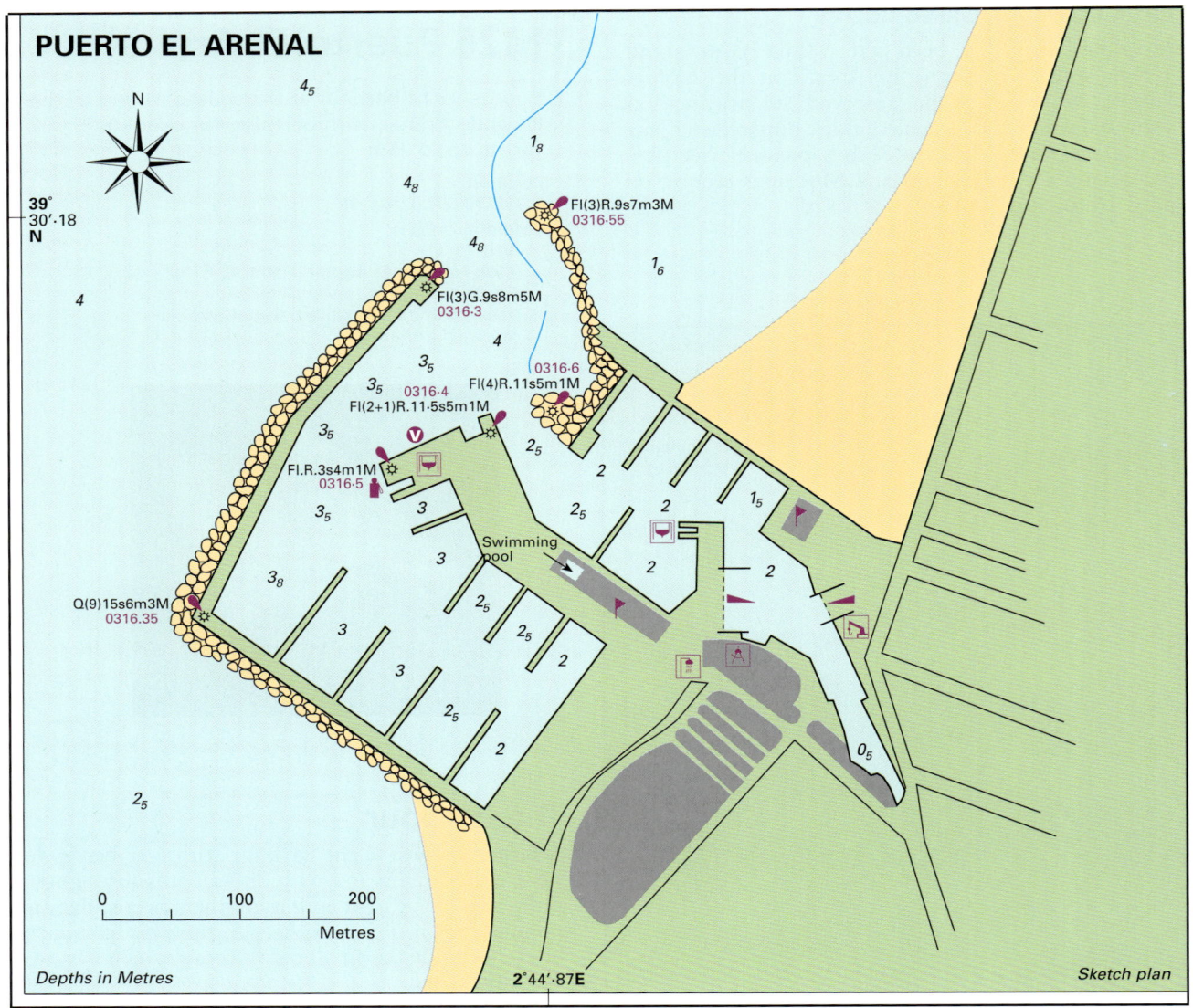

PUERTO EL ARENAL

Fl(3)R.9s7m3M
0316·55

Fl(3)G.9s8m5M
0316·3

0316·6

Fl(4)R.11s5m1M

Fl(2+1)R.11·5s5m1M
0316·4

Fl.R.3s4m1M
0316·5

Q(9)15s6m3M
0316·35

Swimming pool

0 100 200
Metres

Depths in Metres 2°44'·87E Sketch plan

39°
30'·18
N

39° 30'·18 N

PILOTAGE

Approach

⊕69 39°30'.3N 02°44'.5E Off El Arenal

For outer approach see *Puerto Colonia de Sant Jordi* on page 161 and plan on page 158.

From west (as above) Round the very prominent Punta Cala Figuera which has a lighthouse (Fl(4)20s45m15M, white round tower with black diagonal stripes on building 24m) and radio masts on its steep cliffs. Cross the Bahía de Palma heading just north of east towards Cabo Enderrocat, with an inconspicuous tower on its summit, at the northern end of a line of high cliffs. El Arenal lies two miles northeast of this headland, at the southeast end of a sandy beach backed by solid high-rise development.

From east From Cabo Blanco follow the cliffs north-northwest round Cabo Enderrocat, keeping well clear of the new Marine Reserve buoys. See page 167. El Arenal lies two miles northeast off this headland, at the southeast end of a sandy beach backed by a solid high-rise development.

Anchorage in the approach

Anchor either side of the harbour in 3m+ over sand and weed, open southwest–west–northwest.

Entrance

The entrance is easily seen and without hazards, other than those posed by (or to) stray bathers, snorkellers, sailboards and pedalos. The entrance is regularly dredged to 4–5m with 3m throughout the yacht harbour. It is still wise to keep close to the southern breakwater head on entering. There is a 2-knot speed limit.

Berthing

Visitors lie stern-to against the head of the central mole, between the slipway and the fuel berth. Lazy lines are provided, tailed to the quay.

Facilities

Water Water points on the pontoons and quays.
Electricity 220v AC available on all quays and pontoons plus some 380v points.
Fuel Diesel and petrol from pumps at the west end of the central mole.

Puerto El Arenal looking southeast

Provisions Everyday supplies from nearby shops and supermarkets, with many more in Palma six miles away. Hypermarket less than five miles away on the road between Palma and the airport. A market is held in the town on Tuesday and Friday, with a clothes market on Thursdays.

Ice From the *club náutico* bar.

Chandlery Just outside the main gate to the harbour.

Repairs Layup area on the central mole with some services available. Fully fledged boatyards in Palma. For repairs and general maintenance Renav is recommended locally. A 50-tonne travel-lift at the west end of the central mole. A smaller lift and 3-tonne mobile crane in the old harbour. Two slipways in the old harbour and one at the end of the central mole. Engineers available through the *club náutico*.

Yacht club The Club Náutico El Arenal has an elegant clubhouse with restaurant, TV room, bar, terraces, large swimming pool and laundry. Use of the club facilities, including the pool, is a bonus here. The old clubhouse to the northeast also has a restaurant and is used by fishermen and dinghy sailors.

Showers At the east and southeast corners of the harbour area.

Communications Free Wi-Fi available.

Banks In the town.

Medical services In the town. Hospital in Palma six miles away.

Transport

Car hire/taxis In the town.

Buses Frequent bus service to Palma.

Ferries From Palma to the other islands and mainland Spain.

Air services Busy international airport three miles away.

Sights ashore locally

Palma and all its charms are only a short bus ride away.

Eating out

Many restaurants, cafés and bars along the beach.

ANCHORAGES NORTHWEST OF PUERTO EL ARENAL IN THE BAY OF PALMA

⚓ BAHÍA DE PALMA, NORTHEAST SIDE

In settled weather it is possible to anchor off the shore virtually anywhere between El Arenal and Palma itself; the coast is in the main gently sloping, with wide sandy beaches (see plan on page 158). Anchor to suit draught off the open beach. If swimming buoys are laid, ensure you do not encroach on them. Vessels doing so are fined heavily.

Bahía de Palma looking northwest over Puerto de San Antonio. Palma beyond

III. MALLORCA

M27 Puerto de San Antonio de la Playa (Ca'n Pastilla)

Offering excellent protection and facilities for nearly 400 berths up to 15m, this new port is close to the airport and its accompanying noise, being directly under the flight path

Location
39°31'.8N 02°43'.0E

Communications
VHF Ch 09
Club Marítimo San Antonio de la Playa ☎ 971 74 50 76/ 26 35 12 *Fax* 971 26 16 38.
Email cmsap@cmsap.com
www.cmsap.com

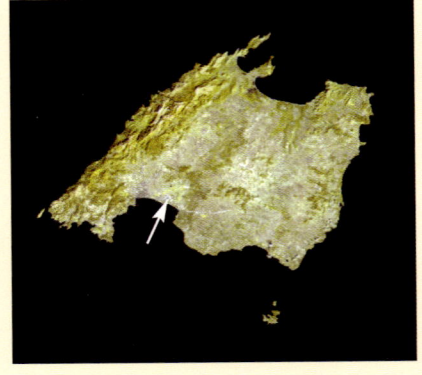

The harbour/marina

A good-sized yacht harbour with nearly 400 berths, handy for the airport (though paying the price with a good deal of aircraft noise) and with better than average facilities. It is easy to approach and enter in normal conditions though with strong onshore winds and swell it could become dangerous due to shallows in the close approach.

Puerto de San Antonio de la Playa lies very close to the large tourist resort of Ca'n Pastilla with its many high-rise hotels and apartment blocks, and is occasionally referred to by this name. An excellent sandy beach stretches for over two miles to the southeast.

PILOTAGE

Approach

⊕70 39°31'.7N 2°43'.0E Puerto de San Antonio

For outer approach see *Puerto Colonia de Sant Jordi* on page 161 and plan on page 158.

From west (as above) Round the very prominent Punta de Cala Figuera which has a lighthouse (Fl(4)20s45m15M, white round tower with black diagonal stripes on building 24m) and radio masts on its steep cliffs. Cross the Bahía de Palma on a northeast course; planes taking off and landing from Palma airport give a good indication of the position of this harbour. In the closer approach the long sandy Playa del Arenal, which is backed by a line of high-rise buildings, will be seen. Near the northwest end of this beach is a separate group of high-rise buildings with the harbour in front. The small, low Islote Galera which has reefs extending 100m southwest, lies 0.5 miles northwest of the harbour entrance.

From east Round cabos Blanco and Enderrocat into Bahía de Palma. Once past the Marine Reserve, Puerto San Antonio lies almost 3.3 miles distant.

Anchorage in the approach

Anchor southeast of the entrance in 5m over sand, or in nearby Cala Estancia (39°32'.1N 2°42'.8E), a small *cala* just west of the port. This is protected by two short breakwaters but is shallow (1–1.5m) and open to the south. A particularly large hotel overlooks it from the west and there is a busy road nearby.

Entrance

An extension to the north end of the southwest breakwater has improved protection, particularly at the visitors' quay, but has turned the entrance into an S-bend. Observe the 2-knot speed limit.

PUERTO DE SAN ANTONIO DE LA PLAYA

Ca'n Pastilla

0   100
Metres

0316·72
Fl(4)G.13s6m3M

Visitors

Fl(4)R.13s8m5M
0316·7

39°
31'·91
N

Sketch plan   2°42'·97E   Depths in Metres

Puerto de San Antonio de la Playa looking north. It is very close to the airport

Berthing

Preferably call ahead on VHF Ch 09 to check that a berth will be available. Otherwise secure to the inner side of the southwest breakwater and visit the harbour office at the *club marítimo* building. There is no more than 2.5m at the visitors' quay, shoaling to 1.5m in places.

Note The visitors' berth becomes virtually untenable in conditions likely to create a swell from the southerly quadrant due to reflection from the eastern breakwater. Also the marina staff are loathe to allow visitors to use empty berths in the marina as they are all private. It is recommended that this port be avoided during strong south winds.

Facilities

Water Taps on all quays and pontoons, including the visitors' quay.
Electricity 220v AC points on all quays and pontoons, including the visitors' quay. 380v AC in the boatyard.
Fuel Diesel and petrol from pumps at the head of the east breakwater; the green column marking the starboard side of the entrance emerges from the fuel cabin's roof.
Provisions Many shops and supermarkets nearby, with more in Palma three miles away. Hypermarket about two miles away on the road between Palma and the airport. Market Tuesdays and Thursdays in Ca'n Pastilla.
Ice From the bar.
Chandlery Near the harbour. Several large chandleries in Palma.

Repairs Boatyard on the west side of the harbour, equal to most work. Otherwise large boatyards in Palma. A 60-tonne travel-lift in the boatyard, 6-tonne mobile crane and several smaller ones. A small slipway near the club maritimo building.
Engineers, electronic & radio repairs at the boatyard. Several sailmakers in Palma.
Yacht club The Club Marítimo San Antonio de la Playa has a large clubhouse with restaurant, bar, terrace, showers, etc.
Showers Below the *club marítimo* building.
Laundrette In Ca'n Pastilla.
Banks In Ca'n Pastilla, directly behind the yacht harbour.
Medical services In Ca'n Pastilla. Hospital in Palma 3½ miles away.

Transport

Car hire/taxis In the town.
Buses Frequent bus service to Palma.
Ferries From Palma to the other islands and mainland Spain.
Air services Busy international airport three miles away.

Sights ashore locally

A short distance from Palma, with a regular bus service.

Eating out

Restaurant at the *club marítimo* and many more restaurants, cafés, and bars in the town.

III. MALLORCA

M28 Puerto de Cala Gamba

A small shallow well protected harbour with 275 berths, occupied with local vessels. Silting has reduced depths in the marina to 1.4m (July 2010)

Location
39°32'.8N 2°41'.8E

Communications
VHF Ch 09
Club Náutico Cala Gamba ☎ 971 26 18 49
Fax 971 49 19 00
Email info@cncalagamba.com

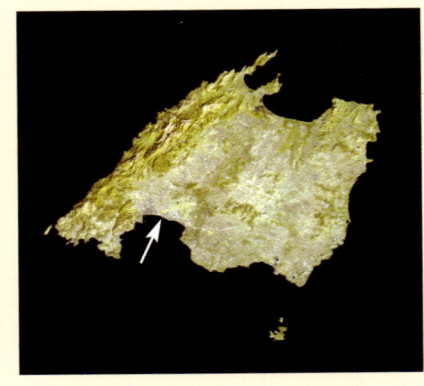

The harbour

The addition of new breakwaters and pontoons has turned this pleasant little fishing harbour into a flourishing yacht harbour with 275 berths, but both depth and facilities are still limited. Much of the harbour carries less than 2m, though 2.5m may be found against parts of the southwest breakwater. The entrance has been known to silt-up, reducing to 1.5m. It cannot be entered with any swell from southeast, south or southwest due to very shallow water in the approach, but otherwise approach and entry offer no difficulties. The noise generated by nearby Palma airport is considerable.

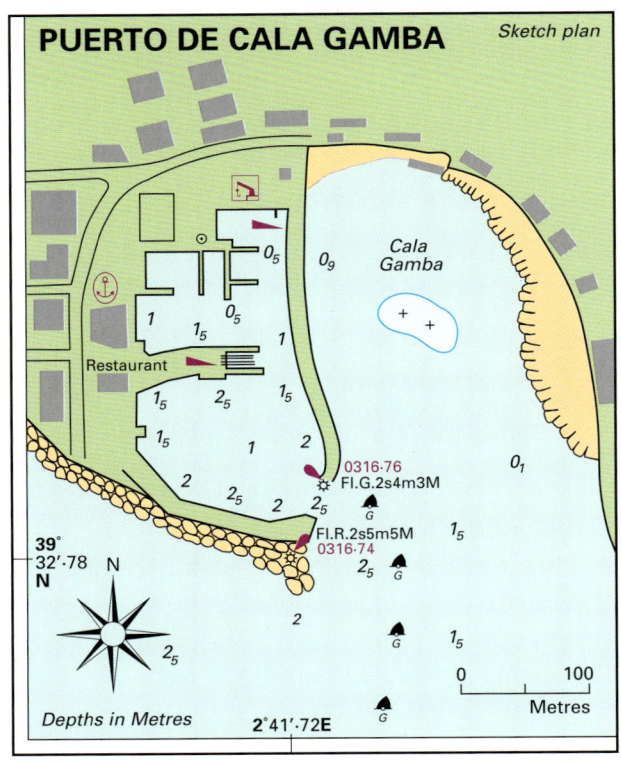

PUERTO DE CALA GAMBA *Sketch plan*

Cala Gamba

Restaurant

0316·76
Fl.G.2s4m3M

Fl.R.2s5m5M
0316·74

39°
32'·78 N
N

0 100
Metres

Depths in Metres   2°41'·72E

PILOTAGE

Approach

⊕71 39°32'.7N 2°41'.7E Puerto de Cala Gamba

For outer approaches see *Puerto de San Antonio de la Playa* on page 170 and plan on page 158.

From west Puerto de Cala Gamba lies 1.3 miles northwest of Puerto de San Antonio de la Playa and slightly north of the airport main runway. A tall, solid, black and white buoy with an × topmark (Fl.Y.3s3M) 650m south of the harbour entrance marks the water inlet for a power station, the chimney of which will be seen. A west cardinal beacon with topmark (Fl(9)15s5m5M) marks the end of a short breakwater 550m northwest of the harbour, with a second west cardinal beacon, also (Fl(9)15s5m5M), a further 600m to the northwest. All three must be passed on the seaward side. Four small conical green buoys and a conical red buoy are the stb entrance channel markers to the harbour.

From east Steer north-northwest from Cabo Enderrocat, being certain to leave both Islote Galera, 0.5 miles northwest of Puerto de San Antonio de la Playa, and the black and white buoy to starboard.

Anchorage in the approach

Anchor in 4m over stones 400m south of the entrance and some 250m north of the buoy mentioned above. Holding is poor.

Entrance

Approach cautiously heading northeast. Though dredged from time to time the entrance channel is narrow and subject to silting to 1.5M.

Berthing

Seek a vacant berth as draught permits and visit the *club náutico* office for allocation of a visitors' berth.

Puerto de Cala Gamba: shallows to north of harbour can be seen clearly

Facilities

Water Taps on quays and pontoons.
Electricity 220v AC points on quays and pontoons.
Fuel Not available.
Provisions Some small shops nearby, supermarkets and more shops a little further inland and all the resources of Palma 2½ miles away. Hypermarket on the road between Palma and the airport.
Ice From the *club náutico* bar.
Repairs Local craftsmen can carry out simple work. Fully equipped boatyards in Palma. 5-tonne and 1-tonne cranes near the root of the east breakwater. A slipway on the central mole and another in the northeast corner.
Yacht club The Club Náutico Cala Gamba has a clubhouse overlooking the harbour with restaurant, bar, showers, etc.
Showers At the *club náutico*.
Banks Nearby.
Hospital/medical services In Palma, 2½ miles away.

Transport

Car hire/taxis Locally or in Palma.
Buses Frequent bus service to Palma.
Ferries From Palma to the other islands and mainland Spain.
Air services Busy international airport two miles away.

Eating out

Numerous restaurants, cafés and bars nearby.

M29 Puerto del Molinar de Levante (Caló d'en Rigo)

A small fishing harbour in a quaint old village, with berths for 140 craft drawing not much more than half a metre as the entrance is silted

Location
39°33'.4N 2°40'.5E

Communications
Club Marítimo Molinar de Levante ✆ 971 27 34 79
Fax 971 25 04 06

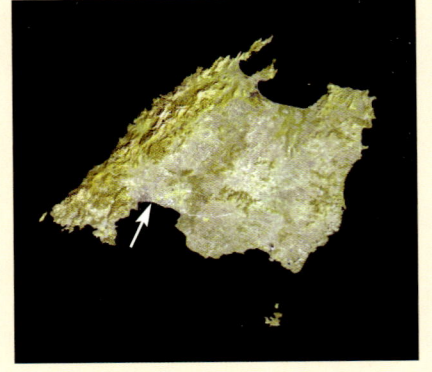

The harbour

A very small fishing harbour built in Caló d'en Rigo, only suitable for craft drawing around half a metre (due to reduced depths in the entrance) and under 9m in length. It is almost exclusively occupied by small speedboats. Facilities are limited to everyday requirements. Approach and entrance are easy but would be dangerous with swell from the southern quadrant.

PILOTAGE

Approach

See *Puerto de Cala Portixol* and page 176 and plan on page 158. Puerto del Molinar de Levante lies 0.3 miles to the southeast.

Anchorage in the approach

Anchor in 2.5m over sand and mud, 400m southeast of the harbour entrance, open southeast–southwest–northwest.

Entrance

Approach the east side of the harbour at slow speed, watching the depth carefully, until the entrance opens up to port.

Puerto del Molinar. Note silting in entrance

View northwest over Puerto del Molinar (bottom left) and
Puerto de Cala Portixol. Puerto de Palma in background

PUERTO DEL MOLINAR
(CALO D'EN RIGO)

Sketch plan

Metres

0317
FI(2)G.7s7m3M

See note

FI(2)R.7s7m5M
0317·2

Note
Depths in entrance
reportedly reduced

39°
33'·46
N

N

2°40'·5E   Depths in Metres

Berthing

Seek a vacant berth and visit the *club náutico* office
for allocation of a visitors' berth.

Facilities

Water Taps around the harbour.
Electricity 220v AC points around the harbour.
Fuel Not available.
Provisioning Shops and supermarkets in El Molinar.
Ice From the Club Marítimo bar.
Chandlery Small chandlery shop nearby.
Repairs Crane on the north side of the harbour and three
    slipways around the harbour.
Yacht club The Club Marítimo Molinar de Levante has a
    clubhouse with restaurant and bar on the west side of
    the harbour.
Banks In El Molinar.
Hospital/medical services In Palma, 1½ miles away.

Transport

See *Puerto de Cala Portixol*, following.

Sights ashore locally

The surrounding area is, as yet, relatively unspoilt
with some attractive older houses and a lofty brick
church directly behind the harbour.

Eating out

A wide selection of restaurants/cafés nearby.

M30 Puerto de Cala Portixol

A large and very safe fishing and yacht harbour less than 2M from Palma with berths for 300 vessels, but it is usually full with local boats and has little space for visitors

Location
39°33'.5N 2°40'.1E

Communications
Club Náutico Portixol ☎ 971 24 24 24

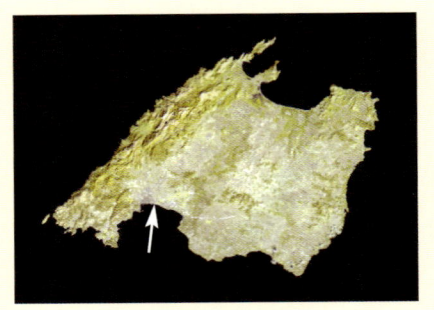

The harbour

An old fishing harbour in a semicircular cove, converted into a combined fishing and yachting harbour by the addition of extra breakwaters and other facilities. Berthing available for 300 vessels, but restricted to not much more than 12m. No space is reserved for visitors. Much of the harbour has depths less than 2m. Traffic noise from the nearby motorway is distinctly audible, as is the nearby airport.

As with the harbours to the southeast, approach and entrance are straightforward other than in heavy swell from the south quadrant, when shoals in the approach could render it dangerous.

Puerto de Cala Portixol: berthing for smaller yachts

PILOTAGE

Approach

⊕72 39°33'.4N 2°40'.1E Off Puerto de Cala Portixol

From west Round the very prominent Punta de Cala Figuera (see plan on page 158) which has a lighthouse (Fl(4)20s45m15M, white round tower with black diagonal stripes on building 24m) and radio masts on its steep cliffs. Cross the Bahía de Palma heading northeast towards Palma Cathedral, a very large building with small twin spires. From a position 0.8 miles off Puerto de Palma south breakwater, the very much smaller breakwaters of Puerto de Cala Portixol will be seen 1.5 miles ahead.

From east Round Cabo Blanco, which is high with steep light brown cliffs topped by a lighthouse (Oc.5s95m15M, white tower and building 12m) and an old watchtower, and set a course northwest until the buildings of Palma come into view. Puerto de Cala Portixol will be seen to starboard when still a mile short of the entrance to Puerto de Palma.

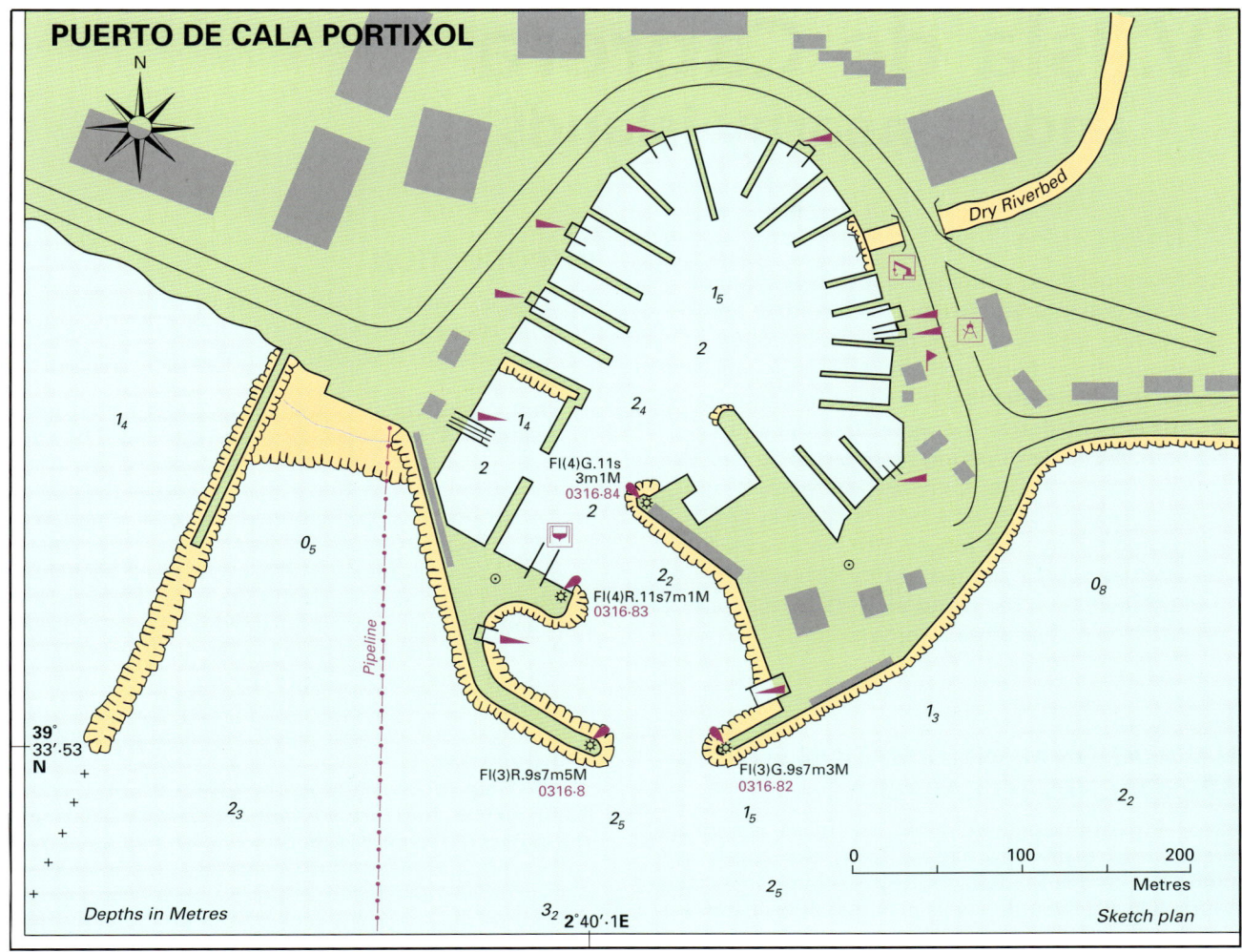

PUERTO DE CALA PORTIXOL

N

Dry Riverbed

FI(4)G.11s
3m1M
0316·84

FI(4)R.11s7m1M
0316·83

Pipeline

39°
33'·53
N

FI(3)R.9s7m5M
0316·8

FI(3)G.9s7m3M
0316·82

0   100   200
Metres

Depths in Metres

2°40'·1E

Sketch plan

Anchorage in the approach

See *Cala Portixolet* below.

Entrance

Approach and enter on a northerly course between the outer breakwaters and then the inner moles, to enter the main harbour. There is a 2-knot speed limit.

Berthing

Local yachts berth on the west side of the harbour just inside the inner mole, but it is unlikely that there will be a space available.

Facilities

Water Water taps around the harbour.
Electricity 220v AC points around the harbour.
Fuel Not available.
Provisions Some shops nearby, with a vast range in Palma, less than two miles away.
Ice Ice machine at the *club náutico*.
Chandlery Two chandlery/fishing tackle shops on the road opposite the harbour gate.
Repairs Simple work possible. Fully equipped boatyards in Palma. A 4-tonne crane to the northeast of the harbour. Nine slipways, mostly very small.
Yacht club The Club Náutico Portixol has a pleasant clubhouse on the east of the harbour with restaurant, bar, terrace, etc.

Showers At the *club náutico*.
Banks In Palma.
Hospital/medical services In Palma.

Transport

Car hire/taxis In Palma.
Buses Frequent bus service to Palma.
Ferries From Palma to the other islands and mainland Spain.
Air services Busy international airport three miles away.

Sights ashore locally

As for Palma.

Eating out

Many eating houses in the area.

⚓ CALA PORTIXOLET
39°33'.6N 2°40'.4E

A shallow and somewhat bleak anchorage, with the rocky breakwaters of Puerto de Cala Portixol on one side and a road backed by houses at the head. Anchor in 1.5m over sand, open to the southern quadrant.

IV. Isla de Cabrera
and its nearby islands

As a National Park, Cabrera is a restricted zone of great natural interest due to its rich wildlife and several rare species of flora, fauna and birdlife unique to the archipelago. The island may only be visited if a permit has first been acquired through its offices in Mallorca. There are 50 buoys in the harbour, available to permit holders and limited to one or two nights. Unsupervised walks are limited to the foreshore and castle but other walks are conducted by the park ranger. There are virtually no facilities but the rugged beauty, rich wildlife and tranquillity of the island await those who are prepared to accept these inconveniences

NAVIGATIONAL INFORMATION FOR APPROACHES TO CABRERA

Since a permit obtained from the main islands is required to visit, approaches from the south are unlikely. The only dangers approaching from the south side are the unlit rocks around Islotes Estels on the southernmost tip. To the north, Isla Conejera and the passages between the island and Cabrera are described in this volume.

Magnetic variation

Negligible: less than 0°00'· (2010).

Approach and coastal passage charts
See *Appendix* for full list of Balearic charts.
Approach lights
0338 **Punta Anciola** 39°07'.8N 02°55'.4E Fl(3)15s121m19M
Red and white chequered tower on white building 21m
277.5°-vis-169°
0338.3 **Cabo Llebeig** 39°09'.7N 02°55'.1E Fl(4)14.5s74m7M
Black and white chequered angular tower 7m
0340 **Isla Horadada** 39°12'.5N 02°58'.8E Fl(2)12s42m13M
White round tower, five black bands, on white round house 13m 047°-vis-0001°

ISLA DE CABRERA WAYPOINTS
⊕73	Puerto de Cabrera	39°09'.5N 02°55'.6E
⊕74	Between Pta de Sa Corrent and	
	Isla Redonda	39°09'.8N 02°58'.4E
⊕75	Off Islote Imperial (SE)	39°07'.5N 02°57'.7E
⊕76	Pta Anciola	39°07'.6N 02°55'.0E
⊕77	Cabo Llebeig	39°09'.7N 02°54'.9E
⊕78	Pta de la Escala	39°11'.0N 02°57'.0E
⊕79	Isla Horadada	39°12'.6N 02°58'.7E

INTRODUCTION

Cabrera is a rugged and hilly island with numerous offlying islets, stretching north-northeast like giant stepping stones towards Mallorca, just over five miles away.

The archipelago was declared a National Maritime and Terrestial Park in April 1991 by the Spanish government in order to preserve the rare indigenous plant and animal life. Access is restricted and a permit must be obtained before visiting (see below). The main island measures some three miles in each direction, indented by several deep bays and rising to 172m at Alto de Picamoscas. There is an excellent sheltered bay on the northwest side, known as Puerto de Cabrera despite having no port facilities beyond a couple of short jetties. Anchoring is forbidden but fifty visitors' moorings have been laid. Access to the many other small, secluded anchorages is also restricted.

The only other island in the group of any size is Isla Conejera, measuring about one mile by 0.6 miles and separated from Isla de Cabrera by a channel 0.7 miles wide and more than 20m deep. Seven smaller islands lie north of Isla de Cabrera, with others close inshore to the south. In general Isla de Cabrera and its islets are all steep-to, and in most places deep water runs close inshore.

No tourist developments, no jet-skis, no noise and only other seafarers for company: this place is as near to heaven as it gets in the Baleares!

WILDLIFE

There are several species of fauna, flora and lizards unique to the archipelago, which is also a haven for seabirds including the rare Audouins gull (see *Flora and Fauna* in the *General Introduction* on page 7) and birds of prey such as the osprey and both peregrine and Eleonora's falcon. The surrounding waters are home to fish, turtles, dolphins, whales and a variety of corals. Booklets describing the history and wildlife of the Cabrera group are available in several languages from the Cabrera National Park Office (see below).

Permits

In August 2010 the National Park was taken over by local government, who now administer it from Palma: Cabrera National Park Office, Calle Gremi de Corredors, 10 first floor, Poligono Son Rossinyol, Palma de Mallorca ☏ 971 177641 (Direct), ☏ 971 176613 (Main office), *Fax* 971 176617 office hours; so closed weekends and bank holidays.

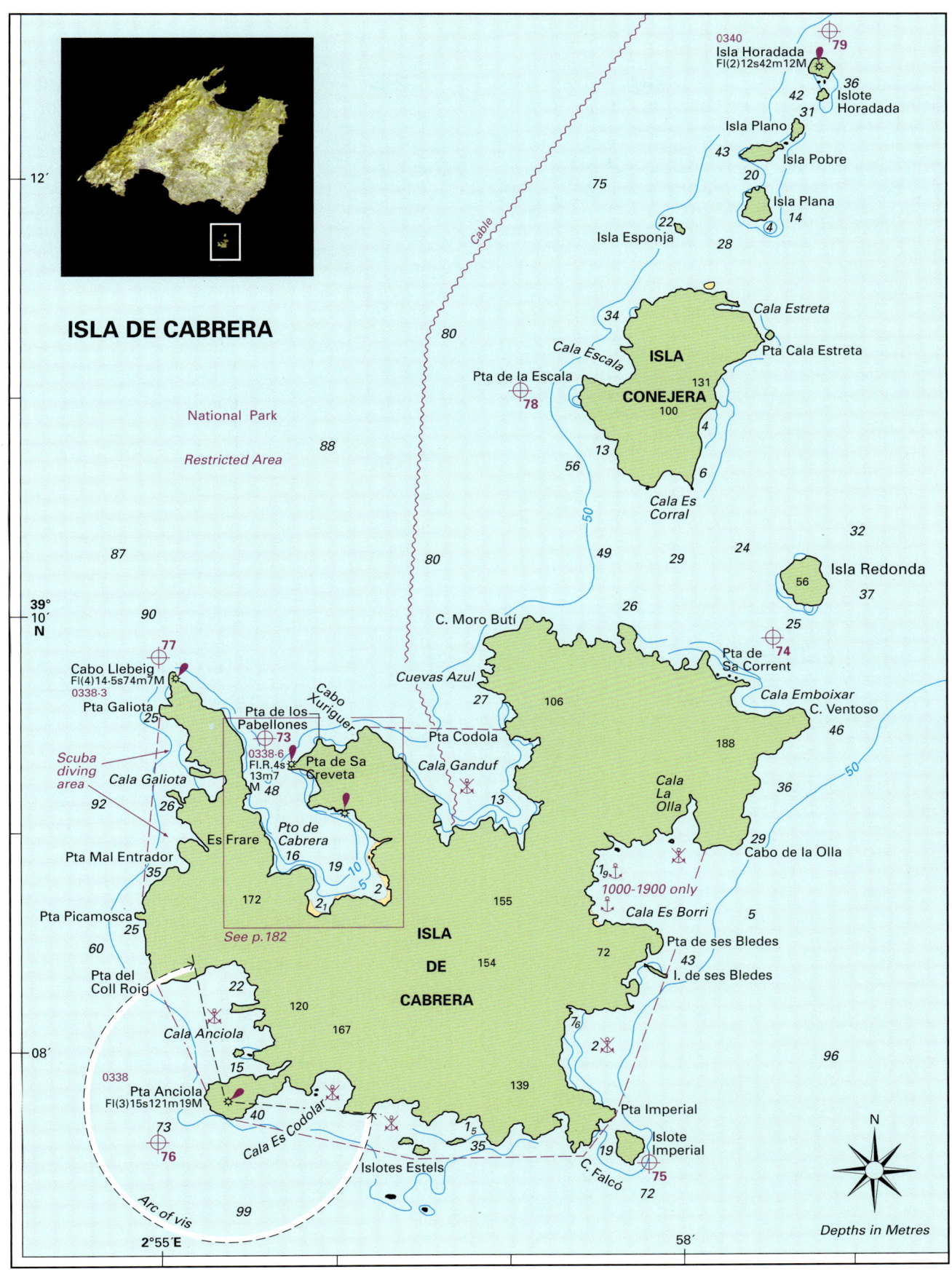

ISLA DE CABRERA

National Park

Restricted Area

0340
Isla Horadada
Fl(2)12s42m12M
79
36
Islote
Horadada
42
31
Isla Plano
43
Isla Pobre
20
Isla Plana
4   14
Isla Esponja
28
75
80
88
Cable

34
Cala Estreta
Cala Escala
ISLA
Pta Cala Estreta
CONEJERA
131
Pta de la Escala
78
100
4
13
56
6
Cala Es
Corral

87
90
77
Cabo Llebeig
Fl(4)14·5s74m7M
0338·3
Pta Galiota
25
Scuba
diving
area
Cala Galiota
92   26
Pta Mal Entrador
35
Pta Picamosca
25
60
Pta del
Coll Roig
22
Cala Anciola
120
15
0338
Pta Anciola
Fl(3)15s121m19M
40
73
76
Cala Es Codolar
Arc of vis
99
2°55′E

32
Isla Redonda
56   37
25
Pta de   **74**
Sa Corrent
Cala Emboixar
C. Ventoso
46
188
50
36
29
Cabo de la Olla
1 9
1000-1900 only
Cala Es Borri
5
Pta de ses Bledes
43
I. de ses Bledes
72
7 6
2
96
Pta Imperial
Islote
19   Imperial
75
72
58′

Pta de los
Pabellones
73
0338·6
Fl.R.4s
13m7
M 48
Es Frare
Pto de
Cabrera
16
172
See p.182
Cabo
Xuriguer
Pta de Sa
Creveta
19 10
5
2 1
2
C. Moro Butí
Cuevas Azul
27
Pta Codola
Cala Ganduf
13
ISLA
DE
CABRERA
154
167
139
1 5
35
C. Falcó

106
Cala
La
Olla

155
72
2

N

Depths in Metres

Permits are dated and can be applied for by fax two days in advance in summer; in winter they can be issued the same day but best allow 24 hours and bear in mind the office is closed on weekends and bank holidays, see page 178 for contact details. Nearby yacht clubs, marinas and harbourmasters in Mallorca will provide a blank Solicitud de Autorizacion and, when completed, will fax it through (a small fee is sometimes charged for this service, though the permit itself is free). Details of the yacht (registration document), skipper (passport and certificate of competence), owner and number aboard are required. A scuba-diving permit is available from the same office, though fishing is strictly prohibited. Animals may not be landed from boats and all rubbish must be taken back aboard.

No more than fifty yachts can use the harbour, Puerto de Cabrera, at any one time and visits are limited to one night in July and August, two nights in June and September and up to seven nights for the rest of the year. The permit is dated, and only valid for the date(s) shown, but if not all the buoys are occupied it may be possible to remain an extra night. (Equally, if all fifty buoys are already allocated a last minute application will be refused.) Weekends are inevitably in greatest demand.

Although sailing around the island in certain areas is allowed, nights have to be spent in the harbour on the allocated buoy.

Each permit is accompanied by a map with details of permitted daytime (1000–1900) anchorages – currently two areas in the entrance to Puerto de Cabrera and Cala Es Borri on the east coast – and prohibited areas, which at present include Cala Ganduf, Cala Anciola, Cala Es Codolar and others on the south coast: Cala La Olla and Cala Emboixar. Even so, brief details of these *calas* are included below in case the restrictions are lifted. There is a 5-knot speed limit in the entire Maritime Park area and a 2-knot speed limit in the harbour.

The boundary of the National Park is indicated by five pillar buoys, all lit and with × topmarks, in positions 39°13'.5N 02°58'E (Fl.Y.2s5M); 39°13'.5N 03°00'E (Fl(2)Y.5M); 39°06'.5N 03°00'E (Fl.Y. 2s5M); 39°06'.5N 02°53'.5E (Fl(2)Y.5M); and 39°10'N 02°53'.5E (Fl(3)Y.5M).

HISTORY

It is probable that Isla de Cabrera (Goat Island) and Isla Conejera (Rabbit Island) were inhabited in prehistoric times: traces of an ancient building have been identified at Clot des Guix, and Roman and Byzantine ceramics and coins have also been found. The castle overlooking Puerto de Cabrera is thought to date back to the end of the 14th century and was probably built as a defence against pirates. During the Peninsular Wars some 9,000 French prisoners were interned on the island, where nearly two-thirds died of disease and starvation. They are buried near the castle and a memorial was erected in 1847 in the centre of the island.

Recent history

Prior to the first world war the island was privately owned, but was requisitioned by the Spanish government in 1915 to prevent it falling into enemy hands. A small army garrison was established (which still exists) and at various times the area has been used as a gunnery range. Landing on any of the smaller islands could be *dangerous*, due to the presence of unexploded shells or other ammunition (as well as being contrary to the rules of the park).

Tourist offices

Sightseeing is limited on Cabrera as it is a National Park, but there is a Park Information Office in the harbour (see harbour plan on page 182). Their head office is in Palma, where permits are issued, details of which are above.

Embassies

None on Cabrera, but see *Appendix* for contact details of embassies on the other islands.

ISLA DE CABRERA NATURE RESERVE

C1 Puerto de Cabrera

This is a large sheltered bay laid with 50 buoys for which a permit must be obtained prior to entry (see note on Permits on page 178)

Location
39°09'.3N 02°55'.6E

Communications
Cabrera National Park Office VHF Ch 09
☎ 971 17 76 41/17 66 13 *Fax* 971 72 55 85

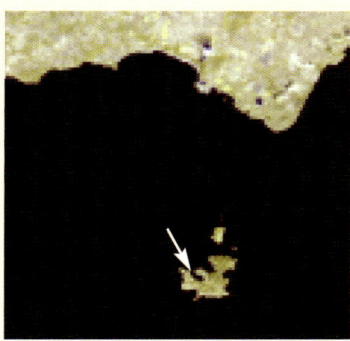

The harbour

A large natural harbour which can be entered under virtually any conditions apart from in strong northwest winds, which are rare. Shelter is good, though a swell rolls in with north or northwest winds. Gusts blowing down into the harbour from the surrounding hills can also be fierce. However, in normal conditions it is one of the few truly peaceful spots in the Balearics, without jet-skis, waterskiers and speedboats, though tourist ferries from Palma (Colonia de San Jordi) arrive daily in the summer.

PILOTAGE

⊕73 39°09'.5N 02°55'.6E Puerto de Cabrera

Approach

From north When approaching from this direction the chain of islands running north/south does not appear separated from Isla de Cabrera itself until quite close (see plan on page 179). Leave these islands to port, heading for a position slightly east of Cabo Lleibeig (Fl(4)14.5s74m7M, black and white chequered angular tower 7m, ⊕77). The entrance lies close under this headland, with Punta de Sa Creveta (Fl.R.4s13m7M, red and white chequered angular tower 5m) to the east.

From west The hills of Isla de Cabrera can be seen from some distance away, with the line of smaller islands running towards the north visible on closer approach. Set a course to round Cabo Lleibeig ⊕77, the northwest tip of the island, after which the entrance will open up beyond.

From east or northeast Pass either side of Isla Redonda to round Cabo Moro Butí and cross the wide and deep Cala Ganduf towards Cabo Xuriguer and Punta de los Pabellones. The entrance will open up on rounding Punta de Sa Creveta beyond.

Puerto de Cabrera. The peace and tranquility here is palpable

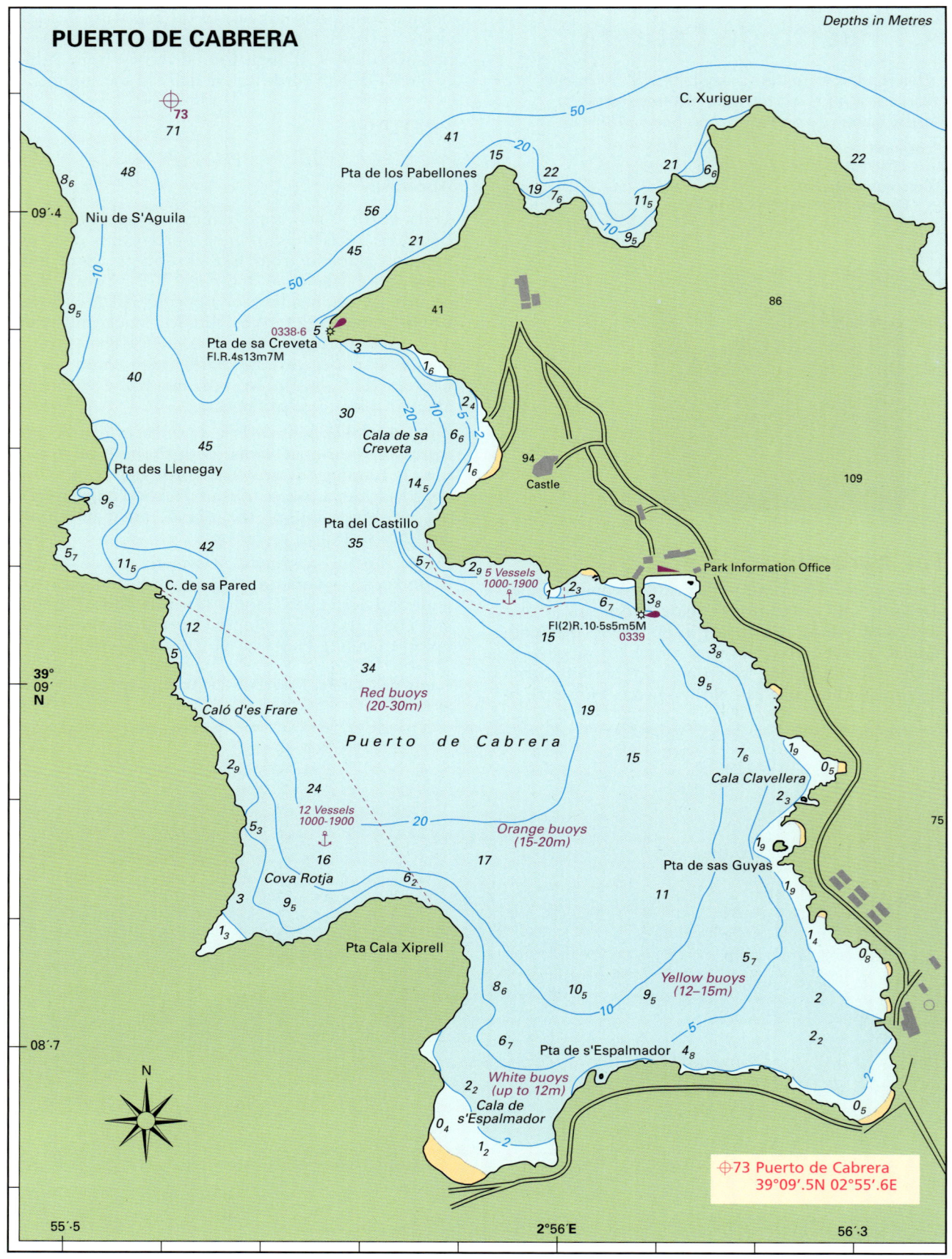

PUERTO DE CABRERA

Depths in Metres

C. Xuriguer

50

Pta de los Pabellones

41

15

20

22

21

6₆

22

19

7₆

11₅

8₆

48

9₅

56

21

09′·4

Niu de S'Aguila

45

50

86

40

0338·6 5

41

Pta de sa Creveta
Fl.R.4s13m7M

3

1₆

2₄

30

2₅

45

Pta des Llenegay

6₆

2

Cala de sa
Creveta

94

9₆

1₆

Castle

109

5₇

14₅

11₅

42

Pta del Castillo

35

C. de sa Pared

5₇

2₉ 5 Vessels
1000-1900

2₃

Park Information Office

1

6₇

3₈

12

15

Fl(2)R.10·5s5m5M
0339

3₈

5

34

9₅

39°
09′
N

Caló d'es Frare

Red buoys
(20-30m)

19

15

7₆

1₉

0₅

2₉

P u e r t o d e C a b r e r a

15

Cala Clavellera

2₃

24

12 Vessels
1000-1900

20

Orange buoys
(15-20m)

17

7₆

1₉

5₃

Pta de sas Guyas

1₉

16

11

75

Cova Rotja

6₂

1₄

0₈

3

9₅

5₇

2

1₃

Pta Cala Xiprell

8₆

10₅

9₅

Yellow buoys
(12–15m)

2₂

08′·7

6₇

Pta de s'Espalmador

4₈

N

White buoys
(up to 12m)

2₂

0₅

Cala de
s'Espalmador

0₄

1₂

2

⊕73 Puerto de Cabrera
39°09′.5N 02°55′.6E

55′·5

2°56′E

56′·3

Currents

Strong wind-induced currents may be experienced around the islands, the direction and strength dependent on that of the wind.

Entrance

The entrance, which is deep but relatively narrow, lies between Cabo Llebeig and Punta de Sa Creveta. Wind conditions in both the entrance and harbour can be very fluky due to the high surrounding hills. Mooring buoys lie south of a line between Cabo de sa Pared and Punta del Castillo. As well as the 5-knot speed limit in the entire Maritime Park area there is a 2-knot speed limit in the harbour itself.

Berthing

Lying alongside the jetty is only possible with a military permit or in an emergency.

Moorings

Secure to one of the 50 visitors' moorings, colour-coded according to yacht size as follows:

White	up to 12m
Yellow	12–15m
Orange	15–20m
Red	20–30m

No charge is made for mooring use. Smaller yacht moorings are tucked into Cala de s'Espalmador and are the most sheltered but also furthest from the main (northeast) jetty, the only place where landing is permitted.

Secure to the mooring by putting a loop of line through the eye on the end of the mooring rope and paying out until the pick-up buoy is back in the water. If it is left out of the water the guard will correct it.

Anchoring

Anchoring in the harbour is generally forbidden. However, relaxation to the rule has been known, to allow 12 vessels to anchor between the hours of 1000 and 1900 on the west side of the harbour between C. de sa Pared and Pta Cala Xiprell and for five craft on the east side in the cove southeast of Pta del Castillo, as marked on the plan.

A third anchorage, possibly available between these hours, lies in Cala Es Borri (described right). However, in November 2010 it was not permitted to anchor anywhere on Cabrera; only use of the mooring buoys. But check with the Park Information Office when applying for your permit before arrival: ② 971 17 76 41/17 66 13 *Fax* 971 17 66 17.

Formalities

A guard visits each yacht every evening to check that a valid permit is held. Landing by dinghy is only allowed at the main jetty, and the permit must be shown at the Park Information Office on embarking ashore. Scuba permits should also be presented before diving.

Isla de Cabrera Park Buildings *Henry Buchanan*

Facility

Water Small quantities of non-drinking water can usually be collected from the army *cantina* (take containers).

Sights ashore

It was once possible to roam over the island unsupervised, but yachtsmen, having landed on the main jetty, are now restricted to the road by the foreshore and a walk to the castle. All other walks (minimum four people) are conducted by Park Rangers at designated times available from the Park Information Office.

The walk up the steep track leading to the castle ruins will be rewarded with spectacular views and it is also possible to visit the memorial to the French prisoners of war.

The Cuevas Azul (Blue Caves) in Cala Ganduf some 600m south–southwest of Cabo Moro Butí are also most attractive but are only accessible by sea. Anchoring in the *cala* is not permitted, but at some 1.4 miles from the buoys in Puerto de Cabrera, a visit by dinghy is feasible.

There are a few houses near the south mole, some used by the owners of the sheep and pigs pastured on the island which keep the vegetation down.

Eating out

The army *cantina* welcomes visitors and has a bar, though food is not available.

ANCHORAGES AROUND CABRERA

⚓ CALA ES BORRI
39°08′.7N 02°57′.5E

This is the only anchorage which may be available to yachts, apart from those within Puerto de Cabrera if permitted (see Anchoring left). All are restricted to use between 1000 and 1900 daily. Anchor in the central and southern parts of the bay. Cala Es Borri is actually the small inlet at its southwest corner. No more than twenty boats can be present at any one time in the *cala*.

Anchor as space permits in 5m+ over sand and rock, open to the east quadrant and to swell from the south. There is a fine sandy beach in Cala Es Borri itself.

IV. ISLA DE CABRERA

Calas and features around Isla de Cabrera

Anchoring is prohibited in the *calas* listed below. Some, as noted, can be sailed in, whereas others can only be admired from afar. These brief details are included for interest.

CALA GANDUF

39°09'.2N 02°56'.7E

A protected and deep bay with several separate indentations, open for sailing, but nothing more.

Passage between Isla de Cabrera and Isla Redonda

⊕74 39°09'.8N 02°58'.4E Between Pta de Sa Corrent and Isla Redonda

An 800m wide passage with a minimum depth of 21m. Transit in a northwest–southeast direction.

CALA EMBOIXAR

39°09'.6N 02°58'.3E

An attractive small bay under cliffs, with a rocky ledge looking like a breakwater to the northwest. Open for sailing, but not for anchoring. There are two small beaches, one rocky and one of sand.

Cala Es Borri looking north. Isla Redonda in view over peninsula with Isla Conejera left top of photo. Isla Plana and Mallorca just in view

CABO VENTOSO (CAP VENTÓS)

39°09'.5N 02°58'.6E

A high (188m), steep, rocky-cliffed promontory with good water at its base.

CALA LA OLLA

39°09'.0N 02°57'.9E

An interesting *cala* amidst wild scenery at the mouth of the eastern of two small calas, themselves at the northern end of a wide bay. Sailing (only) allowed in the *cala*. Several islets lie close to the west.

⊕75 39°07'.5N 02°57'.7E Off Islote Imperial (SE)

Passage between Islote Imperial and Isla de Cabrera

A 100m wide, 18m deep passage between dramatic cliffs, for use in settled weather.

Sailing is permitted along the south coast from Islote Imperial west to Punta Anciola.

ISLOTES ESTELS

39°07'.3N 02°56'.4E (Southernmost: Estels de Fuera)

Five scattered, rocky islands up to 750m off the south coast of Isla de Cabrera.

PUNTA ANCIOLA
39°07'.8N 02°55'.3E

⊕76 39°07'.6N 02°55'.0E Pta Anciola

A rounded headland connected to Isla Cabrera by a low, narrow neck. The paintwork on its lighthouse (Fl(3)15s121m19M, red and white chequered tower on white building 21m) may well be unique.

NORTH OF PUNTA MAL ENTRADOR
39°09'.1N 02°55'.1E

A small bay open to the western quadrant. This area is currently reserved for licensed scuba diving.

CALA GALIOTA
39°09'.2N 02°55'.3E

An attractive *cala* under high cliffs. As above, Cala Galiota is also part of an area restricted for licensed Scuba diving.

CABO LLEBEIG 39°09'.7N 02°55'.1E
⊕77 39°09'.7N 02°54'.9E Cabo Llebeig

A large (60m) conspicuous rocky hummock with a not very prominent lighthouse (Fl(4)14.5s74m7M, black and white chequered angular tower 7m).

The smaller islands of the Isla de Cabrera group

ISLA REDONDA
Centred on 39°10'.1N 02°58'.6E

A roughly circular island some 450m in diameter and 56m high. No anchoring or landing allowed.

Passage between Isla Redonda and Isla Conejera

A 1,000m-wide passage with a minimum depth of 20m.

ISLA CONEJERA (ILLA DES CONILLS)
Centred on 39°11'.1N 02°57'.9E

The second-largest island at one mile long by 0.6 miles wide and reaching 131m high. There are potential landing places on the east coast and several *calas* (see below) but their use is currently prohibited.

CALA ES CORRAL, ISLA CONEJERA
39°10'.6N 02°57'.9E

Two small *calas* side by side at the south end of the island. There are two small offlying islets on either side.

⊕78 39°11'.0N 02°57'.0E Pta de la Escala

Passage between Isla Conejera and Isla Esponja or Isla Plana

A passage 400m wide, with a minimum depth of 11m if midway between Isla Conejera and the two smaller islands.

ISLA ESPONJA
39°11'.7N 02°57'.9E

200m by 40m, and 23m high, Isla Esponja is steep-to and inaccessible.

ISLA PLANA
39°11'.8N 02°58'.4E

400m by 125m, 26m high.

Passage between Isla Plana and Isla Pobre

A 150m wide passage with depths shoaling to 2.5m.

ISLA POBRE
39°12'.1N 02°58'.4E

400m by 100m, 27m high.

Passage between Isla Pobre and Isla Plano

Foul.

ISLA PLANO (ILLOT PLÁ)
39°12'.2N 02°58'.6E

200m by 100m, 27m high.

Passage between Isla Plano and Islote Horadada

A passage 200m wide with 12m minimum depth.

ISLOTE HORADADA (ILLOT FORADADA OR FORADAT)
39°12'.3N 02°58'.8E

100m by 80m, 12m high.

Passage between Islote Horadada and Isla Horadada

Foul.

ISLA HORADADA (ILLA FORADADA OR FORADAT)
39°12'.5N 02°58'.8E

210m by 120m and 42m high, with a lighthouse (Fl(2)12s42m13M, white round tower with five black bands on white round house 13m) on its summit.

⊕79 39°12'.6N 02°58'.7E Isla Horadada N

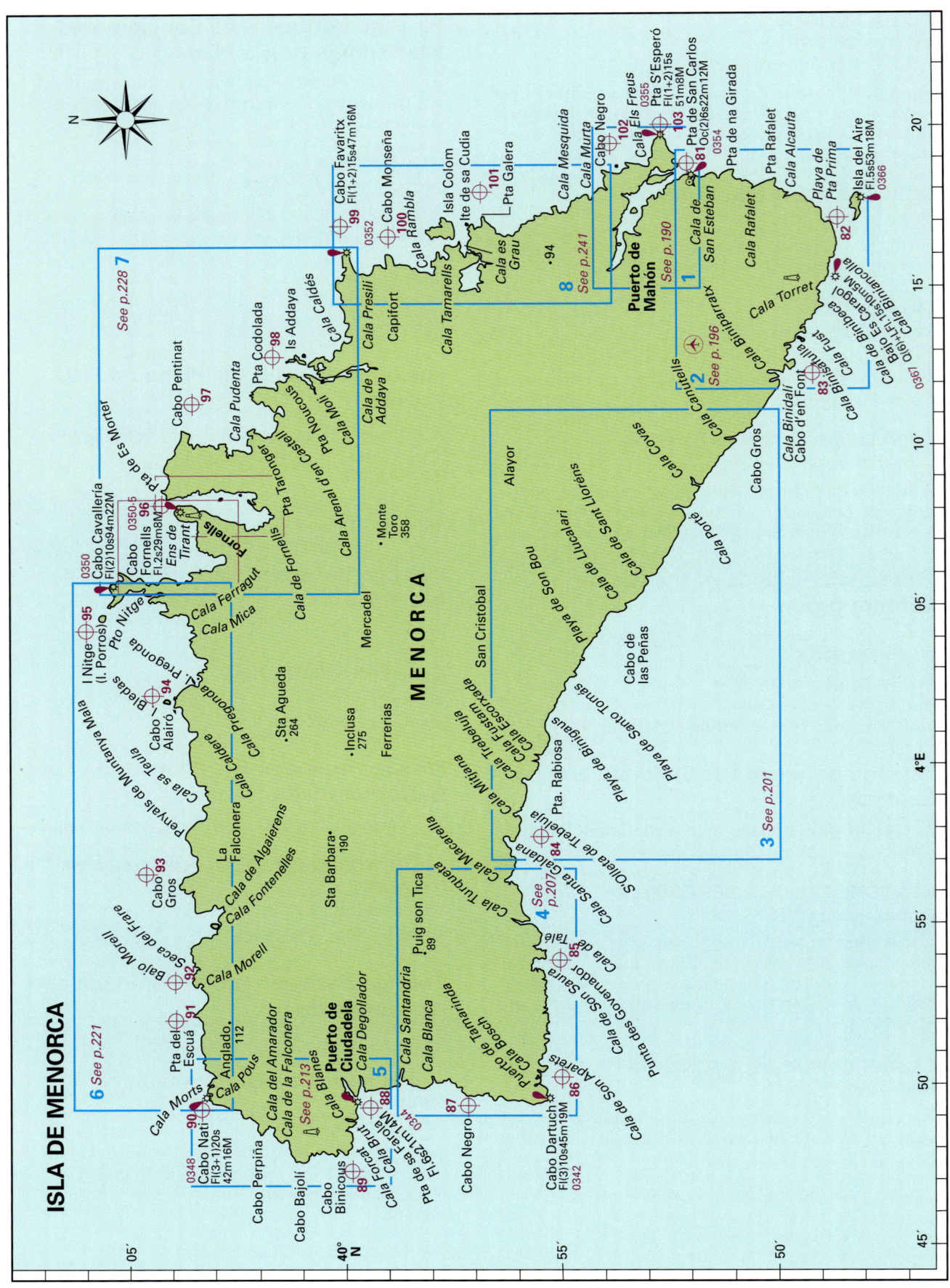

ISLA DE MENORCA

MENORCA

Puerto de Mahón

Puerto de Ciudadela

6 See p.221
7 See p.228
8 See p.241
1 See p.190
2 See p.196
3 See p.201
4 See p.207
5 See p.213

V. Menorca

The oldest of the Balearic islands, Menorca abounds in ancient monuments and relics. It also boasts the largest natural harbour, Mahón, offering excellent berthing and nautical facilities as well as historical sites to visit. There is a strong British influence because of their previous occupations of the island. There are 4 other ports, and numerous delightful bays in which to sojourn, only a few miles apart.

SECTIONS

The coastline is considered in a clockwise direction around the island beginning at Puerto de Mahón

1. **Puerto de Mahón to Punta de San Carlos**
2. **Punta de San Carlos to Cala Binidali**
3. **Cabo Gros to Cala Santa Galdana**
4. **Cala Macarella to Cala Santandria**
5. **Punta Degollador to Cabo Nati**
6. **Cala Pous to Isla Nitge**
7. **Cabo Cavallería to Cabo Favaritx**
8. **Cabo Favaritx to Punta S'Espero**

NAVIGATIONAL INFORMATION FOR APPROACHES TO MENORCA

Menorca is an excellent departure point when heading east and northeast to France, Italy or to Corsica and Sardinia. Space for berthing in Puerto de Mahón while awaiting favourable winds can be found, even in summer. Unlike the other islands, it is less crowded and often cheaper.

Magnetic variation

Negligable: less than 0°00' (2010).

Approach and coastal passage charts

(See *Appendix* for full list of Balearic charts).

Imray	M3
Admiralty	1703, 2833
Spanish	48E, 6A, 428A
French	5505, 7117

MENORCA WAYPOINTS

⊕81	Puerto de Mahón fairway	39°52'.0N 04°18'.6E
⊕82	Isla del Aire Passage	39°48'.4N 04°17'.0E
⊕83	Off Cabo d'en Font	39°49'.1N 04°12'.1E
⊕84	Cala Santa Galdana	39°56'.0N 03°57'.4E
⊕85	Cala Son Saura	39°55'.1N 03°53'.6E
⊕86	Puerto de Tamarinda	39°55'.4N 03°50'.1E
⊕87	Off Cabo Negro	39°57'.2N 03°49'.1E
⊕88	Puerto de Ciudadela	39°59'.6N 03°49'.5E
⊕89	Cabo Binicous (de Banyos)	40°00'.0N 03°47'.1E
⊕90	Cabo Nati	40°03'.1N 03°49'.0E
⊕91	Punta del Escuá	40°03'.8N 03°52'.0E
⊕92	Bajo Morell rock	40°04'.0N 03°53'.0E
⊕93	Off Cabo Gros	40°04'.7N 03°56'.0E
⊕94	Isla Bledas N	40°04'.7N 04°01'.9E
⊕95	Off Isla Nitge	40°05'.8N 04°04'.1E
⊕96	Puerto de Fornells	40°04'.0N 04°08'.0E
⊕97	Cabo Pentinat	40°03'.6N 04°10'.6E
⊕98	Addaya Approach	40°01'.4N 04°12'.4E
⊕99	Cabo Favaritx	39°59'.8N 04°16'.4E
⊕100	Cabo Monseña	39°59'.1N 04°16'.4E
⊕101	Punta Galera	39°56'.7N 04°17'.5E
⊕102	Cabo Negro	39°54'.0N 04°18'.7E
⊕103	Punta S'Esperó	39°52'.6N 04°19'.9E

Approach lights

0355 **Punta S'Esperó** 39°52'.7N 04°19'.7E Fl(1+2)15s51m8M White round tower, two black bands, on white building 11m

0354 **Punta de San Carlos** 39°52'N 04°18'.5E Oc(2)6s22m12M White round tower, three black bands, on square white base 15m 183°-vis-143°

0366 **Isla del Aire** 39°48'N 04°17'.6E Fl.5s53m18M White tower, black bands, on white building 38m 197°-vis-111°

0367 **Bajo d'es Caragol** 39°48'.6N 04°15'.3E Q(6)+LFl.15s10m5M South cardinal beacon with s topmark 10m

0342 **Cabo Dartuch (D'Artrutx)** 39°55'.4N 03°49'.5E Fl(3)10s45m19M White tower, three black bands, on white building 34m 267°-vis-158°

0348 **Cabo Nati** 40°03'.1N 03°49'.5E Fl(3+1)20s42m16M White tower, aluminium cupola, on white building with red roof 19m 039°-vis-162°

Note The characteristics of Cabo Nati are very similar to those of Cabo Formentor, Mallorca

0350 **Cabo Cavallería** 40°05'.3N 04°05'.5E Fl(2)10s94m22M White tower and building 15m 074°-vis-292° Racon

0352 **Cabo Favaritx** 39°59'.8N 4°16'E Fl(1+2)15s47m16M White tower, black diagonal stripes, on white building 28m

Ancient monastery with a church built in 1595 on the highest point in Menorca, Mount Toro

INTRODUCTION

Twenty miles east-northeast of Mallorca lies Menorca. It is the most easterly of the Islas Baleares and is 26 miles long and 11 miles wide. It is not as mountainous as the other two main islands, being for the most part a low plateau with a few small hills near the north coast and the lone Monte Toro (358m) near the centre of the island. This 'mountain' can be seen from afar and makes a useful landmark.

Geologically the island is interesting, in that it consists of two parts. That north of a line drawn from near Cala Morell to Mahón is the oldest part of the Islas Baleares and was apparently originally joined to Corsica, mainland Europe and Catalonia. The southern part of the island was created later by a process of overlaying and folding: part of the same upheaval which formed the Alps. Menorca was also the first of the Baleares to become separated as an island, but this was much later. It lies in the path of the northwest *tramontana* or *mestral* gales and is sometimes referred to as the 'Windy Isle'. The north coast is dangerous when this wind is blowing and should be given a wide berth.

Viewed from offshore many parts of Menorca have a barren appearance, due to the rocky cliffs, despite a considerable amount of arable and wooded land behind the coast. However, these cliffs are broken by innumerable *calas* which offer many attractive anchorages.

Puerto de Mahón (Maó) on the east coast is the major port and can be entered under most conditions. On the west coast lies the much smaller (and often very crowded) Puerto de Ciudadela, which offers shelter in all conditions other than westerly or southwesterly gales. The remaining harbours should not be entered with strong onshore winds and are mostly very uncomfortable, if not downright dangerous, at such times. Cala de Addaya is a notable exception, offering excellent shelter once inside, though the entrance itself may become impassable.

Menorca has noticeably fewer tourist developments than the other main Islas Baleares, and where such facilities exist they generally cater more for the 'quality' than the 'quantity' market. It is certainly less commercialised than the other islands. Mahón is, to a certain extent, an exception because it has been an important naval base for many years and has absorbed the influences, habits and behaviour of the various occupying forces (including the British who were there for much of the 18th century). The island population is currently some 60,000, of whom more than a third live in either Mahón or Ciudadela. Local industries of long standing include leatherwork (mainly shoes), jewellery, and the production of a hard mature cheese which is enjoyed throughout Spain.

Although not as spectacularly beautiful as much of Mallorca, Menorca has its own attractions and has much to offer those who prefer to avoid major centres of tourism.

For the serious navigator interested in cruising around the coast of Menorca the book *Menorca; Atlas Náutico* by Alfonso Buenaventura is an absolute must, as it shows the coastline in 67 chartlets in extreme detail.

There is a growing tendency in some of the calas, as in mainland Spain, to exclude pleasure craft entirely by laying swimmer buoys in high season. In general this applies mainly to *calas* having adjacent hotels: the bigger the hotel, it seems, the greater the exclusion.

HISTORY

Menorca has the greatest concentration of prehistoric remains in the entire Mediterranean, including what is claimed to be the oldest building in Europe. There are a number of Neolithic caves and villages on the island and many megalithic monuments such as *talayots* (towers), *navetas* (burial mounds) and *taulas* (T-shaped monuments) – probably built for religious and funerary purposes by the Bronze Age civilisation which inhabited the land before the Iberians established themselves. Unfortunately very little has been discovered about this Bronze Age tribe, or about the construction and use of the 400 or so large buildings and monuments which are scattered around the island.

In due course, as in large parts of the Mediterranean basin, Menorca saw successive waves of invasion and colonisation by Phoenicians, Carthaginians, Greeks, Romans, Vandals, Byzantines, Visigoths and Moors. During the occupation by the Carthaginians the towns of Maguén (Mahón) and Yamma (Ciudadela) were founded, though doubtless both inlets had been used by seafarers since time immemorial. The period of Roman occupation from 123BC to AD427 was relatively peaceful and prosperous, Mahón

Prehistoric remains at Torralba d'en Salord, near Cala en Porter *GW*

becoming Municipio Flavio Magontano and Ciudadela, Lamnona. Amongst other legacies, the Romans built the island's first road system.

The successive waves of invasion and colonisation by Vandals, Byzantines and Visigoths left fewer permanent traces. After many years of raids, the island was finally occupied by the Moors in about 913. They remained until driven out by King Alfonso III of Aragon in 1287, by which time Menorca was the last Muslim territory in eastern Spain, although in theory it had owed allegiance to the crown of Aragon since 1232. The common prefix 'Bini', as in Binidalí and Binibeca, is from the Arabic, meaning 'belonging to the son of'.

The following centuries were even more difficult for the islanders, with devastating pirate raids, droughts and epidemics. In 1535 Mahón lost much of its population to a raid by the Turkish pirate Barbarossa; in 1558 it was the turn of Ciudadela, which withstood a nine-day siege before being overrun and almost completely destroyed by a force of 15,000 Turks.

Due to the strategic position of Mahón as a naval base in the western Mediterranean, it was coveted by all maritime nations and Menorca changed hands frequently. In 1708 it was occupied by the British, who had supported the Carlist cause in the War of the Spanish Succession, and in 1713 the island was officially ceded by the Treaty of Utrecht (as was Gibraltar). One of their most lasting legacies was the road built by the Governor, Sir Richard Kane, from Ciudadela to Mahón – the first good road linking the two towns since Roman times – and his moving of the capital from Ciudadela to Mahón in 1722. The island remained in British hands for more than forty years, during which Mahón grew as a fortified naval base and the island prospered.

In 1756 a French army landed near Ciudadela and marched across the island to lay siege to the fortress of San Felipe, near Mahón, which was eventually forced to surrender. It was following this episode that the unfortunate Admiral Byng was executed by firing squad at Portsmouth, on the quarterdeck of HMS *Monarque*, for failing to engage the French fleet and thereby lift the siege. This provoked Voltaire's famous quip: '*Dans ce pays-ci, il est bon de tuer de temps en temps un amiral pour encourager les autres.*' ('In this country, it is wise from time to time to kill an admiral in order to encourage the others').

However, the French only held the island until 1763 when it was returned to Britain by the Treaty of Paris.

Richelieu, who had commanded the successful French invasion in 1756, had a sauce called *mahon-ésa* – based on the local *aïoli* (*alioli*) sauce – served at the victory banquet in Paris. This delicacy, which his chef had invented while on the island, has become the ubiquitous 'mayonnaise'.

In 1782 a Franco-Spanish force once more laid siege to the garrison, which after another heroic resistance was forced to surrender. Not surprisingly one of the first things the victors did was to demolish the fortress, first built in the 1500s as a defence against Corsairs. Sixteen years later the British recaptured the island but had to return it to Spain in 1802 under the Treaty of Amiens. A direct result of this ongoing rivalry was the construction of forts and other large defensive works in and around the port of Mahón, many of which are still to be seen. Under Spanish rule the island reverted to a simple pastoral and fishing existence, though in 1830 the French were permitted to establish a base at Mahón for use during their campaign in Algeria. The limited opportunities and employment for young people during the 19th century encouraged emigration, particularly to the west coast of America. During the Spanish Civil War Menorca remained in the hands of the Republicans and much damage was done to the island's churches.

Recent history

Only recently has any attempt been made to cater for the tourist trade, but today considerable development can be seen, bringing not only income but outside influences and values into the lives of the islanders.

TOURIST INFORMATION

Places of interest in Menorca

In addition to the places of interest described in the harbour sections there are many other sites inland which can be visited by taxi, bus or on foot. One not to be missed is Monte Toro, near the village of Es Mercadal, for the panoramic view, the church (built in 1595) and the restored 17th-century monastery founded by Augustine monks. The name Monte Toro comes not from the Spanish 'Bull Mount', but from Arabic 'The Highest (point)' which indeed it is, at 358 metres.

Of the many Megalithic remains, the following are easy to reach from the two main harbours:
- One mile south of Mahón, the *taula* and *talayot* of Trapuco: a megalithic tower and monument
- Two miles southwest of Mahón, the *talayot* of Torellonet (near the airport)
- Five miles west of Mahón, the Torralba group of *taulas* (T-shaped monuments)
- Three miles east of Ciudadela, the *naveta* burial mound at Nau d'es Tudóns (claimed to be the oldest building in Europe)
- Four miles east of Ciudadela, the *poblado* and *taulas* of Torre Llafuda
- Four miles south of Ciudadela, the *talayot* of Son Olivaret.

The Euro-Map of Mallorca, Menorca, Ibiza published by GeoCenter International shows many of the historic and prehistoric sites, as does a multilingual map available locally.

For details of tourist offices see *General Introduction*.

Embassies

For details of embassies see *Appendix*.

ME1 Puerto de Mahón (Maó)

A long and deep *cala* leads into a natural and well-protected harbour hosting a naval base, fishing fleet and many yachting facilities along its shores, with berthing for over 1,000 vessels

Location
39°52'.1N 04°18'.6E

Communications
Pilots (Mahón Prácticos) VHF Ch 12, 14, 16, 20, 27
Port authority ① 971 22 81 50 *Fax* 971 72 69 48
Puerto de Mahón ① 971 35 48 44
Fax 971 35 43 27
Email portsdebaleares@portsdebalears.com
www.portsdebalears.com
S'Altra Banda VHF Ch 09, ① 971 59 40 62 *Fax* 971 36 82 81
Email info@portsaltrabanda.com
www.portsaltrabanda.com
See text for further internet information on other options

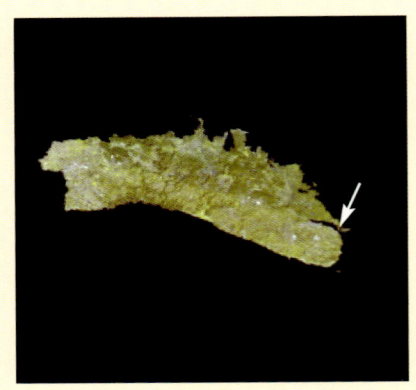

The port

An attractive and interesting commercial, naval, fishing and yachting port up a long deep *cala*. The approach and entrance are straightforward and entry can be made in storm conditions, with good shelter available once inside. There are excellent facilities for yachtsmen including a first-class, expensive yacht club and many lesser facilities.

PILOTAGE

Approach

⊕81 39°52'.10N 4°18'.6E Puerto de Mahón fairway

From south The tall lighthouse on Isla del Aire (Fl.5s53m18M, white tower with black bands on white building 38m), 4M south of the *cala* entrance is easily identified and the island can safely be left on

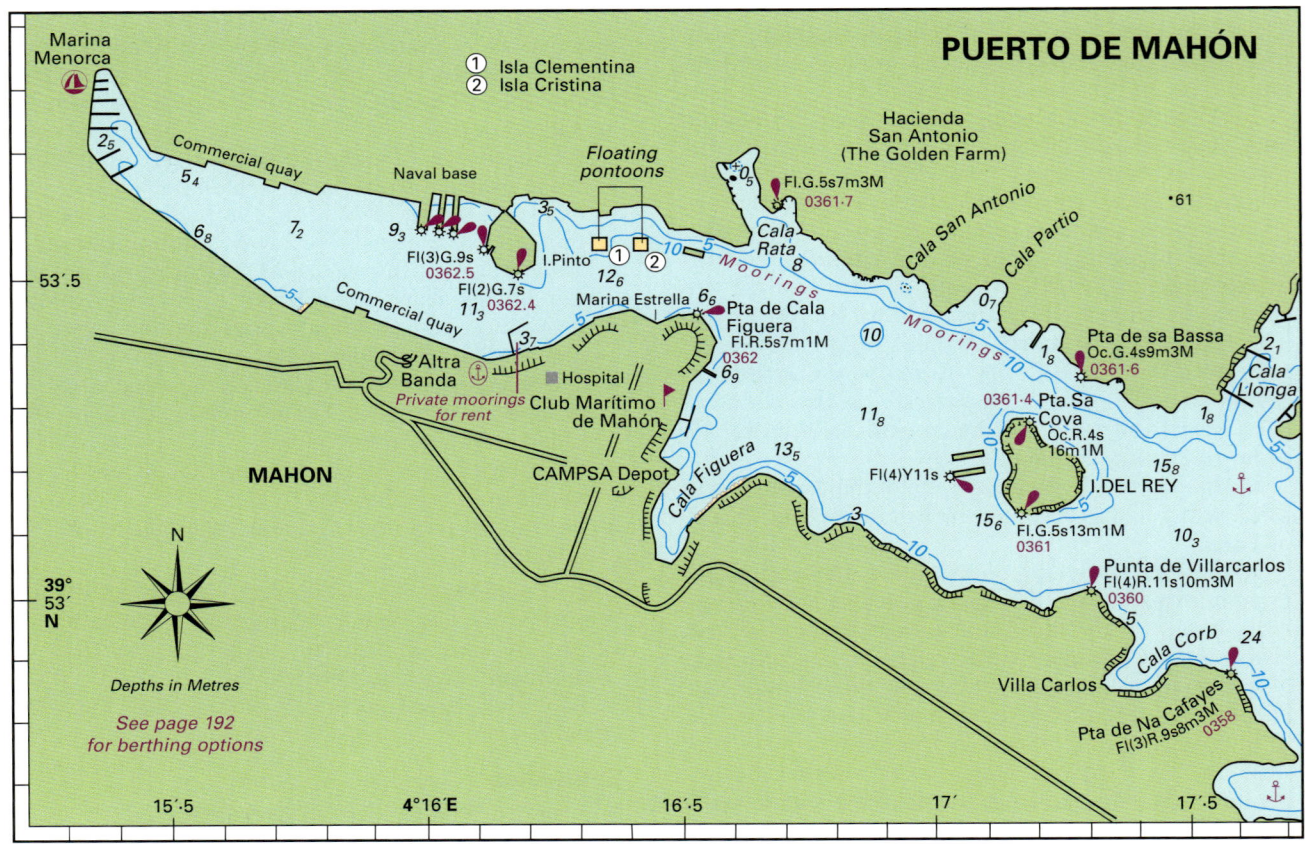

either side (see plan on page 196). The few hazards between Isla del Aire and Puerto de Mahón will be avoided by following a track at least 250m off Punta Rafalet and Punta de Na Girada. The lighthouse (Oc(2)6s22m12M, white tower with three black bands on square white base 15m) and nearby radio towers on Punta de San Carlos are also conspicuous, and the high (78m) peninsula of La Mola ahead easily recognised. The harbour entrance lies between the two.

From north From Cabo Favaritx (Fl(1+2)15s47m16M, white tower with black diagonal stripes on white building 28m) southwards the coast is very broken; Isla Colom may be recognised if sailing inshore (see plan on page 241). The high peninsula of La Mola (78m) with buildings on its summit and a lighthouse on Punta del Esperó

(Fl(1+2)15s51m8M, white tower with two black bands on white building 11m) are conspicuous from this direction. The entrance to Puerto de Mahón lies just beyond.

Currents

There is normally a southwest current past the entrance to Puerto de Mahón. North or northeast winds increase its speed while winds from south or southwest either slow or reverse the flow.

Anchorages in the approach

Just south of the entrance lies Cala de San Esteban. To the north lie Clot de la Mola and Cala Taulera. Clot de la Mola is a small horseshoe bay with 10m over rock and stone, exposed to the south quadrant. Cala Taulera, in contrast, is a long narrow inlet between La Mola and Isla del Lazareto, offering

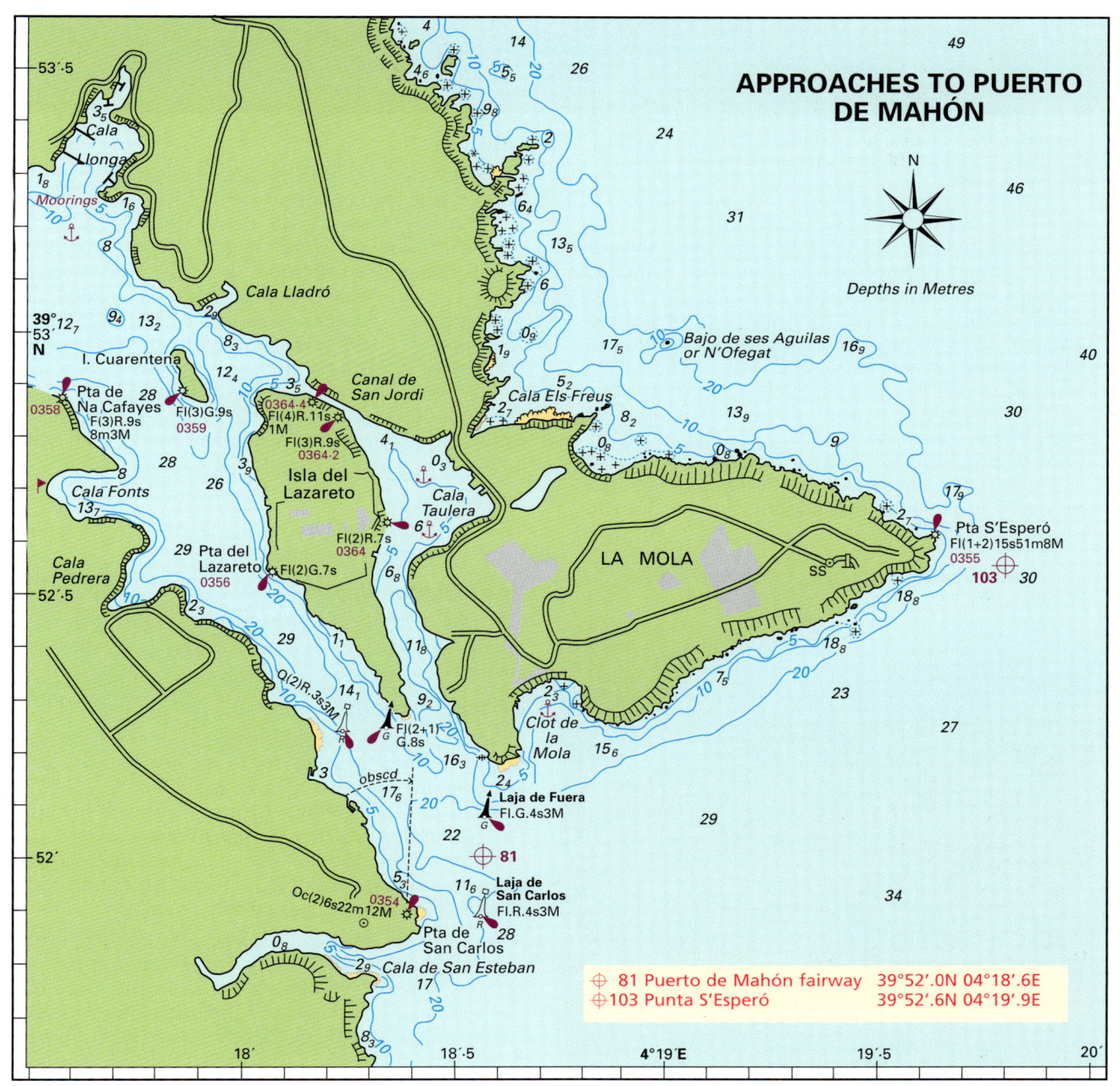

⊕ 81 Puerto de Mahón fairway 39°52'.0N 04°18'.6E
⊕ 103 Punta S'Esperó 39°52'.6N 04°19'.9E

Approach to Mahón looking northwest. Pta de San Carlos left, La Mola right and Isla del Lazareto all clearly seen, along with buoys

total protection in 6m or less over sand though shallow along its north edge. If coming from the east, turn in close past Laja de Fuera buoy to avoid the spit running out from the south end of Isla del Lazareto. The *cala* can easily accommodate 20 or 30 yachts at anchor and is popular with both visitors and locals, even though a charge is sometimes made. Avoid the west side of the *cala* as this is used, at speed, by the tourist boats. An artificial channel, the Canal de San Jordi (sometimes referred to as Canal del Lazareto) provides a 'back door' into the harbour. The canal has a minimum depth of 3m and there are no overhead wires.

Cala Taulera viewed from south-southwest over Isla del Lazareto

Entrance

Enter Puerto de Mahón on a northwest course between the high peninsula of La Mola to starboard and the low rocky-cliffed Punta de San Carlos to port. Lit buoys mark the channel, which is used by commercial vessels of some size and should offer a yacht no difficulties, day or night, provided the buoyage is complied with. However, note that Mahón is a naval, ferry and commercial port and that these vessels have right of way over yachts and small craft. A 3-knot speed limit is in force throughout the *cala* and harbour, but beware of speeding ferries, port officials and motor craft who ignore it.

Sea levels

The sea level falls prior to and during strong winds from southwest, west and northwest.

Note: charted depths

Editions of BA charts 2833 pre 1997 show incorrect depths for Mahón. Subsequent editions have been corrected.

Berthing options

Other than a few visitors' berths offered by the *club marítimo* and Marina Estrella, nearly all yacht berthing in the port is now controlled by S'Altra Banda (of the Ocibar group), licensed by the harbour authorities to administer visitors' berths and moorings. See their website for details of mooring charges and services www.portsaltrabanda.com. They have four principal berthing areas:

a. Stern-to on the quayside just east of their office (see plan on page 190), lines tailed to quay.
b. Two floating 'islands' Isla Clementina and Isla Cristina, moored east of Isla Pinto. They can take up to 25m and 18m yachts respectively, moored stern-to (lazy lines are provided). A rubbish

Private moorings (hidden)

Private moorings opposite Isla Pinto *Graham Hutt*

collection service is provided and electricity is available. Water is now available on the pontoon.

c. Five pontoons in Cala Llonga, able to take 100 yachts up to 15m. Rubbish collection is laid on and water, electricity and showers are available.

d. The former designated anchorage area west of Isla del Rey has been replaced with two extended pontoons with lazy lines. This is now designated for yachts up to 25m (see plan on website). Water and electricity are available, plus rubbish and sewage disposal. The pontoon is now lit with Q(9)15s2m1M on a 1m yellow structure.

S'Altra Banda VHF Ch 09
℡ 971 59 40 62 *Fax* 971 36 82 81
Email info@portsaltrabanda.com
www.portsaltrabanda.com

- **Marina Estrella** Sunseeker Menorca is still up and running in the new guise of Marina Estrella Menorca, still offering 56 moorings from 12m up to 40m with electricity and water supplies, plus Wi-Fi, included. Shower and washing facilities available at the office to all visiting boaters. Frontline moorings with the best situation in this picturesque port. (See plan on page 190.)

  ℡ 971 35 33 20 *Fax* 971 35 33 50
  Email for moorings
  mooringsmenorca@marinaestrella.com
  www.marinaestrella.com

- **Club Marítimo de Mahón** Their mooring area extends from the Punta de Cala Figuera down to their fuelling berth near the south end of Cala Figuera. They have a small pier and floating pontoons but all their moorings are occupied by local members and there is seldom room for visitors. Anchoring is no longer permitted in the *cala*.

  Club Marítimo ℡ 971 36 50 22 *Fax* 971 36 07 62
  Email cmahon@terra.es
  www.clubmaritimomahon.com

- **Marina Menorca** A newish yacht harbour in the extreme west end of the harbour. It has berths for at least 100 yachts of up to 15m, though many of the slots will be for smaller boats with less

draught. Water and electricity are available on the pontoons. This is the furthest marina from the city. Staff are on duty from 0800 to 2100 daily.

VHF Ch 09 or Ch 69
℡ 971 35 98 21
www.marinamenorca.com

- **Pedro's Boat Centre** has a large hardstanding area, crane and chandlery. Offers boat maintenance, repairs and support services (see website for details). It has a fleet of fast RIBs and is always willing to help out in emergencies, though not offering berthing as previously.

  ℡ 971 36 69 68 *Fax* 971 36 24 55
  www.pedrosboatcentre.com

- **Public Quay** The Port Authority, which runs the public quay not already leased to the firms mentioned above, will not allow yachts to berth on the quay as it is now for commercial and ferry traffic only.

- Several private moorings lie along the *cala* between the Commercial Quay and Marina Menorca. It is sometimes possible to find an empty berth in this area and negotiate a price if the owner returns.

Note It is difficult to contact any of the mooring options after 2100. It is therefore best to take any available space and sort out a better option in the morning, if no prior arrangement has been made. I have always been lucky enough to find a private berth available opposite Isla Pinto, with water and electricity. Price negotiable with owner – usually not more than €30 per night off season, for 12m yacht.

Mooring buoys

Private moorings occupy most of the northern shore, with some visitors' moorings (bright yellow) off Cala Llonga, around Cala Partio and off Cala Rata, extending westwards toward Isla Clementina (but they may be out of bounds, 2010). All are administered by S'Altra Banda. A rubbish collection service is provided and there is a dinghy landing stage east of the Banda S'Altra office (a floating restaurant is currently moored to the end of the pontoon).

There are new mooring areas in Cala Font (Fons) and Cala Corp (Corb) which are understood to be administered by S'Altra Banda.

Anchorages within the cala

- In Cala Taulera just inside the entrance to the harbour (see *Anchorages in the approach*) for which a charge is sometimes made
- In the designated anchorage close west of Isla del Rey (see plan) for craft over 20m. Again there is a fee, but this includes rubbish collection and use of a dinghy landing stage in Cala Figuera
- In the mouth of Cala Llonga, outside the moorings.

Prohibited anchorages

Anchoring is prohibited everywhere other than the three areas mentioned above.

Viewed from south, Cala Fonts, Cala Llonga, Cala Pedrera

Facilities

Water At the Club Marítimo; on the quay near both the Marina Estrella and S'Altra Banda offices; at the western end of the commercial quay; on Isla Clementina and its sister island; on the pontoons in Cala Llonga; on the pontoons at Marina Menorca; from the Club Náutico de Villacarlos at the head of Cala Font. Water is metered other than on the commercial quay, where it is coin-operated. The minimum charge can be quite high for small quantities.

Electricity At the Marina Estrella berths, on Isla Clementina and the pontoons in Cala Llonga, and Marina Menorca.

Fuel Diesel and paraffin from the CAMPSA depot on the west side of Cala Figuera (where bunkering facilities are also available). At first sight the CAMPSA depot does not look like a fuel station. Diesel and petrol from the Club Marítimo.

Bottled gas Camping Gaz is readily available in chandleries and hardware stores.

Viewed from south: Cala Figuera across to Cala Rata. Rafts and moorings on far side of bay

Provisioning Small supermarket behind the S'Altra Banda office. A larger one near the CAMPSA depot and another just up the hill from Cala Fonts. The largest supermarkets are on the industrial estates outside the town. General shops of every description are to be found in Mahón. Excellent produce and fish markets near the large church of Santa María, open every morning except Sunday.

Shopping Delivery service Alberto offers a delivery service to all yachts ☎ 0034 655 463862.

Wi-Fi Wi-Fi cards can be purchased from Mangalam (dress shop on the front) but Mo.net is unreliable at the artificial islands. Café in Clostre des Carmes has Wi-Fi.

Ice From the Club Marítimo and Marina Estrella as well as nearby bars and supermarkets.

Chandlery There are several chandlers around the commercial quay area. Some items from Marina Estrella. It is possible to berth for an hour or so near the chandleries on the commerial quay to load heavy items.

Charts From the chandlers; however, there is no official Spanish chart agent in Menorca.

Repairs Major repairs to wood, GRP and aluminium hulls can be undertaken by local yards. Both S'Altra Banda and Marina Estrella are willing to assist in arranging repairs or maintenance. Pedro's Boat Centre, opposite the new Marina Menorca, has a large area of hardstanding and can facilitate repairs. ☎ 971 36 69 68 *Fax* 971 36 24 55 www.pedrosboatcentre.com
There are two travel-lifts (50 and 35-tonne capacity) and a mobile crane at Pedro's Boat Centre. Several more cranes on the commercial quays. Marina Estrella has a 12-ton crane, the Club Marítimo has 10 and 2-tonne models, also a slipway. There is a slipway on the west side of Cala Figuera, 20-tonnes and 14m maximum (enquire at S'Altra Banda or Marina Estrella regarding its use).

Engineers Many around the harbour, including the English-run Marine & Auto Power ☎ 971 35 44 38 and MenMar ☎ 971 35 48 35 *Fax* 971 35 33 50.
Official service agents include the following (telephone and fax numbers should be prefixed 971).)
Marina Estrella ☎ 35 33 20 *Fax* 35 33 50 – Volvo Penta; Auto Recambios Union ☎ 36 01 13 – Yamaha; Motonáutica Menorca ☎ 36 89 17 *Fax* 35 27 25 – Detroit diesel, Honda, Man, Mariner, Perkins; NauticCentreMenorca ☎ 36 05 50 *Fax* 35 12 50 – Ecosse, Mercury/MerCruiser, Solé diesel, Yanmar; Nautic Reynes ☎ 36 59 52 *Fax* 35 34 98 – Force, Mariner, Mercury/MerCruiser, Yanmar; Pedro's Boat Centre ☎ 36 69 68 *Fax* 36 24 55 – Mercury/ MerCruiser.

Electronic & radio repairs Enquire at S'Altra Banda or Marina Estrella.

Sailmaker At the Club Marítimo.

Yacht clubs The Club Marítimo de Mahón has now completed rebuilding and is a magnificent building with showers, toilets, restaurant and all facilities. The Club Náutico de Villacarlos ☎ 971 36 58 84 *Fax* 36 58 84 at the tip of Cala Fonts is a smaller concern, offering a bar and water but no berths.

Showers At the Club Marítimo for €5. Also on the pontoons in Cala Llonga and on Isla Clementina (outdoor shower). Showers in a portacabin are also available at Marina Menorca.

Launderette Several in the town, also at the Club Marítimo and in the S'Altra Banda building.

Banks Several banks in the town, mostly with credit card facilities.

Water taxi A water taxi is available for yachts moored on the islands and pontoons in the *cala*. ☎ +34 616 428891.

Hospital In the town.

Looking west across Islas Pinto, Cristina and Clementina to Marina Menorca and the commercial port *GW*

Transport

Car hire/taxis Numerous car hire and taxi companies.
Buses Bus service to Ciudadela and elsewhere.
Ferries To Palma and mainland Spain.
Air services Smallish international airport, with services direct to major capitals, less than three miles southwest of Mahón.

History

The whole area is steeped in history, some of it from the British occupation.

The ancient Portús Magonis (Mahón) was once thought to have been named after Mago, the younger brother of Hannibal, who founded it in about 206BC. There is, however, no evidence for this and the name could also have come from the Phoenician *maguén* meaning 'shield' or 'fortress', which would have been equally apt. Due to its excellent harbour and its position in the centre of the Mediterranean, Mahón has been a prize that many nations have coveted, and traces of the long British occupation during the 18th century are unmistakable. Many of the older streets and houses with sash windows have a very English appearance, and various English words have gained a place in the Menorquín language. There is even a gin distillery near the harbour. The island changed hands six times between 1708 and 1802 and each time it was Mahón that was the prize.

During the last period of British occupation Lord Nelson, who was in temporary command of the Mediterranean Fleet, spent a few days at the Golden Farm on the north side of the harbour, some time between 12 and 22 October 1799. Local tradition declares (without evidence) that Lady Hamilton was a guest in the house at the same time. Villa El Fonduco, near the southeast side of Cala Figuera and now a hotel, was the residence of Lord Collingwood while he was Flag Officer in Mahón during the early 19th century.

Sights ashore locally

Among places of interest near Mahón, the Golden Farm (now a terracotta colour, not yellow!) should be visited for the view – the house is privately owned and not open to the public. The church of Santa María with its superb early 19th-century organ and the Casa Mercadel Museum are in the town itself. For those interested in the underwater world there is an aquarium near the ferry wharf. The old fortifications around the mouth of the harbour are worth exploring and the fort of Isabel II at La Mola is open for guided walks, lasting two and a half hours, at 1000 and 1700 at a price of €4. It is quite difficult to get to the gate where the tickets are sold by road without a car, but for yachts anchored in Cala Taulera simply land on the small beach and walk the 100m to the ticket office. Apparently the Vickers cannons are a highlight of the tour. The prehistoric *taula* (T-shaped monument) and *talayot* (ancient tower) at Trepuco, about a mile to the south, are typical of many throughout the island. If prepared to stroll a little further, the village of San Luis, founded by the French and still with a definite Gallic feel, is on the same road.

Local events

Fiestas are held on 5–6 January with the arrival by boat of Los Reyes Magos (the Three Wise Men) with toys for the children, followed by a procession. On Good Friday there is a procession and medieval parade. On 15–16 July a sea procession is held in honour of Our Lady of Carmen, and on 7–8 September the fiesta of Nuestra Señora de Gracia includes processions, music, sailing races and other sports. In the third week of September a fair is held to showcase local products.

Eating out

A wide selection of restaurants and many quayside bars and cafés. Bar/restaurant at Cala Llonga. A walk up the steps near the Commercial Quay takes you into town where there are many excellent eating places, some friendly family run businesses and other more expensive restaurants.

⚓ CALA DE SAN ESTEBAN (SANT ESTEVE)

39°51'.9N 04°18'.4E

A narrow but deeply indented *cala* surrounded by a fringe of houses, just south of Puerto de Mahón and easily identified by Punta de San Carlos lighthouse (Oc(2)6s22m12M, white tower with three black bands on square white base 15m), two radio masts and a large house all close north of the entrance (⊕81). Depths of 2m or more lead almost to its head: favour the deeper north side and sound carefully as the bottom is rocky. Good protection is gained deeper in the *cala*.

⚓ CALA RAFALET

39°50'.4N 04°18'.1E

One of the most beautiful of the islands' small calas, narrow with steep rocky cliffs and ideal for a fantastic yacht photograph. Investigate by dinghy first and approach with great caution to anchor in 4–6m, open to the east quadrant. The narrow valley running inland from the head of the *cala* is most attractive and shows signs of ancient cave dwellers. There is a track to the main road and a housing estate on the high ground several hundred metres to the south. A *talayot* (ancient tower) lies 1½ miles to the northwest.

⚓ CALA ALCAUFA (D'ALCAUFAR)

39°49'.7N 04°17'.9E

One of the first *calas* to be developed, with many houses on the north side but virtually nothing to the south. Easy to identify by virtue of a large pale stone tower just south of the entrance. Enter leaving Illot d'es Torn to starboard and anchor in 2–4m over rock and sand, open to the southeast. Holding is poor. There are many moorings and space to anchor is restricted – it may be necessary to moor fore-and-aft or take a line ashore. There are a few shops, restaurants and bars in the village.

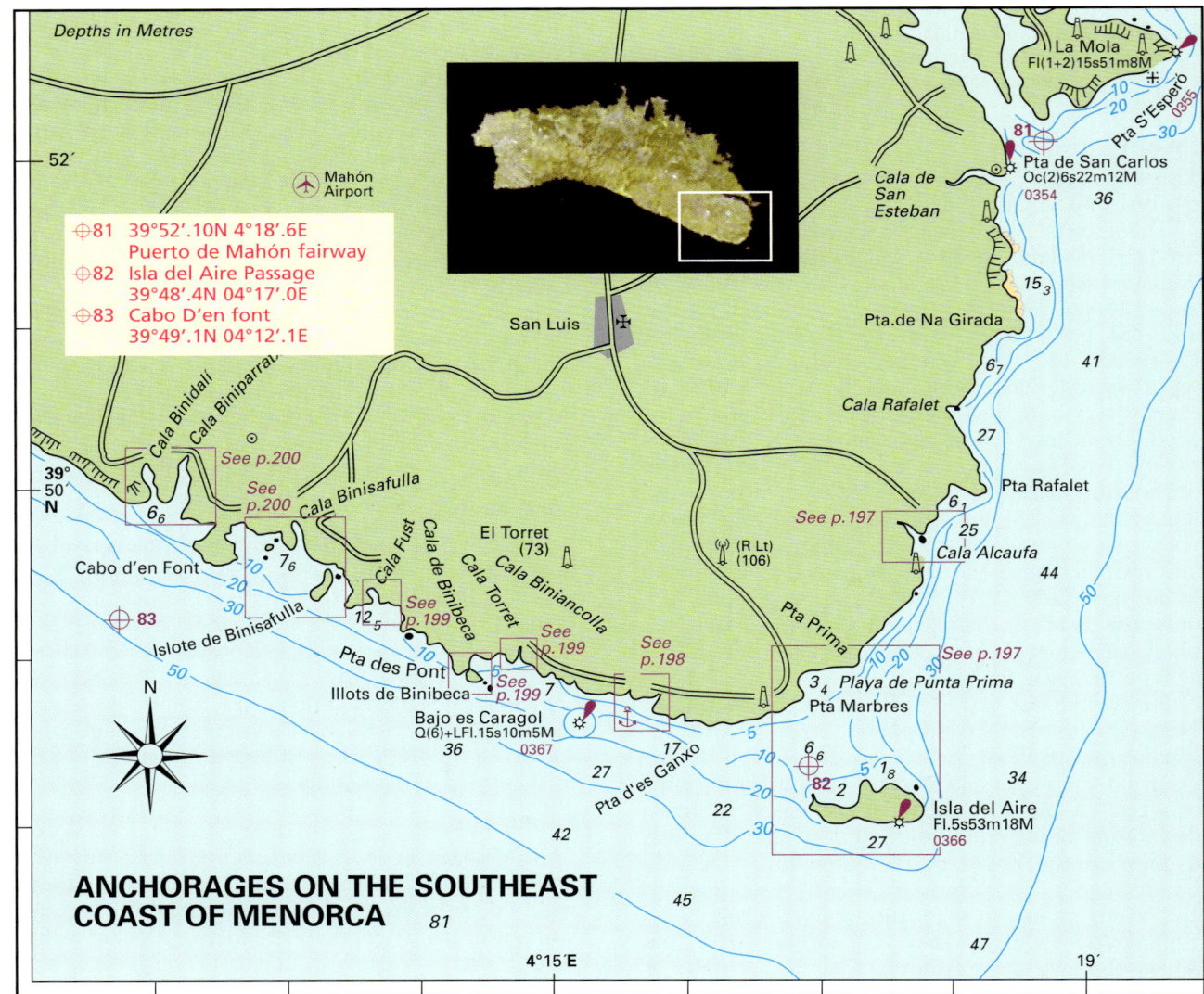

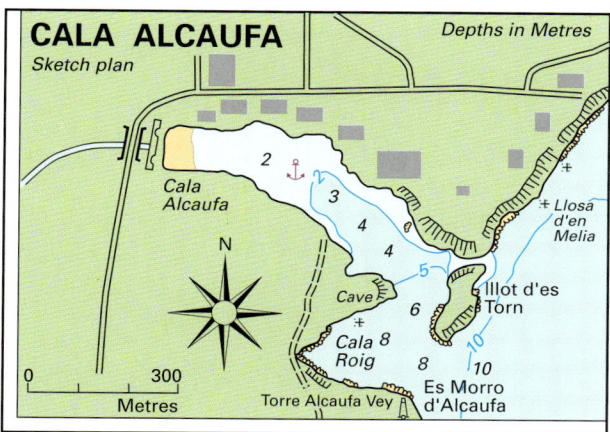

CALA ALCAUFA
Sketch plan
Depths in Metres

Cala Alcaufa
Llosa d'en Melia
Cave
Illot d'es Torn
Cala Roig
Torre Alcaufa Vey
Es Morro d'Alcaufa

0   300
Metres

⚓ PLAYA DE PUNTA PRIMA (ENSENADA ARENAL DE ALCAUFA)

39°48'.8N 04°17'.1E

An exposed anchorage in a wide bay off a superb sandy beach. Anchor in 2m+ of turquoise water. Somewhat protected from the south by Isla del Aire. The bay is backed by houses and apartment blocks together with the usual shops, bars and restaurants. A submarine cable runs in a southeast direction from a point near the head of the bay.

The British landed here under Admiral Sir John Leake and General Stanhope when they captured the island in 1708. Later it was used again by Spanish troops under the Duc de Crillon, landing in 1781 to recapture the island.

Playa de Punta Prima

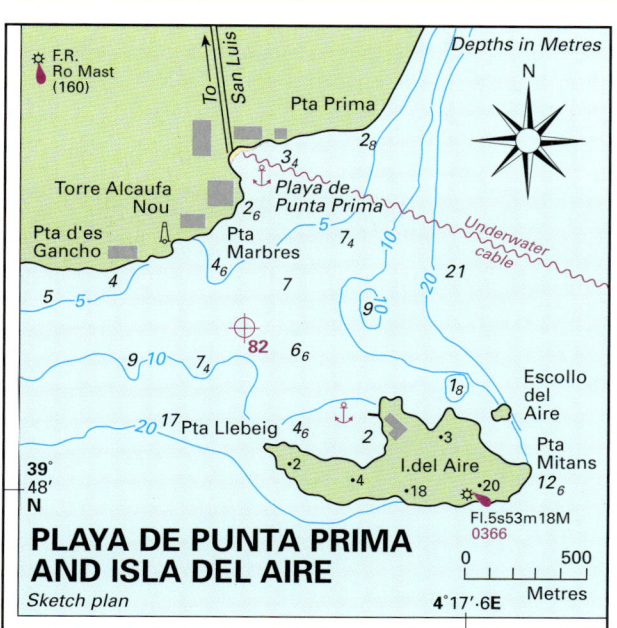

Cala Alcaufa viewed from southeast. Often deserted even in summer

⊕82   Isla del Aire Passage   39°48'.4N 04°17'.0E

PLAYA DE PUNTA PRIMA AND ISLA DEL AIRE
Sketch plan

F.R. Ro Mast (160)
To San Luis
Pta Prima
Depths in Metres
Torre Alcaufa Nou
Pta d'es Gancho
Playa de Punta Prima
Pta Marbres
Underwater cable
82
Pta Llebeig
Escollo del Aire
I.del Aire
Pta Mitans
Fl.5s53m18M
0366

0   500
Metres

4°17'.6E

⚓ ISLA DEL AIRE

Bisected by 39°48'.1N 04°17'.4E

A low, flat island just over 1,000m long by 400m wide but much of it less than 4m high, with a couple of hillocks (18m) and (20m) to the southeast, one topped by a lighthouse (Fl.5s53m18M white tower, black bands, on white building 38m).

Anchor in the bay on the northwest side of the island in 2–4m over sand, weed and some rocks, about 150m west of the landing pier from which there is a track to the lighthouse. Watch for rocky pinnacles and use a tripline.

The island is uninhabited – other than by rabbits and a unique race of black lizards (*Lacerta lilfordi*) – but is visited by tourist boats during summer. It is said that the lizards particularly enjoy tomatoes and will approach quite close if pieces are offered.

Admiral Byng's unsuccessful battle against the French fleet under Galissonnière took place off Isla del Aire in May 1756. This is where Byng failed to close and engage the enemy and fled to Gibraltar. He was court-martialled and executed, as Voltaire said: '*pour encourager les autres*' ('to encourage the others').

Isla del Aire viewed from southeast. Note anchorage north side of island

Passage between Isla del Aire and Menorca

⊕82 39°48'.4N 04°17'.0E Isla del Aire passage

An unimpeded passage 1,000m wide exists between Isla del Aire and Menorca with a minimum central depth of 6.6m. Yachts drawing 2–5m or less can follow the Menorcan coast at 200m. The sandy bottom can usually be seen quite clearly.

⚓ CALA BINIANCOLLA

39°48'.7N 04°15'.7E

A small *cala* with low rocky sides and a village at its head, suitable for small yachts only. A large, conspicuous apartment block stands behind the hamlet and can be seen from afar. If approaching

from the west give the rocky Bajo Es Caragol a generous berth, and enter with care to avoid the outlying rocks on either side. Anchor in sand, rock and weed in ±3m. There are restaurants and cafés in the village.

BAJO ES CARAGOL

39°48'.6N 04°15'.2E

A breaking, rocky bank about 800m southwest of Cala Biniancolla, marked by a south cardinal beacon (Q(6)+LFl.15s10m5M with ⬇ topmark) at its northwest corner. Although there is good water about halfway between the beacon and the shore, the *bajo* should be given a generous berth as rocks extend up to 100m east and south.

Biniancolla viewed from south. Rocky patches just visible

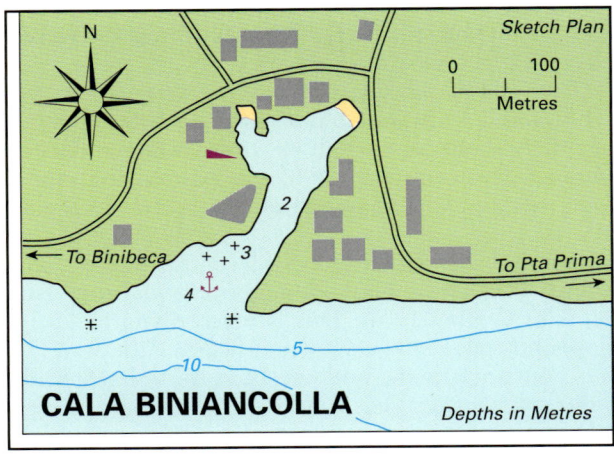

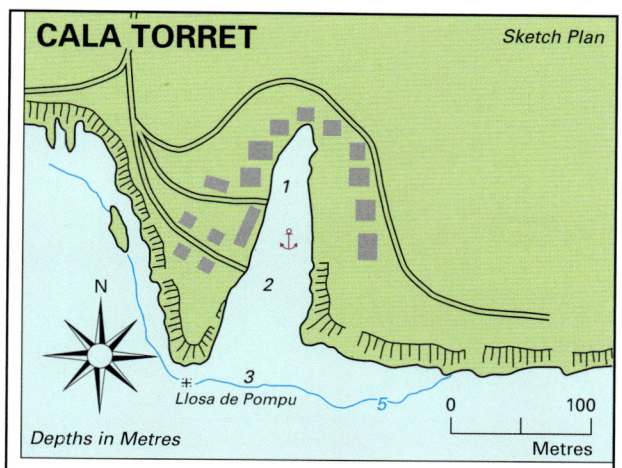

CALA TORRET   Sketch Plan

N

1

2

3
Llosa de Pompu

5

0   100

Metres

Depths in Metres

⚓ CALA TORRET

39°49'N 04°14'.8E

A small, developed *cala* surrounded by houses, only suitable for smaller yachts in good weather. The El Torret tower on the skyline about ¾ mile northeast is a useful mark, as is a line of arched doorways along the west side of the *cala*. Enter with care and anchor in the middle of the *cala*, open southeast through to southwest. The usual cafés, restaurants and small shops will be found ashore.

⚓ CALA DE BINIBECA (BINIBEQUER)

39°48'.9N 04°14'.4E

A large, well-known 'developed' *cala* tucked behind Punta des Pont and the Illots de Binibeca (see plan on page 196), and overlooked by the tourist development of Binibeca Nou. Approach and entrance are straightforward: anchor near the middle in 3–7m over hard sand and weed, open from east to south. There is an excellent beach, very crowded in the season; with a pier, slipway and dinghy crane a short walk east. A *club náutico*, restaurants, shops and a hotel will be found in Binibeca Nou.

⚓ CALA FUST (D'EN FUST)

39°49'.3N 04°13'.7E

Occasionally, and confusingly referred to as Binibeca Vell, Cala Fust is small with many houses and a conspicuous church spire to the east (the village of Binibeca Vell). It is suitable only for smaller yachts. There is an awash rock (Llosa d'en Fust) close east of the entrance. Local fishing craft are moored at the shallow head of the *cala*. There are the usual facilities ashore and some good examples of local rural architecture in Binibeca Vell.

Cala Torret right and Binibeca left, viewed from south

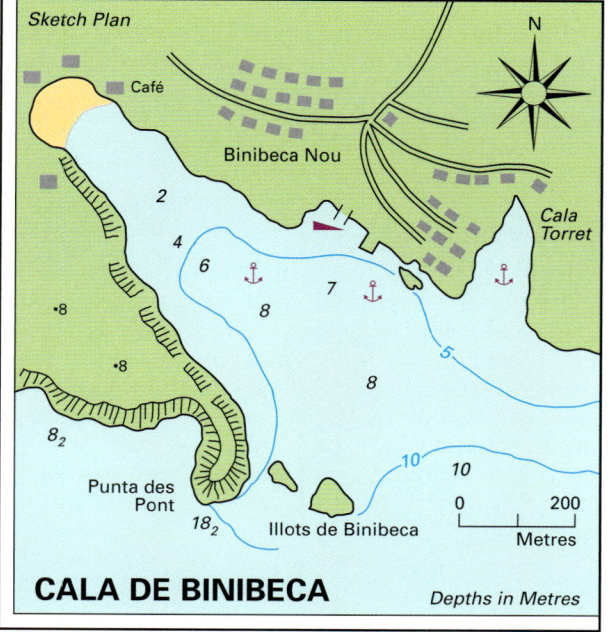

Sketch Plan   N

Café

Binibeca Nou

Cala Torret

2

4

6

7

8

8

•8

•8

8₂

10

10

10

Punta des Pont

18₂   Illots de Binibeca

0   200

Metres

CALA DE BINIBECA   Depths in Metres

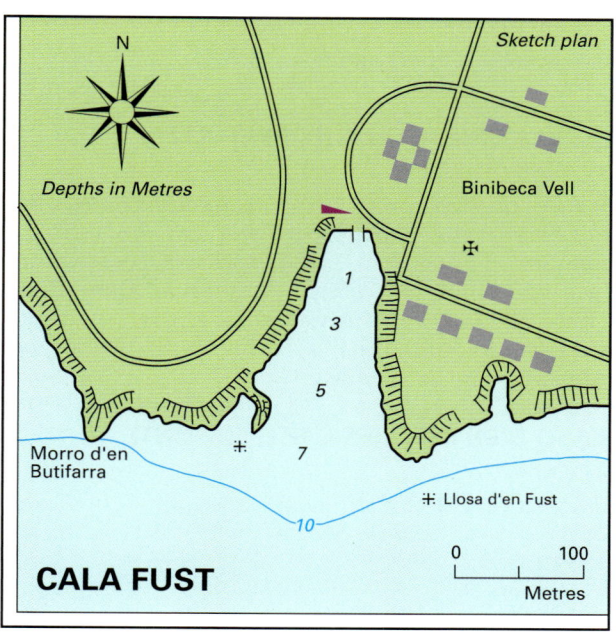

N   Sketch plan

Depths in Metres

Binibeca Vell

1

3

5

7

Morro d'en Butifarra

Llosa d'en Fust

10

0   100

Metres

CALA FUST

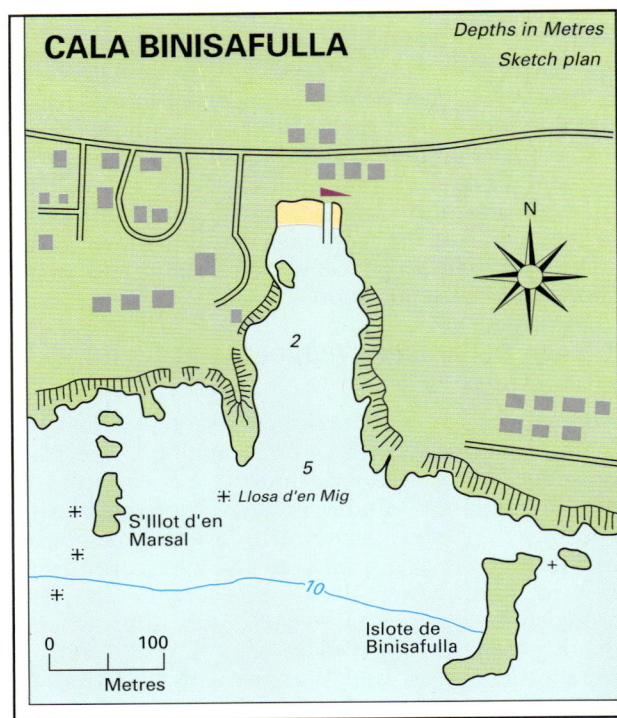

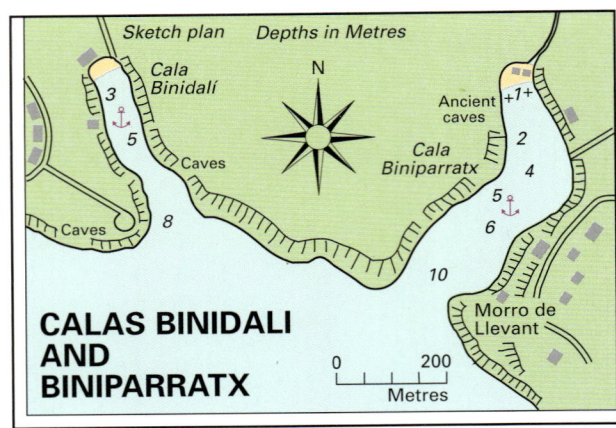

Cala Biniparratx from south

Cala Binisafulla from south

⚓ CALA BINISAFULLA (BINISAFULLER)

39°49′.5N 04°13′.1E

A medium-sized *cala* with some adjacent houses but not overdeveloped. Approach with care because of a number of islets and awash rocks: a course from near the southwest corner of Illot de Binisafuller clears all dangers. Anchor in 2.5m over sand and weed. Cala Binisafulla is in line with the airport runway so it can be noisy.

CABO D'EN FONT (ES CAP D'EN FONT)

39°49′.5N 4°12′.6E

A low (12m) but prominent rocky-cliffed headland covered with houses. Several rocky islets lie to the southeast.

⊕83 39°49′.1N 04°12′.1E Off Cabo d'en Font

⚓ CALA BINIPARRATX

39°49′.8N 04°12′.1E

An attractive small *cala* with high rocky sides, easy to approach and enter. Though inconspicuous from offshore, Cabo d'en Font (some 750m to the east) is prominent. Anchor just short of the 'elbow' in 4–6m over sand and rock. There are rocky patches beyond the corner, and depths shoal rapidly towards the sandy beach. A few houses stand on the east bank of the *cala*, but there are no real facilities.

⚓ CALA BINIDALÍ

39°49′.9N 04°12′.0E

A pretty but very small *cala* just west of Cala Biniparratx, with high rocky cliffs, a sandy beach and a few houses well set back. Strictly a fair-weather anchorage but now closed off by buoys for most of the summer. When open the approach and entrance present no problems; use one or two anchors in 3–5m over sand and rock with possibly a line ashore. The head is shallow. There are no facilities.

3. Cabo Gros to Cala Santa Galdana

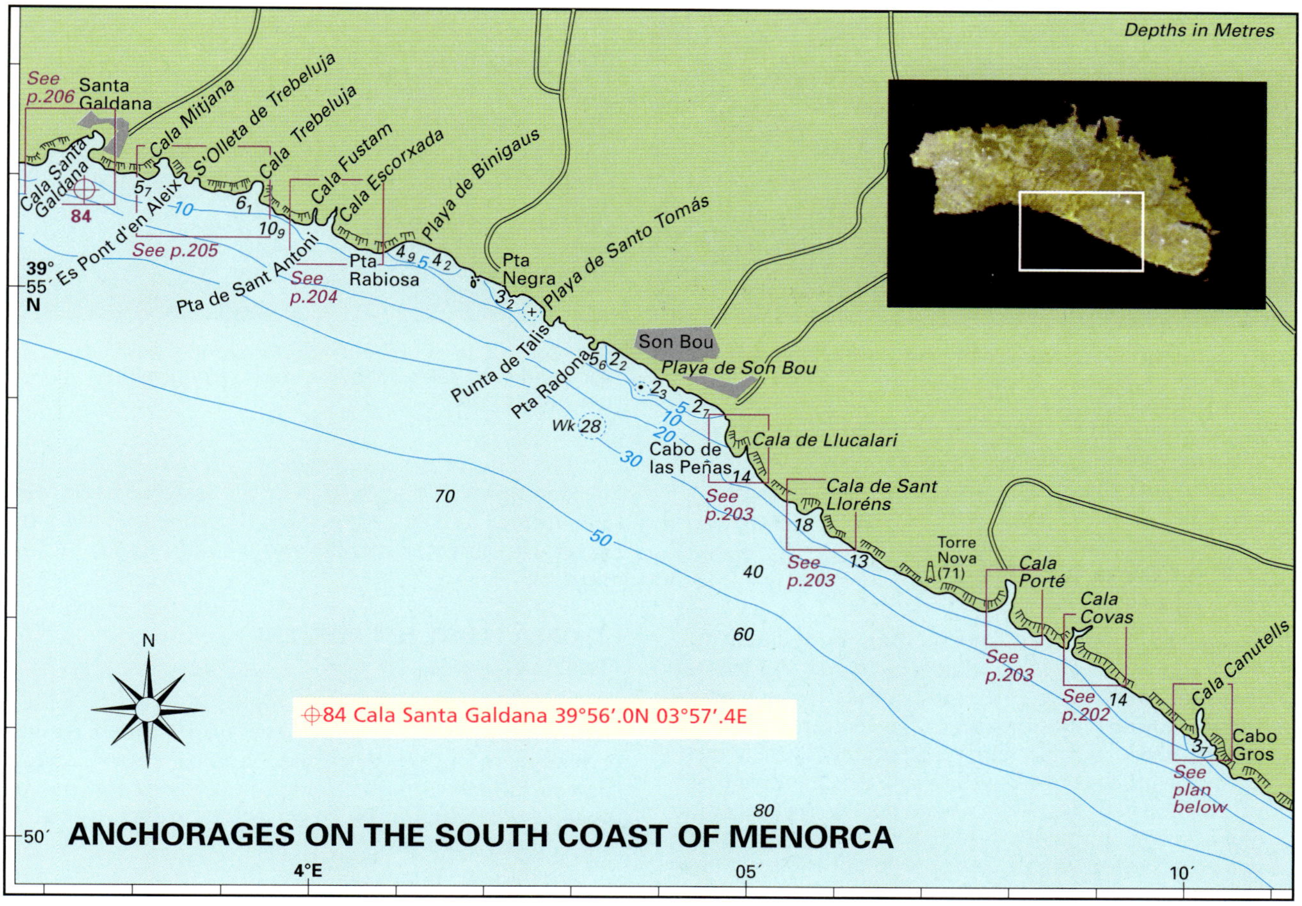

ANCHORAGES ON THE SOUTH COAST OF MENORCA

Depths in Metres

See p.206 Santa Galdana

Cala Mitjana

S'Olleta de Trebeluja

Cala Trebeluja

Cala Fustam

Cala Escorxada

Playa de Binigaus

Playa de Santo Tomás

Cala Santa Galdana

84

Es Pont d'en Aleix

See p.205

Pta de Sant Antoni

See p.204

Pta Rabiosa

Pta Negra

39° 55′ N

Punta de Talis

Pta Radona

Wk 28

Son Bou

Playa de Son Bou

Cabo de las Peñas

See p.203

Cala de Llucalari

Cala de Sant Lloréns

See p.203

Torre Nova (71)

See p.203

Cala Porté

Cala Covas

See p.202

Cala Canutells

Cabo Gros

See plan below

⊕84 Cala Santa Galdana 39°56′.0N 03°57′.4E

50′

4°E 05′ 10′

CABO GROS

39°50′.6N 04°10′.5E

A high (39m), rocky-cliffed headland with some houses on the top. Even so it is not very prominent and can only be seen if coasting close in. There are some prehistoric caves cut into the cliffs, including a very large one on the west face.

⚓ CALA CANUTELLS

39°50′.8N 04°10′.1E

A large and attractive S-shaped *cala* between sloping rocky cliffs, with a large tourist development to the east and many local craft on permanent moorings. Enter down the centre of the *cala*, keeping well clear of the awash rock at the western entrance point, and anchor as space permits in 4–6m over sand. The upper part of the *cala* is very shallow, with a shelving sandy beach at its head which is deservedly popular with tourists. There is a café/restaurant on the beach and at the top of the hill (200m past the café) there is a supermarket, hotel, post, car hire and an English-speaking doctor in attendance every day.

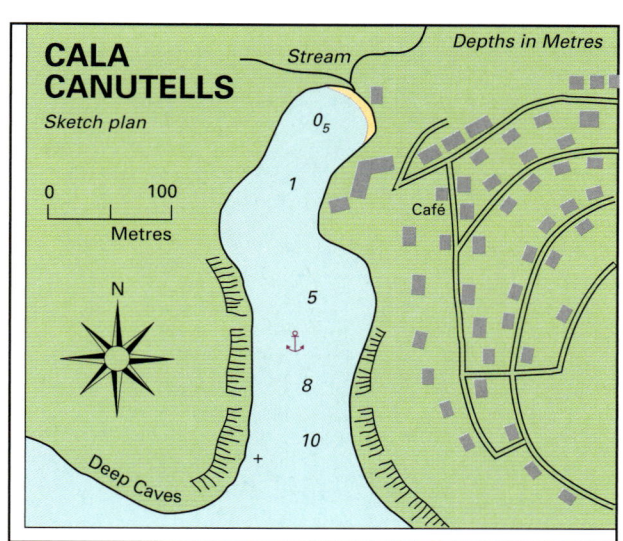

CALA CANUTELLS
Sketch plan

Depths in Metres

Stream

Café

Deep Caves

0 100
Metres

Cala Canutells viewed from southwest: caves visible left of picture

The surrounding cliffs are riddled with caves, including two tall, arched recesses close west of the entrance and the Covas d'es Castella 800m to the east.

⚓ CALA COVAS (COVES)

39°51'.7N 04°08'.6E

Considered the most spectacular and beautiful anchorage in the Islas Baleares, Cala Covas is surrounded by nearly 150 caves, some of which were occupied during prehistoric times. The entrance between two high rocky cliffs lies ¾ mile east of Cala Porté, which is easily identified by the huge housing development to its east. Anchor in 3–5m with two anchors or a line ashore to limit swinging: there are several convenient posts on the west side of the small central promontory (see plan), but investigate first by dinghy as there are fringing rocks. Much of the bottom is rocky, making a tripline advisable. The anchorage is open to southwest and south, depending on the spot chosen.

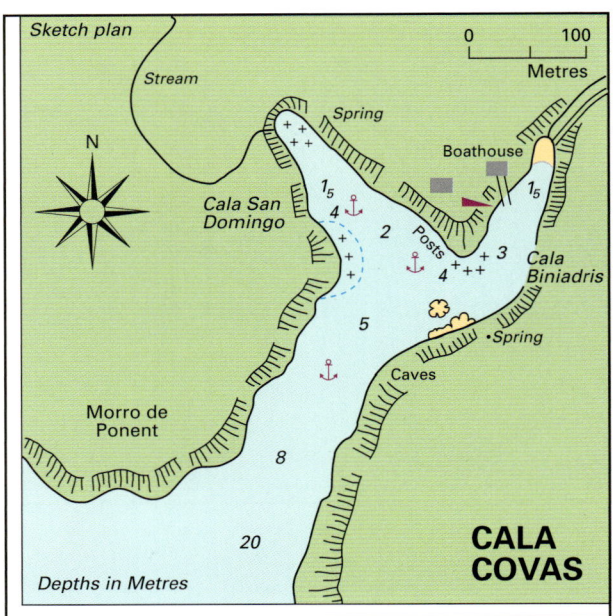

Cala Covas: one of the most spectacular in the Islands, surrounded by caves, many of which were dwellings in prehistoric times

The *cala* is deserted except for two houses, but large numbers of tourists visit the beaches every day in summer and litter has been a problem. There are several freshwater springs and a road inland, but no facilities.

⚓ CALA PORTÉ (EN PORTER)

39°52'.1N 04°07'.9E

A large *cala* lying between high (48m) rocky cliffs. The valley and hillside to the north and east are covered by holiday homes, hotels, shops, cafés, restaurants and discos, which make the *cala* easy to locate. The 8m Torre Nova tower stands about ¾ mile northwest.

Anchor in 3m+ over sand, open to the south and southwest. A line (sometimes two lines) of buoys may be laid to mark off the bathing area in front of the beach. There are two beach cafés, and most everyday requirements are available in the tourist area.

It is worth walking along the cliffs on the eastern side of the entrance to Cova d'en Xeroni, a succession of natural caves with openings through

Cala Porté: buoys near the beach restrict anchoring

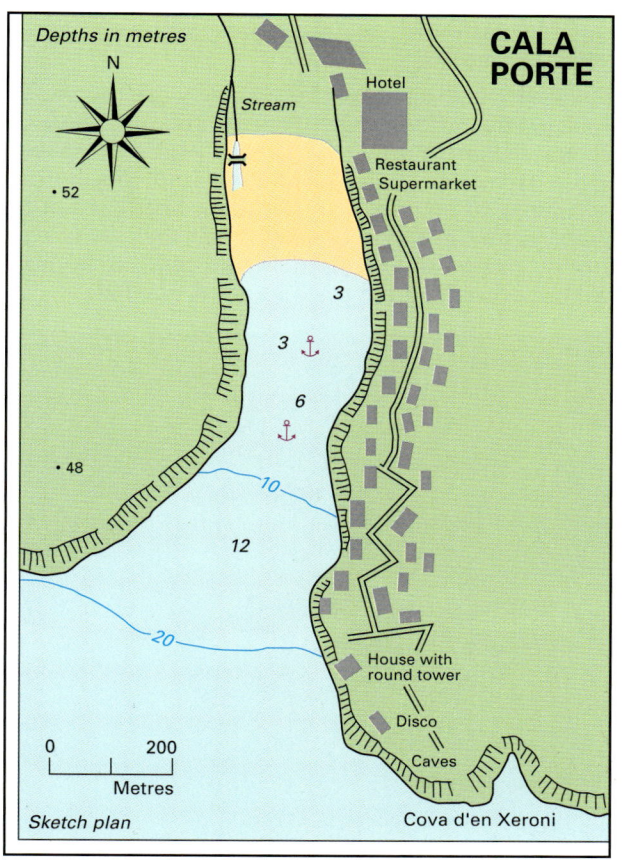

the cliffs, now occupied by a bar and restaurant (and a nightly disco). There are several important *talayots* (towers) and other ancient ruins on the road to Alayor.

TORRE NOVA

39°52'.3N 04°07'.0E

A ruined ancient lookout tower 8m high on the edge of a 63m rocky cliff, about ¾ mile northwest of Cala Porté. It is not very conspicuous.

⚓ CALA DE SANT LLORÉNS (SANT LLORENÇ)

39°52'.9N 4°05'.7E

A very small, deserted *cala* surrounded by sheer rocky cliffs with a steep-sided river valley behind. Only suitable for use by small yachts in settled conditions. Care is necessary in the approach due to several fringing rocks. Moor with two anchors over sand and rock.

⚓ CALA DE LLUCALARI

39°53'.4N 4°04'.9E

A very small, deserted *cala* similar to Cala de Sant Llorens, with high sloping rocky sides. It is tucked behind Cabo de las Peñas (Cap de ses Penyes; see plan on page 201) and backed by a dried-up river valley with a track inland. Its use is limited to small yachts in good weather. Anchor in the centre of the *cala* in 3–4m over rock and sand. There is a small rocky beach but no facilities.

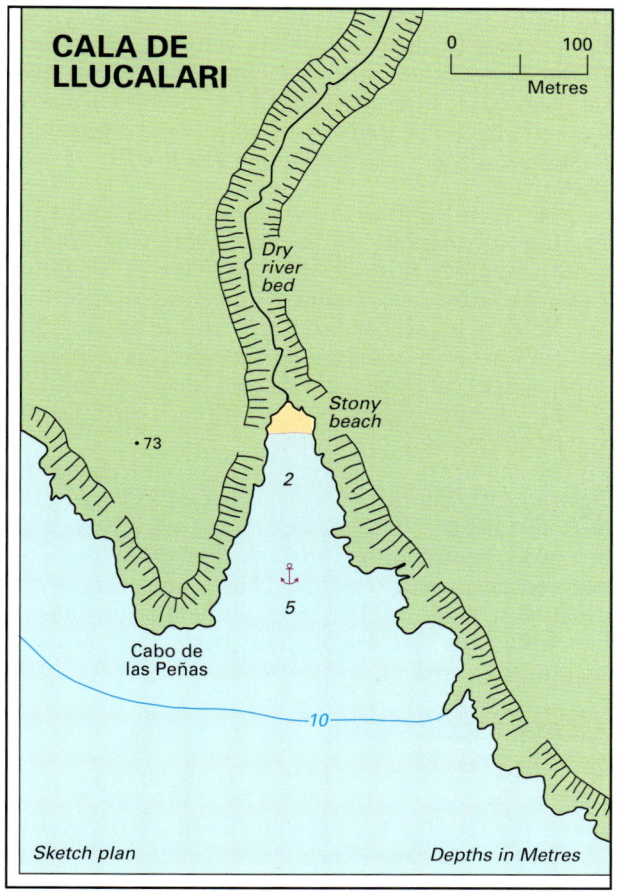

Cala de Llucalari from southeast: narrow with a stony beach

⚓ PLAYA DE SON BOU, PLAYA DE SANTO TOMÁS (PLAYA DE TALIS OR ATALIX) AND PLAYA DE BINIGAUS

Stretching from 39°53'.8N 4°04'.6E to 39°55'.3N 4°01'.1E

A 3-mile stretch of sandy beaches between Cabo de las Peñas (Cap de ses Penyes) and Punta Rabiosa, broken only by the low rocky promontories of Punta Radona, Punta de Talis and Punta Negra (see plan on page 201). They are backed by apartment blocks and hotels and a number of tourist developments, including those of San Jaime Mediterráneo and Santo Tomás.

The 10m contour runs some 400m offshore, making it possible to anchor over sand almost anywhere along this stretch of open coast. There are two small islands and some rocks close inshore.

The San Jaime Mediterráneo resort at Son Bou includes a bank amongst its facilities, as well as a supermarket and the usual bars and restaurants. Santo Tomás has beach bars, restaurants, supermarkets and gift shops.

The ruins of an early Christian church dating from the 5th century overlook the eastern end of the Son Bou beach while two *talayots* (towers) lie near the road from Santo Tomás to Ferrerías, together with other ancient remains. There is a spring at the northwest end of Playa de Binigaus, which is generally less built up than the other beaches mentioned above.

⚓ CALA ESCORXADA

39°55'.5N 04°00'.2E

A deserted *cala* with low rocky cliffs and a large sandy beach, about ¾ mile northwest of the end of Playa de Binigaus. Anchor in 2–5m over sand. Ashore there is a track to San Cristóbal but nothing else.

⚓ CALA FUSTAM

39°55'.5N 04°00'.0E

A smaller and narrower version of Cala Escorxada lying 300m further northwest, on the other side of Punta de Sant Antoni (see plan on page 201). Moor with two anchors in 3–4m over sand, open from southeast to southwest. The sandy beach is not as large as that at Cala Escorxada, but the *cala* is very pretty and totally deserted. Again there is nothing ashore other than the track to San Cristóbal.

Cala Fustam (left) and Cala Escorxada, viewed from southeast

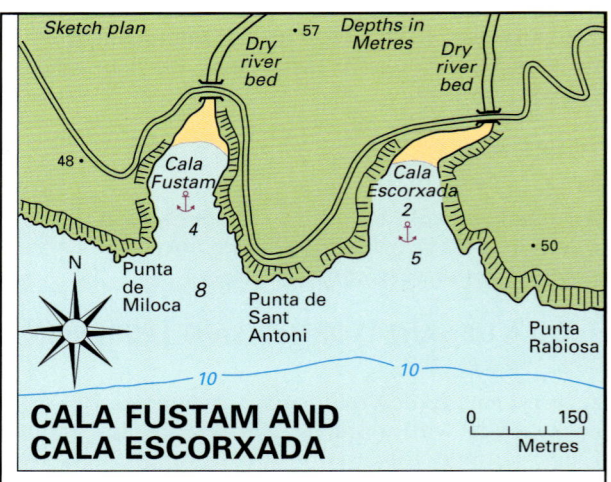

West of Cala Fustam is Cala Trebalújer and then Cala Mitjana (both page 205). Between them lie S'Olleta de Trebalújer and Es Pont d'en Aleix. These are little more than breaks in the cliff line. Although charts show them to be anchorages they are most suited to entering and exploration by dinghy.

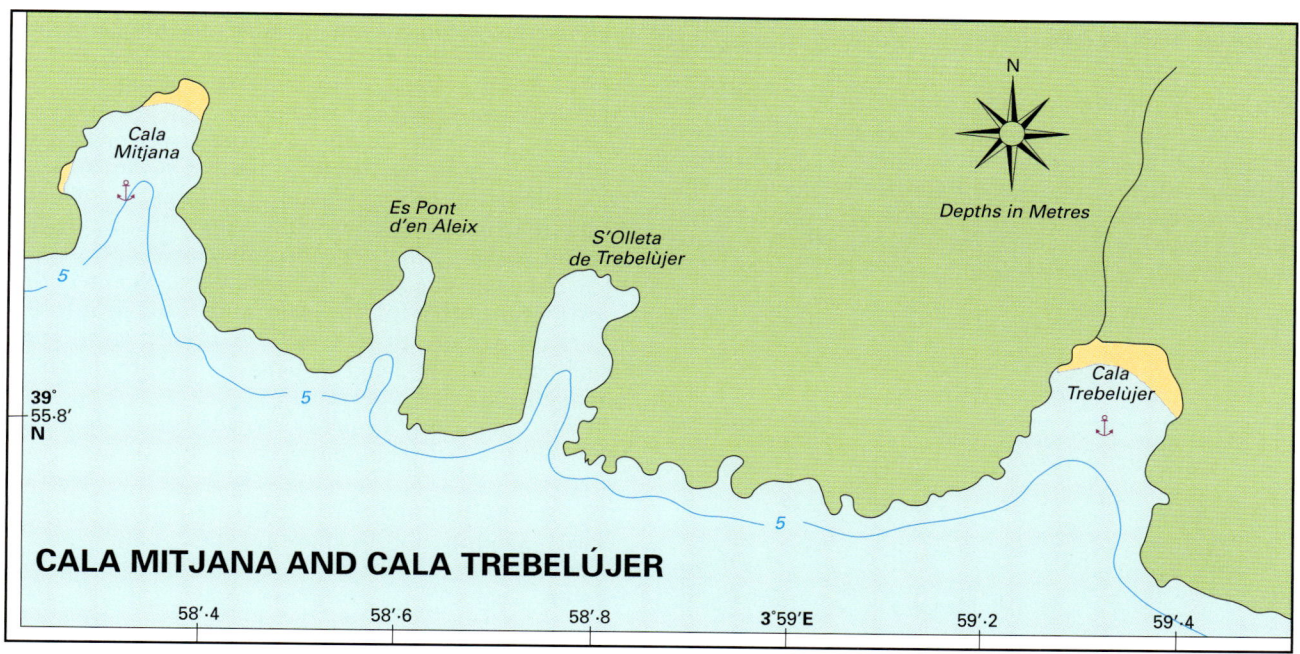

CALA MITJANA AND CALA TREBELÚJER

Cala Trebalùjer

Cala Mitjana from the southwest

⚓ CALA TREBALÙJER

39°55'.7N 03°59'.3E

A large, wide cala with a pinkish sandy beach. there are high (64m) sloping rocky caves on the southeast side and lower, tree-covered cliffs on the northwest side. Anchor in 4–6m over sand. A small freshwater river enters the northwest corner of the cala. It has a low sand bar over which a dinghy can be pulled or carried, allowing one to row a mile upstream with the chance of seeing turtles, fish and various birds. There is a track to San Cristóbal but otherwise the cala is deserted.

⚓ CALA MITJANA

39°56'N 03°58'.3E

A large cala more than 100m wide, surrounded by rocky cliffs but with two good sandy beaches, lying just under ¾ mile east of Cala Santa Galdana (easily recognised by its large hotels and apartment blocks). Anchor in 3–6m over sand and weed. A track connects with the road to Ferrerías.

⊕84 39°56'.0N 03°57'.4E Cala Santa Galdana

⚓ CALA SANTA GALDANA

39°56'.2N 03°57'.5E

Once one of the most beautiful large *calas* in Menorca, and still the largest and most sheltered anchorage on the south coast (see plan on page 201). The construction of several high-rise hotels make it easy to recognise, especially if approaching from the west. However, if arriving from the east little is seen until abreast of the entrance.

A series of buoys linked by a thin line stretches from the central promontory across the *cala* to near the end of the beach, protecting the bathing area but seriously restricting the anchorage. Anchor as space permits, probably in 5m or more, over sand and weed. It may be necessary to lie to two anchors or take a long line ashore when the harbour is crowded. Note that in strong southwest winds the swell rolls in and makes this a very uncomfortable anchorage. The river Barranco de Cala Santa Galdana enters the northwest corner of the *cala* and is navigable by dinghy for more than ½ mile. A bridge some 10m long and 3m in height spans its mouth, with a smallcraft pontoon beyond.

The long sandy beach is crowded in season and the shouts of the bathers echo around the surrounding cliffs. There is also a lot of noise during the evening from bars and discos, but these usually cease around 2200. Restaurants, cafés, bars, supermarkets and tourist shops flourish in the resort.

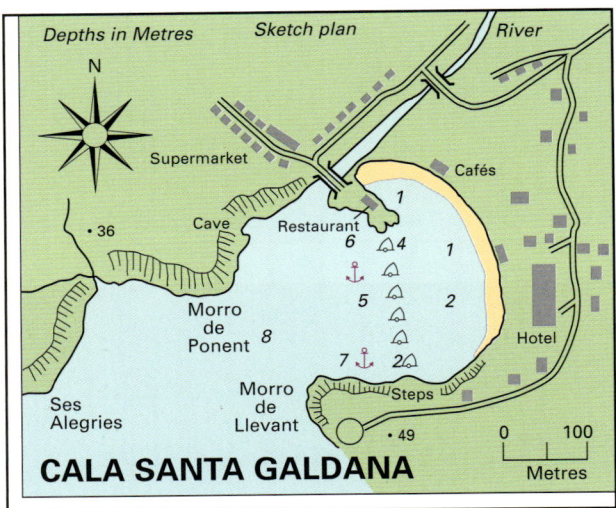

Cala Santa Galdana from southwest. An excellent anchorage in clear waters, though the buoys placed to protect swimmers restrict the anchoring to deeper water

4. Cala Macarella to Cala Santandria

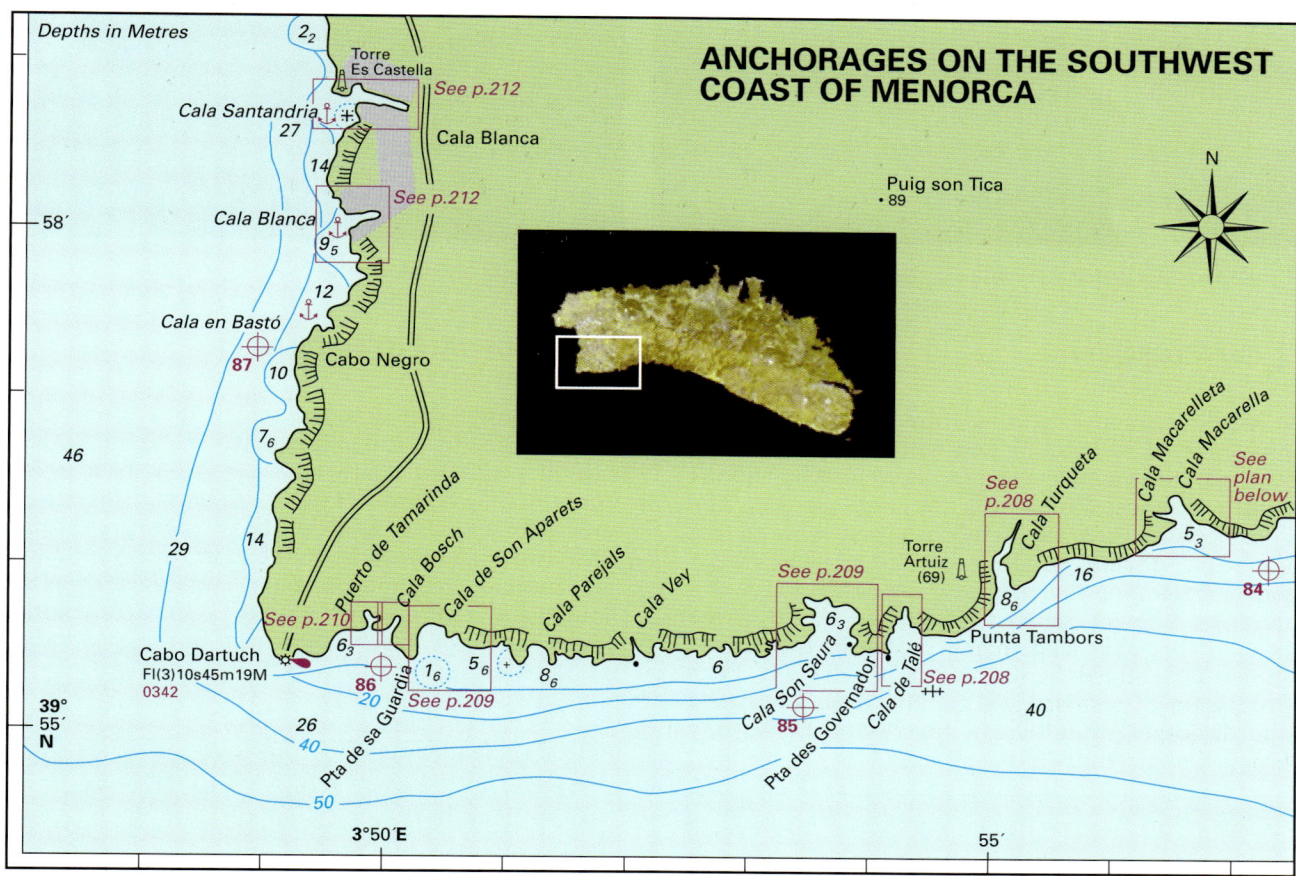

ANCHORAGES ON THE SOUTHWEST COAST OF MENORCA

⚓ CALA MACARELLA AND CALA MACARELLETA

39°56'.1N 03°56'.3E

A large double *cala* with two sandy beaches, surrounded by sloping rocky cliffs, scrub and trees, and easy to spot just under a mile west of Cala Santa Galdana. Anchor in 3–6m over sand and a few weed patches. The anchorage is often crowded and it may be necessary to use two anchors or to take a line ashore. Keep clear of the west end of the *cala* which is roped off for swimmers.

Three tracks bring in day tourists and there is a popular camp site nearby (caves overlooking the *calas* may also be inhabited in summer). The stream flowing into Cala Macarella is embanked with what could be Moorish masonry; the water appears clean and is recommended locally. There is a café/bar on the beach and an ancient ruined village to the west. These calas, together with those further east, were used as hideouts by Barbary pirates in medieval times.

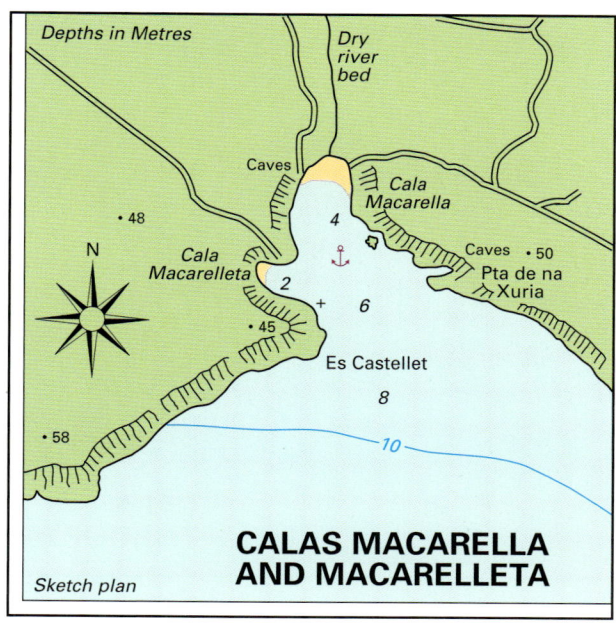

CALAS MACARELLA AND MACARELLETA

Sketch plan

Calas Macarella and Macarelleta

Cala Turqueta and the caves around its entrance

⚓ CALA TURQUETA

39°55'.7N 03°54'.9E

A small, attractive *cala* surrounded by scrub and pine-covered rocky cliffs and with a sandy beach at its head. It lies a mile west of Cala Macarella and the same distance from Cala de Son Saura. The conspicuous Torre de Artuiz lies just west of the entrance. Anchor in 3m+ over sand with weed patches, taking a line ashore if necessary (there is a mooring ring on the east side). Two tracks at the head of the *cala* lead inland. Peace in the *cala* is somewhat spoiled in the middle of the day by a procession of tourist craft coming from Ciudadela and disgorging hundreds of tourists on to the tiny beach. Calm returns in the evening.

⚓ CALA DE TALÉ (D'ES TALAIER)

39°55'.5N 03°54'.1E

A small and often deserted *cala* with a low rocky shore backed by scrub and pine woods, about ½ mile east of Cala Son Saura and separated from it by Punta des Governador. Enter with care as there is a small islet on the west side of the entrance and a lone rock awash close inshore to the east. Anchor in 2m+ over sand, open to southeast and south. Space is very limited and it may be necessary to lie to two anchors. There is a sandy beach at the head of the *cala* and a track inland.

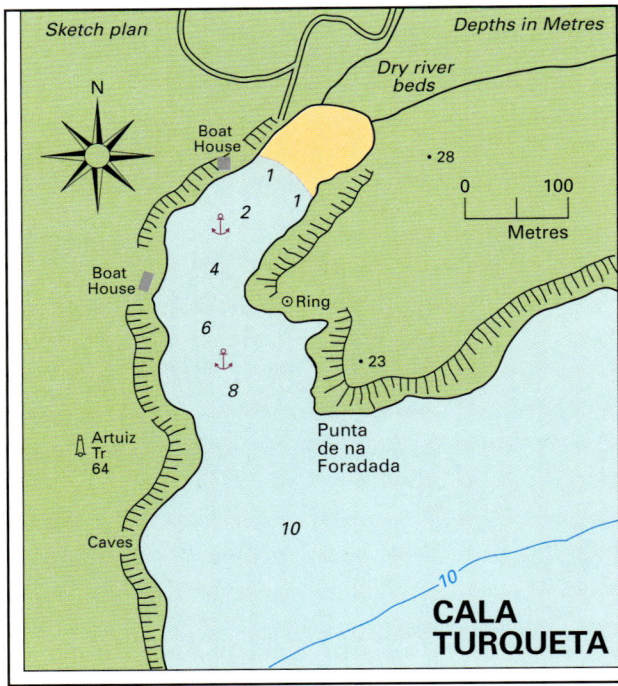

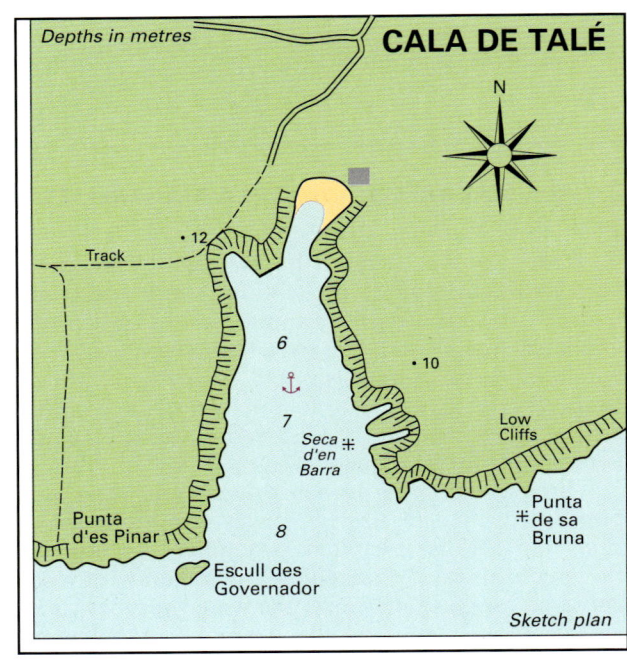

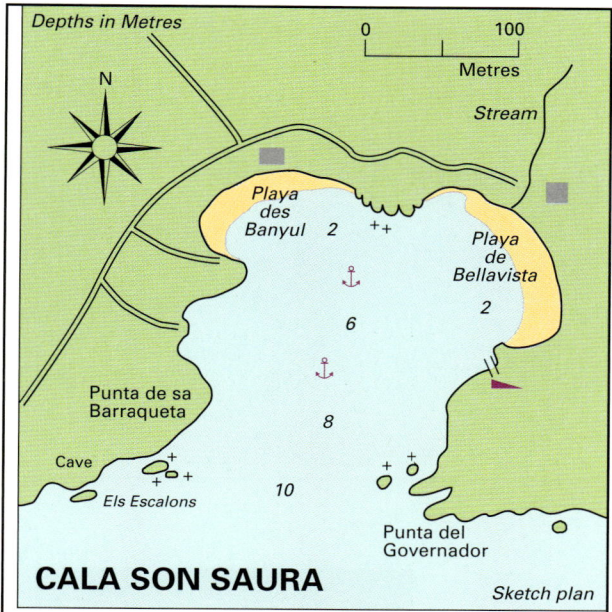

CALA SON SAURA — Sketch plan — Depths in Metres

Ashore there is a long pinkish sandy beach divided into two parts (Playa de Bellavista to the east and Playa des Banyul to the west), by a low rocky area, with a small stream crossing the eastern beach after wet weather. There is a small fishing boat slipway, a few houses well set back and a road leading inland, but nothing else.

⚓ CALA VEY (DE SON VELL) AND CALA PAREJALS

39°55'.3N 03°52'.1E

Two small *calas* with rocky sides on the much-indented stretch of coast between Cala Son Saura and Cala de Son Aparets. There are numerous inshore rocks and islets, and the area should only be explored with considerable care and by experienced navigators.

⚓ CALA DE SON APARETS (PLAYA DE SON XORIGUER)

39°55'.4N 03°50'.6E

A large rounded bay surrounded by low rocky cliffs, behind which lie houses and some apartment blocks. The *cala* is easy to find, being a little under a mile east of Cabo Dartuch (see plan on page 207) and close east of Puerto de Tamarinda and Punta de sa Guardia (na Cap de Porc). On the approach watch out for the isolated Bajo Dartuch (Seca de na Cap de Porc) which lies 400m east of the west entrance point and carries 1.6m, but otherwise there are no hazards. Anchor in 2m+ over sand and weed. The beach is good but often very crowded and in season the swimmers' buoys are laid out to the 5m contour (the major part of the *cala*). There are several beach cafés and roads inland. The Puerto de Tamarinda tourist complex is a short walk away.

Cala de Talé and Cala Son Saura (larger bay on left) viewed from southeast

⊕85 39°55'.1N 3°53'.6E Cala Son Saura

⚓ CALA SON SAURA

39°55'.5N 03°53'.6E

A large, semi-enclosed bay surrounded by a low, sloping rocky foreshore with dark pine trees and scrub behind. It lies close west of Punta Governador (Gobernadó) and is easily recognized by its sheer size – the entrance is 500m wide and it broadens out further inside. There are two small islets on the west of the entrance and two isolated rocks near the east side, but the bay itself is clear. Anchor in 3–8m over sand and weed.

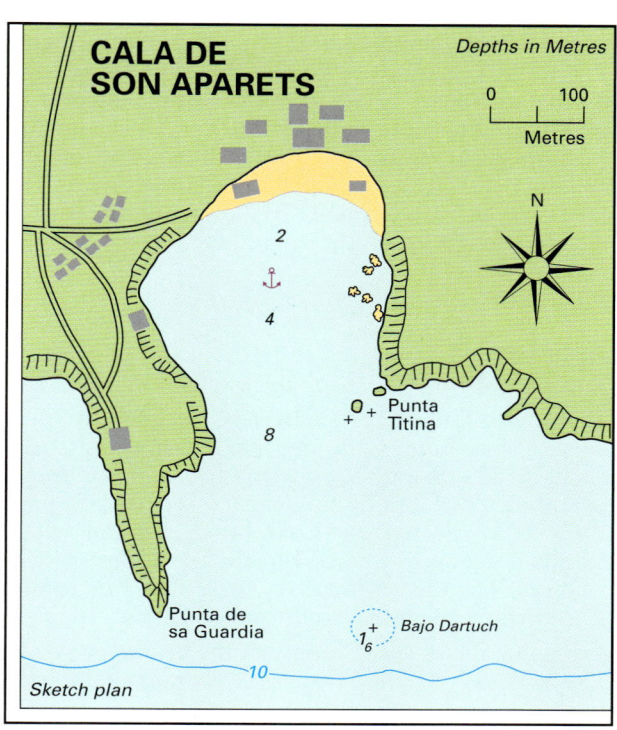

CALA DE SON APARETS — Depths in Metres — Sketch plan

⚓ CALA BOSCH (EN BOSC)

39°55'.5N 03°50'.2E

A small *cala* with low rocky edges and a crowded sandy beach at its head, just east of Puerto de Tamarinda and west of Punta de sa Guardia (na Cap de Porc). Anchor in 2m+ over sand and weed, keeping clear of the swimmers' buoys off the beach. In season swimmers' buoys exclude craft from entry into this *cala* as they stretch from headland to headland. There are low-rise tourist apartments behind the *cala* and it is only a step across to the Puerto de Tamarinda tourist complex where there are shops and other facilities.

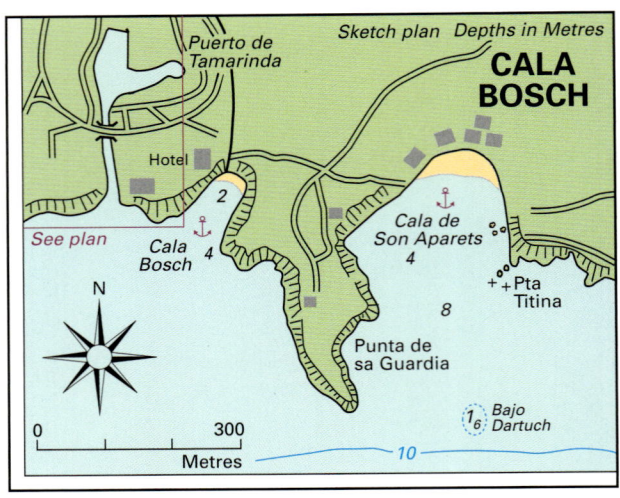

ME2 Puerto de Tamarinda (Marina Cala'n Bosch)

A small harbour with 264 moorings accessed via a narrow canal, but with a bridge restricting height to 10m. Only suitable for motor boats and dinghies

Location
39°55'.5N 03°50'.1E

Communications
Club Deportivo Cala'n Bosch ☎ 971 38 71 70/38 52 38
Fax 971 38 71 71
Email darbosch@teleline.es

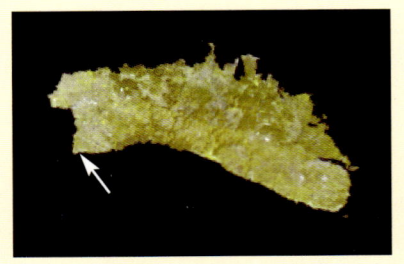

The harbour

A small man-made lagoon dredged from a low-lying area. Approached via a narrow channel spanned by a footbridge reminiscent of a willow-pattern plate, Puerto de Tamarinda is inaccessible to sailing vessels as the stated air height is only 6.8m. However, it makes an interesting visit by dinghy and is suited to medium-sized motor yachts, speedboats and smaller sailing craft. It is also used by sailboarders. The harbour is surrounded by a growing tourist development with all the related facilities.

PILOTAGE

Approach

⊕86 39°55'.4N 3°50'.1E Puerto de Tamarinda

From east Follow the coast past a series of small calas. The large Cala de Son Aparets is easily recognized, being separated by a low rocky promontory (Punta de sa Guardia, see plan on page 207) from the narrow Cala Bosch, behind which stands a group of apartment blocks. 200m west of this *cala* lies the entrance to Puerto de Tamarinda. The entrance is not obvious until close by.

From north and west Approach the prominent Cabo Dartuch with its black-and-white-banded lighthouse

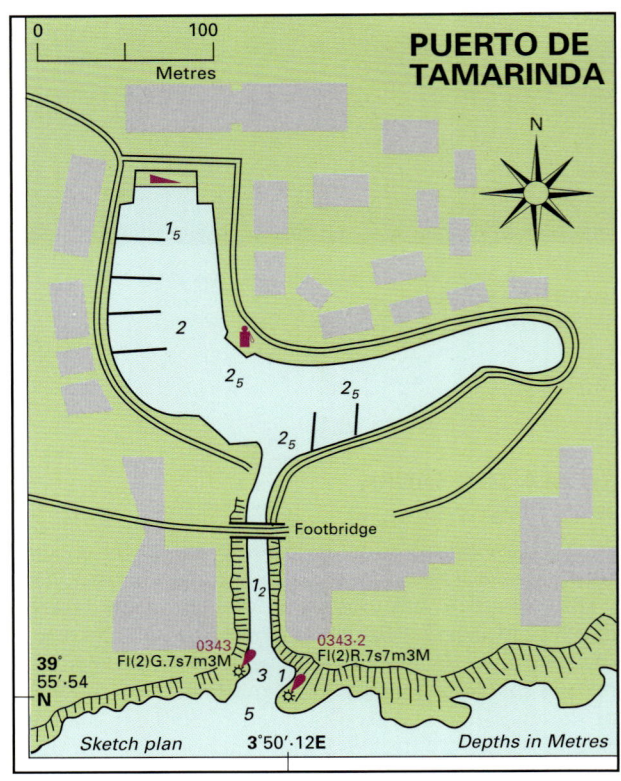

Cabo Dartuch with its distinctive lighthouse, viewed from south. Cala Bosch and Puerto de Tamarinda just behind peninsula centre of picture

(Fl(3)10s45m19M, white tower with three black bands on white building 34m surrounded by a low white wall). The entrance to Puerto de Tamarinda lies around 1,000m east-northeast of the lighthouse and west of Cala Bosch, which will be recognised by its narrow sandy beach surrounded by apartment blocks.

Anchorages in the approach

Anchor in Cala Bosch or Cala de Son Aparets (see pages 209 and 210) if possible; later in the season the *calas* are closed off with swimmer buoys.

Entrance

The entrance is less than 10m wide – too narrow for anything larger than dinghies to pass each other, and much too narrow to turn. It is therefore essential to

Puerto de Tamarinda with its quaint bridge, Cala Bosch to right just out of picture

check that the way is clear before committing oneself. Approach heading north into the channel with its conspicuous white footbridge and enter at slow speed. The water is often muddy and depths are unreliable, so keep a close eye on the echo-sounder. If in any doubt about mast clearance it would be wise to anchor in Cala Bosch and walk round to measure the bridge. In strong winds and swell from the southerly quadrant it would be dangerous to attempt entry into Puerto de Tamarinda.

Berthing

Secure in any vacant berth: the harbour is unlikely to be full. An official will allocate one in due course.

Facilities

Water At the base of some of the pontoons, otherwise from one of the cafés.
Electricity On some (but not all) of the pontoons.
Fuel Available.
Provisioning Small supermarket and other shops in the complex, a chemist and tourist shops.
Ice From the nearby bars and cafés.
Repairs A very wide slipway at the head of the harbour.
Bank In the tourist complex.
Hospital/medical services In Ciudadela, about 4½ miles away.

Transport

Taxis By telephone from Ciudadela, or enquire in the tourist complex.
Buses Buses to Ciudadela.

Sight ashore locally

There is a *talayot* (ancient tower) at Son Olivaret about a mile north on the road to Ciudadela.

Eating out

A choice of restaurants, cafés and bars within the tourist complex.

PUERTO TAMARINDA TO CALA SANTANDRIA

CABO DARTUCH (CAP D'ARTRUTX)

39°55'.3N 03°49'.5E

A prominent headland of low (10m) dark cliffs surmounted by a conspicuous lighthouse (Fl(3)10s 45m19M, white tower with three black bands on white building 34m surrounded by a low white wall). The headland is steep-to.

⊕87 39°57'.2N 3°49'.1E Off Cabo Negro

CABO NEGRO (CAP NEGRE)

39°57'.1N 03°49'.5E

A relatively inconspicuous headland of black rock, 12m high and steep-to. Easily seen if coasting close inshore.

⚓ CALA EN BASTÓ

39°57'.4N 03°49'.7E

A very small *cala* close north of Cabo Negro and about two miles north of Cabo Dartuch, surrounded by low (8m) black rocky cliffs and to be used with extreme caution. A small breaking rock lies on the south side of the entrance. The *cala*, which is open from west to north, has no beach and is generally deserted.

⚓ CALA BLANCA

39°58'N 3°50'E

A narrow *cala* between low rocky sides, Cala Blanca is easy to identify due to an unusual building with deep verandas on its northern side and a huge white apartment block/hotel in the background. Anchor in 4–8m over sand. In high season swimmers' buoys virtually exclude craft from this *cala*. The sandy beach at its head is often crowded, and there are hotels, restaurants, cafés and houses nearby. The Caves of Parella a few hundred metres inland are worth visiting.

⚓ CALA SANTANDRIA

39°58'.8N 03°49'.9E

A long *cala* with several shorter branches, Cala Santandria lies between low, pinkish, rocky cliffs just over a mile south of Puerto de Ciudadela (see plan on page 207). The entrance is not easily picked out, but the Torre Es Castella (a restored defensive tower) on the north headland helps. A small islet off the east side of the entrance is the only hazard on entering. Anchor in 3m+ over sand and weed as space permits, either lying to two anchors or taking a line ashore. Two cables run down the centre of the *cala*, so care is needed when picking a spot. This anchorage has been reported as uncomfortable even in light winds and it is difficult to keep clear of the cables.

Lines of buoys mark off all three bathing beaches with their bars and cafés. Supermarkets, hotels and restaurants are located slightly further back. There are pleasant walks on either side of the *cala* and the Torre Es Castella is worth a visit. Maréchal Richelieu, commander of the French invasion, landed here with his troops on 18 April 1756, en route to capture Ciudadela.

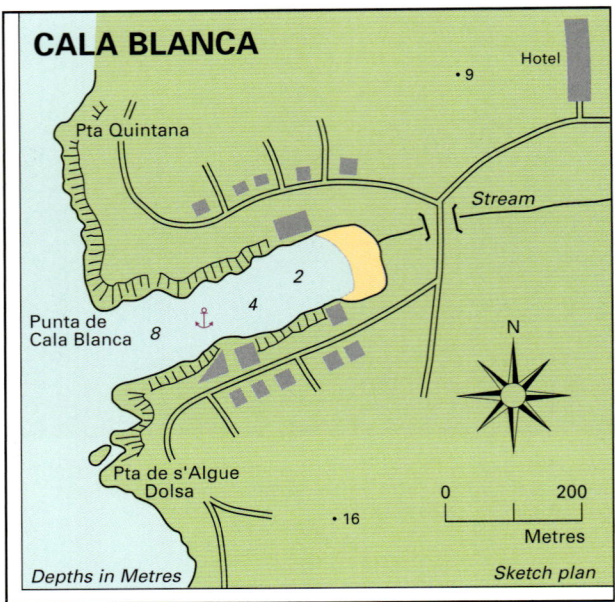

Cala Santandria viewed from west

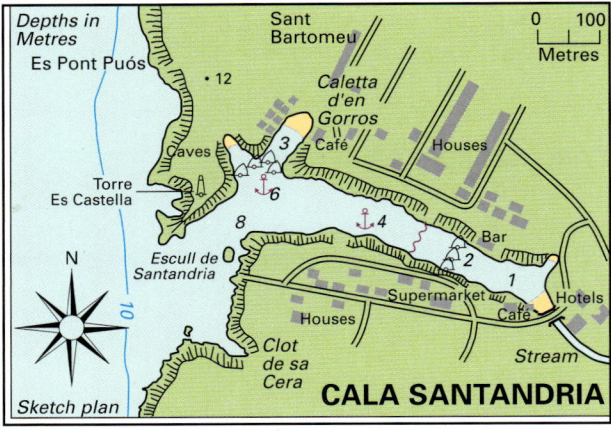

⚓ CALA DEGOLLADOR

39°59'.6N 03°49'.7E

A narrow *cala* just south of the entrance to Puerto de Ciudadela, surrounded by low rocky cliffs and with two popular (and often crowded) sandy beaches at its head (see plan on page 213). Islote de la Galera, a small islet 4m high, lies in the middle of the entrance with a 4.1m shoal extending 80m northwards. Anchor in 4m+ over sand with weed patches. It may be necessary to use two anchors to restrict swinging room as the *cala* is very narrow (see plan on page 214).

Cala Degollador forms a useful alternative to Ciudadela when the latter is crowded, and has all its shoreside facilities within easy reach. Plans for turning the *cala* into a yacht harbour behind protective breakwaters seem to have been shelved. Pontoons have been added in Cala d'en Busquets on the north side of Puerto de Ciudadela.

A commercial harbour with a ferry terminal is under construction south of the *cala* (October 2010).

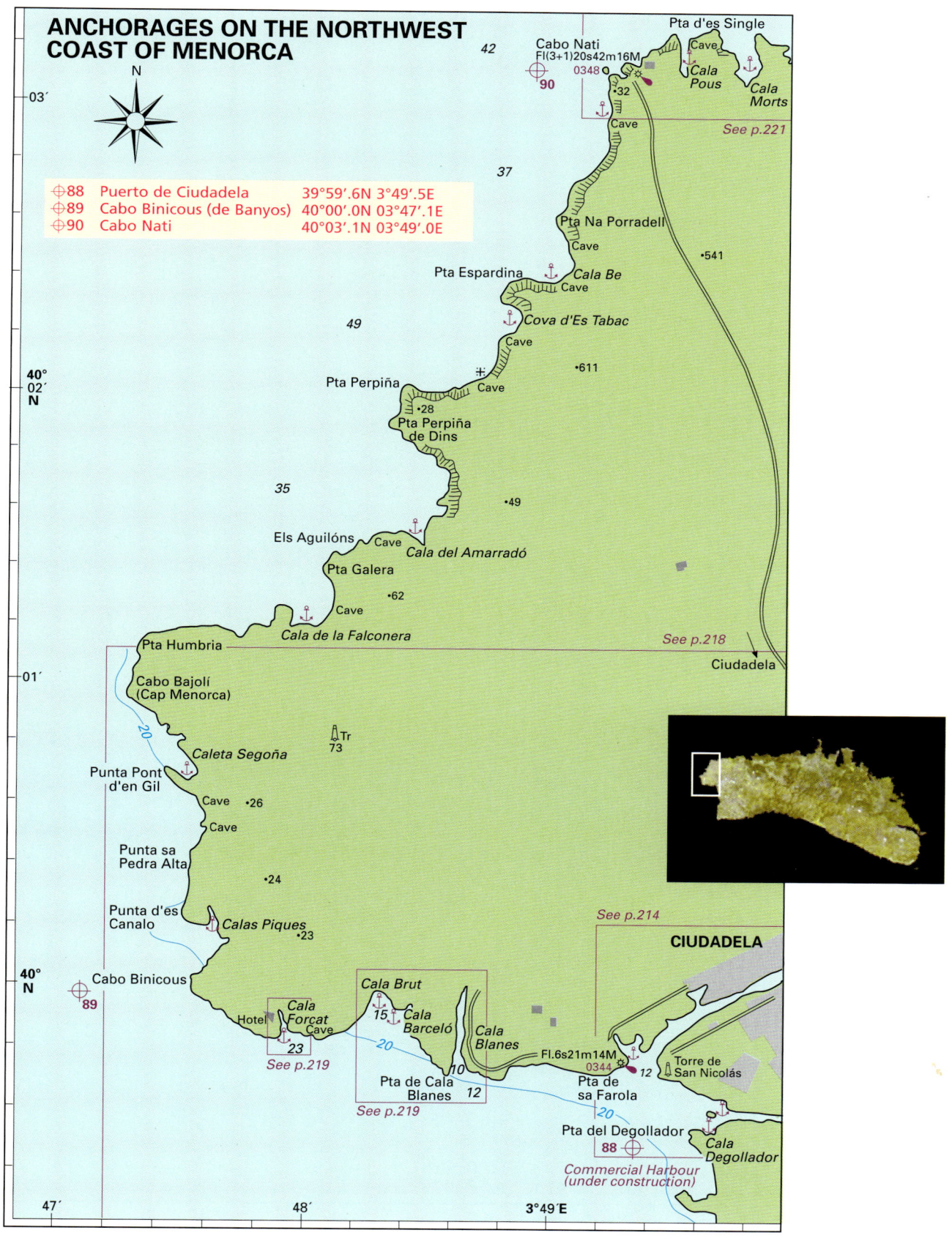

ANCHORAGES ON THE NORTHWEST COAST OF MENORCA

N

⊕88	Puerto de Ciudadela	39°59'.6N 3°49'.5E
⊕89	Cabo Binicous (de Banyos)	40°00'.0N 03°47'.1E
⊕90	Cabo Nati	40°03'.1N 03°49'.0E

42

Cabo Nati
Fl(3+1)20s42m16M
0348
90
•32

Pta d'es Single
Cave
Cala Pous
Cala Morts

See p.221

Cave

37

Pta Na Porradell
Cave

•541

Pta Espardina
Cala Be
Cave

49

Cova d'Es Tabac
Cave

Pta Perpiña
Cave
•611

•28
Pta Perpiña
de Dins

35

•49

Els Aguilóns
Cave
Cala del Amarradó
Pta Galera
•62
Cave
Cala de la Falconera

See p.218

Ciudadela

Pta Humbria

Cabo Bajolí
(Cap Menorca)

20

Caleta Segoña

Tr
73

Punta Pont
d'en Gil
Cave
•26
Cave

Punta sa
Pedra Alta
•24

Punta d'es
Canalo
Calas Piques
•23

See p.214

CIUDADELA

40°
N
89
Cabo Binicous

Cala Brut

Hotel
Cala
Forcat
Cave
23
See p.219

15
Cala
Barceló

Cala
Blanes

20

Pta de Cala
Blanes
12
See p.219

10

Fl.6s21m14M
0344
12
Pta de
sa Farola

Torre de
San Nicolás

20

Pta del Degollador
88
Cala
Degollador

Commercial Harbour
(under construction)

47'
48'
3°49'E

V. MENORCA

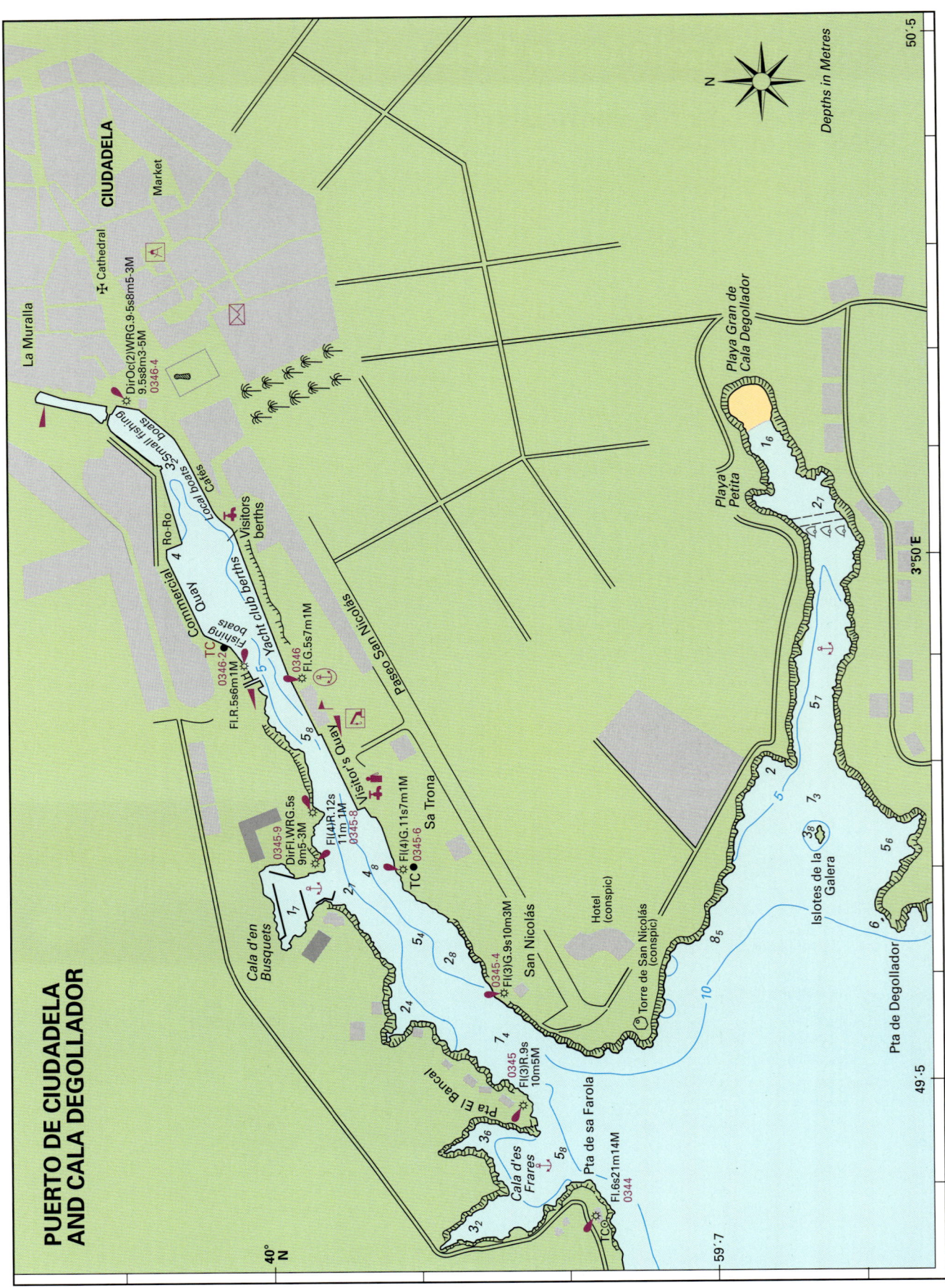

PUERTO DE CIUDADELA AND CALA DEGOLLADOR

CIUDADELA

La Muralla

✠ Cathedral

Market

DirOc(2)WRG.9.5s8m5-3M
9.5s8m3-5M
0346.4

Small fishing boats
Ro-Ro
3

Commercial Quay
4
TC ☆
0346-2
Fl.R.5s6m1M

Fishing boats

Local boats Cafés

Visitors berths

Yacht club berths
5
0346 ☆
Fl.G.5s7m1M

Visitor's Quay
5₈

Paseo San Nicolás

DirFl.WRG.5s
9m5-3M
0345-9

Fl(4)R.12s
11m.1M
0345-8
2₄

☆ Fl(4)G.11s7m1M
TC● 0345-6
4   8

Cala d'en Busquets
1₇

Sa Trona

San Nicolás
Fl(3)G.9s10m3M
0345-4
☆ Fl(3)G.9s10m3M

2₄

5₄

2₈

Hotel (conspic)

Torre de San Nicolás (conspic)
○

7₄

Pta El Bancal

3₆

Fl(3)R.9s
10m5M
0345
☆

Cala d'es Frares
5₈

Pta de sa Farola
Fl.6s21m14M
0344
TC○ ☆

3₂

N

Depths in Metres

Playa Gran de Cala Degollador

Playa Petita
1₆

2₇

3°50′E

5₇

5   2
7₃

5₆

Islotes de la Galera
3₈

8₅

6₂

10

Pta de Degollador

50′·5

49′·5

59′·7

ME3 Puerto de Ciudadela (Ciutadella)

A natural harbour up a long *cala,* with berthing for 100 vessels

Location
  39°59'.8N 03°49'.5E

Communications
  Port Authority (Puerto de Ciudadela)
  VHF Ch 09, 14, 16
  Club Náutico de Ciudadela ① 971 38 39 18
  Fax 971 38 58 71
  Email cnciutadella@cncuitadella.com
  www.cnciutadella.com

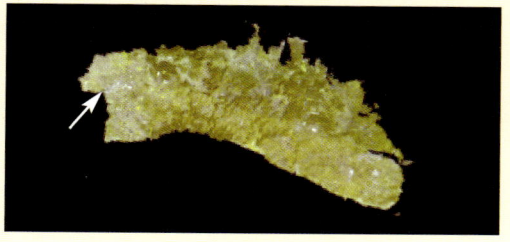

The harbour

A most attractive natural harbour consisting of a long narrow *cala* leading to a small inner area edged with ancient quays. Only in the last decade has a new public quay for visitors been added nearer the entrance.

Approach and entrance are straightforward but, from some angles and in some light conditions, it is virtually impossible to see the entrance itself until very close in. Entry is not advisable in strong southwest winds as seas break across its mouth. Once inside, good shelter is available, but swell finds its way up the *cala* with winds from southwest or west. During the summer season both harbour and town become very crowded.

PILOTAGE

Approach

⊕88 39°59'.6N 3°49'.5E Puerto de Ciudadela

From south or southwest Cabo Dartuch, a low rocky-cliffed promontory topped by a very conspicuous lighthouse (Fl(3)10s45m19M, white tower with three black bands on white building 34m surrounded by low white wall), is easily recognised (see plan on page 207). The entrance to Puerto de Ciudadela lies 4.4 miles to the north and there are no offshore hazards. The buildings of Ciudadela (in particular the Torre de San Nicolás) together with the large curved hotel behind, can be seen from afar.

From north or northwest Cabo Nati and its conspicuous lighthouse (Fl(3+1)20s 42m16M, aluminium cupola on white tower above white building with a red roof 13m), Cabo Bajolí with its 10m tower and 20m brick signal station, and Cabo Binicous further south, are all prominent headlands (see plan on page 213). Follow them round at 400m until heading east-southeast, when the buildings of Ciudadela will be seen less than two miles away.

Anchorages in the approach

Major works have been continuing during 2009 and into 2010 around the port. Some of this is to reduce the *resaca* (undercurrent). Other works include laying visitors' moorings. This has drastically reduced the option of anchoring, as in many places around the coast. Some Port Authority moorings may be available at the head of the harbour. See below.

Entrance

The entrance can be difficult to identify until close in, but the Punta de Sa Farola lighthouse on the north side and the Torre de San Nicolás to the south are good landmarks. Southwest gales produce breaking seas across the entrance and swell inside the harbour. In these conditions an alternative destination should be sought. See also the note regarding sea levels below. Due to the steep cliffs on either side the wind can be very variable and fluky.

There are three sets of six lights set up at the south end of the commercial quay (marked TC on plan) for harbour traffic control. There are three vertical red, and vertical green, white, green. If the three red lights are lit you must clear the harbour channel within a maximum of 10 minutes. If the GWG plus flashing red are on then access to the channel is prohibited to all craft except for those expressly authorised. When lights are off, navigation is open to any user and to enter the harbour simply follow the centre line of the *cala.*

Sea levels

The level of the sea rises with a southwest wind and falls with north and northeast winds by as much as 0.5m. Under certain meteorological conditions, usually when a depression and spring tide coincide, a phenomenon known as *resaca* or *seiche* occurs, causing the level to rise and fall by as much as 1.5m every 10 or 15 minutes, an oscillation which may continue for several days. Local fishermen often give warning when they expect it to occur.

Berthing

Although there are a variety of berthing possibilities, Puerto de Ciudadela is often full to capacity during the summer. On the starboard side just short of the *club náutico* is a stretch of quay capable of taking seven or eight yachts in line, rafted two or three deep. Although owned by the Port Authority this is franchised to the *club náutico*, who admister the area and collect mooring fees.

Beyond the *club náutico* local yachts and small craft lie bow or stern-to, with Port Authority moorings for a few visiting yachts, also stern-to, at the far end just short of where the harbour narrows. The Iris Jet service from Ratjada uses the quay on the north side which was previously used by fishermen. The fishermen consequently now use the south quay (with much bad grace as their storage spaces are still on the north quay!) which means there is even less room for visitors. Much of the port side is taken up by the commercial quay (often occupied by large fishing vessels) and the RoRo ferry

Ciudadela viewed from southwest. Cala Degollador to right. The 17th-century torre de San Nicholas seen centre of picture and Cala d'es Frares left

berth. However, if no ship is due, yachts may be allowed to lie alongside overnight. The wash caused by ships passing can cause surge problems on the western quay, particularly if rafts have grown to more than three yachts deep, in which case the outer yachts will be told to leave in order to clear the channel.

Anchorage in the harbour

Anchoring is now impossible in Cala d'en Busquets. Pontoons have been laid for yachts up to 12m and with a maximum draught of 1.7m. Currently it is still possible to go bows-/stern-to where *visitors' berths* is marked on the plan on page 214.

Facilities

Water At all three quays listed above.
Electricity On the *club náutico* and Port Authority quays.
Fuel Diesel and petrol pumps on the *club náutico* quay.
Provisions A good selection of supermarkets and specialist food shops. A small open-air market in the town, with a fish market in its centre.
Ice From nearby bars.
Chandlery About 200m east of *club náutico* on Paseo San Nicolas. Menorca Yachting ✆ 971 48 20 44 *Fax* 971 48 20 12 on the waterfront above the restaurant, Sa' Figura is also willing to assist yachtsmen in need.
Repairs Small boatyard by the slipway west of the commercial quay. Cranes on the commercial quay and at the *club náutico* (5 tonnes). Slipway at the west end of the commercial quay. The slightly rustic cradle can handle up to 5 tonnes.
Engineers Centre Nautic Ciudadela ✆ 971 38 26 16 *Fax* 971 38 56 79 are agents for Ecosse, Volvo Penta and Yanmar.
Yacht club The Club Náutico de Ciudadela has a fine clubhouse fronting the harbour with bar, lounge, terrace, restaurant and showers.
Showers At the *club náutico*. A small charge is made, payable at the bar.
Laundry In the town.

Banks Several in the town, with credit card facilities.
Hospital/medical services In the town.

Transport

Car hire/taxis Available in the town.
Buses Bus service to Mahón, Fornells and elsewhere.
Ferries Car ferries to Alcudia, Mallorca.

History

Ciudadela harbour has been in use since prehistoric times, long before the Phoenicians settled in 1600–1200BC and gave it its first name, Yamma, meaning 'western' or 'west town'. The Greeks and Romans followed, and Pliny the Elder referred to it as Iama or Iamnona. The next name on record was that of the Arabs, to whom it was Medina Minurka. With the expulsion of the Arabs by the Aragonese it received its current name of Ciudadela meaning 'little city', though very little from that time remains due to repeated attacks by pirates and Corsairs. The

Looking up the *cala* to visitors' berths *GW*

Ancient walls of Ciudadela *GW*

most notorious assault was led by the Turkish pirate Barbarossa who, in 1558, laid siege to the town and, when it fell, destroyed its buildings and took many of the inhabitants away as slaves. Even so, Ciudadela remained the capital of the island (and the see of a bishop) until 1722 when the British transferred the administration to Mahón, the better natural harbour.

Ciudadela looking northeast across Pta de sa Farola. Yachts on the visitors' quay further up the *cala* can just be seen on the right *GW*

Sights ashore locally

The fascinating old town is unspoilt and can answer most needs. It is a delight to explore, with pavement cafés under the arches of Ses Voltes and a contrast between the palaces of the old families fronting the open squares and the tiny houses of the artisans, packed apparently at random (intended, it is said, to confuse the all-too-frequent intruders with a succession of blind alleys and unexpected turns). The 14th-century cathedral merits a special visit, but Ciudadela is a town oozing antiquity and interest on every side.

Three miles out of Ciudadela, just off the road to Mahón, lies the Naveta d'es Tudóns, which lays claim to being the oldest building in Europe and is undoubtedly the oldest in Spain. The Naveta (so-called because the ground plan resembles a ship) is built of large stone blocks and has two storeys. It measures 14m by 6.5m and was used over many centuries as a communal tomb.

Local speciality

Ciudadela's final distinction lies in its fiesta of San Juán on 23–24 June, famed for its daring equestrian displays to which the usual drinking and merrymaking are only a sideshow. The build-up to the fiesta begins the previous Sunday and it can be guaranteed that there will not be a free berth in the harbour. On 2 July the Fiesta Patriótica is celebrated, commemorating the town's resistance to Turkish pirates in 1558.

Eating out

Many restaurants, cafés and bars.

V. MENORCA

ANCHORAGES WEST AND NORTHWEST OF PUERTO DE CIUDADELA

⚓ CALA D'ES FRARES

39°59'.8N 03°49'.4E

A short double *cala* on the north side of the entrance to Puerto de Ciudadela, surrounded by low (6m) sloping rocky cliffs. Anchor near the entrance in ±4m over sand. The west arm of the *cala* has a small sandy beach.

⚓ CALA BLANES

39°59'.7N 03°48'.7E

A long narrow *cala* between low (9m) undercut cliffs leading to a crowded sandy beach, about ½ mile west of Punta de Sa Farola lighthouse and the entrance to Puerto de Ciudadela. There is a large hotel with a small white tower on its roof near the head of the *cala* which can be seen from the entrance. Anchor in 5m+ over sand and weed, open to the south: it may be necessary to use two anchors or to take a line to

Cala Brut (left of centre), Cala Barceló (centre) and Cala Blanes (right) viewed from south

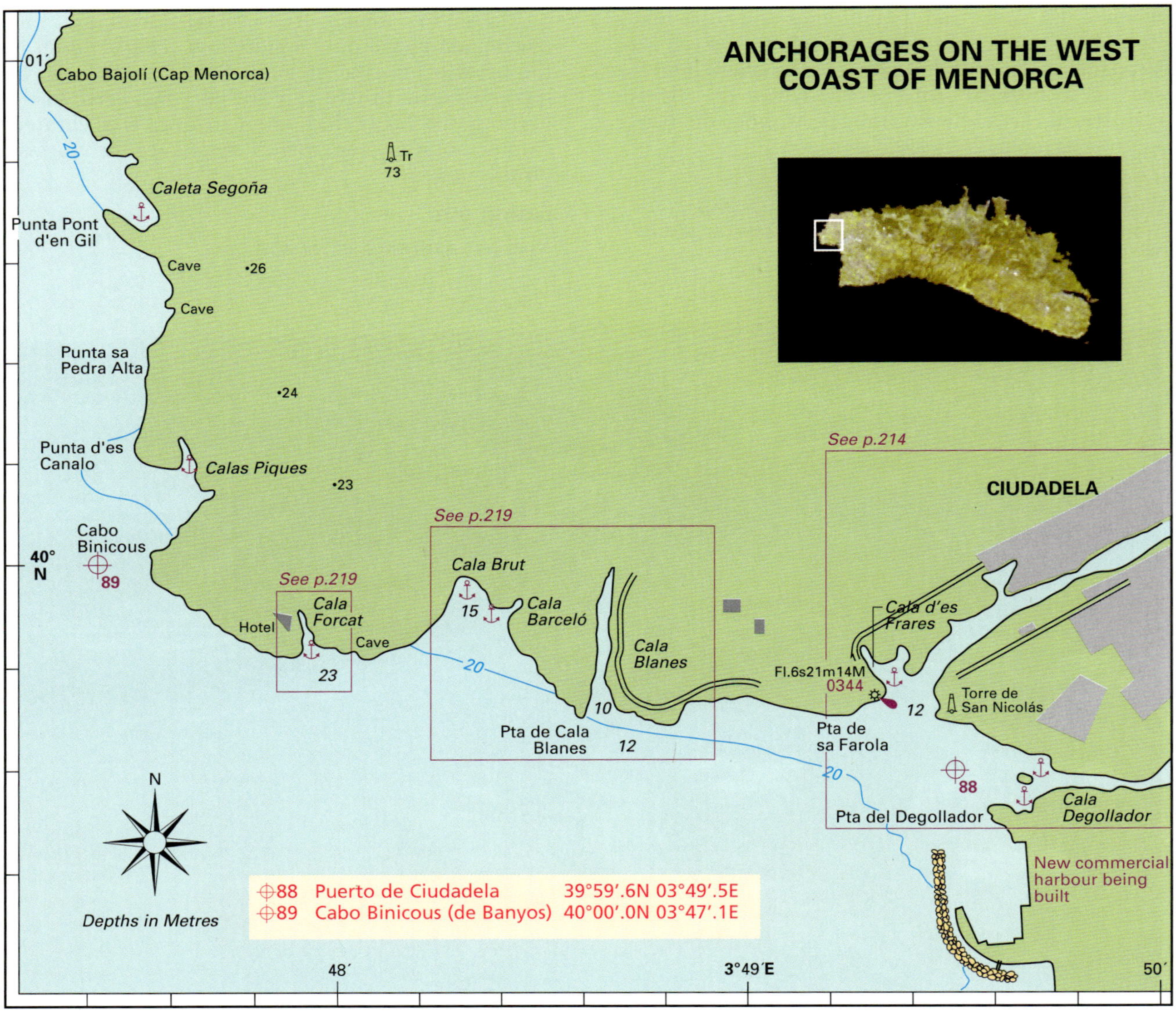

ANCHORAGES ON THE WEST COAST OF MENORCA

01'
Cabo Bajolí (Cap Menorca)

Tr
73

Caleta Segoña

Punta Pont
d'en Gil

Cave   •26

Cave

Punta sa
Pedra Alta

•24

See p.214

CIUDADELA

Punta d'es
Canalo   Calas Piques

•23

Cabo
Binicous
40°   ⊕
N   89

See p.219

Hotel

Cala
Forcat

23

Cave

See p.219

Cala Brut

15   Cala
Barceló

Cala
Blanes

Cala d'es
Frares

Fl.6s21m14M
0344   12

Torre de
San Nicolás

Pta de
sa Farola

20

10

Pta de Cala
Blanes   12

⊕
88

Cala
Degollador

Pta del Degollador

New commercial
harbour being
built

N

Depths in Metres

48'   3°49'E   50'

| ⊕88 | Puerto de Ciudadela | 39°59'.6N 03°49'.5E |
| ⊕89 | Cabo Binicous (de Banyos) | 40°00'.0N 03°47'.1E |

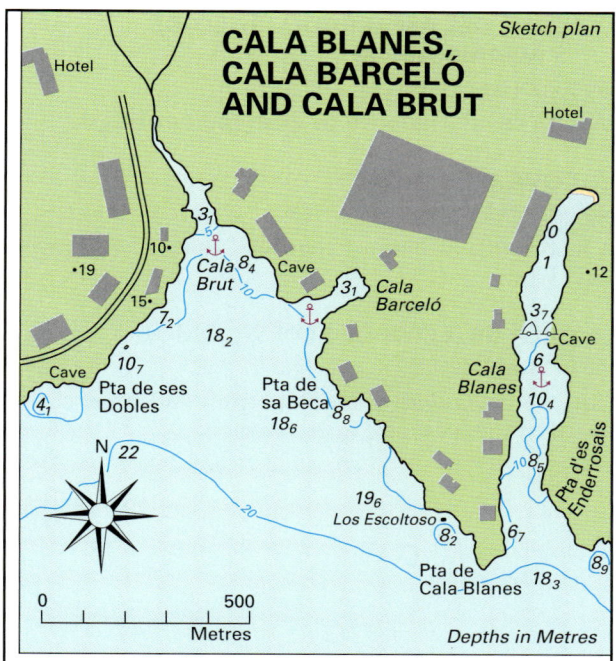

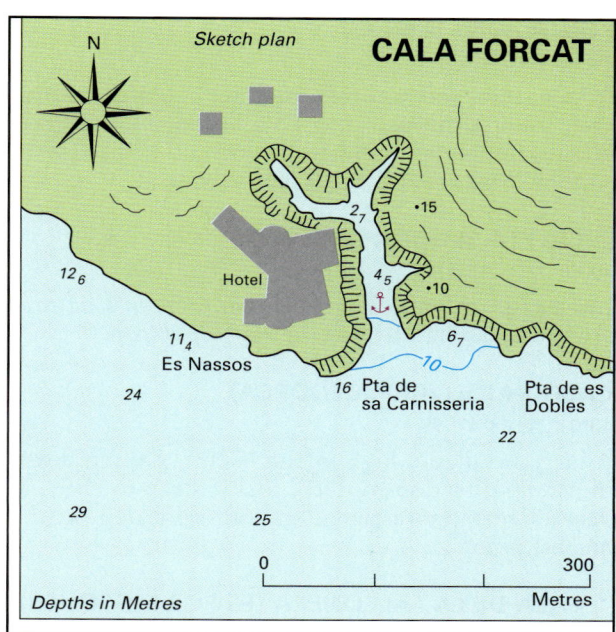

one of the rings ashore. In summer a line of buoys marks off the bathing area and virtually excludes craft from using this *cala*.

A tourist resort is growing around Cala Blanes, complete with the usual hotels, restaurants, beach bars, etc. Most day-to-day items can be purchased in the resort, though it may be simpler (and cheaper) to go into Ciudadela.

Cala Forcat bottom right, looking northwest over Cabo Binicous (left). Calas Piques and Caleta Segoña on far side of peninsula

⚓ CALA BARCELÓ

39°59′.9N 03°48′.5E

A very small, almost circular *cala* surrounded by 10m rocky cliffs, open to the southwest. Mooring buoys occupy most of the space available. There is no beach or other attractions.

⚓ CALA BRUT

40°00′N 03°48′.4E

A small narrow *cala* at the head of a wider inlet about 0.75M west of the entrance to Puerto de Ciudadela. Anchor in 5–10m over sand in the entrance to the *cala*. There are rocky bathing terraces on either side and a large hotel near the head. Again note that in high season swimmers' buoys exclude craft from most of this *cala*.

⚓ CALA FORCAT

39°59′.9N 03°48′.1E

A very small Y-shaped *cala* dwarfed by an immense reddish-orange hotel, Cala Forcat is suitable only for smaller yachts and dinghies. It is surrounded by low (10m) rocky cliffs and is open to the south. Anchor in 4–5m over sand and rock, using two anchors. All the usual facilities of a large modern hotel are available.

⊕89 40°00′.0N 03°47′.1E Cabo Binicous (de Banyos)

CABO BINICOUS (CAP DE BANYOS) TO CABO NATI

The anchorages between Cabo Binicous (Cap de Banyos) and Cabo Nati should not be attempted in anything less than settled weather and by experienced navigators. Most are deep and surrounded by high rocky cliffs (24–64m) and there are no beaches, houses or roads. The bottom is mostly rocky and 10–15m deep.

PUNTA PONT D'EN GIL

40°00'.7N 3°47'.6E

A long, thin, rocky-cliffed point with a large natural arch leading through into Cala Segoña. The arch is about 10m high and 8m wide and can be used with care by dinghies and small motor boats.

⚓ CALETA SEGOÑA (CIGONYA)

40°00'.7N 3°47'.7E

Just north of Punta Pont d'en Gil there is a natural archway leading through the rocky outcrop.

CABO BAJOLÍ (CAP MENORCA)

40°01'.1N 03°47'.5E

A large headland, high inland (72m), sloping down in a west direction to dark, rocky, steep-to cliffs. A disused semaphore signal station is located on the highest point.

⚓ CALA DE LA FALCONERA (ES POP MOSQUER)

40°01'.4N 03°48'.0E

A small *cala* under very high cliffs on the north side of Cabo Bajolí.

⚓ CALA DEL AMARRADÓ (RACO DE S'ALMARRADOR)

40°01'.7N 03°48'.4E

A very small *cala* open to west and northwest.

⚓ COVA D'ES TABAC

40°02'.3N 03°48'.9E

Close south of Punta Espardina, open to southwest and west.

⚓ CALA BE (COVA DE SON SALOMÓ)

40°02'.4N 03°49'.0E

An open *cala* with a sandy bottom and some caves, open to the west and northwest.

Rugged coastline looking east-southeast from Cabo Nati, with several calas

V. MENORCA

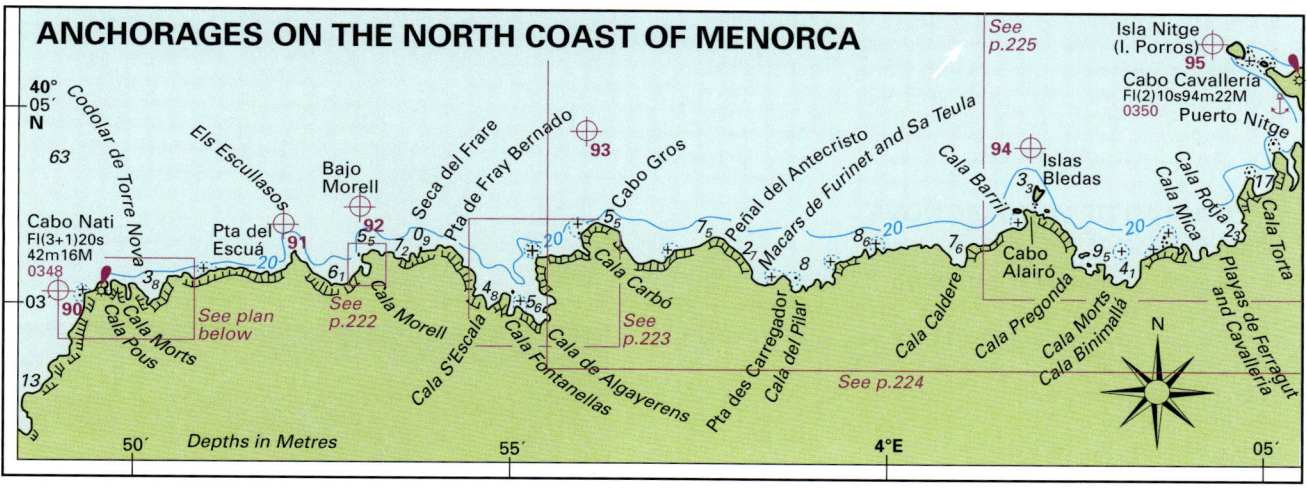

ANCHORAGES ON THE NORTH COAST OF MENORCA

⊕90 40°03'.1N 03°49'.0E Cabo Nati

CABO NATI

40°03'.1N 03°49'.2E

A prominent 32m headland of dark cliffs sloping to the northwest, with a conspicuous white lighthouse (Fl(3+1)20s42m16M, aluminium cupola on white tower above a white building with a red roof 13m) set inside a white-walled enclosure a hundred metres or so inland. The cliffs are steep-to, but with several small rocky islets close inshore. A road runs from the lighthouse to Ciudadela.

⊕90	Cabo Nati	40°03'.1N 03°49'.0E
⊕91	Punta del Escuá	40°03'.8N 3°52'.0E
⊕92	Bajo Morell Rock N	40°04'.0N 3°53'.0E
⊕93	Off Cabo Gros	40°04'.7N 03°56'.0E
⊕94	Isla Bledas N	40°04'.7N 04°01'.9E
⊕95	Off Isla Nitge	40°05'.8N 04°04'.1E

⚓ CALA POUS

40°03'.2N 03°49'.6E

A small, narrow, rocky *cala* amidst rugged surroundings 300m northeast of Cabo Nati lighthouse, with a small high islet on the east side of

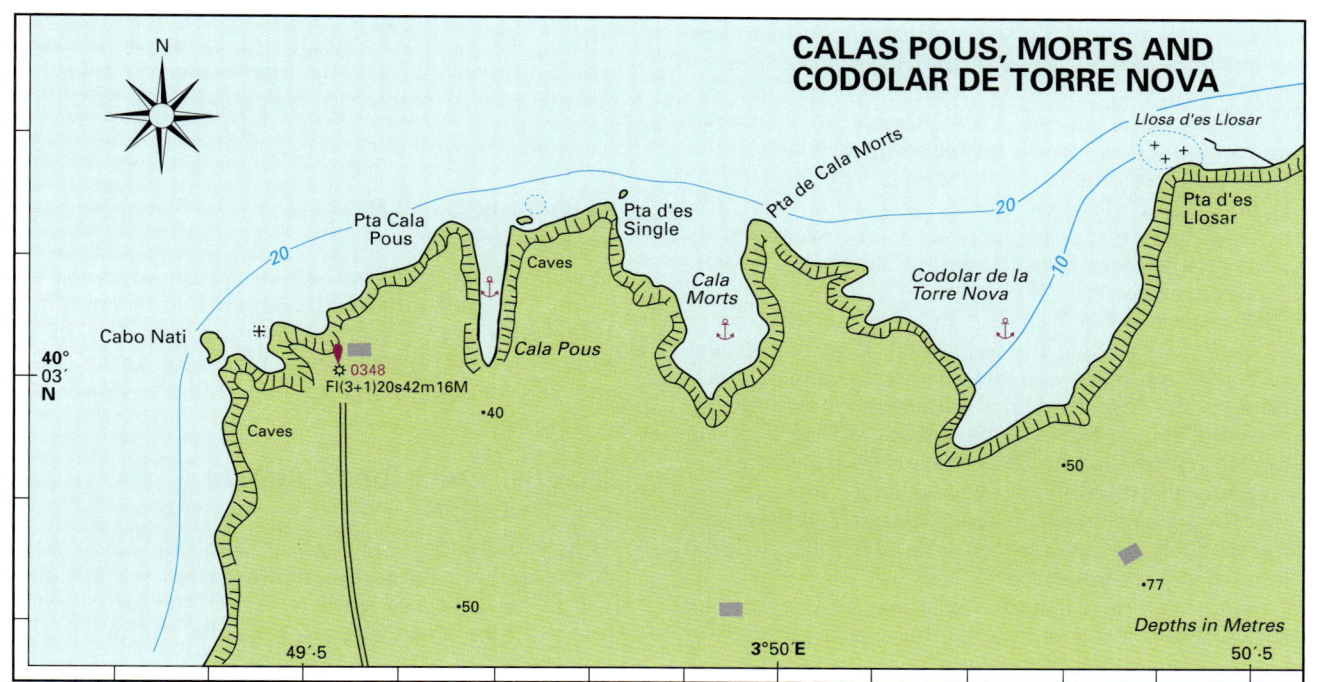

CALAS POUS, MORTS AND CODOLAR DE TORRE NOVA

the entrance. The inlet lies between 30m sloping cliffs and has a small stony beach at its head. Anchor over rock, weed and sand.

⚓ CALA MORTS
40°03'.2N 03°49'.8E

A larger, wider *cala*, again between 30m rocky cliffs and with a stony beach at its head, separated from Cala Pous by Punta d'es Single. Two conspicuous islets to the west of the entrance and a *talayot* (ancient tower) on the skyline, make identification easy. Anchor in sand, rock and weed, open to the north sector. There are a great many *talayots*, large and small, but nothing else.

⚓ CODOLAR DE LA TORRE NOVA
40°03'.1N 03°50'.2E

A large, open deserted *cala* with 40m rocky cliffs, some rocky beaches and several caves, one of which can be entered by dinghy. There are several rocky islets off Punta d'es Llosar on the east side of the entrance and two *talayots* (ancient towers) on the skyline. Anchor in 10m or less over sand, rock and weed, open to the north.

⊕91 40°03'.8N 3°52'.0E Punta del Escuá

PUNTA DEL ESCUÁ AND ELS ESCULLASOS
40°03'.5N 03°52'.1E

Three small rocky islets lie close inshore under the high (79m) sloping cliffs of Punta del Escuá (Punta de s'Escullar). 100m to the north lie two breaking rocks (Els Escullasos) with foul ground extending for 100m around them.

⚓ CALA MORELL
40°03'.4N 03°52'.9E

This small, almost landlocked *cala* with sloping rocky cliffs gives a very beautiful anchorage. The entrance is difficult to spot until well into the outer bay. If coming from the west, on rounding Els Escullasos a group of white houses will be seen above Punta d'es Elefant on the southwest side of the entrance. Coming from the east a few houses on Punta de Cala Morell will be seen. The *cala* only opens after this point is astern. Allow generous clearance to Seca d'es Frare and Bajo d'en Morell rocks (see right).

Anchor in 4–6m over sand and weed near the centre of the *cala*, avoiding the unmarked 0.3m reef on the east side (see plan) and the swimmers' buoys which take up the east third of the *cala* and now actually enclose the reef. Most people anchor with a long line to the western shore (if tying to a ring make sure it is a secure one!). Holding is patchy and a few summer moorings are usually laid for local boats. If winds from the north sector are forecast it is adviseable to leave immediately, as a nasty swell rolls in.

There is a small sandy beach at the head of the *cala* where a seasonal stream enters, and a miniature quay, slipway, crane and boat park for dinghies. A

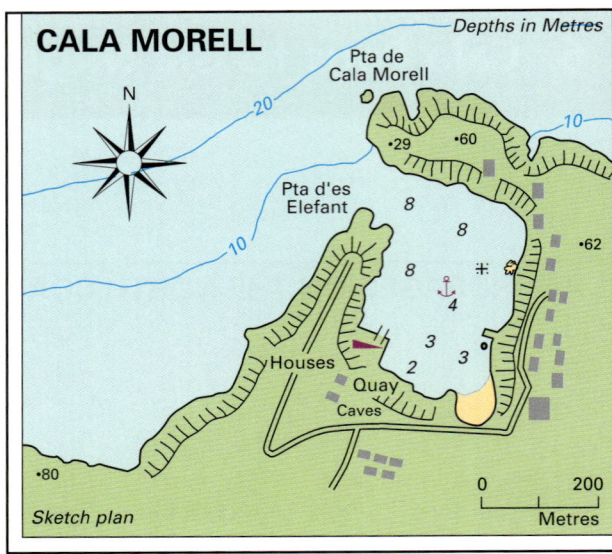

Cala Morell: a very pleasant and safe anchorage in most conditions

restaurant and basic shopping can be found in the village. There are a number of caves in the area which are second only in importance to those at Cala Covas. A main road leads to Ciudadela.

⊕92 40°04'.0N 3°53'.0E Bajo Morell Rock N

BAJO (BAIX D'EN) MORELL
40°03'.7N 03°53'.0E

This breaking rock lies 400m north–northeast of Punta de Cala Morell with foul ground reaching for 100m around it. There are two other similar rocks very close inshore. There is a passage 150m wide and 16m deep between the *bajo* and the shore; use with caution.

SECA DEL FRARE (DE CORNIOLA)
40°03'.7N 03°53'.7E

An isolated rock, carrying less than 1m, 250m west of Pta de Fray Bernardo (Punta de Fra Bernat) and not to be confused with a rocky islet, Escull des Frares, 50m from the shore some 200m to the southwest.

Cala S'Escala right, with Cala Fontanellas just behind the rock and the larger Cala de Algayerens beyond

⚓ CALA S'ESCALA (CODOLAR DE BINIATRAM)
40°03'.1N 03°54'.7E

An open bay surrounded by a sloping rocky shore with a stony beach, Cala S'Escala can be identified by the bleak Escull de ses Vinjoles Island (14m) off the headland to the east. Anchor over sand and rock, open to the north quadrant. There is a track leading inland but otherwise the bay is deserted.

⚓ CALA FONTANELLAS
40°03'.1N 03°55'E

A pleasant anchorage surrounded by green shrub-covered hills, with a small sand and rock beach. Escull de ses Vinjoles (14m) lies on the northwest side of the entrance. Anchor over sand, rock and weed near the head of the *cala*, which is open to the north but also feels swell from northwest and northeast. A few seasonal moorings may be laid for local boats.

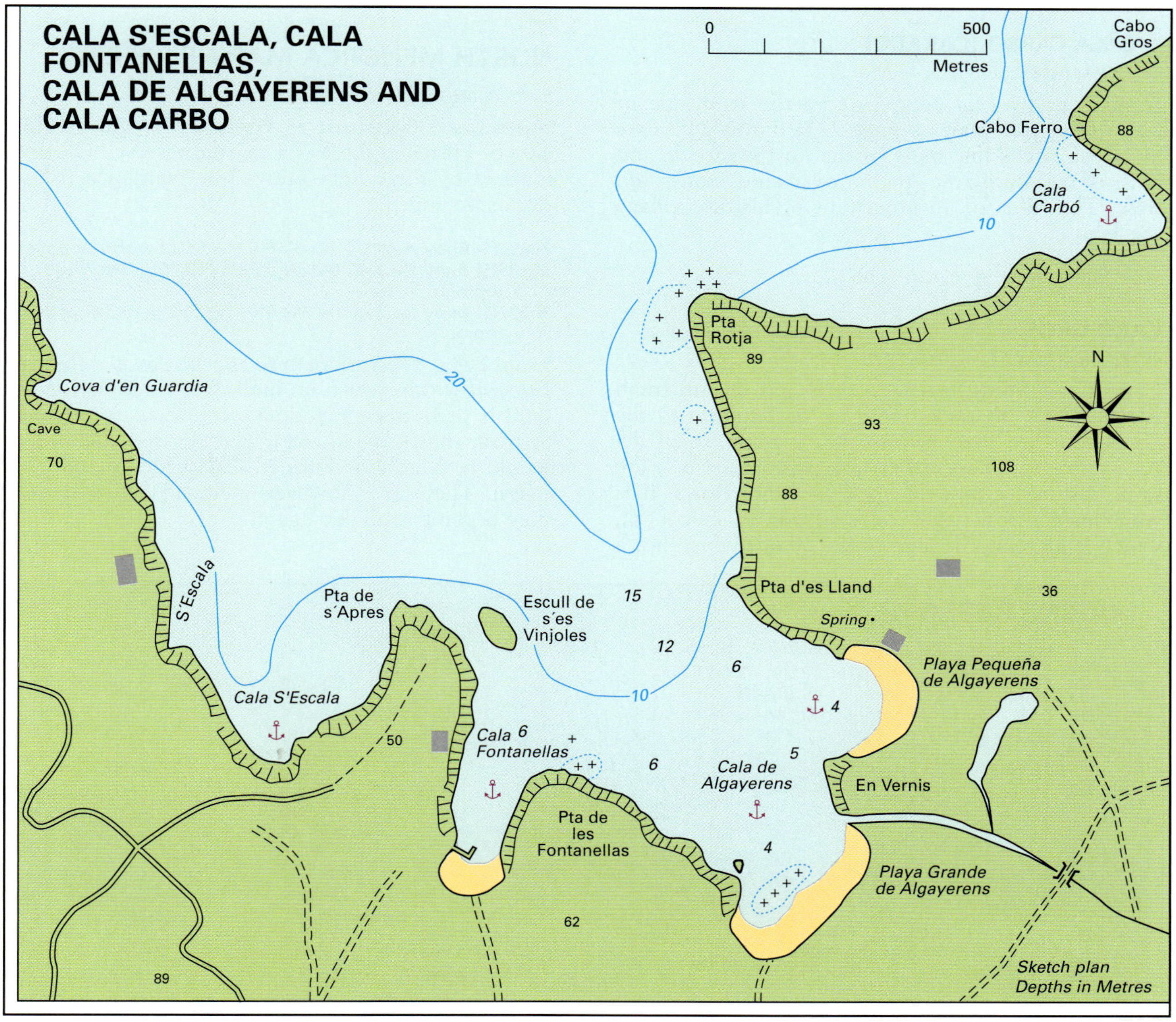

CALA S'ESCALA, CALA FONTANELLAS, CALA DE ALGAYERENS AND CALA CARBO

0   500
Metres

Cabo Gros

Cabo Ferro   88

Cala Carbó

10

Pta Rotja   89

N

Cova d'en Guardia

Cave
70

93

108

20

88

Pta d'es Lland   36

Spring

S'Escala

Pta de s'Apres

Escull de s'es Vinjoles

15

Playa Pequeña de Algayerens

Cala S'Escala

12

6

4

50

Cala Fontanellas 6

10

6

5

Cala de Algayerens

En Vernis

Pta de les Fontanellas

4

Playa Grande de Algayerens

62

Sketch plan
Depths in Metres

89

There are one or two houses in the vicinity and fishermen's huts on the north side. Much of the beach at the head of the *cala* is taken up by a short stone quay and slipway for the use of small motorboats kept on the foreshore.

⚓ CALA DE ALGAYERENS (D'ALGAIARENS)

40°03'N 03°55'.3E

A wide bay with two good beaches, Playa Grande de Algayerens (Platja des Tancats) to the southeast and Playa Pequeña de Algayerens (Platja des Bot) to the northeast, divided by an angular headland. If approaching from the north keep well off Punta Rotja which has foul ground extending up to 200m from its base. Anchor off either beach over sand with weed patches in 2–6m. A rocky reef lies close to the beach of Playa de Grande Algayerens.

There is a boathouse on Playa de Pequeña Algayerens with a spring, the Font d'en Cumar, nearby, but no houses. Several roads and tracks allow visitors to reach the beaches which are popular in summer. A large lagoon with much wildlife lies inland.

⚓ CALA CARBÓ (CARABÓ)

40°03'.5N 03°55'.7E

A small rocky *cala* tucked under the west side of Cabo Gros (see plan on page 223). Enter with care as awash rocks line most of the northeast side and parts of the southwest. Anchor over sand, stones and rock. The ruins of an important prehistoric village are ashore.

⊕93 40°04'.7N 03°56'.0E Off Cabo Gros

CABO GROS

40°03'.8N 03°56'.1E

Cabo Gros (96m) has steep cliffs and several small islets and awash rocks close in, particularly to the northwest (see plan below). Both it and Peñal del Anticristo 1.2 miles further east are composed of the same distinctive rust-red rock as Punta Rotja. It is sometimes erroneously referred to as Falconera, which is actually the high peak (205m) which lies a

Cala Carbó

mile south-southeast. A ruined prehistoric village and wall lie south of the headland, not far from Cala Carbó.

NORTH MENORCA MARINE RESERVE

Reserve area shown on plan below

From Cabo Gros east to Punta de Es Morter (just east of Fornells) there is a marine reserve. The area marked by three light buoys (see plan) is a fishing exclusion zone.

36690(S) **Buoy A** 40°04'.3N 3°56'E Fl.Y.5s5M with × topmark
36695(S) **Buoy No.1** 40°04'.2N 3°58'E Fl(2)Y.10s3M with × topmark
36697(S) **Buoy No.2** 40°04'.4N 4°01'.6E Fl(2)Y.10s3M with × topmark

From Peñal del Anticristo to Isla Bledas is a *Reserva Integral* within which no underwater activity of any kind is permitted (including, according to the latest Spanish charts, anchoring). The affected anchorages would be Macar de Furinet, Cala Caldere and Cala Barril. These are, however, included below in case they become available again.

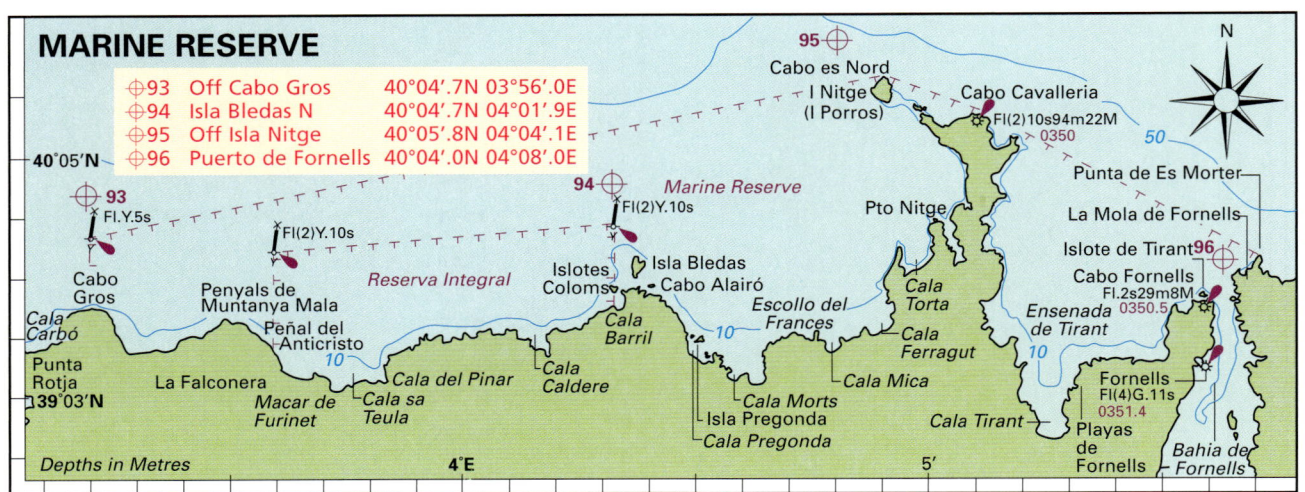

⚓ MACARS DE FURINET AND SA TEULA

40°03'.5N 03°58'.4E (see Anchoring Note left)

Two ends of an open bay surrounded by sandy and rocky cliffs, to be used with care. There are rocks off the west beach (Macar de Furinet), while Punta des Carregador to the east has rocks and islets extending at least 100m northwest. Anchor off either beach over sand and rock, open to the north quadrant. There is a hut behind the stony east beach but otherwise the area is deserted.

⚓ CALA DEL PINAR

40°03'.3N 03°58'.7E

A small bay between high (69m), sloping reddish cliffs. Numerous awash rocks and small islets line the coast to the east, but an approach on a southerly course leaving Illa d'es Pilar 150m to port clears all dangers. Anchor over sand and rock, open to northwest round to northeast.

⚓ CALA CALDERE

40°03'.6N 04°00'.9E (see Anchoring Note left)

A wide *cala* with sloping reddish cliffs on either side and scrub-covered hills (57m) above. There are two awash rocks close inshore, one each side of the *cala*, and at its head a sandy beach crossed by a stream bed. Anchor off the beach over sand and rock, open to the northwest and north. There is a track leading inland with a few houses and two prehistoric *navetas* (burial mounds) at Sant Jordi about ½ mile away.

⚓ CALA BARRIL

40°03'.8N 04°01'.7E (see Anchoring Note left)

An anchorage off a rock and sand beach close west of Cabo Alairó (Cap de s'Alarió) and the Isla Bledas (Illa Bledas), easy to locate by a track embanked with a stone wall. Careful navigation is necessary due to a small island, an awash rock and an islet to port of the approach. From a position 200m north of Isla de'sColoms, avoiding an awash rock (Baix d'es Coloms) 120m to the northwest of the *isla*, enter on a southerly course between the *isla* and Cabo Alairó, aiming for the centre of the beach at the head of the *cala*.

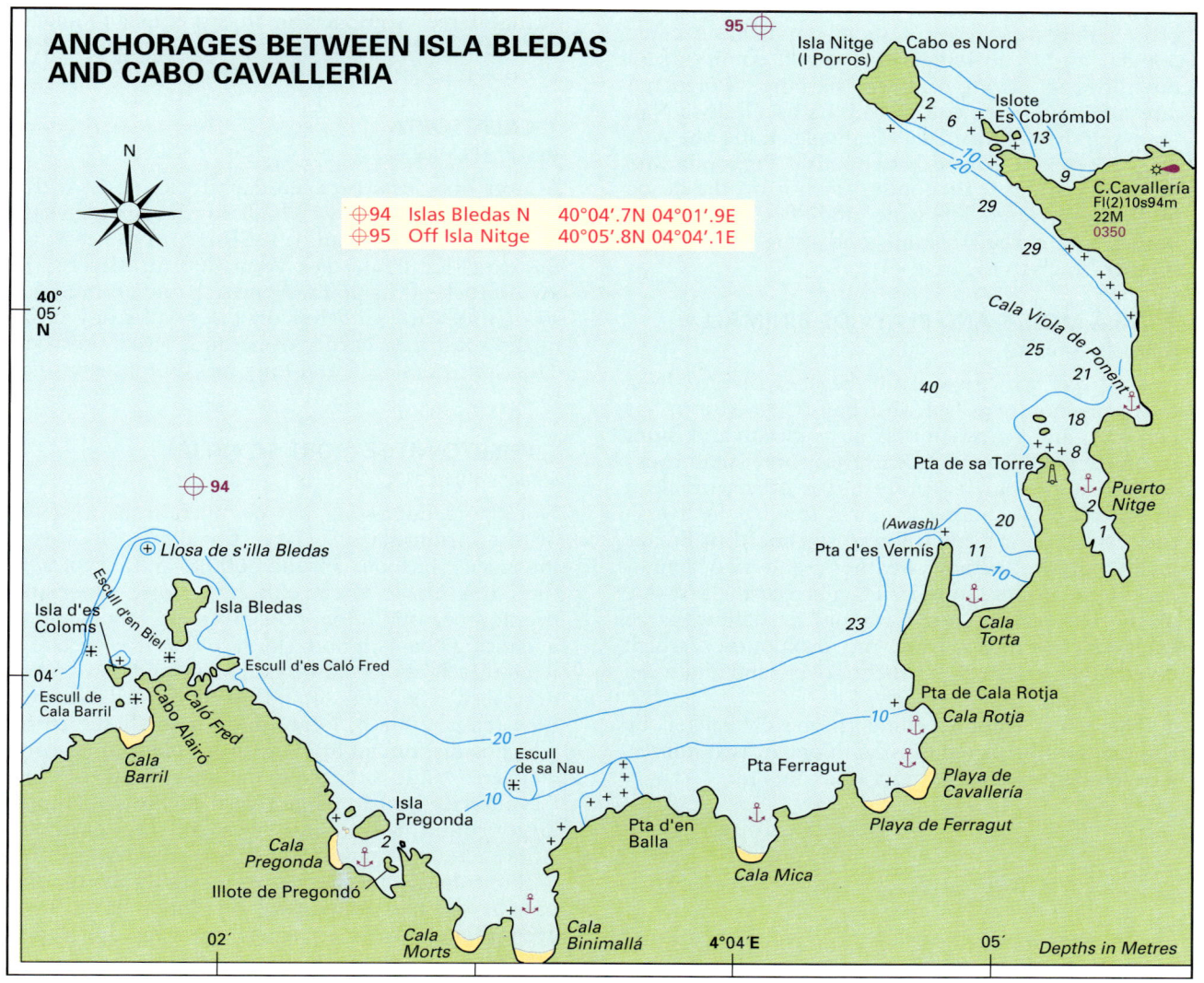

ANCHORAGES BETWEEN ISLA BLEDAS AND CABO CAVALLERIA

⊕94	Islas Bledas N	40°04'.7N 04°01'.9E
⊕95	Off Isla Nitge	40°05'.8N 04°04'.1E

Depths in Metres

ISLA BLEDAS
40°04'.2N 04°02'.0E

Normally pass north of the Nature Reserve buoy to the north of Isla Bledas – although an offing of at least 250m will clear the isolated Llosa de s'illa Bledas, which lies 120m northwest of the northwestern point of the isla (see plan on page 225).

There is said to be a fair-weather passage 100m wide and 5m deep inside Isla Bledas but this area is reported as a maze of barely submerged rocks. Rock hoppers should rely on eyeball navigation if attempting this passage.

⚓ CALÓ FRED
40°03'.9N 04°02'.1E

A very small *cala* hidden away behind the Escull d'es Caló Fred, only for use by experienced navigators in good weather. More a place to explore than to anchor, the *cala* is open to the northeast, has a rocky bottom and no beach. There are just a few houses and a road ashore.

⚓ CALA PREGONDA
40°03'.4N 04°02'.6E

A pleasant anchorage in a large bay and partially protected by rocky islets, Cala Pregonda has become popular and is no longer deserted. If coming from the northeast having rounded Isla Nitge (Porros), a direct course for the entrance clears Escull de sa Nau – an awash rock off Cala Binimallá. Enter the *cala* on a southwest course between Isla Pregonda and the smaller Illot de Pregondó. Anchor off the beach in ±4m over sand. The wide sandy beach has a few houses and a road behind, and there is a second smaller beach to the east.

⚓ CALA MORTS AND PLAYA DE BINIMALLÁ
40°03'.3N 04°03'.0E

A wide bay with two sandy beaches divided by a rocky promontory. The west bay (Cala Morts) has two islets and an awash rock at its mouth and is not recommended. The east beach has some small rocks close inshore near its centre but is otherwise clear. Approach on a southerly course leaving the awash rock Escull de sa Nau 100m to starboard (it breaks in all but the calmest weather), and two similar rocks close inshore to port. Then favour the east side of the bay, taking care to avoid a shallow patch extending northeast from the promontory which divides the two beaches. Anchor over sand and weed in 4m or less.

There is a lagoon behind the beach backed by sloping, scrub-covered hills, with one or two houses, a beach bar/restaurant and a track inland.

⚓ CALA MICA
40°03'.5N 04°04'.0E

A wide and deep *cala* with a sandy beach. It has a number of islets and awash rocks both in the approach (up to 200m from the shore) and fringing either side of the entrance. Anchor near the middle of the *cala* over sand, weed and rocks. There is very little ashore: a house and a track inland, and some of the surrounding hills are terraced.

⚓ PLAYA DE FERRAGUT, PLAYA DE CAVALLERÍA AND CALA ROTJA
40°03'.6N 04°04'.5E

Three possible anchorages in a large bay broken by rocky outcrops. Approach Playa de Ferragut on a south course to anchor off the beach over sand and weed. At the east end of the beach there are two small rocky islets dividing it from Playa de Cavallería, which is popular with visitors in summer. Take care on final approach to this latter as there is an isolated awash rock 200m off the middle of the beach (see plan on page 225) – favour the east end, to anchor over sand and rock.

Beyond the distinctive reddish point known as Punta de Cala Rotja (Rotja means 'red'), lies the *cala* of that name. Approach on an east course to anchor off the beach, avoiding a patch of rocky islets. Various tracks run inland but there is little else.

⚓ CALA TORTA
40°04'.2N 04°04'.9E

A large open *cala* between dark rocky cliffs, with a large conspicuous tower built by the British in the 18th century on Punta de sa Torre, to the east. On the west side Punta d'es Vernís has an islet and an awash rock off its point. Approach and entrance are straightforward – anchor off the small stony beach in the southwest corner over sand, weed and rock. The *cala* is deserted and only has footpaths leading to it.

⚓ PUERTO NITGE (PORT SA NITJA)
40°04'.5N 04°05'.2E

Not a port, but a long, narrow inlet on the west side of the peninsula of Cabo Cavallería. It was a Phoenician harbour around 1600BC and is typical of the sites they often chose: a low, defensible promontory with the possibility of launching or anchoring boats on both sides, so that irrespective of wind direction they could escape, defend or attack as necessary. The Romans occupied the *cala* in their turn (circa 200BC), establishing a small settlement which is mentioned by Pliny in his *Natural History*.

Puerto Nitge is tucked in on the west side of Cabo Cavalleriá with Isla Nitge (Illa d'els Porros), and its large round tower just west of the entrance. Approach and entrance are straightforward, but without local knowledge it is advisable to pass outside the two islets lying off Punta de sa Torre even though a 50m passage carrying 5m depths exists between the islets and the point.

Favour the east side of the entrance as rocks fringe the west point, and watch the echo-sounder carefully – the inner part of the inlet has silted up – though 2m can usually be carried for 200m, and 1m for the same distance again. Anchor in 2m+ over sand, weed and rock, open to the northwest and north. The sides of the *cala* are of dark rock and the surroundings somewhat low and windswept.

There are three short piers or jetties in the upper part of the *cala*, used by small motor and fishing boats, and some seasonal moorings may be laid. A stream, largely blocked by a sandbank, flows into the southwest corner. A few houses and fishermen's huts lie to the east with a large farm to the south. There is a road out to the lighthouse on Cabo Cavalleriá. A large- scale plan of Puerto Nitge appears on Spanish chart 4262.

⚓ CALA VIOLA DE PONENT

40°04'.6N 04°05'.3E

This tiny *cala*, which lies near the east side of the entrance to Puerto Nitge, might be visited by experienced navigators in good conditions, but has a number of isolated rocks, on the northeast side of the *cala*. Open to the west and northwest.

⊕95 40°05'.8N 04°04'.1E Off Isla Nitge

Passage inside Isla Nitge (Illa d'els Porros)

40°05'.5N 04°04'.5E

There is a passage 150m wide with a minimum depth of 6m between Isla Nitge and Cabo Cavallería with its offlying rocks and islets. Head north-northeast (or south-southwest), equidistant between Isla Nitge and Islote Es Cobrómbol, keeping to the centre of the passage as the sides are lined with just-covered and awash isolated rocks.

A very narrow fishermen's passage, the Pas d'es Cobrómbol, exists between the islet of that name and Menorca. However, it should not be attempted without local knowledge or first making a detailed recce by dinghy.

Looking west from Ensenada de Tirant towards Isla Bledas and Cabo Gros

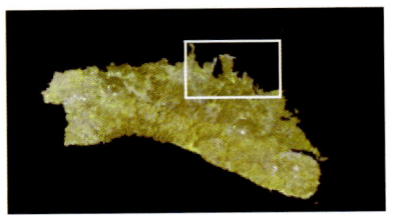

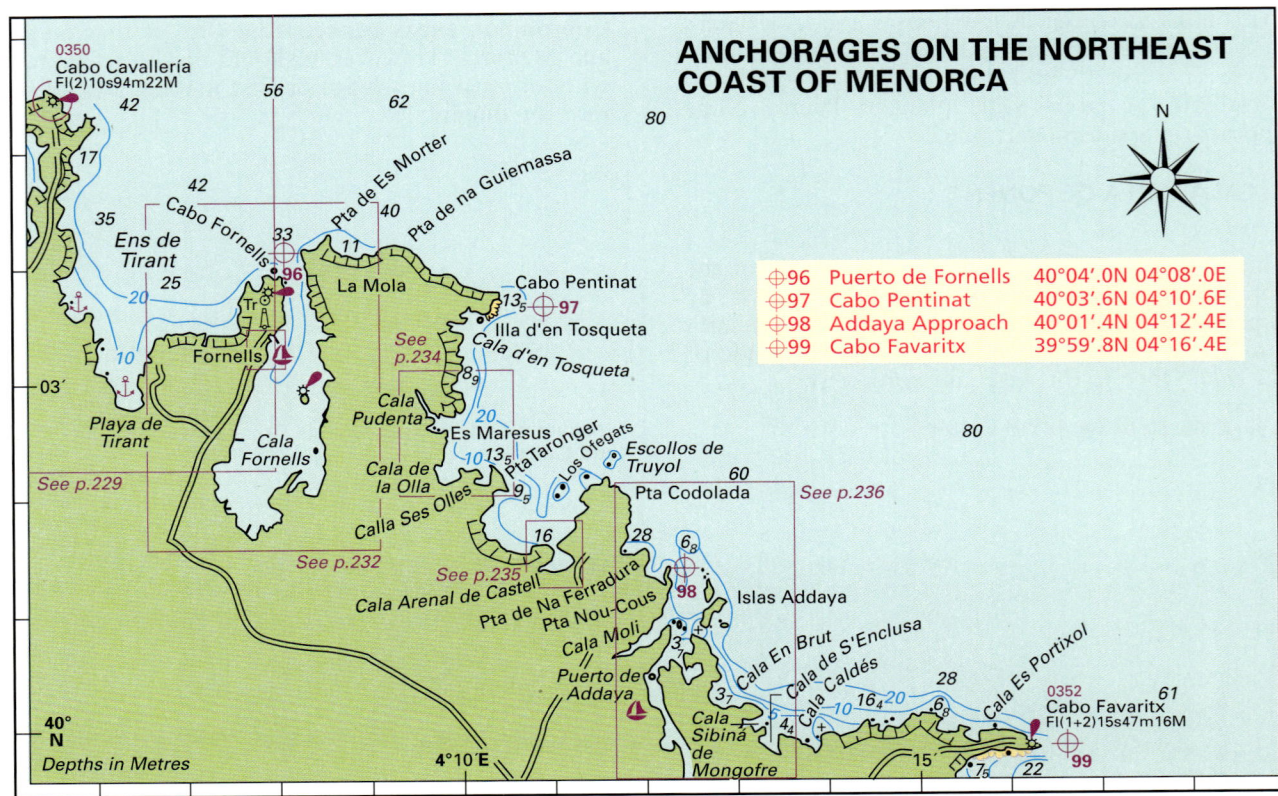

ANCHORAGES ON THE NORTHEAST COAST OF MENORCA

⊕96	Puerto de Fornells	40°04'.0N 04°08'.0E
⊕97	Cabo Pentinat	40°03'.6N 04°10'.6E
⊕98	Addaya Approach	40°01'.4N 04°12'.4E
⊕99	Cabo Favaritx	39°59'.8N 04°16'.4E

CABO CAVALLERÍA

40°05'.4N 04°05'.5E

A very prominent and conspicuous peninsula and headland sloping from 80m at the north end down to 5m where it joins Menorca. A lighthouse (Fl(2)10s94m22M, white tower and building 15m) stands on the northeast point. There is very deep water up to the cliffs but watch out for the one 6.5m outlier, Llosa dels Ocelliers, just north of the lighthouse (see plan on page 229).

ANCHORAGES BETWEEN CABO CAVALLERÍA AND PLAYA DE TIRANT

A series of anchorages open to northeast through to southeast, on the east side of the peninsula of Cabo Cavallería. All have isolated rocks close inshore and a rock and sand bottom, and should be used only with great care in settled conditions. From Cova des Vell Mari southwards they appear on the large-scale Bahía de Tirant and Cala Fornells insert on BA 2833.

⚓ CALA S'OLLA

40°05'.1N 04°05'.7E

A wide, high-cliffed (74m) *cala* close east of Cabo Cavallería lighthouse, which is deep close inshore.

⚓ CALA VIOLA DE LLEVANT

40°04'.5N 04°05'.7E

Two awash rocks on the south side of the entrance.

⚓ COVA DES VELL MARI

40°04'.2N 04°05'.7E

Surrounded by low rocky cliffs; open north through to east.

⚓ CALA MACAR GRAN

40°03'.5N 04°05'.8E

A wide shallow bay with some offshore rocks, open from north to northeast.

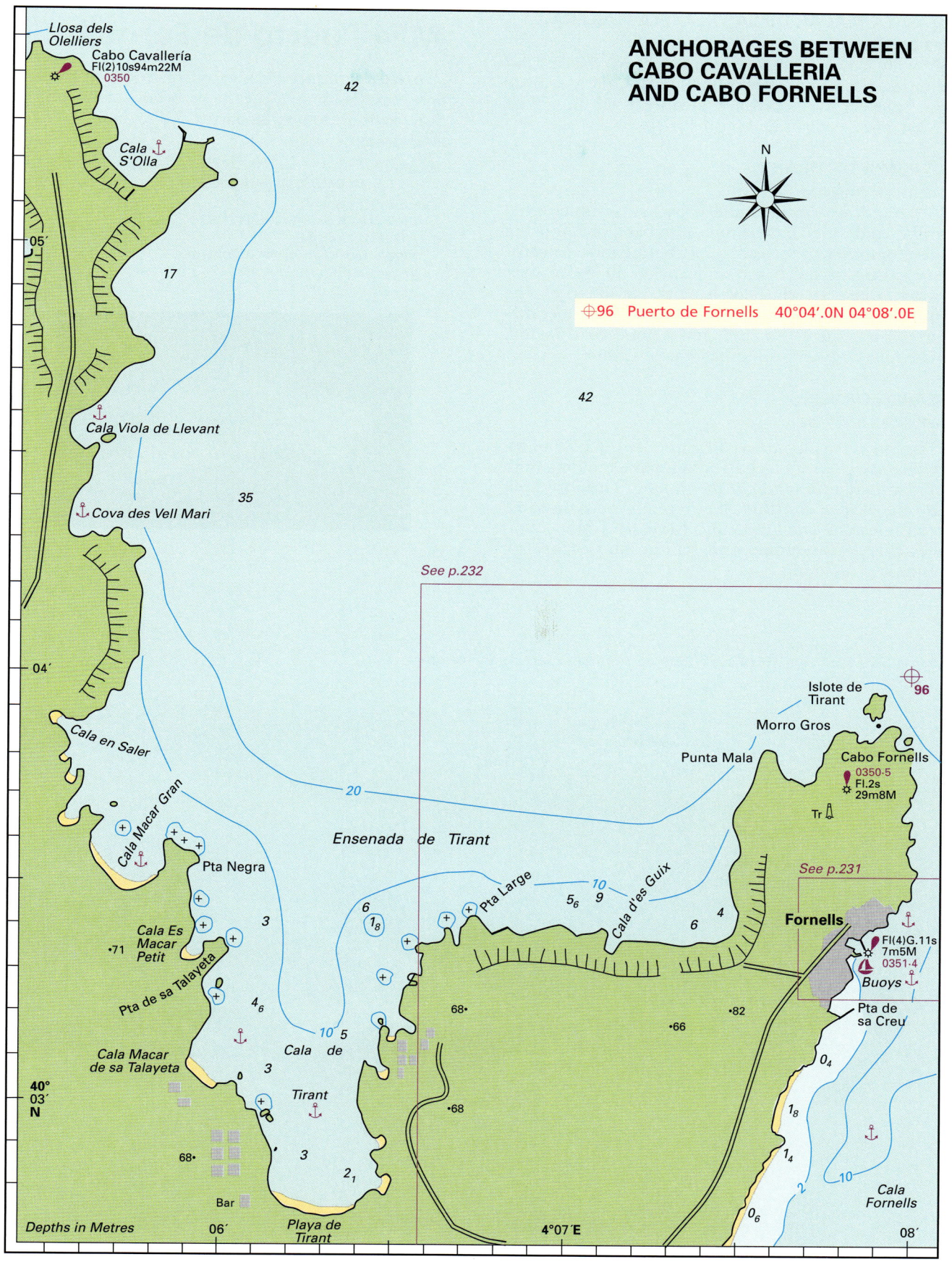

Llosa dels
Olelliers
Cabo Cavallería
Fl(2)10s94m22M
0350

ANCHORAGES BETWEEN
CABO CAVALLERIA
AND CABO FORNELLS

N

42

Cala
S'Olla

⊕96   Puerto de Fornells   40°04′.0N 04°08′.0E

05′

17

42

Cala Viola de Llevant

35

Cova des Vell Mari

See p.232

04′

Islote de
Tirant

Morro Gros

Cala en Saler

Punta Mala

Cabo Fornells
0350·5
Fl.2s
29m8M
Tr

20

Cala Macar Gran

Ensenada de Tirant

See p.231

Pta Negra

10

Cala d'es Guix

Fornells

Pta Large

5 6

9

4

6

Fl(4)G.11s
7m5M
0351·4

3

6
1 8

Cala Es
Macar
Petit

•71

Buoys

Pta de sa Talayeta

Pta de
sa Creu

4 6

68•

•82

•66

0 4

10 5

Cala Macar
de sa Talayeta

3

Cala   de

1 8

**40°
03′
N**

Tirant

1 4

68•

•68

3

2

10

Cala
Fornells

68•

3

2 1

0 6

Bar

V. MENORCA

⚓ CALA MACAR DE SA TALAYETA (TAILERA)

40°03'.0N 04°06'.0E

A wide bay with a large sandy beach backed by houses, open to north through east. (Cala Macar de sa Talayeta is incorrectly identified on BA chart 2761 inset as Cala Es Macar Petit).

⚓ PLAYA DE TIRANT

40°02'.9N 04°06'.3E

A large deep bay surrounded by low scrub-covered hills and an increasing number of housing developments. Approach on a south course towards the centre of the beach and anchor in 4–5m over sand, open to the north with swell from the northeast. The long sandy beach is sometimes crowded – there is a café, and a good road inland. The huge lagoon behind has much wildlife.

CABO FORNELLS

40°03'.8N 04°07'.8E

This rocky headland has a lighthouse (Fl.2s29m8M, white tower with black band on white building 6m), and a small fort a little further inland. This fort, built by the British in 1801, has recently been restored and houses a small museum. Islote de Tirant (20m) lies close off its point with foul ground between it and the headland.

ME4 Puerto de Fornells

A narrow entrance gives excellent shelter in this long *cala*, leading to several mooring possibilities for yachts, including 88 berths and several anchorages

Location
   40°03'.9N 04°08'.1E (entrance)

Communications
   Club Náutico de Fornells ① 971 37 63 28
   Fax 971 37 63 58
   Email nauticfornells@compusoft.es
   www.nauticfornells.com

Fornells viewed from north over Islote de Tirant. Isla Sargantana centre

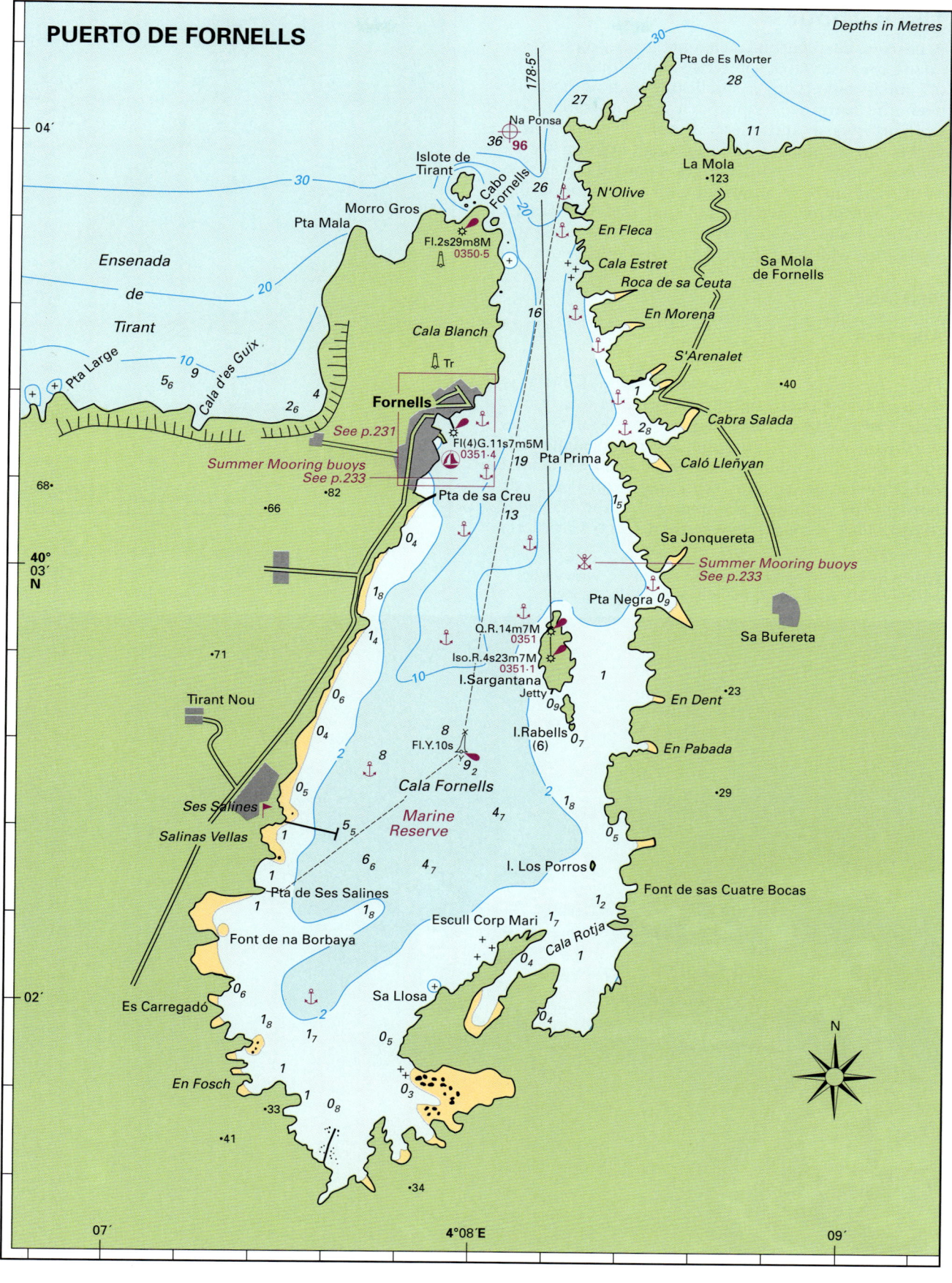

PUERTO DE FORNELLS

Depths in Metres

178·5°

Pta de Es Morter

27   28

Na Ponsa
36 **96**   11

Islote de
Tirant

Morro Gros   26   N'Olive   La Mola
•123

Pta Mala   Cabo Fornells   En Fleca

Ensenada   Fl.2s29m8M   Cala Estret   Sa Mola
de Fornells

0350·5   Roca de sa Ceuta

de   20   16   En Morena

Tirant   S'Arenalet

Pta Large   10   9   Cala Blanch   •40

5 6   Tr   1

Cala d'es Guix   Cabra Salada

2 6   4   **Fornells**   2 8   Caló Lleñyan

See p.231

68•   *Summer Mooring buoys*   Fl(4)G.11s7m5M   19   Pta Prima

See p.233   0351·4   1 5

•82   Pta de sa Creu   Sa Jonquereta

•66   13   *Summer Mooring buoys*

See p.233

40°   0 4   Pta Negra 0 9   Sa Bufereta

03'   1 8   Q.R.14m7M

N   0351

•71   1 4   Iso.R.4s23m7M   1

0351·1

Tirant Nou   0 6   I.Sargantana   En Dent •23

Jetty

0 4   0 9

2   1

8   I.Rabells   0 7   En Pabada

Ses Salines   0 5   8   Fl.Y.10s   (6)   0 7

Salinas Vellas   9 2   2   1 8   •29

Cala Fornells   4 7

1   5 5   *Marine*   0 5   Font de sas Cuatre Bocas

Reserve

1   6 6   4 7   I. Los Porros

Pta de Ses Salines   1 2

1   1 8   Escull Corp Mari 1 7

Font de na Borbaya   Cala Rotja

0 4   1

0 6   N

Es Carregadó   2   Sa Llosa   0 4

1 8   1 7   0 5

1   0 3

En Fosch   1   0 8

•33

•41

•34

07'   4°08'E   09'

The harbour

A narrow, deep entrance channel gives access to an inland area of water some two miles long by up to 0.7 miles wide, with a small and shallow harbour near the entrance. Approach and entrance are straightforward and there is a large area where yachts can anchor in solitude, though holding is very poor in places. Two anchorages – one on either side of the harbour – are now laid with summer mooring buoys. See plan on page 231 and the Anchorages section on page 233. A swell finds its way into the anchorage with gales from north and northwest.

PILOTAGE

Approach

⊕96 40°04'.0N 04°08'.0E Puerto de Fornells

From west The very prominent Cabo Cavallería with its conspicuous lighthouse projects nearly two miles out to sea and has two outlying islands to its northwest (see plan on page 229). Immediately to the east of this promontory lies the deeply indented Bahía de Tirant which is separated from Puerto de Fornells by another promontory, Cabo Fornells (41m). This is much smaller than Cabo Cavallería

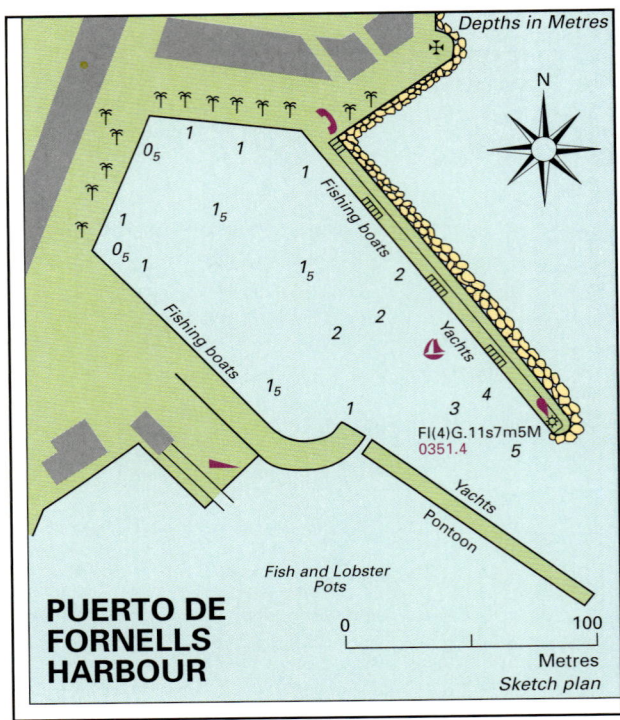

PUERTO DE FORNELLS HARBOUR

Depths in Metres

Fishing boats

Yachts

Fl(4)G.11s7m5M
0351.4

Yachts
Pontoon

Fish and Lobster Pots

0   100
Metres
Sketch plan

Puerto de Fornells harbour looking northeast, with yachts anchored off. Shallows in the area can be clearly seen

and has a very conspicuous isolated tower on its top. To the east of the entrance lies La Mola (123m) and Punta de Es Morter, composed of steep, angular cliffs falling to a gentler slope below. Approach when the entrance bears due south.

From east After rounding Cabo Pantinat (25m) follow the coast past Punta de na Guiemassa (50m) to Punta de Es Morter with the lofty La Mola (123m) behind (see plan on page 228). On rounding Punta de Es Morter the entrance lies to the south.

Entrance

When positive identification of the entrance has been made, approach on a course due south. Isla Sargantana with its two white beacon towers will be visible in the middle of the bay just over a mile away. Line up the towers on 178.5° to enter (or alternatively keep the island bearing 180°). The sides of the entrance channel are steep-to.

Entrance at night should present no problems providing the leading lights are identified before entering the channel and followed until opposite or beyond the small harbour.

Anchorages

There are many possible anchorages in Cala Fornells (see plan), though holding is poor in the more popular areas due to over-use and elsewhere because of beds of long, dense, grassy weed. For close access to the town, anchor about 100m east or southeast of the harbour in 5m over soft mud and weed. An area just south of the harbour is used to moor lobster-keep boxes, which float just level with the water and are difficult to see.

Southwest of the harbour are summer mooring buoys which may be reserved at www.balearslifeposidonia.eu/index.php?register_vars[lang]=en between the 1st June and 30th September. See plan on page 231 and the Anchoring and Moorings section on page 16 for further details.

The area between Punta Prima and the Isla Sargantana, previously taken up with fish farms, is also now taken up with mooring buoys, which can be reserved via the website above. See the plan on page 231. It is possible to anchor further N off Calo Llenyan in 4m but this should be used with caution as holding has been reported as poor; reasonably good holding can be found equidistant between the harbour and Isla Sargantana in about 8m over mud and weed.

The Club Náutico de Fornells has its clubhouse and dinghy jetty at Ses Salines in the southwest part of the bay, near which there are several further anchorages particularly favoured by those who carry sailing dinghies or windsurfers.

If entering and anchoring after dark, follow the leading lights until the single harbour light (Fl(4)G.11s7m5M) bears 230°, alter course onto 215°, and drop anchor in 8m or so when the light bears due west.

Berthing

The harbour is small with room for fewer than 20 yachts not exceeding 10m or so; check by dinghy first as it becomes very crowded in summer and there is little chance of a vacant berth. If space permits, berth stern-to the northeast mole or on the pontoon extending from the southwest quay. Several buoys have been laid just north of the stone mole; these are available for visitors and from here it is only a very short row into town. Berthing is inexpensive here and anchoring is still free.

Facilities

Water and electricity On the southern pontoon and all berths.
Fuel No fuel available.
Provisions Supermarket and other shops in the village. It may be possible to buy fish at the co-operative southwest of the harbour.
Ice From the fishermen's co-op southwest of the harbour (likely to be icebox quality only) or from a bar opposite the north corner of the harbour.
Chandlery A small chandlery near the harbour.
Repairs Carried out on local craft at the head of the wide shallow slipway which lies southwest of the harbour. Crane available but no information on specifications.
Yacht club The Club Náutico de Fornells, located at Ses Salines about 1¼ miles south of the harbour and main anchorage, has a bar, restaurant, lounge, terrace and showers.
Bank In the village (open mornings only).
Post office In the village.

Transport

Car hire/taxis One car rental company in the village.
Buses Buses to Mahón and Ciudadela.

History

The fishing village of Fornells (pronounced Fornays) dates back to time immemorial, but its claim to historic fame comes from having been used as one of the secondary invasion ports during the first British expedition of 1798. They had intended to land at Fornells, but a headwind prevented this so the first landing took place at Addaya. When the wind changed the following day Commodore Duckworth captured Fornells.

Sights ashore locally

Most of the surroundings are of unspoilt natural beauty and development is restricted to a few areas. The village is small and picturesque but offers simple facilities.

The anchorage is surrounded by some enjoyable walks, such as to the defence tower and museum on Cabo Fornells or, for the really energetic, up to La Mola (123m) on the east side of the entrance. Both offer excellent views. Isla Sargantana makes an interesting dinghy expedition, partly to observe the unique breed of lizard which has evolved there (though you have to be an expert to know the difference). At the south end of Cala Fornells are the ruins of an ancient Christian church.

Local event

A fiesta is held in Fornells during the last week of July in honour of San Antonio.

Eating out

Many restaurants and cafés. Fornells has long been famous for its lobsters, served either with *mahonésa* or as *caldereta de langosta* (lobster stew).

ANCHORAGES AND FEATURES EAST OF PUERTO DE FORNELLS

PUNTA DE ES MORTER (DES MURTER), PUNTA DE NA GUIEMASSA AND CABO PENTINAT

(See plan on page 228)
40°04'.2N 04°08'.5E to 40°03'.7N 04°10'.5E

A 1.7-mile-wide promontory with three distinct headlands, the westernmost backed by the heights of La Mola (123m). As a whole the headland slopes downwards from west to east and steep-to other than two rocks awash close inshore off Punta Na Guiemassa. However, when rounding Cabo Pentinat (Punta d'en Pentinar), you should give the point a berth of at least 200m to avoid Lloses d'en Pentinar, awash rocks that lie 100m northeast of the point and two smaller awash rocks east of the point. There is also a lot of turbulence around the headland.

⊕97 40°03'.6N 04°10'.6E Cabo Pentinat

⚓ CALA D'EN TOSQUETA

40°03'.4N 4°10'E

A well-protected *cala* tucked away under Cabo Pentinat, with a sand and shingle beach and rocky cliffs. Approach leaving Illa d'en Tosqueta to starboard (rocks also extend off the headland to the northeast) to anchor off the beach over sand and rock, open to the southeast. A second beach lies 100m southwest and there are two more further south. There is a fine view from the headland and two caves to explore. Cala d'en Tosqueta is a popular anchorage which often becomes crowded in summer.

View looking west-northwest over Peninsula La Mola. Cala de la Olla with Cala Pudenta on right, Isla Sargantana in the background

⚓ CALA PUDENTA AND ES MARESUS

40°02'.5N 04°09'.8E

A smallish double *cala* with low rocky sides and small sandy beaches. The approach is straightforward, but look out for two awash rocks either side of Es Maresus. Anchor in sand over 3m or less, open to northeast through southeast. There is a spring behind the northwest beach, a track inland and a parking area, but little else.

Arenal d'en Castell

⚓ CALA DE LA OLLA (ARENAL DE SON SAURA)

40°02'.2N 04°09'.8E

A nearly circular *cala* with a large sandy beach and sloping rocky sides. A small islet lies off the northwest corner, and there are awash rocks close inshore on the northwest and southeast sides. Anchor in 3–5m over sand. There is an extensive tourist development on the eastern headland, and a large lagoon with much wildlife about ¼ mile to the southwest.

⚓ CALA SES OLLES

40°02'.1N 04°10'.1E

A small, rounded *cala* close east of Cala de la Olla, surrounded by low cliffs and with no beach. Enter with care sounding carefully: an awash rock, Escull d'en Tarouger, and several islets lie up to 150m off the point on the east side of the entrance and there are some small rocks close to the shore to the southwest. Anchor in 3–6m over rock, open north and northeast and to swell from the east. There is a large tourist development between the two calas.

⚓ ARENAL D'EN CASTELL

40°01'.5N 04°10'.9E

A large, almost circular bay with a long sandy beach, surrounded by large apartment blocks, hotels and houses. If approaching from the east, round Punta Codolada with a least offing of 400m and continue due west until the entrance bears 160° before turning south. This avoids three small islets off the headland, plus the low rocks to the west known as Los Ofegats (Esculls d'es Augegats). In most conditions the latter's breaking crests will be clearly visible.

Anchor off the beach in 4–8m over sand and weed, open only to the north. There are small-craft moorings on the west side of the bay and the north

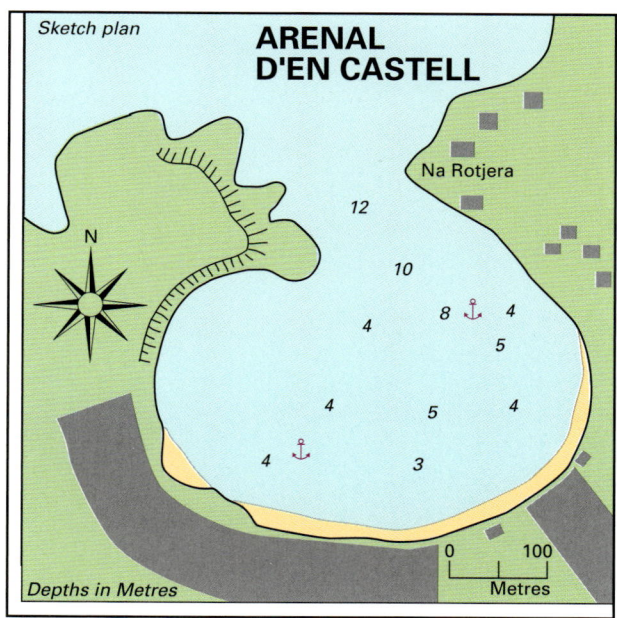

part has a rocky bottom. There is a considerable amount of development behind the beach, with all the usual tourist shops, restaurants and cafés.

PUNTA CODOLADA

40°02'.1N 04°11'.5E

A low rocky headland with outlying rocks and islets but it can be identified when coming from the east by an isolated white house 200m from the point. The island na Joanassa lies close north of the point, with two rocks, Escollos de Truyol, some 350m north of the point. If rounding to visit Arenal d'en Castell keep well clear of Los Ofegats, lying some 550m southwest of the point (see *Arenal d'en Castell* above).

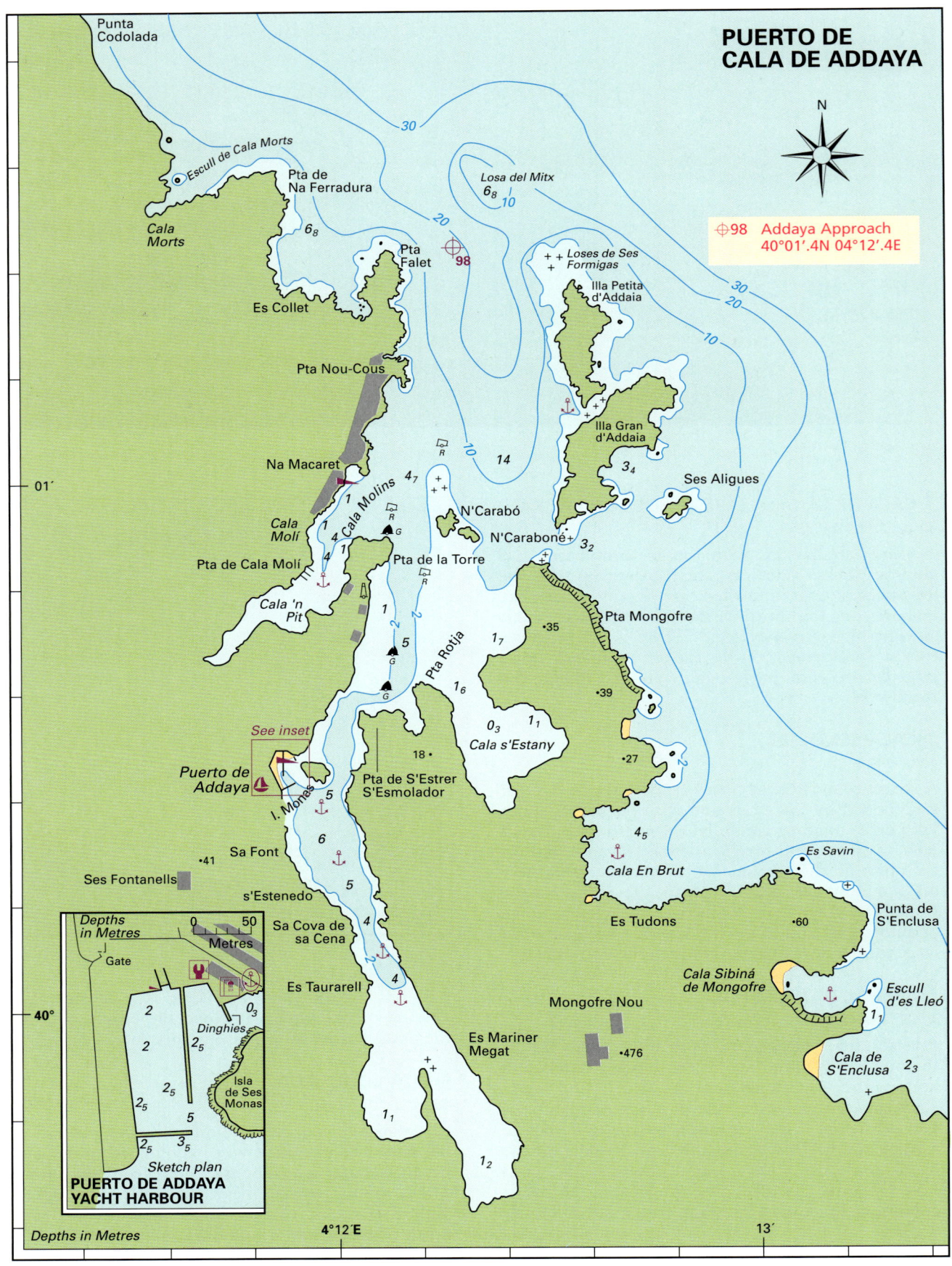

PUERTO DE
CALA DE ADDAYA

N

⊕98 Addaya Approach
      40°01'.4N 04°12'.4E

Punta
Codolada

Escull de Cala Morts

Pta de
Na Ferradura

Cala
Morts

6₈

Pta
Falet

98

Es Collet

Losa del Mitx
6₈ 10

20

Loses de Ses
Formigas

Illa Petita
d'Addaia

30

20

10

Pta Nou-Cous

Illa Gran
d'Addaia

3₄

Ses Aligues

Na Macaret

4₇

10

14

R

Cala
Molí

Cala Molins

4

R   G

N'Carabó

N'Caraboné

3₂

Pta de Cala Molí

4

Pta de la Torre

R

Cala 'n
Pit

1

2

Pta Mongofre

•35

•39

G

5

Pta Rotija

1₇

1₆

1₁

See inset

G

0₃
Cala s'Estany

•27

Puerto de
Addaya

18 •

Pta de S'Estrer
S'Esmolador

4₅

I. Monas

5

6

Cala En Brut

Es Savin

Sa Font

•41

5

Es Tudons

•60

Punta de
S'Enclusa

Ses Fontanells

s'Estenedo

4

Sa Cova de
sa Cena

Cala Sibiná
de Mongofre

Escull
d'es Lleó

1₁

Es Taurarell

4

Mongofre Nou

Cala de
S'Enclusa

2₃

Es Mariner
Megat

•476

1₁

1₂

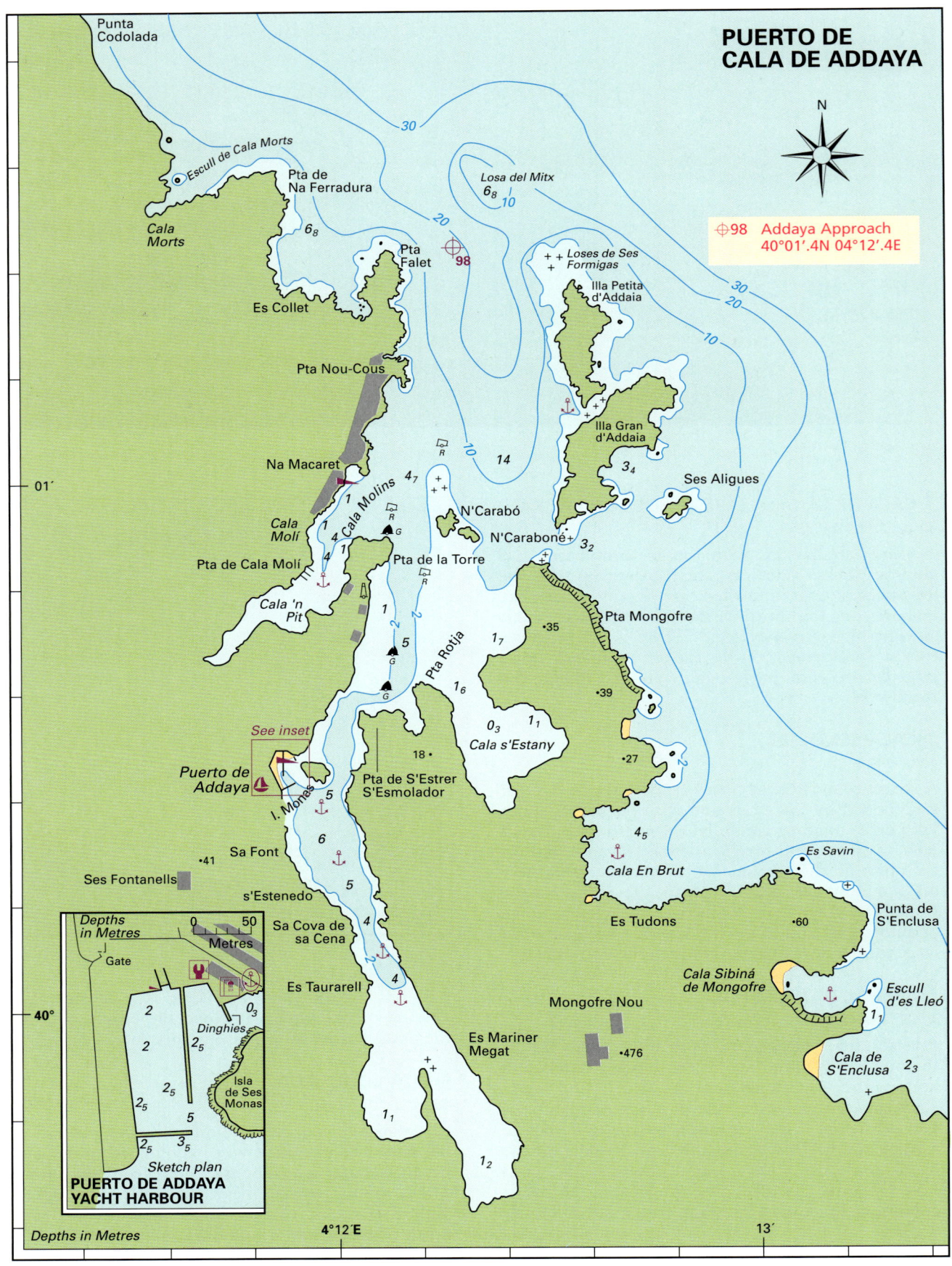

Depths in
Metres

0   50

Metres

Gate

2

2

2₅

2₅

2₅

5

2₅   3₅

0₃

Dinghies

2₅

Isla
de Ses
Monas

Sketch plan
**PUERTO DE ADDAYA
YACHT HARBOUR**

40°

Depths in Metres

4°12'E

13'

ME5 Puerto (Deportivo) de Cala de Addaya

A very safe friendly harbour deep in a long *cala*, with berthing for 150 vessels. Requires accurate navigation to enter with larger vessels. Berthing for 150 vessels up to 20m in a beautiful location

Location
40°01'N 04°12'.3E (entrance)
40°00'.4N 04°12'E (yacht harbour)

Communications
Puerto Deportivo de Addaya VHF Ch 09
Marina office ✆/*Fax* 971 18 88 71

V. MENORCA

The harbour and anchorage

A long, narrow estuary, its entrance guarded by a line of islands, Cala de Addaya (or Addaia) is a very pleasant, secluded and sheltered anchorage with a small and helpful yacht harbour in one corner. Considerable tourist development is taking place around the *cala* overlooking the yacht harbour, together with a yacht club building and sports club.

The entrance to the *cala* requires care and in some light conditions it is difficult to see. Entrance would be impossible in strong winds from northwest round to east, though vessels already in the lagoon would be both safe and comfortable.

Facilities are limited, but adequate for everyday needs.

Cala Molí moorings for shallow-draught vessels. Shallows easily seen here

PILOTAGE

Approach

⊕98 40°01'.4N 4°12'.4E Addaya Approach

From northwest Round the wide promotory comprising Punta de Es Morter, Punta de Na Guiemassa and Cabo Pentinat (see plan on page 228), which are without offlying hazards, then head south-southeast for Punta Codolada 1.8 miles away. There are a number of *calas* in the intervening bay (see plan on page 236). On rounding Punta Codolada, leaving it at least 400m to starboard, the Islas Addaya (Illes d'Addaia) will open up ahead, with Punta de Na Ferradura and Punta d'en Falet to starboard. In heavy weather Losa del Mitx (Losa d'Emmig), a rock with 6.8m depth, may break about 550m offshore but at other times it poses no threat. Aim to pass Punta d'en Falet about 200–300m off,

rounding the headland at this distance to take a south and then southwest course into the channel between Punta Nou-Cous (mis-spelt Punta Na Cous on BA 2833 and 2761, as well as being somewhat misplaced) and Illa Petita d'Addaia.

From southeast After rounding Cabo Favaritx (see plan on page 228), a low headland with a conspicuous lighthouse of black and white diagonal stripes, steer 300° towards a position off Punta Codolada. Stand on well past the Islas Addaia and the offlying Loses de Ses Formigas rocks, only heading in towards the coast when Punta d'en Falet bears 235° or less. Close the headland to a distance of 300m before taking a south and then south-southwest course into the channel between Punta Nou-Cous and Illa Petita d'Addaia (see plan on page 236).

Note Although fishermen use the passage between Punta Mongofre and the Islas Addaya as a short cut if heading east, it is far from straightforward and requires local knowledge.

Anchorage in the approach

There is a good daytime anchorage just west of the gap between Illa Gran d'Addaia and Illa Petita d'Addaia in 5m+ over rock and weed, open to the north and northwest.

Entrance

Once past Punta Nou-Cous the channel is buoyed approximately as on the plan, though the buoys may be positioned slightly differently each season. Head for Punta de la Torre (low, with houses and a car park; the tower itself is well back from the point), passing one small red port-hand buoy. This is not always on station, and note that both the existence and/or positions of some of the inner channel buoys appear somewhat erratic: see warning following. If in doubt favour the west side of the channel: the chief danger is posed by rocks north of the islets of N'Carabó and N'Caraboné.

A slightly larger red buoy is laid in summer off Punta de la Torre and should be left to port. A green starboard-hand buoy sits within a stone's throw of the headland. Turning to port through this 'gate', a red buoy may be seen ahead marking the southwest side of N'Carabó and this should be left fairly close to port. One or more green buoys show the extent of the shoals and mudbank fringing the east side of Punta de la Torre (some indication is also given by the extent of smallcraft moorings). Proceed slowly towards Punta de S'Estrer in the centre of the channel. (Note that the shallows can be clearly seen in most conditions but a good lookout is recommended.)

A little short of Punta de S'Estrer a mudbank, normally marked by two small green buoys, extends out from the west shore putting an S-bend in the channel. If these two buoys are *not* in place, once past the tower (see plan) steer for the centre of Punta de S'Estrer ahead, turning west only when depths off the headland begin to shoal. In calm conditions the mudbank will be clearly visible as a brownish patch,

but should a mistake be made the bottom is soft and the position sheltered.

Keep to the centre of the gap between Illa de ses Monas and the eastern bank before turning into the yacht harbour or coming to anchor in the lagoon beyond. Round Isla Monas about 50m off and Puerto Deportivo de Addaya will open to the northwest.

Warning

The channel buoys mentioned previously may not be laid until well into the season (May or June) and are unlit. If cruising the area for the first time earlier in the year do not attempt the entrance unless conditions are favourable. If the buoys are not in position proceed very slowly as described, with a lookout on the bow and a careful watch on the echo-sounder.

Night approach, without good local knowledge, is not advisable: for preference a first visit should be made in light winds and good visibility.

Berthing

Visitors normally berth bow or stern-to outside the south pontoon, though space is at a premium during the high season, and if in doubt about space or depth anchor off and investigate by dinghy. Alternatively consult the yacht harbour staff on VHF Ch 09.

Puerto Deportivo de Addaya is one of the Balearics' smallest (and many would say nicest) marinas, with just over 150 berths covering all sizes up to about 20m. As with everywhere in the islands there are plans to expand but they are unlikely to be approved.

Anchorages

Anchor in 6m or less in the lagoon south of Isla Monas, which has good holding and all-round shelter. It is also possible to anchor further up the *cala* (see plan) in 4–6m, north of the narrows. (Note: a mud bank sticks out from the east shore almost to the centre of the narrows so keep to the west side). The inner lagoon is silting and depths are now reported as being less than 2m: proceed with caution and keep a good lookout at the bow. Much of the bottom is weed covered and holding is thus suspect. The land around the *cala* is privately owned.

There is a small pontoon directly in front of the harbour office where crews of anchored yachts may land by dinghy. There has been no charge for anchoring, though this is being considered.

Owners of shallow-draught yachts may wish to investigate Cala Molí (Molins) on the west side of Punta de la Torre. Proceed with care (the bottom is uneven and there are many moorings). The birdwatching is excellent.

Moorings

There are a number of mooring buoys in the lagoon but all are private.

Facilities

Water On the pontoons; yachts anchored off are charged to come in and fill tanks. If asked politely the harbour staff usually allow portable carriers to be filled gratis.
Electricity 220v AC points on the pontoons.

Puerto de Cala de Addaya from northeast, tucked in behind Isla Monas

Fuel Not available, though it may be possible to arrange small quantities via the harbour office.

Provisions The supermarket up the hill to the west of the harbour, plus shops at Na Macaret (west of Cala Molí) can provide everyday requirements.

Ice From the harbour office.

Repairs Mardaya SC ☎ 971 18 88 05 *Fax* 971 37 22 90, based at the yacht harbour, can handle repairs, maintenance, painting, etc. A cross between a travel-lift and a trailer, since it uses the slipway, of approximately 10-tonne capacity. Also a shallow slipway on the north side of the harbour.

Engineers Addaya Motor Servicios ☎/*Fax* 971 18 87 96, based at the yacht harbour.

Sailmaker Mardaya SC handle canvas work.

Showers By the harbour office. Free if berthed in the yacht harbour, otherwise €2.

Launderette Up the hill from the harbour.

Banks In Mahón, though there is an exchange bureau up the hill from the harbour.

Hospital/medical services In Mahón.

Transport

Car hire/taxis Car hire agency nearby, ☎ 971 367111 or can be arranged from Mahón.

Buses Bus service to Mahón and elsewhere along the nearby main road (ask for directions in the harbour office).

History

The harbour has been in use since Roman times and many amphoras and other remains have been found. The last British expedition to Menorca landed near Na Macaret on 7 November 1798 under the command of General Sir Charles Stuart, mainly because the three frigates and troop transports were unable to enter Fornells in adverse winds. The Highland Scots troops were amazed to find the hills covered with heather similar to that at home. In five days the 3,000 British troops captured Menorca from 3,600 Spanish without the loss of a single British soldier. In 1861 three Dutch ships carrying bullion (the warship *Wasaner* and two escorts, the *Sint Laurens* and *Sint Joris*) were wrecked off Cala de Addaya.

Sights ashore locally

There is a small sandy beach off the holiday village of Na Macaret, where there are restaurants and basic shops.

Mahón is less than 10 miles away by bus.

Eating out

Restaurants and cafés up the hill from the harbour and a bar in the harbour itself.

ANCHORAGES EAST AND SOUTHEAST OF PUERTO DE ADDAYA

⚓ CALA EN BRUT

40°00′.3N 4°12′.7E

An open bay on the east side and south of Punta Mongofre, surrounded by high sloping rocks, recognisable by a conspicuous white building with a tower on the hill behind. There are a few islets close inshore on the north side. Anchor over sand (see plan on page 236).

⚓ CALA SIBINÁ (SIVINAR, SAVINAR) DE MONGOFRE AND CALA DE S'ENCLUSA

40°00′N 4°13′.1E

Twin *calas* surrounded by high (40–63m) rough hills and separated by a rocky point. Cala Sibiná is the smaller of the two and has rocks awash close inshore on both sides of the entrance. Cala de S'Enclusa has an islet with an outlying rock, Llosa de S'Enclusa, east of the entrance and a single breaking rock in the southeast part of the *cala* itself. Both *calas* are mainly sand and are open to the north and northeast. A conspicuous white building with a tower and red roof, stands on the hill to the east. There are several sandy beaches and some tracks inland, but otherwise nothing.

View southeast over Cabo Favaritx

⚓ CALA CALDÉS

39°59′.8N 4°13′.7E

A small *cala* at the mouth of a narrow valley with high (30 to 70m) hills each side and a small stony beach. A group of five rocky islets lies to the west of the entrance and four awash rocks plus an islet to the east. Enter on a south course midway between the two groups to anchor off the beach over sand and rock, open to the north. There is one small house in the valley with a track inland.

⚓ CALA ES BARRANC GROS

40°00′.0N 4°15′.2E

A large open *cala* amongst rocky cliffs and hills, with a smaller *cala* in the southwest corner in which there is a sand and stone beach. Several islets lie close inshore on either side of the entrance. Anchor off the beach over rock with sand patches. The road from Cabo Favaritx to Mahón lies only 200m inland.

⚓ CALA ES PORTIXOL

40°00′N 4°15′.5E

A small round *cala* with an islet in the middle of the entrance, surrounded by low rocky cliffs and sloping hills (15–21m). Inshore islets line either side of the entrance; enter with care favouring the east side, and anchor off the beach, taking care to avoid three awash rocks in the south centre of the *cala*. Open to the north. There is a small sandy beach backed by sand dunes in the southeast corner, and the road to Mahón 100m inland.

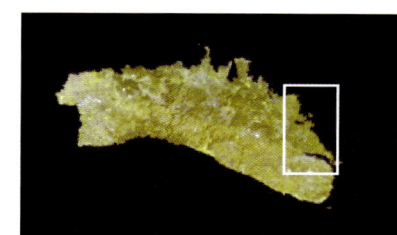
8. Cabo Favaritx to Punta S'Esperó

⊕99 39°59'.8N 04°16'.4E Cabo Favaritx

CABO FAVARITX

39°59'.8N 04°16'.2E

A very prominent low (12m), broken rocky headland with a conspicuous lighthouse (Fl(1+2)15s47m16M, white tower with black diagonal stripes on white building 28m) set slightly back from the point itself. It is steep-to but with two islets on its south side.

⚓ CALA PRESILI

39°59'.4N 04°15'.4E
(Incorrectly identified as Cala Algaret on BA 2833)

A very open *cala* with sandy beach, dunes and small sloping hills behind. Anchor off the beach over sand and stone, open to the northeast through southeast. Three rocks with some 2m over them are reported to lie about 100m off the beach. If approaching from the south see the note regarding Punta de las Picas and Cabo Monseña, below.

Cala Presili looking northwest

PUNTA DE LAS PICAS

39°59'.2N 04°15'.7E

Punta de las Picas (Cap de ses Piques) is a wide headland with offliers and awash rocks some 150m offshore. An islet, Escull d'en Tortuga (39°59'.1N 04°15'.8E), lies 350m to the east of the point with clear water all around it.

⚓ CALA MORELLA NOU

39°59'N 04°15'.7E

A *cala* with two sandy beaches separated by a rocky point. Enter on a southwest course between the islets and reefs off Cabo Monseña (Cap Monsenyar Vives) to port, and Punta de las Picas (Cap de Ses Piques)

⊕99	Cabo Favaritx	39°59'.8N 04°16'.4E
⊕100	Cabo Monsena	39°59'.1N 04°16'.4E
⊕101	Punta Galera	39°56'.7N 04°17'.5E
⊕102	Cabo Negro	39°54'.0N 04°18'.7E
⊕103	Punta S'Espero	39°52'.6N 04°19'.9E

to starboard. The latter has a small island, Escull d'en Tortuga, some 350m offshore which should be left to starboard. Anchor off either beach in sand. There is a track inland and a few houses.

⊕100 39°59'.1N 04°16'.4E Cabo Monseña

CABO MONSEÑA
39°59'N 04°16'.1E

Cabo Monseña (Cap de Mossèn Vives) is a narrow headland with a reef of awash rocks, Baix des Ferros, running off some 450m to the northeast. It is advisable to keep at least 600m off this point especially in rough weather, to avoid the overfalls.

⚓ CALA EN CAVALLER
39°58'.7N 04°15'.7E

A small *cala* just south of Cabo Monseña, with a sand and shingle beach and a small islet on the south side of the entrance. Enter on a northwest course, keeping closer to the south side to avoid a couple of groups of awash rocks extending some 100m from the cliffs, on the north side. Anchor off the beach: open to east and southeast. A tree-lined valley with sloping rocky sides runs inland. If approaching from the north, see Cabo Monseña and Punta de las Picas, above.

Looking west, Menorca centre and Isla Colom right. Left is Cala Grao with S'Albufera lagoon behind. Left foreground is Islota de sa Cudia

⚓ CALA RAMBLA (CALA SA TORRETA)
39°58'N 04°15'.5E

A large double *cala* with low rocky cliffs on either side and the Llosa de Rambles reef some 400m north of the entrance. Enter on a southwest course to anchor over sand off the west beach, open to north and northeast. The east side of the *cala* has some awash rocks scattered across its entrance though there is a good sandy beach behind. There is a single house between the beaches and a track inland. A standing *taula* and a *talayot* (ancient monument and tower) and burial ground will be found just over 0.5M inland, together with a ruined village at Sa Torre Blanca.

ISLA COLOM NORTH END
39°58'.0N 04°16'.6E

An almost deserted island with rocky cliffs, Isla Colom is 0.6M long by 0.5M at its widest point and up to 42m high. The northeast coast between Cap de Mestral and Cap de Llevant has many rocky outliers, many just below the surface. One, Llosa des Cap de Mestral, is no less than 450m north of the central headland and a similar distance north-northeast of Cap de Mestral itself. Some 75m north of Cap de Llevant, (although it has been reported further offshore by several people who have grounded there) lies Llosa de ses Eugos, a rock with

S'Albufera lagoon   Islota de sa Cudia   Isla Colom

Cala Grao

ANCHORAGES AND PASSAGES BETWEEN ISLA COLOM AND MENORCA [14]

39° 58′ N

Cap de Mestral

Llosa des Cap de Mestral

•36

S'Arenal d'es Moro

7

11

Ses Planes

Cap de Llevant

Llosa de Ses Eugos

Isla Colom

•37

•38

Pta de sa Torre d'es Tamarells

11₆

Torre Rambla •27

2

Summer mooring buoys See below

10

Pta d'es Tamarells

12

•33

3

2

64•

Cala Tamarells d'es Nord

5

7

8

Pta Negra 16

Cala Tamarells d'es Sud

5

8

Pte de la Pastera

3

Cala de s'Isla

2

Macar de Dins

29

1₅

2

10

13₆

1

MENORCA

Pta Fra Bernal

Baix d'es Pas

7

Islote de sa Cudia

Cala Grao

4

5

6

2

Es Grao

Caleta Avellana

Pta de sa Cudia

S'Albufera lagoon

57′

4°16′E

Depths in Metres

Pta Galera

17′

N

V. MENORCA

only 1.3m over. It is recommended that an offing of at least three cables (550m) is maintained along this section of the island coast. There are two attractive small beaches to which daily boat trips are run from Es Grao, and one large house, Lloc de s'Illa, plus a hut. Inevitably, the island has its own unique species of lizard.

Passage inside Isla Colom

A dog-legged passage between Isla Colom and Menorca, little more than 1m deep and about 100m wide makes a short cut for shallow draught vessels. However, the passage is prone to shifting sands following gales and depths are unreliable.

ANCHORAGES BEHIND ISLA COLOM

Apart from Mahón and Addaya, the anchorages behind Isla Colom offer the best shelter on the northeast coast. They are, however, open to the northwest and to swell from the north, and are therefore not suitable in heavy weather or in winds with a north component, since the two anchorages that might be thought to give all-round shelter (Cala Tamarells d'es Nord and S'Arenal d'es Moro) are too small to provide adequate swinging room in a blow. Mooring buoys have been placed south of Punta de sa Torre d'es Tamarells and east of Punta d'es Tamarells, which can be reserved in advance for 1st June to 30th September at www.balearslifeposidonia.eu/index.php?register_var s[lang]=en. See plan above and the Anchoring and Moorings section on page 16 for further details.

The next four anchorages all have an interesting phenomenon: sandy weed-covered tufts stick up abruptly giving unreliable depth readings. Clumps of weed can be as high as 3m, reducing depths displayed on the echo-sounder to practically nothing. For reliable depths avoid these areas.

⚓ CALA TAMARELLS D'ES NORD
39°57'.8N 04°15'.8E

The north, and smaller, of a pair of *calas* divided by a rocky promontory. The conspicuous Torre Rambla (Es Colomar) stands on the north side of the entrance. Rocky islets and awash rocks lie close inshore around this point and off the central promontory – favour the south side of the entrance to anchor in ±5m over sand and rock. Shelter is good from all directions, but there is restricted swinging room even for a single yacht and it may be necessary to moor using two anchors at the bow.

⚓ CALA TAMARELLS D'ES SUD
39°57'.6N 04°16'E

A much larger anchorage than its twin to the north, with better protection than might be expected. There are offlying rocks around both headlands as well as the central promontory – keep to the south and west sides where there are a couple of sandy beaches. Anchor in 5–8m over sand and rock. Depths reduced to 2m have been reported, with an uneven bottom.

⚓ S'ARENAL D'ES MORO, ISLA COLOM
39°57'.8N 04°16'.5E

A small *cala* on the northwest side of Isla Colom surrounded by sloping, scrub-covered hills. A small islet, Illot d'es Moro (also called Islote Pardals), lies just off the north side of the sandy beach, which itself has an offlying ridge of rock, carrying less than 1m. Anchor in 5–7m over sand and weed in good shelter. There is little swinging room and in all but the lightest winds it may be necessary to moor using two anchors at the bow. S'Arenal d'es Moro is a popular spot with daytime visitors but is deserted at night.

⚓ CALA DE S'ISLA, ISLA COLOM
39°57'.5N 04°16'.4E

A small, shallow, but very pretty *cala* just northeast of the passage between Isla Colom and Menorca, surrounded by low sloping hills and with a house set back from the northeast corner. A large rock just below water level lies in the central part of the anchorage, while the south side is fringed with rocks merging into those of the southwest headland. Approach the centre of the *cala* with care on an east course to anchor in the outer part of the bay in 3m over sand. Like the beach further north, Cala de s'Isla is a popular destination for tourist boats from Cala Grao but is very quiet at night.

⚓ MACAR DE DINS, ISLA COLOM
39°57'.3N 04°16'.6E

Strictly a fair-weather stop on the south side of Isla Colom, off a small beach with rocks awash near its centre. In settled northerly weather it is possible to anchor almost anywhere between Macar de Dins and the southwest promontory.

⚓ CALA GRAO (CALA DE LA ALBUFERA)
39°57'.1N 04°16'.1E

A popular anchorage in a large, rounded *cala* scattered with moorings and overlooked by the holiday village of Es Grao. Approach and enter on a west course keeping near the centre of the *cala*, which shoals rapidly towards the beach – keep an eye on the echo-sounder after crossing the 10m line. See also note below. Anchor in 3m+ off the beach, open to the east. There are slipways and quays for dinghies and small boats. Es Grao has a supermarket, restaurants and cafés (which also sell ice).

A broad stream leading from the vast Albufera lagoon drains into the southwest corner of the *cala* and would make an interesting dinghy excursion. The lagoon and marshes, which extend more than a mile inland, are a wildlife and nature reserve.

⚓ CALETA AVELLANA (CALA VELLANA)
39°57'.1N 4°16'.5E

A small *cala* between sloping rocky sides close east of Cala Grao, with an isolated rock in the middle of the entrance.

Note This rock, with about 1.2m over, has been reported some 100m further north, than the position shown on the chart, which can be a problem if a little too far south when entering Cala Grao. Approach from slightly west of north, sounding carefully to anchor over sand, weed and rock.

⊕101 39°56'.7N 04°17'.5E Punta Galera

⚓ CALA BINILLANTÍ
39°55'.5N 04°17'.0E

A very small, deserted *cala* inshore of Islote Bombasa (En Bombarda) and north of Punta Sansá. Approach on a southwest course and anchor off the beach. Do not confuse Cala Binillantí with one of a series of five even smaller *calas* to the north (see plan on page 241).

⚓ CALA S'ARENAL GRAN (GRAU)
39°54'.9N 04°17'.3E

This large *cala* lies immediately north of Cala Mesquida and Punta de sa Torre (topped by a large pale stone tower), and south of Punta Pá Gros. To the east lies Islota Mesquida. Punta Pá Gros has groups of offlying rocky islets of which the outermost, the Illots d'es Mesquida, are 400m offshore. Leave all these islets to starboard on the approach and anchor over sand off the north end of the beach, open to the east and southeast. The south

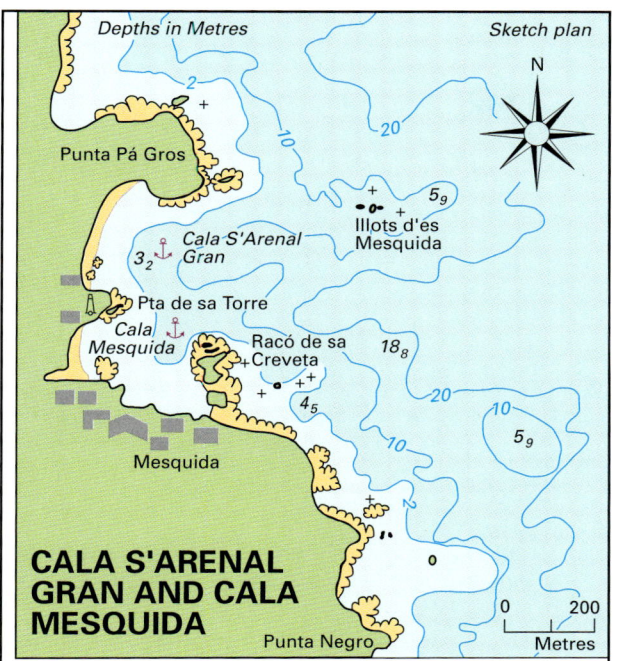

Depths in Metres · Sketch plan · N

Punta Pá Gros

Cala S'Arenal Gran

Illots d'es Mesquida

Pta de sa Torre

Cala Mesquida

Racó de sa Creveta

Mesquida

CALA S'ARENAL GRAN AND CALA MESQUIDA

Punta Negro

0   200

Metres

part of the beach has rocky outcrops running out into the *cala*. There are a few houses and a road, but no facilities (see plan above).

⚓ CALA MESQUIDA

39°54'.8N 04°17'.3E

An angular *cala* with a small beach, close south of Cala S'Arenal Gran and Punta de sa Torre and its prominent tower (which has the proportions of a medieval castle keep). Leave the Illots d'es Mesquida to starboard and steer southwest towards the small beach, leaving Racó de sa Creveta and its associated rocks to port. If approaching from the south keep at least 500m offshore until due east of Punta de sa Torre before heading in. Anchor between Racó de sa Creveta and the tower in 5–6m over sand and rock. Do not approach the beach without a previous recce by dinghy, as a reef runs most of the way across it in a northwest direction from the rocks near the further buildings. A shallow river flows into the head of the *cala*. There is a dinghy harbour and slipway in the southeast corner, in front of a café/restaurant backed by several streets of houses.

It was here that the heavy siege train of the Duc de Richelieu was finally landed in April 1756. It had originally been landed at Ciudadela, but was held up by the destruction of the road to Mahón and was re-embarked.

PUNTA NEGRO

39°54'.3N 4°17'.8E

A low (12m) headland with houses on its summit, not to be confused with the much more prominent Cabo Negro (37m) 0.7M to the southeast. Rocks lie southeast off the point (see plan on page 241).

⚓ CALA MURTA (ES MURTAR)

39°54'.2N 04°17'.7E

A wide *cala* just south of Punta Negro, with a series of rocky beaches and many houses to the north. Approach the middle of the *cala* on a west course to anchor in the northwest corner over rock and sand, open to the east and southeast. Care is necessary because the coast is foul in parts.

⊕102 39°54'.0N 04°18'.7E Cabo Negro

CABO NEGRO (CAP NEGRE)

39°54'N 04°18'.5E

A high (37m), prominent point of black rock with steep sides sloping seawards. A small islet and awash rock lie close to the promontory, which has some sea caves.

⚓ CALA ELS FREUS

39°52'.9N 04°18'.7E

A narrow *cala* on the north side of the isthmus of La Mola, which is foul on its south side. Bajo de las Aguilas (N'Ofegat), a low islet with awash rocks, guards the approach 500m to the east-northeast (see plan on page 191).

⊕103 39°52'.6N 04°19'.9E Punta S'Espero

PUNTA S'ESPERÓ

39°52'.6N 04°19'.7E

A high (78m), conspicuous, flat-topped promontory with sheer cliffs, sloping gently downwards towards Puerto de Mahón. A large fort and other conspicuous buildings occupy the plateau, with a lighthouse (Fl(1+2)15s51m8M, white round tower with two black bands on white building 11m) at the eastern tip. There are two awash rocks close to this point but it is otherwise steep-to (see plan on page 191).

Looking southeast over Isla Colom to Cala Grao and S'Albufera lagoon. Es Grao is on the left

Appendix

1. List of Lights

IBIZA

IB1 PUERTO DE IBIZA (EIVISSA)
Approach
0262 **Islote Dado Grande** 38°53'.5N 1°27'.2E Fl(2)5s13m6M Black tower, red band, ⁇ topmark 6m
0264 **Islote Botafoch** 38°54'.2N 1°27'.2E Oc.WR.7s31m14M Siren(2)10s White tower above a white house 16m 034°-R-045°(over Islas Malvines and Esponja)-W-034°(obscured over N Llados by Isla Grossa)
Entrance
0263 **Botafoch breakwater head** 38°54'.2N 1°26'.9E Fl.G.3s14m7M Green post 4m
0264.4 **NE (Marina Botafoch) breakwater head** 38°54'.7N 1°27'E Fl(2+1)G.11s6m3M Green column, red band, on white base displaying green ▲ 3m
0264.5 **T-jetty hd** 38°54'.7N 1°27'E Fl(2)R.5s2m1M Black post 1m
0264.6 **Marina Botafoch, inner mole** 38°54'.7N 1°27'E Fl(2)G.5s2m1M Green post 1m
0265 **SW breakwater** 38°54'.7N 1°26'.6E Fl(2)R.7s12m5M White truncated conical tower on building, red cupola 11m Obsc W of Islotes Malvins
0265.6 **Puerto Deportivo Ibiza Nueva, S mole** 38°54'.8N 1°26'.6E Fl(2)G.7s12m1M Green column on white base 11m
0265.8 **Puerto Deportivo Ibiza Nueva, N mole** 38°54'.8N 1°26'.7E Fl(4)R.11s7m1M Red tower on office building 6m
0265.9 **SW head** 38°54'.9N 1°26'.6E Fl(2+1)G.21s5m1M Green column, red band 4m
0266 **Contramuelle, NE corner** 38°54'.8N 1°26'.3E Fl(3)R.9s6m1M Red post 4m
0266.2 **NW corner** 38°54'.7N 1°26'.4E Fl(4)R.11s6m1M Red post
0267 **Commercial mole, E corner** 38°54'.8N 1°26'.4E Fl(2+1)G.8s6m1M Green pole red band 4m
0267.2 **Commercial mole, W corner** 38°54'.8N 1°26'.3E Fl(4)G.11s6m1M Green metal column 4m

PASSAGES BETWEEN IBIZA AND ESPALMADOR
0260 **Islote Ahorcados, S end (Illa des Penjat)** 38°48'.9N 1°24'.7E Oc(1+2)14s27m12M White tower, three black bands, on white building 17m
0258 **Bajo de'n Pou** 38°48'.4N 1°25'.2E Q.9m4M N cardinal beacon, ⁇ topmark 9m
0254 **Los Puercos or Los Pou** 38°48'N 1°25'.3E Fl(3+1)20s28m11M White tower, two black bands, 27m
0256 **Isla Espardel, N point** 38°48'.2N 1°28'.6E Fl(3)7.5s37m8M White truncated conical tower 16m
32540(S) **Boya Bajo Ahorcades** 38°48'.7N 1°24'.5E Q(6)+LFl.15s5M ⁇ card

IB2 PUERTO DE SAN ANTONIO
Approach
0274 **Isla Conejera** 38°59'.7N 1°12'.9E Fl(4)20s85m18M White tower and building 18m

0273 **Punta Xinxó** 38°58'.5N 1°17'.1E Fl(2)G.7s9m5M Green column on white base displaying green ▲ 8m 075°-vis-275°
Entrance
0273.3 **N breakwater head** 38°58'.6N 1°17'.8E Fl(2)R.7s11m3M Red column on white base displaying red ■ 9m
Club Náutico pontoons 38°58'.8N 1°18'.2E F.R.3.5m1M Blue metal posts at end of each of the five *club náutico* pontoons
Buoys
32465(S) **Buoy 1** 38°58'.5N 01°17'.7E Fl(3)G.9s3M lateral stbd ▲ topmark
32475(S) **Buoy 2** 38°58'.4N 01°17'.9E Fl(4)G.11s1M lateral stbd ▲ topmark
32480(S) **Buoy 3** 38°58'.7N 01°18'.3E Fl.G.5s1M lateral stbd ▲ topmark

IB3 PUERTO DE SANTA EULALIA DEL RIO (SANTA EULARIA DES RIU)
Approach
31970(S) **Buoy** 38°58'.7N 1°35'.5E Fl(2)5s5M ⁇ topmark
Entrance
0267.8 **Dique de Abrigo head** 38°58'.9N 1°32'.3E Fl(3)G.9s11m5M Green pyramidal tower 6m
0267.85 **Contradique head** Fl(3)R.9s4m3M Red pyramidal tower 3m

FORMENTERA

F1 PUERTO DE SABINA
Approach
0252 **Isla Sabina** 38°44'.2N 1°25'E Fl(4)16s13m7M White truncated conical tower 11m
Entrance
0253 **Dique de Abrigo** 38°44'.2N 1°25'.2E Fl(2)G.6s11m3M Green column on white base displaying green ▲, 8m
0253.2 **Dique Pesquera head** Fl(4)R.15s5m1M Red tower 3m

MALLORCA

M1 PUERTO DE PALMA DE MALLORCA
Approach
0330 **Punta de Cala Figuera** 39°27'.5N 2°31'.4E Fl(4)20s45m15M Siren(2)12s Aero RC White round tower, black diagonal stripes, on building 24m
0316 **Cabo Blanco** 39°21'.9E 2°47'.3E Oc.5s95m15M White tower and building 12m 336°-vis-115°
0318.8 **Puerto de Palma** 39°32'.7N 2°37'.9E Fl(2)15s41m22M Square brown stone tower, visible outside Bahía de Palma 327°-040°
Entrance
0318 **S breakwater head** 39°33'.2N 2°38'.4E Fl.R.5s19m7M Red column on white hut displaying red ■ 13m F.R. on radio masts 4.5M E and E–SE
0318.3 **S breakwater outer elbow** 39°33'.1N 2°38'.4E VQ(3)5s16m5M E cardinal tower 10m Obscd inside harbour Siren Mo(P)30s
0318.6 **S breakwater inner elbow** 39°32'.7N 2°37'.9E VQ(6)+LFl.10s16m5M S card tower 8m

0319 **Muelles de Poniente** 39°33'.3N 2°38'.0E
Fl(2+1)R.14·5s2m3M Red pyramidal column, green band
4m

0320 **W mole N elbow** 39°33'.3N 2°37'.8E Fl(2)R.10s4m1M
Red metal column 5m

0328.42 **Club de Mar central mole, S head** 39°33'.4N
2°37'.7E FlY5s5m1M Yellow post 4m

0328.39 **Club de Mar N mole, S head** 39°33'.5N 2°37'.8E
Fl(2+1)R.12s5m1M Red column 4m

0322 **NE breakwater, SW corner** 39°33'.6N 2°38'.1E
Fl(2)G.10s6m5M Green column on white hut displaying
green ▲ 15m

0322.2 **NE breakwater, NW corner** 39°33'.7N 2°38'.1E
Fl(2)G.10s5m3M Green tower 6m

0328.38 **Club de Mar N mole, N head** 39°33'.6N 2°37'.8E
Fl(4)R.11s5m3M Red metal post 4m

0328.36 **Pantalán del Mediterraneo, S head** 39°33'.7N
2°37'.8E Fl(2+1)R.15s3m1M Red metal post 1m

0328.34 **Pantalán del Mediterraneo, N head** 39°33'.8N
2°37'.8E Fl.R.3s5m1M Red metal column 4m

0328.08 **Réal Club Náutico, S extremity** 39°33'.9N 2°38'E
Fl(2+1)R.12s6m1M Red post, green band 5m

0323 **NE breakwater spur, W corner** 39°33'.8N 2°38'.1E
Fl(3)G.9s6m1M Green post 5m

Numerous other lights exist in the NE of the harbour.

M2 PUERTO DE CALA NOVA

0328.7 **S breakwater** 39°32'.9N 2°36'E Fl(2)R.7s7m5M Red
post 3m

0328.75 **N mole** 39°33'N 2°36'E Fl(2)G.7s7m3M Green post
2m

M3 PUERTO PORTALS

0328.8 **S breakwater** 39°31'.8N 2°33'.9E Fl(3)G.14s9m4M
Green column on white base displaying green ▲ 6m

0328.85 **N mole** 39°31'.9N 2°34'E Fl(3)R.14s4m3M Red
column 2m

M4 PUERTO DE PALMA NOVA

0329 **S mole** 39°31'.5N 2°32'.6E Fl(4)G.11s7m5M Green
column on white base displaying green ▲ 6m

0329.2 **N mole** 39°31'.5N 2°32'.6E Fl(4)R.11s6m3M Red
column on white base displaying red ■ 6m

M5 PORTO ADRIANO

Approach

0332 **Islote El Toro** 39°27'.8N 2°28'.4E Fl.5s31m8M White
round tower 7m

Entrance

0332.5 **NW breakwater** 39°29'.4N 2°28'.6E
Fl(2+1)G.14·5s3m1M Green post, red band 2m

0332.6 **E mole** 39°29'.4N 2°28'.7E Fl(2)R.5s6m1M Red metal
post 2m

M6 PUERTO DE SANTA PONSA

0333 **NW breakwater** 39°30'.9N 2°28'E Fl(3)G.9s10m5M
Green column on white base displaying green ▲ 5m

0333.2 **Punta de la Caleta** 39°30'.8N 2°28'E Fl(3)R.9s10m3M
Red column on red base 4m

M7 PUERTO DE ANDRAITX

Approach

0334 **Cabo de la Mola** 39°32'N 2°21'.9E Fl(1+3)12s128m12M
White column, black bands, on white square tower 10m

Entrance

0336 **Outer breakwater** 39°32'.6N 2°22'.8E Fl(4)R.12s12m5M
Stone tower, red top 9m

35191(S) **Buoy No.1** 39°32'.6N 2°22'.9E Fl(4)G.12s3M Green
pillar buoy

35192(S) **Buoy No.1** 39°32'.7N 2°22'.9E Fl.R.4s1M Red pillar
buoy

35193(S) **Buoy No.2** 39°32'.7N 2°23'E Fl(2)R.6s1M Red pillar
buoy,

35195(S **Buoy No.2** 39°32'.6N 2°22'.9E Fl.G.4s1M Green pillar
buoy

35197(S) **Buoy No.3** 39°32'.7N 2°23'E Fl(2)G.6s1M Green
pillar buoy

35198(S) **Buoy No.4** 39°32'.7N 2°23'.1E Fl(3)G.12s1M Green
pillar buoy

0336.6 **YC Dique de Abrigo head** 39°32'.8N 2°23'.1E
Fl(3)R.10s6m1M Red column on white hut displaying red
square 4m

0336.7 **YC Spur W head** 39°32'.8N 2°23'.1E Fl.G.4s3m1M
Green post 2m

0336.8 **YC Spur E head** 39°32'.8N 2°23'.2E Fl(4)R.12s6m1M
Red column 3m

0337 **S mole** 39°32'.8N 2°23'.2E Fl(4)G.12s7m1M Green
column on white base.

Note The fish keeps may be marked by one or more yellow
lights (Fl.Y.4s) and several unlit reflectors, but they are out
of the channel to the N.

ISLA DRAGONERA AND THE DRAGONERA PASSAGE

0282 **Cabo Llebeitx** 39°34'.5N 2°18'.3E Fl.7.5s130m20M
Masonry tower on stone building with red roof 15m
313°-vis-150°

0284 **Cabo Tramontana** 39°36'N 2°20'.4E Fl(2)12s67m14M
Round masonry tower on stone building with red roof
15m 095°-vis-230° and 346°-vis-027°

0286 **Isla Mitjana** 39°35'.2N 2°20'.6E VQ(9)10s10m3M Ɪ Y
beacon, black band 5m

M8 PUERTO DE SÓLLER

Approach

0289 **Cabo Gros** 39°47'.9N 2°41'E Fl(3)15s120m18M White
tower and house, red roof 22m 054°-vis-232°

Entrance

0288 **Punta de Sa Creu** 39°47'.9N 2°41'.4E Fl.2.5s35m13M
White conical tower, three black bands 13m 088°-vis-
160°

0290 **Ldg Lts on 126.5° Front** 39°47'.6N 2°41'.9E Q.R.49m5M
Aluminium ◆ on white round tower 7m

0290.1 **Rear 36m from front**, Iso.R.4s60m5M Aluminium ◆
on white round tower 7m

0291 **Dique E head** 39°47'.8N 2°41'.6E Fl.R.4s7m5M Red post
2m

0292 **NW Mole head** 39°47'.9N 2°41'.7E Fl(2)R.7s4m3M Red
post, green band 5m

0293.2 **Commercial mole head** 39°47'.9N 2°41'.8E
Fl(3)R.9s4m1M Red post 5m

0293 **Commercial mole elbow** 39°47'.9N 2°41'.7E
Fl(2+1)G.9s4m1M Green post 5m

M9 PUERTO DE POLLENSA

Approach

0296 **Cabo Formentor** 39°57'.7N 3°12'.8E Fl(4)20s210m21M
White tower and house 22m

0303.7 **Punta Sabaté (Cabo del Pinar)** 39°53'.6N 3°11'.8E
Fl(3)13s47m5M White tower, black band 15m

0298 **Punta de la Avanzada** 39°54'.1N 3°06'.7E
Oc(2)8s29m15M Octagonal stone tower on building 18m
234°-vis-272°

Entrance

0299.2 **Breakwater head** 39°54'.4N 3°05'.1E Fl(2)G.6s6m5M
Green tower, white base and top 4m

0299.5 **Dique de Abrigo elbow** 39°54'.3N 3°05'.3E
Q(3)G.10s3m3M ◆ on black beacon, yellow band 2m

0299.7 **Contradique head** 39°54'.2N 3°05'.1E Fl(2)R.8s2m3M
Red column 1m

0300 **Service mole S head** 39°54'.3N 3°05'.2E Fl(3)R.9s2m1M
Red column 1m, synchronised with 0300.2

0300.2 **Service mole N head** Fl(3)R.9s2m1M Red column 1m,
synchronised with 0300.

0300.5 **Yacht Club Spur** Fl(3)G.12s5m1M Green tower white
base and top 4m

M10 PUERTO DE BACARES

The light was withdrawn in 1997 but the structure is still
there and now painted white.

M11 PUERTO MARINA DE BONAIRE

Approach

0296 **Cabo Formentor** 39°57'.7N 3°12'.8E Fl(4)20s210m21M
White tower and house 22m

0303.7 **Punta Sabaté (Cabo del Pinar)** 39°53'.6N 3°11'.8E
Fl(3)13s47m5M White tower, black band 12m

Entrance
0303 **N breakwater** 39°52'.1N 3°08'.7E Fl(3)R.10s5m5M Red column, white base and top 4m
0303.2 **W mole** 39°52'.1N 3°08'.7E Fl(3)G.10s5m3M Green column on white base 4m

M12 PUERTO DE ALCUDIA
Approach
0304 **Isla Aucanada** 39°50'.2N 3°10'.3E Fl.5s25m11M White tower and house 15m F.R. on chimney 4M W-SW
Commercial harbour
0306 **SE (commercial) breakwater** 39°50'N 3°08'.5E Fl.G.3s10m5M Green column on white base 5m
33122(S) **Buoy** 39°50'N 03°08'.3E Fl(2)10s3M RGR pillar with ╏ topmark
0306.5 **W mole SE head** 39°50'.1N 03°08'.4E Fl(2+1)R.12s4m3M Red tower with green band 3m
0306.55 **Pantalan head, NW** 39°50'·1N 3°08'·3E Fl.Y.5s4m1M Yellow x on yellow post 2m
0306.56 **W mole NW head** Fl(2)G.6s4m1M Green post 2m
Marina and fishing harbour
33140(S) **Buoy** 39°50'.3N 3°08'.3E Fl(3)G.9s1M
0306.6 **Dique SE head** 39°50'.3N 3°08'.2E Fl(3)R.9s5m3M Red pyramidal tower 4m
0307 **Old N mole** 39°50'.3N 3°08'.2E Fl(4)G.11s4m1M Green pyramidal tower 3m

M13 PUERTO DE CA'N PICAFORT
Approach
0307.16 **Escollo de Ca'n Barret** 39°46'.1N 3°09'.5E VQ(3)5s3m4M Black column, yellow band, 3m
Entrance
0307.1 **E breakwater** 39°46'.1N 3°09' Fl(2)R.7s8m5M Red pyramidal tower 4m
0307.15 **W mole** 39°46'.1N 3°09'.6E Fl(2)G.6.5s5m3M Green tower 4m
Beacons
Seventeen pairs of tall day-marks, about 1000m apart and numbered from N to S, were erected along the coast from a point just S of the Gran Canal to the NE of Colonia de San Pedro. Though some pairs are now missing, the remaining beacons are still useful navigationally.
Beacon Nos 1 and 2 mark an area of obstructions 1.5 miles NW of the harbour. Beacon No 4 (which is white with a red top, but does not display its number) is located just W of the entrance to Ca'n Picafort. Some of the remaining beacons are white, others natural stone.

M14 PUERTO DE SERRA NOVA
0307.17 **NE breakwater** 39°44'.4N 3°13'.5E Fl(3)R.10s6m5M Red column 2m
0307.19 **W mole** 39°44'.4N 3°13'.4E Oc.G.8s3m1M Green column 2m

M15 PUERTO DE COLONIA DE SAN PEDRO
0307.2 **Breakwater head** 39°44'.3N 3°16'.4E Fl(4)R.12s6m5M Red column 3m
0307.25 **W mole head** 39°44'.3N 3°16'.5E Fl(4)G.12s4m3M Green column 3m

M16 PUERTO DE CALA RATJADA
Approach
0308 **Cabo de Pera** 39°43'N 3°28'.7E Fl(2+3)20s76m16M White tower on white building with dark corners and red roof 21m 148°-vis-010°
Entrance
0308.2 **Breakwater head** 39°42'.6N 3°27'.9E Fl.G.5s12m5M Green post 3m
0308.3 **Breakwater spur (fishermen's quay)** 39°42'.7N 3°27'.9E Fl(2)G.6s6m1M Green post 5m
0308.32 **W mole** 39°42'.7N 3°27'.9E Fl.R.3s6m3M Red post on white base 5m
0308.34 **NW mole** 39°42'.7N 3°27'.9E Fl(2)R.6s6m1M Red post 5m

M17 PUERTO DE CALA BONA
0308.6 **S breakwater** 39°36'.8N 3°23'.6E Fl(2)R.10s5m5M Red column on white base displaying red ■ 2m

0308.7 **N breakwater** 39°36'.8N 3°23'.6E Fl(2)G.10s5m3M Green column on white base displaying green ▲ 2m

M18 PORTO CRISTO
0309 **Cabo del Morro de sa Carabassa** 39°32'.2N 3°20'.5E Fl.5s20m7M White tower, black vertical stripes 6m
0309.4 **NE mole** 39°32'.5N 3°20'.3E Fl(3)R.10s5m3M Red octagonal column 2m

M19 PORTO COLOM
Approach
0310 **Punta de ses Crestas (Punta de la Farola)** 39°24'.9N 3°16'.3E Fl(2)10s42m10M White round tower, black bands, on white building with red roof 25m 207°-vis-006°
Entrance
0310.4 **Punta de sa Batería** 39°25'.0N 3°16'.2E Fl(4)R.11s12m5M Red tower on white base 7m
0311 **W mole** 39°25'.3N 3°15'.8E Fl(3)R.10s5m1M Red tower on white base with red square 3m
0311.2 **Yacht harbour S mole** 39°25'.5N 3°15'.8E Fl(4)R.11s3m1M Red column 2m
33622(S) **Buoy 1** 39°25'.2N 3°16'.1E Fl.G.4s1M Green pillar, ▲ topmark
33624(S) **Buoy 2** 39°25.1N 3°16'.1E Fl.R.3s1M Red pillar, ■ topmark
33625(S) **Buoy 3** 39°25'.3N 3°16'E Fl(2)G.6s1M Green pillar, ▲ topmark
33626(S) **Buoy 4** 39°25'.2N 3°15'.9E Fl(2)R.6s1M Red pillar, ■ topmark
33628(S) **Buoy 5** 39°25'.4N 3°15'.9E Fl(3)G.8s1M Green pillar, ▲ topmark
Buoys
In addition to the starboard-hand buoys, ten unlit white buoys with green triangular topmarks indicate the starboard side of the dredged channel into the yacht harbour, and two white buoys with red triangular topmarks mark a shoal near the root of the yacht harbour S mole. A line of yellow buoys marks the swimming area off the beach at Arenal Gran.

M20 PUERTO DE CALA LLONGA
0311.4 **Punta del Fortin** 39°22'.1N 3°14'.1E Fl(1+2)20s17m7M Round white column on square white base, both with vertical black stripes 6m
0311.45 **Cala Llonga N side** 39°22'.2N 3°13'.9E Fl.G.5s9m5M Green column on white base 6m
0311.5 **Marina S mole** 39°22'.2N 3°13'.7E Fl.R.5s5m1M Red column on white base 3m

M21 PORTO PETRO
0311.8 **Punta de sa Torre** 39°21'.4N 3°13'E Fl(3+1)10s22m7M White tower on square base with two vertical black stripes 9m
0311.9 **Yacht harbour S mole** 39°21'.7N 3°12'.8E Fl(2)R.7s7m5M Red column 3m
0312.2 **Yacht harbour hammerhead, N end** 39°21'.8N 3°12'.8E Fl(2+1)G.12s6m3M Green column with red band on white base
0312.25 **Yacht harbour hammerhead, S end** 39°21'.7N 3°12'.7E Fl(2)G.7s4m1M Green post 3m

M22 PUERTO DE CALA FIGUERA
0312.6 **Torre D'en Beu** 39°19'.8N 3°10'.7E Fl.5s32m12M White octagonal tower, vertical black stripes 6m
0313 **Molehead** 39°20'N 3°10'.3E Fl(3)R.10s6m5M Red column on white base displaying red ■ 5m

M23 PUERTO COLONIA DE SANT JORDI
Approach
0315 **Punta Sa** 39°18'.8N 2°59'.7E Fl(3)10.5s18m7M White round tower, three black bands 12m
0314.2 **Isla de na Guardia** 39°18'.7N 3°00'E Fl(4)G.12s7m5M Green tower on white base 5m
Entrance
0314.4 **SE Breakwater head** 39°19'N 3°00'E Fl(4)R.12s5m3M Red column on white base
0314.6 **Marina N mole** 39°19'N 2°59'.9E Fl.G.4s4m1M Green column on white base 3m

0315.8 **Punta Plana** 39°21.2N 2°54.9E Fl(1+3)12s16m7M
White round tower, black bands 12m

M24 PUERTO DE LA RÁPITA
Approach
0315.8 **Punta Plana** 39°21'.2N 2°54'.9E Fl(1+3)12s16m7M
White tower, black bands, on building 12m
Entrance
0315.4 **W breakwater head** 39°21'.8N 2°57'.4E
Fl.R.2.5s7m5M Red column 6m
0315.5 **E breakwater head** Fl.G.4.5s8m3M Green column 6m

M25 PUERTO DE S'ESTANYOL
Approach
0315.8 **Punta Plana** 39°21'.2N 2°54'.9E Fl(1+3)12s16m7M
White tower, black bands, on building 12m
Entrance
0315.6 **S breakwater** 39°21'.7N 2°55'.3E Fl(2)R.6s7m5M Red
column on white base 6m
0315.7 **N Mole head** 39°21'.7N 2°55'.2E Fl(2)G.7s8m1M
Halfway up black lamp post 8m

M26 PUERTO EL ARENAL
0316.3 **Dique de Abrigo head** 39°30'.2N 2°44'.8E
Fl(3)G.9s8m5M Green column, with white top and base
4m
0316.35 **Dique de Abrigo elbow** 39°30'N 2°44'.7E
Q(9)15s6m3M Yellow tower black band 2m
0316.55 **Contradique head** 39°30'.2N 2°44'.9E
Fl(3)R.9s7m3M Red post 4m
0316.6 **Contradique spur** Fl(4)R.11s5m1M Red tower on
white base 6m
0316.4 **Interior mole NE corner** 39°30'.1N 2°44'.9E
Fl(2+1)R.11.5s5m1M Red column, green band, white top
7m
0316.5 **Interior mole SW corner** Fl.R.3s4m1M Red tower 3m

M27 PUERTO DE SAN ANTONIO DE LA PLAYA
0316.7 **W breakwater head** 39°32'N 2°43'.E Fl(4)R.13s8m5M
Red column on white base 6m
0316.72 **E breakwater head** Fl(4)G.13s6m3M Green column
on building 5m

M28 PUERTO DE CALA GAMBA
0316.74 **Dique de Abrigo** 39°32'.8N 2°41'.7E Fl.R.2s5m5M
Red post 3m
0316.76 **Contradique head** Fl.G.2s4m3M Green post 3m

M29 PUERTO DEL MOLINAR DE LEVANTE
0317.2 **SW breakwater head** 39°33'.5N 2°40'.5E
Fl(2)R.7s7m5M Red tower 4m

M30 PUERTO DE CALA PORTIXOL
0316.8 **SW breakwater** 39°33'.5N 2°40'.1E Fl(3)R.9s7m5M
Red column on white base displaying red ■ 6m
0316.82 **SE breakwater** 39°33'.5N 2°40'.2E Fl(3)G.9s7m3M
Green column on white base displaying green ▲ 6m
0316.83 **SW inner mole** 39°33'.6N 2°40'.1E Fl(4)R.11s7m1M
Red column on white base displaying red ■ 4m
0316.84 **SE inner mole** 39°33'.6N 2°40'.1E Fl(4)G.11s3m1M
Green column on white base displaying green ▲ 5m

CABRERA

C1 PUERTO DE CABRERA
Approach
0338.3 **Cabo Llebeig** 39°09'.7N 2°55'.1E Fl(4)14.5s74m7M
Black and white chequered angular tower 7m
Entrance
0338.6 **Punta de Sa Creveta** 39°09'.3N 2°55'.8E
Fl.R.4s13m7M White and red chequered angular tower
0339 **Jetty** 39°09'.1N 2°56'.1E Fl(2)R.10.5s5m5M Red column
on building 4m

MENORCA

ME1 PUERTO DE MAHÓN
Approach
0366 **Isla del Aire** 39°48'N 4°17'.6E Fl.5s53m18M White
tower, black bands, on white building 38m 197°-vis-111°
0355 **Punta S'Esperó** 39°52'.7N 4°19'.7E Fl(1+2)15s51m8M
White round tower, two black bands, on white building
11m
0352 **Cabo Favaritx** 39°59'.8N 4°16'E Fl(1+2)15s47m16M
White tower, black diagonal stripes, on white building
28m
Entrance
0354 **Punta de San Carlos** 39°52'N 4°18'.5E Oc(2)6s22m12M
White round tower, three black bands, on square white
base 15m 183°-vis-143°
35970(S) **Laja de San Carlos** 39°51'.9N 4°18'.6E Fl.R.4s3M
Red pillar buoy, ■ topmark
35990(S) **Laja de Fuera** 39°52'.1N 4°18'.6E Fl.G.4s3M Green
pillar buoy, ▲ topmark
36010(S) **Punta San Felipet** 39°52'.3N 4°18'.4E Q(2)G.3s3M
Green pillar buoy, ▲ topmark
36030(S) **Laja del Moro** 39°52'.3N 4°18'.3E Q(2)R.3s3M Red
pillar buoy, ■ topmark
0356 **Punta del Lazareto** 39°52'.6N 4°18'.2E Fl(2)G.7s13m3M
White column displaying green ▲ 9m
0359 **Isla Cuarentena or Plana** 39°53'N 4°18'E
Fl(3)G.9s9m3M Green column, white top and base 6m
0358 **Punta de Na Cafayes** 39°53'N 4°17'.7E Fl(3)R.9s8m1M
Red column on white hut displaying red ■
0360 **Punta de Villacarlos** 39°53'.1N 4°17'.4E
Fl(4)R.11s10m3M Red column on white hut displaying
red ■ 4m
0361 **Isla del Rey or del Hospital, S side** 39°53'.2N 4°17'.3E
Fl.G.5s13m3M White column displaying green ▲ 13m
0361.2 **Pontoon head** 39°53'.2N 4°17'.1E Fl(4)Y.11s2m1M
Yellow column, black band 1m
0361.4 **Isla del Rey, N side (Punta Sa Cova)** 39°53'.3N
4°17'.3E Oc.R.4s16m3M Red tower 6m
0361.6 **Punta de Sa Bassa** 39°53'.4N 4°17'.4E Oc.G.4s9m3M
Green ▲ on green metal tripod on white hut 3m
0361.7 **Cala Rata** 39°53'.6N 4°16'.8E Fl.G.5s7m3M
Green ▲ on green post
0362 **Punta de Cala Figuera** 39°53'.5N 4°16'.6E Fl.R.5s7m1M
Red ■ on red metal post 5m
0362.4 **Isla Pinta, S side** 39°53'.6N 4°16'.3E Fl(2)G.7s4m1M
Green ▲ on green metal post 3m F.R on tower 650m
N-NW
0362.5 **Isla Pinta, W side** 39°53'.6N 4°16'.2E Fl(3)G.9s4m1M
Green ▲ on green metal post 3m
0363 **Naval base, E jetty** 39°53'.6N 4°16'.2E Fl.Y.5s3m1M
Green ▲ on green metal post 3m
0363.2 **Naval base, central jetty** 39°53'.6N 4°16'.1E
Fl.Y.5s3m1M Green ▲ on green metal post 3m
0363.4 **Naval base, W jetty** 39°53'.7N 4°16'.1E Fl.Y.5s3m1M
Green ▲ on green metal post 3m
0364.2 **Canal de San Jordi E end** 39°52'.9N 4°18'.3E
Fl(3)R.9s7m1M Red tower 6m
0364.4 **Canal de San Jordi W end** Fl(4)R.11s7m1M Red tower
6m
0364 **Isla del Llatzeret E coast** 39°52'.6N 4°18'.4E
Fl(2)R.7s7m1M Red round tower

ME2 PUERTO DE TAMARINDA
0343 **Entrance canal (E)** 39°55'.6N 03°50'.1E Fl(2)G.7s7m5M
Green column on white base with green ▲ 5m
0343.2 **Entrance canal (W)** Fl(2)R.7s7m3M Red column white
base with red ■ 5m

ME3 PUERTO CIUDADELA
Approach
0342 **Cabo Dartuch (D'Artruitx)** 39°55'.4N 3°49'.5E
Fl(3)10s45m19M White tower, three black bands, on
white building 34m 267°-vis-158°
0348 **Cabo Nati** 40°03'.2N 3°49'.5E Fl(3+1)20s42m16M White
tower, aluminium cupola, on white building with red
roof 13m 039°-vis-162°

Entrance

0344 Punta de Sa Farola 39°59'.8N 3°49'.4E Fl.6s21m14M
White tower, black vertical stripes, on white building
13m 004°-vis-094°

0345 Punta El Bancal 39°59'.9N 3°49'.5E Fl(3)R.9s10m5M
Red tower on white base displaying red ■

0345.4 San Nicolás 39°59'.9N 3°49'.6E Fl(3)G.9s10m3M
Green square structure on white base displaying
green ▲ 4m

0345.6 Sa Trona 39°59'.9N 3°49'.7E Fl(4)G.11s7m1M Green
square structure on white base displaying green
▲ 4m

0345.9 Cala d'en Busquets, Dir Lt 40°N 3°49'.8E
DirFl.WRG.5s9m5-3M White square tower 3m (044°-W-
046° marks centre of channel, red sector to the N, green
sector to the S)

0345.8 Cala d'en Busquets, E light 40°N 3°49'.8E
Fl(4)R.12s11m1M Red column on white base displaying
red ■ 4m

0346.2 Slipway 40°00'.1N 3°49'.9E Fl.R.5s6m1M Red tripod
on white base displaying red ■ 5m

0346 Club Náutico 40°00'.0N 3°49'.9E Fl.G.5s7m1M Green
column on white base displaying green ▲ 5m

0346.4 La Muralla 40°00'.1N 3°50'.2E
DirOc(2)WRG.9.5s8m5-3M White square tower 6m.
(064°-W-065° marks centre of channel, red sector to the
N, green sector to the S)

ME4 PUERTO DE FORNELLS

0350.5 Cabo Fornells (Cap de Sa Paret) 40°03'.8N 4°08'E
Fl.2s29m8M White tower, black band, on white building
6m

0351 Ldg Lts 178.5° (Isla Sargantana) *Front* 40°02'.9N
4°08'.2E Q.R.14m7M White pyramidal tower 6m

0351.1 *Rear* 110m from front Iso.R.4s23m7M White
pyramidal tower 9m

0351.4 Harbour, NE mole 40°03'.3N 4°08'E Fl(4)G.11s7m5M
Green column 6m

ME5 PUERTO DE CALA DE ADDAYA

No lights.

2. Waypoints

IBIZA WAYPOINTS

⊕1	E Approach to Puerto de Ibiza	38°53'.7N 01°27'.5E
⊕2	Puerto de Ibiza	38°53'.9N 01°26'.7E
⊕3	Isla Sal Rossa	38°52'.2N 01°24'.8E
⊕4	Freu Grande channel	38°48'.6N 01°25'.6E
⊕5	Punta Rama	38°49'.5N 01°22'.0E
⊕6	Cabo Llentrisca	38°51'.0N 01°14'.7E
⊕7	Isla Vedrá W	38°51'.7N 01°10'.8E
⊕8	Islote Espardel W	38°57'.5N 01°10'.4E
⊕9	Isla Conejera NW	38°59'.7N 01°12'.5E
⊕10	Puerto de San Antonio	38°58'.8N 01°17'.0E
⊕11	Islas Margaritas (Margalides) W	39°03'.0N 01°18'.6E
⊕12	Cabo Eubarca W	39°04'.6N 01°21'.4E
⊕13	Isla Murada	39°05'.8N 01°25'.9E
⊕14	Punta Charracó	39°06'.7N 01°29'.4E
⊕15	Punta Moscarté	39°07'.4N 01°32'.0E
⊕16	Islas Hormigas	39°06'.3N 01°35'.5E
⊕17	Punta Grosa	39°05'.0N 01°37'.0E
⊕18	Between Punta Valls and Isla Tagomago	39°02'.2N 01°37'.7E
⊕19	Isla de Santa Eulalia	38°58'.8N 01°35'.3E
⊕20	Puerto de Santa Eulalia	38°58'.6N 01°32'.5E
⊕21	Cabo y Escollo Llibrell	38°56'.6N 01°32'.0E
⊕22	Lladó del Norta	38°55'.4N 01°29'.5E

FORMENTERA WAYPOINTS

⊕23	Puerto de Sabina	38°44'.2N 01°25'.3E
⊕24	Isla del Gastabí (SW)	38°46'.3N 01°24'.7E
⊕25	Pta Single Mal	38°39'.8N 01°36'.0E
⊕26	Cabo Berbería	38°37'.7N 01°23'.2E
⊕27	Pta Gabina	38°43'.1N 01°22'.1E
⊕28–30	unallocated	

MALLORCA WAYPOINTS

⊕31	Puerto de Palma	39°33'.4N 02°38'.5E
⊕32	Puerto de Cala Nova	39°32'.8N 02°36'.1E
⊕33	Las Illetas	39°31'.8N 02°35'.5E
⊕34	Puerto Portals	39°31'.5N 02°33'.8E
⊕35	Isla del Sech	39°28'.7N 02°32'.8E
⊕36	Punta de Cala Figuera	39°27'.2N 02°31'.5E
⊕37	Islote el Toro	39°27'.5N 02°28'.0E
⊕38	Isla Malgrats	39°29'.5N 02°26'.5E
⊕39	Cabo de la Mola	39°31'.6N 02°21'.4E
⊕40	Isla Dragonera (S)	39°33'.8N 02°18'.5E
⊕41	Punta de na Foradada	39°38'.5N 02°25'.2E
⊕42	Punta S'Aliga	39°42'.4N 02°31'.5E
⊕43	Peninsula de la Foradada	39°45'.6N 02°37'.2E
⊕44	Approach to Sóller	39°48'.0N 02°41'.2E
⊕45	Morro de la Vaca	39°52'.0N 02°48'.3E
⊕46	Punta Beca	39°55'.6N 02°57'.0E
⊕47	Cabo de Cataluña	39°58'.0N 03°10'.7E
⊕48	Cabo de Formentor	39°57'.8N 03°13'.0E
⊕49	Isla de Formentor (S)	39°55'.0N 03°09'.0E
⊕50	Puerto de Bonaire	39°52'.2N 03°08'.5E
⊕51	Cabo del Pinar	39°53'.5N 03°12'.7E
⊕52	Isla de Aucanada (S)	39°49'.9N 03°10'.3E
⊕53	Off Ca'n Picafort	39°46'.2N 03°09'.5E
⊕54	Off Puerto de Colonia de San Pedro	39°44'.5N 03°16'.3E
⊕55	SW of Cala es Calo	39°46'.3N 03°19'.8E
⊕56	Farayó de Aubarca (W)	39°46'.2N 03°24'.3E
⊕57	Cabo del Freu	39°45'.0N 03°28'.0E
⊕58	Cabo de Pera	39°43'.0N 03°29'.2E
⊕59	Cabo d'es Piná (Del Pinar)	39°38'.0N 03°26'.5E
⊕60	Punta de Amer	39°34'.8N 03°24'.5E
⊕61	Cala Manacor (Porto Cristo)	39°32'.2N 03°20'.5E
⊕62	Punta de ses Crestas (Approach to Puerto Colom)	39°24'.7N 03°16'.2E
⊕63	Cala Llonga (Approach to Puerto de Cala d'or)	39°22'.0N 03°14'.2E
⊕64	Off Porto Petro	39°21'.3N 03°13'.2E
⊕65	Punta Salinas	39°15'.5N 03°03'.2E
⊕66	Off Puerto Colonia de Sant Jordi	39°18'.5N 02°59'.7E
⊕67	Puerto de la Rápita	39°21'.7N 02°57'.3E
⊕68	Cabo Blanco	39°21'.6N 02°47'.0E
⊕69	Off El Arenal	39°30'.3N 02°44'.5E
⊕70	Puerto de San Antonio	39°31'.7N 02°43'.0E
⊕71	Puerto de Cala Gamba	39°32'.7N 02°41'.7E
⊕72	Off Puerto de Cala Portixol	39°33'.4N 02°40'.1E

ISLA DE CABRERA WAYPOINTS

⊕73	Puerto de Cabrera	39°09'.5N 02°55'.6E
⊕74	Between Pta de Sa Corrent & Isla Redonda	39°09'.8N 02°58'.4E
⊕75	Off Islote Imperial (SE)	39°07'.5N 02°57'.7E
⊕76	Pta Anciola	39°07'.6N 02°55'.0E
⊕77	Cabo Llebeig	39°09'.7N 02°54'.9E
⊕78	Pta de la Escala	39°11'.0N 02°57'.0E
⊕79	Isla Horadada	39°12'.6N 02°58'.7E
⊕80	unallocated	

MENORCA WAYPOINTS

⊕81	Puerto de Mahón fairway	39°52'.0N 04°18'.6E
⊕82	Isla del Aire Passage	39°48'.4N 04°17'.0E
⊕83	Off Cabo d'en Font	39°49'.1N 04°12'.1E
⊕84	Cala Santa Galdana	39°56'.0N 03°57'.4E
⊕85	Cala Son Saura	39°55'.1N 03°53'.6E
⊕86	Puerto de Tamarinda	39°55'.4N 03°50'.1E
⊕87	Cabo Negro	39°57'.2N 03°49'.1E
⊕88	Puerto de Ciudadela	39°59'.6N 03°49'.5E
⊕89	Cabo Binicous (de Banyos)	40°00'.0N 03°47'.1E
⊕90	Cabo Nati	40°03'.1N 03°49'.0E
⊕91	Punta del Escuá	40°03'.8N 03°52'.0E
⊕92	Bajo Morell rock	40°04'.0N 03°53'.0E
⊕93	Off Cabo Gros	40°04'.7N 03°56'.0E
⊕94	Isla Bledas N	40°04'.7N 04°01'.9E
⊕95	Off Isla Nitge	40°05'.8N 04°04'.1E
⊕96	Puerto de Fornells	40°04'.0N 04°08'.0E
⊕97	Cabo Pentinat	40°03'.6N 04°10'.6E
⊕98	Addaya Approach	40°01'.4N 04°12'.4E
⊕99	Cabo Favaritx	39°59'.8N 04°16'.4E
⊕100	Cabo Monseña	39°59'.1N 04°16'.4E
⊕101	Punta Galera	39°56'.7N 04°17'.5E
⊕102	Off Cabo Negro	39°54'.0N 04°18'.7E
⊕103	Punta S'Esperó	39°52'.6N 04°19'.9E

3. Charts

Charts and other publications may be corrected annually by reference to the Admiralty *List of Lights and Fog Signals* Volume D (NP 77) or weekly via the *Admiralty Notices to Mariners*.

Note A few charts appear twice in the following list under different island headings. The index diagrams only show large-scale charts where the diagram's scale permits.

BRITISH ADMIRALTY CHARTS

Chart	Title	Scale
Approaches from the Spanish coast		
1701	Cabo de San Antonio to Villaneuva y Geltrú including Islas de Ibiza and Formentara	300,000
Ibiza		
1702	Ibiza, Formentera and southern Mallorca	300,000
2834	Islas Baleares, Ibiza and Formentera	120,000
	Channels between Ibiza and Formentera	50,000
	San Antonio Abad	20,000
	Ibiza	10,000
Mallorca		
1703	Mallorca and Menorca	300,000
2831	Mallorca: Punta Salinas to Cabo de Formentor including Canal de Menorca	120,000
	Puerto de Alcudia	20,000
2832	Mallorca – Punta Salinas to Punta Beca including Isla de Cabrera	120,000
3034	Approaches to Palma	25,000
3035	Palma	10,000

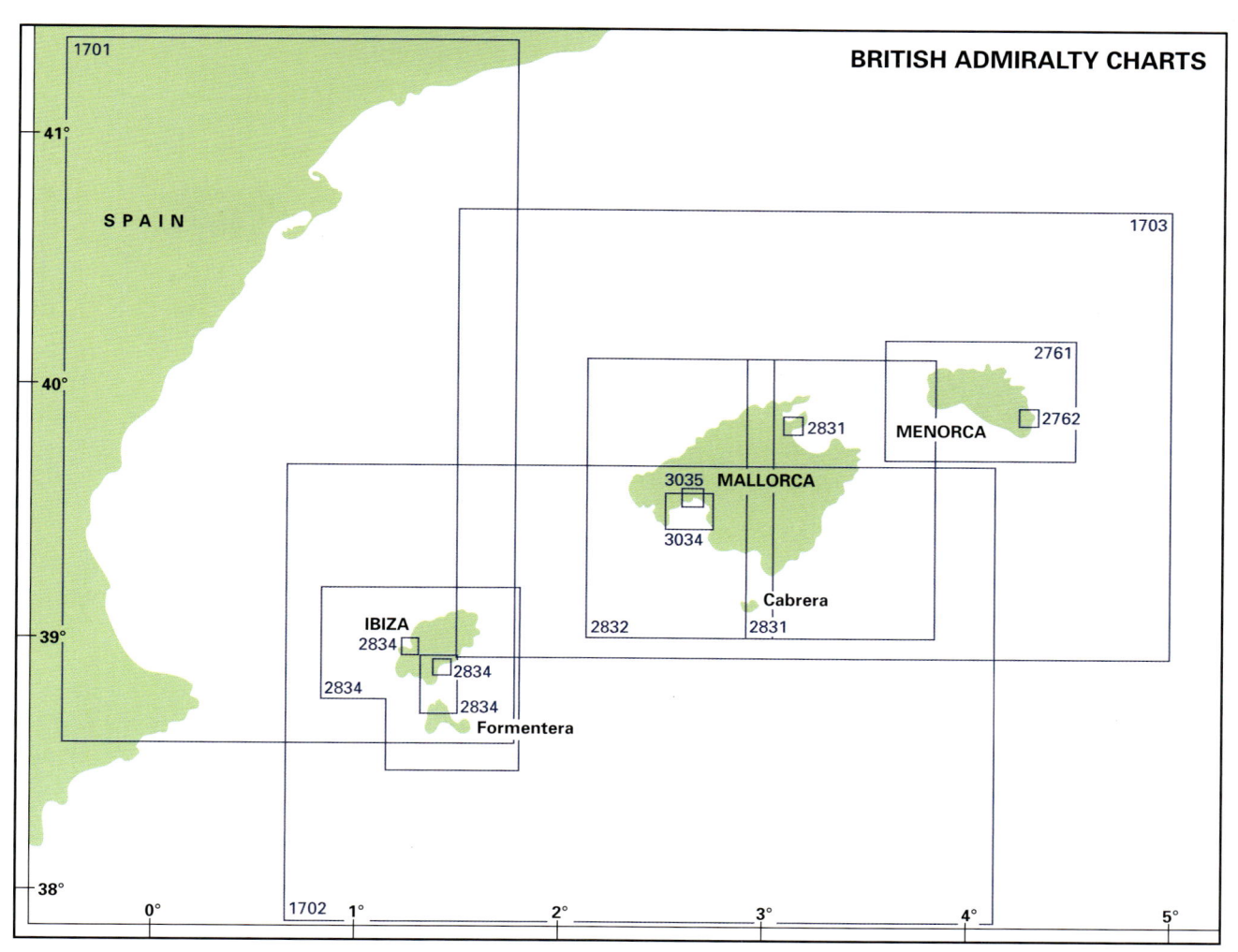

BRITISH ADMIRALTY CHARTS

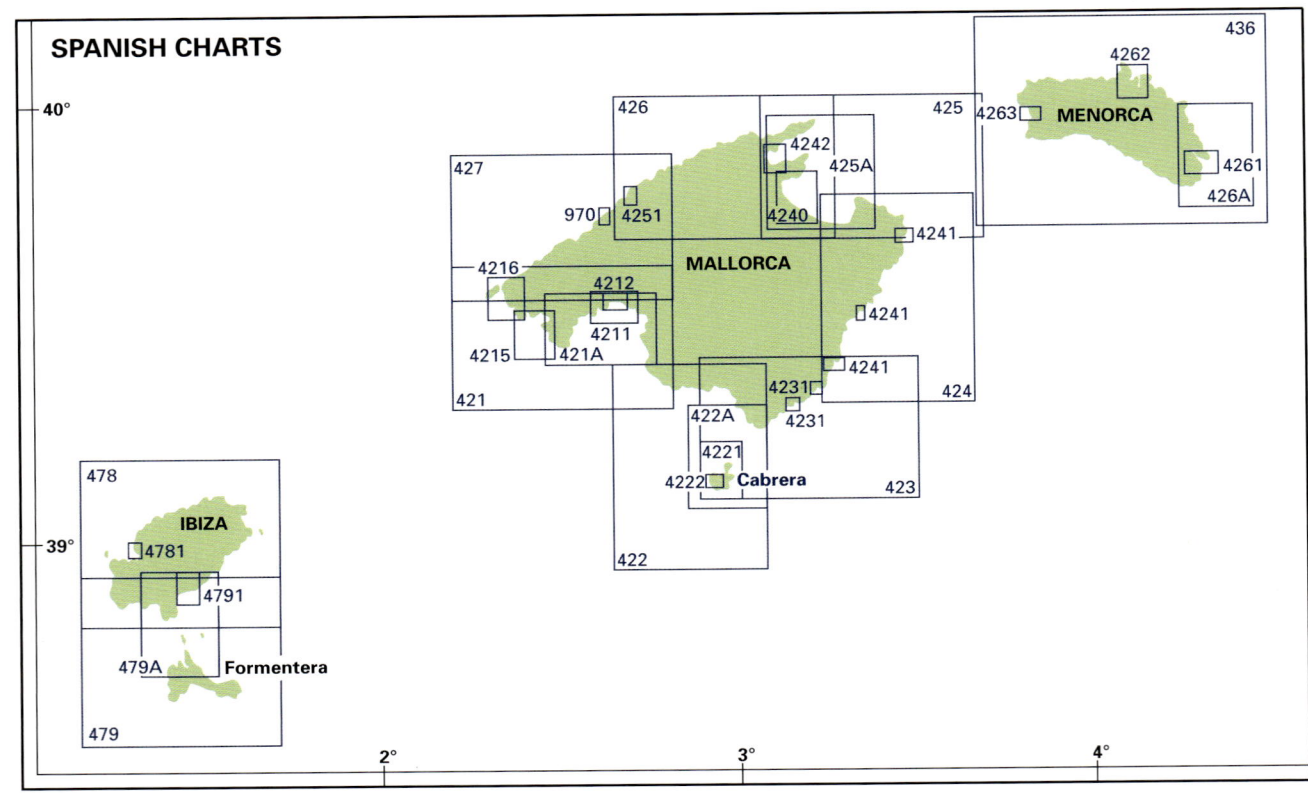

SPANISH CHARTS

40°
426
4242
425
436
4262
425A
4263
MENORCA
427
4251
970
4240
4261
4241
426A
MALLORCA
4216
4212
4211
4241
4215
421A
4241
424
421
4231
422A
4231
4221
478
4222 Cabrera
423
IBIZA
39°
4781
422
4791
479A Formentera
479
2°
3°
4°

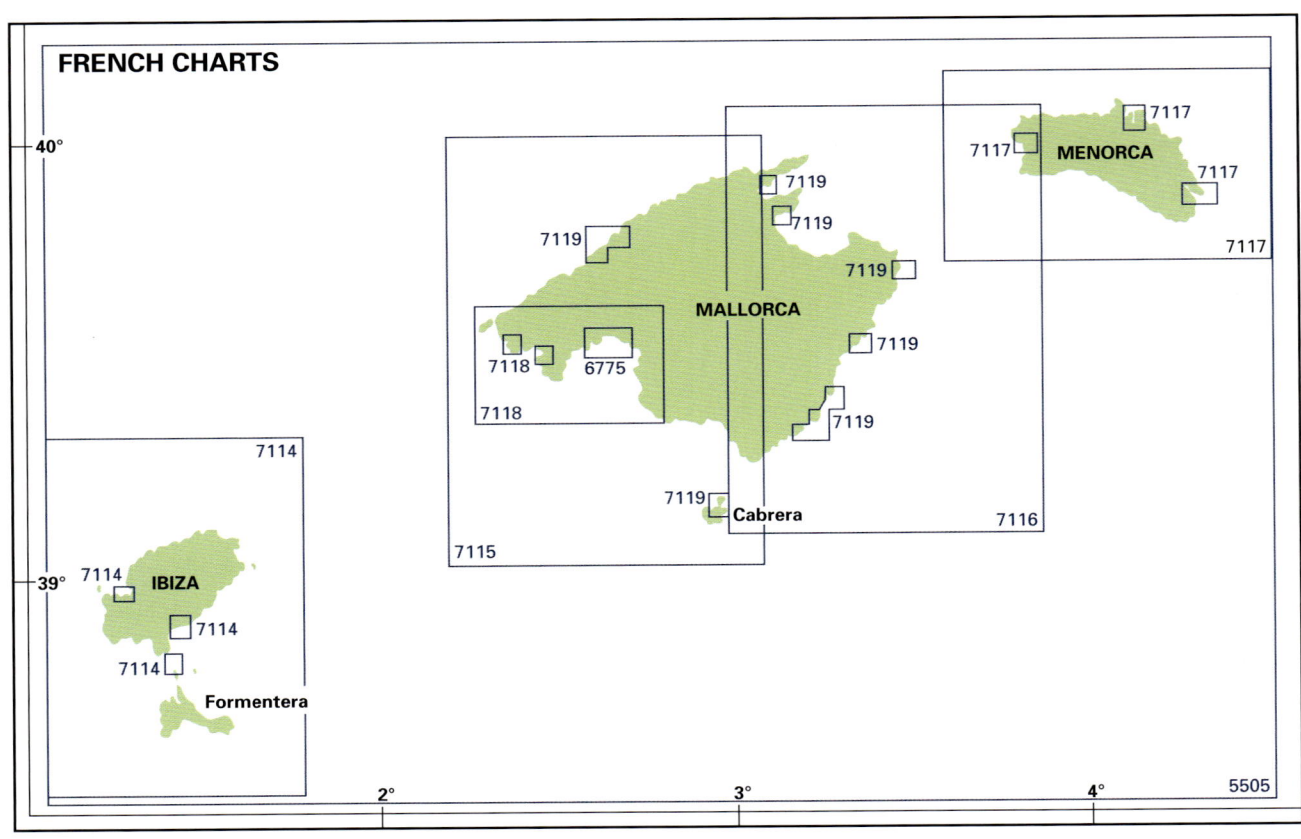

FRENCH CHARTS

40°
7117
7117
MENORCA
7117
7119
7119
7117
7119
7119
7119
MALLORCA
7119
7118
6775
7119
7118
7119
7119
7114
7116
7119 Cabrera
7115
7114
IBIZA
39°
7114
7114
Formentera
2°
3°
4°
5505

Menorca
1703	Mallorca and Menorca	300,000
2761	Menorca	60,000
2762	Mahón	7,500

SPANISH CHARTS

Ibiza
478	De Cabo Negret a Cabo Berberia	50,000
479	De Cabo Berberia a Punta Arabi	50,000
479A	Freus entre Ibiza y Formentera	25,000
4781	Puerto de San Antonio Abad	5,000
4791	Puerto de Ibiza	10,000

Mallorca
48E	Islas de Mallorca y Menorca	175,000
421	De isla Dragonera a Cabo Blanco	50,000
421A	Bahía de Palma. De islote El Toro a Cabo Regana	25,000
422	De Cabo Regana a Punta Salinas	50,000
422A	Freu de Cabrera	25,000
423	De Punta Plana a Porto Colom con la Isla de Cabrera y adyacentes	50,000
424	De cala Llonga a Cabo Farrutx	50,000
425	De Cabo Pera a Cabo Formentor	50,000
425A	Bahía de Alcudia	25,000
426	De la Bahía de Alcudia al Puerto de Sóller	50,000
427	De Cala de la Calobra a Isla Dragonera	50,000
4211	Bahía de Palma. De las Illetas a islote Galera	10,000
4215	Ensenada de Santa Ponsa	10,000
4216	Freu de Dragonera y Puerto de Andraitx	15,000
4221	Isla de Cabrera y adyacentes	12,500
4222	Puerto de Cabrera	5,000
4231	Porto Petro y Cala Llonga	7,500
	Cala Figuera	2,500
4240	Bahía de Alcudia	12,500
4241	Porto Colom	5,000
	Porto Cristo o Cala Manacor	5,000
	Cala Ratjada	5,000
4242	Bahía de Pollença	7,500
4251	Puerto de Pollensa	7,500

Menorca
48E	Islas de Mallorca y Menorca	175,000
426A	Approaches Puerto de Mahón	25,000
428A	De Punta Binibeca a Cabo Favaritx	25,000
436	Isla de Menorca	60,000
4261	Puerto de Mahón	7,500
4262	Puerto de Farnells y Bahía de Tirant	10,000
4263	Puerto de Ciudadela	5,000

FRENCH CHARTS

Ibiza
7114	Ibiza et Formentera	
	Cartouche: A – Ibiza et Formentera	100,000
	Cartouche: B – San Antonio Abad	20,000
	Cartouche: C – Puerto de Ibiza	10,000
	Cartouche: D – Passages entre Ibiza et Espalmador Abords de Puerto de Ibiza	30,000

Mallorca
6775	Baie de Palma – De Las Illetas à l'îlot Galera	10,000
7115	Mallorca – Partie Ouest – De Punta Beca à Punta Salinas	100,000
7116	Mallorca – Partie Est –De Punta Salinas à Cabo de Formentor	100,000
7118	Abords de Palma – De Isla Dragonera à Cabo Blanco	40,000
	Cartouche: A – Puerto de Andraitx	10,000
	Cartouche: B – Cala de Santa Ponsa	10,000
7119	Ports et mouillages de Mallorca et Cabrera	
	Cartouche: A – Puerto de Pollensa	12,500
	Cartouche: B – Puerto de Alcudia	10,000
	Cartouche: C – Puerto de Sóller	10,000
	Cartouche: D – Puerto Colom	15,000

	Cartouche: E – Cala Ratjada	10,000
	Cartouche: F – Surgidero de la Foradada	12,500
	Cartouche: G – Cala Figuera	5,000
	Cartouche: H – Puerto Cristó ou Calá Manacor	5,000
	Cartouche: I – Puerto de Cabrera	12,500
	Cartouche: J – Porto Petro et Cala Llonga	12,000

Menorca
7117	Menorca – Ports et Mouillages de Menorca	
	Cartouche: Menorca	100,000
	Cartouche: A – Puerto de Ciudadela	10,000
	Cartouche: B – Bahía de Tirant et Cala Fornells	15,000
	Cartouche: C – Puerto de Máhon	15,000

NAVICARTE CHARTS
(PUBLISHED BY BLOC MARINE)

| E01 | Majorque Est – Minorque |
| E02 | Majorque Ouest – Ibiza – Formentera |

IMRAY

| M3 | Islas Baleares | 356,000 |

4. Further reading
PILOTS AND TOURIST GUIDES

Many navigational publications are reprinted annually, in which case the latest edition should be carried. Others, including most cruising guides, are updated by means of supplements available from the publishers. Further corrections or amendments are always welcome.

Admiralty publications
Mediterranean Pilot Vol I (NP 45) and supplement covers the S and E coasts of Spain, the Islas Baleares, Sardinia, Sicily and the N coast of Africa
List of Lights and Fog Signals Vol E (NP 78) (Mediterranean, Black and Red Seas)
List of Radio Signals
Vol 1, Part 1 (NP281/1) Coast Radio Stations (Europe, Africa and Asia)
Vol 2 (NP 282) Radio Navigational Aids, Electronic Position Fixing Systems and Radio Time Signals
Vol 3 Part 1 (NP 283/1) Radio Weather Services and Navigational Warnings (Europe, Africa and Asia)
Vol 4 (NP 284) Meteorological Observation Stations
Vol 5 (NP 285) Global Maritime Distress and Safety Systems (GMDSS)
Vol 6, Part 2 (NP 286/2) Vessel Traffic Services, Port Operations and Pilot Services (The Mediterranean, Africa and Asia)

English language
Imray Mediterranean Almanac Rod Heikell (Imray Laurie Norie & Wilson Ltd). A biennial almanac with second year supplement, packed with information. Particularly good value for yachts on passage when not every cruising guide is likely to be carried.
Mediterranean Cruising Handbook Rod Heikell (Imray Laurie Norie & Wilson Ltd). General information on cruising areas, passages etc. some of which is now slightly out of date.
Guia del Navegante – La Costa de España y el Algarve (PubliNáutic Rilnvest SL, revised annually) in colloquial English with a Spanish translation. Not a full scale pilot book, but an excellent source of up-to-date information on local services and facilites (partly via the advertisements) with phone numbers, etc.
Guia Náutica Turistica y Deportiva de España by the Asamblea de Capitánes de Yate. An expensive and colourful guide book covering all the Spanish coasts and including some useful data on harbours but no pilotage information. The plans are

in outline only. Written in Spanish with a partial English translation. Because symbols are lavishly used, much of it can be understood with only a limited knowledge of Spanish.

Guia Náutica de España. Tomo II, Costa del Azahar, Blanca and Baleares. One of a series of books featuring attractive colour pictures, some of which are out of date, and some text. Written in Spanish but an English version is sometimes available.

El Mercado Náutico (The Boat Market). A free newspaper published every two or three months and available from yacht clubs, marina offices, etc. Written in Spanish, English and German it includes, amongst other things, a useful (though by no means comprehensive) listing of current marina prices.

Menorca. Atlas Náutico Alfonso Buenaventure. A book of 67 double page chartlets showing the coastline of Menorca in extreme detail – a must for anyone thinking of cruising around Menorca.

Nuevos Aeroguias – El Litoral de Mallorca (Editorial Planeta S.A) It has aerial photographs of the whole coastline of Mallorca. Ensure you get a recent edition as most shops only hold the old one.

North Africa RCC/Graham Hutt (Imray)

French

Votre Livre de Bord – Méditerranée (Bloc Marine) French almanac covering the Mediterranean, including details of weather forecasts transmitted from France and Monaco. An English/French version is also published which translates some, though by no means all, the text. Published annually.

Ports & Mouillages – Baléares (SHOM). French guide in a series which also covers western Italy, Sardinia and the Lesser Antilles. Colour photos and plans.

Les Guides Nautiques – Baléares J C Alvarez (Edition Eskis). Written in French in colloquial style, lacking in detail and with basic plans.

German

Spanische Gewässer, Lissabon bis Golfe du Lion K Neumann (Delius Klasing). A seamanlike guide and semi-pilot book, which includes sketch plans of most harbours. Harbour data is limited but it contains much good general advice on sailing in this area.

Die Baleares Bernhard Bartholmes (Edition Maritim). Well laid-out with good detail and some excellent, though out of date, aerial photographs.

Häfen und Anker Plätze Gerd Radspieler. A useful book but with very basic plans and lacking in detail.

Background

The Birth of Europe Michael Andrew (BBC Books). An excellent and comprehensive work which explains in simple terms how the Mediterranean and surrounding countries developed over the ages from 3000 BC.

The First Eden, David Attenborough (William Collins). A fascinating study of 'The Mediterranean World and Man'.

The Inner Sea Robert Fox (Sinclair-Stevenson, 1991). An account of the countries surrounding the Mediterranean and the forces which shaped them, written by a well known BBC journalist.

Sea of Seas H Scott (van Nostrand). A half-guidebook half-storybook on the western Mediterranean. Very out of date and now out of print, but a delight to read.

TRAVELLERS' GUIDES

Essential Mallorca, Ibiza and Menorca Tony Kelly (Automobile Association, 2004). A handy, pocket-sized tourist guide with a little bit of everything – what to see, where to shop, restaurant recommendations, countryside and wildlife, etc. Excellent colour photos. Highly recommended and very user friendly, this series is available at some UK airports and via www.theAA.com/bookshop

The AA Map & Guide to Mallorca, Twinpack series Tony Kelly (AA publishing 2005). Similar in size and content to *Essential Mallorca*, it includes, 'Top 25 sights', 'Where to:

eat, shop, etc.' and 'Practical Matters'. It comes with an OS map of the island. Also highly recommended, as is *Twinpack Menorca* and the AA *Spiral Guide Mallorca* (Carol Baker 2001).

Baedeker's Majorca (which also covers Menorca) and *Baedeker's Ibiza* Peter M Nahm (Automobile Association, 1994). Serious, informed guides, well illustrated and particularly strong on culture – history, architecture, etc. – though with some notable omissions and many errors in the index. A pocket in the plastic cover carries an island map.

Landscapes of Ibiza Han Losse; *Landscapes of Mallorca* Valerie Crespí-Green; *Landscapes of Menorca* Rodney Ansell (Sunflower Books, 1995, 1994 & 1996). Three pocket-sized volumes of car tours, walks and picnic suggestions, plus some public transport schedules.

The Rough Guide: Mallorca & Menorca Phil Lee (Rough Guides, distributed by the Penguin Group, 1996). A new addition to the worldwide series for land-based budget travellers, but useful to anyone wanting practical information. Town plans, no photographs. Also 46 pages on the Islas Baleares in the Spain volume (1994).

The Balearic Islands Helen Thurston (Batsford, 1977). Not so much a travel guide as a detailed history of the influences which have shaped the islands over the centuries. Slightly out of date but highly readable.

The Balearic Islands (Nagel Publishers, 1969). Thumbnail descriptions of places in the Islas Baleares, with historic details and suggestions for visits. Companion volume on Spain. Getting distinctly out of date.

Mallorca and Menorca Berlitz Travel Guide. By 1995 this book had reached its 24th edition – what more can one say!

PERIOD ACCOUNTS

Jogging Round Majorca Gordon West (Black Swan Books, 1994). First published in 1929 when 'jogging' meant a leisurely stroll, this is a charming glimpse of the island before tourism arrived. Also available on cassette. Highly recommended.

A Cottage in Majorca Lady Margaret Kinloch (Skeffinton, 1936). Another mirror into the past written with great affection. Long out of print, so not an easy book to track down.

Majorca Observed Robert Graves and Paul Hogarth (Cassells, 1965). Probably the most famous author to live and write in Mallorca before mass tourism.

ROAD MAPS

Road maps are indispensable when making a journey inland. As usual, Michelin produce an excellent road map which is available throughout the islands.

Euro-Map – Mallorca, Menorca, Ibiza (GeoCenter International). Detailed but comprehensible road map giving contours, place names (sometimes both Castilian and local versions) historic sites, street plan of Palma, etc. Scale 1:150,000. Useful for any form of travel.

The Firestone road map of the Islas Baleares is also reported to be excellent, but may be difficult to obtain in the UK.

COOKERY BOOKS

Mediterranean Seafood Alan Davidson. Penguin. A handbook with all the names of Mediterranean fish, crustaceans and molluscs in several languages and over 200 recipes from Mediterranean countries. Indispensable in the markets and fishing harbours with their unfamiliar fish. The recipes are practical and do not require ingredients exotic to the Mediterranean.

Mediterranean Cookery Claudia Roden. It contains 250 delicious and easy recipes of traditional Mediterranean cooking prepared with locally available ingredients.

5. Spanish glossary

The following limited glossary relates to the weather, the abbreviations to be found on Spanish charts and some words likely to be useful on entering port. For a list containing many words commonly used in connection with sailing, see Webb & Manton, *Yachtsman's Ten Language Dictionary* (Adlard Coles Nautical).

WEATHER

On the radio, if there is a storm warning the forecast starts *aviso temporal*. If, as usual, there is no storm warning, the forecast starts *no hay temporal*. Many words are similar to the English and their meanings can be guessed. The following may be less familiar:

Viento (wind)

calm calm
ventolina light air
flojito light breeze
flojo gentle breeze
bonancible moderate breeze
fresquito fresh breeze
fresco strong breeze
frescachón near gale
temporal fuerte gale
temporal duro strong gale
temporal muy duro storm
borrasca violent storm
huracán, temporal huracanado hurricane
tempestad, borrasca thunderstorm

El cielo (the sky)

nube cloud
nubes altas, bajas high, low clouds
nubloso cloudy
cubierto covered, overcast
claro, despejado clear

Names of cloud types in Spanish are based on the same Latin words as the names used in English.

El mar (sea state)

calma calm
marizada ripples
marejadilla slight sea (choppy)
marejada rough sea
fuerte marejada very rough
mar corta short seas
mar gruesa steep seas

Visibilidad (visibility)

buena, bueno, buen good
regular moderate
malo, mala, mal poor
calima haze
neblina mist
bruma sea mist
niebla fog
Precipitación Precipitation
aguacero shower
llovizna drizzle
lluvia rain
aguanieve sleet
nieve snow
granizada hail

Sistemas del Tiempo Weather Systems

anticiclón anticyclone
depresión, borrasca depression
vaguada trough
cresta, dorsal ridge
cuna wedge
frente front
frio cold
cálido warm
ocluido occluded
bajando falling
subiendo rising

LIGHTS AND CHARTS – MAJOR TERMS AND ABBREVIATIONS

A	*amarilla*	yellow
Alt	*alternativa*	alternative
Ag Nv	*aguas navegables*	navegable waters
Ang	*angulo*	angle
Ant	*anterior*	anterior, earlier, forward
Apag	*apagado*	extinguished
Arrc	*arrecife*	reef
At	*atenuada*	attenuated
B	*blanca*	white
Ba	*bahía*	bay
	bajamar escorada	chart datum
Bal	*baliza*	buoy, beacon
Bal. E	*baliza elástica*	plastic (elastic) buoy
Bco	*banco*	bank
Bo	*bajo*	shoal, under, below, low
Boc	*bocina*	horn, trumpet
Br	*babor*	port (i.e. left)
C	*campana*	bell
Card	*cardinal*	cardinal
Cañ	*cañon*	canyon
	boya de castillete	pillar buoy
cil	*cilíndrico*	cylindrical
C	*cabo*	cape
Cha	*chimenea*	chimney
Cno	*castillo*	castle
cón	*cónico*	conical
Ct	*centellante*	quick flashing (50{80/minute)
CtI	*centellante interrumpida*	interrupted quick flashing
cuad	*cuadrangular*	quadrangular
D	*destello*	flash
Desap	*desaparecida*	disappeared
Dest	*destruida*	destroyed
	dique	breakwater, jetty
Dir	*direccional*	directional
DL	*destello largo*	long flash
E	*este*	east
edif	*edificio*	building
	ensenada	cove, inlet
Er	*estribor*	starboard
Est	*esférico*	spherical
Esp	*especial*	special
Est sñ	*estación de señales*	signal station
ext	*exterior*	exterior
Extr	*extremo*	end, head (of pier etc.)
F	*fija*	fixed
Fca	*fabrica*	factory
FD	*fija y destello*	fixed and flashing
FGpD	*fija y grupo de destellos*	fixed and group flashing
Flot	*flotador*	float
Fondn	*fondeadero*	anchorage
GpCt	*grupo de centellos*	group quick flashing
GpD	*grupo de destellos*	group flashing
GpOc	*grupo de ocultaciones*	group occulting
GpRp	*grupo de centellos rápidos*	group very quick flashing
hel	*helicoidales*	helicoidal
hor	*horizontal*	horizontal
Hund	*hundida*	submerged, sunk
I	*interrumpido*	interrupted
Igla	*iglesia*	church
Inf	*inferior*	inferior, lower
Intens	*intensificado*	intensified
Irreg	*irregular*	irregular
Iso	*isofase*	isophase
L	*luz*	light
La	*lateral*	lateral
	levante	eastern
M	*millas*	miles
Mte	*monte*	mountain
Mto	*monumento*	monument
N	*norte*	north

Naut	*nautófono*	foghorn
NE	*nordeste*	northeast
No	*número*	number
NW	*noroeste*	northwest
Obst	*obstrucción*	obstruction
ocas	*ocasional*	occasional
oct	*octagonal*	octagonal
oc	*oculta*	obscured
Oc	*ocultación sectores*	obscured sectors
Pe A	*peligro aislado*	isolated danger
	poniente	western
Post	*posterior*	posterior, later
Ppal	*principal*	principal
	prohibido	prohibited
Obston	*obstrucción*	obstruction
Prov	*provisional*	provisional
prom	*prominente*	prominent, conspicuous
Pta	*punta*	point
Pto	*puerto*	port
PTO	*puerto deportivo*	yacht harbour
	puerto pesquero	fishing harbour
	puerto de Marina de Guerra	naval harbour
R	*roja*	red
Ra	*estación radar*	radar station
Ra+	*radar + suffix*	radar + suffix (Ra Ref etc.)
RC	*radiofaro circular*	non-directional radiobeacon
RD	*radiofaro dirigido*	directional radiobeacon
rect	*rectangular*	rectangular
Ra	*rocas*	rocks
Rp	*centeneallante rápida*	very quick flashing (80-160/min)
RpI	*cent. rápida interrumpida*	interrupted very quick flashing
RW	*radiofaro giratorio*	rotating radiobeacon
s	*segundos*	seconds
S	*sur*	south
SE	*sudeste*	southeast
sil	*silencio*	silence
Silb	*silbato*	whistle
Sincro	*sincronizda con*	synchronized with
Sir	*sirena*	siren
son	*sonido*	sound, noise, report
Sto/a	*Santo, Santa*	Saint
SW	*sudoeste*	southwest
T	*temporal*	temporary
Te	*torre*	tower
trans	*transversal*	transversal
triang	*triangular*	triangular
troncoc	*troncocónico*	truncated cone
troncop	*troncopiramidal*	truncated pyramid
TSH	*antena de radio*	radio mast
TV	*antena de TV*	TV mast
U	*centellante Ultra-rápida*	ultra quick flashing (+160/min)
UI	*cent. Ultra-rápida interrumpido*	interrupted ultra quick flashing
V	*verde*	green
Vis	*visible*	visible
	vivero	shellfish raft or bed
W	*oeste*	west

PORTS AND HARBOURS

puerto' is applied to any landing place from a beach to a container port.

a popa stern-to
a proa bows-to
abrigo shelter
al costado alongside
amarrar to moor
amarradero mooring
ancho breadth (see also manga)
anclar to anchor

botar to launch (a yacht)
boya de amarre mooring buoy
cabo warp, line (also cape)
calado draught
compuerta lock, basin
dársena dock, harbour
dique breakwater, jetty
escala ladder
escalera steps
esclusa lock
escollera jetty
eslora total length overall
espigón spur, spike, mole
fábrica factory
ferrocarril railway
fondear to anchor or moor
fondeadero anchorage
fondeo mooring buoy
fondo depth (bottom)
grua crane
guia mooring lazy-line (lit. guide)
nudo knot (i.e. speed)
longitud length (see also eslora), longitude
lonja fish market (wholesale)
manga beam (i.e. width)
muelle mole, jetty, quay
noray bollard
pantalán jetty, pontoon
parar to stop
pila estaca pile
pontón pontoon
práctico pilot (i.e. pilot boat)
profundidad depth
rampa slipway
rompeolas breakwater
varadero slipway, hardstanding
varar to lift (a yacht)
vertedero (verto) spoil ground

Direction
babor port
estribor starboard
norte north
este east
sur south
oeste west

Around the port
aceite oil (including engine oil)
agua potable drinking water
aseos toilet block
astiller shipyard
duchas showers
efectos navales chandlery
electricidad electricity
gasoleo diesel diesel
hielo (cubitos) ice (cubes)
lavandería laundry
lavandería automática launderette
luz electricity (lit. light)
manguera hosepipe
parafina, petróleo, keroseno paraffin, kerosene
gasolina petrol
velero sailmaker (also sailing ship)

Phrases useful on arrival
Donde puedo amarrar? Where can I moor?
A donde debo ir? Where should I go?
Que es la profundidad? What is the depth?
Cuantos metros? What is your length?
Para cuantas noches? For how many nights?

Formalities
aduana customs
capitán de puerto harbourmaster
derechos dues, rights
dueño, propietario owner
guardia civil police
patrón skipper (not owner)
título certificate

Documentation

It has been found useful to have the following list available for registering at each port or marina to be visited:

Nombre de Yate Yacht's name
Bandera Flag
Lista y folio Yacht's number
Reg. bruto Registered weight
Tipo Type of vessel
Palos Number of masts
Motor, marca y potencia Engine make and capacity
Eslora total L.O.A.
Maga Beam
Calado Draught
Puerto base Home port
No. cabinas No. of cabins
Seguro Insurance company
Proprietario Skipper
Nacionalidad Nationality
Telefono Telephone
Pasaporte Passport
Tripulante y pasajero Passengers on board

6. Charter regulations

Any EU-flag yacht applying to charter in Spanish waters must be either VAT paid or exempt (the latter most commonly due to age). Non-EU flag vessels must have a valid Temporary Import Licence and may also have to conform to other regulations.

Applying for a charter licence can be a tortuous business. Firstly the Director General de Transportes at the Conselleria d'Obres Publiques i Ordenacio del Territorio must be approached with a pre-authorisation application. This obtained, the application itself is sent to the Capitanias Maritimas together with ships' papers and proof of passenger insurance and registration as a commercial activity. A safety and seaworthiness inspection will be carried out. Finally a fiscal representative must be appointed and tax paid on revenue generated.

It will probably be found simpler to make the application through one of the companies specialising in this type of work. Try NETWORK, Edificio Torremar, Passeo Marítimo, 44 - 07015 Palma de Mallorca ② 971 403903/403703 *Fax* 971 400216, who will also deal with VAT and legal matters.

7. Repair and maintenance facilities in Palma de Mallorca

All telephone and fax number have a prefix of 971.
Companies are normally listed alphabetically.
Chandleries
   Yacht Centre Palma ② 971 715612 *Fax* 971 711246 at the Club de Mar, also La Central ② 971 731838 and others.
Liferaft servicing
   GDR ② 971 760798 *Fax* 971 430787
Charts Admiralty
   Rapid Transit Service ② 971 401210 / 405325 *Fax* 971 404511
   Spanish – Librería Fondevila ② 971 725616 *Fax* 971 713326
   Casa del Mapa ②/*Fax* 971 466061
Generators
   Salva ② 971 730303 *Fax* 971 450906
Repairs
Audax Marina ② 971 720474 *Fax* 971 720475 Repair yard at the Réal Club Nautico *Email* info@audaxmarina.com
   Astilleros de Mallorca boatyard ② 971 710645 *Fax* 971 721368: a shipyard with four slipways able to take yachts up to 100m on the Contramuelle Mollet opposite the Réal Club Náutico.
   Boat Yard Palma ② 971 718302 *Fax* 971 718611 and Carpinser ② 971 725079 on the Muelles Viejo and Nuevo near the root of the NE breakwater and several others.
   A 150-tonne travel-lift at Boat Yard Palma, 90 and 30-tonne lifts on the Muelle Viejo, 60-tonne lift at the Réal Club Náutico. A 9-tonne crane at the Réal Club Náutico, 5-tonne crane at Club de Mar, plus many others in the commercial areas of the port. A commercial slipway in the Dársena de Porto Pi able to handle 350 tonnes, for which a docking plan is required. Several in the shipyard E of the Réal Club Náutico.
Engineers
   C-Tec SA ② 971 405712
   Marine Machine ② 971 462660 *Fax* 971463693
   Talleres Guidet ② 971 718643 *Fax* 971 720577
Official service agents include:
   C-Tec SA (*see above*) – Caterpillar, Man
   Marine Machine (*see above*) Ford/Lehman, Perkins, Sabre, Volvo Penta
   Salva ② 971 730303 *Fax* 971 450906
   Volvo Penta España SA ② 971 430343 Volvo Penta
Metalwork
   Ruben Doñaque ② 971 760796 *Fax* 971 202313
   Talleres Guidet (*see above in Engineers*).
Electronic & radio repairs, autopilots, watermakers etc
   C-Tec SA ② 971 405712
   Vetus Mallorca ② 971 713050 *Fax* 971 713054
   Yacht Electronic Services ② 971 400213 *Fax* 971 405873
Sailmakers and canvaswork
   Valería Orion ② 971 757688
   Valera J Matheu ② 971 273887.

APPENDIX

8. Official addresses

SPANISH NATIONAL EMBASSIES AND CONSULATES

UK 39 Chesham Place, London SW1X 8SB ☎ 020 7235 5555
  Fax 020 7259 5392
Consulate 20 Draycott Place, London SW3 2RZ ☎ 020 7589
  8989 *Fax* 020 7581 7888
US 2375 Pennsylvania Avenue NW, Washington, DC 20037
  ☎ 202 452 0100/728 2340 *Fax* 202 833 5670
  Email embespus@mail.mae.es
Consulate 150 E. 58th St, New York, NY 10155
  ☎ 212 355 4080/2/5/6 *Fax* 644 3751/90
  Email spainconsulny@mail.mae.es

BRITISH AND AMERICAN EMBASSIES IN MADRID

UK Calle Fernando el Santo 16, 28010 Madrid
  ☎ 91 700 8200/524 9700 *Fax* 91 700 8309
  www.madridconsulate@ukinspain.com
US Calle Serrano 75, 28006 Madrid
  ☎ 91 587 2240/5872240 *Fax* 91 587 2243/2303

BRITISH REPRESENTATION IN ISLAS BALEARES

Mallorca British Consulate, Plaza Mayor 3D, 07002 Palma de
  Mallorca, ☎ 971 712445, 716048 *Fax* 971 717520
  Email consulate@palma.mail.fco.gov.uk
Menorca British Vice-Consulate, SA Casa Nova, Cami de
  Biniatap 30, 07720 Es Castell, Menorca ☎ 971 367818
  Fax 971 354690 www.fco.gov.uk
Ibiza British Vice-Consulate, Avenida Isidoro Macabich
  45-1, Apartado 307, 07800 Ibiza ☎ 971 301816/8
  Fax 971 301972 *Email* BritishConsulate.Ibiza@fco.gov.uk

AMERICAN REPRESENTATION IN ISLAS BALEARES

Mallorca Vice-Consulate, Edificio Reina Constanza, Porto Pi,
  8,9D 07015 Palma de Mallorca ☎ 971 403707/403905
  Fax 971 403971

SPANISH NATIONAL TOURIST OFFICES

UK PO Box 4009 London W1A 6NB ☎ +44 020 74868077
  Fax 020 74868034 *Email* info.londres@tourspain.es
  www.tourspain.co.uk
US 666 Fifth Avenue, New York, NY 10103
  ☎ 212 265 8822/6577246 *Fax* 212 2658864
  Email oetny@tourspain.es
  www.okspain.org

9. Government moorings website

www.balearslifeposidonia.eu/index.php?register_vars[lang]=en
This website is a helpful guide to the new mooring buoys in
Balearics.

Summer season
- This is a free service of the Govern de les Illes Balears and the buoys can be booked from 1 June until 30 September 2010.
- Before your first booking, we recommend you to read the rules of use.
- You must register yourself and your boat to make a booking.
- Bookings can be made between 20 and one day in advance of your arrival at the area (until 1900).
- A maximum of two consecutive nights every six natural days at the same area can be booked.
- The reserved buoys have to be taken between 1300 and 1830 of the arriving day.
- The latest the buoys can be left is at 1200 of the departure day.

Index

INDEX

INDEX

Index